SuperVision and Instructional Leadership

A Developmental Approach

SEVENTH EDITION

Carl D. Glickman
University of Georgia

Stephen P. Gordon
Texas State University

Jovita M. Ross-Gordon
Texas State University

PEARSON

Boston   New York   San Francisco
Mexico City   Montreal   Toronto   London   Madrid   Munich   Paris
Hong Kong   Singapore   Tokyo   Cape Town   Sydney

Senior Series Editor: *Arnis E. Burvikovs*
Editorial Assistant: *Erin Reilly*
Marketing Manager: *Tara Kelly*
Editorial Production Service: *Omegatype Typography, Inc.*
Composition Buyer: *Linda Cox*
Manufacturing Buyer: *Linda Morris*
Electronic Composition: *Omegatype Typography, Inc.*
Interior Design: *Carol Somberg*
Cover Administrator: *Linda Knowles*

For related titles and support materials, visit our online catalog at
www.ablongman.com.

Between the time website information is gathered and then published, it is not
unusual for some sites to have closed. Also, the transcription of URLs can result in
typographical errors. The publisher would appreciate notification where these errors
occur so that they may be corrected in subsequent editions.

Library of Congress Cataloging-in-Publication Data

Glickman, Carl D.
    SuperVision and instructional leadership : a developmental approach / Carl D.
Glickman, Stephen P. Gordon, Jovita M. Ross-Gordon. — 7th ed.
      p. cm.
    Includes bibliographical references and index.
    ISBN 0-205-48953-2
    1. School supervision. I. Gordon, Stephen P. II. Ross-Gordon, Jovita M. III.
Title.
LB2806.4.G56 2007
371.2'03—dc22

                                  2006041657

Printed in the United States of America

10 9 8 7 6   RRD-VA   11 10 09 08

Contents

part **three**

Interpersonal Skills   115

chapter **6** **Supervisory Behavior Continuum:
Know Thyself**   117

chapter **7** **Developmental Supervision:
An Introduction**   131

chapter **8**   **Directive Control Behaviors**   143

chapter **9**   **Directive Informational Behaviors**   155

chapter **10** **Collaborative Behaviors**   167

part **five**

Tasks of SuperVision 299

chapter **16 Direct Assistance to Teachers** 301

chapter **17 Group Development** 321

chapter 18 Professional Development   351

chapter 19 Curriculum Development   375

chapter **20** Action Research: The School as the
Center of Inquiry   405

part **six**

Function of SuperVision   427

chapter **21** SuperVision, Change,
and School Success   429

chapter **22 SuperVision for What? Democracy and the Good School** 449

Appendix A: What Is Your Educational Philosophy?   467

Appendix B: Skill Practices Using Directive Control, Directive Informational, Collaborative, and Nondirective Approaches   473

Name Index   481

Subject Index   487

Preface

One might suppose the seventh edition of any book would allow its authors a certain level of comfort as they went about revising a familiar and popular text. Contrary to that supposition, we worked on this edition with a great sense of urgency. This sense of urgency was based on two realities. First, educators are increasingly losing their authority to make decisions about education—including decisions about the content of the curriculum, how students should be taught, and how student learning should be assessed. Second, as the economic gap between the "haves" and "have-nots" in our society increases, there is a corresponding widening of the educational gap. Low-income students, minority students, and other students placed at risk are failing and dropping out of school at an alarming rate. The field of supervision has a moral obligation to address both of these realities. Regarding the loss of decision making, our colleague John Smyth (2005) argues that supervision needs to become a "firewall" between harmful policies and authentic instructional improvement at the district, school, and classroom levels. Put somewhat more gingerly, supervisors can assist teachers to meet external mandates while using best practices to meet the learning needs of students, but they must also work with teachers and others to change policies that are harmful to students. Regarding the second reality, supervision can assist teachers to work for social justice at the school and classroom levels, and through that work influence their communities and the larger society.

In view of the concerns described, this seventh edition **places considerable emphasis on school and teacher empowerment as well as diversity and social justice.** It also emphasizes supervisor reflection and self-critique as a means of improving the supervisory process.

Readers familiar with previous editions will note updating of the following topics:

- A proposal for a new paradigm for supervision calling for supervision to be collegial rather than hierarchical, the province of teachers as well as supervisors, focused on teacher growth rather than compliance, based on teacher collaboration, and characterized by continuous reflective inquiry (Chapter 1)
- Effective schools research and the transition to school improvement research (Chapter 3)
- Connections between school and community development (Chapter 3)

- The integration of adult learning and adult development theories with instructional supervision (Chapter 4)
- Developmental supervision, the supervisory behavior continuum, and four interpersonal approaches to supervision (directive control, directive informational, collaborative, and nondirective) (Chapters 7–12)
- Technical skills of supervision: assessing, planning, observing, research, program evaluation, and teacher evaluation (Chapters 13–15)
- The tasks of supervision: direct assistance, group development, professional development, curriculum development, and action research (Chapters 16–20)
- Examples of model professional development (Chapter 18) and action research programs (Chapter 20)
- Shared governance for instructional improvement: premises, principles, and models (Chapter 20)
- Change, including discussions of change from the leader's view, change from the teacher's view, chaos theory applied to school and classroom change, and creating a culture for change (Chapter 21)

There is also new material that:

- Addresses issues of equity in school and classroom practice (Chapters 2, 3, 5, 12, 16, 19, 20, 22)
- Discusses the need to improve classroom and school culture (Chapters 1, 2, 3, 5, 16, 19, 20, 21, 22)
- Describes how supervisors can critique their own performance (Chapters 5, 6, 8, 9, 10, 11, 12)
- Cautions against reductionist approaches to instructional improvement (Chapter 5), conferencing (Chapter 7), planning (Chapter 13), observing (Chapter 14), the change process (Chapter 21), and educational reform (Chapter 22)
- Critically examines No Child Left Behind and legislated learning (Chapters 13, 19, 21, 22)
- Presents new forms of action research (Chapter 20)
- Argues for radically changing the conditions of teaching (Chapter 21)

One new feature that cuts across this edition is the "Practitioner Reflection" at the end of each chapter. We asked practitioners of supervision to write reflective essays that connected one or more major topics in an assigned chapter to their own work as a supervisor. For these essays, we defined the term *practitioner* broadly. Essay writers include associate superintendents, district coordinators, principals, assistant principals, consultants from state intermediate units, private consultants, and others. Not all of the practitioner-writers agree with everything that the authors say in the assigned chapter, and this is how it should be. Alternative positions presented by practitioners add to the range of ideas for readers to consider and discuss. Our intent is that the practitioners' essays generate reflection and dialogue among those who read this book. We hope that this seventh edition continues to signal the need for all of us—writers and readers—to think, challenge, and practice the promise of schools, education, and democracy.

Acknowledgments

It is impossible to acknowledge all those who have contributed to the development of this book. We would like to acknowledge the contribution of our colleague Edward Pajak, who developed with Glickman the directive informational supervisory approach in the early 1980s; he continues to provide a guiding influence on the field of supervision. A host of colleagues—school practitioners, graduate students, and university faculty members—have provided us with settings, collaborations, and discussion for field-testing developmental and democratic propositions about supervision. We are grateful to Miguel G. Guajardo and Sarah Nelson of Texas State University for reviewing new material for this edition. Many thanks to honors student Megan Dvorsky for typing and organizing revisions, and to doctoral student and graduate assistant Julie Diehl for her outstanding research and editing. We are grateful to the reviewers of this edition: Loucrecia Collins, University of Alabama at Birmingham; Alicia Cotabish, University of Arkansas at Little Rock; and Dan Gutmore, Seton Hall University. Special thanks to the instructional leaders from around the nation who contributed to the practitioner essays—their contributions have made this a better book!

To the Instructor

At the end of each chapter, you will find exercises that might be assigned to your graduate students. The first six editions of this text have been used in universities and colleges throughout the United States and Canada. Based on the experience of many colleagues who have used the text with their supervision classes, we would like to offer some suggestions. For those who teach on a semester system, the first three chapters are relatively brief and can be read as one assignment; students can then complete one or two chapters for each subsequent week. For those who teach on a quarter system, it is recommended that the first three chapters be assigned the first week, and two or three chapters each subsequent week.

Exercises are categorized as academic, field, and developmental. *Academic exercises* are those done primarily through library research, reading, writing, and constructing. *Field exercises* are those done in practice within school settings and with other professionals. Academic exercises are suitable for graduate students who do not hold supervisory positions and/or are seeking more knowledge of theory and research. Field exercises are suitable for practitioners who wish to make immediate improvements in their professional situations. Regardless of whether students are in supervisory positions, we suggest that students do both field and academic exercises at a ratio weighted toward their interests, situations, and needs. Students periodically can be asked to choose and complete one academic or field exercise from a set of related chapters. A short sharing session is useful at the beginning of the subsequent class, to give students an opportunity to discuss the results of their exercises.

Developmental exercises are done as sustained projects that can be used as a term or an extra-credit project. Developmental exercises are written with the purpose of encouraging students to continue their professional growth. If used as a term assignment, please allow students during the first week of classes to scan *all* the developmental activities in each chapter before asking them to make a choice for the academic term.

The exercises (academic, field, and developmental) are numerous and provide students a wide arena of choice. Likewise, we encourage the instructor to make his or her own choices according to his or her own expertise and experience. The sequence of chapters is consistent with the proposed model of supervision, but an individual instructor might find another order more suitable. Similarly, the instructor might wish to adapt, revise, or discard suggestions for using chapter exercises. Our purpose in writing this book was to increase supervisory success in schools. However an instructor can use this book to bring about such success, it will make our efforts worthwhile.

PowerPoint® presentations that highlight issues in every chapter accompany this text. These slides can be accessed online by contacting your local representative.

Reference

Smyth, J. 2005. *New direction for supervision: When teachers give students power over their learning.* Paper presented at the annual meeting of the Council of Professors of Instructional Supervision, Athens, GA, October.

part one
Introduction

SuperVision for Successful Schools

Take a walk with us. First, let's step into Finnie Tyler High School, with a student body of 1,200, in a lower- to middle-class urban neighborhood. A sign by the entrance tells all visitors to report to the office. In the halls, we see students milling around, boys and girls talking in groups, couples holding hands, one couple intertwined romantically in a corner. The bell rings and students scurry to the next class. We find the school office and introduce ourselves to the secretary and school principal, who are expecting our visit. They welcome us and assure us that we may move around the school and talk to students, teachers, and other staff. The school population has been notified of our visit and understands that we have come to see how Tyler High School operates. The principal tells us we will find Tyler a pleasant place. Equipped with a floor plan of classrooms and other facilities, we continue on our way.

The principal's description is accurate: Students seem happy and uninhibited, socializing easily with each other even during instruction time. Teachers joke with students. In the faculty lounge, we hear laughter that rises, falls, and then rises again. Several teachers have told us about the traditional Friday after-school gatherings at the local pizza parlor, where teachers and administrators socialize over a drink.

Classrooms vary considerably from each other; teachers tell us they can teach however they wish. Most teachers stand at the front of the room, lecturing, asking questions, and assigning seatwork. Some, however, take a less structured approach, allowing students to work alone or in small groups. There is an unhurried atmosphere. Students move at a leisurely pace, and classes seldom start on time. Teachers of the same subjects use the same textbooks but otherwise seem to have discretion to function as they please. As one seven-year veteran teacher at this school sums it up: "We have an ideal situation. We like each other, and the administration leaves us alone. I am observed once a year. I have one faculty meeting a month to attend. I love the other teachers and we have a great time together. The kids are fine, not as academic as they should be, but this school is a nice place for them. I wouldn't want to teach anyplace else."

Now let's drive across town to Germando Elementary School, with 600 students, located in a wealthy, suburban part of the city. Again, we follow the sign to the office. A few students are standing with their noses against the wall by their classroom doors. Otherwise, the halls are vacant and still; all classroom doors are shut. In the principal's office sit two students with tears in their eyes, obviously fearful of their impending conference with the principal. The principal welcomes us and hands us a preplanned schedule of times to visit particular teachers. She tells us not to visit any classroom during instructional time. "I think you will find that I run a tight ship," she says. "Teachers and students know exactly what is expected of them and what the consequences are for ignoring those expectations. Teachers are here to teach, and I see to it that it happens."

Moving down the halls, we are struck by the similarity of the classrooms. The desks are in rows; the teacher is in front; the school rules are posted on the right of the chalkboard. At the first recess time, the students seem to erupt onto the playground. Expecting to find a group of teachers in the faculty lounge, we are surprised to find only two people. One is knitting and the other is preparing a cup of coffee. All the other teachers have remained in the classrooms, either alone or with one other teacher.

Continuing our observation after recess, we find that teachers at each grade level not only work with the same textbooks but are on the same pages as well. When we ask about this, one teacher tells us that the principal has standardized the entire curriculum and knows what is being taught in every classroom at each moment of the day. At the first faculty meeting in August, the principal lays out materials, schedules, and time lines developed by the central office. We ask how the principal can enforce such procedures, and the teacher replies, "She asks for weekly lesson plans, visits my room at least once every two weeks, and has other central office personnel visit and report back to her."

In the classrooms we visit, students are generally quiet but restless. They appear attentive; those who are not are disciplined. Teachers are mostly businesslike; some show warmth toward their students, others do not. We conclude our visit with three separate interviews of teachers. It seems that teaching in Germando is perceived as a job to do. Whether one likes them or not, the principal's rules and regulations are to be followed. Teachers mention that when they have attempted to make modest changes in their instruction, they have been told to drop the changes and return to the school plan. All three mention the teacher who last year refused to follow the reading textbook and was subsequently forced to resign.

Finnie Tyler High School and Germando Elementary School are examples of real schools. Which is the successful school? Which has better attendance, attitudes, and achievement? *Neither does!* Both are ineffective, mediocre schools. The successful schools in the same system are quite different from either. Our first conclusion might be that these schools are very different. Tyler High School appears to have little supervision of instruction, whereas Germando has too much. According to the definition of instructional supervision presented in this book, however, *neither* school has effective instructional supervision. It also might appear that Tyler meets teachers' individual needs, whereas Germando meets organizational goals set by the principal. In successful schools, however, individual needs are fulfilled through organizational goals. In these two schools, *neither* need is being met. Finally, the working environments in these two schools only appear to be dissimilar; soon we will see how similar they really are.

The last school on our tour is Progress Middle School. Our first stop at Progress is the school office, where we are informed by the school secretary that the principal will meet with us at the end of the period. The principal is teaching Mr. Simmons's class while Simmons observes another teacher as part of a peer coaching program involving a number of teachers. The secretary invites us to wait for the principal in the teachers' lounge, where several teachers are spending their preparation period. As we relax with a soda, we listen to an animated discussion among the teachers concerning an interdisciplinary unit of instruction they are planning. The teachers are brainstorming alternative teaching and assessment strategies for the unit, and discussing how these strategies could be connected to the unit's theme.

Soon the principal joins us and invites us on a tour of the school. During the tour, we note that classroom environments are work oriented, as well as warm and supportive. In some classrooms, students are involved in hands-on inquiry. In other classrooms, cooperative learning is taking place. In still others, teachers are challenging students to reflect on lesson content by using higher-level questioning and inviting student opinions on the lesson topic. A commonality across all classrooms is students engaged in active learning. Teachers give students feedback on their performance, and provide alternative learning opportunities and special attention to those experiencing difficulties.

After school, we attend a meeting of the school leadership council, made up primarily of teachers. The council is considering action research proposals submitted by faculty liaison groups. Each proposal is focused on improvement of curriculum and instruction. Much of the debate among council members is concerned with whether or not the proposed research will assist in meeting the school's vision, mission, and goals agreed upon two years earlier by the entire faculty. At times the debate becomes heated. Clearly the council is taking its decision making seriously. The principal is a voting member of the council, but does not have veto power over council decisions, which are made by majority rule.

Germando Elementary is an example of a *conventional school*—characterized by dependency, hierarchy, and professional isolation. Finnie Tyler is an example of a *congenial school*—characterized by friendly social interactions and professional isolation. A successful school like Progress Middle School is a *collegial school*—characterized by purposeful adult interactions about improving schoolwide teaching and learning. Professional respect is a byproduct of discussing issues with candor, accepting disagreements as integral to change, and respecting the wisdom and care of all for arriving at educational decisions for students.

Collegial schools establish learning goals for all students consistent with the responsibility of education in a democratic society. These schools are always studying teaching and learning, setting common priorities, making decisions about internal changes and resource allocations, and assessing effects on student learning. These schools are driven by (1) a covenant of learning—mission, vision, and goals; (2) a charter for schoolwide, democratic, decision making; and (3) a critical study process for informing decisions and conducting action research (Glickman, 1993, 2003). In effect, successful schools create a "SuperVision" of instruction, democratically derived and studied, that gives purpose and direction to the common world of adults.

SuperVision: A New Name for a New Paradigm

Like schools, supervision can be conventional, congenial, or collegial. Throughout most of its history supervision has operated from within a conventional paradigm (worldview), attempting to control teachers' instructional behaviors. Based on what we know about successful schools, the time has come to move from conventional schools (still dominant in the United States) and congenial schools (less prevalent but still present throughout the nation) toward collegial schools (growing in number and success). *A "paradigm shift" toward the collegial model, if it is to succeed, must include a shift away from conventional or congenial supervision toward collegial supervision.* This view of supervision includes all of the following:

1. A collegial rather than a hierarchical relationship between teachers and formally designated supervisors
2. Supervision as the province of teachers as well as formally designated supervisors
3. A focus on teacher growth rather than teacher compliance
4. Facilitation of teachers collaborating with each other in instructional improvement efforts
5. Teacher involvement in ongoing reflective inquiry (Gordon, 1997, p. 116)

Jo Blase captures the spirit of this new, collegial approach to supervision in the following description:

> Leadership is shared with teachers, and it is cast in coaching, reflection, collegial investigation, study teams, explorations into the uncertain, and problem solving. It is position-free supervision wherein the underlying spirit is one of expansion, not traditional supervision. Alternatives, not directives or criticism, are the focus, and the community of learners perform professional—indeed, moral—service to students. (cited in Gordon, 1995)

Collegial supervision, then, stands in sharp contrast to traditional approaches to supervision (Keedy and Simpson, 2002).

Given the fact that the historic role of supervision has been inspection and control, it is not surprising that most teachers do not equate supervision with collegiality. When teachers have been asked to make word associations with the term *instructional supervision,* most of the associations have been negative, as indicated by the following list (Gordon, 1997, p. 118):

Control	Directive
Step-by-step	Irrelevant
Lack of creativity	Waste of time
Lack of free choice	Restricting
Evaluation	Rules
Negative	Dog and pony show
Nonexistent	Big brother
Jumping through hoops	Intimidating
Boring	Constantly under watch
Paperwork	Anxiety
Bureaucrat	Boss
Monitoring instruction	Stress
Guidelines for testing	Need for detailed lesson plans
Authority	Administrative micro management
Unrealistic	Yuck!

The dictionary definition of *supervision* is to "watch over," "direct," "oversee," "superintend." The history of instructional supervision is viewed most often as an instrument for controlling teachers. In a series of recent studies, Richard Ingersoll (2003) concludes that the flight from education of both new and experienced educators is due to the external control of teachers' work lives. It seems that a new term for describing the collegial model of instructional leadership espoused in this book is in order. Therefore the first word in the title of this new edition is

SuperVision, a term that denotes a common vision of what teaching and learning can and should be, developed collaboratively by formally designated supervisors, teachers, and other members of the school community. The word also implies that these same persons will work together to make their vision a reality—to build a democratic community of learning based on moral principles calling for all students to be educated in a manner enabling them to lead fulfilling lives and be contributing members of a democratic society.

Supervisory Glue as a Metaphor for Success

We can think of supervision as the *glue* of a successful school. Supervision is the function in schools that draws together the discrete elements of instructional effectiveness into whole-school action. Research shows that those schools that link their instruction and classroom management with professional development, direct assistance to teachers, curriculum development, group development, and action research under a common purpose *achieve their objectives* (Bernauer, 2002; Calhoun, 2002; MacKenzie, 1983). In other words, when teachers accept common goals for students and therefore complement each other's teaching, and when supervisors work with teachers in a manner consistent with the way teachers are expected to work with students, then—and only then—does the school reach its goals. Regardless of a school's grade span, socioeconomic setting, or physical characteristics, successful schools have a common glue that keeps a faculty together and creates consistency among a school's various elements. The glue is the process by which some person or group of people is responsible for providing a link between individual teacher needs and organizational goals so that individuals within the school can work in harmony toward their vision of what the school *should* be (Bernstein, 2004).

Effective supervision requires knowledge, interpersonal skills, and technical skills. These are applied through the supervisory tasks of direct assistance to teachers, curriculum development, professional development, group development, and action research. This adhesive pulls together organizational goals and teacher needs and provides for improved learning.

Who Is Responsible for SuperVision?

Mark Zelchack, an experienced teacher, has been appointed as a mentor for a beginning teacher in his elementary school. At the beginning of the school year, Mark oriented the new teacher to the school, the curriculum, and the new teacher's responsibilities. Mark visits the new teacher's classroom on a regular basis, has conferences with his mentee, and is helping him to carry out an instructional improvement plan that they designed collaboratively.

Jane Simmons is a school principal. She has recently initiated a clinical supervision program with a group of volunteer teachers. In a typical clinical cycle, Jane holds a preconference with a teacher in which they discuss the teacher's plan for a future lesson. They also discuss nonjudgmental data that the teacher wishes Jane to collect while observing the lesson. After observing the class and collecting the desired data, Jane shares the data with the teacher during a postconference. The postconference is non-evaluative, aimed at interpreting the data and helping the teacher to plan improvement goals and strategies for reaching those goals.

Michele Carver is a lead teacher. She is released from teaching for three periods a day to help other teachers improve their instruction. This year Michele has conducted professional development programs on cooperative learning and teaching thinking skills, and has provided expert coaching to teachers who are attempting to transfer their new instructional skills to their classrooms. Recently, Michele has been elected chairperson of her school's instructional improvement committee.

Briget Myers is a first-grade teacher. She is a member of a collegial peer-coaching triad. This week she is scheduled to observe two other first-grade teachers who are attempting to use some of the same balanced literacy strategies that Briget is trying out with her own first-graders. She hopes not only to provide her colleagues with useful observation data, but also to pick up ideas on how she can better implement balanced literacy in her own classroom.

The educators discussed here carry out a variety of roles within their schools. However, they all participate in supervision during at least part of their working day. SuperVision, for us, is identical to leadership for the improvement of instruction. This definition allows for instructional leadership to be viewed as a function and process rather than a role or position. Educators throughout the school system—from the top to the bottom of its organizational chart—can engage in the function and process of supervision.*

Organization of This Book

Figure 1.1 demonstrates the scope and organization of this book. For those in supervisory roles, the challenge to improving student learning is to apply certain knowledge, interpersonal skills, and technical skills to the tasks of direct assistance, group development, curriculum development, professional development, and action research that will enable teachers to teach in a collective, purposeful

---

*To avoid awkwardness of writing, from here on we will use the spelling SuperVision only in particular headings. But the point is that SuperVision and instructional leadership are integrated and interchangeable concepts.

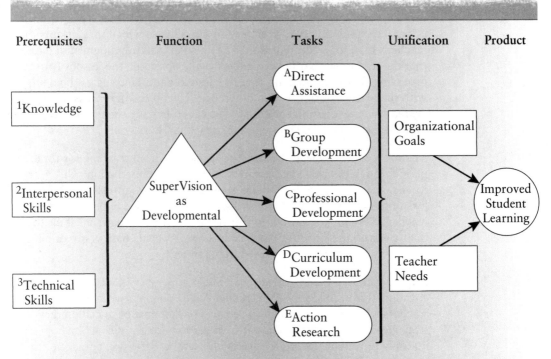

| Prerequisites | Function | Tasks | Unification | Product |

¹Knowledge

²Interpersonal Skills

³Technical Skills

SuperVision as Developmental

^ADirect Assistance

^BGroup Development

^CProfessional Development

^DCurriculum Development

^EAction Research

Organizational Goals

Teacher Needs

Improved Student Learning

FIGURE 1.1 *SuperVision for Successful Schools*

manner uniting organizational goals and teacher needs. As the supervisor allows teachers to take greater control over their own professional lives, a school becomes a dynamic setting for learning.

To facilitate such collective instructional improvement, those responsible for supervision must have certain prerequisites. The first is a *knowledge* base. Supervisors need to understand the exception—what teachers and schools can be—in contrast to the norm—what teachers and schools typically are. They need to understand how knowledge of adult and teacher development and alternative supervisory practices can help break the norm of mediocrity found in typical schools. Second, there is an *interpersonal skills* base. Supervisors must know how their own interpersonal behaviors affect individuals as well as groups of teachers and then study ranges of interpersonal behaviors that might be used to promote more positive and change-oriented relationships. Third, the supervisor must have *technical skills* in observing, planning, assessing, and evaluating instructional improvement. Knowledge, interpersonal skills, and technical competence are three complementary aspects of supervision as a developmental function.

Supervisors have certain educational tasks at their disposal that enable teachers to evaluate and modify their instruction. In planning each task, the supervisor needs to plan specific ways of giving teachers a greater sense of professional power to teach students successfully. Those supervisory tasks that have such potential to affect teacher development are direct assistance, group development, professional development, curriculum development, and action research. Direct assistance *(A)* is the provision of personal, ongoing contact with the individual teacher to observe and assist in classroom instruction. Group development *(B)* is the gathering together of teachers to make decisions on mutual instructional concerns. Professional development *(C)* includes the learning opportunities for faculty provided or supported by the school and school system. Curriculum development *(D)* is the revision and modification of the content, plans, and materials of classroom instruction. Action research *(E)* is the systematic study by a faculty of what is happening in the classroom and school with the aim of improving learning.

By understanding how teachers grow optimally in a supportive and challenging environment, the supervisor can plan the tasks of supervision to bring together organizational goals and teacher needs into a single fluid entity. The unification of individual teacher needs with organizational goals in "a cause beyond oneself" has been demonstrated to promote powerful instruction and improved student learning.

Figure 1.1, therefore, presents the organization of this textbook in a nutshell. Part II will be devoted to essential knowledge. Part III will deal with interpersonal skills. Part IV will explain technical skills the supervisor needs, and Part V will discuss the application of such knowledge and skills to the tasks of supervision. Finally, Part VI will suggest ways of applying knowledge, skills, and tasks to integrate individual needs with organizational goals to achieve needed change and instructional success.

Supervision and Moral Purpose

SuperVision based on moral purpose begins with the school community asking two broad questions:

1. What type of society do we desire?
2. What type of educational environment should supervision promote in order to move toward the society we desire?

If even part of the answer to the first question involves a democratic society in which all members are considered equal, then the answer to the second question must involve creating an educational environment that prepares students to be members of that democratic society. We can take this one step further and say that the answer involves creating a school that mirrors the democratic society that we desire.

We ground this book in a SuperVision of a good school, one that delivers on the promise of education that promotes a better democracy for all (see Glickman, 2003; Gordon, 2001). To do so, we cannot think of ourselves as first-grade teachers, high school mathematics teachers, middle school counselors, central office specialists, high school principals, or superintendents. These positions are reflections of where we locate our bodies to go to work, but the names don't reflect where we need to locate our minds and our hearts. Educators are the primary stewards of the democratic spirit. The total of our efforts is far greater than the particulars of our job (Glickman, 1998b).

The democratic impulse for renewing education continues to resonate in the thoughts of many local teachers, parents, administrators, and citizens in schools throughout this country—perhaps among more people than ever before. However, schools blessed with such far-sighted people are still in the margin. The challenge to bring an inclusive definition of democracy as the guiding principle into public education is enormous (Glickman, 1998a, 1999; Scheurich, 1998). We have been here before and we might fall short once again. But, whether we succeed or simply keep the spirit alive, we will have let other generations of educators and citizens know that this is the most important fight in which to engage—the democratic education of our students for a just and democratic society.

PRACTITIONER REFLECTION

When Is Collegiality Real?

Edward F. Tobia, *Executive Director, Center for Teacher Renewal*

Early in my career, as a newly appointed middle school assistant principal, I was determined to be as collegial as possible; in my own teaching career I had a "history of being mistreated by supervisors," and I was going to be different. As with many things, the implementation of my beliefs was harder than I thought.

I was responsible for supervising a seventh-grade interdisciplinary team at the school and I had some concerns about the harsh disciplinary tactics being used by an experienced teacher who, in his own words, could have taught me in his seventh-grade class. Mr. Fox was passionate about social studies and wouldn't tolerate students who didn't hold to his high academic standards. I wanted to work out a plan with him that would help integrate his high expectations for academic achievement and behavior with the developmental needs of the "tweens" he was teaching. I had experienced a difficult time with my own son in seventh grade just a year prior to my new appointment and I had read extensively about adolescent development so I thought I knew a few things. However, in the eyes of Mr. Fox, I had three strikes against me—I was young, I was new to the school and the community, and I had just completed my doctorate (I was one of two people in the district with a doctorate at the time). The lessons I learned in working with this teacher were not taught in any course I took or found in any book or journal article I had read.

I scheduled a time to meet with him (that was already out of the ordinary for him). He came in to the meeting with a self-assured air that his years of experience would trump anything I could possibly have to offer. I opened the conversation with some ice-breaking comments but it was clear that he wanted to get right down to whatever I had on my mind. Looking back on the conversation, he was setting the stage for playing on my naiveté and agreeing with anything I might suggest. I had the sense that what looked like a collegial conversation was in reality just "going through the motions." I did not have the presence of mind to ask, "I'm uncertain why you're agreeing with me. Please tell me what you think." Instead, I ended the meeting as gracefully as I could, determined to find some way of genuinely communicating with this teacher.

Predictably, the teacher did not change his behavior, putting me on shaky ground as his supervisor. If I said or did nothing I would lose all credibility with him, and if I tried to confront him I was sure to face a repeat of the earlier conversation. The solution came by accident when another seventh-grade teacher had to go home and I had to cover her classroom. She was on the same interdisciplinary team, so she and Mr. Fox shared the same students. Teaching has always been my love and I had a great time that day. The fact that I was not shut away in my office and could work well with the same students Mr. Fox had difficulty with seemed to break the ice with him. I can't say that our relationship improved right away, but that opportunity began the process of trust building. He began to see me not as some young kid with little experience and lots of book knowledge but as a colleague who could relate to students and still have high academic expectations. Changes took place in the hallway conversations we had and over time our interactions became more collegial. I never revisited that original conversation with him but something from that meeting must have taken hold. I met with the team often and heard his tone toward students change over time. I'm sure that it had much more to do with his trusting me as a teacher than my knowledge of preadolescent developmental needs.

In their study of trust in school, Bryk & Schneider (2003) found a strong connection between relational trust among stakeholder groups and student achievement. In their words,

> Relational trust is grounded in the social respect that comes from the kinds of social discourse that take place across the school community. Respectful exchanges are marked by genuinely listening to what each person has to say and by taking these views into account in subsequent actions. Even when people disagree, individuals can still feel valued if others respect their opinions. (p. 42)

I had entered the initial conversation with Mr. Fox with the idea that my noble intentions to collaborate would shine through and we would be able to come to agreement on the best way to work with students. However, I came to the meeting with some false assumptions:

- I knew the best way to work with middle school students.
- Mr. Fox didn't care about the students.
- I could enter a new system and on the basis of my credentials pass over the need to build relationships before trying to collaborate.

By entering an adjoining classroom for a day (and other classrooms on other days) I entered into a social discourse with which Mr. Fox could relate. From that point, we were able to listen to one another, even though that listening took place in team meetings, in hallway conversations, and over lunch. Those interactions opened the door to more genuine collegial conversations about teaching and learning.

EXERCISES

Academic

1. Compare this chapter's definition of instructional supervision with at least four definitions of instructional supervision found in other supervision texts.

2. This chapter lists five tasks of instructional supervision. Rank these tasks according to what you consider their order of importance. Write a rationale for your ranking.

3. Several recent national studies have cited shortcomings in U.S. public education and have called for educational reforms. After reviewing one of these studies, discuss the major educational problems the study cites and the major reforms it recommends.

4. This chapter describes two ineffective schools: Finnie Tyler High School and Germando Elementary School. For both schools, discuss at least three instructional problems likely to result from the type of supervision practiced by the respective principals. Discuss how each probable instructional problem could be avoided or better managed through more appropriate supervision.

5. Review three journal articles that deal with the tasks, roles, or responsibilities of instructional supervision. Write a summary of each article.

Field

1. Prepare five questions to be asked during an interview with a school supervisor, focusing on problems the supervisor confronts in his or her attempts to facilitate instructional improvement and how he or she attempts to manage such problems. Conduct the interview and write a brief report on the supervisor's responses.

2. Arrange to visit a school that has a reputation for being exemplary. If possible, include visits to the school office, a few classrooms, the teachers' lounge, the cafeteria, and the school playground. Write a description of the learning climate of the school, including examples of how the type of supervision present in the school affects the learning climate.

3. Ask three supervisors and three teachers to list what they consider the five most important tasks of instructional supervision. Write a report comparing supervisors' perceptions and teachers' perceptions with the five tasks of supervision outlined in Chapter 1.

4. Ask two supervisors, two teachers, two students, and two parents to write one or two paragraphs on "What Makes a Successful School." After reviewing the responses, write a report discussing and comparing the respondents' perceptions.

5. Arrange a panel interview of four persons on the topic "What Makes a Successful School." The panel might include supervisors, teachers, parents, students, and perhaps business and community leaders. Record the discussion on a tape recorder.

Developmental

1. Write down any questions concerning instructional supervision that you have raised while reading Chapter 1. Refer to these questions as you read appropriate chapters in the remainder of this book.

2. Review Figure 1.1 and the model of instructional supervision it implies. As you continue to explore this book and other readings in supervision, begin to formulate your own proposed model of educational supervision.

3. Begin a file (to be kept throughout your reading of this book) on knowledge, skills, and procedures gained from the text and related activities that can be used by you as a supervisor—either now or in the future—to help teachers improve their instructional performance.

REFERENCES

Bernauer, J. 2002. Five keys to unlock continuous school improvement. *Kappa Delta Phi Record, 38*(2), 89–92.

Bernstein, E. 2004. What teacher evaluation should know and be able to do: A commentary. *NAASP Bulletin, 88,* 80–88.

Bryk, A., and Schneider, B. 2003. Trust in schools: A core resource for school reform. *Educational Leadership, 60*(6), 40–45.

Calhoun, E. F. 2002. Action research for school improvement. *Educational Leadership, 59*(6), 18–24.

Glickman, C. D. 1993. *Renewing America's schools: A guide for school-based action.* San Francisco, CA: Jossey-Bass.

Glickman, C. D. 1998a. Educational leadership for democratic purpose: What do we mean? *The International Journal of Leadership in Education, 1*(1), 45–53.

Glickman, C. D. 1998b. *Revolutionizing America's schools.* San Francisco: Jossey-Bass.

Glickman, C. D. 1999. A response to the discourse on democracy: The dangerous retreat. *The International Journal of Leadership in Education, 2* (1), 43–46.

Glickman C. D. 2003. *Holding sacred ground: Courageous leadership for democratic schools.* San Francisco: Jossey-Bass.

Gordon, S. P. (Ed.). 1995, April. *Newsletter of the Instructional Supervision Special Interest Group of the American Educational Research Association.*

Gordon, S. P. 1997. Has the field of supervision evolved to a point that it should be called something else? *Yes.* In J. Glanz and R. F. Neville (Eds.), *Educational supervision: Perspectives, issues, and controversies* (pp. 114–123). Norwood, MA: Christopher-Gordon Publishers.

Gordon, S. P. 2001. The good school. *Florida Journal of Educational Leadership, 1*(2), 13–15.

Ingersoll, R. 2003. *Who controls teachers' work: Power and accountability in America's schools.* Cambridge, MA: Harvard University Press.

Keedy, J. L., and Simpson, D. S. 2002. Principal priorities, school norms, and teacher influence: A study of sociocultural leadership in the high school. *Journal of Educational Administration and Foundations, 16*(1), 10–41.

MacKenzie, D. E. 1983. Research for school improvement: An appraisal of some recent trends. *Educational Researcher, 12*(4), 8.

Scheurich, J. J. 1998. The grave dangers in the discourse on democracy. *The International Journal of Leadership in Education, 1*(1), 55–60.

SUGGESTED READINGS

Glanz, J., and Neville, R. (Eds.). 1997. *Educational supervision: Perspectives, issues, and controversies.* Norwood, MA: Christopher Gordon.

Glickman, C. D. (Ed.). 1992. *Supervision in transition.* Alexandria, VA: Association for Supervision and Curriculum Development.

Gordon, S. P. 1992. Paradigms, transitions, and the new supervision. *Journal of Curriculum and Supervision, 8*(1), 62–76.

Pajak, E. 1993. Conceptions of supervision and leadership: Change and continuity. In Gordon Cawelti (Ed.), *Challenges and achievements of American education.* 1993 ASCD Yearbook. Alexandria, VA: Association for Supervision and Curriculum Development.

Sergiovanni, T. J., and Starratt, R. J. 1993. *Supervision: A redefinition.* New York: McGraw-Hill.

Sullivan, S., and Glanz, J. 2005. *Supervision that improves teaching: Strategies and techniques.* Thousand Oaks, CA: Corwin Press.

Waite, D. 2000. Identity, authority, and the heart of supervision. *International Journal of Educational Reform, 9*(4), 282–291.

part two
Knowledge

P art II examines the prerequisite knowledge for supervision. Chapter 2 will consider the pessimistic news—why schools are typically ineffective. The causes of ineffectiveness will be traced to the teaching career and the school environment. Chapter 3 will explain the optimistic news found in school research on characteristics of successful schools, with particular attention to those work environment factors within the province of supervision. Chapter 4 will explain how optimal adult development contrasts with the teaching career. Chapter 5 will look at how supervisory practices might respond to helping teachers develop and eliminate the causes of ineffectiveness. While moving from pessimism to optimism to realism, we will be riding through highly explosive grounds. Reactions of delight, anger, chagrin, hope, and disagreement are to be expected as current research challenges us to rethink current supervisory practices.

chapter 2

The Norm
Why Schools
Are as They Are

Dan Lortie (1986) wrote about the concept of structural strain, describing teachers of today who still work under school conditions of long ago (see Kottkamp, Provenzo, and Cohn, 1986). He and others have studied the work environment of schools and how work conditions promote or inhibit teacher development and instructional improvement. Our eyes must be wide open as we examine historical aspects of schools, teachers, and leadership. We must acknowledge that schools cannot be left alone to do business as usual, if we are serious about lasting instructional improvement.

The Work Environment or Culture of Schools

The study of values, beliefs, myths, rituals, symbols, heroes, shamans, and storytellers in organizations is well documented in the literature (Deal, 1985; Bolman and Deal, 2002). It may seem technically incorrect to apply the term *culture* to professional settings; the term is appropriated from the anthropological studies of largely intact and isolated communities of people. However, the concept of culture helps us reexamine schools as places of human community with peculiar histories and stories. When we grasp the underlying values of our particular school as a work environment, we can consciously act to reshape the organization into a purposeful collection of individuals who believe that schools are for students, for learning, and for improvement rather than for insularity, self-protection, and complacency.

How does it happen that in the same school district, teachers in two schools view their work so differently from each other? In Meadow Valley Middle School, teachers come to school within 15 minutes of the required arrival time and leave school 15 minutes after the last bell. If a teacher arrives earlier or stays later, other teachers' questions and glances make that teacher feel as if he or she shouldn't be working more than the required time. To do so is to violate an unspoken norm that teachers have come to accept about the proper amount of time to spend in school. Yet, one and a half miles across town, at the other middle school in the same district, the norms about proper time are different. At Mountain View Middle School, teachers are in their classrooms 45 minutes ahead of time, sharing coffee with each other, organizing materials, and conferring with individual students. One hour after school each day, the majority of staff are still there, working industriously in their own rooms, conducting tutorials, calling parents, and checking on tomorrow's plans. If a teacher arrives later or leaves earlier, the questions and glances of other teachers make him or her feel that a taboo is being violated.

Teachers in both schools work under the same district regulations, yet their expectations about work in their particular school are quite different. Why is this so? How does this come about? What have been the enduring norms of schools and how have they been established? The answers to these questions are quite important if we are to know how to intervene in our own schools so as to minimize resistance and capitalize on school beliefs that give impetus to student learning.

The Legacy of the One-Room Schoolhouse

Discussing the present work environment of schools without discussing the one-room schoolhouse would be comparable to talking about issues in Western democracies without acknowledging the Magna Carta. Much of what exists in beliefs and expectations about schools can be traced to the idyllic-looking, clapboard, one-room schoolhouses of pioneer times. The teacher was responsible for the total instruction of all students, the maintenance of the building, keeping the stove filled with wood, and cleaning the floors. Our first schoolteachers were seen as working in an honorable but menial profession, poorly paid but second only to the preacher in prestige (Lortie, 1975).

In the one-room schoolhouse, the teacher was responsible for all that transpired within its four walls; therefore, collective action in a school was automatic. What the teacher wanted to do about curriculum and instruction was what the school did! This legacy of independence, isolation, and privatization of teaching remains alive and well in many schools today. Instead of having physically separated one-room schoolhouses, we often see the one-room schoolhouses repeated every few yards down a school corridor. Each teacher sees his or her students, within the four walls, as his or her own school. Although the old one-room school is physically gone, it still holds a pervasive grip on the minds and actions of many teachers and schools.

The sense of classrooms as being private places is in direct contrast to the research on norms of improving schools.

> Research suggests that the schools with the greatest student learning going on are those which do not isolate teachers, but instead encourage professional dialogue and collaboration. Teaching in effective schools is a collective, rather than individual enterprise. (Freiberg and Knight, 1987, p. 3)

The one-room schoolhouse of pioneer times has spawned a deep-seated institutional belief among educators that is characterized by isolation, psychological dilemmas, routine, inadequate induction of beginning teachers, lack of career stages, lack of professional dialogue, lack of involvement in school decisions, lack of a shared technical culture, and conservatism. Many educators accept that these characteristics are simply part of a school culture, and there is little doubt that they pervade the minds and beliefs of most teachers and administrators. However, instructional leaders question whether beliefs and practices acceptable in the past are appropriate for the present, when we need to initiate a new culture based on purposeful and collective beliefs about school, students, and teaching. Let's look at the characteristics of today's education that are derived from the one-room schoolhouse of bygone days.

Isolation

The isolation and individualism of teachers has been observed in all major studies of their work environment. As an example of this isolation, Dreeben (1973) noted:

> Perhaps the most important single property of classrooms, viewed from a schoolwide perspective, is their spatial scattering and isolation throughout school buildings; and because teachers work in different places at the same time, they do not observe each other working . . . the implications of this spatial isolation are far reaching. (p. 468)

Dreeben further wrote:

> Unlike hospitals and law firms, for example, where new recruits to medicine and law learn their trade as apprentices by performing work tasks of gradually increasing difficulty under close supervision, schools provide a less adequate setting—the classroom—for work and training activities to occur simultaneously. (p. 470)

As Dreeben pointed out, classrooms are set up structurally in such a way that teachers are difficult to supervise, do not receive feedback from others, and cannot work collaboratively. During a typical workday, a teacher will talk to only a few other adults—on the way to the classroom in the morning, for 20 minutes or so at lunch and recess, and at the end of the day on the way out of the building. While teaching, teachers in most schools are invisible to each other and lack any concrete knowledge of what other teachers are doing in their classrooms.

Sarason (1996) points out that *physical* teacher isolation can lead to *psychological* isolation:

> What does it mean to go through a work day with no sustained personal contact with another adult? Being and talking with children is not psychologically the same as being and talking with peers. . . . When one is almost exclusively with children—responsible for them, being vigilant in regard to them, "giving" to them—it must have important consequences. *One of the consequences is that teachers are psychologically alone even though they are in a densely populated setting.* It is not only that they are alone, but they adapt to being alone. (p. 133; emphasis in original)

Teachers who have experienced long-term psychological isolation tend to view their work environment as limited to *their* classroom, *their* students, and *their* teaching. Although their isolation was initially involuntary, over time they have adapted to and accepted the tradition of isolation (Sarason, 1996); they now resist opportunities for professional dialogue and collaboration with other teachers that might arise.

Psychological Dilemma and Frustration

The teacher's work environment is marked by incessant psychological encounters. In just a few minutes of observation, one might see a teacher ask a question, reply with a smile to a student's answer, frown at an inattentive student, ask a student to be quiet, put a hand on a student's shoulder, and begin to lecture. Teachers have thousands of such psychological encounters in a normal schoolday (Jackson, 1968). A look, a shrug, and a word all have intended meanings between teacher and students.

Each day an elementary teacher meets with 25 to 35 students for six and one-half hours. A secondary teacher meets with 100 to 150 students for five to seven 50-minute periods. All this human interaction takes place in a 900 square-foot room, where a teacher must instruct, manage, discipline, reinforce, socialize, and attend to multiple occurrences. This crowded professional life makes teachers wish for smaller classes to reduce the psychological demand of constant decision making. Sarason (1996) described this incessant demand as a psychological dilemma:

> The teacher feels, and is made to feel, that one's worth as a teacher will be judged by how much a class learns in a given period of time. The strong feeling that teachers have about the complexity of their tasks stems from the awareness that they

are expected to bring their children (if not all, most) to a certain academic level by a time criterion in regard to which they have no say. Faced with numbers and diversity of children and the pressure to adhere to a time schedule presents the teacher not with a difficult task but an impossible one. *I say impossible because I have never met a teacher who was not aware of and disturbed by the fact that he or she had not the time to give to some children in the class the kind of help they needed.* (p. 187; emphasis in original)

To maintain their own sanity in the face of an overload of psychological encounters and an inability to attend to the psychological needs of each student in a confined and regulated workplace, teachers often cope by routinizing classroom activity. The classroom routine for students becomes similar to the outside routine for teachers. For example, a science teacher might have students listen to a 20-minute presentation, followed by a 10-minute question-and-answer period and then by 20 minutes of seatwork. An elementary teacher might have three reading groups who rotate to him or her for 15 minutes each; each group reads aloud, responds to teacher questions, and then does worksheets. By routinizing what happens within the classroom, a teacher avoids making hundreds of decisions. The routinization of teaching allows the teacher to avoid the inherent conflict between being overwhelmed psychologically by the responsibility for teaching a large number of students, and being aware of neglecting the personal needs of individual students. In interpersonal terms, teaching closely resembles clinical psychology, but it takes place in an environment more like that of factory production.

Routine

The routine of the teaching day is imposed by administrative fiat, school board policy, and state guidelines. Every classroom teacher is required to be at school before students enter and to remain until they have departed. In primary or elementary schools, a teacher has specific times for recess and lunch, as well as approximate time allocations for teaching a given subject (for example, 45 minutes for reading, 30 minutes for mathematics, 30 minutes twice a week for social studies). The teacher is assigned a certain number of students and has responsibility for them for the entire day and school year. He or she is expected to remain physically in the assigned classroom for the entire schoolday, with the exception of recess, lunch, or special classes. Outside the classroom, teachers also have scheduled responsibilities for lunch, recess, and dismissal. In middle schools, junior high schools, and senior high schools, the schoolday is different from that of elementary schools but still has a set routine. A secondary teacher will have four to seven different classes of students meeting at specific times each day for an extended period (11, 18, or 36 weeks). Again, the teacher begins and dismisses each class at a prescribed time and has regular duties outside the classroom (for example, monitoring the lunchroom, halls, or bathrooms).

Regardless of grade level, teachers do not schedule their own time or determine the number or type of students. Unlike more autonomous professionals, teachers do not put up a shingle on the door, ask clients to arrange for appointments, or take Wednesday mornings off. Teachers do not have the right to make changes in their schedule. Imagine a teacher asking the school secretary to clear his or her schedule for several hours so he or she can attend to other business. School goes on, students keep coming, the bells keep ringing, and teachers cannot make individual readjustments of their professional time.

Of course, elementary and secondary teachers often do make readjustments within the assigned time, within their four walls, with their assigned students, and with instruction. School time, however, is imposed. Starting and ending times, numbers of students, physical locations for teaching, and extra duties are set for the duration, and a teacher has little control. The routines the school as a workplace imposes are more like those of the factory than like those of high-status professions. The punch-in, punch-out clock may not be visible in the entering hallway of the school, but nonetheless it exists.

Sarason (1996) raises a critical question concerning the effects of routine on teachers and students:

> *If teaching becomes neither terribly interesting nor exciting to many teachers, can one expect them to make learning interesting or exciting to children?* If teaching becomes a routine, predictable experience, does this not have inevitable consequences for life in the classroom? The model classroom does not allow me other than to conclude that children and teachers show most of the effects of routinized thinking and living. (p. 200; emphasis in original)

Inadequate Induction of Beginning Teachers*

Teaching has been a career in which the greatest challenge and most difficult responsibilities are faced by those with the least experience—a strange state of affairs indeed! Beginning teachers in many schools are faced with a number of environmental difficulties: inadequate resources, difficult work assignments, unclear expectations, a sink-or-swim mentality, and reality shock (Gordon, 1991; Gordon and Maxey, 2000; Colley, 2002; Johnson and Kardos, 2002). As we describe these difficulties, we invite you to reflect on your own first year of teaching and to recall if they were part of your entrance to the profession.

Inadequate Resources. If a teacher makes known that he or she will not be returning in the fall, then after the last day of school other teachers will often descend on the vacant classroom and remove materials that will be useful to them. Not only are instructional materials removed but also desks, tables, and chairs! In their place are put those discarded items and furniture that no one else wants. Additionally, teachers may jockey around for the more spacious, better lighted class-

---

*Parts of this section are adapted from Stephen P. Gordon, *How to Help Beginning Teachers Succeed,* pp. 1–6. Reprinted by permission of the Association for Supervision and Curriculum Development. Alexandria, VA. Copyright © 1991 by the Association for Supervision and Curriculum Development. All rights reserved.

rooms. Thus, for the incoming year, the neophyte teacher with the least amount of experience often steps into the physically least desirable classroom in the school, with discards for furniture and equipment, and few instructional materials.

Difficult Work Assignments. Experienced staff and administration will often arrange for the "problem" children and/or lowest-achieving groups of students to be assigned to the newest teacher. In addition, the least interesting and most difficult courses usually are assigned to beginners (Kurtz, 1983; Johnson, 2001; Stansbury, 2001). New teachers are often given larger classes and more duties than experienced teachers (Romatowski, Dorminey, and Van Voorhees, 1989; Birkeland and Johnson, 2002).

Unclear Expectations. A common complaint among first-year teachers is that they are never sure what is expected of them as professionals (Kurtz, 1983; Johnson and Kardos, 2002). Administrators, other teachers, parents, and students express conflicting expectations of the beginner, leaving the neophyte in a quandary about whose expectations he or she should try to meet. A failure to socialize novice teachers into a professional community leads to what Corcoran (1981) has called the "condition of not knowing" (p. 20).

Sink-or-Swim Mentality. For a variety of reasons, beginning teachers are left on their own to "sink or swim." Administrators and experienced teachers tend to view the first year of teaching as a necessary "trial by fire" through which all neophytes must pass. Many experienced colleagues are reluctant to provide assistance to beginning teachers. Some veterans think it is only fair that new teachers should pass through the same trials and tribulations that they navigated when they were beginners. Some see it as a process that "weeds out" weak teachers, allowing only the strong to survive. Other experienced teachers are reluctant to assist beginners because of the norms of individualism and privacy that pervade the school culture.

Beginners often are reluctant to ask the principal or colleagues for help when they are experiencing management or instructional problems. This is due to the fact that teaching is the only profession in which a novice is expected to assume the same (or more) responsibilities at the same level of competence as experienced colleagues. Novice teachers often do not ask for help because they fear that a request for assistance will call into question their professional competence. In fact, neophytes often go to great lengths to conceal their classroom problems (Newberry, 1978).

Reality Shock. Veenman defined *reality shock* as "the collapse of the missionary ideals formed during teacher training by the harsh and rude reality of classroom life" (1984, p. 143). Individuals tend to enter teaching with idealized visions of what it will be like. Classroom management problems, student learning difficulties, and the environmental difficulties already discussed tend to destroy those ideals rather quickly. Moreover, neophytes are faced with the numbing realization that they are unprepared to deal with the harsh realities of teaching. This realization can lead to disillusionment and professional paralysis (Corcoran, 1981).

Effects of Environmental Difficulties. The environmental problems just discussed can cause tremendous stress and eventually lead to physical and emotional problems. Novice teachers tend to have more negative attitudes about themselves, their teaching, their profession, and students at the end than at the beginning of their first year of teaching (Gordon, 1991). Between one-third and one-half of teachers drop out of the profession within their first seven years of teaching (Metropolitan Life, 1985), with up to 15 percent leaving each of the first two years (Schlechty and Vance, 1981). Many of the most promising teachers are the ones who leave the profession early in their careers (Harris and Collay, 1990; Schlechty and Vance, 1983). America's schools may need to hire 2.2 million teachers over the next several years to replace approximately two-thirds of the teaching profession (Barth, 2001). Finally, as a result of their initial negative experiences, many teachers who stay in the profession develop a survival mentality, a narrow set of teaching methods, and resistance to experimentation and change that may last throughout their teaching careers (Romatowski, Dorminey, and Van Voorhees, 1989; Huling-Austin, 1986).

In recent years many school districts have initiated beginning teacher assistance programs (sometimes called teacher induction programs) in an effort to address the problems discussed here. These programs often include the assignment of experienced teachers as mentors of novice teachers. Chapter 18 includes a description of a successful beginning teacher assistance program.

Inequity

The inequity between experienced and beginning teachers is not the only type of disparity often found in conventional districts and schools. Schools located in lower-income communities often are not provided the same resources as other schools in the same district. The physical facilities in low-income schools may be in ill repair and even present health and safety hazards. Class sizes often are larger than those in middle- or upper-class schools. Textbooks and instructional materials may be woefully out of date or nonexistent. Low-income schools may be shortchanged on human resources as well. Many teachers in low-income schools are teaching outside of their field (Ingersoll, 2002). New teachers often stay at low-income schools only until they are eligible to transfer to other schools, creating problems with faculty and school stability. The personnel problems in low-income schools often are blamed on the difficulty and frustration of teaching low-achieving students, but the major cause of the problem is that districts often provide neither sufficient resources and incentives to attract the most qualified teachers nor sufficient support to retain them.

Inequity for low-income, minority, and students in at-risk situations also can be a problem within conventional schools that include a diverse student body. Large percentages of low-income groups often are placed in remedial tracks where they miss out on the richer, higher-level curriculum taught to other students. In many conventional schools, there is little or no attempt to consider the culture or learning styles of minority students when designing curriculum, selecting instructional materials, or preparing lessons. Worse still, both unconscious and overt racism go unchallenged by supervisors and teachers in some schools. It may not be easy or comfortable for educators in conventional schools to critically examine inequity, but admitting the presence of inequity is the first step toward removing it from our schools.

Unstaged Career

More prestigious professions avoid such an abrupt transition from student to full professional. Physicians, lawyers, engineers, and scientists all experience several transition years of apprenticeship, internship, and junior membership on the job before they qualify for full rights and responsibilities in the profession.

This set of circumstances leads to the negative characteristic of the teaching profession that perhaps most significantly differentiates it from others—an unstaged career. More prestigious occupations have rigorous screening and requirements. Furthermore, they have a transitional or proving-ground stage; only when an aspirant has been judged competent by senior members does the junior member step into the next stage of the career, which provides high visibility, greater challenge, a substantial increase in salary, and responsibility for monitoring and judging the next wave of junior members. For example, a law school graduate must pass the bar exam and then serve as a clerk, as a legal aide, or as a junior member of a law firm. He or she works behind the scenes on writing and research that are credited to his or her superior. After proving competence over time, however, the lawyer then becomes a partner in a firm, a public prosecutor or defender, or an independent attorney. This movement brings visibility and stature in the profession and the right to have one's own apprentices to do the less challenging, less exciting work.

Teaching, on the other hand, has been unstaged from entry to exit. Education majors take courses, spend time in schools, perform as student teachers, and then graduate from college into their own classrooms as teachers. After that, no matter how many years they continue to teach, they do not move into another stage. The 20-year veteran teacher has the same classroom space, number of students, and requirements as the first-year teacher. Furthermore, for each year of experience, a teacher realizes a salary increase identical to that received by all others of comparable experience.

Lack of Dialogue about Instruction

Generally, people in schools do not talk about their work—teaching—with each other. DeSanctis and Blumberg (1979) found that the length of instruction-related discussion among teachers in a typical schoolday in a high school in New York was two minutes. Little's (1982) study of schools, Rosenholtz's (1985) review of effective schools, and Pajak and Glickman's (1987) study of 15 exemplary elementary and secondary schools in three improving districts pointed to one essential dimension of successful schools: Professionals constantly talk with each other, in a problem-solving, action-oriented way, about teaching. This talk is generated through faculty and committee meetings, in-service workshops, observations and conferences, faculty lounge contacts, and other informal occasions. This talk is of a specific nature: teaching and learning of students. Of course, teachers talk with each other in all schools, but the talk is of a more social nature—telling stories about students, parents, administrators, community, and school events.

For teachers to talk often and seriously with each other about the core of their job—instruction and curriculum—is a rarity in many schools. Time is not planned for it to occur. Faculty meetings are information giving, and when school concerns are raised, they are often deflected to noninstructional matters such as schedules, district policies, extracurricular responsibilities, and building maintenance.

The public school as a work institution is unique in that a collection of adults can be employed as professionals within the same physical setting, with a common responsibility for providing their particular services to the same group of clients (students), and not be frequently and intensively engaged with each other in discussions on how to improve their services. Again, the lack of such dialogue is related to the one-room schoolhouse legacy, which accepts isolation, privacy, and lack of career stages as the norms of teaching.

Lack of Involvement in Schoolwide Curriculum and Instructional Decisions

If teachers don't see each other at work, don't talk with each other about their work, and see teaching as what goes on within their own four walls, it is not surprising that they are not given the opportunity, time, or expectations to be involved in decisions about curriculum and instruction beyond their four walls. Goodlad's (1984) study of schooling found that teachers' involvement in decisions about curriculum and instruction was virtually nil. Blumberg (1987) has referred to one of the basic problems with public schools as "situations premised on having mature, competent adults as employees, yet treating these same adults as children when it comes to deciding and operationalizing their work." Boyer (1983) has been even more adamant, referring to schools as impoverished intellectual climates for adults. The norm in most schools is that teachers are not expected to contribute experience, knowledge, and wisdom to decisions about the common good of educating students.

Lack of a Shared Technical Culture

Colleagues within a shared technical culture possess common purpose, expertise, and methods for analyzing and solving problems. They have developed sophisticated performance standards and communicate through a shared technical language. Imagine that a team of surgeons is about to perform a heart transplant operation. Each member of the team shares extensive knowledge of the cardiovascular system as well as state-of-the-art surgical procedures that will be used during the operation. The purpose of the surgery, as well as the technical means for achieving that purpose, are clear to each team member. Both in planning and performing the operation, the surgeons communicate in a complex technical language, much of which would be difficult for a layperson to understand. During the operation, the surgeons receive precise feedback from advanced technology and each other on the patient's condition. Should complications arise during the operation, the surgeons will rely on their expertise and each other to analyze the problem and take corrective action. The patient's survival is never assured, but the shared technical culture of the surgical team greatly enhances the patient's chances for recovery.

Unlike advanced professional communities, most schools are not characterized by shared technical cultures. Isolation, lack of dialogue, inadequate induction, and lack of involvement in schoolwide decisions all inhibit the development of such cultures among teachers. Based on his classic sociological study of schools and teachers, Lortie's (1975) description of school culture is in sharp contrast to the shared technical culture we have been discussing.

> There is little "state of the art". . . . The image projected is more individualistic, teachers are portrayed as an aggregate of persons each assembling practices consistent with his experience and peculiar personality. It is not what "we the colleagues" know and share which is paramount, but rather what I have learned from experience. (p. 79)

Lortie concluded that the lack of a shared technical culture means that "the teacher's craft . . . is marked by the absence of concrete models for emulation, unclear lines of influence, multiple and controversial criteria, ambiguity about assessment timing, and instability in the product" (p. 136). Lortie's seminal research about nontechnical school cultures and their effects on teachers was carried out in the mid-1970s. Unfortunately, more recent studies have found that most schools still lack sophisticated technical cultures and are still characterized by unclear goals, uncertainty about what constitutes effective instruction, idiosyncratic teaching, and ambiguous assessment (Rosenholtz, 1989).

Conservatism

The lack of a shared technical culture and the resulting ambiguity and uncertainty foster teacher conservatism. One aspect of this conservatism is a set of restricted, teacher-centered instructional methods. After reviewing data from observations of more than 1,000 classrooms, John Goodlad (1984) concluded the following:

> The domination of the teacher is obvious in the conduct of instruction. Most of the time the teacher is engaged in either frontal teaching, monitoring, students' seat work, or conducting quizzes. Relatively rarely are students actively engaged in learning directly from one another or in initiating processes of interaction with teachers. When students work in smaller groups, they usually are doing the same thing side by side, and these things tend to be determined by the teacher. (pp. 123–124)

Beyond reliance on traditional teaching methods, less obvious aspects of conservatism can be observed in most schools, including the following:

- An emphasis on short-range rather than long-range instructional goals
- Satisfaction with successes with individual lessons, students, and projects rather than with the continuous growth of all students
- Reliance on personal experience rather than educational research
- Narrow limits on the types and degree of collegiality and collaboration in which teachers are willing to engage
- A reflexive resistance to curricular or instructional innovations

Such conservatism is not surprising considering the isolation and psychological dilemma found in the traditional school environment. The irony is that conservatism, which results largely from the other environmental problems we have described, tends to hinder efforts to solve those very same problems!

Blaming the Victim and Structural Strain

A Nation at Risk (National Commission on Education, 1983), a report highly critical of public education in the United States, intensified a tendency for politicians, policy makers, and the general public to blame educators for the low academic achievement of many K–12 students. This and similar national reports reinforced the perception that problems in public education were caused by incompetent, inconsiderate, and self-serving teachers and administrators. The general consensus among elected officials that public education was in deep trouble was not accompanied by a will to increase funding for teacher education, teacher pay, or school improvement. Rather, the solution of choice across the nation was legislation designed to control and monitor the work of educators and the curriculum taught to students. This "legislated learning" (Wise, 1988) includes state-mandated curriculum, statewide teacher evaluation systems, and high-stakes achievement tests.

Researchers on school reform and student learning are telling us loud and clear that we cannot improve education by simply legislating higher standards and higher stakes. To this point, policy makers do not appear to be listening. Moreover, none of the popular legislated reforms are aimed at improving the school as a culture or workplace. Thus, the problems described earlier in this chapter remain largely unaddressed. In fact, these problems are aggravated by the external control brought about by legislated reform and the diminishing ability of teachers to engage in professional decision making.

Either the work environment of schools must be altered or we must accept that, regardless of extrinsic rewards, schools are not the place for our best teachers and thinkers. Supervision of instruction can play a strong role in reshaping the work environment to promote norms of collegiality and collective action, or supervision can remain another control apparatus "to keep teachers in their place." We can then continue to blame the victims for not shaking the institutional chains that shackle every attempt to work together in the instructional interest of all students.

Viewing School Culture in the Context of the Larger Culture

Our discussion of legislated learning opens the door to consideration of how other forces in the larger culture affect schools, and how educators should respond to these forces. In one sense, of course, we want our public schools to serve our culture, inculcating students with democratic values, preparing them to be contributing members of society, and so forth. We would be naïve, however, if we did not realize that there are factors in our culture than can have negative effects on teachers and their students. Donald Thomas and William Bainbridge (2002), for example, have argued that there are a variety of public policies that harm children's education:

- Millions of children in the United States live in poverty and without proper health care, which prevents them from developing their full cognitive potential.
- Most U.S. schools are underfunded. Schools in low wealth states and districts are especially hard hit, with inadequate instructional materials, little technology, unsafe buildings, and less-qualified teachers.
- Poorly regulated child-care centers across the nation damage childrens' creativity and development.
- The federal government, although requiring special accommodations for students with disabilities, provides inadequate funding for such assistance.

Beyond harmful public policies, we must not forget that many of the social evils that have long victimized so many of our citizens are still present, and still harming our nation's children. These include racism, classism, sexism, homophobia, and religious prejudice, to name a few. We would be foolish to ignore the fact that these evils exist, not only in the larger culture, but also inside our schools (Weiner, 2003; Kao, 2004).

How should schools address the societal problems that impinge on our children's growth and development? There are increasing calls for educators to become more politically active regarding policy issues that affect student learning. Political action can start with local educators forming partnerships with parents, the community, nearby universities, and the corporate sector (Fullan, 1999). Political action might take the form of working with the media to assure accurate reporting on policy issues, or communicating concerns to state and national legislators (Biddle and Berliner, 2002). Perhaps the most effective means of political action for educators, not surprisingly, is educating fellow citizens and policy makers on critical issues that relate to teaching and learning. Some harmful policies, of course, will stay in place despite the best efforts of educators and their allies to bring about change. In these cases, educators must use their creativity to meet ill-advised government mandates in ways that will not interfere with quality curriculum and instruction.

Regarding the deeper societal problems of prejudice and discrimination, in the short term it is possible for schools to become oases of equity and social justice. However, this can happen only as a result of the school community critiquing its structures, curriculum, instruction, and assessment practices; continuously reflecting on the relationships and interactions of administrators, teachers, students and parents; and critically examining assumptions at the deepest levels of school culture. The school community must engage in continuous identification and analysis of aspects of the school culture that work against democratic learning and personal empowerment (Weiner, 2003).

In the long term, our schools can become society's primary vehicle for developing a more democratic and just society. Students can develop understanding and tolerance for others, and a commitment to democratic principles, the common good, and the well-being of all men and women. This can be accomplished through developing schools as moral communities characterized by democratic learning, with opportunities for applying that learning locally, and connecting it to communities across the nation and around the globe.

TO SUMMARIZE AND PROPOSE

If supervision is to improve instruction in a school, then it must be an active force that provides focus, structure, and time for matters of curriculum and instruction. Supervision is intended to reduce the norms of the one-room schoolhouse—isolation, psychological dilemma, routine, inadequate teacher induction, inverted beginner responsibilities, lack of career stages, and absence of shared technical culture—and increase the norms of public dialogue and action for the benefit of all students. If supervision is to improve instruction, it must reshape norms and beliefs about the work culture of schools.

PRACTITIONER REFLECTION

Peace as a New Environmental Norm

Cheryl Sirois, *Assistant Principal, Luling Junior High School*

As a child, my favorite hymn was *A Prayer to St. Francis.* I remember singing part of the refrain, "Let peace begin with me." I believed then and now that there was nothing more important than making it possible for people to live in harmony. The whole idea of being a school leader came about because of this dream of peace.

In third grade I noticed a boy in my class who was having a difficult time during our "round robin" reading time. I offered to help him during the silent reading time before lunch.

He agreed and started to read to me during this time. It seemed to help him be more comfortable when he was reading in class. This memory returned to me when I saw him again when I was in college. He introduced me to his group of friends as the "girl who taught him how to read." The words impacted me immediately, even though I knew I did not "teach him to read." I know that I did help him and he obviously appreciated my efforts. I helped give him some peace when he was truly unsure of his abilities as a reader, and that allowed him time and space to practice and become a better reader. On that day he delivered to me the peace of mind that, at some level, I could impact other's lives and that impact could be long lasting. I decided to make the dream I had flirted with throughout my life come true—I would change my major and become a teacher.

As a teacher, I wanted to give students the peace required for learning by caring about them and meeting their needs. As I entered the profession, I started hearing teachers complain about students, parents, and administration. I felt I could create a greater peace for students and teachers by becoming an administrator. Students, teachers, support staff, parents, and the community can all be affected positively by an administrator who creates the peace necessary for true dialogue and collaboration. The instructional improvement process must include providing teachers with a safe environment for examining their own beliefs, collaborating with other teachers to develop a common vision, and taking risks as they work toward making that vision a reality.

Teachers need peace in order to engage their hearts and minds in a continuous, long-term improvement process. Improvement is more likely to happen if we change incrementally and maintain a high level of emotional and professional support throughout the change process. To create "peaceful" change we can collaboratively make selective change, see what effects the change has on the educational environment, tweak the change if necessary, and then move on to the next change.

I am in education for the good of all children. I believe that we supervisors cannot take the weight of instructional improvement on our individual shoulders, but as a team working with teachers we can make great gains in school performance while providing each other peace along the way. Then we will have our own peace, knowing that we are effective educators, knowing that we are improving continuously, and knowing that we are doing the best we can for our students.

EXERCISES

Academic

1. Choose a period of American history (for example, the colonial period or the early twentieth century) and research the state of teaching as a profession during that era. Prepare a report comparing the role, functions, working conditions, and status of teachers in the selected era and the current era.

2. Research the state of teaching as a profession in an industrialized nation other than the United States. Prepare a report comparing the role, functions, working conditions, and status of teachers from the selected nation with those of U.S. teachers.

3. The chapter lists routine, psychological dilemma, and isolation as three factors associated with the work environment of teachers. Interview a supervisor about the work environment of teachers in his or her school. How does he or she attempt to improve conditions? Write a summary of your interview.

4. In most school systems, a teacher's career is unstaged. Outline a plan for a staged teaching career. Include recommended entry requirements, screening methods, a description of an apprenticeship period (other than student teaching), and suggested requirements and rewards for promotion to full membership in the teaching profession. Suggest ways in which teachers who have attained full professional status can be presented with new challenges and rewarded for meeting such challenges.

5. Write an autobiographical essay in which you discuss your experiences with the daily routine, psychological encounters, and isolation you have confronted as a teacher or observed as a visitor in a school.

Field

1. Interview three teachers of various experience levels about why they chose teaching as a career. Write a report that includes a brief description of each teacher, a summary of his or her reasons for becoming an educator, and a comparison of the various teachers' responses.

2. Conduct interviews with a veteran and a first-year teacher in which you ask them to compare their written job descriptions with the duties they actually carry out. During both interviews, write out a list of duties the teacher carries out that are not listed on the formal job description. Prepare a report summarizing your findings and drawing conclusions.

3. Interview a member of a graded profession (physician, attorney, college professor, scientist, engineer, or the like) who has reached full professional status. Ask the professional about the stages and challenges he or she had to pass through to attain such status, the extent to which having to pass through these grades increased his or her professional performance, and the rewards of reaching full professional status. Prepare a report summarizing the interviewee's responses and giving your opinion of whether aspects of such a graded career could be adapted to the teaching profession.

4. Interview a veteran instructor or supervisor in a teacher preparation program. Ask him or her to compare students who are preparing for a career in education today with teacher candidates of 10 years ago in terms of academic preparation, performance, and commitment to a teaching career. If the interviewee perceives significant differences between present and past teacher candidates, ask for his or her perceptions of why such differences exist and how they are likely to affect the future of education. Prepare a report summarizing the interview and drawing your own conclusions.

5. Interview an individual who was a teacher for at least five years and voluntarily left teaching for a new career. Request (a) his or her reasons for entering the teaching field, (b) his or her reasons for leaving teaching, and (c) a comparison of the teaching profession with his or her present career. Prepare a written report on the interview.

Developmental

1. Begin a diary of how the major characteristics of your work environment affect your job performance over a period of time.

2. Begin a notebook of ideas for breaking up the inertia of the teaching profession and environment. Over time, note your own ideas and also record the ideas and actions of teachers and supervisors you observe attempting to counter the routine, psychological dilemma, and isolation of the teaching environment. Include ideas for promoting teacher autonomy and encouraging teachers and supervisors to focus on a cause beyond oneself.

REFERENCES

Barth, R. S. 2001. Teacher leader. *Phi Delta Kappan, 82*(6), 443–449.

Biddle, B. J., and Berliner, D. C. 2002. Unequal school funding in the United States. *Educational Leadership, 59*(8), 48–59.

Birkeland, S., and Johnson, S. M. 2002. What keeps new teachers in the swim? *Journal of Staff Development, 23*(4), 18–21.

Blumberg, A. 1987. *A discussion on the effects of local, state, and federal mandates on supervisory practices.* Annual conference of the Council of Professors of Instructional Supervision, Philadelphia, November.

Bolman, L. G., and Deal, T. E. 2002. Leading with soul and spirit. *School Administrator, 59*(2), 21–26.

Boyer, E. L. 1983. *High school: A report on secondary education in America.* New York: Harper & Row.

Colley, A. C. 2002. What can principals do about new teacher attrition? *Principal, 81*(4), 22–24.

Corcoran, E. 1981. Transition shock: The beginning teacher's paradox. *Journal of Teacher Education, 32*(3), 19–23.

Deal, T. E. 1985. The symbolism of effective schools. *Elementary School Journal, 85*(5), 601–620.

DeSanctis, M., and Blumberg, A. 1979. *An exploratory study into the nature of teacher interactions with other adults in the schools.* Paper presented at the annual meeting of the American Educational Research Association, San Francisco, April.

Dreeben, R. 1973. The school as a workplace. In R. M. Travers (Ed.), *Second handbook of research on teaching* (pp. 450–473). Chicago: Rand McNally.

Freiberg, H. J., and Knight, S. 1987. *External influences of school climate.* Paper presented at the

annual meeting of the American Educational Research Association, Washington, DC, April.

Fullan, M. 1999. *Change forces: The sequel. Philadelphia.* Philadelphia: Falmer Press.

Goodlad, J. I. 1984. *A place called school.* New York: McGraw-Hill.

Gordon, S. P. 1991. *How to help beginning teachers succeed.* Alexandria, VA: Association for Supervision and Curriculum Development.

Gordon, S. P., and Maxey, S. 2000. *How to help beginning teachers succeed.* Alexandria, VA: Association for Supervision and Curriculum Development.

Harris, M. M., and Collay, M. P. 1990. Teacher induction in rural schools. *Journal of Staff Development, 11*(4), 44–48.

Huling-Austin, L. 1986. What can and cannot reasonably be expected from teacher induction programs. *Journal of Teacher Education, 37*(1), 2–5.

Ingersoll, R. M. 2002. Deprofessionalizing the teaching profession: The problem of out-of-field teaching. *Educational Horizons, 80*(1): 28–31.

Jackson, P. W. 1968. *Life in classrooms.* New York: Holt, Rinehart & Winston.

Johnson, H. R. 2001. Administrators and mentors: Keys in the success of beginning teachers. *Journal of Instructional Psychology, 28*(1), 44–49.

Johnson, S. M., and Kardos, S. M. 2002. Keeping new teachers in mind. *Educational Leadership, 59*(6), 12–16.

Kao, G. 2004. Social capital and its relevance to minority and immigrant populations. *Sociology of Education, 77*(2): 172–175.

Kottkamp, R. B., Provenzo, E. F., Jr., and Cohn, M. M. 1986. Stability and change in a profession: Two decades of teacher attitudes. 1964–1984. *Kappan, 67*(8), 559–567.

Kurtz, W. H. 1983. Identifying their needs: How the principal can help beginning teachers. *NASSP Bulletin, 67*(459), 42–45.

Little, J. W. 1982. Norms of collegiality and experimentation: Workplace conditions of school success. *American Educational Research Journal, 19*(3), 325–340.

Lortie, D.C. 1975. *School teacher: A sociological study.* Chicago: University of Chicago Press.

Lortie, D.C. 1986. Teacher status in Dade County: A case of structural strain. *Kappan, 67*(8), 568–575.

Metropolitan Life. 1985. *Former teachers in America.* New York: Author.

National Commission on Education. 1983. An open letter to the American people. A nation at risk: The imperative for educational reform. *Education Week, 2*(31), 12.

Newberry, J. 1978. The barrier between beginning and experienced teachers. *The Journal of Educational Administration, 16*(1), 46–56.

Pajak, E., and Glickman, C. 1987. *Dimensions of improving school districts.* Presentation to the annual conference of the Association for Supervision and Curriculum Development, New Orleans, March.

Romatowski, J. A., Dorminey, J. J., and Van Voorhees, B. 1989. *Teacher induction programs: A report.* (ERIC ED 316 525)

Rosenholtz, S. J. 1985. Effective schools: Interpreting the evidence. *American Journal of Education, 93*(3), 352–388.

Rosenholtz, S. J. 1989. *Teachers' workplace: The social organization of schools.* New York: Longman.

Sarason, S. B. 1996. *Revisiting the culture of the school and the problem of change.* New York: Teachers College Press.

Schlechty, P. C., and Vance, V. S. 1981. Do academically able teachers leave education? The North Carolina case. *Kappan, 63*(2), 106–112.

Stansbury, K. 2001. What new teachers need. *Leadership, 30*(3), 18–21.

Thomas, M. D., and Bainbridge, W. L. 2002. No child left behind: Facts and fallacies. *Phi Delta Kappan, 83,* 781–782.

Veenman, S. 1984. Perceived problems of beginning teachers. *Review of Educational Research, 54*(2), 143–178.

Weiner, L. 2003. Why is classroom management so vexing to urban teachers? *Theory into Practice, 42*(4): 305–312.

Wise, A. E. 1988. The two conflicting trends in school reform: Legislated learning revisited. *Kappan, 69*(5), 328–333.

SUGGESTED READINGS

Gordon, S. P., and Maxey, S. 2000. *How to help beginning teachers succeed.* Alexandria, VA: Association for Supervision and Curriculum Development.

Hargreaves, A. 1994. *Changing teachers, changing times: Teachers work and culture in the postmodern age.* London: Cassel.

Reyes, P. (Ed.). 1990. *Teachers and their workplace.* Newbury Park, CA: Sage.

Sarason, S. B. 1996. *Revisiting "The culture of the school and the problem of change."* New York: Teachers College Press.

Sashkin, M., and Walberg, H. 1993. *Educational leadership and school culture.* Berkeley, CA: McCutchan.

Smith, S. C. 1990. *The collaborative school: A work environment for effective instruction.* Eugene, OR: ERIC Clearinghouse on Educational Management.

Waite, D., and Allen, D. 2003. Corruption and abuse of power in educational administration. *The Urban Review, 35*(4), 281–296.

Yee, S. M. 1990. *Careers in classroom: When teaching is more than a job.* New York: Teachers College.

Zehm, S. J., and Kottler, J. A. 1993. *On being a teacher.* Newbury Park, CA: Sage.

chapter 3

The Exception
What Schools Can Be

When we analyze the definitions of school success, we find great divergence in goals and practices. What do we mean by school success, and how do we measure it? Is the measure of school success short term—higher achievement scores on standardized basic-skills tests? Is school success measured by improved student attitudes toward learning, social behavior, displays of creative work, critical writing or thinking, attendance, grades, promotion, retention, or community or extracurricular participation? The instructional goals that a school sets and how these goals are measured reflect how the staff members collectively understand and prioritize their beliefs about education. A successful school is foremost an organization that defines good education for itself, through its goals and desired practices, and then engages in collective action to achieve that vision (Glickman, 1987).

Early Effective Schools Research

Beginning in the mid-1970s, research began to focus on individual schools that are exceptional, that consistently achieve results far superior to those of schools in general. In composition of student body, location, socioeconomic setting, and

37

per-pupil expenditure, these schools do not differ from schools in general. Yet whether they are in poor urban areas or in wealthy suburbs, they succeed while others fail.

Ronald Edmonds (1979), after discovering that the results of his own research were consistent with those of other independent investigations, was confident enough to predict that *all schools could be effective.*

> It seems to me, therefore, that what is left of this discussion are three declarative statements: (a) We can, whenever and wherever we choose, successfully teach all children whose schooling is of interest to us; (b) We already know more than we need to do that; and (c) Whether or not we do it must finally depend on how we feel about the fact that we haven't so far. (p. 22)

Edmonds conducted three different studies. His first study was of 2 inner-city schools in Detroit; the second was of 55 effective schools in the Northeast; and the third included 20 schools in inner-city New York. Edmonds's findings were consistent with those of other early effective schools studies. He found that effective schools were distinguished by the presence of:

- Strong leadership
- A climate of expectation
- An orderly but not rigid atmosphere
- Communication to students of the school's priority on learning the basics
- Diversion of school energy and resources when necessary to maintain priorities
- Means of monitoring student (and teacher) achievement

The Second Wave of Effective Schools Research

Beginning in the latter half of the 1980s a new wave of effective schools research was carried out. These new studies, relying on more sophisticated research designs and new statistical analysis techniques (Creemers, 1996), tended to result in longer lists of correlates than the early effects research (Mortimore et al., 1988; Levine and Lezotte, 1990; Teddlie and Stringfield, 1993). After reviewing "second wave" effective schools research generated in a number of countries, Austin and Reynolds (1990, pp. 168–174) reported the following characteristics of effective schools:

- Site management
- Leadership
- Staff stability
- Curriculum and instructional articulation and organization

- Staff development
- Maximized learning time
- Widespread recognition of academic success
- Parental involvement and support
- Collaborative planning and collegial relationships
- Sense of community
- Clear goals and expectations commonly shared
- Order and discipline

Although agreeing with the early effective schools research on the need for such things as strong leadership, order, and agreed upon priorities, the second wave of research introduced new correlates such as site-based management, professional development, parental involvement, and teacher collaboration and collegiality.

Context Studies in Effective Schools Research

Traditional effective schools research has been criticized for reporting characteristics common to effective schools while ignoring differences between schools from various contexts (Hannaway and Talbert, 1993). Examples of context include location (urban, suburban, rural), socioeconomic status (SES), students' ethnicity and race, and school level (elementary, middle, or high school).

Makedon (1992) has maintained that schools identified as effective have not closed the achievement *gap* between students of low and middle socioeconomic status. Cook, Semmel, and Gerber (1995) reported that in schools seeking to apply effectiveness research, general student achievement increased, but special education student achievement decreased. Pierce (1991) concluded that implementation of factors identified in effective schools research has failed to bring about significant achievement gains for language minority students. The fact that implementation of "traditional" effective schools correlates has often failed to raise the achievement of low-income (Gustafson, 2002), minority, and special needs students has led to effectiveness research aimed specifically at these groups. Context studies on schools with high-achieving, low-income, and minority students (Pierce, 1991; Scribner, 1999; Stedman, 1987) have identified a number of school characteristics, including:

- Respect for racial pluralism
- A culture of caring
- Basic skills supplemented with rich academic programs
- Shared governance involving leaders, teachers, parents, and students
- Professional development to help teachers address cultural and special needs
- Teaching aimed at preventing academic problems

Has Effective Schools Research Outlived Its Usefulness?

Soon after publication of the first effective schools studies, school districts across the nation began to plan and implement programs designed to apply the research to their own schools. By the early 1990s over half of the school districts in the United States were implementing programs based on effective schools research (Reynolds and Stoll, 1996). Such efforts are still going on today. Yet many educators have raised concerns about using the effective schools research as the basis of school reform. One concern is that effective schools have usually been identified by student scores on standardized literacy and mathematics tests, despite the fact researchers have warned against using such tests to judge a school's performance (Cuban, 1998). Another concern is that effective schools research is *correlational;* there is a significant positive correlation between the identified characteristics and the chosen measure of school effectiveness, but the research has not shown that these characteristics *cause* the effectiveness they have been associated with. Yet another problem with the effectiveness research is discussed by Hill (1998):

> School effectiveness research has not found a satisfactory way of dealing with the fact that schools and school education are essentially about growth, progress, and change. Researchers have been reduced to taking snapshots of phenomena, to focusing on achievement rather than rates of progress of students, and on measuring current status rather than charting change over time. (p. 428)

For these reasons as well as continuing problems in research design and methodology, many experts believe that effective schools research has outlived its usefulness and that it is time to base school reform efforts on a new research paradigm (Cuban, 1998; Hill, 1998; Slavin, 2002).

The Legacy of Effective Schools Research

Despite criticism of effects research, it has left a positive legacy (Taylor, 2002). It has disproven the earlier conclusions by Coleman, Jencks, and others that socioeconomic status determines student achievement and that schools and teachers have little effect on student learning. Larry Cuban (1998) has pointed out that basic values of effective schools reformers of the early 1970s—that all children can learn, the importance of academic achievement, the need for accountability—have now been adopted by those who make and influence public policy.

Joseph Murphy (1992) suggested that since effective schools correlates tend to change in different studies and contexts, educators need to move beyond a narrow interpretation of school effectiveness to a set of broad principles that underlie the various correlates. Murphy maintained that these principles constitute the real legacy of the effective schools research and include the following:

1. All students can learn.
2. Schools should focus on student outcomes and rigorously assess progress toward reaching those outcomes.
3. Schools should assume a fair share of the responsibility for student learning.
4. Schools should be structurally, symbolically, and culturally linked, providing for consistency and coordination throughout the school community (pp. 165–168).

Although the legacy of effective schools research is secure, the prevalent opinion of researchers is that this body of research, *by itself,* provides an insufficient basis for school reform. Additional research beyond the effects studies is necessary. This leads us to the topic of school improvement research.

From Effective Schools to School Improvement

Although effective schools research is still being carried out, over the last several years *school improvement research* has taken center stage. Before reviewing the research in this area, let's discuss differences between the two types of research. As noted by Bennett and Harris, effects research asks the question "What do effective schools look like?" and school improvement research asks "How do schools improve over time?" Effects research examines inputs, throughputs, and outputs and emphasizes organizational structure, whereas school improvement research is focused on school culture and the change process (Bennett and Harris, 1997; Bernauer, 2002; Fullan, 2002, 2005; Harris, 2002; Rust and Friedus, 2001). Effects research takes statistical snapshots of performance measures and their correlates, whereas school improvement research is concerned with long-term growth, often examined through case studies (Bollen, 1996). In short, school improvement research is concerned with the *how* of successful schools. Although the specific characteristics of successful school improvement efforts vary somewhat across the research on school improvement (see Hopkins, Ainscow, and West, 1994; Joyce, Calhoun, and Hopkins, 1999; Levine, 1991; Little, 1982; Rosenholtz, 1989; Teddlie and Stringfield, 1993; Wasley, Hampel, and Clark, 1997), a consensus has emerged on the most important factors. Figure 3.1 provides a composite list of these characteristics.

After reviewing both the effective schools and the school improvement research, it becomes clear that these are not entirely separate types of research. Rather, effects research has informed and provided a foundation for school

- Varied sources of leadership, including teacher leadership
- Consideration of individual school context and culture
- Parental involvement
- Shared vision and continuous revisioning
- External and internal support, including time, moral, and technical support
- Focus on teaching and learning
- Ongoing professional development, including continuous analysis, reflection, and growth
- Instructional dialogue
- Teacher collaboration
- Democratic, collective inquiry, including action research
- Integration of improvement efforts into a coherent program
- Data-based feedback on improvement efforts using multiple measures

FIGURE 3.1 *Characteristics of Improving Schools*

improvement research. Together, the two types of studies provide us with a knowledge base for developing successful schools.

Studies have pointed out that a successful school can vary considerably from other successful schools in the degree of community involvement, school leadership, and change initiation (Hallinger and Murphy, 1987; Purkey and Smith, 1983; Davies, 2002). There is ample research on school improvement to inform us of the different paths, factors, and actors of school success. However, we can say with confidence that participants in successful schools show a remarkable tendency to see themselves as being involved in "a moral equivalent of war" or "a cause beyond oneself."

A Cause Beyond Oneself

Later chapters on observation, direct assistance, professional development, and curriculum development will explain how a supervisor can use the research on effective classroom practice with teachers. For now, however, the outside-the-classroom but within-the-school factors that correlate with or predict school success provide the more significant issue. *Every major research study on successful schools has noted the organizational phenomenon of collective action, agreed-on purpose, and belief in attainment* (Pratzner, 1984). On the other hand, every major research study on ineffective schools has noted an absence of such purpose. Successful schools do not happen by accident: Supervision is the force that shapes the organization into a productive unit.

Clearly, one characteristic of successful schools is that each teacher has "a cause beyond oneself." Teachers do not view their work as simply what they carry out within their own four walls. In successful schools, teachers see themselves as part of the larger enterprise of complementing and working with each other to educate students. For successful schools, education is a collective rather than an individual enterprise.

Connecting School Improvement to the Local Community and Larger Society

Successful school improvement efforts extend beyond school walls. School improvement needs to connect to the community in a number of ways. First, it is important that parents and other community members be involved in planning, implementing, and assessing school improvement efforts. The days of limiting parent and community involvement in schools to parent-teacher conferences, bake sales, and chaperoning field trips quickly is coming to an end. Parents and community members need to be involved in decision making about the school's mission and goals, and in helping educators and students reach improvement goals. This shared decision making can be accomplished in a number of ways, including parent and community representatives on school councils, open forums with parent and community members, and parent surveys on school needs and improvement efforts (Doyle, 2004; Sanders and Lewis, 2005).

Successful schools do not treat parents and community members as outsiders. Rather, parents are welcome in successful schools and invited to participate in a variety of school and classroom activities. Many successful schools now include parent councils, as well as parent centers coordinated and staffed by parents and serving as hubs for parent and community involvement in the school. In addition to sharing school turf and decision making with parents, educators need to interact with parents and families on a regular basis in community centers, neighborhoods, and homes. Many parents are unable to visit schools on a regular basis because of work schedules, transportation problems, or anxiety based on past negative experiences with schools. Educators need to reach out to parents in such circumstances, to collaborate not only in the education of individual children but also in decisions about school improvement.

It is important to connect school improvement and community development. Davies (2002) argued that "school success and community success are linked. Public schools are seldom able to be much better than neighborhoods and surrounding communities. Neighborhoods and communities are seldom able to stay healthy and attractive without good schools" (p. 392). Schools and community agencies can coordinate community services such as health care, social services, recreation programs, and community activities. Proponents of "full-service community schools" propose that schools become hubs of education *and* community services (Dryfoos, 2002).

According to Arrington and Moore (2001), "When we purposely involve students in learning experiences that stretch far beyond the school walls into the community and the world, we provide motivation and relevance that can make a difference in children achieving school success" (p. 56). A number of teaching and learning models that connect students to the community and larger society are being incorporated into school improvement efforts. Three such models are service learning, place-based learning, and democratic learning.

Service Learning. The service learning model integrates the curriculum with community service, and occurs only when service is accompanied by academic learning. In service learning, students analyze community issues, choose a service project, plan activities, perform the service, and engage in individual and group reflection on the project (Arrington and Moore, 2001). Service learning can take place within any content area, and often cuts across several content areas.

Place-Based Learning. The place-based learning model uses social, cultural, and natural aspects of the students' local environment as the context for learning. Smith (2002) has provided a snapshot of place-based learning:

> When Environment Middle School students go to Brookside Wetlands . . . their water samples and inventories of macro invertebrates, collected and compiled over the course of the year, become part of a report on the Portland's Bureau of Environmental Studies. The project allows for a direct rather than mediated experience of the world. The water is cold—the mud, slippery. And when the class spots two geese threatening with outstretched necks a third who tries to cross the invisible boundary that marks their territory, everyone watches in silence. (p. 31)

In place-based learning, students produce rather than consume knowledge, teachers are co-learners and guides rather than instructors, and students solve real-world problems (Smith, 2002; Powers, 2004).

Democratic Learning. The democratic learning model asks students to integrate their self-concerns with concerns about the larger world and the common good. Students decide on a common theme, often dealing with race, class, gender, or issues of diversity. Within the common theme, small groups and individuals can develop their own questions and projects. The questions that students ask in democratic learning tend to focus on serious social issues, such as war and peace, the environment, and the family. As students explore issues, they engage in rigorous academic work, display high-level cognitive skills, show mutual respect, and build community (Beane, 2002; Marri, 2005).

The connections between school and community development recently were illustrated to one of the authors serving on a blue-ribbon panel asked to select the most outstanding school systems from a large number of nominated districts. The selection process included on-site visits to finalists' district offices as well as elementary, middle, and high schools. One topic the panel asked educators, parents, and community members in each district to discuss was school-community relationships. The panel was surprised that interviewees in the most outstanding districts and schools initially had significant difficulty answering this question. The reason interviewees gave for this difficulty was most interesting: The schools were such an integral part of the communities they served, and the communities were so closely associated with their schools, it was difficult to consider school and community as separate entities, thus difficult to talk about their "relationship"! The panel received this type of response in visits to outstanding schools in urban, suburban, and rural communities. The schools were considered the centers of their communities. The schools' educators felt a strong obligation to serve the communities in which they were located, and community members felt an equally strong obligation to serve their schools. In short, the educators, parents, and other community members the panel interviewed considered school and community development less as two separate processes to be linked and more as one and the same process.

The supervisor's role in connecting schools with their communities and the larger society should mirror the role of teachers in that same venture. The supervisor becomes a co-learner and facilitator as teachers, students, and communities explore ways to use partnership to improve student learning, develop communities, and, ultimately, improve society.

SUMMARY

Supervision must be viewed as developmental if schools are to become more successful. Supervision must not only respond to current teacher performance but also encourage greater involvement, autonomous thinking, and collective action by teachers. The first order of business for a supervisor is to build the staff into a team. In order to improve school instruction, a supervisor has to work with staff to create a professional togetherness. They must share a common purpose for their instruction and they must have confidence that their collective action will make a difference in their students' lives.

Gaining knowledge of successful schools and effective classrooms is only the first step in improving schools. Using such knowledge in one's own school demands skill and practice. Skill and practice flow from knowledge. We have seen that the research on school success converges on the concept of a cause beyond oneself or a belief in collective action. To use that knowledge, a supervisor needs further understanding about teaching and the teaching profession to understand why such a cause beyond oneself does not occur naturally in schools.

PRACTITIONER REFLECTION

A Case for Engaging Parents in School Improvement Initiatives

Gary Davison, *Principal, Settles Bridge Elementary School*

In this age of educational accountability, teachers, parents, and supervisors are looking for leadership that can propel students to higher levels of success. Many have hoped that increased student success will be brought about through a simple panacea. Educational "quick fixes" have set many teachers, supervisors, and policy makers on the search for "the solution." The holy grail of school improvement has yet to be found, but researchers (Davies, 2002; Lawrence-Lightfoot, 2003) have begun to identify ways that effective school leaders may engage parents and the community in school improvement. Improving schools use data every day to make instructional and curricular decisions for children. Here is how one school uses data gathered from parents to make decisions for children.

How Do We Engage Parents?

In our setting, parent involvement is a reality to be embraced. Understanding parents' perspectives is essential for us if we are to move forward toward our goals. We have found that input and knowledge are two variables parents require. Several endeavors have been instituted to best utilize parents' talents to meet collective ends. Our endeavors include focus groups, Parent Academy, surveys, neighborhood chats, and curricular planning sessions. Each of these strategies has a different purpose.

Parent Focus Groups. Parents are invited to attend focus groups on a variety of topics coordinated by the principal and the school leadership team. Each year, the school leadership team selects the agenda and topics to be covered. These topics are aligned with the school improvement plan for the year. Data from the focus groups are analyzed to identify themes and implications for the work of the school. These themes and implications are then shared with the school community at large to be used in planning and coordinating future initiatives. This involvement in the school program gives parents opportunities to be heard on topics that often are viewed as outside of their domain.

Parent Academy. Parents attend classes taught by the principal using school processes, curriculum, and education at large as the context. These classes meet once a week in the school and are open in regard to topics discussed. Needs assessments are mailed to participants prior to the first meeting and their suggestions are integrated into session agendas. Typical topics covered are reading instruction, standards-based reporting, educational trends, homework ideas for parents, school structure, and school procedures and policies. The outcome of Parent Academy has been improved collaboration among parents, principal, and teachers. Parents feel involved in the school and have a better understanding of the purpose of our efforts. As one parent recently wrote, "I now know how things are done administratively, how decisions are made, what special programs and technology are available, and how to handle common issues like homework, conflict resolution, and peer problems."

Surveys. Parents are sent surveys each year to assess the entire parent body on a variety of topics. Survey data, of course, are more general than focus group data. The benefit of surveys, compared to focus groups, is the wider participation. Survey data are compiled and analyzed along with the more in-depth focus group information. Surveys are viewed as another source of data to help generate wise decisions.

Neighborhood Chats. Neighborhood clubhouses are common gathering places in the community where we meet with families on "their turf" to discuss topical issues or just keep them informed. We take notes and disaggregate the data into the same form used during the previously mentioned focus groups. The intimate nature of these smaller settings provides warmth and builds trust. Parents are excited about our discussions, which have been well attended. Data generated have been helpful to our future planning.

Curriculum and Instruction Sessions. Parents are involved in long-term curriculum and instructional planning. They are consulted on the pace of instruction, efficacy of students, student engagement, and homework assignments. Additional topics include fund-raising and collaborations with PTA and other parent groups. "Buy-in" made possible by these sessions has made our 21st Century Classroom initiative a tremendous success. Parents, students, and teachers, for example, now are excited about integrating technology with writing and other content areas.

What Effects Have We Seen from Parent Engagement?

Parents have indicated they now have a better idea of how to assist their children's learning. Improved relationships with parents have meant less stress for all members of the school community. Parents have a better feeling when communicating with teachers, who they view as "on their side." When they feel included, parents are willing to stand up for the school's commitment to raise student-learning standards. This trust and commitment is invaluable, and well worth our school's effort to involve parents in the decision-making process!

EXERCISES

Academic

1. This chapter summarizes the results of several studies of successful schools but also suggests that the majority of schools are not successful. Prepare a report expressing your agreement or disagreement.

2. Review three journal articles that deal with research on successful schools. Based on these readings and your reading of the text, compile a composite list of probable characteristics of a successful school.

3. Read single chapters dealing with the same topic from two books listed as references for Chapter 3. Write a paper comparing and contrasting the authors' conclusions concerning the chosen topic.

Field

1. This chapter asserts that effective supervision must provide for both completing tasks and meeting individual and social needs. Observe an administrator or supervisor who is able to balance task and human needs effectively. Write a report on your observations, including a description of the knowledge, skills, and procedures the supervisor draws on in meeting both organizational goals and teacher needs.

2. Prepare a slide or transparency presentation on a summary of successful-schools research. Make your presentation to a group of educators. Ask for and record reactions to your presentation.

3. Visit a school that is perceived to be a successful school by both educators and community members. Seek and observe examples of effective leadership, communication, instruction, and other factors that researchers have found to be present in successful schools. Take photographs representative of the effective characteristics observed. Mount selected photographs on poster board, along with brief written descriptions of how the scene in each photograph relates to effective education. Display your photo essay to interested parties.

4. Conduct an interview with a supervisor or administrator in a business, industrial, government, or military setting, focusing on how he or she attempts to integrate organizational goals (task emphasis) with employees' individual and social needs (human emphasis). Write a summary of his or her attitudes, strategies, and methods as well as your opinion about whether they can be applied to a school setting.

Developmental

1. Maintain an ongoing review of prominent educational journals for reports on future successful-schools research. With each new research study, look for (a) findings not already indicated in the review of research in Chapter 3 and (b) any findings that tend to contradict the research cited in Chapter 3.

2. Monitor any major changes in leadership style, curriculum, professional development, or instruction within a local school system over the next few months. Examine such changes to determine which are at least partially based on recent research on successful schools.

3. Over the next few months, examine statements made by prominent educational, political, and civic leaders that include proposals for educational reform. To what extent do such proposals reflect what we have learned from research on successful schools?

REFERENCES

Arrington, H. J., and Moore, S. D. 2001. Infusing service learning into instruction. *Middle School Journal, 32*(4), 55–60.

Austin, G., and Reynolds, D. 1990. Managing for improved school effectiveness: An international survey. *School Organization, 10*(2/3), 167–178.

Beane, J. A. 2002. Beyond self-interest: A democratic core curriculum. *Educational Leadership, 59*(7), 25–28.

Bennett, N., and Harris, A. 1997. *Hearing truth from power? Organization theory, school effectiveness, and school improvement.* Paper presented at the annual meeting of the American Educational Research Association, Chicago, March.

Bernauer, J. 2002. Five keys to unlock continuous school improvement. *Kappa Delta Pi Record, 38*(2), 89–92.

Bollen, R. 1996. School effectiveness and school improvement: The intellectual and policy context. In D. Reynolds, R. Bollen, B. Creemers, D. Hopkins, L. Stoll, and N. Lagerweij (Eds.), *Making good schools: Linking school effectiveness and school improvement.* New York: Routledge.

Cook, B. G., Semmel, M. I., and Gerber, M. M. 1995. *Are recent reforms effective for all students?* Paper presented at the annual meeting of the American Educational Research Association, San Francisco, April. (ERIC ED 385 012)

Creemers, B. 1996. The school effectiveness knowledge base. In D. Reynolds, R. Bollen, B. Creemers, D. Hopkins, L. Stoll, and N. Lagerweij (Eds.), *Making good schools: Linking school effectiveness and school improvement* (pp. 36–58). New York: Routledge

Cuban, L. 1998. How schools change reforms: Redefining reform success and failure. *Teachers College Record, 99*(3), 453–477.

Davies, D. 2002. The 10th school revisited: Are school/family/community partnerships on the reform agenda now? *Phi Delta Kappan, 83,* 388–392.

Doyle, L. H. 2004. Leadership for community building: Changing how we think and act. *The Clearing House, 77*(5), 196–199.

Dryfoos, J. 2002. Full-service community schools: Creating new institutions. *Phi Delta Kappan, 83,* 398–399.

Edmonds, R. 1979. Effective schools for the urban poor. *Educational Leadership, 37*(1):15–24.

Fullan, M. 2002. The change leader. *Educational Leadership, 59*(8), 16–20.

Fullan, M. 2005. Turnaround leadership. *The Educational Forum, 69*(2), 174–181.

Glickman, C. D. 1987. Good and/or effective schools: What do we want? *Kappan, 68*(8): 622–624.

Gustafson, J. P. 2002. Missing the mark for low-SES students. *Kappa Delta Pi Record, 38*(2), 60–63.

Hallinger, P., and Murphy, J. 1987. *Social context on school effects.* Paper presented at the annual meeting of the American Educational Association, Washington, DC, April.

Hannaway, J., and Talbert, J. 1993. Bringing context into effective schools research: Urban-suburban differences. *Educational Administration Quarterly, 29*(2):164–186.

Harris, A. 2002. *School improvement: What's in it for schools?* New York: Routledge Falmer.

Hill, P. W. 1998. Shaking the foundations: Research driven school reform. *School Effectiveness and School Improvement, 9*(4), 419–436.

Hopkins, D., Ainscow, M., and West, M. 1994. *School improvement in an era of change.* New York: Teachers College Press.

Joyce, B., Calhoun, E., and Hopkins, D. 1999. *The new structure of school improvement: Inquiring schools and achieving students.* Philadelphia: Open University Press.

Lawrence-Lightfoot, S. 2003. *The essential conversation: What parents and teachers can learn from each other.* New York: Random House.

Levine, D. V. 1991. Creating effective schools: Findings and implications from research and practice. *Phi Delta Kappan, 72,* 389–393.

Levine, D. V., and Lezotte, W. 1990. *Unusually effective schools: A review and analysis of research and practice.* Madison, WI: National Center for Effective Schools Research and Development.

Little, J. W. 1982. Norms of collegiality and experimentation: Workplace conditions of school success. *American Educational Research Journal, 19*(3), 325–340.

Makedon, A. 1992. *Is Alice's world too middle class?* Recommendations for effective schools research. (ERIC ED 346 612)

Marri, A. R. 2005. Building a framework for classroom-based multicultural democratic education: Learning from three skilled teachers. *Teachers College Record, 107*(5), 1036–1059.

Mortimore, P., Sammons, P., Stoll, L., Lewis, D., and Ecob, R. 1988. *School matters.* Berkeley, CA: University of California Press.

Murphy, J. 1992. Effective schools: Legacy and future directions. In D. Reynolds and P. Cuttance (Eds.), *School effectiveness: Research, policy, and practice* (pp. 164–170). London: Cassell.

Pierce, L. V. 1991. *Effective schools for national origin language minority students.* Washington, DC: The Mid-Atlantic Equity Center.

Powers, A. L. 2004. An evaluation of four place-based education programs. *The Journal of Environmental Education, 35*(4), 17–32.

Pratzner, F. C. 1984. Quality of school life: Foundations for improvement. *Educational Researcher, 13*(3), 20–25.

Purkey, S. C., and Smith, M. S. 1983. Effective schools: A review. *Elementary School Journal, 83,* 427–452.

Reynolds, D., and Stoll, L. 1996. Merging school effectiveness and school improvement: The knowledge bases. In D. Reynolds, R. Bollen, B. Creemers, D. Hopkins, L. Stoll, and N. Lagerweij (Eds.), *Making good schools: Linking school effectiveness and school improvement* (pp. 94–112). London and New York: Routledge.

Rosenholtz, S. J. 1989. *Teachers' workplace: The social organization of schools.* New York: Longman.

Rust, F. O., and Freidus, H. (Eds.). 2001. *Guiding school change: The role and work of change agents.* New York: Teachers College Press.

Sanders, M. G., and Lewis, K. C. 2005. Building bridges toward excellence: Community involvement in high schools. *The High School Journal, 88*(3), 1–9.

Scribner, A. P. 1999. High performing Hispanic schools: An introduction. In P. Reyes, J. D. Scribner, and A. P. Scribner (Eds.), *Lessons from high performing Hispanic schools: Creating learning communities.* New York: Teachers College Press.

Slavin, R. E. 2002. Evidence-based education policies: Transforming educational practice and research. *Educational Researcher, 31*(7), 15–21.

Smith, G. A. 2002. Going local. *Educational Leadership, 60(*1), 30–33.

Stedman, L. C. 1987. It's time we change the effective schools formula. *Kappan, 69*(3), 215–224.

Taylor, B. O. 2002. The effective schools process: Alive and well. *Phi Delta Kappan, 83*(5), 375–378.

Teddlie, C., and Stringfield, S. 1993. *Schools make a difference: Lessons learned from a 10-year study of school effects.* New York: Teachers College Press.

Wasley, P., Hampel, R., and Clark, R. 1997. The puzzle of whole-school change. *Phi Delta Kappan, 78,* 690–697.

SUGGESTED READINGS

Becker, M. 1992. *An effective schools primer.* Arlington, VA: American Association of School Administrators.

Garcia, E. 1994. *Understanding and meeting the challenge of student cultural diversity.* Boston: Houghton Mifflin.

Glickman, C. D. 1993. *Renewing America's schools. A guide for school-based action.* San Francisco: Jossey-Bass.

Harris, A. 2002. *School improvement: What's in it for schools?* New York: Routledge Falmer.

Hopkins, D., Ainscow, M., and West, M. 1994. *School improvement in an era of change.* New York: Teachers College Press.

Joyce, B., Calhoun, E., and Hopkins, D. 1999. *The new structure of school improvement: Inquiring schools and achieving schools.* Philadelphia: Open University Press.

Levine, D. V., and Lezotte, W. 1990. *Unusually effective schools: A review and analysis of research and practice.* Madison, WI: National Center for Effective Schools Research and Development.

Reyes, P., Scribner, J. D., and Scribner, A. P. (Eds.). 1999. *Lessons from high performing Hispanic*

schools: Creating learning communities. New York: Teachers College Press.

Reynolds, D., Bollen, R., Creemers, B., Hopkins, D., Stoll, L., and Lagerweij, N. (Eds.). 1996. *Making good schools: Linking school effectiveness and school improvement.* New York: Routledge.

Rosenholtz, S. J. 1989. *Teachers' workplace: The social organization of schools.* New York: Longman.

Senge, P. M., McCabe, N. H., Lucas, T., Kleiner, A., Dutton, J., and Smith, B. 2002. *Schools that learn. A fifth discipline fieldbook for educators, parents, and everyone who cares about education.* New York: Doubleday.

Teddlie, C., and Stringfield, S. 1993. *Schools make a difference: Lessons learned from a 10-year study of school effects.* New York: Teachers College Press.

Wasley, P., Hampel, R., and Clark, R. 1997. The puzzle of whole-school change. *Phi Delta Kappan, 78,* 690–697.

chapter 4

Adult and Teacher Development within the Context of the School

Clues for Supervisory Practice

This chapter will serve as a core for thinking and practicing supervision in a developmental framework. So far, we have defined "a cause beyond oneself" as a demarcation between the collective, thoughtful, autonomous, and effective staffs of successful schools and the isolated, unreflective, and powerless staffs of unsuccessful schools. Knowledge of how teachers can grow as competent adults is the guiding principle for supervisors in finding ways to return wisdom, power, and control to both the individuals and the collective staff in order for them to become true professionals. With the understanding of how teachers change, the supervisor can plan direct assistance, professional development, curriculum development, group development, and action research at an appropriate level to stimulate teacher growth and instructional improvement.

The research on adult learning and development has been prolific. We have attempted to distill the knowledge of adult and teacher development that has direct applications for supervision and supervisors. Readers who desire more detail should refer to the references at the end of the chapter. The use of such readily available and potentially rich knowledge about human growth can be extremely valuable to those who work with adults. If schools are to be successful, supervision must respond to teachers as changing adults.

Adults as Learners

Instructional improvement takes place when teachers improve their decision making about students, learning content, and teaching. The process of improving teacher decision making is largely a process of adult learning. Thus, research and theory on adult learning is an important component of the knowledge base for instructional supervision.

Intelligence

Two basic questions drove much of the early research on adult learning ability: Does ability to learn diminish with age? Are there differences between the learning process of adults and children? Thorndike (1928) was among the first to suggest that adult learning did not peak in youth and diminish steadily thereafter (a common belief of his day).

Horn and Cattell (1967) identified two categories of intelligence: *fluid* and *crystallized*. Fluid intelligence, which depends heavily on physiological and neurological capacities, peaks early and explains why youth excel on tasks requiring quick insight, short-term memorization, and complex interactions (Merriam and Caffarella, 1999). Crystallized intelligence, assessed by untimed measures calling for judgment, knowledge, and experience, is more heavily influenced by education and experience. Hence, older individuals show an advantage when it is measured.

Contemporary theories of intelligence have extended the notion that intelligence consists of multiple components or factors. Most readers of this text will be familiar with Howard Gardner's theory of multiple intelligences (1983, 1999). Gardner initially posited seven types of intelligence (linguistic, logical-mathematical, musical, spatial, bodily kinesthetic, intrapersonal, and interpersonal). He later added naturalistic intelligence, and suggested there are likely other forms of intelligence. Gardner's ideas are also relevant to supervision. Supervisors can identify and utilize the learning strengths of individual teachers when assisting them with instructional improvement efforts. Supervisors can also assist teachers to gradually expand their repertoire of learning strategies.

Sternberg (1985, 1990) likewise has proposed a theory of intelligence that may be helpful in thinking about the cognition of teachers. His is called a *triarchic theory of intelligence* because it consists of three subtheories. The first subtheory is referred to as *componential*; it deals with cognitive processing. This part of the theory deals with what has traditionally been discussed in trying to understand intellectual ability. The second subtheory is *experiential*, which suggests that assessing intelligence requires consideration not only of the mental components but of the level of experience at which they are applied. Sternberg, intrigued by the differences between novices and experts, has suggested that experience promotes both the ability to respond automatically to routine situations and to deal effectively with novel situations. Thus, novice teachers can be expected to require different types of supervision than those who are more experienced.

Although the first two subtheories deal with universal processes, Sternberg's third *contextual* subtheory deals with socially *influenced abilities*. Individuals are said to cope with life's challenges by adapting to the environment, shaping the environment, or selecting a different environment—all the while being influenced by what is considered appropriate and intelligent behavior within one's cultural milieu. This last contextual subtheory becomes important when one looks at how teachers deal with challenging situations. Some obviously have greater capacities than others to adapt to or change the classroom and school environment. Through appropriate supervision, teachers can be assisted in broadening their array of adaptation and change strategies. It is this kind of practical intelligence that intrigues Sternberg and other theorists who propose that not enough attention has focused on the demonstration of adult intelligence through the identification and solution of real-world problems.

Theories of Adult Learning

As research increasingly put to rest the question of whether adults could continue to learn, attention focused on how their learning differed from that of children. The focus of the following overview of adult learning theories will be on those theories that have received particular attention over recent decades as adult educators sought to answer this question. A chronological review of the literature on adult learning would reveal in greater detail what this brief overview will suggest—a shift from a psychological orientation (Knowles, 1980; Tough, 1971) toward a sociocultural orientation (Amstutz, 1999; Hansman, 2001; Hayes and Flannery, 2000).

Andragogy

The *theory of andragogy*, popularized in this country by Malcolm Knowles, has become one of the better-known theories of adult learning in recent years. Knowles (1980) proposed four basic assumptions of adult learning:

1. Adults have a psychological need to be self-directing.
2. Adults bring an expansive reservoir of experience that can and should be tapped in the learning situation.
3. Adults' readiness to learn is influenced by a need to solve real-life problems often related to adult developmental tasks.
4. Adults are performance centered in their orientation to learning—wanting to make immediate application of knowledge.

Later, Knowles added a fifth assumption—that adult learning is primarily intrinsically motivated (Knowles, 1984). The theory of andragogy no longer receives the uncritical acceptance that it once did, with questions increasingly raised about the extent to which these assumptions are exclusively true of adults (Tennant, 1986), the extent to which self-direction is an actual versus a desirable preference of adult learners (Brookfield, 1986), and the conditions under which andragogy may or may not apply (Pratt, 1988; Rachal, 2002). Knowles himself, before his death in 1997, came to acknowledge that differences between adults and children as learners may be a matter of degree and situation rather than a rigid dichotomy. Nevertheless, the theory of andragogy is still accepted by many as a broad guide to thinking about adults' learning (Merriam, 2001; Rose, Jeris, and Smith, 2005).

Self-Directed Learning. Even as self-direction in learning was emerging as one of the most challenged assumptions within andragogy, a distinct body of theory and research on adults' self-directed learning (SDL) was evolving. Allen Tough (1971) is generally credited with providing the first comprehensive description of self-directed learning—learning that adults engage in systematically as part of everyday life and without benefit of an instructor. A long-standing body of research on this topic has documented the ubiquitousness of adults' self-directed learning and led to the development of numerous models of self-directed learning as well as several instruments intended to measure it (Merriam, 2001).

Self-direction has been alternatively conceptualized as a goal for adult learning, a process through which learning occurs, a characteristic of learners that may be enduring or situational, and an instructional model through which instructors in formal classrooms foster student control of learning. The implications of the concept of self-directed learning are numerous for those who seek to foster teachers' growth and development through developmental supervision. Supervision should foster rather than inhibit self-directed learning by matching supervisory behaviors with teachers' readiness for self-direction. It is important to recognize that not all adults appear to be equally ready for self-directed learning, nor is an individual equally prepared for self-directed learning in every situation. Variables like background knowledge and degree of confidence affect the level of support adults may need in their learning efforts (Pratt, 1988). Just as Grow (1991) recommended that instructors match their teaching style to the estimated stage of self-direction of adult learners, so too the effective supervisor will adapt his or her supervisory style in response to the degree of self-directed readiness exhibited by the teacher in a given context.

Transformational Learning. For some who question whether either andragogy or SDL theory represent a learning theory that is uniquely adult, transformative learning theory—proposed and revised most prominently by Jack Mezirow (2000)—offers an appealing alternative. This theory grew out of Mezirow's research with reentry women in higher education. He has offered the following definition of transformative learning:

> Transformative learning refers to the process by which we transform our taken-for-granted frames of reference (meaning perspectives, habits of mind, mind-sets) to make them more inclusive, discriminating, open, emotionally capable of change, and reflective so that they may generate beliefs and opinions that will prove more true or justified to guide action. (pp. 7–8)

Kegan (2000) contrasts transformative learning (changes in *how* we know) with informative learning (changes in *what* we know), adding that we all experience potentially important kinds of change that do not bring about a fundamental shift in our frames of reference.

Perspective transformation often is described as triggered by a significant life event, originally referred to by Mezirow as a disorienting dilemma. Perspective transformation also can occur in response to minor events that create an opportunity for reflection and redirection, or may occur when an accumulation of internal dilemmas creates a growing sense of disillusionment (Taylor, 2000; English, 2005). A teacher's trigger for transformative learning may occur in a situation as obvious as experiencing failure for the first time when she accepts a new position in an urban setting, or as subtle as having a conversation with a gay student about the impact of other students' homophobic jokes on his learning.

Cranton (1994) recommended that the educator should critically reflect on his or her own meaning perspective of being an educator. She also described the processes by which the educator might accomplish this:

> The educator, in order to develop the meaning perspective of being an educator would: increase self awareness through consciousness-raising activities, make his or her assumptions about beliefs about practice explicit, engage in critical reflection on those assumptions and beliefs, engage in dialogue with others, and develop an informed theory of practice. (p. 214)

The strategies Cranton suggested that may be useful in this process are varied, including writing journals, visiting the classrooms of colleagues, conducting criteria analysis of incidents which epitomize their notions of success or failure in practice, experimenting with practice, eliciting feedback from learners, and consulting or engaging in dialogue with colleagues.

Experience and Learning: Situated Cognition, Informal and Incidental Learning

At the heart of numerous conceptions of adult learning and education dating back to Dewey (1938) and Lindeman (1926) is the centrality of experience to learning. This concern with experience is reflected in Knowles's (1980) inclusion of the importance of adult experience as one of his original four assumptions about adult learning (Gorard and Selwyn, 2005). It is also reflected in Kolb's inclusion of two phases focusing on experience (concrete experience and active experimentation) as part of his four-phase model of the adult learning cycle (1984).

The centrality of experience to learning takes on new dimensions when the emerging body of work on situated cognition is applied to consideration of adult learning. Many cite Brown, Collins, and Duguid (1989) as a seminal work in proposing a theory of situated cognition. Essentially, they propose that education is misconceived to the degree that it emphasizes the acquisition of decontextualized, abstract knowledge. They insist that lasting knowledge emerges as learners engage in authentic activity embedded in specific situations. Referring specifically to adult learning, Hansman (2001) stated, "The nature of the interactions among learners, the tools they use within these interactions, the activity itself, and the social context in which the activity takes place shapes learning" (p. 45). Linking situated cognition to Schon's (1983) work on acquisition of professional knowledge through "knowing-in-action," Wilson (1993) suggested that adults learn *in* experience as they act in situations and are acted upon by situations, rather than the traditional assumption that adults learn *from* experience.

Extending the parallel with craft apprenticeships, Brown, Collins, and Duguid (1989) and others emphasized the cognitive *apprenticeship* as a means for learners to acquire knowledge as participants in a community of practice (Gonzales and Nelson, 2005). Wilson (1993) made an analogy between the cognitive apprenticeship and Schon's (1983) reflective practicum (Lea and Griggs, 2005). Lave and Wenger (1991) have described the role of communities of practice, or self-organized groups who share a common sense of purpose and a desire to learn from one another. Each of these strategies offers a valuable approach for fostering professional development of teachers, particularly those who are new to the field or to a particular school culture. In line with situated cognition theory, teachers would most effectively acquire knowledge useful in a new situation by being directly immersed in real practice situations, with support from experienced colleagues whose methods might include modeling and coaching.

Most recently, interest in the ties between adult learning and experience have been explored in examinations of learning in the workplace, which have found that much of the meaningful learning that occurs in that context is of the informal and incidental variety rather than the highly structured learning traditionally associated with workplace training (Kerka, 1998; Uys, Gwele, McInerney, Rhyn, and Tanga, 2004). Marsick and Watkins (1990, 2001) have offered a theory of informal and incidental learning. Informal learning is usually intentional but less structured than formal learning. Examples include self-directed learning, networking, informal coaching, and mentoring. Incidental learning, on the other hand, is defined as a byproduct of some other activity, and is most often tacit or unconscious at the time. The model they proposed describes a progression of meaning making which they warn is neither as linear or sequential as their model might suggest. They described this progression as follows:

1. Learning typically begins with a trigger event that is framed in light of the person's worldview.
2. The experience itself is interpreted, assessing what is problematic or challenging about it. The context of the experience is interpreted simultaneously.
3. Alternative actions are considered and chosen.
4. Learning strategies are used to implement the desired solution. Context influences options here.
5. A proposed solution is produced.

6. Outcomes are assessed.
7. Lessons are learned.
8. Concluding thoughts become a part of the framework for analyzing subsequent situations.

Marsick and Watkins suggested that those wishing to help adults improve their informal learning (i.e., supervisors) might assist adults in identifying conditions in the sociocultural context that help them learn more effectively or that stand in the way of learning. Once such factors are identified, supervisors can help the learner deal with or change them.

Critical and Postmodern Theories of Adult Learning. Kilgore (2001) has offered a brief synopsis of the critical and postmodern perspectives of adult learning, analyzing both their similarities and differences. As she notes, each of these perspectives challenges pillars of adult learning theory such as andragogy and self-directed learning as exclusionary and overly focused on the individual. Both critical and postmodern perspectives share assumptions that knowledge is socially constructed, along with an interest in power as a factor in learning. They differ, however, in other significant ways. Critical theorists argue that hegemony (dominant influence or authority wielded by those in power) operates to preserve inequities linked to structures of privilege and oppression based on categories like race, ethnicity, gender, class, and age. In this view, learning involves reflecting on the hegemonic assumptions that often guide our practices and perhaps acting to change the practices as well as the assumptions (an example given by Kilgore is that of use and misuse of standardized tests). Social justice is viewed as a core value. Postmodern theorists, on the other hand, resist embracing *any* universal truth, emphasizing that knowledge is multifaceted and truths shift according to the experience and context of the knower. Even the same individual can hold multiple perspectives on a topic based on situational variables or in their multifaceted identities (what Sheared, 1999, refers to as polyrhythmic realities).

Power is a consideration for each framework, but in different ways. For instance, critical theories are interested in how the status quo (e.g., an individualistic focus on learning that research suggests may be culturally biased toward certain groups) can be interrupted to create more emancipatory knowledge (e.g., a greater emphasis on group learning, which research suggests is more culturally relevant for some groups of learners). Power is seen as held by some over others; for instance, the traditional role of principals invests them with greater power than teachers. From the postmodern perspective, power is present in every relationship and can be exercised by anyone to one degree or another. We must analyze (or deconstruct) the situation to know how power is being used (whether for repressive or liberating purposes) and by whom. In this view, teacher and parent participation in site-based management or participatory action research projects become tools both for producing knowledge collaboratively and for negotiating and rearranging power relationships.

Teachers as Adult Learners

Fullan (1991) pointed out that "educational change is a learning experience for the adults involved" (p. 66). Our knowledge of adult learning tells us that it is important to link learning about instructional innovations to teachers' past experiences, and to allow them ample time to integrate innovations gradually into their teaching repertoire. Yet, in recent years, teachers have been bombarded with a plethora of innovations as part of the educational reform movement. Fullan (1991) concluded that "many decisions about the kinds of educational innovations introduced in school districts are biased, poorly thought out, and unconnected to the stated purposes of education" (p. 8). This is no doubt why many innovations have failed. Other innovations potentially of significant value and technically sound have also failed. One reason for these failures may be that supervisors have not helped teachers to integrate the innovations with their past experiences or adapt the innovations to their current teaching practice. Moreover, teachers often simply are not provided sufficient time to learn about and adapt the innovation before a new innovation is given precedence by administrators and supervisors (Zepeda, 2004).

Sternberg's (1985, 1990) work on the experiential component of adult intelligence indicates that novice teachers need to be supervised differently than experienced teachers. One example of this need for differentiation is that many beginning teachers have more difficulty assessing and responding to novel teaching situations and problems than their experienced colleagues, and thus are in need of more intensive support. Both Sternberg's (1985, 1990) and Gardner's (1983) research on multiple intelligences take us beyond differences between novice and experienced teachers and point to the need for identifying and utilizing different learning strengths of teachers at all levels of experience.

The need to individualize teacher learning, indicated by the literature on adult learning, stands in sharp contrast to the actual treatment of teachers. Many supervisors treat teachers as if they were all the same, rather than individuals in various stages of adult growth. In most schools, teachers receive the same inservice workshops, the same observations, and the same assessments. It is as if teachers were stamped out of teacher training institutes as identical and thereafter have no further need to be viewed as individual learners. The research on adults shows the lack of wisdom of such assumptions (Mathis, 1987).

Sternberg's (1985, 1990) discussion of socially influenced abilities points to the need for teachers to engage in learning aimed at developing a variety of strategies for adapting to or changing their classroom and school environment. Both Mezirow (1981, 1990) and Brookfield's (1986) work on adult learning indicate that in order to learn and grow, teachers need to participate in a continuous cycle of collaborative activity and reflection on that activity, and need to develop the powers of critical thinking. Finally, the writings of Knowles (1980, 1984), Mezirow (1981, 1990, 2000), and Brookfield (1986) have all supported the notion of the supervisor facilitating teacher growth toward empowerment and self-direction.

Unfortunately, many schools do not foster collaborative action, reflection, critical thinking, or teacher empowerment. Rather, the hierarchical structure of many school systems—as well as the environmental problems of isolation, psychological dilemma, and lack of a shared technical culture discussed in Chapter 2—tends to work against the type of growth described in the adult learning literature.

Adult and Teacher Development

Literature on adult development can be seen as reflecting several distinct but related approaches. Just a few decades ago, the study of human development focused on children, and adulthood was either not a consideration or was thought to represent a period of stability. Theory and research on adult development for several decades emphasized development as an orderly progression. Because much of the work in this area was done by developmental psychologists, there was an emphasis on the change processes occurring in the individual with relatively little consideration to his or her interaction with the environment. Early approaches to adult development were rooted in such a tradition. Over time, alternative views of adult development evolved, with less concern for a universal progression and greater interest in the interaction between the individual and the social environment. Subsequent sections of this chapter will discuss adult development according to these five subtopics: (1) stage development, (2) life cycle development, (3) transition events, (4) role development, and (5) sociocultural influences on adult development.

Stage Theories of Adult and Teacher Development

We will begin discussion of adult development by focusing on developmental stage theories. Levine (1989) delineated the characteristics of stages:

> First and foremost is their structural nature. Each stage is a "structured whole," representing an underlying organization of thought or understanding. Stages are qualitatively different from one another. All emerge in sequence without variation; no stage can be skipped. Finally stages are "hierarchically integrated"; that is, progressive stages are increasingly complex and subsume earlier stages. Individuals always have access to the stages through which they have passed. Under ordinary circumstances or with proper supports, people will generally prefer to use the highest stages of which they are capable. (p. 86)

It may be helpful to look more closely at several specific stage theories.

Cognitive Development. Piaget described four stages of cognitive development: sensorimotor, preoperational, concrete operations, and formal operations (Ginsburg and Opper, 1979). The person at the formal operations stage has already progressed beyond reasoning only for the "here and now" and can project into and relate time and space. A person at the formal operations stage uses hypothetical reasoning, understands complex symbols, and formulates abstract concepts.

Some researchers have found that formal thought is not demonstrated by all adults. Others question the extent to which cultural bias in the traditional Piagetian tasks plays a role in differential findings, particularly in non-Western cultures (Neimark, 1987). There has been considerable exploration of characteristic adult forms of thinking that go beyond Piaget's fourth stage to a postformal operations stage (Arlin, 1975; Kitchener, Lynch, Fischer, and Wood, 1993; Merriam and Caffarella, 1999; Riegel, 1973), with some positing alternative cognitive frameworks to describe adult thought (Perry, 1970, 1981). Terms like *dialectical thought* (Riegel, 1973; Kramer, 1983), *integrative thought* (Kramer, 1987), and *epistemic cognition* (Taranto, 1987) have been used to describe the highest stage of cognition observed in adults. A related strand of research has examined the meaning of wisdom (Clayton and Birren, 1980; Holliday and Chandler, 1986) often seen as the hallmark of advanced adult thinking. Taranto (1987) and Neimark (1987) pointed out that in real life, unlike in the typical Piagetian assessment tasks, adults must focus on ill-defined problems without definitive answers. Neimark contended that such thinking is best assessed by giving adults problems without clear-cut answers on which to make judgments. Figure 4.1 represents the adult cognitive developmental continuum.

Teachers' cognitive development was explored by Ammon and associates in a study of a two-year graduate teacher education program with an emphasis on Piagetian theory (Ammon, 1984). This emphasis was intended to teach the adult preservice and in-service teachers about child development as well as to promote the teachers' own development. As the teachers studied Piagetian and related developmental theory, their conceptions of students, learning, and teaching changed. They progressed from simplistic to more complex, interactive explanations of student behaviors, development, and learning. These teachers also moved from a conception of teaching as "showing and telling" to creating a learning environment designed to foster the students' learning and development. The teachers' views on learning shifted from passive reception to active construction. They also came to think of their roles differently, as facilitating learning rather than imparting knowledge.

FIGURE 4.1 *Adult Cognitive Development Continuum*

Conceptual Development. One developmental framework that is closely related to cognitive development and that has been studied significantly with teachers is that of conceptual development. Hunt and others defined *conceptual level (CL)* "in terms of (1) increasing conceptual complexity, as indicated by discrimination, differentiation, and integration and (2) increasing interpersonal maturity, as indicated by self-definition and self-other relations" (Hunt, Butler, Noy, and Rosser, 1978). Hunt placed individuals on a continuum from most concrete (lowest CL) to most abstract (highest CL).

Persons of *low CL* evaluate things in a simple, concrete fashion. They tend to view issues in "black and white." Individuals of low CL have difficulty defining a problem they are experiencing and respond to the same problem in a habitual manner despite the fact that the repeated response is not solving the problem. They need to be shown how to solve the problem. Persons of *moderate CL* are becoming more abstract in their thinking. They can define the problem and generate a limited number of possible solutions but have difficulty formulating a comprehensive plan. They still need some assistance in solving a complex problem. Persons of *high CL* are abstract thinkers. They are independent, self-actualizing, resourceful, flexible, and possess a high capacity of integration. Figure 4.2 represents the conceptual development continuum.

High-concept teachers have been found to differ from low-concept teachers in terms of both teaching approach and teacher-generated classroom atmosphere. High-concept teachers rate higher on what are generally considered to be more positive characteristics (such as warmth, perceptiveness, empathy, flexibility, ingenuity, task effectiveness, smoothness, and consistency) and low-concept teachers rate higher on more educationally negative characteristics (such as innovativeness, rule orientation, punitiveness, and anxiety) (Harvey, White, Prather, Alter, and Hoffmeister, 1966; Heck and Davis, 1973; Reiman and Thies-Sprinthall, 1998). Hunt and Joyce (1967) found correlations between teacher conceptual level and ability to use learners' needs as a basis for planning and evaluation. High-concept teachers used a greater range of learning environments and teaching methods. Similarly,

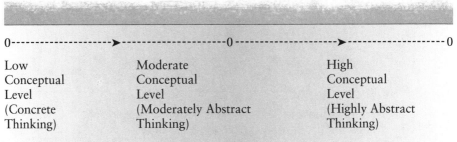

0-------------------▶--------------------0--------------------▶------------------- 0

| Low Conceptual Level (Concrete Thinking) | Moderate Conceptual Level (Moderately Abstract Thinking) | High Conceptual Level (Highly Abstract Thinking) |

FIGURE 4.2 *Conceptual Development Continuum*

Hopkins (1990) found that high-stage teachers employed new methods of teaching at a rate four times greater than their counterparts at lower stages. Parkay (1979), in a study of inner-city high school teachers, found that high-concept teachers stimulated positive student attitudes and student achievement gains, and were less susceptible to professional stress. A study of 52 teachers by Calhoun (1985) found that teachers with high conceptual thought provided more corrective feedback to students, gave more praise, and were less negative and punitive. These teachers were more varied in their instructional strategies and were able to elicit more higher-order conceptual responses from their students than teachers of moderate and lower levels of conceptual thought.

Moral Development. Kohlberg and Armon (1984) identified three broad categories of morality: the preconventional level, the conventional level, and the postconventional level. They further delineated two stages of development within each of these levels, with the second stage more advanced and organized than the first. Across the three levels, reasoning shifts from a self-centered perspective to one that increasingly considers the perspectives and rights of others. The individual at Level I makes decisions from a self-centered orientation. At Level II, individuals "do the right thing" because that is what is expected according to social norms. Finally, at Level III, moral decisions serve to recognize the social contract and to uphold individual rights. Although conflicts between these principles and legal mandates are recognized as problematic in the lower stage of Level III, moral principles come to take precedence by the time an individual reaches the highest stage of moral development. Kohlberg sees the higher stages as superior, and he sees enhancing development as an appropriate aim for education. Figure 4.3 represents the moral development continuum.

It is important here to give mention to the work of Carol Gilligan (1979, 1982). Gilligan compared conclusions from Kohlberg's model of moral development with conclusions from her own research with women discussing personal decisions. People at the top of Kohlberg's stages worry about interfering with others' rights, whereas those at the top of Gilligan's stages worry about errors of omission, such as not helping others when you could. At Gilligan's highest stage, morality is conceived in terms of relationships, and goodness is equated with helping

0----------------->----------------0----------------->----------------0

| Preconventional | Conventional | Postconventional |
| Level | Level | Level |

FIGURE 4.3 *Moral Development Continuum*

others. Gilligan proposed that a different conception of development emerges from the study of women's lives:

> This conception of morality as fundamentally concerned with the capacity for understanding and care also develops through a structural progression of increasing differentiation and integration. This progression witnesses the shift from an egocentric through a societal to the universal moral perspective that Kohlberg described in his research on men, but it does so in different terms. The shift in women's judgment from an egocentric to a principled ethical understanding is articulated through their use of a distinct moral language, in which the terms "selfishness" and "responsibility" define the moral problem as one of care. Moral development then consists of the progressive reconstruction of this understanding toward a more adequate conception of care. (1979, p. 442)

Several small-scale studies have investigated relationships between teachers' moral development and their understandings of teaching and learning. Johnston (1985) found that teachers scoring low on the same test of moral reasoning possessed a narrow conception of the on-task students (working quietly and individually on an assignment provided by the teacher). Teachers with the highest scores on moral reasoning considered students' perspectives and the complex, continuous nature of learning while resisting classifying students as on task or off task based solely on behavioral observation. Reiman and Parramore (1994) found first-year teachers at higher moral reasoning levels to exhibit greater concern for the instructional needs of their students.

Ego Development. Ego is both a process of striving for coherence and meaning in one's life, and a structure with its own internal logic (Levine, 1989). This is one of the few developmental theories derived from the study of women, but it has been applied subsequently to numerous samples of women and men. Loevinger (1976) has identified 10 stages of ego development that individuals can pass through. Orientations toward symbiotic, impulsive, and self-protective behaviors are manifest in the early stages. In these lower stages, a person depends on others for solutions to problems. In the middle stages of ego development, the individual exhibits conventional behaviors. At the higher stages, the adult becomes individualistic, autonomous, and integrated. The person at the highest stage of ego development is able to synthesize what seem to be unrelated or opposing concepts to individuals at lower stages (Witherell and Erickson, 1978). Adults at the beginning point on the continuum might be classified as *fearful*. Those at the midpoint on the continuum can be called *conforming*. Adults at the end of the continuum (those with the most mature egos) are referred to as *autonomous*. Figure 4.4 represents the ego development continuum.

Cummings and Murray (1989) found that teachers at different levels described different roles of a teacher, with those at lower levels of ego development focusing on the role of the teacher as information disseminator and caregiver, and those at higher levels emphasizing the role of the teacher in helping students learn

Fearful   Conforming   Autonomous

FIGURE 4.4 *Ego Development Continuum*

to learn. Based on their findings, they concluded that lower-level teachers may not have the resources to cope with the intricacies of the student-teacher relationships or deal with the complexity of the learning process. Levine (1989) suggested that higher levels of teacher ego development can be stimulated by providing experiences that require teachers to take the perspectives of different persons (including students) within the school. She recommended activities in which conflicts between school rules and individual rights are resolved and principles are formulated that recognize and reconcile the claims of both.

Levels of Consciousness. Robert Kegan (1994), a self-acknowledged neo-Piagetian, is a more recent entrant on the scene of adult developmental psychology with his theory of levels of consciousness.

As with the Piagetian shift from concrete to formal operations, the development of abstract thinking is a key characteristic of movement from the adolescent stage of durable category level to a more mature *cross-categorical* (or *third-order*) *consciousness*. The person functioning at the cross-categorical level is capable of thinking abstractly, reflecting on his or her own emotions, and being guided by beliefs and values that ensure loyalty to the larger community. At this stage the adult experiences a new construction of reality, with the needs, wants, and desires of others figuring as prominently as her own (Taylor and Marienau, 1995). Only with the transition from cross-categorical to *systems* (or *fourth-order*) *consciousness*, however, does the individual move beyond defining himself or herself in terms of those duties, devotions, and values to become a truly independent and autonomous person. At this level we can look objectively at our own perspective, compare it with that of others, and work to reconcile differences. It is the systems level of consciousness which is said to be necessary to meet the various demands of modern adult life (parenting, partnering, working, continued learning), but Kegan contends many do not reach this stage until their 30s or 40s, if at all. Finally, as is common with stage theories Kegan posits a level rarely achieved, *Trans-systems* (or *fifth-order*) *consciousness*. Dialectical thinking is associated with this level of consciousness, said to be rare before midlife.

Kegan's model suggests our expectations may be high, both for ourselves and others. In the preface to his book *In Over Our Heads: The Mental Demands of Modern Life* (1994), he especially appealed to those who provide education, training, and supervision for other adults to be mindful of the mental demands we place on others. An example would be our expectation that teachers, even those recently graduated as traditional-age students, exhibit high levels of critical thinking and metacognitive skills, although he speculates these skills may not be fully evolved for many until their 30s and 40s. The emphasis Kegan placed on continuing adult learning in the workplace as well as in other domains of adult life, along with his suggestion that teaching/coaching can stimulate developmental growth, makes this a promising model for future examination with practicing teachers. It also provides a framework that is consistent with the principles of developmental supervision. Figure 4.5 depicts the continuum of adult consciousness.

Stages of Concern. In the 1960s and early 1970s, Frances Fuller (1969) conducted pioneer studies of teacher concerns. In analyzing both her own studies and six others, she found that the responses by hundreds of teachers at various stages of experience showed different concerns.

Kimpston (1987), in a study examining both teacher and principal stages of concern, substantiated a steady increase in the stage of concern for most teachers. Kimpston also discovered that the nature of teachers' participation in staff development (sustained and active versus brief and episodic) had an impact on the emergence of higher stages of concern.

Teachers at the *self-adequacy* stage are focused on survival. They are concerned with doing well when a supervisor is present, getting favorable evaluations, and being accepted and respected by students and other teachers (Adams and Martray, 1981). Their primary concern is making it through the schoolday.

With survival and security assured, teachers think less of their own survival needs and begin to focus on *teaching tasks*. At this stage, teachers become more concerned with issues related to instructional and student discipline. They begin to think about altering or enriching the classroom schedule, the teaching materials, and their instructional methodology. Instructional concerns include the pressures of teaching, routinization and inflexibility of the teaching environment, student load, workload, and lack of academic freedom. Discipline concerns include class control, conflict between student and adult values and attitudes, and disruptive students (Adams and Martray, 1981). Concerns at this stage can be characterized as focused on the teaching environment and teaching responsibilities.

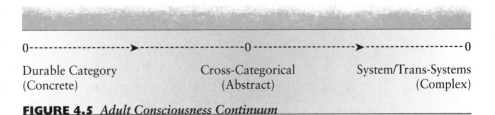

0--------------------▶---------------------0---------------------▶-------------------0

Durable Category   Cross-Categorical   System/Trans-Systems
(Concrete)   (Abstract)   (Complex)

FIGURE 4.5 *Adult Consciousness Continuum*

Superior teachers are at the highest stage of concern, referred to as the *teaching impact* stage. At this stage, teachers are most concerned with the impact on students' learning and students' well-being, even if it means departing from rules and norms. Academic concerns at this stage include diagnosing and meeting individual needs, sparking unmotivated students, and facilitating the intellectual and emotional development of students. The teacher with mature concerns also tends to be interested in the whole child, including interest in student health and nutrition, use of drugs by students, dropout prevention, and so on (Adams and Martray, 1981). The unfolding of teachers' concerns evolves on a continuum reflecting a shifting perspective, from "I" concerns to concerns for "my group" to concerns for "all students." Figure 4.6 represents the continuum of teacher concerns.

Integrating Stage Development Theories. Investigators of adult and teacher development have postulated that the various developmental characteristics are related (Oja and Pine, 1984; Sullivan, McCullough, and Stager, 1970). Although still somewhat speculative, these findings suggest that many teachers at a given level (low, moderate, or high) in one developmental characteristic may operate at the same general level in another developmental characteristic. The probable relationship of various developmental characteristics allows one to make tentative composite descriptions of teachers of generally low, moderate, and high levels of stage development. Figure 4.7 reviews the six adult/teacher development continuums.

The majority of teachers appear to be in relatively moderate to low stages of cognitive, conceptual, moral, and ego development—probably no different from the adult population at large (Oja and Pine, 1981; Rest, 1986; Wilkins, 1980). So what? What difference does it make that many teachers are not complex or autonomous? Perhaps one does not need higher-ordered thinking to teach. One could argue that if teaching is a simple enterprise with no need for decision making, then it would make little difference. In fact, if most teachers were autonomous and abstract, then trying to do a simple job would create great tension, resentment, and noncompliance. If teaching is a simple activity, schools need people who can reason simply. If teaching is complex and ever-changing, however, then higher levels of reasoning are necessary. A simple thinker in a dynamic and difficult enterprise would be subjected to overwhelming pressures.

Sociologists have documented the environmental demands posed by making thousands of decisions daily, by constant psychological pressure, and by expectations that the teacher must do the job alone—unwatched and unaided. A teacher

0- - - - - - - - - - - - - - - - - -> - - - - - - - - - - - - - - - - - -0- - - - - - - - - - - - - - - - - -> - - - - - - - - - - - - - - - -0

Self-Adequacy   Teaching Tasks   Teaching Impact

FIGURE 4.6 *Teacher Concerns Continuum*

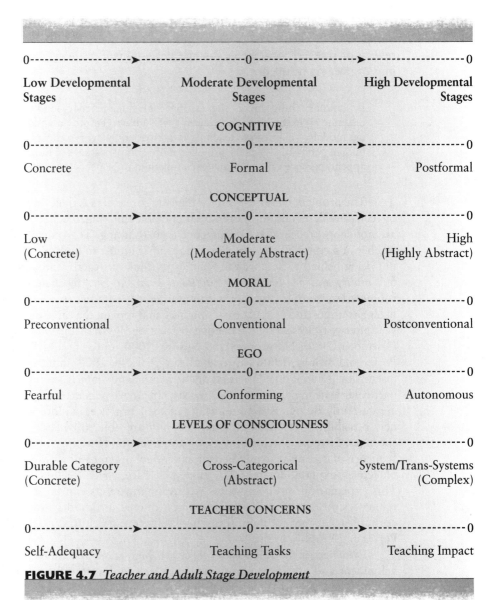

0------------------►------------------0------------------►------------------0

Low Developmental   Moderate Developmental   High Developmental
Stages   Stages   Stages

COGNITIVE

0------------------►------------------0------------------►------------------0

Concrete   Formal   Postformal

CONCEPTUAL

0------------------►------------------0------------------►------------------0

Low   Moderate   High
(Concrete)   (Moderately Abstract)   (Highly Abstract)

MORAL

0------------------►------------------0------------------►------------------0

Preconventional   Conventional   Postconventional

EGO

0------------------►------------------0------------------►------------------0

Fearful   Conforming   Autonomous

LEVELS OF CONSCIOUSNESS

0------------------►------------------0------------------►------------------0

Durable Category   Cross-Categorical   System/Trans-Systems
(Concrete)   (Abstract)   (Complex)

TEACHER CONCERNS

0------------------►------------------0------------------►------------------0

Self-Adequacy   Teaching Tasks   Teaching Impact

FIGURE 4.7 *Teacher and Adult Stage Development*

Source: Figures 4.1 through 4.5 and 4.7 are adapted from Stephen P. Gordon, *Assisting the Entry Year Teacher: A Leadership Resource.* Published 1990 by the Ohio Department of Education, Columbus, Ohio. Used with permission.

daily faces up to 150 students of various backgrounds, abilities, and interests, some of whom succeed while others fail. Concrete, rigid thinking on the part of the teacher cannot possibly improve instruction. As Madeline Hunter (1986) has noted, "Teaching . . . is a relativistic situational profession where *there are no absolutes*" (italics in original).

Teacher improvement can only come from abstract, multiinformational thought that can generate new responses toward new situations. Glassberg's (1979) review of research on teachers' stage development as related to instructional improvement concluded:

> In summary these studies suggest that high stage teachers tend to be adaptive in teaching style, flexible, and tolerant, and able to employ a wide range of teaching models. . . . effective teaching in almost any view is a most complex form of human behavior. Teachers at higher, more complex stages of human development appear as more effective in classrooms than their peers at lower stages.

The problem with the need for high-stage teachers is that, although the work by its nature demands autonomous and flexible thinking, teachers in most schools are not supported in ways to improve their thinking. The only alternative for a teacher in a complex environment who cannot adjust to multiple demands and is not being helped to acquire the abilities to think abstractly and autonomously is to *simplify and deaden the instructional environment.* Teachers make the environment less complex by disregarding differences among students and by establishing routines and instructional practices that remain the same day after day and year after year. Research on effective instruction (Berman and McLaughlin, 1978; Glatthorn, 2000; Hargreaves and Moore, 2000; O'Keefe and Johnston, 1989; Porter and Brophy, 1988; Rutter et al., 1979; Tieso, 2000) indicates that effective instruction is based on adaptation of curriculum and materials to local settings and particular learning goals. In other words, effective teachers think about what they are currently doing, assess the results of their practice, explore with each other new possibilities for teaching students, and are able to consider students' perspectives. Effective teaching has been misunderstood and misapplied as a set and sequence of certain teaching behaviors (review previous day's objectives, present objectives, explain, demonstrate, guided practice, check for understanding, etc.). This explanation of effectiveness is simply untrue, as can be seen in the prior references to Hunter (1986) and Berliner (quoted in Brandt, 1986). Rather, successful teachers are thoughtful teachers (Elliott and Schiff, 2001; Ferraro, 2000; Porter and Brophy, 1988).

Evidence of the relationship between high-stage attainment of teacher development and effective instructional practice can be found in several research studies. The works of Thies-Sprinthall and Sprinthall (1987), Phillips and Glickman (1991), Oja and Pine (1981), and Parker (1983) are particularly important because they suggest that teachers, when provided with a stimulating and supportive environment, can reach higher stages of development, yet, other research indicates that most teachers do not reach those higher stages. Why, if optimal adult learning suggests a continued capability to learn, are teachers characterized by a lack of such cognitive growth?

One possible explanation is found in the nature of the work environment. Schooler (1989) found through a 10-year longitudinal study of 687 subjects that "occupational conditions that promote occupational self-direction or otherwise involved dealing with complex environments would increase intellectual flexibility, while conditions that limit occupational self-direction and environmental complexity would decrease intellectual flexibility" (p. 5). Indicators of environmental complexity (measured through detailed interviews about what people do when working with things, data, and people) included the degree of routinization on the job, the closeness of supervision, and the substantive complexity of work—the degree to which the work demands thought and independent judgment. Schooler concluded from this study, as well as others investigating working men and women, that jobs that limit self-direction actually decrease intellectual flexibility. Schooler's research is consistent with conclusions made by O'Keefe and Johnston (1989) after reviewing teacher stage development research: "Development is unlikely in environments that are repressive or restrictive. Dialogue, reflection, and challenge embedded in organizational and personal support systems are critical components of growth producing contests" (p. 24).

Teachers who are isolated in their classrooms, receive no systematic feedback, attend monthly faculty meetings only to listen to monologues of announcements, and spend a few minutes each day chatting idly in the lounge may be viewed as remarkable specimens of survival. Such teachers, however, are not contributors to a successful school.

Life Cycle Development, Teachers' Life Cycles, and the Teaching Career

The next area of adult development to be discussed is research on age-linked life cycle development. These theorists too have sought to define sequential and normative patterns of development. The pioneering theorists in this tradition tended to look at very broad age periods and the patterns or issues for resolution associated with them (Buhler, 1956; Erikson, 1950), whereas later theorists have tended to posit a greater number of specific age periods (Gould, 1978; Levinson et al., 1978).

The study by Daniel Levinson and his colleagues (1978) of 40 men aged from mid-30s to mid-40s is among the most frequently cited studies of life cycle development. This research described how individuals alternate through periods of stability and transition in a life structure whose critical components typically revolve on work and family. An occupational dream is said to be formed during young adulthood and nurtured, frequently with the assistance of the spouse and a mentor. Levinson's work is a coherent treatment of changes in a person's life but has limitations in that the subjects were all middle-class males from a limited set of occupations. A number of subsequent studies of women have substantiated the model in part, but differences have been found in the timing and quality of transitions and the ages associated with transitional periods among women (Levinson and Levinson, 1996; Roberts and Newton, 1987). Some of the variability among women is related to whether they have followed a more traditionally female orientation to family versus a more typically masculine orientation to career during early adulthood (Lieblich, 1986; Roberts and Newton, 1987).

Occupational development of teachers appears to run counter to the needs of teachers as they progress through the adult life cycle. The work of Levinson (1978) and Neugarten (1977) has pointed to early adulthood as a period of bravado, romance, and the pursuit of dreams. The young adult aged 20 to 35 is on an exciting search for status, comfort, and happiness in work, family, and friends. The middle years, ages 35 to 55, provide some disillusionment, reflection, and reordering of priorities according to a reassessment of one's capabilities and opportunities. In teaching, however, the young adulthood period, which should be one of romance, quickly becomes one of disillusionment. The young person of age 24 or 25 who has entered teaching to pursue his or her dreams often finds after three years that work life is going nowhere. The job does not excite; the advancements do not exist; and the variety of work is nonexistent. The result can be intense boredom, leading to resignation—either *from* the job or *on* the job. What does it mean to education when a young teacher's natural inclination toward excitement and idealism is bound by a straitjacket of repetition?

Let's ask the next question. What happens when the natural inclination of the middle-aged teacher to reflect and reorder his or her teaching priorities confronts the same six periods of 30 students that he or she has faced for the past 20 years? One might expect a further despair of any impulse to change and to improve. Finally, what about the older teacher who is perceived by many as an anomaly, a relic who has remained in teaching because of inability to advance into administration or supervision. The acquisition of 30 years of experience coincides with the natural time for consolidating achievements and identifying one's remaining career objectives. Instead, there is only the same job—the same job as that of the new teacher down the hall, who might be the age of the older teacher's grandchild. Where is the sense of responsibility, generativity, and accomplishment in seniority? Old and new teachers are treated the same, accorded the same status, and expected to conform to the same routines.

Teaching appears to be a topsy-turvy occupation, running against the natural adult life cycle. Those who continue to make lasting improvement and enhance their students' educational lives should have our utmost respect. If not fortunate enough to be in a school that responds to and supports phases of the adult life cycle, the effective teacher truly transcends the system and educates in spite of, not because of, the school.

A small but growing body of literature focuses on the links between teacher development and issues related to the adult lifespan. Gehrke (1991) argued that we should more fully incorporate our understanding of adult development in developing programs for new teachers. This means both fostering the generative motivations of mature teachers and being sensitive to the fact that many young teachers are dealing with needs for intimacy. Levine (1987) argued that profitable activities that capitalize on young teachers' enthusiasm might include opportunities to work on new teaching methods, to develop curricula, and to initiate projects. The key is nurturing their need for innovation and adventure and helping them establish and cultivate close collegial relationships that meet their needs for intimacy.

Levine (1987) encouraged placing midlife teachers in situations permitting "a combination of teaching and administrative responsibilities that expands an adult's authority and mobility without sacrificing his or her expertise with children" (p. 16). Work on decision-making committees and mentorship of younger colleagues can provide such an outlet. Krupp (1987) argued that lack of career centrality and on-the-job retirement can be countered by bringing the older teachers' interests into the school. For instance, older teachers' interests in computers, photography, and gardening can be brought into the curriculum or extracurricular programs for students.

Transition Events

A third approach to adult development focuses more explicitly on the kinds of events associated with life transitions. Some theorists resist accepting the study of what are variably called *life events, critical events,* or *marker events* as part of the rubric of adult development because such a focus does not attempt to describe a universal, orderly sequence of development. However, Fiske and Chiriboga (1990) noted that just as the assumption of adult stability has given way to models of adult development "as a progression of orderly transformations over time," more recent models emphasize the role of transition events in our lives.

Life events have been typologized in a variety of ways. One typology, offered by Willis and Baltes (1980), seems to relate directly to the salience of the event for the individual. They talk about *normative age-graded events*—events that occur in many people's lives and that are anticipated around certain ages (such as marriage, birth of first child, and widowhood), *normative history-graded events*—those that affect large numbers of people in a given age cohort simultaneously (such as World War II and the Depression), and *non-normative events*—those personal events that are not anticipated as part of the life course even though they may occur for many (such as divorce, unemployment, and unexpected illness). Events can be positive or negative, anticipated or unanticipated. Although events associated with expected transitions in adult lives are often the impetus for adult growth (Aslanian and Brickell, 1981), it appears to be the unanticipated event, even if negative, that may provide the greatest opportunity for change and growth (Fiske and Chiriboga, 1990; Krupp, 1982).

Neugarten (1977, 1987) studied the timing of events such as childbearing, occupational advancement and peaking, children leaving home, retirement, personal illness, and death of a spouse or close friend. Many of these events are common to all or most adults; the time of their occurrence, according to Neugarten, influences how the person responds and continues with life. For example, the Blum and Meyer (1981) study of the recovery of adult men from severe heart attacks highlighted the difference in timing of critical events. Young men were bitter and hostile toward their heart attack and couldn't wait to resume their previous lives. Middle-aged men were reflective about the heart attack and seriously weighed whether they wanted to continue to live as they had before. They contemplated changes in family relations, job, and living environments. Older men were accepting and grateful that the heart attack had left them alive with the opportunity to finish some of their desired retirement plans. As one can see, the same event—a heart attack—resulted in quite different reactions, depending on the time and age of the adult.

Neugarten's interpretation of these differential responses relates to the experience of the events as "on time" versus "off time"—that is, occurring at an age considered socially appropriate or not. Certainly recent years have seen increasing variability in the timing of many common events. As Merriam and Caffarella (1999) observed, not having children, returning to school in later life, and beginning a new career in midlife are all more viable options today than decades ago. The growing number of teacher preparation programs aimed at adults choosing teaching as a second career gives testimony to her claim. Yet, the authors noted that timing still matters when it comes to many life events, given the powerful influence age norms exert on our thinking.

Both personal transition events (marriage, birth of a child, divorce, death of a loved one) and professional transition events (entry into the profession, tenure, transferring schools, becoming a lead teacher or department chairperson) can have a significant impact on a teacher's career and teaching. Traditionally, personal and transitional events have been ignored and professional transitions have been given pro forma recognition by the school organization. Krupp (1987) has suggested that staff development programs providing an environment of trust and collegiality, as well as adult transition support networks within schools, can be an important means of assisting teachers as they prepare for anticipated change events, such as retirement, or cope with unanticipated changes, such as the sudden dependency of a parent. The support networks and professional development recommended by Krupp to assist teachers have been largely nonexistent in schools.

One exception in recent years has been the emergence of beginning teacher assistance programs, including the assignment of support teams and mentors to novice teachers. Hopefully, beginners' assistance programs will become the foundation on which career-long support for personal and professional transitions becomes available. Beyond formal support programs, schools need to become the type of collegial, caring, growth-oriented communities that sustain teachers in times of transition.

Role Development

One of the most recent directions in work on adult development has emphasized adult social roles, generally examining how adult lives are characterized by interacting roles related to work or career, family life, and personal development. Juhasz (1989) has developed a model of adult roles that incorporates each of three major roles: family, work, and self. These roles are depicted as intertwining, sometimes in synchrony, sometimes with different momentum and force. This model emphasizes the active involvement of adults who take roles and choose which roles they will place emphasis on at given points in their lives, with self-esteem as the driving force "directing energies toward roles that will best enhance feelings of worth" (p. 307).

Merriam and Clark (1991, 1993) designed a questionnaire to study the relationship between life events in the domains of "work and love" (here broadly defined as in the instrumental and expressive components of life) and adult learning. In essence, people graphed their life patterns, using two separate lines to show the ups and downs in these two domains of life. Respondents were asked next to list major events occurring in the last 20 years of their adult life (age 18 or older) and to describe learning experiences. From their analysis of 405 respondents, they found evidence for three different models used to characterize linkages between work and family life: (1) segmentation—when there is little or no connection, (2) compensatory—where individuals seek in one area the satisfaction or activities that are lacking in the other, and (3) generalization—where attitudes formed in the work setting spill over into family life or vice versa.

One of Merriam and Clark's most significant findings was the predominance of work-related learning for both men and women and the evidence that more learning occurs when things are going well in both arenas (work and family life). However, learning that led to a real perspective transformation most often was associated with coping with the difficult times in either work (e.g., being fired) or family life (e.g., losing a parent). Since much of the most significant adult learning appears to be from life experience, the role of the supervisor may be critical in helping teachers to experience growth as an outcome of unsettling life experiences in the professional, personal, or family domains. Although the supervisor need not and should not assume the role of therapist, one implication of the social roles models of adult development is that a teacher's personal, family, and professional roles interact with and affect each other, and need to be addressed holistically by supervision.

School systems and supervisors traditionally have been concerned only with teachers' professional roles, ignoring their personal and family roles. The few efforts intended to address the relationship of the three domains have been criticized as being beyond the scope of supervision, an inappropriate use of school resources, and superfluous to the improvement of teaching and learning. Yet, the literature on adult role development tells us that we cannot compartmentalize the personal, family, and professional aspects of a teacher's life. Put succinctly, teachers' other adult roles have direct effects on their instruction. Supervision, however, has largely failed to provide teachers with support to help them understand the interaction of their various adult roles, cope with role conflict and resulting stress, or develop the proper balance and synergy among alternative roles.

Beyond Universal Conceptions of Development: The Sociocultural Context of Adult Development

From the 1980s and through the present a significant body of research has emerged examining the impact of social structural variables (e.g., race, class, gender, disability, or sexual orientation) on adult development (Clark and Caffarella, 1999), with greatest emphasis on the effects of gender and race/ethnicity. The intent of some researchers has been to develop more robust and inclusive theories, describing a broader range of people than earlier theories. In other cases, especially for researchers informed by the postmodern resistance to "grand" theories, there has been no such attempt at "umbrella" theories of adult development (Kilgore, 2001). The latter researchers have been interested in offering previously unavailable pictures of adult development for individuals from groups marginalized in the construction of knowledge about adult development, as well as in illustrating how structural variables like gender, race, and class intersect in the construction of our identities (Sheared, 1999; Tisdell, 2000; Graue, 2005).

The Role of Gender in Adult Development. Much of the literature examining the relationship of gender and adult development has looked specifically at women, in response to the initial claim that their lives and experiences were not accounted for in the early development of adult development theory. Emerging theory and research have taken two forms, in some cases extending or adapting earlier work based primarily on men, and in other cases starting afresh with female or mixed gender samples. In the first strand is the work of Gilligan (1982), challenging Kohlberg's model of moral development (Kohlberg and Turiel, 1971). Her work suggested men and women base their moral decisions on different criteria, with women using an ethic of caring and men an ethic of justice. Similarly, Josselson (1987) reexamined Erikson's stage theory of psychosocial development, postulating four potential outcomes of Erikson's identity stage for women. Primary among her findings was that maintaining a sense of connectedness and affiliation with others was crucial for women.

The second strand of research consists of studies based specifically on the lives of women. One of the most cited sources in this strand is *Women's Ways of Knowing* by Belenky, Clinchy, Goldberger, and Tarule (1986). Resisting the notion of hierarchical stages, Belenky and colleagues pointed to the development of *voice* as central to women's development, and delineated five positions or categories in the development of women's knowledge: silence, received knowledge, subjective knowledge, procedural knowledge, and constructed knowledge. The developmental ideal is the integration of all five categories. Also representing this strand of research is the work of Peck (1986). She theorized women's lives as consisting of three contiguous layers, including an outermost core of socio-historical context; a flexible, bi-directional "sphere of influence," consisting of the sum of multiple relationships; and, finally, a center core of self-definition. These spheres are presumed to be constantly interacting as women move through their lives. Caffarella and Olson (1993) summarized the research on women's development in terms of four themes: the centrality of relationships, the importance and interplay of social roles, the dominance of role discontinuities and change as the norm for women, and the diversity of experience across age cohorts. Given the predominance of women in the teaching workforce, it seems important that supervisors become familiar with those models of adult development that reveal the distinctive developmental concerns women may bring.

More recently, models of adult development whether based on men's or women's lives have been critiqued for their universalizing character, tending to ignore or discount diversity *among* men and women, and the degree to which individuals of each gender exhibit patterns described as typical of the opposite sex. For example, Anderson and Hayes (1996) found that both men and women value achievement as well as relationships, derive self-esteem from similar sources, and struggle with ongoing issues of holding on (connection) and letting go (separation). The tendency of these models to ignore diversity related to race, class, and culture has also been criticized. Harris (1996) examined how men from different subcultures viewed each of 24 cultural messages about masculinity, and described differences related to class, race, sexual orientation, and community of origin (city, urban, rural). This literature may help understand why some men are more willing to break mainstream cultural norms that discourage their entry into the elementary education teaching force.

The Role of Race and Ethnicity in Adult Development

Chavez and Guido-DiBrito (1999) have provided an excellent overview of models of racial and ethnic identity, two prominent stands of work contributing to an understanding of the impact of race and ethnicity on adult learners. Cross (1971, 1995) developed one of the earliest of these models, focusing on the development of racial identity among African Americans. According to this model, Blacks move from a stage of limited awareness of race (a stage Chavez and Guido-DiBrito question) to later stages of embracing first an Afrocentric identity and finally a multicultural identity. Similarly, Parham (1989) has focused on how experiences with negative differential treatment by others become the trigger for formation of racial identity among Blacks. Chavez and Guido-DiBrito, on the other hand, posited that immersion in one's own racial group acts as the primary trigger for such identity development. Similarly they take issue with the focus on perceptions of other groups inherent in the most prominent model of White racial identity development, that of Helms (1993, 1995). Helms stressed interracial exposure as a powerful trigger for the development of a White racial identity that moves beyond a dominant group assumption of White superiority toward a nonracist frame. Chavez and Guido-DiBrito argue that Helms's model places inordinate emphasis on the intersection of racial perceptions of others and racial perception of self. They are more intrigued by models of ethnic identity development.

A model of White ethnic identity by Katz (1989) identifies values and perspectives of White American cultural identity. These values include autonomy, competitiveness, and a linear sense of time, and can be contrasted with values such as harmony, balance, and respect for the wisdom of elders identified in Garrett and Walking Stick Garrett's (1994) model of Native American identity. Phinney (1990), on the other hand, developed a model describing an ethnic identity process that can be applied to all groups. She emphasized two issues faced by members of nondominant group members: (1) dealing with stereotyping and prejudicial treatment by the dominant group and (2) resolving the clash between the value systems of their own ethnic culture and that of the dominant culture by negotiating a bicultural value system.

Several implications for adult learning can be drawn from these models. The models generally suggest that although most individuals from White ethnic groups typically experience learning that is grounded in their own cultural norms, they may struggle with or resist learning in less familiar multicultural environments. This has implications for efforts in the area of diversity training. On the other hand, persons from nondominant cultural groups often have to learn to be at least bicultural in their learning if they are to succeed in "mainstream" learning environments. For instance, Alfred (2001) has pointed to the development of bicultural competence as a factor in the career development of successful (tenured) African American women faculty. She also has pointed to the assistive role that White male mentors played in some cases. Similarly teachers from nondominant groups are likely to find that they must learn to successfully navigate two or more cultures; their mentors need to remain sensitive to the challenges this presents.

Recent research on women's development and research on the place of race and ethnicity in identity development have challenged our thinking about the degree to which any single theory of adult development can adequately describe all adult lives. Yet, these models can still provide a useful heuristic for thinking about the many ways in which adults continue to change throughout the course of their lives and the myriad forces which come to influence these changes. For those who seek to provide assistance to teachers, familiarity with this literature serves as a reminder of the tremendous degree of difference that exists among the adult learners who constitute the teaching force.

Review of Adult/Teacher Development Models

Table 4.1 presents a schematic review of the five conceptual frameworks for adult development. One thing all five approaches have in common is the supposition that adult lives are characterized by change and adaptation. For teachers, as with all adult learners, the one thing we can be certain of is that things will not remain the same; thus, individuals will need to cope with changes as they arise. Supervision provides the opportunity for ascertaining the levels, stages, and issues of adult development in schools and assisting the teacher's professional development in the context of these realities.

Development: Ebb and Flow

Cognitive researchers have shown that stages of thinking vary according to the domain or topic (Gardner, 1983; Case, 1986; Sternberg, 1988). Fred loves to teach art to his second-grade youngsters. He's constantly looking for ideas, finding

TABLE 4.1	Conceptual Models of Adult Development			
Universal, Orderly, Sequential		**Interactive, Socially Contexted**		
Hierarchical Stages	*Life Cycle Phases*	*Transition Events*	*Role Development*	*Sociocultural Variables*
Cognitive Piaget, Perry	*Goal Phases* Buhler	*Critical Events* Brim and Ryff	*Family, Work, and Self* Juhasz	*Spheres of Influence* Peck
Moral Gilligan, Kohlberg	*Critical Issues* Erikson	*Stressful Events* Fiske et al.	*Love, Work, and Learning* Merriam and Clark	*Women's Ways of Knowing* Belenky et al.
Conceptual Hunt	*Stability vs. Transition* Levinson	*On Time/Off Time* Neugarten		*Ethnic Identity Development* Phinney
Ego Loevinger				
Levels of Consciousness Kegan				
Concern Fuller				

materials, and expending energy to improve his art program. Yet, when it comes to teaching mathematics, he puts in the required time, uses the worksheets, and muddles through the material. He never liked mathematics as a student and doesn't care to spend extra time on it. Suffice it to say that teachers, like all humans, are not static in their levels of thinking and commitment about all endeavors.

Furthermore, development can regress, recycle, or become blocked. Because one has reached a high level of development in one arena does not mean that level of development is consolidated eternally. *Experience* is a relative term—a teacher (or supervisor) with 30 years of teaching (or supervising) can still be inexperienced in many ways. Change the expectations of the jobs and/or change the clientele served, and suddenly there is an inexperienced person trying to figure out how to survive. Likewise, a first-year teacher may, after only a few months, be experienced and able to reason according to concerns beyond his or her own survival.

Alterations to a person's personal or professional situation can usher in regression in levels of thinking and levels of motivation. A highly committed and thoughtful faculty, who had made their school an exciting and successful place, was jolted when negotiations between the teachers' union and the school board resulted in a bitter strike. The immediate result on the school was that teachers retreated within their four walls, carrying out the letter of their contract and removing themselves from involvement in school curriculum and instruction issues. Most teachers retreated to a self-survival stage.

Teacher or adult development is not monolithic, linear, or eternal. The research on developmental stages provides lenses for viewing teachers individually and collectively as to their current levels of thinking and commitment. Through such lenses, we can explore possible interventions to assist teachers individually and collectively to move into higher stages of development.

Influences on Teacher Development

In helping teachers grow, supervisors must consider characteristics of the teacher as a client. We can view teacher development against the background of adult learning and development, influences on the work environment of the school, and characteristics of the teaching profession. The context of teacher development is illustrated in Figure 4.8. Imagine a large felt board representing the context of a teacher's life. At the center is the individual with his or her unique development embedded into the work environment of the school, which is in turn embedded into characteristics of the teaching profession. When viewing a teacher's growth (or lack of growth), we must consider both the characteristics of the individual and the influences of the work environment and the teaching profession.

For example, a teacher may be resistant because of previous negative experiences within the work environment of the school. Perhaps at one time the teacher was concerned with improving her class and used abstract thought to implement a new classroom design. Perhaps other teachers or a supervisor frowned on such experimentation and threatened the teacher with the loss of her job. This teacher, needing to keep the job for financial reasons, therefore gave up trying to change. She retreated from improvement because of adverse pressure. This teacher might now be resistant, but she still has the ability to improve. Improvement will not occur, however, until changes occur in her immediate work environment.

Another example might be a willing teacher who has found a satisfactory maintenance level of group instruction and can live comfortably with the school norms. The reasons he does not demonstrate further improvement might be traced to characteristics of the teaching profession. The teacher may see no future prospects for increased status, income, or responsibility. Without any prospects for career advancement, he may rationally decide to remain adequate but nothing more. The supervisor must develop ways to provide advancement, recognition, and/or status in this teacher's career in order to realize further growth.

The point is that characteristics of the individual teacher may not be fixed, but rather function as a part of the teacher's perceptions of the larger environment. Research on adults has demonstrated that teachers can become more committed and more thoughtful about their work. Every person has the potential to improve:

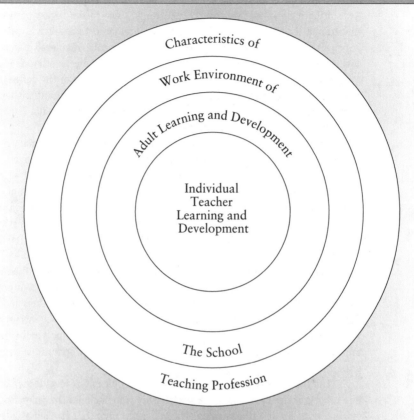

FIGURE 4.8 *Influences on Teacher Development*

Such potential might be blocked, slowed down, or even reversed, but it still exists. The challenge for the supervisor is to treat teachers as individual adult learners to enable them to use their potential.

PRACTITIONER REFLECTION

Adult Learning for Student Learning

Lauralee Pankonien, *Coordinator, Leadership Development, Region XIII Education Service Center*

In the summer of 2000, I made the transition from my position as an elementary campus principal in a large, urban school district to serving as a teacher of adults and professional developer for one of the 20 Regional Education Service Centers in Texas. The Region XIII ESC serves

60 Central Texas school districts. Initially, my department's offerings to facilitate administrators' professional growth were almost entirely one-day workshops presented on site at the ESC. Most of those workshops were organized around some sort of review of recent publications on educational leadership, and all of them were targeted to individual principals or assistant principals. At the end of the day, workshop participants completed a short evaluation (most of them indicating that they enjoyed the chance to dialogue together on leadership topics and commenting on the temperature of the room or the quality of the coffee), received a certificate documenting their "seat time" for the day, and left our building without being challenged to put much thought into how the ideas we discussed might actually impact their work. A lot has changed in a relatively short amount of time.

The disconnect between what we had been offering and what campus leaders truly needed in a climate of increased accountability became increasingly obvious to us over the last few years. We recognized that a new model of professional development—one that represented a convergence of response to demands of the increasing layers of accountability and research on best practice in adult learning—had to be developed. The Leadership Institute for School Improvement was the result. This essay describes the design of the Institute and illustrates the various ways in which principles of adult learning have been translated into collaborative implementation of best practices in classroom teaching.

One principle of adult learning is that readiness to learn is influenced by the need to solve real-life problems. Clearly, teachers and administrators have an unprecedented need for an effective support system to cultivate school-based leadership teams and prepare them with the skills and knowledge to advocate for effective practices that will raise student achievement. The goal of the Institute is to develop the capacity for individuals and teams to lead and sustain improvement through data-driven, job-embedded interventions supported by ongoing professional development.

The Institute is designed for participation by campus-level leadership teams organized into cohorts of five to six teams. Each leadership team includes the campus principal, lead teachers, and possibly other key campus leaders. Each cohort is designed as a learning community in which supportive professional networks and collegial relationships can be established and developed over time, both within and across campus teams. Cohorts work together for a period of three years, creating a powerful opportunity for members to learn from one another. Cohort members participate in several common learning modules as well as additional professional development customized to meet the needs of their individual campus. Leadership Institute learning modules focus on issues critical to classroom practice and student success, including the following:

> *Prioritizing, mapping, and monitoring the curriculum.* This module challenges teams to answer key questions such as: What learning is important? How can we develop and align curriculum that includes such learning? How do we know if the planned curriculum is being taught? In a world of accountability, it is imperative for schools to keep their curriculum on target.

> *Using data to lead change.* Many data are available in schools, but often they are not used to examine the effectiveness of curriculum and instruction. Inquiry processes are taught as participants learn how gathering and reflecting on data are vital parts of the

school improvement process. Participants learn how to use a problem-solving process to tackle tough issues in a system whose parts are interrelated and deeply affect one another.

Leading assessment and instruction. Participants learn how curriculum, instruction, and assessment are linked, and how to recognize good instruction. Research-based strategies, tools, and processes are taught to help school leaders facilitate the improvement of instruction and assessment.

Standards in practice. Schools may adopt standards that promote higher-level learning, but do learning activities match the standards? Participants learn how to analyze student work to determine if students are really being asked to do high-quality work.

In addition to the learning modules, former principals or superintendents trained in instructional coaching support Leadership Institute principals as they apply newly learned knowledge and skills in their schools. This on-site application with coaching results in the situated cognition discussed earlier in this chapter. Coaches become a key resource in sustaining the implementation of the concepts and strategies presented in the learning modules. Additionally, the coaches model the facilitative behaviors that the principals need to use with teachers implementing school improvement strategies.

Campus leadership teams participating in the Institute have the opportunity to share their successful school improvement stories and disseminate information about the Institute modules through presentations to peer cohort campuses.

Today, the demands of state and federal accountability systems cannot be ignored in considering the professional development of educational leaders. Principals' and teacher leaders' participation in learning activities must not only incorporate principles of best practice in adult learning but it must also result in improved student performance in a clear and measurable way. The Leadership Institute for School Improvement aims to effectively accomplish both ends.

EXERCISES

Academic

1. Review the theories of a major author on adult development, as found in the list of references that follows these exercises. Write a paper summarizing the author's theories and any research on which those theories are based.

2. Review the research of a prominent investigator of teacher development. Write a paper summarizing the major conclusions that researcher has drawn from his or her studies.

3. Review literature and/or research on adult learning. On the basis of your review, discuss in writing several generally accepted principles of adult learning. For each principle, infer and discuss implications for supervision.

Field

1. Visit the classrooms of a teacher you perceive to be functioning at high stages of development and one you perceive to be at low stages of development. Write a report comparing the teachers in terms of teaching methods, interaction with students, classroom management, attention to individual student needs, and general teaching effectiveness. (Use fictitious names in your report.)

2. On the basis of observations of leader-teacher, teacher-teacher, and teacher-student interactions, faculty meeting activities, posted communications, and the like, infer a group of *social norms* that prevail at a selected school. Write a paper stating your perceptions of the school's social norms and your opinion of whether those norms are positive or negative influences on teachers' stage development.

3. Interview a veteran teacher who is nearing retirement. Ask the teacher to discuss the major transitions that have taken place during his or her career. Summarize the interview in writing.

4. Reflect on your own career and the major transitions that have taken place during your career. Choose an artifact that symbolizes each major transition. Prepare a display of your artifacts and an oral or written report explaining the relationship between your career transitions and these artifacts.

5. Ask a first-year teacher, a third-year teacher, and a teacher with at least 10 years of experience to list their concerns about teaching. Prepare a report comparing the various responses and drawing relevant conclusions.

Developmental

1. For the time that you will be reading this book, keep a diary of weekly decisions you have made. You might want to include the possible choices for each decision, the factors important in resolving your problems, and the success with which you carried out your decisions. Review your diary after six weeks or more. Do you see any trends? What appear to be the most important considerations you use in making your decisions?

2. Begin a career scrapbook with the purpose of documenting your own professional development.

3. Begin an in-depth study of a major topic discussed in Chapter 4 (for example, adult learning, adult development, teacher development, the teaching career, or teacher motivation).

REFERENCES

Adams, R. D., and Martray, C. 1981. *Teacher development: A study of factors related to teacher concerns for pre, beginning, and experienced teachers.* Paper presented at the annual meeting of the American Educational Research Association, Los Angeles, April.

Alfred, M. V. 2001. Expanding theories of career development: Adding the voices of African American women in the White academy. *Adult Education Quarterly, 51,* 108–127.

Ammon, P. 1984. Human development, teaching and teacher education. *Teacher Education Quarterly, 11*(4), 95–108.

Amstutz, D. 1999. Adult learning: Moving toward more inclusive theories and practices. In T. C. Guy (Ed.), *Providing culturally relevant adult ed-*

ucation: A challenge for the twenty-first century. *New Directions for Adult and Continuing Education, 82.* San Francisco: Jossey-Bass.

Anderson, D. Y., and Hayes, C. L. 1996. *Gender, identity and self-esteem: A new look at adult development.* New York: Springer.

Arlin, P. K. 1975. Cognitive development in adulthood: A fifth stage. *Developmental Psychology, 11,* 602–606.

Aslanian, C. B., and Brickell, H. M. 1981. *Americans in transition.* New York: College Entrance Examination Board.

Belenky, M. F., Clinchy, B. M., Goldberger, N. R., and Tarule, J. M. 1986. *Women's ways of knowing: The development of self, voice, and mind.* New York: Basic Books.

Berman, P., and McLaughlin, M. W. 1978. *Federal programs supporting educational change, Vol. 8. Implementing and sustaining innovations.* Santa Monica, CA: Rand Corporation. (ERIC ED 159 289)

Blum, L. S., and Meyer, R. 1981. *Developmental implications of myocardial infarction for mid-life adults.* Paper presented at the annual meeting of the American Educational Research Association, Los Angeles, April.

Brandt, R. S. 1986. On the expert teacher: A conversation with David Berliner. *Educational Leadership, 44*(2), 4–9.

Brookfield, S. 1986. *Understanding and facilitating adult learning.* San Francisco: Jossey-Bass.

Brown, J. S., Collins, A., and Duguid, P. 1989. Situated cognition and the culture of learning. *Educational Researcher, 18*(1), 32–42.

Buhler, C. 1956. *From childhood to maturity.* London: Routledge and Kegan Paul.

Caffarella, R. S., and Olson, S. K. 1993. Psychosocial development of women: A critical review of the literature. *Adult Education Quarterly, 43*(3), 125–151.

Calhoun, E. F. 1985. *Relationship of teachers' conceptual level to the utilization of supervisory services and to a description of the classroom instructional improvement.* Paper presented at the annual meeting of the American Educational Research Association, Chicago, April.

Case, R. 1986. The new stage theories in intellectual development. In M. Perlmutter (Ed.), *Perspectives on intellectual development,* Vol. 19. Hillsdale, NJ: Lawrence Erlbaum.

Chavez, A. F., and Guido-DiBrito, F. 1999. Racial and ethnic identity and development. In M. C. Clark and R. S. Caffarella (Eds.), *An update on adult development theory: New ways of thinking about the life course. New Directions for Adult*

and Continuing Education, 84. San Francisco: Jossey-Bass.

Clark, M. C., and Caffarella, R. S. 1999. *An update on adult development theory: New ways of thinking about the life course. New Directions for Adult and Continuing Education, 84.* San Francisco: Jossey-Bass.

Clayton, V., and Birren, J. 1980. The development of wisdom across the lifespan: A reexamination of an ancient topic. *Lifespan Development and Behavior, 3,* 103–135.

Cranton, P. 1994. *Understanding and promoting transformative learning.* San Francisco: Jossey-Bass.

Cross, W. E., 1995. The psychology of Nigrescence: Revising the Cross model. In J. G. Ponterott, J. M Casa, L. A. Suzuki, and C. M. Alexander (Eds.), *Handbook of multicultural counseling.* Thousand Oaks, CA: Sage.

Cross, W. E., Jr. 1971. Toward a psychology of Black liberation: The Negro-to-Black convergence experience. *Black World, 20*(9), 13–27.

Cummings, A. L., and Murray, H. G. 1989. Ego development and its relation to teacher education. *Teaching and Teacher Education, 5*(1), 21–32.

Dewey, J. 1938. *Experience and education.* New York: Collier.

Elliott, V., and Schiff, S. 2001. A look within. *Journal of Staff Development, 22*(2), 39–42.

English, L. M. 2005. Historical and contemporary explorations of the social change and spiritual directions of adult education. *Teachers College Record, 107*(6), 1169–1192.

Erikson, E. H. 1950. *Childhood and society.* New York: Norton.

Erikson, E. H. 1963. *Childhood and society* (2nd ed.). New York: Norton.

Ferraro, J. M. 2000. Reflective practice and professional development. Washington, DC: *ERIC Clearinghouse on Teaching and Teacher Education.* (ERIC ED 449 120)

Fiske, M., and Chiriboga, D. A. 1990. *Change and continuity in adult life.* San Francisco: Jossey-Bass.

Fullan, M. G. 1991. *The new meaning of educational change* (2nd ed.). New York: Teachers College Press.

Fuller, F. F. 1969. Concerns of teachers: A developmental conceptualization. *American Educational Research Journal, 6*(2), 207–266.

Gardner, H. 1983. *Frames of mind: The theory of multiple intelligences.* New York: Basic Books.

Gardner, H. 1999. *Intelligence reframed: Multiple intelligences for the 21st century.* New York: Basic Books.

Garrett, J. T., and Walking Stick Garrett, M. 1994. The path of good medicine: Understanding and counseling Native American Indians. *Journal of Multicultural Counseling and Development, 22,* 134–144.

Gehrke, N. J. 1991. Seeing our way to better helping of beginning teachers. *Educational Forum, 55* (3), 233–242.

Gilligan, C. 1979. Woman's place in man's life cycle. *Harvard Educational Review, 49*(4), 431–446.

Gilligan, C. 1982. *In a different voice.* Cambridge, MA: Harvard University Press.

Gilligan, C. 1998. Remembering Larry. *Journal of Moral Education, 27*(2), 125–140.

Ginsburg, H., and Opper, S. 1979. *Piaget's theory of intellectual development* (2nd ed.). Englewood Cliffs, NJ: Prentice Hall.

Glassberg, S. 1979. *Developing models of teacher development.* (ERIC ED 171 685)

Glatthorn, A. A. 2000. *The principal as curriculum leader: Shaping what is taught and tested* (2nd ed.). Thousand Oaks, CA: Corwin Press.

Gonzales, A. H., and Nelson, L. M. 2005. Learner-centered instruction promotes student success. *T.H.E. Journal, 32*(6), 10, 12, 14–15.

Gorard, S., and Selwyn, N. 2005. What makes a lifelong learner? *Teachers College Record, 107*(6), 1193–1216.

Gould, R. L. 1978. *Transformations.* New York: Touchstone Books.

Graue, E. 2005. Theorizing and describing preservice teachers' images of families and schooling. *Teachers College Record, 107*(1), 157–185.

Grow, G. 1991. Teaching learners to be self-directed: A stage approach. *Adult Education Quarterly, 41*(3), 125–149.

Hansman, C. A. 2001. Context-based adult learning. In S. Merriam (Ed.), *The new update on adult learning theory. New Directions for Adult and Continuing Education,* 89. San Francisco: Jossey-Bass.

Hargreaves, A., and Moore, S. 2000. Curriculum integration and classroom relevance: A study of teachers' practice. *Journal of Curriculum and Supervision, 15*(2), 89–112.

Harris, I. 1996. *Messages men hear: Constructing masculinities.* London: Taylor.

Harvey, O. J., White, B. J., Prather M., Alter, R., and Hoffmeister, J. 1966. Teachers' belief systems and preschool atmospheres. *Journal of Educational Psychology, 57,* 373–381.

Hayes, E., and Flannery, D. D. 2000. *Women as learners: The significance of gender in adult learning.* San Francisco: Jossey-Bass.

Heck, E. J., and Davis, C. S. 1973. Differential expression of empathy in a counseling analog. *Journal of Counseling Psychology, 20,*101–104.

Helms, J. E. 1993. Introduction: Review of racial identity terminology. In J. E. Helms (Ed.), *Black and White racial identity: Theory, research and practice.* Westport, CT: Praeger.

Helms, J. E. 1995. An update of Helms' White and people of color racial identity models. In J. G. Ponterott, J. M. Casas, L. A. Suzuki, and C. M. Alexander (Eds.), *Handbook of multicultural counseling.* Thousand Oaks, CA: Sage.

Holliday, S. G., and Chandler, M. J. 1986. *Wisdom: Explorations in adult competence.* Basel: Karger.

Hopkins, D. 1990. Integrating staff development and school improvement: A study of personality and school climate. In B. Joyce (Ed.), *ASCD Yearbook: Changing school culture through staff development.* Alexandria, VA: Association for Supervision and Curriculum Development.

Horn, J. L., and Cattell, R. B. 1967. Age differences in fluid and crystallized intelligence. *Acta Psychological, 26,* 107–129.

Hunt, D. E., Butler, L. F., Noy, J. E., and Rosser, M. E. 1978. *Assessing conceptual level by the paragraph completion method.* Toronto: Ontario Institute for Studies in Education.

Hunt, D. E., and Joyce, B. R. 1967. Teacher trainee personality and initial teaching style. *American Educational Research Journal, 4*(3), 253–255.

Hunter, M. 1986. To be or not to be—Hunterized. *Tennessee Educational Leadership, 12,* 70.

Johnston, M. 1985. How elementary teachers understand the concept of "on-task": A developmental critique. *The Journal of Classroom Interaction, 21,* 15–24.

Josselson, R. 1987. *Finding herself: Pathways to identity development in women.* San Francisco: Jossey-Bass.

Juhasz, A. M. 1989. A role-based approach to adult development: The triple helix model. *International Journal of Aging and Human Development, 29*(4), 301–315.

Katz, J. H. 1989. The challenge of diversity. In C. Woolbright (Ed.), *College unions at work.* Monograph, No. 11, 1–17. Bloomington, IN: Association of College Unions-International.

Kegan, R. 1994. *In over our heads: The mental demands of modern life*. Cambridge, MA: Harvard University Press.

Kegan, R. 2000. What "form" transforms?: A constructive-developmental perspective on transformational learning. In J. Mezirow and Associates (Eds.), *Learning as transformation: Critical perspectives on a theory in progress*. San Francisco: Jossey-Bass.

Kerka, S. 1998. *New perspectives on mentoring*. ERIC Digest No. 194. (ERIC ED 418249)

Kilgore, D. W. 2001. Critical and postmodern perspectives on adult learning. In S. B. Merriam (Ed.), *The new update on adult learning theory. New Directions for Adult and Continuing Education, 89*. San Francisco: Jossey-Bass.

Kimpston, R. D. 1987. Teacher and principal stage of concern regarding implementation of benchmark testing: A longitudinal study. *Teaching and Teacher Education, 3*(3), 205–217.

Kitchener, K. S., Lynch, C. L., Fischer, K. W., and Wood, P. K. 1993. Developmental range of reflection judgment: The effect of contextual support and practice on developmental stage. *Developmental Psychology, 29*(5), 893–906.

Knowles, M. S. 1980. *The modern practice of adult education: From pedagogy to andragogy* (2nd ed.). Chicago: Association/Follett.

Knowles, M. S. 1984. *Andragogy in action: Applying modern principles of adult learning*. San Francisco: Jossey-Bass.

Kolb, D. A. 1984. *Experiential learning*. Englewood Cliffs, NJ: Prentice Hall.

Kohlberg, L., and Armon, C. 1984. Three types of stage models used in the study of adult development. In M. Commons, F. A. Richards, and C. A. Armon (Eds.), *Beyond formal operations: late adolescent and adult cognitive development*. New York: Praeger.

Kohlberg, L., and Turiel, E. 1971. Moral development and moral education. In G. Lessor (Ed.), *Psychology and educational practice*. Chicago: Scott, Foresman.

Kramer, D. A. 1983. Post-formal operations? A need for further conceptualization. *Human Development, 26*(2), 91–105.

Kramer, D. A. 1987. *Improved learning in aging: Implications for education*. Paper presented at Information and Aging: Coalitions for the Future, New Brunswick, NJ, April. (ERIC ED 283 098)

Krupp, J. 1982. *The adult learner: A unique entity*. Manchester, CT: Adult Development and Learning.

Krupp, J. 1987. Understanding and motivating personnel in the second half of life. *Journal of Education, 169*(1), 20–47.

Lave, J., and Wenger, E. 1991. *Situated learning: Legitimate peripheral participation*. New York: Cambridge University Press.

Lea, V., and Griggs, T. 2005. Behind the mask and beneath the story: Enabling students-teachers' to reflect critically on the socially-constructed nature of their "normal" practice. *Teacher Education Quarterly, 32*(1), 93–114.

Levine, S. L. 1987. Understanding life cycle issues: A resource for school leaders. *Journal of Education, 169*(1), 7–19.

Levine, S. L. 1989. *Promoting adult growth in schools*. Boston: Allyn and Bacon.

Levinson, D. J., et al. 1978. *The seasons in a man's life*. New York: Knopf.

Levinson, D. J., and Levinson, J. D. 1996. *The seasons of a woman's life*. New York: Knopf.

Lieblich, A. 1986. Successful career women at midlife: Crises and transitions. *International Journal of Aging and Human Development, 23*(4), 301–312.

Lindeman, E. 1926. *The meaning of adult education*. New York: New Republic.

Loevinger, J. 1976. *Ego development*. San Francisco: Jossey-Bass.

Marsick, V. J., and Watkins, K. 1990. *Informal and incidental learning in the workplace*. New York: Routledge.

Marsick, V. J., and Watkins, K. E. 2001. Informal and incidental learning. In S. Merriam (Ed.), *The new update on adult learning theory. New Directions for Adult and Continuing Education, 89*. San Francisco: Jossey-Bass.

Mathis, C. 1987. Educational reform, the aging society and the teaching profession. *Journal of Education, 169*(1), 80–88.

Merriam, S., and Caffarella, R. 1999. *Learning in adulthood* (2nd ed.). San Francisco: Jossey-Bass.

Merriam, S. B. 2001. Something old, something new: Adult learning theory for the twenty-first century. *New Directions for Adult and Continuing Education, 89*, 93–96.

Merriam, S. B., and Clark, M. C. 1991. *Lifelines: Patterns of work, love and learning in adulthood*. San Francisco: Jossey-Bass.

Merriam, S. B., and Clark, M. C. 1993. Learning from experience: What makes it significant? *International Journal of Lifelong Education,* 12(2), 129–138.

Mezirow, J. D. 1981 A critical theory of adult learning and education. *Adult Education,* 32(1), 3–24.

Mezirow, J. D., and associates. 1990. Fostering critical reflection in adulthood. *A guide to transformative and emancipatory learning.* San Francisco: Jossey-Bass.

Mezirow, J. M. 2000. Learning to think like an adult: Core concepts of transformation theory. In J. M. Mezirow & Associates (Eds.), *Learning as transformation: Critical perspectives on a theory in progress.* San Francisco: Jossey-Bass.

Neimark, E. D. 1987. *Toward a cross-cultural examination of adult thought.* Paper presented at the Satellite Conference of the International Society of the Study of Behavior Development, Beijing, May. (ERIC ED 291 869)

Neugarten, B. L. 1977. Personality and aging. In J. E. Birren and K. W. Schaie (Eds.), *Handbook of the psychology of aging.* New York: Van Nostrand Reinhold.

Neugarten, B., and Neugarten, D. 1987. The changing meaning of age. *Psychology Today,* 21(5), 29–33.

O'Keefe, P., and Johnston, M. 1989. Perspective taking and teacher effectiveness: A connected thread through three developmental literatures. *Journal of Teacher Education,* 40(3), 20–26.

Oja, S. N., and Pine, G. J. 1981. *Toward a theory of staff development.* Paper presented at the annual meeting of the American Educational Research Association, Los Angeles, April.

Oja, S. N., and Pine, G. J. 1984. *Collaborative action research: A two-year study of teachers' stages of development and school contexts.* Durham, NH: University of New Hampshire.

Parham, T. 1989. Cycles of psychological Nigrescence. *The Counseling Psychologist,* 17(2), 187–226.

Parkay, F. W. 1979. *Inner-city high school teachers: The relationship of personality traits and teaching style to environmental stress.* Paper presented to the Southwest Educational Research Association, Houston.

Parker, W. C. 1983. *The effect of guided reflection and role-taking on the interactive decision making of teachers.* Paper presented at the annual meeting of the American Educational Research Association, Montreal, April.

Peck, T. A. 1986. Women's self-definition in adulthood: From a different model? *Psychology of Women Quarterly,* 10(3), 274–284.

Perry, W. G. 1970. *Forms of intellectual and ethical development in the college years.* New York: Holt, Rinehart and Winston.

Perry, W. G. 1981. Cognitive and ethical growth: The making of meaning. In A. Chickering (Ed.), *The modern American college.* San Francisco: Jossey-Bass.

Phillips, M. D., and Glickman, C. D. 1991. Peer coaching: Developmental approach to enhance teacher thinking. *Journal of Staff Development,* 12(2), 20–25.

Phinney, J. S. 1990. Ethnic identity in adolescents and adults: Review of the research. *Psychological Bulletin,* 108, 499–514.

Porter, A. C., and Brophy, J. 1988. Synthesis of research on good teaching: Insights from the work of the Institute for Research on Teaching. *Educational Leadership,* 45(7), 78–85.

Pratt, D. D. 1988. Andragogy as a relational construct. *Adult Education Quarterly,* 38, 160–181.

Rachal, J. R. 2002. Andragogy's detectives: A critique of the present and a proposal for the future. *Adult Education Quarterly,* 52(3), 210–227.

Reiman, A. J., and Parramore, B. 1994. The first year of teaching: Assignment, expectations, and development. In S. Odell and M. O'Hair (Eds.), *Diversity and teaching.* Orlando, FL: Harcourt Brace Jovanovich.

Reiman, A. J., and Thies-Sprinthall, L. 1998. *Mentoring and supervision for teacher development.* New York: Longman

Rest, J. 1986. *Moral development: Advances in research and theory.* New York: Praeger.

Riegel, K. 1973. Dialectical operations: The final period of cognitive development. *Human Development,* 16, 346–370.

Roberts, P., and Newton, P. M. 1987. Levinsonian studies of women's adult development. *Psychology and Aging, 2,* 154–163.

Rose, A. D., Jeris, L., and Smith, R. 2005. Is adult education a calling? Shaping identity and practice in steel mill learning centers. *Teachers College Record,* 107(6), 1305–1334.

Rutter, M., Maughan, B., Mortimore, P., Ouston, J., and Smith, A. 1979. *Fifteen thousand hours. Secondary schools and their effects on children.* Cambridge, MA: Harvard University Press.

Schön, D. A. 1983. *The reflective practitioner: How professionals think in action.* New York: Basic Books.

Schooler, C. 1989. *A sociological perspective in intellectual development.* Paper presented at the biennial meeting of the Society for Research in Child Development. (ERIC ED 308 932)

Sheared, V. 1999. Giving voice: Inclusion of African American students' polyrhythmic realities in adult basic education. In T. C. Guy (Ed.), *Providing culturally relevant adult education: A challenge for the twenty-first century. New Directions for Adult and Continuing Education,* 82. San Francisco: Jossey-Bass.

Sternberg, R. J. 1985. *Beyond IQ: A triarchic theory of human intelligence.* New York: Cambridge.

Sternberg, R. J. 1988. *Triarchic mind: A new theory of human intelligence.* New York: Viking.

Sternberg, R. J. 1990. *Metaphors of mind: Conceptions of the nature of intelligence.* New York: Cambridge.

Sullivan, E. V., McCullough, G., and Stager, M. A. 1970. Developmental study of the relationship between conceptual, ego, and moral development. *Child Development, 41,* 399–411.

Taranto, M. 1987. *Wisdom and logic.* Paper presented at the annual symposium of the Jean Piaget Society, Philadelphia, May. (ERIC ED 282 099)

Taylor, K. 2000. Teaching with developmental intention. In J. Mezirow and Associates (Eds.), *Learning as transformation: Critical perspectives on a theory in progress.* San Francisco: Jossey-Bass.

Taylor, K., and Marienau, C. 1995. Bridging practice and theory for women's adult development. In *New Directions for Adult and Continuing Education, 65,* San Francisco: Jossey-Bass.

Tennant, M. 1986. An evaluation of Knowles' theory of adult learning. *International Journal of Lifelong Education, 5*(2), 113–122.

Thies-Sprinthall, L., and Sprinthall, N. A. 1987. Experienced teachers: Agents for revitalization and renewal as mentors and teacher educators. *Journal of Education, 169*(1), 65–79.

Thorndike, E. L., et al. 1928. *Adult learning.* New York: Macmillan.

Tieso, C. 2001. Curriculum: Broad brushstrokes or paint-by-the-numbers? *The Teacher Educator, 36*(3), 199–213.

Tisdell, E. 2000. Feminist pedagogies. In E. Hayes and D. Flannery (Eds.), *Women as learners: The significance of gender in adult learning.* San Francisco: Jossey-Bass.

Tough, A. 1971. *The adult's learning projects: A fresh approach to theory and practice in adult learning.* Toronto: Ontario Institute for Studies in Education.

Uys, L. R., Gwele, N. S., McInerney, P., Rhyn, L., and Tanga, T. 2004. The competence of nursing graduates from problem-based programs in South Africa. *Journal of Nursing Education, 43*(8), 352–361.

Wilkins, R. A. 1980. If the moral reasoning of teachers is deficient, what hope for pupils. *Kappan, 61*(8), 548–549.

Willis, S. L., and Baltes, P. B. 1980. Intelligence in adulthood and aging: Contemporary issues. In L. W. Poon (Ed.), *Aging in the 1980s: Psychological issues.* Washington DC: American Psychological Association.

Wilson, A. L. 1993. The promise of situated cognition. In S. Merriam (Ed.), *An update on adult learning theory. New directions for adult and continuing education, 57.* San Francisco: Jossey-Bass.

Witherell, C. S., and Erickson, V. L. 1978. Teacher education as adult development. *Theory and Practice, 17,* 229–238.

Zepeda, S. J. 2004. Leadership to build learning communities. *The Educational Forum, 68*(2), 144–151.

SUGGESTED READINGS

Brown, J. S., Collins, A., and Duguid, P. 1989. Situated cognition and the culture of learning. *Educational Researcher, 18*(1), 32–42.

Clark, M. C., and Caffarella, R. S. 1999. *An update on adult development theory: New ways of thinking about the life course. New Directions for Adult and Continuing Education, 84.* San Francisco: Jossey-Bass.

Cross, K. P. 1991. *Adults as learners.* San Francisco: Jossey-Bass.

Fessler, R. 1992. *The teacher career cycle: Understanding and guiding the professional development of teachers.* Boston: Allyn and Bacon.

Grow, G. 1991. Teaching learners to be self-directed: A stage approach. *Adult Education Quarterly, 41* (3), 125–149.

Hargreaves, A., and Fullan, M. D. (Eds.). 1992. *Understanding teacher development.* New York: Teachers College.

Knowles, M. S., Holton III, E. F., and Swanson, R. A. 2005. *The adult learner: The definitive classic in adult education and human resource development* (6th ed.). San Diego, CA: Elsevier.

Levine, S. L. 1989. *Promoting adult growth in schools.* Boston: Allyn and Bacon.

Merriam, S. B. (Ed.). 2001. *The new update on adult learning theory. New Directions for Adult and Continuing Education,* 89. San Francisco: Jossey-Bass

Merriam, S., and Caffarella, R. 1999. *Learning in adulthood* (2nd ed.). San Francisco: Jossey-Bass.

Mezirow, J., and Associates. 2000. *Learning as transformation: Critical perspectives on a theory in progress.* San Francisco: Jossey-Bass.

Zehm, S. J., and Kottler, J. A. 1993. *On being a teacher.* Newbury Park, CA: Sage.

chapter 5

Reflections on Schools, Teaching, and SuperVision

As we seek ways to improve school and classroom instruction, we need to understand how present thinking, beliefs, and practices in the field of supervision interact with instruction and the assumptions about students and teachers as learners. This chapter will show how issues of school and teaching effectiveness are not clearly answered by research, but instead must be resolved by human judgments about goals and purposes. Next, we will look at how supervisory beliefs are related to a particular educational philosophy or platform. An instrument will then be provided to help clarify each person's own supervisory belief, and we will examine how one's own supervisory belief fits along a control continuum. Finally, some propositions about supervisory belief and consequences for teacher development will be presented.

How do we reconcile the uncertainties of supervision, teaching, and instructional improvement? How do we know whether we are progressing in the desired direction? Unless we reflect on our own beliefs, there is little to steer us.

Sergiovanni and Starrat (1983) noted the importance of understanding one's own supervisory beliefs:

What is needed is some firm footing in principle. Some have called our often unexpressed constellation of principles a platform. Just as a political party is supposed to base its decisions and actions on a party platform upon which it seeks election, so, too, supervisory personnel need a platform upon which, and in the light of which, they can carry on their work. With a clearly defined platform, they can begin to take a position relative to educational practices, looking beyond the surface behavior to probe for the real consequences of a variety of school practices. (pp. 226–227)

Knowing oneself as a supervisor is necessary before considering alternative practices and procedures. To move from a platform, we must first know where we are standing. Let's look at the human decisions that a supervisor must make about school improvement, teaching effectiveness, and one's purpose in working with teachers.

Effective Teaching Research: A Historical Perspective

Beginning in the 1970s, various studies, collectively known as *effective teaching research,* were carried out. These studies were the classroom equivalent of the effective schools research discussed in Chapter 3. They identified correlates between student performance on standardized achievement tests and teaching variables. One type of effectiveness research concerned the correlation between *teachers' attitudes and beliefs* and student achievement. These findings were summarized by Brophy and Evertson (1976):

1. Effective teachers have a sense of being in charge, a "can do" attitude. Although effective teachers face the same types of problems as ineffective teachers, they see them as challenges to be met, not suffering to be endured.
2. Effective teachers spend whatever time and effort is necessary to assure that all students learn. They give special attention, including reteaching and extra practice, to slower students.
3. Effective teachers have realistic, professional attitudes toward students. They possess neither romantic nor cynical views of their students. They see themselves as "diagnosticians and problem solvers," rather than as "mother-substitutes" or "disciplinarians" (Brophy and Evertson, 1976, p. 45).
4. Effective teachers expect their students to achieve. They believe that all students can learn essential knowledge and skills.

Another area of research examined the *classroom climate* created by the teacher. After reviewing the effectiveness research, Barnes (1981) identified two broad characteristics of a positive classroom climate: a work-oriented atmosphere and a warm, supportive environment. A work-oriented atmosphere is created by the teacher focusing on academics and explicitly communicating expected behaviors and attitudes to students. A warm, supportive environment is fostered by the teacher who provides specific praise when deserved, respects students' contributions, exhibits confidence and enthusiasm, engages in positive interactions with students, and maintains an orderly classroom with limits on social conversation.

In the area of *academic learning time,* researchers found that the more teacher and student class time spent on successful academic task performance, the higher was the level of student achievement (Denhan and Lieberman, 1980; Ybarra and Hollingsworth, 2001). In the area of *student diagnosis and evaluation,* Brophy and Evertson (1976) found that effective teachers relied less on frequent student testing than on techniques like observation of students, detailed note taking on student performance, and correcting daily student work.

The most widely disseminated results of the effective teaching research were findings concerning the *instructional process.* Researchers found strong positive correlations between higher scores on standardized achievement tests and "direct" or "explicit" instruction. Brophy (1979) summarized these findings: "Learning gains are more impressive in classrooms in which students receive a great deal of instruction from and have a great deal of interaction with the teacher, especially in public lessons and recitations that are briskly paced but conducted at a difficulty level that allows consistent success" (p. 747).

Based on his review of process-product research, Rosenshine (1983) identified a set of six instructional "functions":

1. Review, including checking of previous day's work and reteaching if necessary
2. Presentation of new content/skills
3. Initial student practice (and checking for understanding)
4. Feedback and correctives (and reteaching if necessary)
5. Student independent practice
6. Weekly and monthly reviews (p. 337)

Many interpreted Rosenshine's findings as confirming direct instruction as the one best instructional process, regardless of the students or content to be taught. Additionally, Rosenshine's six functions (or variations thereof) were extolled as the "essential elements" of any effective lesson. We will dispute these interpretations as our discussion of effective teaching continues.

Cautions Concerning Effective Teaching Research

Gary Griffin (1985) has cautioned educators against overreliance on the effective teaching research:

> Much research is correlational; the teaching behaviors associated with positive pupil outcomes were discovered in existing classroom settings. They were, if you will, naturally occurring phenomena in an untampered-with context. Few studies have been designed to determine if the same behaviors, when introduced

experimentally into classrooms, result in the same pupil outcomes. . . . Also, much of the effective teaching research is situation specific, tied to certain grade levels with certain student populations in specific demographic and social contexts. Therefore, the results may not be generalizable to other situations. (p. 44)

Barak Rosenshine, the synthesizer of what has become commonly termed *effective instruction,* stated that the body of research on instruction that results in short-term basic-skills acquisition should be more aptly referred to as "teachers' effects" research.

My main point is that it is difficult to apply some of the major findings which we have learned from the teaching of skills to lessons which teach content. Some of these findings include checking for student understanding, providing for active student participation, providing for a high success rate, correcting errors, and providing for guided practice and independent practice. But such findings do not, and will not, transfer easily to the teaching of content, and we haven't faced this problem. (1986, p. 14)

Furthermore, Rosenshine has written that explicit teaching is "less relevant for teaching compositions, writing of term papers, reading comprehension, analyzing literature, historical trends . . . discussion of social issues, or for teaching entangled concepts" (1986, p. 60). Therefore, it is inappropriate to view explicit, direct instruction as the model for effective teaching, valid for the majority of instruction in a classroom. Yet many school districts and states use this very misapplication of research in evaluating teachers against a template of "effective" instruction. Lest this explanation be seen as a polemic against explicit or direct instruction, remember that the critics of its overgeneralization and prescriptive applications are the researchers who conducted the actual studies and developed the instructional theory.

The Coast of Britain

Correct answers to questions about even physical matters are human decisions. Answers about social and educative matters are even more clearly human judgments (see Glickman, 1987b). An example from geometry is illustrative. To the question, "How long is the coast of Britain?" the geometer Benoit Mandelbrot answered that the coast has no real length apart from human judgment (Hardison, 1986). If one uses a measurement scale of 100 miles to an inch to draw the British coastline, that coastline has large bays and capes. If one uses a scale of 10 miles to an inch, then new inlets and promontories appear. The coast becomes longer or shorter, depending on the scale used. Furthermore, what happens when measurement of the coast begins when the tide is coming in? Each incoming wave reduces the coast, and each outgoing wave lengthens the coast. Therefore, how does one find the length of the British coast? The question can be answered only by agreeing on the purpose of the measurement, the perspective and the unit of measurement to be used, and the particular time at which the measurement is to be made. The length of the coast is a mathematical fiction created so that humans can find a representation that will accomplish their purpose.

Effective and Good Schools: The Same?

In discussing questions about supervision, teaching, and school improvement, as in measuring the coast of Britain, there is no certainty about how to arrive at an answer. The issue of effective schools highlights the human values that drive school decisions and actions (Glickman, 1987a).

Many of the clarion calls for school reform cite the findings from research on effective teaching and effective schools as examples of how schools and classrooms should change. The reformers tell us that the goal of all schools should be effectiveness—as measured by such factors as students' scores on high-stakes achievement tests. Furthermore, we ought to narrow the academic focus of the curriculum, test students more frequently, raise standards for promotion, and have teachers state specific, measurable objectives and follow a prescribed instructional approach that involves reviewing, explaining, demonstrating, guiding practice, checking for understanding, and summarizing. The findings of the recent research on effective teaching and effective schools are treated as scientific laws that apply to *all* teachers and *all* schools.

The findings of the research on effective teaching and effective schools are too often equated with what is desirable or good. By failing to distinguish between *effectiveness* and *goodness,* we avoid two central questions in education. The first question with which schools and school systems must deal is: What is good? Only after that question has been answered should we deal with the second question: How do we become effective? The current fascination with findings from the research on effectiveness has blinded schools and school systems to the more basic question of goodness.

Do higher test scores justify labeling a school "good" if the price for those higher scores has been an increase in the dropout rate? Are higher scores in reading and mathematics "good" if students gain them at the expense of time spent in studying science, social studies, art, or music? Is an average gain of eight points on reading test scores worth the increased allocation of time and resources to direct instruction in reading? Is that gain more desirable than maintaining current achievement levels in reading but devoting a greater proportion of class time to a whole-language approach that emphasizes creative writing or critical thinking? The research on effective schools and effective teaching does not answer these questions for us. The research is neutral: It does not choose our goals but simply tells us how to accomplish certain things (which may or may not be among our goals). Educators who care about the fate of all children must define *goodness* before they worry about *effectiveness;* as supervisors, we must first clarify our own definitions.

Changing Views: New Emphasis on Constructivist Teaching and Learning

In recent years the constructivist view has had increasing influence over teaching and learning in our nation's classrooms. Constructivism is an epistemology (a theory of the nature of knowledge) based on the work of a variety of philosophers, psychologists, and educators. Luminaries associated with constructivism include Immanuel Kant, Lev Vygotsky, John Dewey, Jean Piaget, Jerome Bruner, and Howard Gardner. Constructivism holds that people create new knowledge as a result of the interaction of their existing knowledge, beliefs, and values with new ideas, problems, or experiences. To the constructivist, knowledge is not universal, objective, or fixed, but is constructed or co-constructed by learners.

Although there are several different models of constructivism, these models can be classified into one of two broad categories. *Cognitive constructivism* is focused on the individual's intellectual development. It holds that learning is stimulated when the individual encounters an idea or experience that contradicts his or her present conception of reality. This discrepancy causes "cognitive conflict" and "disequilibrium," which stimulates the person to develop and assimilate new knowledge as a means of dealing with the discrepancy. The other broad category is social constructivism, which proposes that knowledge is not created by the individual but is constructed as a result of the individual's interaction with his or her social context. Furthermore, that interaction brings about changes to both the individual and the social context (Null, 2004).

What are the practical implications of constructivism for instruction? Although constructivism does not contradict all of the teaching effectiveness research, it clearly conflicts with that part of the effectiveness research that supports direct teaching characterized by teacher presentation, student practice, and teacher correctives. Airasian and Walsh (1997) have discussed what a constructivist approach means for teachers and students:

> In a constructivist approach, teachers will have to learn to guide, not tell; to create environments in which students can make their own meanings, not be handed them by the teacher; to accept diversity in constructions, not search for the one "right" answer; to modify prior notions of "right" and "wrong," not stick to rigid standards and criteria; to create a safe, free, responsive environment that encourages disclosure of student constructions, not a closed, judgmental system. (p. 148)
>
> Students will also have to learn new ways to perform. They will have to learn to think for themselves, not wait for the teacher to tell them what to think; to proceed with less focus and direction from the teacher, not to wait for explicit teacher directions; to express their own ideas clearly in their own words, not to answer restricted-response questions; to revisit and revise constructions; not to move immediately on to the next concept or idea. (p. 448)

Table 5.1 further illuminates the constructivist approach to teaching and learning by comparing traditional to constructivist classrooms.

TABLE 5.1	Comparing Constructivist and Traditional Classrooms

	Traditional Classroom	**Constructivist Classroom**
Educational Purpose	• Transmission of knowledge	• Construction of knowledge
Curriculum	• Content centered • Rigid, sequential	• Problem centered • Flexible, webbed
Instructional Focus	• Discreet pieces of information • Breadth	• Big ideas • Depth
Planning	• By teacher	• By teacher and students
Instructional Methods	• Lecture • Teacher questions with "correct" student responses • Student recitation • Student practice with teacher feedback • Independent student practice	• Open-ended discussion • Student-initiated questions • Problem solving • Inquiry, experimentation • Active learning • Cooperative learning • Self and group reflection on constructions
Assessment	• Distinct from learning • Intended to measure learning and grade students • Objective quizzes and tests • Designed externally or by teacher	• Integrated with learning • Co-planned by teacher and students • Seeks to understand student constructions • Authentic • Assessment of process and product equally important • Includes self, peer, and group assessment

Instructional Improvement and Effective Teaching

Let's continue this reflection on practice by taking an innocuous statement about supervision that virtually no one would take issue with: The goal of supervision is to improve instruction. It sounds nice, until we ask for a definition of what type of instruction we wish to improve. Effective teaching, to a large extent, depends on what you are trying to teach. Consider the following examples:

- If the goal is for students to master basic skills, then effective teaching might involve explanation, demonstration, practice, feedback, and more practice.
- If the goal is for students to learn classical culture, then effective teaching might consist of reading the great works, lecture, and Socratic discussion.
- If the goal is for students to become problem solvers, then effective teaching might call for exposing students to real-world problems and active student involvement in testing possible solutions and reaching resolutions.
- If the goal is social development, then effective teaching might consist of structuring cooperative learning and community building activities.

- If the goal is personal development, then effective teaching might mean facilitation of students' self-directed learning and self-assessment.
- If the goal is critical inquiry, then effective teaching might require the teacher to challenge students' current values and assumptions, and ask students to critique dominant belief systems, social structures, and power relationships.

In the final analysis, what constitutes instructional improvement and successful teaching can be defined only within the context of particular instructional goals, local learning environments, and individual students. This means that the search for a single instructional model—effective for all learning content, students, and situations—is futile.

A more productive course of action is to identify various instructional strategies that are effective in relation to identified instructional goals and individual students. If this proposition is accepted, the supervisor's role becomes one of assisting teachers to clarify school and classroom instructional goals, develop a variety of instructional strategies (direct instruction, constructivist teaching, cooperative learning, classroom dialogue, service learning, and so on), "mix and match" instructional strategies to learning goals and students, and assess the effects of instruction for the purpose of continuous improvement. With such a supervision emphasis, effective instruction is seen as the teacher's ability to use various ways of teaching according to a variety of learning goals and student learning styles.

To the mix of multiple learning goals and multiple instructional models, Ornstein (1990) has added the concept of *teaching style:*

> Teaching style is a truncated version of a personality and philosophical type. Everyone must develop his or her own style of teaching and feel comfortable in the classroom. In short, teachers must develop their own repertoire, relative to their own physical and mental characteristics and their students. Thus, there is no one ideal type but a multiple set of teacher types or styles. Teacher style is a matter of choice and comfort, and what works for one teacher with one set of students may not work for another. (p. 84)

Teaching styles, of course, can change and broaden over time, allowing for the expansion of a teacher's repertoire of instructional strategies. However, attempting to force teachers to immediately adopt strategies that strongly conflict with their current teaching style is inconsistent with both the principles of adult learning and the concept of the teacher as a professional. It is better to initially invite teachers to learn and try out new strategies which are consistent with their current style, and then facilitate teachers' continued development of teaching style and repertoire over time.

Instructional improvement can be defined as helping teachers acquire teaching strategies consistent with their instructional goals and compatible with their general teaching styles that increase the capabilities of students to make wise decisions in varying contexts (with regard to peers, adults, academics, and life). Effective teaching consists therefore of those teaching decisions about actions, routines, and techniques that increase the decision-making capabilities of students.

Beliefs about Education

We've discussed how the definition of effective instruction depends on school and teacher instructional goals. Instructional goals, in turn, are ultimately based on beliefs concerning such things as the purpose of education, what should be taught, the nature of the learner, and the learning process. Whether or not they are conscious of it, teachers' and supervisors' educational philosophies have a significant impact on instruction and instructional improvement efforts. The following are summaries of educational platforms of three teachers with different beliefs about education.

> Joan Simpson believes that the purpose of education should be to transmit a prescribed body of basic knowledge, skills, and cultural values to students. To do this effectively, the teacher must exercise control over the classroom, lesson content, and students. Content should be broken first into discreet academic areas and then into small elements, and learning should take place in a series of small, sequential steps. All students should be expected to master the same content. Grades and other types of external motivation are necessary to assure student learning.

> Bill Washington believes that the purpose of education should be student growth, especially in inquiry and problem-solving skills. To promote such growth, the teacher conveys existing knowledge, but also encourages students to experiment in order to test old ideas and find solutions to new problems. Bill believes that since inquiry is most successful in a democratic environment, the teacher should share control of the learning environment with students. Because problem solving often takes place within a social context, students should learn social skills as well as academic content.

> Pat Rogers believes that each child is unique and that the primary purpose of education should be to meet students' individual needs. The teacher should foster the development of each student toward his or her fullest potential. This means addressing students as whole persons by fostering their physical, emotional, cognitive, moral, and social development. Such holistic education includes facilitating student self-inquiry. Pat believes that students should have as much control over their own learning environment as their maturity level permits. Teachers should base lessons on students' experience, concerns, and interests. Students should be allowed to participate in assessing their own learning.

The three educational platforms just described do indeed represent contrasting beliefs. Based on their educational beliefs, Joan Simpson, Bill Washington, and Pat Rogers, no doubt, have quite different definitions of instructional improvement and effective teaching! You may view one of these educational platforms as quite similar to your own, you may agree with parts of each, or you may have an entirely different set of beliefs. In any case, it is important for you to clarify your own educational beliefs. By reflecting on the following questions, you can begin to build your educational platform:

1. What should be the purpose of education?
2. What should be the content of the school curriculum?
3. Who should control the learning environment?
4. What should be the relationship of teacher and students?
5. Under what conditions is student learning most successful?
6. What motivates students to do their best in school?
7. What is your definition of effective teaching?
8. What personal characteristics are possessed by a successful teacher?
9. How should the teacher assess student learning?
10. What is your definition of a good school?

Supervision Beliefs

Most supervisors, of course, are former teachers. As a result, their views about learning, the nature of the learner, knowledge, and the role of the teacher in the classroom influence their view of supervision. After all, supervision is in many respects analogous to teaching. Teachers wish to improve students' behavior, achievement, and attitudes. Supervisors similarly wish to improve teachers' behavior, achievement, and attitudes. The supervisory platforms of three supervisors are described next. As you read these platforms, note the relationship between the beliefs they contain and the teacher beliefs present in the three educational platforms discussed earlier in this chapter.

> Bob Reynolds believes that the purpose of supervision is to monitor teachers to determine if their instruction includes the elements of effective instruction. If those elements are observed, the supervisor should provide positive reinforcement to assure that they continue to be included in the teacher's lessons. Bob believes that if a teacher is not using, or is incorrectly using, the elements of effective instruction, the supervisor has a responsibility to provide remedial assistance by explaining and demonstrating correct instructional behaviors, setting standards of improvement, and monitoring and reinforcing the teacher's improvement efforts. In short, the supervisor should have primary responsibility for instructional improvement decisions.

> Jan White believes that the purpose of supervision is to engage teachers in mutual inquiry aimed at the improvement of instruction. The supervisor and teacher should share perceptions of instructional problems, exchange suggestions for solving those problems, and negotiate an improvement plan. The improvement plan becomes a hypothesis to be tested by the

teacher with the supervisor's assistance. Thus, Jan believes that supervisors and teachers should share the responsibility for instructional improvement.

Shawn Moore believes that the purpose of supervision should be to foster teacher reflection and autonomy and to facilitate teacher-driven instructional improvement. The supervisor should be concerned with the teacher's self-concept and personal development as well as the teacher's instructional performance. It is critical for the supervisor to establish a relationship with the teacher characterized by openness, trust, and acceptance. Shawn believes that the supervisor should allow the teacher to identify instructional problems, improvement plans, and criteria for success. The supervisor can assist the teacher's self-directed improvement through active listening, clarifying, encouraging, and reflecting. Thus, the teacher should have primary responsibility for instructional improvement decisions, with the supervisor serving as an active facilitator.

These descriptions show that supervisory platforms can be as varied as educational platforms. When we compare the educational platforms of Joan Simpson, Bill Washington, and Pat Rogers with the supervisory platforms of Bob Reynolds, Jan White, and Shawn Moore, we can see that both types of platforms reveal basic beliefs about knowledge, human nature, and control. By answering the following questions, you can begin the process of clarifying your own beliefs about instructional supervision. We suggest that you write responses to the questions, save your responses, and reassess your supervisory platform after you have finished reading this text.

1. What is your definition of instructional supervision?
2. What should be the ultimate purpose of supervision?
3. Who should supervise? Who should be supervised?
4. What knowledge, skills, attitudes, and values are possessed by successful supervisors?
5. What are the most important needs of teachers?
6. What makes for positive relationships between supervisors and teachers?
7. What types of activities should be part of instructional supervision?
8. What should be changed about the current practice of instructional supervision?

Supervisory Platform as Related to Educational Philosophy

Many educators view discussions of educational philosophy as overly abstract and irrelevant to the real world of supervisors and teachers. Yet, a supervisor's actions in working with teachers are based on supervisory beliefs, which in turn reflect a broader educational philosophy. Many different philosophies exist. Some, such as idealism and realism, date back to ancient times. Others, such as pragmatism and behaviorism, have been developed within the last century. Even more recent has been the emergence of progressivism, reconstructionism, and existentialism. Philosophies are numerous and overlapping, and many have historical roots in each other. To unravel the major philosophical trends in education, one must decipher how philosophies differ from each other and then build overriding conceptual categories. Each conceptual category or superphilosophy is created by grouping various philosophies that have central agreement on the type and scope of education. In other words, there may be disagreement on the specific nature of knowledge, truth, and reality, yet they hang together as a general educational philosophy because they are in agreement on the purpose and treatment of education.*

With educational application in mind, divergent philosophies can be simplified and classified. Three major educational superphilosophies have direct relevance to supervision. These categories have been labeled, according to Johnson, Collins, Dupuis, and Johansen (1973), as essentialism, progressivism, and existentialism. We would like to substitute for progressivism the more general term *experimentalism,* as described by Morris (1961).

Essentialism

Essentialism as a philosophy is derived from idealism and realism. *Idealism,* which dates back to Plato, espouses a belief in absolutes: The world we live in is merely a reflection of reality. Reality, truth, and standards of morality exist beyond our common ways of knowing. Only by training the mind do we glimpse the ultimates. Yet training the mind is not sufficient in itself; it only brings the mind nearer to grasping reality. Divine revelation, insight, and faith are the necessary elements for ultimate knowledge of what exists. Therefore, idealism emphasizes truth and reality existing outside of people. It is absolute and unchanging. *Realism,* developed at the onset of the industrial age, places a similar emphasis on truth and reality being outside of people. Instead of humankind and the outer environment being separated from each other, realism maintains that humanity is part and parcel of that environment. The world is a preordained, mechanistic reality. All of existence operates according to scientific, cause-and-effect relations. It is as if existence is a clock that always runs according to mechanical principles governing levers, gauges, and gears. Humans have no existence apart from this clock; they are a part of the predetermined machine. Knowledge is learning how the machine works; truths are the scientific laws of regulation. Nothing exists outside the principles of nature. The purpose of education is to condition the mind to think in a natural, logical way. The mind should be trained to become consciously aware of the predetermined nature of the world.

*The descriptions of philosophy in Chapter 5 are taken from C. D. Glickman and J. P. Esposito, *Leadership Guide for Elementary School Improvement: Procedures for Assessment and Change* (Boston: Allyn and Bacon, 1979), p. 20.

Essentialism, created by William L. Bagley in 1938, encompassed the educational philosophies of idealism and realism. He took the ideas of knowledge being eternal and outside of humankind (idealism—absolutes; realism—natural laws) to form pedagogy. Essentialists emphasize that there is a body of timeless knowledge, both historical and contemporary, that is of value to the living.

Essentialism in terms of supervision emphasizes the supervisor as the person who teaches truths about teaching to teachers. Supervisors are those most knowledgeable about those absolute standards. Teachers are then handled mechanistically to systematize and feed content to students. As teachers digest these teaching truths, they move closer to being good teachers.

Experimentalism

As Western society became more industrialized, optimism and confidence in human ability to control nature emerged. The philosophy of *pragmatism* developed by Charles S. Pierce and William James emphasized what people can do to nature rather than what nature does to humankind. John Dewey, circa 1920, further expanded on the writings of James by putting the individual squarely in the context of society. Humans can both reform and be reformed by society. Dewey's philosophy is, of course, the well-known school of progressive thought. *Reconstructionism* is a further offshoot of both pragmatism and progressivism. Richard Pratte (1971) cited the pamphlet *Dare the Schools Build a New Social Order,* written by George S. Counts in 1932, as a guiding document for the then radical notion that schools and students were the reformers of society.

Experimentalism emerges from the philosophies of pragmatism, progressivism, and reconstructionism. They hold in common a historical break from the more traditional philosophies of realism and idealism. The essentialist idea that knowledge, truth, and morality exist as absolute and outside of humans was rejected. The emerging faith in the scientific method, the ability of humans to create their own laws, principles, and machines, and the fact that such man-made inventions would work for them demanded an accompanying philosophy. Experimentalism provided that philosophy.

Reality was what worked. If a person could form a hypothesis, test it, and find it to work, then it was regarded as tentatively true. On repeated experimentation with the same results, it became real. Yet experimentalists would never claim an absolute truth. The human environment was believed to be constantly changing, so that what one can do and prove today may not be probable tomorrow. A new situation and a different approach may alter yesterday's reality. Experimentalists point to the historical evidence of Newton's law of gravity as a past truth that has given way to Einstein's theory of relativity; they believe that in time a new theory will replace Einstein's.

Morality is also viewed in relation to what works for humanity and human society. *Morality* is that behavior that promotes one's working with the group to achieve greater ends. To be wise is to understand how the environment (of things and people) affects oneself and how one might affect it. Whether action is moral or not is determined by the degree of progress that has been achieved by the group. The use of trial and error in a laboratory setting is the key to evaluating the outcome of action. Therefore, experimentalists do not view knowledge as absolute or external to human capabilities. Rather, knowledge is a result of the interaction between the scientific person and the environment.

The educational application of experimentalist thinking to supervision is well documented in the writing of Dewey. Teachers (as students) need to learn what are the truths of their time, but they should not rest content with that parcel of knowledge. Supervisors view schools as laboratories for working with teachers to test old hypotheses and to try new ones. Supervisors work democratically with teachers to achieve collective ends that will help everyone. Supervisors are not solely conveyors of age-old wisdom; they are both the conveyors of the rudimentary knowledge of the time and the guiders of trial-and-error, exploratory learning.

Existentialism

Existentialism as a school of thought is derived from the rejection of the other philosophies encompassed in essentialism and experimentalism. As such, it is a large category for many diverse philosophers. They have in common a scorn for rational, empirical, and systematic thinking as the way of knowing reality. As previously mentioned, the essentialists believe in rational thinking to help elevate the mind to uncover the absolutes of the universe. Experimentalists believe in rational, scientific thinking to explore and frame the relevant knowledge of the times. However, the existentialists believe that this same rational thinking restricts humans from discovering existence and therefore keeps them ignorant.

This philosophy has roots in the writings of Sören Kierkegaard in the mid-nineteenth century. It has been popularized in drama and literature by such exponents as Albert Camus and Jean-Paul Sartre. The current popular cults of transcendental thinking, meditation, and introspection (knowing oneself) have a kinship with existentialism. The basic tenet of the philosophy is that the individual is the source of all reality. All that exists in the world is the meaning the individual puts on his or her own experiences. There is no absolute knowledge, no mechanical working of the universe, and no preordained logic. To believe in such inventions is merely the narrow, incorrect way humans interpret their own experiences.

Beyond the individual exists only chaos. The only reality that exists is one's own existence. Only by looking within oneself can one discern the truth of the outside disorder. Humanity is paramount. Human dignity and worth are of greatest importance; they are the source and dispenser of all truth. With this realization, one acquires a profound respect for all human beings and their uniqueness. Human relations become very important, affirming individual worth and protecting the individual's right to discover his or her own truth. Morality is the process of knowing oneself and allowing others the freedom to do likewise. Faith, intuition,

TABLE 5.2	Comparing Three Super Philosophies		
	Essentialism	**Experimentalism**	**Existentialism**
View of Reality (knowledge, truth, morality)	Exists outside of humans, absolute, unchanging	Reality is what works; it is tentative, constantly changing	Individual is source of all reality; individual defines reality
How to Learn about Reality	Train the mind to think rationally	Interact with environment; experiment	Engage in self-discovery; create meaning
Application to Supervision	Supervisor is expert; mechanistically transmits instructional knowledge to teacher	Supervisor works democratically with teachers to test old hypotheses and try new ones	Supervisor facilitates teacher exploration and autonomous decision making

mysticism, imagery, and transcendental experiences are all acceptable ways of discovery. Humans are totally free, not shaped by others or restricted by the flux of the times. They hold within themselves the capacity to form their own destiny.

This philosophy of education, applied to supervision, means a full commitment to individual teacher choice. The supervisor provides an environment that enables the teacher to explore his or her own physical and mental capabilities. Teachers must learn for themselves. The supervisor does not dispense information and shies away from intrusively guiding a teacher. Supervisors help when needed, protect the rights of others to self-discovery, and encounter the teacher as a person of full importance.

Table 5.2 compares the three superphilosophies.

Checking Your Own Supervisory Beliefs

Let's step back and watch ourselves at work. First, we'll consider how we act with individual teachers, and then with groups. Read Box 5.1, the Supervisory Interpersonal Behaviors Questionnaire for Working with Individuals, and select the approach you most often take.

Next, take a look at the interpersonal behaviors you typically use when meeting with groups of teachers (Box 5.2). Please respond to the Supervisory Interpersonal Behavior Questionnaire for Working with Groups.

The supervisory approaches in the Supervisory Interpersonal Behaviors Questionnaires correspond to the philosophies of essentialism, experimentalism, and

BOX 5.1 Supervisory Interpersonal Behaviors Questionnaire
for Working with Individuals: A Scenario

The schoolday has just ended for students at Which-way School. Just as the teacher sits down at the desk, you (the supervisor) appear at the door and the teacher invites you in. "How is everything going?" you ask. Looking at the large stack of papers to correct, the teacher predicts a number of them will reflect that the students did not understand the work. "It's very frustrating working with this class. They have such a wide range of ability!" Then the teacher mentions another source of frustration: "Some of the students are discipline problems and their behavior results in class disruption."

After further discussion, the teacher and you agree that you will come into the classroom to observe what is going on, followed by a conference to discuss the classroom visit.

A few days later, after you have observed in the classroom and carefully analyzed the collected information, you begin to plan for the conference. You consider a number of approaches to use in the conference to help the teacher.

Approach A. Present what you saw in the classroom and ask for the teacher's perceptions. Listen to each other's responses. After clarifying the problem, each of you can propose ideas. Finally, you will agree on what is to be done in the classroom. You will mutually identify an objective and agree to an action plan that both of you will work together to carry out. The plan is for both of you to make.

Approach B. Listen to the teacher discuss what is going on in the classroom. If asked, you offer your perceptions regarding what you observed. Encourage the teacher to analyze the problem further, and ask questions to make sure the teacher is clear about his or her view of the problem. If the teacher requests your views on how to proceed, respond, but only if asked. Finally, ask the teacher to determine and detail the actions he or she will take and

find out if you might be of further help. The plan is the teacher's to make.

Approach C. Share your observations with the teacher and tell the teacher what you believe to be the major focus for improvement. Ask the teacher for input into your observations and interpretations. Based on your own experience and knowledge, carefully delineate what you believe are alternative actions to improve the classroom and ask the teacher to consider and select from the options. The plan to follow is chosen by the teacher from the supervisor's suggestions.

Approach D. Present your beliefs about the situation and ask the teacher to confirm or revise the interpretation. After identifying the problem, offer directions to the teacher on what should be done and how to proceed. You can go into the classroom to demonstrate what you are telling the teacher to do, or tell the teacher to observe another teacher who does well in this particular area. Praise and reward the teacher for following the given assignment. The plan is for you (the supervisor) to make.

Response. Most often, I use Approach ____.

Interpretation.
Approach A: A cluster of *collaborative behaviors* in which the supervisor and teacher share the decision making about future improvement.
Approach B: A cluster of *nondirective behaviors* in which the supervisor helps the teacher formulate his or her own decisions about future improvement.
Approach C: A cluster of *directive informational behaviors* in which the supervisor frames the teacher's choices about future improvement.
Approach D: A cluster of *directive control behaviors* in which the supervisor makes the decision for the teacher.

*Adapted from an instrument developed by Katherine C. Ginkel, 1983. "An Overview of a Study Which Examined the Relationship between Elementary School Teachers' Preference for Supervisory Conferencing Approach and Conceptual Level of Development," a paper presented at the annual meeting of the American Educational Research Association, Montreal, April. Used with permission of Katherine C. Ginkel.

BOX 5.2 Supervisory Interpersonal Behavior Questionnaire for Working with Groups

You (the supervisor) have just called on the science teachers to decide on a policy for allowing students to use laboratory equipment outside of regular class time. Many students have complained about not having enough class time for doing their experiments. The issue is how and when to free up more laboratory time for students (before school, at lunchtime, during study hall, after school) under the supervision of certified teachers. How would you work with the science teachers to make a decision?

Approach A. Meet with the staff and explain that they need to decide what to do about this issue. Present the information you have about the problem and ask for clarification. Paraphrase what they say and, once the teachers verify your summary, ask them to decide among themselves what they are going to do. Remain in the meeting, helping to move the discussion along by calling on people, asking questions, and paraphrasing, but do not become involved in making your own position known or influencing the outcome in any conscious way.

Approach B. Meet with the staff by first explaining that you have to make a decision that will meet the needs of students, teachers, and supervisor. Either by consensus or, if not, then by majority vote, make a decision. You should listen, encourage, clarify, and reflect on each staff member's perception. Afterwards, ask each member, including yourself, to suggest possible solutions. Discuss each solution; prioritize the list; and, if no consensus emerges, call for a vote. Argue for your own solution, but go along with the group's decision.

Approach C. Meet with the staff and explain to them that there are several permissible actions that you have thought about that could remedy this situation. You would like them to discuss and agree on which of these actions or combinations of actions they would like to implement. Lay out the alternatives, explain the advantages and disadvantages of each, and then allow the group to discuss and decide among your alternatives.

Approach D. Meet with the staff and tell them you want their feedback before you make a decision about the issue. Make it clear that the staff's involvement is to be advisory. Ask for their suggestions, listen, encourage, clarify, and paraphrase their ideas. After everyone has had a chance to speak, decide what changes should be made. Tell them what you are going to do, when the changes will be made, and that you expect them to carry out the plan.

Response. Most often, I would use Approach ____.

Interpretation.
Approach A: A cluster of *nondirective behaviors* in which the supervisor assists the group to make its own decision.
Approach B: A cluster of *collaborative behaviors* in which the supervisor works as part of the group in making a group decision.
Approach C: A cluster of *directive informational behaviors* in which the supervisor works as the framer of choices among which the group is to decide.
Approach D: A cluster of *directive control behaviors* in which the supervisor makes the decision for the group.

*Adapted from an instrument developed by Katherine C. Ginkel, 1983. "An Overview of a Study Which Examined the Relationship between Elementary School Teachers' Preference for Supervisory Conferencing Approach and Conceptual Level of Development," a paper presented at the annual meeting of the American Educational Research Association, Montreal, April. Used with permission of Katherine C. Ginkel.

existentialism, and are labeled *directive* supervision, *collaborative* supervision, and *nondirective* supervision. Glickman and Tamashiro (1980) wrote:

> Directive Supervision is an approach based on the belief that teaching consists of technical skills with known standards and competencies for all teachers to be effective. The supervisor's role is to inform, direct, model, and assess those competencies.
>
> Collaborative Supervision is based on the belief that teaching is primarily problem solving, whereby two or more persons jointly pose hypotheses to a problem, experiment, and implement those teaching strategies that appear to be most relevant in their own surroundings. The supervisor's role is to guide the problem-solving process, be an active member of the interaction, and keep the teachers focused on their common problems.
>
> Non-Directive Supervision has as its premise that learning is primarily a private experience in which individuals must come up with their own solutions to improving the classroom experience for students. The supervisor's role is to listen, be nonjudgmental, and provide self-awareness and clarification experiences for teachers. (p. 76)

What Does Your Belief Mean in Terms of Supervisor and Teacher Responsibility?

Beliefs about supervision and educational philosophy can be thought of in terms of decision-making responsibility (see Table 5.3). An essentialist philosophy is premised on the supervisor being the expert on instruction and therefore having major decision-making responsibility. A situation of high supervisor responsibility and low teacher responsibility is labeled *directive supervision*. An experimentalist philosophy is premised on the supervisor and teachers being equal partners in instructional improvement; equal supervisor and teacher responsibility is labeled *collaborative supervision*. Existentialist philosophy is premised on teachers discovering their own capacities for instructional improvement. Low supervisor responsibility and high teacher responsibility is labeled *nondirective supervision*.

TABLE 5.3	Relationship of Philosophy, Control, and Supervisory Belief	
Educational Philosophy	**Decision-Making Responsibility**	**Supervisory Belief**
Essentialism	Supervisor high, teacher low	Directive
Experimentalism	Supervisor equal, teacher equal	Collaborative
Existentialism	Supervisor low, teacher high	Nondirective

As we clarify our own educational philosophy and supervisory beliefs, we rarely find a pure ideological position. Therefore, Sergiovanni's idea of a supervisory platform becomes helpful. What combination of various philosophies and beliefs do we consider important? Perhaps our beliefs are mainly essentialist and directive yet contain parts of experimentalism and collaboration; or perhaps we have another combination of beliefs. A particular platform is not right or wrong; rather, it is an assessment of the bits and pieces we use to create the floor we stand on.

The Authors' Supervisory Platform

Earlier in this chapter we encouraged you to write your supervisory platform. We believe that readers of this book should have a clear idea of what *our* beliefs about supervision are.

Our own supervisory platform is based on the premise that human development is the aim of education. Therefore, supervision should be *eclectic* in practice, directed toward the goal of nondirective, existentialist supervision. Our goal as supervisors is eventually to return control to the teaching faculty to decide on collective, instructional improvements. Such an ideal cannot be achieved suddenly. Instead, the supervisor at times might use behaviors that come from an essentialist-directive belief structure as a point of entry, or might use behaviors that come from an experimentalist-collaborative belief structure as another point of entry. Regardless of the entry point, the supervisor should always strive to shift control to teachers. The supervisor may never allow total autonomy, but moving in that direction is worth the effort. The center of our platform is, therefore, collaborative experimentalism striving toward nondirective existentialism. Other key "planks" in our supervisory platform are listed here. We believe the following:

- All participants in instructional improvement efforts have knowledge to contribute to the supervisory process.
- Supervision should engage participants in reflective inquiry leading to professional growth and renewal.
- Successful supervision produces organizational growth through a synergy of individual and group efforts.
- Successful supervision fosters both common purpose and alternative means to contribute to that purpose; effective supervision recognizes teacher and student diversity.
- Successful supervision integrates various supervision functions into a comprehensive whole.
- Successful supervision is a long-term process; it balances the importance of completing the immediate task with the need to maintain positive long-term interpersonal relationships.
- Successful supervision is built on trust, openness, and mutual respect.
- Successful supervision creates an environment conducive to experimentation and risk taking.

- Successful supervision adapts to changing contexts and cultures within and outside of the school.
- Successful supervision fosters a critical examination of educators' beliefs about teaching and learning as well as movement toward congruence of beliefs and practice.
- Successful supervision requires a wide range of knowledge as well as technical and interpersonal skills.
- Successful supervision takes into consideration principles of adult learning and knowledge about adult and teacher development.

Where You Stand Depends on Where You Sit: Effects of Culture on Beliefs

A person's cultural background is an important aspect of what he or she believes about education. There is a natural tendency for members of the dominant culture to support curriculum and instruction that will transmit that culture to students. Students from minority cultures, however, may find it difficult to adapt to curriculum and instruction intended to convey the dominant culture, and may resist (sometimes passively, sometimes actively) the transmission of that culture. This is not just a question of an unfortunate mismatch between dominant and minority cultures that eventually will be overcome as minority cultures are assimilated. Schools that marginalize the cultures of particular students marginalize those students as well. What is especially insidious about such marginalization is that educators may not realize they are partly responsible for its occurrence.

Educators' beliefs about education often are influenced by cultural assumptions they may not be aware of because the assumptions are so deeply ingrained and taken for granted. These assumptions can influence the curriculum that educators design, their relationships with students and parents, the lessons they plan, and so forth. Because of the influences of our cultural assumptions and beliefs on students, it is not sufficient for us simply to articulate our beliefs and then base educational goals and practices on those beliefs. Rather, we should attempt to identify and critically examine our cultural assumptions. Such critique, often done in dialogue with others, can cause us to change assumptions that have negative effects on colleagues and students.

Identifying and critiquing cultural assumptions is not easy for individuals and schools to do. It usually is necessary to begin with examination of our actions, cultural artifacts, and espoused beliefs, and then begin to search below the surface of those actions, artifacts, and beliefs for underlying assumptions. At the individual level, this might mean reflecting on questions such as the following:

- Do I have more difficulty working with some cultural groups than others? If so, why?
- How congruent are my espoused beliefs and actions when working with cultural groups different from my own?

- How does my cultural background influence my expectations of and interactions with parents?
- How does my cultural background contribute to my perceptions of effective teaching?
- How does my cultural background affect my expectations of students in general? My expectations of different student groups?

These questions provide entry points for critical reflection that can expand our understanding of cultural assumptions. Questions such as the following can assist groups to critically examine cultural effects on the school as an organization:

- How does the dominant culture inform our goals as a school? How do other cultures contribute to our goals?
- How is the dominant culture represented in our curriculum, including textbooks and curriculum materials? Are other cultures reflected positively in our curriculum?
- How do our cultural beliefs affect the way students are grouped and placed in various programs in our school?
- How do our cultural beliefs affect the school's disciplinary practices?
- How do our cultural beliefs affect the way we assess student learning?
- How do our cultural beliefs affect the way we interact with our students' families?

Another catalyst for changing beliefs is a better understanding of cultures different from our own. This can be done by reading literature about other cultures and about multicultural education, talking with students and colleagues from other cultures, interacting with parents and community members from different cultures in various community settings, and sharing educational and leadership roles within the school with representatives of various cultures. Better understanding of cultures, especially when achieved through interaction with those cultures, can overcome personal bias, change educational beliefs, and ultimately inform a different and more diverse educational practice.

SUMMARY AND CONCLUSIONS

We have examined the relationship of educational philosophy to supervisory belief and practice. You were asked to define what is meant by good and effective schools and teaching effectiveness and then to determine your own supervisory platform. We revealed our platform of supervision as collaborative experimentalism striving toward nondirective existentialism within a developmental framework. We believe teachers will become collectively purposeful as they gain greater control over decisions for instructional improvement. Finally, we believe that supervisors and teachers need to critically examine the effects of culture on their educational beliefs.

PRACTITIONER REFLECTION

Supervisory Platform—What's Your Story?

Rosa M. Pena, *Principal, Zavala Elementary School*

I have been trying to live my idea of leadership for the past four years as an elementary school principal, even though I have served as a leader in different capacities throughout my education career. By no means do I feel I have reached my full potential as a Nondirective Existential leader, or as those leaders described in Howard Gardner's *Leading Minds*. The principal position is not about power or prestige for me, it is about being the lead teacher and role model on a campus that serves a population that I can relate to.

This part of my "leadership story" begins with the day I interviewed for the Zavala Elementary principal position. I remember walking into the interview room and seeing a long table with 12 anxious people sitting around it. I greeted everyone in English and in Spanish, which seemed to have broken the ice because I can remember smiles from everyone. As I recall, some of my responses to their questions came in the form of a story. It just seemed natural for them to learn about me and what I stood for as a leader through my stories. I also distinctly remember being open and honest throughout the whole process. Before I left that afternoon, I felt the interview committee had a real picture of who I was and who I was going to be as the principal of their school. It was up to them to decide if I was the right person for the job.

Gardner (1995) identifies four factors that appear to be crucial to the practice of effective leadership and are related to my own supervisory platform. The first factor Gardner proposes is having a tie to the community or audience. He explains that the relationship between the leader and followers must be ongoing and active. They each affect the other and they need to take cues from each other to make the changes necessary for the relationship to continue to grow. This was one of the first steps that I took when I was appointed principal. I made it a point to schedule individual meetings with all the staff members and key parent leaders so that I could learn about their values and the vision for the school. I continue this practice by starting our weekly staff meetings with individuals sharing so that the staff members and I have an opportunity to learn more about each other.

Another practice I encourage is for the staff to complete at least two neighborhood walks during the school year so we can show families that we want to learn more about them. This gives us a chance to learn the issues that our families face and believe need to be addressed as a learning community. This also allows us to embody our common values and maintain positive interpersonal relationships.

The second factor that Gardner feels is needed for effective leadership, and one that I embrace, is for the leader to spend time with his or her followers and be in constant contact with them. Every Friday morning I spend at least one hour with parents discussing any concerns they have about our school and the children's learning. At times I model different teaching strategies they can practice at home with their children. This strengthens our school-home connections and also gives me opportunities to recognize diversity among our students and their families. I am then able to share my learning with the staff.

One supervisory practice mentioned in this chapter is for supervision to allow for reflective inquiry encouraging professional growth and renewal. This reminds me of Gardner's third factor—that there must be evidence of the relationship between stories and embodiments. I feel that this is one of my strongest traits as a leader and as a person. I do my best everyday to live by what I believe. One example of this was when I modeled honesty and openness. I was feeling "stuck" as the leader of the school. I did not believe we were moving student learning in the right direction. I did not know what else to do but to be honest with the staff. I told all of them in small group meetings what I was feeling and that I needed to know how they thought we could move our learning to higher levels. I needed to know if we were still sharing the same vision and values. Since these meetings, I have been able to push each staff member to reflect on individual and whole-school practices. We have had numerous conversations that I believe are the beginning stages of a renewed spirit for teaching and learning.

The final factor presented by Gardner is one that he calls the centrality of choice, whereby the leader and the followers exert some kind of choice and where there is no need for using fear to maintain the leadership position. Only by "leadership through choice" can the other three factors be implemented. As I stated at the beginning of my story, I did not pursue this position so that I could have power and control. On the contrary, as a leader I would like to foster leadership, build a constituency, form collaborations, and strengthen relationships. By doing this, I will be able to create an environment that is conducive to experimentation and risk-taking.

As my leadership story continues to unfold, I will need to work so that the stories and embodiments fuse. I know that through this whole leadership process I will need to understand my leadership position, which at this time can be categorized as collaborative experimentalism. Hopefully, with a better understanding of my own educational and supervisory platforms, I will inspire effective followers to articulate their own stories and become instructional leaders.

EXERCISES

Academic

1. Write your own educational platform. Your platform need not exclusively reflect any of the three major philosophies discussed in this chapter. Reflection on this chapter's open-ended questions about your educational beliefs will help you to build the platform.

2. Write your own supervisory platform. Reflection on this chapter's open-ended questions about your supervisory beliefs will help you to build the platform.

3. Design a chart comparing the three major philosophies discussed in this chapter in terms of what each philosophy assumes about:
   a. Human nature
   b. What constitutes reality
   c. The human relationship to the environment
   d. The human relationship to fellow humans

Design a second chart comparing *implications* of the three philosophies in terms of:

a. How people best learn

b. The proper goal(s) of education

c. The appropriate role of the teacher

d. The appropriate role of the educational supervisor

4. Prepare a report in which you identify one of the three major philosophies discussed in this chapter (essentialism, experimentalism, existentialism) as the one most clearly reflected in U.S. education today. Provide a rationale for your choice.

5. Write a reaction to the authors' supervisory platform. Include your perceptions of problems that might be encountered by a supervisor attempting to make the authors' platform a reality within a public school setting.

Field

1. Ask five teachers from different school districts for single-paragraph descriptions of central office supervisors. Assuming each teacher has given an accurate description of at least one central office supervisor, classify each described supervisor according to his or her probable philosophy (experimentalist, essentialist, existentialist, or other). Summarize your study and conclusions in writing. (Supervisors and school districts should remain anonymous in the teacher descriptions; responding teachers should remain anonymous in your written summary.)

2. Ask five adults to list improvements that should be made in U.S. education. On the basis of the lists, attempt to relate each respondent to one of the major philosophies described in this chapter (essentialism, experimentalism, existentialism). Summarize your study and conclusions in writing.

3. Ask five teachers each to write one or two paragraphs on "What Makes an Effective Supervisor." On the basis of the teachers' responses, predict which supervisory approach each teacher would prefer during classroom supervision or staff development activities.

4. Ask five students to write one or two paragraphs on "What Makes a Good School." Attempt to relate each student response to one of the three major philosophies described in this chapter (essentialism, experimentalism, existentialism). Write a report reviewing the students' responses and showing whether each response relates to one of the three philosophies, and if so, how.

5. Visit or recall the organization and climate of a selected school. On the basis of your observations or recollections, which of the three major philosophies described in this chapter (essentialism, experimentalism, existentialism) does the school's organization and climate most clearly reflect? Prepare a report discussing the school's organizational and climate characteristics and supporting your philosophical classification of the school.

Developmental

1. Begin an in-depth study of one of the philosophies described in Chapter 5. As you carry out the study, continue to relate your inquiry to education and educational supervision.

2. Begin a review of the works of popular authors who present what they consider successful approaches to management, leadership, or interpersonal communication. For each author, consider whether his or her recommended approach or system most nearly resembles a directive, collaborative, nondirective, or eclectic approach. Make a personal evaluation of each author's proposals.

REFERENCES

Airasian, P. W., and Walsh, M. E. 1997. Constructivist cautions. *Phi Delta Kappan, 78*(6), 444–449.

Barnes, S. 1981. *Synthesis of selected research on teacher findings.* Austin, TX: Research and Development Center for Teacher Education.

Brophy, J. 1979. Teacher behavior and its effects. *Journal of Teacher Education, 71,* 733–750.

Brophy, J., and Evertson, C. 1976. *Learning from teaching: A developmental perspective.* Boston: Allyn and Bacon.

Denhan C., and Lieberman, A. (Eds.). 1980. *Time to learn.* Washington, DC: U.S. Department of Education.

Gardner, H. 1995. *Leading minds: An anatomy of leadership.* New York: Basic Books.

Ginkel, K. C. 1983. *An overview of a study which examined the relationship between elementary school teachers' preference for supervisory conferencing approach and conceptual level of development.* Paper presented at the American Educational Research Association, Montreal, Canada, April.

Glickman, C. D. 1987a. Good and/or effective schools: What do we want? *Kappan, 68*(8), 622–624.

Glickman, C. D. 1987b. Unlocking school reform: Uncertainty as a condition of professionalism. *Kappan, 69*(2), 120–122.

Glickman, C. D., and Tamashiro, R. T. 1980. Determining one's beliefs regarding teacher supervision. *Bulletin, 64*(440), 74–81.

Griffin, G. A. 1985. Teacher induction: Research issues. *Journal of Teacher Education, 36*(1), 42–46.

Hardison, O. B., Jr. 1986. A tree, a streamlined fish, and a self squared dragon: Science as a form of culture. *Georgia Review* (Summer), 394–403.

Johnson, J. A., Collins, H. W., Dupuis, V. L., and Johansen, J. H. 1973. *Foundations of American education.* Boston: Allyn and Bacon.

Morris, V. C. 1961. *Philosophy and the American school.* Boston: Houghton Mifflin.

Null, J. W. 2004. Is constructivism traditional? Historical and practical perspectives on a popular advocacy. *The Educational Forum, 68*(2), 180–188.

Ornstein, A. C. 1990. A look at teacher effectiveness research: Theory and practice. *NASSP Bulletin, 74*(528), 78–88.

Pratte, R. 1971. *Contemporary theories of education.* Scranton, PA: T. Y. Crowell.

Rosenshine, B. 1983. Teaching functions in instructional programs. *The Elementary School Journal, 83,* 335–351.

Rosenshine, B. 1986. *Unsolved issues in teaching content: A critique of a lesson on Federalist Paper No. 10.* Paper presented at the annual meeting of the American Educational Research Association, San Francisco, April.

Sergiovanni, T. J., and Starrat R. J. 1983. *Supervision: Human perspectives* (3rd ed.) (pp. 226–227). New York: McGraw-Hill.

Ybarra, S., and Hollingsworth, J. 2001 Increasing classroom productivity. *Leadership, 31*(1), 34–35.

SUGGESTED READINGS

Borich, G. D. 1992. *Effective teaching methods.* New York: Macmillan.

Brandt, R. (Ed.). 1992. *Educational Leadership, 49*(7). Theme issue on "Beyond 'Effective Teaching.'"

Brooks, J. G., and Brooks, M. G. 1993. *The case for constructivist classrooms.* Alexandria, VA: Association for Supervision and Curriculum Development.

Joyce, B. R., and Weil, M. 1996. *Models of teaching* (5th ed.). Boston: Allyn and Bacon.

Kindsvatter, R. 1992. *Dynamics of effective teaching.* New York: Longman.

Lambert, L. 2003. *Leadership capacity for lasting school improvement.* Alexandria, VA: Association for Supervision and Curriculum Development.

Oser, F. K., Dick, A., and Patry, J. (Eds.). 1992. *Effective and responsible teaching.* San Francisco: Jossey-Bass.

Patterson, J. L., and Kelleher, P. 2005. *Resilient school leaders: Strategies for turning adversity into achievement.* Alexandria, VA: Association for Supervision and Curriculum Development.

Power, E. J. 1996. *Educational philosophy: A history from the ancient world to modern America.* New York: Garland.

Waxman, H. C., and Walberg, H. J. 1991. *Effective teaching: Current research.* Berkeley: McCutchan.

part three
Interpersonal Skills

The organization of this book was outlined in Figure 1.1 in Chapter 1. The prerequisites for supervision as a developmental function are knowledge, interpersonal skills, and technical skills. Part II examined the critical knowledge base. Part III will describe interpersonal skills. Chapter 6 will introduce the supervisory behavior continuum, Chapter 7 will introduce the theory of developmental supervision, Chapter 8 will detail the use of directive control behaviors, Chapter 9 will detail the use of directive informational behaviors, Chapter 10 will detail the use of collaborative behaviors, Chapter 11 will detail the use of nondirective behaviors, and Chapter 12 will discuss in detail the theory and practice of developmental supervision.

Knowledge of what needs to be done for teacher growth and school success is the base of a triangle for supervisory action (see Figure III.1). Knowledge needs to be accompanied by interpersonal skills for communicating with teachers and technical skills for planning, assessing, observing, and evaluating instructional improvement. We will now turn to the interpersonal skill dimension.

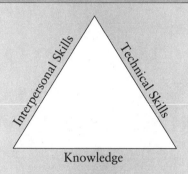

FIGURE III.1 *Prerequisite Dimensions for a Supervisor*

chapter 6

Supervisory Behavior Continuum

Know Thyself

This chapter looks at the range of interpersonal behaviors available to a supervisor who is working with individuals and groups of teachers. It will assess how supervisors typically behave with staff in school settings and then determine other behaviors that might be used skillfully and effectively. Later chapters will provide training in each of four clusters of interpersonal skills.

What are the categories of behaviors? After many years of collecting supervisors' observations in meetings with individuals and groups of teachers for purposes of making classroom or school decisions, broad categories of supervisory behaviors have been derived (Glickman, 1981, 2002; Wolfgang and Glickman, 1980). These categories encompass almost all observed supervisor behaviors that are deemed purposeful. A *purposeful* behavior is defined as one that contributes to the decision being made at the conference or meeting. The derived categories of supervisory behaviors are listening, clarifying, encouraging, reflecting, presenting, problem solving, negotiating, directing, standardizing, and reinforcing. Definitions of each category are as follows:

- *Listening.* The supervisor sits and looks at the speaker and nods his or her head to show understanding. Gutteral utterances ("uh-huh," "umm") also indicate listening.

- *Clarifying.* The supervisor asks questions and statements to clarify the speaker's point of view: "Do you mean that?" "Would you explain this further?" "I'm confused about this." "I lost you on . . . ."
- *Encouraging.* The supervisor provides acknowledgment responses that help the speaker continue to explain his or her positions: "Yes, I'm following you." "Continue on." "Ah, I see what you're saying; tell me more."
- *Reflecting.* The supervisor summarizes and paraphrases the speaker's message for verification of accuracy: "I understand that you mean . . . ." "So, the issue is . . . ." "I hear you saying . . . ."
- *Presenting.* The supervisor gives his or her own ideas about the issue being discussed: "This is how I see it." "What can be done is . . . ." "I'd like us to consider . . . ." "I believe that . . . ."
- *Problem solving.* The supervisor takes the initiative, usually after a preliminary discussion of the issue or problem, in pressing all those involved to generate a list of possible solutions. This is usually done through statements such as: "Let's stop and each write down what can be done." "What ideas do we have to solve this problem?" "Let's think of all possible actions we can take."
- *Negotiating.* The supervisor moves the discussion from possible to probable solutions by discussing the consequences of each proposed action, exploring conflict or priorities, and narrowing down choices with questions such as: "Where do we agree?" "How can we change that action to be acceptable to all?" "Can we find a compromise that will give each of us part of what we want?"
- *Directing.* The supervisor tells the participant(s) either what the choices are: "As I see it, these are the alternatives: You could do A . . . , B . . . , or C . . . . Which of these make the most sense to you and which will you use?" *Or* the supervisor tells the participants what is to be done: "I've decided that we will do . . . ." "I want you to do . . . ." "The policy will be . . . ." "This is how it is going to be." "We will then proceed as follows."

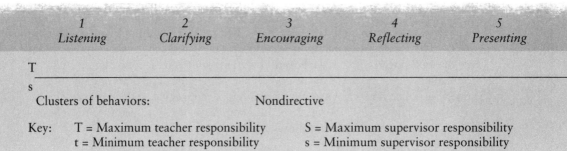

1	2	3	4	5
Listening	Clarifying	Encouraging	Reflecting	Presenting

T _____

s

Clusters of behaviors: Nondirective

Key: T = Maximum teacher responsibility   S = Maximum supervisor responsibility
        t = Minimum teacher responsibility   s = Minimum supervisor responsibility

FIGURE 6.1   *The Supervisory Behavior Continuum*

- *Standardizing.* The supervisor sets the expected criteria and time for the decision to be implemented. Target objectives are set. Expectations are conveyed with words, such as: "By next Monday, we want to see . . . ." "Report back to me on this change by . . . ." "Have the first two activities carried out by . . . ." "I want an improvement of 25 percent involvement by the next meeting." "We have agreed that all tasks will be done before the next observation."
- *Reinforcing.* The supervisor strengthens the directive and the criteria to be met by telling of possible consequences. Possible consequences can be positive, in the form of praise: "I know you can do it!" "I have confidence in your ability!" "I want to show others what you've done!" Consequences also can be negative: "If it's not done on time, we'll lose the support of . . . ." "It must be understood that failure to get this done on time will result in . . . ."

The foregoing categories of interpersonal supervisory behavior move participants toward a decision. Some supervisory behaviors place more responsibility on the teacher(s) to make the decision, others place more responsibility on the supervisor to make the decision, and still others indicate a shared responsibility for decision making. The categories of behaviors are listed in a sequence on the supervisory behavior continuum (Figure 6.1) to reflect the scale of control or power.

When a supervisor *listens* to the teacher, *clarifies* what the teacher says, *encourages* the teacher to speak more about the concern, and *reflects* by verifying the teacher's perceptions, then clearly it is the teacher who is in control. The supervisor's role is that of an active prober or sounding board for the teacher to make his or her own decision. The teacher has high control and the supervisor low control over the actual decision (big *T,* small *s*). This is seen as a *nondirective interpersonal approach.*

When a supervisor uses nondirective behaviors to understand the teacher's point of view but then participates in the discussion by *presenting* his or her own ideas, *problem solving* by asking all parties to propose possible actions, and then

6 *Problem Solving*	7 *Negotiating*	8 *Directing*	9 *Standardizing*	10 *Reinforcing*

t

S

Collaborative   Directive
Informational   Directive Control *negotiating* to find a common course of action satisfactory to teacher and supervisor, then the control over the decision is shared by all. This is viewed as a *collaborative interpersonal approach.*

When a supervisor *directs* the teacher in what the alternatives are from which the teacher might choose, and after the teacher selects, the supervisor *standardizes* the time and criteria of expected results, then the supervisor is the major source of information, providing the teacher with restricted choice (small *t*, big *S*). This is viewed as a *directive informational interpersonal approach.*

Finally, when a supervisor *directs* the teacher in what will be done, *standardizes* the time and criteria of expected results, and *reinforces* the consequences of action or inaction, then the supervisor has taken responsibility for the decision (small *t*, big *S*). The supervisor is clearly determining the actions for the teacher to follow. These behaviors are called a *directive control interpersonal approach.*

Outcomes of Conference

Another way of clarifying the distinctions among supervisory approaches is by looking at the outcomes of the conference and determining who controls the final decision for instructional improvement.

Approach	*Outcome*
Nondirective	Teacher self-plan
Collaborative	Mutual plan
Directive informational	Supervisor-suggested plan
Directive control	Supervisor-assigned plan

In the nondirective approach, the supervisor facilitates the teacher's thinking in developing a self-plan. In the collaborative approach, both supervisor and teacher share information and possible practices as equals in arriving at a mutual plan. In the directive informational approach, the supervisor provides the focus and the parameters of possible actions, and the teacher is asked to choose within the supervisor's suggestions. In the directive control approach, the supervisor tells the teacher what is to be done. Nondirective provides maximum teacher choice; collaborative, mutual choice; directive informational, selected choice; and directive control, no choice in the outcome of the conference.

Valid Assessment of Self

We need to make sure that how we perceive ourselves is consistent with how others perceive us. For example, if we checked that we typically use a collaborative approach with individuals and a nondirective approach with groups, then we need further information to know whether that is true. If not, then later in this chapter we might recommend a continuation, refinement, or discontinuation with a cluster of behaviors that simply do not exist in anyone's mind but our own. As an example, let us give a personal instance of erroneous self-perception.

As a school principal in New Hampshire, one of the authors regarded himself as operating a successful school and being accessible to teachers. He could document success by external evidence—state and national recognition the school had received and complimentary letters from numerous visitors. He documented his accessibility through casual discussions with teachers in the lounge and by having an open-office policy for every staff member who wished to speak with him. In his third year as a principal at this particular school, the superintendent asked all principals in the school system to allow teachers to evaluate principal performance. One item on the evaluation form was "Ability to Listen to Others," followed by a numerical scale of responses from 1 ("rarely listens") to 7 ("almost always listens"). Before giving the form to teachers, the author filled out the same evaluation form according to his own perception of his performance. He confidently circled the number 7 on "ability to listen." Once the teachers' responses were collected and results were received, he was amazed to find that the lowest teacher rating on the entire survey was on that very item on which he had rated himself highest. To the author's chagrin, there was an obvious discrepancy between his own perception of performance and staff perceptions.

Johari Window

The Johari Window (Luft, 1970; Janas, 2001) provides a graphic way to look at what we know and do not know about our behavior (see Figure 6.2). Visualize a window with four windowpanes. In this scheme, there are four windowpanes of the self in which behaviors are either known or not known by self (the supervisor) and others (the teachers). In windowpane 1, there are behaviors that both supervisor and teachers know the supervisor uses. This is the *public self*. For example, the supervisor knows that when he or she is anxious, speech will become halting and hesitant; teachers are also aware of what such speech indicates.

In windowpane 2 is the *blind self*—behaviors the supervisor practices that are unknown to the self but are known to teachers. For example, as a school principal, one of the authors was displaying behaviors toward teachers that he thought were listening behaviors, but teachers saw the same behaviors as a failure to listen. Of course, once one becomes aware of teachers' perceptions of those behaviors, the blind self becomes the public self.

In windowpane 3 is the *private self*—behaviors the supervisor has knowledge about but that teachers do not know. For instance, in new situations a supervisor might mask his or her unsureness by being extroverted in greeting others. Only the supervisor knows that this behavior is covering up insecurity. Once the supervisor discloses this perception to others, the private self becomes public.

	Known to Supervisor	Not Known to Supervisor
Known to Teachers	1. Public self	2. Blind self
Not Known to Teachers	3. Private self	4. Unknown self

FIGURE 6.2 *Adaptation of Johari Window*

Source: Adapted from Joseph Luft, *Group Processes: An Introduction to Group Dynamics* (New York: National Press Books, 1970).

Finally, there is windowpane 4, the *unknown self*. There are actions a supervisor takes of which both supervisors and teachers are unaware. From time to time the supervisor might rapidly shift his legs while speaking behind a table. Neither supervisor nor teachers are aware of this leg movement. Perhaps a supervisor becomes irritated while a certain teacher is speaking. The supervisor may not know why she is irritated or even that she feels this way, and the teacher may not know either. The unknown self is unconscious to all; it becomes private, blind, or public only by circumstances that create a new awareness.

What does the Johari Window have to do with supervision? We cannot become more effective as supervisors unless we know what we are doing. We may, at our discretion, decide to keep parts of ourselves private. (For example, we may not want teachers to know all the details of our life and personality.) Yet we need to understand that by remaining largely private and not sharing the experiences that bind us as humans, we are creating a distance when we work with teachers. We may prefer formality and distance and may be able to document that such privateness accomplishes certain results. On the other hand, we must also accept that our privateness will be reciprocal, and that staff may not easily discuss personal situations that may affect teaching performance. First, we must be aware of how private or public we are with our staff and determine if we desire teachers to be the same way with us. Second, as supervisors, we cannot afford to be blind to our own behaviors and the effect of those behaviors on others. We can improve only what we know; to believe only our own self-perceptions is to court disaster.

The author's perception of his listening behavior as a principal is a case in point. As long as he saw himself as a wonderful, accessible listener, it did not seem probable that teachers were not coming to him with instructional problems. However, he discovered that on two different occasions teachers had gone to the superintendent about instructional problems of which he was unaware. After the superintendent had told him that teachers were going over his head, he angrily confronted the teachers with their "unprofessional" behavior. It did not occur to the author that he might have been the one at fault. After the staff evaluations, he could no longer delude himself. Many teachers were not telling him their concerns because they did not believe that he would really listen. The author had to face the fact that the staff did not see him as accessible. He might have avoided collecting such information, continued with his euphoric self-perception, and then been devastated as the school fell apart.

Cognitive Dissonance

Invalidity of perceptions creates *cognitive dissonance,* according to a model of motivation by psychologist Leon Festinger (1957). The model is based on the premise that a person cannot live with contradictory psychological evidence—that is, thinking of himself or herself in one way while other sources of information indicate that he or she is different. When the author's perception of his listening abilities were contradicted by teacher perceptions, mental turmoil or cognitive dissonance was created. For example, if you believe that you are a collaborative supervisor and then you receive feedback from teachers that you are a directive supervisor, this will cause cognitive dissonance. We must wrestle with disparate perceptions and reconcile them. If not, the two differing sources of information will continue to bother us. This mental anguish strives to resolve the question of what is it that we really do. The resolution can come about in three alternative ways (Hyman, 1975).

First, we can dismiss the source of contrary evidence as biased and untrue. For example, the principal might rationalize, "I really am a good listener; teachers marked me low because they didn't like the way I scheduled bus duties." Or the supervisor might think he or she really is collaborative: "Teachers simply don't understand what collaboration is." By dismissing the other source of information as erroneous, we can continue to believe that we are what we originally thought. No further change is necessary.

Second, we can change our own self-perception to conform to the other source of information and can then live with the new perception of ourselves. We accept that they are right and we are wrong; thus, our perception will now be theirs. For example, "I really was wrong about my listening abilities, and I now reconcile myself to being a poor listener," or "The supervisor is really not collaborative but instead is, as the teachers say, directive." Accepting the other source of information makes dissonance vanish so that no further change is necessary.

Third, we can accept our original self-perception as how we wish to be perceived, use the other source of information as an indicator of how we are currently perceived, and then change our behaviors to be more similar to our wish. In other words, our perception was not accurate, but it still represents what we want to be. In our example, the author thought he was a good listener, but others said that he was not; so he attempted to change his listening behaviors in order to become a good listener. The supervisor thought he or she was collaborative but others said that he or she was directive; so he or she changed behavior to become more collaborative.

The third alternative to resolving cognitive dissonance creates behavioral change. Whenever we have an idea of how we desire to be matched against the reality of how others see us, there exist conditions for individual change. The acknowledged gap between what is and what should be becomes a powerful stimulus to change. We change our behaviors and gather feedback from others to determine whether others are forming new perceptions of us and more positive results are forthcoming.

Comparing Self-Perceptions with Others' Perceptions

Box 6.1 provides an instrument that the supervisor uses to compare self-perceptions with teacher perceptions of supervisor performance. The *Supervisor's Self-Assessment* is divided into four sections: "Professional Characteristics," "Skills," "Individual Assistance," and "Schoolwide Assistance," and yields a sub-score for each section. The process of self-assessment begins with the supervisor completing and self-scoring the instrument. It is important for the supervisor to be totally open when completing the self-assessment, so as a general rule the supervisor should not be expected to share results with superiors or teachers. The supervisor next distributes the instrument to the teachers or a randomly selected sample of the teachers he or she supervises. It's important that the teachers complete and return the completed instruments anonymously. After calculating item, section, and overall means of teacher responses, the supervisor can compare self-perceptions with teacher perceptions. When comparing self-ratings to teacher ratings on any particular item, the supervisor can reach a variety of conclusions, including:

1. Supervisor and teacher satisfaction with supervisor performance
2. Supervisor satisfaction and teacher dissatisfaction with supervisor performance
3. Supervisor dissatisfaction and teacher satisfaction with supervisor performance
4. Supervisor and teacher dissatisfaction with supervisor performance

Any of the last three conclusions can be the basis for supervisor-defined improvement objectives, and supervisor-designed action plans for the improvement of instructional assistance.

BOX 6.1 Supervisor's Self-Assessment

Directions for Completing: Place in the space before each item the number (1, 2, 3, or 4) of the response that most nearly indicates your level of agreement with the item:

1. Strongly disagree
2. Disagree
3. Agree
4. Strongly agree

Section A: Professional Characteristics

___ 1. The supervisor is genuinely concerned with the growth and development of students.

___ 2. The supervisor is genuinely concerned with the growth and development of teachers.

___ 3. The supervisor is trustworthy.

___ 4. The supervisor treats teachers fairly.

___ 5. The supervisor is flexible.

___ 6. The supervisor is ethical.

Section B: Skills

___ 7. The supervisor displays communication skills.

___ 8. The supervisor displays needs assessment skills.

___ 9. The supervisor displays planning skills.

___10. The supervisor displays group facilitation skills.

___11. The supervisor displays problem-solving skills.

___12. The supervisor displays change agency skills.

___13. The supervisor displays observation skills.

___14. The supervisor displays conflict resolution skills.

Section C: Individual Assistance

___15. The supervisor effectively observes teaching and provides helpful feedback.

___16. The supervisor provides useful instructional resources.

___17. The supervisor fosters teacher reflection.

___18. The supervisor demonstrates effective teaching.

___19. The supervisor shares innovative instructional strategies.

___20. The supervisor effectively assists beginning teachers.

___21. The supervisor effectively assists teachers with instructional problems they are experiencing.

___22. The supervisor effectively assists teachers to plan for instruction.

___23. The supervisor effectively assists teachers to assess student learning.

___24. The supervisor effectively assists teachers to individualize instruction.

Section D: Schoolwide Assistance

___25. The supervisor effectively facilitates instructional dialogue among teachers.

___26. The supervisor fosters a positive school culture.

___27. The supervisor facilitates collective vision building.

___28. The supervisor fosters teacher collaboration for schoolwide instructional improvement.

___29. The supervisor fosters teacher empowerment.

___30. The supervisor effectively facilitates teachers' professional development.

___31. The supervisor effectively facilitates curriculum development.

___32. The supervisor effectively facilitates program evaluation.

Directions for Scoring: For the instrument completed by the supervisor, add the ratings for the items in each section to find subtotals. The range of possible subtotals for each section follows:

Section A: Professional Characteristics, from 6–24.
Section B: Skills, from 8–32.
Section C: Individual Assistance, from 10–40.
Section D: Schoolwide Assistance, from 8–32.

The overall rating (the sum of the four subtotals) ranges from 32 to 128.

(continued)

For the instrument completed by teachers, calculate the mean scores for each item, section, and the overall rating. For example, if five teachers responded to the same item with ratings of 2, 3, 4, 4, and 5 respectively, the teachers' mean rating for that item would be 3.6. For an example at the section level, if the subtotals on Section A from five teachers were 16, 18, 19, 21, and 22, the mean ratings for Section A would be 19.2. For the overall mean, if individual overall ratings by five teachers were 83, 92, 100, 112, and 118, the overall mean for teacher ratings would be 101.

Comparing Self-Perceptions to Recorded Behaviors

Another way to create cognitive dissonance as a catalyst for improvement of supervisory practice is for the supervisor to compare his or her perceptions to data gathered on the supervisor's actual behaviors. One of the key processes a supervisor is responsible for is gathering data on classroom behaviors to assist teachers to improve their instruction. It makes sense, then, for the supervisor to analyze data on her or his own performance for the purpose of improved supervision. Data gathering on supervision often takes place while the supervisor is interacting with individual teachers or groups. The data can be gathered in a number of ways. Another supervisor can observe a conference or meeting that the observed supervisor is conducting and gather requested data. The supervisor can tape a supervisory conference or meeting and review the tape. The supervisor can analyze documents that reflect supervisory behaviors, such as e-mails, memos, and observation reports that she or he has prepared. The purpose of analyzing these types of data is to compare the supervisor's perceptions to recorded supervisory behaviors. Comparison of perceptions to data can create the same types of cognitive dissonance as the comparison of supervisor and teacher perceptions discussed in the previous section. In fact, comparing supervisor perceptions to hard data may bring about cognitive dissonance more easily than comparison of supervisors and teacher perceptions. The cognitive dissonance caused by self-analysis of data on supervisory behaviors can lead to changes in supervisory behaviors.

What types of data on supervisory performance should be gathered and analyzed? Data might be gathered on interpersonal behaviors in general. For example, when a supervisor attempts to use a collaborative approach, are collaborative behaviors in evidence, or does the supervisor slip into directive or nondirective behaviors? Data also can be used to compare the supervisor's behaviors with different groups. Does the supervisor treat men and women differently? Hispanics and Whites? Younger and older teachers? If so, why is one group treated differently from the other? If equity is an educational goal, than equitable treatment of teachers by supervisors should be a model for teachers and students. By recording and analyzing supervisory behaviors through the lens of equity, the supervisor can recognize problems in this area and begin to improve her or his own performance.

SUMMARY, CONCLUSIONS, AND PREVIEW

This chapter outlined the supervisory behavior continuum and the clustering of interpersonal behaviors into nondirective, collaborative, directive informational, and directive control approaches. An assessment instrument was provided. A discourse on the Johari Window and cognitive dissonance was given so that we might check the perceptions of our beliefs and behaviors by those who are recipients of our behaviors. To compare our own supervisory beliefs and self-perceived interpersonal behavior with teacher perceptions of our behavior or with objective data is believed to be important in refining and changing behaviors.

We will next examine and practice the skills of each supervisory approach in terms of actual conferencing and meeting behaviors. Understanding how we behave as supervisors and then refining our present behaviors are the first steps toward acquiring new interpersonal behaviors.

PRACTITIONER REFLECTION

Re-Booting

Holly Galloway, *Associate Principal for Curriculum and Instruction,*
John B. Connally High School

I generally do not consider myself religious but spirituality is an important part of my life. One Sunday, not unlike any other Sunday, as I sat in my regular pew, my mind began to wander during the sermon. The sermon was on the need to transform one's self, away from conformity and self-importance toward what is really important in life. I was completely unaware until the moment when my mind began to wander that I needed to be transformed. As a leader I have experience with building master schedules, managing students, and solving technology problems. During all of these activities I frequently use the term *re-boot*. What I did not know was that in my daily rush of high standards, *I* needed to re-boot. My mind had conformed to the world around me. I had become lost in the tasks and pride of my personal accomplishments and forgotten to match my inner self with my outer self. I was suffering from a case of cognitive dissonance.

I have worked at the same school since it opened nine years ago, first as a teacher and now as an assistant principal. The majority of these years have been wonderful experiences of growth, excellence, and touching the lives of students. For the past three years a sense of discord and uneasiness had been present both in my heart and in my mind. When I began my nine-year journey at Connally, I worked for a legend in education and leadership who helped create a profoundly successful school. As legends often do, he retired and I then turned my loyalty and soul to the new leader. The new principal was a legend in his own right but was not worshiped by all as the inaugural principal had been. After the first year with the new leader I began to feel completely overwhelmed. Many of what I considered "principal tasks" were now mine, including making difficult leadership decisions, and I began to resent the new principal. I hate to admit it, but I was quite pleased when he left. For the third principal,

Connally was a one-year stepping-stone. She, unlike the previous two principals, never quite embraced Connally as the best place you could be as an educator. These three years were difficult for me, and when the Connally success began to falter during this time I blamed the top. I never looked at myself as part of the problem. I was the solution. I love Connally. I was part of the original staff. I had a master's degree. I was working on my Ph.D. I was Queen Connally. Sometimes the queen is part of the problem. My realization was that I had been conforming to my surroundings. I realized that I had my own hand in the problems my school was experiencing.

As my mind wandered in church that day I decided to drive out the discord I could no longer ignore. The cognitive dissonance I was experiencing was that my inner professional self was not matching my outer professional self. This experience helped me to formulate three lessons.

Lesson one is to remember who you are. To do this I had to realize that I was not the job I had, and I needed to rediscover my purposeful behaviors. Lesson two is to choose the present and future over the past. Connally must continue to educate students. It should not matter who the leader of Connally is. I should be able to work to reverse problems at Connally and not spend my time blaming the leadership. I must drop the past, stand in the present, and look forward. Lesson three is to choose reason over emotion. This does not mean becoming emotionless, but rather to realize that what you feel today can control your thoughts and can influence how you feel and act in the future. I had to refocus my thoughts on the present and future.

My inner self was guilty of exaggerating my own importance and causing an imbalance between my inner and outer self. Fortunately, the cognitive dissonance I was experiencing had yet to greatly affect the perceptions or behaviors of those around me. Now that I have taken the time to reflect and "re-boot," I am at peace and willing to do whatever it takes to be the best educational leader I can. I can do this because I have been transformed by the resolution of my cognitive dissonance. My inner and outer selves are once again in balance. Well, at least until my mind needs to be re-booted again.

EXERCISES

Academic

1. After reviewing the 10 categories of supervision defined in this chapter, list specific behaviors your supervisor has exhibited while supervising you. For each example, write a brief description of your feelings toward the supervisor while he or she was using the given behavior, as well as your behavioral response to the situation. What does a review of your feelings and responses tell you about the supervisory approach you most prefer? Least prefer?

2. This chapter proposes three possible ways of resolving the mental conflict brought about by cognitive dissonance. Prepare a report in which you cite examples of cognitive dissonance you have personally experienced and your reaction to each resulting dilemma. Based on your recollections, which of the three possible responses to cognitive dissonance has been your typical mode of resolution?

3. Label the left-hand column of a sheet of paper "Public Self" and the right-hand column "Private Self." Think of personality or other characteristics that you intentionally disguise in your work setting. For each characteristic, describe in a few words the image you consciously present to others (left-hand column) and the real you that your public behavior conceals (right-hand column).

4. Locate a research study on the effectiveness of one or more of the following supervisor approaches to supervisor-teacher conferences: (a) directive control, (b) directive informational, (c) collaborative, and (d) nondirective. Summarize the purpose, methods, results, and conclusions of the study in writing.

5. Chapter 6 relates an experience in which a discrepancy between a blind self and a public self led to communication problems with subordinates. Discuss in writing three other situations in which conflicts between a supervisor's blind self and public self might eventually lead to leadership problems.

Field

1. Arrange to visit a teacher's class and for a postobservation conference with that teacher. The postobservation conference should include an analysis of the teacher's instructional performance, the setting of instructional improvement goals, and planning a strategy for meeting those goals. Record the postobservation on audiotape. Refer to the categories of supervisor behavior in this book as you listen to the tape. Write a paper in which you state whether you used a primarily directive, collaborative, or nondirective approach during the postobservation conference. Cite examples of specific behaviors you exhibited during the postobservation conference. Compare those behaviors with your results on the Supervisory Beliefs Inventory (Chapter 5).

2. Carry out the exercises suggested in this chapter. Prepare a written report on the results of the exercises and your reaction to those results.

3. Put yourself in the shoes of an individual you supervise or have supervised. (Even those not in formal supervisory roles have at one time or another been responsible for supervising others.) Write a description of your supervisory style; be careful to describe your supervisory style as the other person would, not as you would. Compare this description of your supervisory style with your results on the Supervisory Beliefs Inventory.

4. Draw a two-frame cartoon for each of the following themes: (a) public self—private self, (b) my message—their perception, (c) cognitive dissonance. Base your cartoons on personal experiences or observations in a school setting. Write narratives explaining each cartoon.

Developmental

1. Begin to make mental notes on behaviors you use when supervising others. Look for patterns of behavior that can be related to an orientation toward supervision (directive, collaborative, nondirective, eclectic) of which you may not now be conscious.

2. Informally observe others in leadership roles. Do their behaviors tend to cluster toward a directive, collaborative, or nondirective approach?

3. Begin to examine discrepancies between your public self and your private self, and consider possible reasons for such discrepancies.

REFERENCES

Festinger, L. 1957. *A theory of cognitive dissonance.* Stanford, CA: Stanford University Press.

Glickman, C. D. 1981. *Developmental supervision: Alternative practices for helping teachers improve instruction.* Alexandria, VA: Association for Supervision and Curriculum Development.

Glickman, C. D. 2002. *Leadership for learning: How to help teachers succeed.* Alexandria, VA: Association for Supervision and Curriculum Development.

Hyman, R. T. 1975. *School administrator's handbook of teacher supervision and evaluation methods* (pp. 46–47). Englewood Cliffs, NJ: Prentice Hall.

Janas, M. 2001. Getting a clear view. *Journal of Staff Development, 22*(2), 32–34.

Luft, J. 1970. *Group processes: An introduction to group dynamics.* New York: National Press Books.

Wolfgang, C. H., and Glickman, C. D. 1980. *Solving discipline problems: Alternative strategies for teachers.* Boston: Allyn and Bacon.

SUGGESTED READINGS

Hoerr, T. R. 2005. *The art of school leadership.* Alexandria, VA: Association for Supervision and Curriculum Development.

Reeves, D. B. 2003. *Assessing educational leaders: Evaluating performance for improved individual and organizational results.* Thousand Oaks, CA: Corwin Press.

chapter 7

Developmental Supervision

An Introduction

This chapter provides an introduction to developmental supervision—a model that will be described in greater detail throughout the remainder of the text. We will begin by sharing four case studies of developmental supervision in action. As you read the four case studies, compare them in relation to the following:

1. The teacher's levels of development, expertise, and commitment to solving the problem
2. The nature of the problem
3. The interpersonal behaviors of the supervisor, including any shifts in supervisory behavior which take place

Case Study One

After receiving complaints about Gerald Watson's teaching methods from students, parents, and other teachers, principal Martha Cozero observed Gerald's science class on several occasions. Regardless of lesson content or student population, all of the observed lessons followed the same pattern. First, seat by seat and row by row, students would take turns reading paragraphs from the science text. Next, Gerald would pass out a worksheet for students to complete independently. If students finished their worksheets before the end of class, they were told to begin their homework assignment, which always consisted of written exercises from the textbook. During independent seatwork, Gerald usually sat at his desk reading sports magazines, looking up only to give an "evil-eye" to students who were talking to each other or out of their seats.

Martha was not surprised by Gerald's "instructional" routine. She *was* surprised that he made no attempt at more active teaching even during her classroom observations. Martha used the first of several conferences with Gerald to try to find out more about his attitudes toward teaching science. He admitted that he rarely graded or returned the written assignments that he required students to complete. Gerald stated that he neither understood nor used the hands-on science program that the middle school science team had agreed to adopt the previous year. He had not attended the science team's after-school meetings that led to the decision to adopt the program. He had taken personal days rather than attend the all-day workshops during which science teachers developed skills necessary to implement the program. Gerald told Martha that he was six years away from retirement and saw no reason to learn new skills or use new teaching methods.

After reflecting on her classroom observations and conference with Gerald, Martha designed an improvement plan that she presented to him during their next conference. During that conference, she told Gerald that his current instructional strategies and failure to learn about or implement the school's science program were detrimental to student learning and that his approach to teaching science was unacceptable. She stated that Gerald's improvement goals would be to engage in more active teaching and make use of instructional strategies consistent with the science curriculum's goals. Martha mandated the following steps on Gerald's part:

1. End excessive reliance on students taking turns reading aloud from the science text.
2. Reduce the use of worksheets as a primary instructional strategy.
3. Review written assignments completed by students, and provide students with feedback on their performance.
4. Review the school district's written curriculum as well as teacher guides for the school's hands-on science program.
5. Visit other science teachers' classrooms to observe the science program in action.
6. Use more hands-on science activities consistent with the adopted science program.

The principal made it clear that the goals and activities she presented were not optional. Martha listened to Gerald's concerns and answered questions about the action plan. She promised to provide him with resources and materials necessary to implement the new science program. Martha scheduled a series of classroom observations that would allow her to monitor Gerald's progress with the plan and provide him with assistance and feedback on the new instructional strategies he would be trying out.

Gerald reluctantly began to implement the mandated improvement plan. Although progress was slow, his teaching methods did begin to change. Some of Gerald's attempts at hands-on learning worked well, others did not. Students were enjoying the hands-on activities and demonstrating levels of interest and learning that Gerald had not thought possible. Eventually, he admitted to Martha that missing the workshops on the new curriculum had been a mistake: There were many gaps in his knowledge of the new curriculum that his readings and observations had not filled.

Martha decided that Gerald needed formal training in how to implement the science program if he was going to continue to improve his teaching. She also decided that the effort and progress he had made warranted allowing Gerald some choice in how that training should be acquired. Martha offered Gerald three options for learning more about the program: attendance at two days of in-service education on the program offered by the program's publisher at a nearby intermediate unit, after-school workshops to be presented by the science supervisor at the district's other middle school, or individualized training by Jim Adams, the science coordinator at Gerald's middle school. Gerald had always liked Jim so he told Martha that he preferred to receive training from a colleague who was just down the hall and who he could call on if he had problems implementing the curriculum. Jim agreed to work with Gerald, and Martha and Jim designed a plan to provide Gerald with several hours of individualized training and intensive classroom coaching.

Case Study Two

Veteran teacher Bill Levin was assigned as beginning teacher Janice Smith's mentor. Janice had joined the middle school teaching staff eager to try out a variety of innovative teaching strategies she had been introduced to during her teacher preparation program. Now, just two months into her teaching career, Janice was considering leaving the profession at the Thanksgiving break. After a few observations of Janice's teaching, Bill was convinced that Janice had considerable potential as a teacher but that her classroom management problems might prevent her from reaching that potential. Although Janice had been exposed to brief discussions of student discipline problems in several of her teaching methods courses, she had never received systematic training in effective classroom management. Her lack of training and inexperience in dealing with middle school students was becoming increasingly apparent. On several visits to Janice's classroom, Bill observed considerable off-task behavior and numerous student disruptions. Rather than attempting to control the high noise level, Janice would first try to yell over the student conversations, then scream at disruptive students who had ignored her pleas to quiet down.

Janice knew she had classroom management problems but was not sure why the students behaved the way they did or what she could do to improve the situation. Based on his observations and discussions with Janice, Bill made the following suggestions to the novice teacher:

1. Establish a set of rules and procedures for classroom behavior and determine natural consequences for students who fail to follow those rules and procedures.
2. Share the rules and procedures with the students, explaining the rationale for each rule, procedure, and natural consequence.
3. Give the students the opportunity to practice each rule and procedure under simulated conditions, and provide them with feedback on their performance.
4. Consistently enforce all rules and procedures, providing positive feedback for student compliance and carrying through on natural consequences for noncompliance.

Bill offered to help Janice develop her rules and procedures, rehearse her presentation and explanation to students, and plan opportunities for students to practice new guidelines and receive feedback on their performance. Bill also suggested that Janice try out a number of nonverbal and verbal interventions to correct minor student misbehaviors before they reached a disruptive stage. He explained how in his own classroom he used nonverbal interventions such as eye contact, physical proximity, and touch control, as well as verbal interventions such as use of students' names, reminder of a rule or procedure, and explicit redirection. Bill invited Janice to visit his classroom and observe his classroom management techniques. He also offered to observe Janice's class as she implemented his suggested strategies and techniques, and to provide her with feedback based on the observations.

Janice agreed to try out Bill's recommendations. With considerable assistance from her mentor, she implemented the suggested strategies and techniques. After several weeks, most of the students in Janice's class had increased their amount of time on task considerably and student disruptions had decreased. Janice had made it through to Thanksgiving and was willing to give teaching another chance, at least until the end of the school year.

Bill was pleased with the progress Janice had made but concerned about three students who seemed to be immune to his protégée's new classroom management strategies and techniques. He knew that even a few students could disrupt Janice's entire class if she was unable to help them change their behavior. The mentor offered two possibilities for dealing with the three disruptive students. One was for Janice to work individually with each of the problem students to develop a behavior contract. In the contract, teacher and student would negotiate specific behavioral improvement goals, a time period for meeting the goals, teacher and student actions, assessment of student progress, and rewards and consequences.

The second possibility suggested by Bill was that Janice keep daily logs of disruptive behaviors by each of the three students. The initial record keeping would last for a period of two weeks, with the students required to sign log entries each day. At the end of the two-week period, Janice could assign the three students individual improvement plans aimed at reducing the types of behaviors recorded in the logs. Once the plan was initiated, Janice could record both positive and disruptive student behaviors in the logs in order to document student progress toward improvement goals.

When Bill asked Janice to select one of the two options, she asked if it would be agreeable to use parts of both strategies by first logging student behaviors for two weeks and then negotiating a behavioral contract with each of the three students. Bill agreed that this would be an appropriate synthesis of the two strategies. He offered to assist Janice in reviewing the log entries and writing the three behavioral contracts—an offer that Janice readily accepted.

Case Study Three

Social studies teacher Mike Phillips had requested a conference with George Cantinni, his department chairperson. Mike was not satisfied with the quality of discussions in his current events class. George asked Mike to describe the type of class discussions he wanted to take place. Mike replied that he wanted to foster students' "higher-level" thinking and open dialogue concerning important social and political issues. When George asked Mike what was preventing such discussion, he replied that he probably hindered class discussions himself by asking too many simple recall questions rather than questions that would spark student interest and discussion. Another problem Mike discussed was that typically only a few students participated in class discussions, and he had done little to encourage those who did not participate to join in.

Based on Mike's description of the problem, George suggested that changes in the way Mike structured class discussions might be in order. He proposed that Mike and he take a few minutes to write down separately ideas for improvement. After both had reflected on and listed potential actions, George asked Mike to share his ideas. Mike's possible actions included asking students more open-ended questions, giving the entire class more time to think about a question before calling on one of the students to respond, and randomly calling on students in order to increase student participation. George responded that he agreed with the first two suggestions. He added that while randomly calling on students to respond was appropriate in some situations, he did not believe that it was a viable way to foster the open, reflective dialogue that Mike was hoping for.

George introduced additional possible actions by building on ideas already suggested by Mike. He suggested that Mike refer to the upper five categories of Bloom's taxonomy when planning discussion lessons, first to help determine the lesson's objectives and then to formulate relevant discussion questions. George reviewed Bloom's cognitive domain, which Mike vaguely recalled from his undergraduate years. To Mike's idea of giving the class time to think about questions before responding to them, George added the option of allowing students to discuss questions in small groups prior to whole-class discussion. Finally, George suggested that during whole-class discussions the class as well as individual students be provided adequate "wait time" to formulate their responses and that appropriate wait time also *follow* individual student responses.

Mike responded that he liked the idea of basing learning objectives and discussion questions on Bloom's taxonomy, but thought he might have trouble formulating the different types of questions. He asked George if he would be willing to help develop some questions for Mike's next few lessons. George agreed, and also offered to observe a few of Mike's lessons in order to record the number of questions asked within each category of Bloom's taxonomy. Mike replied that he would appreciate the feedback. Regarding George's suggestion of beginning discussions with small groups, Mike stated that for the time being he would prefer to lead whole-class discussions throughout his lessons. He said that he had a fairly good understanding of the different types of wait time, but would like to have some feedback on how many seconds he was allowing for each type of wait time. George agreed to collect data on Mike's wait time during the observations they had already agreed to. Mike and George also agreed that in addition to types of questions and wait time, George would track the number of students who participated in each class discussion.

After considerably more discussion, Mike and George had worked out an action plan for instructional improvement. The plan was written as follows:

Goal: to increase student participation in open discussion requiring student interpretation, application, analysis, synthesis, and evaluation.

Mike Phillips's Responsibilities:

1. Participate in the design of student learning objectives within each of Bloom's upper five categories of cognitive objectives (listed in goal statement).
2. Participate in the creation of open-ended discussion questions for each of the five types of learning objectives.
3. Allow at least five seconds after asking an open-ended question for a student to respond. Call on volunteers only.
4. Allow at least five seconds after calling on an individual student for the student to respond.
5. Wait at least five seconds after a student has responded to an open-ended question before continuing the discussion.

George Cantinni's Responsibilities:

1. Assist Mr. Phillips in designing student learning objectives based on the upper five categories of Bloom's taxonomy.

2. Assist in creating open-ended discussion questions corresponding to stated objectives.
3. Periodically observe Mr. Phillips's class discussions. Collect data on:
   a. Frequency of teacher questions inviting student responses requiring interpretation, application, analysis, synthesis, and evaluation
   b. Duration of wait time after teacher questions, after calling on students to answer questions, and after student responses
   c. Frequency of each student's participation in open-ended discussions

Criteria for Success:

1. In selected classes, open-ended questions will be asked and related discussions held at each of the five upper levels of Bloom's taxonomy.
2. When appropriate, at least five seconds of wait time will be provided after asking open-ended discussion questions, after calling on students to respond to questions, and after student responses.
3. Each student will make at least one contribution to each open-ended class discussion.

Working closely with George over a period of several weeks, Mike made steady progress toward his instructional improvement goal. Eventually, George suggested that Mike had developed sufficient skill at writing open-ended discussion questions that he no longer needed George's assistance during his lesson planning. Mike agreed, but asked George if he would review Mike's discussion questions for a few weeks and give him feedback on their quality. George and Mike also decided that in lieu of additional classroom observations by George, Mike would record his next few class discussions on audiotape. He would review his own performance by analyzing the tapes. George agreed to review the tape of any class discussion for which Mike requested expert feedback.

Case Study Four

Stella Simpson was assistant principal for instruction at Kennedy Elementary School. She had developed a professional development option for teachers wishing to participate in an individualized professional development program. Maria Sanchez had some tentative ideas for a program that would provide development opportunities for herself and others, and requested a meeting with Stella to discuss the plan.

During their meeting, Stella listened, reflected, clarified, and encouraged as Maria discussed a problem she saw emerging at the school. With the growing popularity of cooperative learning, a number of teachers had decided to try out cooperative strategies in their classrooms. Unfortunately, few of the teachers had received in-depth training in cooperative learning. Most had attended only a 60-minute awareness session provided at a recent districtwide in-service education day. Maria, who had received 30 hours of training in cooperative learning, was delighted that other teachers were taking an interest in cooperative learning. However, based on her classroom observations as part of the school's peer-coaching program, she was concerned that many teachers did not have a clear grasp of the basic elements of a cooperative learning lesson. Maria was concerned that if teachers did not develop sufficient expertise in cooperative learning, their use of it would be ineffective, and they would soon abandon it as an instructional strategy.

Stella paraphrased Maria's general concerns, then asked her to discuss specific problems teachers were having with cooperative learning. Maria replied that several teachers were attempting cooperative lessons without teaching students prerequisite social skills. She also stated that they were not building positive interdependence or individual accountability—two vital aspects of cooperative learning—into their lessons. Maria added that, based on her conversations with other teachers, these problems were not confined to teachers she had observed as a peer coach.

Stella agreed with Maria's observations. She had attended the same 30-hour training program as Maria, and her classroom observations verified Maria's concerns. Stella asked Maria for her perceptions of what could be done about the problem. As Maria presented her proposal, Stella continued to listen intently, sometimes paraphrasing Maria's statements, sometimes asking clarifying questions, other times encouraging Maria to elaborate. Maria proposed that she attend an advanced training program that would enable her to develop additional expertise in cooperative learning as well as skills necessary to deliver a training program to other teachers. After completing the advanced program, Maria would deliver a series of evening workshops providing 30 hours of basic training on cooperative learning to interested teachers. Maria also suggested that she provide classroom coaching to the teachers attending her workshops in order to assist them to transfer skills learned in the workshops to their classrooms.

Stella asked Maria if she had considered the difficulties she might encounter when attempting to provide instructional assistance to peers. Maria replied that she had considered the issue, but that since she would be working with volunteer teachers only, she did not see her peer status as a major problem. She reminded Stella that as a participant in the school's peer-coaching program she had successfully provided instructional assistance to many of the teachers who would attend the workshops. Also, she would not attempt to lead workshops for peers until she had received extensive leadership preparation.

Stella told Maria that if her plan was accepted, professional development funds could be used to pay for released time, the costs of Maria's leadership training, and the materials for the evening workshops that Maria would deliver. She told Maria that no funds were available to pay her for the considerable amount of personal time and energy Maria would have to spend to make the program a success. Stella asked Maria if she was willing to make the extensive commitment that her new leadership role would require. After receiving an affirmative response, Stella asked Maria to put together a detailed proposal, including goals, activities, needed resources, criteria for success, a time line, and a tentative budget.

Developmental Supervision

We stated in Chapter 5 that the ultimate aim of the supervisor should be reflective, autonomous teachers facilitated by nondirective supervision. However, the fact that many teachers are functioning at developmental levels or in situations in which self-direction is not feasible means that the supervisor often must initially use collaborative, directive informational, or, in rare cases, directive control behavior. Each of the four case studies represents a different entry point for supervision. In each case, the supervisor based his or her initial supervisory approach on the teacher's levels of development, expertise, and commitment and the nature of the situation.

The case studies provide examples of three phases of developmental supervision. In Phase 1, the supervisor diagnoses the teacher's developmental levels, expertise, commitment, and educational situation, and selects the interpersonal approach that creates the best supervisory match. In Phase 2, the supervisor uses the selected interpersonal approach to assist the teacher in instructional problem solving. In Phase 3 (illustrated in the first three case studies), the supervisor changes his or her interpersonal behavior in the direction of less supervisor control and more teacher control. Such a change in supervisory approach occurs only after the teacher has shown readiness to assume more decision-making responsibility.

In Case Study One, Martha Cozero determined that Gerald Watson was functioning at low levels of development, expertise, and commitment. She was convinced that Gerald's purposeless instructional routine was a serious impediment to student learning. Martha decided to use directive control behaviors in her initial supervisory approach. She identified the problem, presented Gerald with the instructional improvement goal, and directed him to carry out actions to reach the goal. Martha followed up by monitoring and providing feedback on Gerald's progress. Once Gerald had shown some improvement in teaching behaviors and motivation, Martha took a first step away from complete control, asking Gerald to choose one of three training formats.

In Case Study Two, novice Janice Smith's lack of classroom management and problem-solving skills created a different type of instructional problem. Janice initially had been highly motivated. She realized she had classroom management problems. What she needed was intensive assistance in identifying causes and solutions. After observing and conferencing with Janice, mentor Bill Levin decided to use directive informational behaviors during his initial assistance to Janice. Bill identified a goal for Janice of improved classroom management. He suggested a number of actions that she and he could take to move toward that goal. It was up to Janice to accept or reject Bill's suggestions. After Janice had made considerable progress under his mentorship, Bill encouraged her to choose from two alternative strategies for working with three students who displayed chronic discipline problems. Janice and Bill's negotiation and mutual agreement to integrate the two strategies represent movement toward a more collaborative relationship between novice and mentor.

In Case Study Three, Mike Phillips was able to define the problem he was experiencing and identify some causes, but he needed assistance in thinking through a plan to solve the problem. Chairperson George Cantinni decided to use a collaborative approach with Mike. After listening to Mike's perceptions, George shared his own point of view, then suggested that he and Mike both develop and exchange options for solving the problem. During the negotiation process, both Mike and George accepted, rejected, and proposed modifications to ideas presented by the other. Eventually, Mike and George reached mutual agreement on an action plan. George's suggestion that Mike independently design his own discussion questions and tape and review his class discussions was an attempt to move away from collaborative and toward nondirective supervision. Their agreement that George would be available to review Mike's discussion questions and audiotapes indicated a transitional phase between collaborative and nondirective supervision.

In Case Study Four, teacher Maria Sanchez was clearly functioning at high levels of personal and professional development. Assistant principal Stella Simpson used nondirective interpersonal behaviors of listening, reflecting, clarifying, and encouraging as Maria discussed her concerns and proposal. Stella asked Maria to consider the consequences of her plan. Stella's request for a written proposal was made to encourage Maria to decide on details and standards and make a formal commitment to the plan.

Stella Simpson used noncontrolling interpersonal behaviors throughout Case Study Four, encouraging Maria Sanchez to assume full decision-making responsibility. Supervisors in the first three case studies used various levels of control, but *in each of the first three cases, the supervisor moved from more to less control and toward more decision-making responsibility on the part of the teacher.* Developmental supervision thus is "developmental" in two ways. First, the entry-level supervisory approach is matched with the teacher's current developmental levels and the immediate situation. Second, supervisory behaviors are gradually modified to promote and accommodate long-range teacher development toward higher levels of reflection and problem-solving ability.

We purposefully provide case studies in this chapter demonstrating a clear match of the teacher's levels of development, expertise, and commitment with the supervisory approach. In the real world, other variables tend to enter the picture and interactions are more complex. The supervisory approach that the teacher is most comfortable with, although not necessarily the determining factor, should be part of the decision on which approach to use. The supervisor's level of comfort and expertise with various supervisory approaches must be considered. The specific problem that the supervisor and teacher are dealing with also should be a determining factor. The past relationship of the teacher and supervisor is yet another variable to be considered. Even if we had a totally valid and reliable way of measuring a teacher's levels of development, expertise, and commitment (which we don't), it is impossible to predict in advance all of the other variables that might need to be considered when selecting the best supervisory approach. This is why deciding on the best approach is a human decision, not the result of a predetermined formula. The decision should be based on observations and discussions with the teacher or group over time, combined with an assessment of the situation at hand.

SUMMARY AND A LOOK AHEAD

This chapter has provided a brief introduction to developmental supervision and case studies of supervisors using alternative supervisory approaches within a developmental frame.

Chapters 8 through 11 provide detailed discussions of the four supervisory approaches encompassed by developmental supervision. Chapter 12 includes in-depth discussions on the theory and application of developmental supervision.

PRACTITIONER REFLECTION

One Size Doesn't Fit All

Leticia Romero Grimaldo, *Reading Technical Assistance Specialist,* *University of Texas System*

When I first began my position as a reading technical assistance specialist, I was excited about the opportunity to be working with an array of school principals, local campus reading coaches, and classroom teachers in a joint effort to support and improve classroom reading instruction in kindergarten through third grade. The first meeting I had with the local campus reading coaches that I would be working with brought faces full of excitement, enthusiasm, and anticipation of what the upcoming school year had in store.

I started the year by giving the reading coaches the essential professional development that I felt was important to begin the year with success. The professional development included topics such as administration of beginning-of-year assessments, using data to guide classroom instruction, and progress monitoring. I held monthly meetings with the reading coaches. As the weeks passed by I noticed a distinct change in the faces that were first full of hope and optimism. Those same faces were now filled with discouragement and worry.

I decided to include in our meetings a time for reflection where we could all talk about the issues that we were facing in schools. I began to hear a common theme of teacher resistance, and teachers not wanting help in the classroom. Story after story came of various educators feeling as though the coaching model was being pushed on them when they did not need it. They felt threatened by the fact that someone was coming in to observe or model teach in their classrooms.

It also became apparent that principals were worried about the climate in their schools. As I visited campuses and talked with principals, several expressed concern about the impact of the campus reading coach on school culture. Teachers did not feel trusted, and they saw the coach as another evaluator.

It became abundantly clear to me. One size doesn't fit all. Teachers are working at various developmental levels, and they all need different levels of support. Although the common goal has always been to empower and build capacity within teachers, the way to get them there is not the same for all. Something needed to be done to make teachers feel safe, valued, and respected. We were here as a support system to improve effective reading instruction, and somehow this message had been lost.

Our focus quickly began to change. With the campuses that I was working with, we focused on teachers who embraced the support and wanted the help. This is where we spent most of our time. Instructional ideas that were implemented in these classrooms caused curiosity to peak with other teachers, and the strategies began to spread. Soon, teachers who were at first resistant began asking questions and slowly began asking for support. When teachers were autonomous in their decision making, then "buy-in" began to take place.

We also began asking teachers in what areas they needed support. We had an open door policy that allowed teachers to ask for help in areas they needed extra assistance in, and we would facilitate in that specific area. Slowly, we began getting different requests that focused on different areas of reading instruction. Teachers began to feel comfortable going to the reading coach with questions as trusting relationships were being built. Some teachers responded best to a directive informational approach; others preferred a collaborative or nondirective approach.

The district had a large number of teachers who were experts in the field of reading instruction, and we began to recognize them. Teachers had a wealth of knowledge to share, and we began setting up model classrooms where new teachers or teachers who asked for this type of support could come in and observe the "expert" teachers in action. This empowered teachers and, in essence, they became the coaches helping other educators refine their own skills.

It is now the second year that I have been working with principals, local campus reading coaches, and classroom teachers, and things look very different from when we first began. Although the change has been a slow process, the climate in schools is now one of warmth, trust, and caring. The majority of teachers now feel respected and valued, and I see smiles across supervisors' faces as I walk through hallways.

chapter 8

Directive Control Behaviors

Supervisor: Have you been using the computers? I haven't seen any students at the desks.

Teacher: Well, I really don't think computers are such an important topic for seventh-grade mathematics. The students need training in basic geometry, not in how to play games with a computer.

Supervisor: As you know, part of the geometry curriculum is on a computer disk. It's not just fun and games. They could be learning geometry as they improve their technology skills.

Teacher: All this computer emphasis is ridiculous! It's another educational fad that's supposed to solve all our problems! I have enough trouble getting kids to learn what's in the book.

Supervisor: I understand your reservations about using the computer, but our school curriculum states that computers are to be used in seventh-grade mathematics. We're committed to doing so, particularly after spending so much money on the equipment and software.

Teacher: I think it's ridiculous.

Supervisor: That's beside the point. I want to see your kids using them.

Teacher: I'd rather not. Couldn't they teach computers in science class? After all, computers are science.

Supervisor: We're now using computers throughout the curriculum, including in science and in mathematics. I'd like to see at least one-third of your class begin the software program on plotting graphs by next Friday.

Teacher: Who's going to show them how to operate the program? I don't know how to.

Supervisor: Mrs. Techno, you were a participant in the computer class last summer. You know how to do it.

Teacher: I didn't understand the foggiest bit of it. Professor Wallenwood was a terrible teacher. He just paid attention to all those teachers who already had a computer background.

Supervisor: Well, I wasn't aware that you were unsure of how to use the computer in class. I'll call Fred Tirtial, director of media, to come into your class next week to demonstrate how to use the equipment. I'll see to it that he gets the program started in your class, and then you continue with it.

Teacher: Any help would be appreciated.

Supervisor: You keep me posted, and we'll shoot for at least one group of your students working on the graphing program by a week from Friday.

Directive Control Continuum of Behaviors

It is evident in the foregoing scenario that the supervisor has taken over the teacher's problem. At first, the supervisor identified the problem by gathering information from his own observations and discussing this information with the teacher. Next, he told the teacher what to do and provided an explanation of why his suggestion would work. He concluded by reviewing the proposed action and reiterating his expectations for the teacher. The teacher was left with a concrete understanding of what she was expected to do. As we look at a typical sequence of behaviors along the supervisory behavior continuum (Figure 8.1), keep in mind that the sequence and frequency of behaviors will vary, especially in the beginning of the conference, but the directive control approach will end with the supervisor making the final decisions for the teacher. This chapter will accentuate directive behaviors that control teacher actions.

1. Presenting: *Identifying the problem.* The supervisor begins with a general idea of what the needs and difficulties are. Having used observations and gathered information from other sources, the supervisor tells the teacher what seems to be the problem: "I understand that there is a problem with . . . ."

2. Clarifying: *Asking teacher for input into the problem.* The supervisor wants to gather direct information from the teacher about the problem prior to the solution stage. This is done by using the teacher in an advisory capacity, asking the teacher such questions as: "How do you see the problem?" "Why do you think these conditions exist?"

3. Listening: *Understanding the teacher's point of view.* To gather maximum information in the shortest amount of time, the supervisor must attend carefully to what the teacher says. He or she listens both to the surface messages—"Computers are a waste of time"—and to underlying messages—"I don't know how to use them"—in formulating a complete problem.

4. Problem solving: *Mentally determining the best solution.* The supervisor processes the information and thinks, "What can be done?" After considering various possibilities, he or she selects the needed actions. The supervisor should be confident of indeed having a good, manageable solution to the problem before conveying it to the teacher.

5. Directing: *Telling expectations to the teacher.* The supervisor tells the teacher in a matter-of-fact way what needs to be done: "I want to see you do the following . . . ." The phrasing of the directive is important. Avoid timid, circular expectations: "Well, maybe you might consider doing . . . ." "Don't you think it would be a good idea to . . . ?" The supervisor is not asking or pleading with the teacher, but *telling.* On the other hand, directing does not mean being vindictive, overbearing, condescending, or insulting. Avoid personal slights or paternalistic references: "I don't know why you can't figure out what needs to be done." "Why can't you get it right in the first place?" "Now listen, honey, I'm going to help you by . . . ." A supervisor should state actions as *I* statements, not as what others think. Tell the teacher what *I* want to happen, not what parents, other teachers, or the superintendent would want to see. A statement such as "If the superintendent saw this, he would tell you to do . . . ." is hiding behind someone else's authority. The supervisor needs to make statements based on his or her own position, credibility, and authority.

6. Clarifying: *Asking the teacher for input into the expectations.* Possible difficulties with the supervisor's directive should be known before the teacher leaves the conference. For example, if circumstances exist that make teacher compliance with the directive impossible, it is better to adjust to those circumstances during the conference than to find out two weeks later why the plan failed. Therefore, after telling the teacher what is expected—"I want one-third of your students using the computers"—the supervisor needs to ask such questions as: "What do you need to carry out this plan?" "How can I help you carry out the plan?"

7. Standardizing: *Detailing and modifying expectations.* After considering the teacher's reactions to the directive, the supervisor solidifies the plan by building in the necessary assistance, resources, time lines, and criteria for expected success. The teacher is then told the revisions: "I can rearrange the visit time to . . . ," "I will find those materials for you," "I will arrange for you to attend . . . ," "I will change the time to three weeks."

8. Reinforcing: *Repeating and following up on expectations.* The supervisor reviews the entire plan and establishes times for checking on progress. The supervisor closes the meeting by making sure the teacher clearly understands the plan: "Do you understand what you're to do?" "Tell me what it is you're now going to do."

1	2	3	4	5
Listening	*Clarifying*	*Encouraging*	*Reflecting*	*Presenting*

T
s

1. Identifying the problem

2. Asking teacher for input into the problem

3. Understanding the teacher's point of view

6. Asking teacher for input into the expectations

Key: T = Maximum teacher responsibility   S = Maximum supervisor responsibility
      t = Minimum teacher responsibility   s = Minimum supervisor responsibility

FIGURE 8.1 *The Supervisory Behavior Continuum: Directive Control Behaviors*

A History of Overreliance on Control

Historically, control has been used by supervisors as a first rather than last resort. The tradition has been to rely on controlling behaviors with all teachers in all situations (Gordon, 1992; Harpaz, 2005). At times, this has been done by tying supervision to summative evaluation systems requiring certain teaching behaviors. At other times, social pressure has been applied to force teachers to conform to generic "research-based" teaching methods (the research cited during such efforts often has been misinterpreted and oversimplified). Even worse, some supervisors wishing to reduce teacher resistance have combined control and manipulation, hoping to convince teachers that they have participated in a decision when in fact the supervisor knew all along what the decision would be.

6	7	8	9	10
Problem Solving	*Negotiating*	*Directing*	*Standardizing*	*Reinforcing*

t

S

4. Mentally determining best solution

5. Telling expectations for teacher

7. Detailing and modifying expectations

8. Repeating and following up on expectations

We strongly disagree with supervisors using directive control behaviors with all teachers and in all situations. We also oppose using directive control behaviors indefinitely. Finally, in all cases, we oppose control through *manipulation*. Although we admit that directive control is necessary with some teachers and groups in some situations, we believe that it should be used only when no other supervisory approach is feasible. When using a directive control approach with a teacher or group, the supervisor should be ready to move away from directive control toward noncontrolling behaviors as soon as possible.

Issues in Directive Control

Two of three major issues with using directive control behaviors have already been mentioned. One has to do with being forthright, the other with source of authority. The third issue is a consideration of time, which includes the need for directive control in response to emergencies. When the flow of school life is interrupted by irate parents, student defiance, malfunctioning heaters, or media investigations, the supervisor may have to be unilaterally decisive. He or she will simply not have time to meet with teachers before responding. For example, a middle school principal was called at home by a newspaper reporter who sought her reaction to a fire marshal's report about unsafe cardboard partitions in a classroom of her school. The principal, totally unaware of the marshal's visit, refused comment and called the fire marshal to confirm the report. The marshal told her that all cardboard in classrooms was to be removed by the following morning. Deciding not to fight the fire marshal's orders and thus to avoid further newspaper attention, the principal told each teacher arriving at school the next morning of the fire marshal's report and told them to have their rooms cleared of all cardboard partitions before ten o'clock. She also informed them that they would meet later that afternoon to discuss the fire marshal's ruling and determine whether they wanted to appeal it. For the moment, she had used her own judgment. Later, when there was time to review the matter, she and the staff decided collaboratively to meet with the marshal about a proposal to reinstall cardboard partitions covered with fire-resistant plastic.

When to Use Directive Control Behaviors

Since directive behaviors raise issues of power, respect, expertise, and line and staff relationships, the following guidelines are given with caution. Directive control behaviors should be employed:

1. When teachers are functioning at very low developmental levels.
2. When teachers do not have awareness, knowledge, or inclination to act on an issue that a supervisor, who has organizational authority, thinks to be

of critical importance to the students, the teachers, or the community, then the directive control approach should most likely be used.

3. When teachers will have no involvement and the supervisor will be involved in carrying out the decision. If the supervisor will be held totally accountable and the teachers will not, then the directive control approach should probably be used.

4. When the supervisor is committed to resolving the issue and the teachers are not. When decisions do not concern teachers, and they prefer the supervisor to make the decision, the directive control approach should most likely be used.

5. In an emergency, when the supervisor does not have time to meet with teachers, the directive control approach should be used.

To develop skills in the four supervisory approaches demands real-life practice. Item B2 in Appendix B provides a format for practicing directive control behaviors.

Moving from Directive Control toward Directive Informational Behaviors

In long-term supervisory situations and relationships, the supervisor should begin to shift from a directive control to a directive informational approach as soon as possible. Stabilizing an unstable situation or giving a teacher or group intensive support will tend to foster limited professional growth. Such growth is likely to continue only if the supervisor then begins to give the teacher or group limited opportunities to make decisions and assume some responsibility. One way to do this is to begin to allow the teacher or the group *restricted choice*. For example, the supervisor might mandate an instructional improvement goal and then allow the teacher or group to choose from two or three clearly defined alternatives for meeting the goal. By doing this, the supervisor has begun movement toward directive informational supervision—an approach that is discussed in detail in the next chapter.

Critical Reflection on Directive Control Supervision

The supervisor should reflect critically on directive control behaviors both during and after their use. Questions that might assist critical reflection include the following:

- Are teacher developmental levels low enough or the situation critical enough to require my use of directive control behaviors?
- What effects will my use of directive control behaviors have on my long-term professional relationship with the teacher or group?

- Are the decisions made through the use of directive control behaviors likely to be implemented?
- What is my plan for moving away from directive control behaviors as soon as possible?

SUMMARY

Directive control supervision is used to transmit supervisor expectations to teachers clearly. Supervisors in a line position *over* teachers can use directive controlling language and enforce via hierarchical control. Supervisors in a staff position can only hope for compliance based on trust and credibility with teachers. Directive control supervision consists of behaviors of presenting, clarifying, listening, problem solving, directing, standardizing, and reinforcing (with line authority). The direction of presenting, problem solving, and directing is mostly from supervisor to teacher. Directive control behaviors are useful in limited circumstances when teachers possess little expertise, involvement, or interest with respect to an instructional problem and time is short. In these circumstances, directive control is not an adversarial or capricious set of behaviors, but an honest approach with teachers to an emergency.

PRACTITIONER REFLECTION

Directive Control Behaviors—When Other Leadership Styles Haven't Made an Impact

Karin Pogna Johnson, *Principal, Running Brushy Middle School*

In my experience as a school administrator, I have been compelled to use Directive Control Supervision on several occasions. Obviously, the first question I need to ask myself is, "Does the teacher's action warrant my directive control behavior?" The answer is "yes" when other supervisory approaches will not work and when I believe without a doubt that I have the expertise and experience to improve the situation.

When it's time to schedule a directive control conversation with a teacher I first gather as much information about the situation as possible. I list on paper all the concerns I've collected and I leave room on the paper to write the teacher's responses to each concern. I spend a great deal of time reflecting on how to approach the teacher with my concerns—control is not an easy approach for a leader who typically manages with a collaborative or nondirective style. I remind myself that this is a professional issue; it is not personal. I also consider the personality of the individual with whom I'm conferencing. If I anticipate certain teacher behaviors, I can be better prepared and less likely to be caught off guard. Will the teacher interrupt? Try to derail the meeting? Become defensive? Argue? If I expect these behaviors, then I will set ground rules before we even begin:

> Mr. Jones, I need to make you aware of some concerns I have. I am going to talk about one issue at a time, and allow you to respond after each issue, but only after I have finished. I will not interrupt you, and you may not interrupt me.

If my suspicions are correct, and he begins inserting information that is not on topic, I will stop him and calmly remind him, "This is not relevant to this meeting; please stay on topic." If I can expect him to begin blaming other professionals, I will again stop him and say, "Right now we're discussing your actions. If you want to talk about Mrs. Davis, we can do that at another time. We need to get back to why we're here." I am responsible for controlling the situation, and for not allowing the teacher to attempt to monopolize the meeting. However, I must listen carefully to try to sift out what he is really trying to say.

Next, I consider the seating arrangement in my office. In a collaborative or nondirective meeting, I may sit with this person at my round table. However, in a directive control situation, I sit behind my desk and the teacher sits on the other side. This sends the message that the issue has been elevated to a higher degree of formality. Finally, I create my list of directives. I will go over each of the directives with the teacher after I have finished sharing my concerns. These directives are aligned with my expectations for changes in the teacher's behavior.

I don't allow very much time before scheduling and holding a meeting with a teacher. If I schedule too far in advance, I can almost guarantee that the teacher will frantically try to find me, fear in his voice, asking me what the meeting is about, is he in trouble, and so on. My goal is not to frighten the teacher. I have my secretary call the teacher to set up the meeting. That, too, sends a message of importance. In addition, I usually try to schedule these visits right after school. That way the teacher won't go back to his class in a negative frame of mind.

When I begin the meeting, I thank the teacher for coming in. During the meeting, I remain focused on my objective, express my concerns about the teacher's actions, listen carefully to his responses, get his input, offer any type of support I can, document accurately, and make certain he understands my directives:

> Mrs. Simpson, I want to share some concerns I have about your record keeping. When we met last spring, we talked about the importance of meeting your deadlines with regard to Special Education paperwork. You assured me things would improve. You also said that you were struggling because you didn't understand how to manage the documents, and colleagues often interrupted you when you were working in your classroom alone. I sent you to some valuable training to help you better understand how to manage the paperwork. I also suggested that you tell your colleagues to please respect your prep time. Now I've received word that you have missed two deadlines for ARD paperwork, and you did not attend a Special Education department meeting. Tell me about the problems you're having with meeting your deadlines.

After listening to the teacher's concerns, I provide directives for improvement.

At the end of the meeting, I reiterate my concerns and each of my directives. Then I tell the teacher that I will put these items in writing for his signature. I tell him this paperwork is for my records only, and it will not be sent to the personnel department.

When the meeting concludes, I thank the teacher for coming, remind him that I expect these changes to begin immediately, and escort him to the door. Once he is gone, I debrief and jot down anything that I might have missed. Within two to three days I write a memo to the teacher reviewing the problem, my directives for addressing the problem, a time line for implementation, and criteria for improvement.

My goal is not to terminate a teacher. If I value him as an educator, I strive to support his growth—but I need to help him understand that his behaviors must change. After the meeting, it is incumbent on me to set the tone for our professional relationship. When we encounter each other in the hall or office, I will make it a point to smile and say hello. I realize that he may feel uncomfortable because I gave him some directives to follow, but we still must maintain a professional relationship.

I prefer not to operate in a Directive Control mode; it is not a comfortable role for me. Usually, I am much more collaborative and informal, and I want to give teachers as much autonomy as possible. The key to moving out of directive control supervision is to provide frequent follow-up and feedback with the teacher, and offer praise when improvements are made. I want the teacher to feel comfortable as he strives to learn. The process of helping someone grow professionally is about changing behaviors, providing support, listening to concerns, and giving directives when necessary.

EXERCISES

Academic

1. Write an imaginary dialogue between a supervisor and a teacher during a conference in which the supervisor successfully uses a directive control approach. Be sure to include examples of each of the eight behaviors discussed in Chapter 8.

2. This chapter suggests that a sequence of eight directive control behaviors takes place during a directive conference. Think of a situation in which a successful directive control conference would start with the first suggested behavior (identifying the problem) and end with the eighth (repeating and following up on expectations), but have a different sequence of six intermediate behaviors. Describe the situation and modified sequence of directive behaviors in writing. Include a rationale for the suggested sequence.

3. Write an imaginary dialogue between a supervisor and a teacher in which the supervisor implements directive control procedures with mechanical precision but fails to be directive in an effective sense.

4. Write a paper comparing the directive control approach as described in this book with manipulative control that you have experienced or observed.

5. Assume you have recently attended a seminar at which a university professor argued against educational supervisors using the directive control approach with any teacher. The professor proposed that the supervisor should play the role of a helper, not attempt to control a teacher's behavior. The speaker argued that successful change cannot be brought about unless the teacher perceives the need for change and has had a part in deciding how to bring about the needed change. He concluded that a directive control supervisory approach will only alienate

teachers and make supervisors unwelcome in many classrooms. You have been asked to reply to the professor's arguments at an upcoming seminar. Write a paper in which you present an argument for using directive control behaviors with some teachers and under some circumstances.

Field

1. Assume the role of a supervisor using a directive control approach by conducting a simulated postobservation conference with a teacher. Assume that the teacher is in clear violation of a policy and has refused to change his or her practice. Prepare a written report in which you (a) evaluate your success in displaying control behaviors, (b) summarize the problems discussed and decisions made during the conference, (c) give your perceptions of the teacher's responses to your directive control efforts, and (d) judge the conference in terms of overall success.

2. Observe an educational supervisor or other leader whom you know to possess a directive control orientation in dealing with individuals and/or groups. On the basis of your observations and/or an interview with the leader, write a paper describing both successes and failures the selected leader has experienced while using directive control behaviors. Include possible reasons why the directive leader has been more successful in some situations than in others.

3. Observe three teachers or staff members who clearly respond positively to directive control supervision. Write a paper examining personal and social characteristics of these individuals that may account for their positive response to a directive control approach.

4. Prepare a photo album entitled "Supervisory Direction for Instructional Improvement." Each photograph should be accompanied by a written explanation of how it relates to the album theme.

5. Videotape or audiotape a conference or professional development activity led by a supervisor who typically uses a directive control approach. As you review the tape, compare the recorded activities with the sequence of behaviors that, according to this chapter, exemplify the directive process. Prepare a report on your findings.

Developmental

1. Through interaction with various individuals in a variety of situations, begin to establish a set of personal guidelines that will indicate when the directive control approach is most appropriate for your own use in carrying out present or anticipated leadership functions.

2. Begin an in-depth study of assertiveness training (see the Suggested Readings). As you progress through your study, note how training in assertiveness can be used by supervisors when they find themselves with teachers or in situations requiring a directive control approach.

3. Record a simulated or actual supervisor-teacher conference in which you, as supervisor, attempt to display directive control behaviors. Review the tape for analysis of your performance. Record another simulated or actual conference in four weeks. Review both tapes to discover any improvement in terms of successfully displaying behaviors this chapter describes as directive control.

REFERENCES

Gordon, S. P. 1992. Paradigms, transitions, and the new supervision. *Journal of Curriculum and Supervision, 8*(1), 62–76.

Harpaz, Y. 2005. Teaching and learning in a community of thinking. *Journal of Curriculum and Supervision, 20*(2), 136–157.

SUGGESTED READINGS

Bower, S. A. 1991. *Asserting yourself: A practical guide for positive change.* Reading, MA: Addison-Wesley.
Townend, A. 1991. *Developing assertiveness.* London: Routledge.

Wilson, K. 1993. *Assertion and its social context.* New York: Pergamon.

chapter 9

Directive Informational Behaviors

Supervisor: So, in conclusion, what I've observed is that 7 of your 26 students had little involvement in the discussion or question-and-answer period.

Teacher: Well, those seven who you are referring to show no interest in class. At least, if they are quiet, they don't interfere with the learning of others. However, I am surprised that they had such little involvement. I guess if they are quiet, I've just learned to tune them out.

Supervisor: I believe that a goal might be to involve those seven students actively in your future classes.

Teacher: I'd agree. None of my other classes are like this. If I only knew how to do that! When I call on them, they don't respond. When I give the class a controversial topic in U.S. history, most students jump right in, but Sheila, Aliendra, and the rest of them go blank, giggle, and seem not to care.

Supervisor: Well, based on my own experiences as a teacher and what I've seen others do with seemingly apathetic students, let me give you a list of possible actions. Think about them, and determine which of these are worth trying. First, you might establish individual contracts with each of those seven students, that they will be expected to participate at least twice in each class and can earn extra homework points for their participation. Second, you might move to the back and corners of the room during question-and-answer sessions. This is where most of these nonparticipating kids sit. In your lesson plans, make notes to call on each of these students at least once. Your physical presence close to them might help. Third, when you know that a topic to be introduced can be controversial, you might prep the students by using a cooperative learning format. Break the class into groups of three—put each of the nonparticipants with two active participants and ask each group to formulate a group position, with each member being responsible for reporting the position. Monitor the groups while they are working. At discussion times, occasionally call the nonparticipants to speak for the group. What do you think of these possibilities?

Teacher: Individual contracts for students aren't practical—other students would think I'm playing favorites. Moving around to the back and corners of the room is obvious, I could become more aware of doing that. The last idea of cooperative groups is one that I hadn't thought of with this class. I do that with my honors classes but never thought of using small groups here. I guess I assumed that it would be too confusing.

Supervisor: Which of these activities would you like to try?

Teacher: Moving to the back of the room, for sure! The cooperative learning, I'd like to try on a small scale to see how it would work. What do I need to do to prepare the groups to work together and how do I introduce the topic and task?

Directive Informational Continuum of Behaviors

The scenario, transcribed from a tape of an actual conference, shows a supervisor acting as the information source for the goal and activities of the improvement plan. The supervisor, through her observations, has determined a clear classroom goal for the teacher and directs the teacher to those activities she believes to have a high degree of probability in achieving the goal. Notice that, through each step of the conference, the supervisor remains the information source but always asks and considers teacher feedback. Furthermore, the supervisor provides a range of alternatives from which the teacher is asked to choose. The scenario concludes with the teacher committing himself to using several activities. The supervisor then will detail with the teacher the what, when, and how of implementing the activities, set criteria for improvement, and reinforce the understanding of what is to be done. As we look at a sequence of directive informational behaviors (see Figure 9.1), keep in mind that the supervisor is constantly framing the direction and choices for the teacher.

1. Presenting: *Identifying the goal.* Based on the observation and previous experience she has with the teacher, the supervisor begins by reviewing her summarized observations and concluding with an interpretation that seven students being nonparticipants throughout a class period is problematic. Therefore, she sees an important goal as "involving all students."

2. Clarifying: *Asking the teacher for input into the goal.* The supervisor is careful not to move too quickly into a planning phase until she checks to see what the teacher thinks of her interpretation and goal. The teacher is surprised, agrees, and explains why these seven students have been neglected.

3. Listening: *Understanding the teacher's point of view.* The supervisor listens to determine if the teacher accepts the goal as an important one or if she needs to provide further explanation.

4. Problem solving: *Mentally determining possible actions.* The supervisor has given thought to some alternative actions that might be considered by the teacher. When the teacher explains the reasons for students being uninvolved and what has been done, the supervisor mentally prepares to lay out the alternative actions or suggestions.

5. Directing: *Telling alternatives for teachers to consider.* The supervisor carefully words the alternative actions as possibilities, based on her experience and knowledge, for the teacher to judge, consider, and respond.

6. Listening: *Asking the teacher for input into alternatives.* The supervisor asks the teacher to react to her suggestions. The teacher has the opportunity now to give the supervisor information to modify, eliminate, and revise before finalizing the choices.

7. Directing: *Framing the final choices.* In a straightforward manner, the supervisor lays out what the teacher could do: "So, in the final analysis, these are the actions you could take . . . ."

8. Clarifying: *Asking the teacher to choose.* The supervisor asks the teacher to decide and clarify which activities or combinations he will use.

9. Standardizing: *Detailing the actions to be taken.* At this juncture, the supervisor assists the teacher in developing the specifics of the activities (i.e., introduce cooperative learning, set up threesomes, identify one controversial topic, try for 15 minutes next Tuesday, etc.) and the criteria for success (i.e., "Let's see, when I come in next Thursday, whether four of these seven students can be called upon and give prepared, on-target responses").

10. Reinforcing: *Repeating and following up on the plan.* The supervisor concludes the conference by restating the goal, the activities to be taken, the criteria for success, and the follow-up time for the next observation and/or conference.

1 Listening	2 Clarifying	3 Encouraging	4 Reflecting	5 Presenting

T
s

1. Identifying the goal

2. Asking teacher for input into the goal

3. Understanding the teacher's point of view

6. Asking teacher for input into the expectations

8. Asking teacher to make a choice

Key: T = Maximum teacher responsibility   S = Maximum supervisor responsibility
        t = Minimum teacher responsibility   s = Minimum supervisor responsibility

FIGURE 9.1 *The Supervisory Behavior Continuum: Directive Informational Behaviors*

Comparing Directive Control and Directive Informational Statements

Students in supervision courses using this text often have difficulty distinguishing between directive control and directive informational behaviors, especially when practicing the different behaviors during role plays. This is not surprising, since there is often a thin line between controlling and informational language. And yet that thin line is a critical one. The seminal work on this by Pajak and Seyfarth (1983), Glickman and Pajak (1986), and Pajak and Glickman (1989) underscores this point. The precise language used by a supervisor using a directive approach

6	7	8	9	10
Problem Solving	*Negotiating*	*Directing*	*Standardizing*	*Reinforcing*

t

S

4. Mentally
   determining
   best solution

5. Telling
   expectations
   for teacher

7. Framing the
   final choices

9. Determining
   the actions
   to be taken

10. Repeating
    and following
    up on plan

can be the difference between a successful and unsuccessful supervisory conference or group meeting. The following examples will help you distinguish directive control from directive informational statements by a supervisor.

Directive Control (DC): It is essential that you improve your classroom management during your first-period math class.

Directive Informational (DI): I suggest the goal of improving your classroom management during your first-period math class.

DC: One of my expectations is that you attend the classroom management workshop being offered by the district.

DI: One alternative is for you to attend the classroom management workshop being offered by the district.

DC: You need to have a written lesson plan prepared for each class. Each plan must include the following elements . . . .

DI: You could prepare more detailed lesson plans for this group. Each plan might include these additional elements . . . .

DC: You must include a wider range of instructional strategies in your lessons.

DI: In my own teaching, I've found that using a wide range of instructional strategies improves student behavior and learning. You may wish to include a wider range of teaching strategies in your lessons.

DC: Do you have any questions concerning these new expectations?

DI: Do you have any questions concerning these possible actions?

DC: You will be required to make the changes we've discussed in accordance with this written timeline.

DI: Which of the alternatives that we have discussed do you wish to try out?

DC: I will be observing your class again in four weeks, and I expect to see the following changes . . . .

DI: I would be willing to visit your class again in four weeks to observe your progress in implementing the changes you have selected.

To summarize, the supervisor using directive control behaviors is analogous to a judge or policeman giving directives which must be followed (although the analogy eventually breaks down because we know of no district where teachers go directly to jail for failing to follow a supervisor's suggestions for instructional improvement!). On the other hand, the supervisor using directive informational behaviors can be compared to a physician or attorney giving expert advice to a patient or client. The person receiving the advice does not have to follow it, but if they respect the expertise of the professional giving the advice they will probably conclude that it is in their best interest to act on the professional's suggestions. (If you begin to compare the salaries of physicians or attorneys with instructional supervisors, once again our analogy falls apart, but we've made our point!).

Issues in the Directive Informational Approach

Anyone who uses a directive informational approach needs to be aware of the degree of expertise that he or she has when delineating the choices available to others. Since the supervisor is placing himself or herself in the role of expert, the issues of confidence and credibility are crucial. The supervisor must be confident that he or she knows what practices will work in helping the teacher, because when the teacher chooses to use one or more of the supervisor's suggestions, the person ultimately responsible for the success or failure of the various practices will be the supervisor, not the teacher. After all, if I consider and select from your proposed actions, implement what you've suggested, and those actions don't work, I'm probably going to tell you the next time we meet, when we note that the goal is no closer to being achieved, "After all, I just did what you told me to do!"

The teacher is correct in holding the supervisor accountable for the results. Thus, the issue of credibility hovers above the directive informational approach. Not only must the supervisor be confident that his or her own knowledge and experience are superior to and different from those of the teacher, but the teacher must also believe that the supervisor possesses a source of wisdom that he or she does not have. When confidence and credibility in the supervisor's knowledge are shared by both parties, and the teacher is either unaware, inexperienced, or stumped about what changes can be made, then the directive informational approach can be a most valuable set of behaviors to use. When we begin on a path where we have not ventured before, there is much to be learned from a person who has explored that trail successfully many times in the past. This might be the reason why directive informational approaches are seen as most helpful to teachers when they are inexperienced, confused, unaware, or simply at a loss for what to do about a particular classroom or school goal. Finally, with a directive informational approach, it is imperative to remember that the teacher exercises some control in choosing which practice(s) to use. (This is not the case when we look at the directive control approach.)

When to Use Directive Informational Behaviors

Directive informational behaviors revolve on expertise, confidence, credibility, and limiting choice (Grainer, 1967). Therefore, they should be employed under the following circumstances:

1. When the teacher is functioning at fairly low developmental levels.
2. When the teacher does not possess the knowledge about an issue that the supervisor clearly possesses.
3. When the teacher feels confused, inexperienced, or is at a loss for what to do, and the supervisor knows of successful practices.
4. When the supervisor is willing to take responsibility for what the teacher chooses to try.
5. When the teacher believes that the supervisor is credible—a person who has the background and wisdom to know whereof he or she speaks.
6. When the time is short, the constraints are clear, and quick, concrete actions need to be taken.

Item B3 in Appendix B provides a format for practicing directive informational behaviors. Despite the similarities between directive control and directive informational behaviors, they do require different interpersonal skills. We recommend that after you have practiced both directive control and directive informational behaviors, some time be taken to reflect on and discuss the differences between the two approaches in action.

Moving from Directive Informational toward Collaborative Behaviors

In directive informational supervision, the teacher or group is given some choice but the supervisor still assumes *primary* decision-making responsibility. In the collaborative approach, the teacher and supervisor share decision-making responsibility equally. Movement from directive informational to collaborative is thus a matter of degree. The supervisor might begin that movement by suggesting an instructional improvement goal, asking the teacher or group to suggest one or two activities for moving toward the goal, and then suggesting a detailed action plan incorporating some of the teacher or group's proposed actions. Hopefully, the supervisor eventually will be able to enter a fully collaborative relationship with the teacher.

Critical Reflection on Directive Informational Supervision

Considering the following questions can assist the supervisor in reflecting critically on the use of directive informational behaviors:

- Is my interaction with the teacher or group truly informational rather than controlling, both in terms of technical language I use and the overall environment I create?
- Is the teacher or group provided alternative actions to consider that are clearly defined but also provide meaningful choice?
- Is the directive informational approach resulting in any unanticipated consequences?
- Is the directive informational approach working well with this teacher or group? Would another approach work better?

SUMMARY

Directive informational supervision is used to direct teacher(s) to consider and choose from clearly delineated alternative actions. The supervisor is the major source of information, goal articulation, and suggested practices. However, the supervisor is careful to solicit teacher input as he or she revises and refines the choices;

ultimately, the teacher is asked to make a judgment as to which practices or combinations are feasible and realistic. Such an approach is useful when the expertise, confidence, and credibility of the supervisor clearly outweigh the teacher's own information, experience, and capabilities.

PRACTITIONER REFLECTION

The Lesson Plan

Julie N. Diehl, *Doctoral Student, Ph.D. Program in School Improvement and Graduate Assistant, National Center for School Improvement, Texas State University–San Marcos*

Being a first-year teacher is very overwhelming. You start the day feeling prepared, imagining all the seeds of information that you will plant in your garden of students. At the end of the day, you feel like your garden has been trampled by a herd of wild horses. This is how I felt most days during my first year teaching first-graders.

In college, I excelled at my coursework. My student teaching experience was great. I loved being with the kids, reading stories, playing games, listening to their stories. But when I was finally employed in an urban elementary school with high numbers of minorities and low socioeconomic students, I began to feel that I had lost my way. My 22 students were looking to me to provide all of the guidance and instruction.

I began to lose confidence in my abilities and I did not know who to turn to for help. My mentor had told me to check with her for questions about school policies, but she did not seem open to discussing instructional issues and concerns. The five other teachers on my team seemed to have many years of experience under their belts. They would whoosh into their classrooms 15 minutes before the bell and be gone soon after the children left. I began to feel very alone, wondering if I had chosen the right profession.

Meanwhile, I felt like my classroom was falling apart. The confluence of varied abilities, temperaments, and disabilities seemed more than I could handle. One area in which I felt especially lacking was my instructional planning. I would plan a great reading lesson; however, my math lesson would bomb. I would prepare all of the materials for my perfect spelling lesson, but I would forget to gather all the items needed for science. I would introduce a math concept one day and the students seemed to have clear understanding, but then they had no clue when I would bring up the concept the next day. What was I doing wrong?

I continued on in this fashion for a couple of months, wondering if it would get better. My principal approached me one day and informed me that she would like to observe my teaching. I felt a great deal of apprehension because I had spent minimal time interacting with my principal. Would she think that I was an inept teacher?

The dreaded observation day arrived. The principal sat in at one of the children's tables as the students gathered around me on the floor for our reading lesson. The principal began writing even before I began teaching the lesson. My sense of fear heightened. Luckily, the children must not have sensed my anxiety and followed along with the lesson. After the lesson, the principal thanked me. She asked me to bring my lesson plan book and meet with her in her office during my conference time.

I headed down to the principal's office, armed with my lesson plan book and a pencil. I felt like a child again, marching toward some impending gloom and doom. The principal waved me in as she finished her telephone call. I sat down gingerly, as if the chair might have nails that would help drive home what a poor teacher I really was. The principal smiled and began to share positive comments about my lesson. I was in shock. I had expected to hear about how Tim was standing on his seat and how June could not read the word *day*.

Then my principal asked to see my lesson plan book. She flipped through the pages without saying a word. When she finally spoke, I could hear the concern in her voice. She questioned me about the content of the plans, or perhaps the lack of content. I had been unsure how to fit my plans in those tiny boxes, so many boxes were filled with just a few words to remind me about my focus for the day. She empathized that I must have been feeling overwhelmed every day with teaching and material preparation, but she was concerned that my lack of detailed lesson plans was hurting my instruction. I agreed with her assessment of the problem. She provided me with three possible options to remedy the situation. The choices included the following: use the lesson plans outlined in our basal reading, math, and science books; utilize a standard district template for lesson planning; or find a teammate to coordinate lesson planning. I decided to choose the third option. The principal offered to sit in on a planning meeting to make sure that my teammate was providing me with ample structure and resources. She promised to follow up with me in two weeks to check my lesson planning progress.

The problem turned out to be a blessing for our team. Once I asked one of the teachers for help with lesson planning, the rest of the team also offered to help. We scheduled a weekly afternoon planning time where we wrote detailed lesson plans for the upcoming week. The principal joined one of our planning sessions, in which the team shared concerns about lack of leveled reading materials for our students. This led to the acquisition of more leveled reading books. The team appreciated the principal's interest in our instructional planning. When the principal came into my room two weeks later, I was able to show her my new lesson plans with great pride, knowing that that they were thorough and well thought out. Without this intervention by my principal, my already overwhelming year would have caused me to fail and perhaps leave the teaching profession.

Looking back on this experience nine years later, I am able to realize the profound impact that my principal's actions had on my teaching. She provided me direction when I did not know who to turn to for help. She gave me structure when I was lacking a definitive shape. Her influence was one factor in my decision to pursue my master's in educational leadership. As an aspiring supervisor, I hope that I will one day be an influential and guiding light to teachers.

EXERCISES

Academic

1. Write an imaginary dialogue between a supervisor and a teacher during a conference in which the supervisor successfully uses a directive informational approach. Be sure to include examples of each of the 10 behaviors discussed in Chapter 9.

2. This chapter delineates six examples in which it is appropriate to use the directive informational approach. Write a description of a situation for each example. Can you think of any other circumstances, other than the six given, for which the directive informational approach would be appropriate? If so, include such an example in your answer.

3. Write an imaginary dialogue between a supervisor and a teacher during a conference in which the supervisor implements directive informational procedures with mechanical precision but fails to be successful for one or more reasons.

4. Explain what you would do if you as a supervisor worked with a teacher who always wanted you to use the directive informational approach with him or her. This experienced teacher is quite comfortable in the classroom and when asked can clearly articulate concerns or problems he or she has for his or her students and the school. Yet, unlike his or her peers, who prefer the collaborative or nondirective approach, this teacher favors being given a choice from your suggestions. Do you feel you should continue using the directive informational approach with this teacher? Write a summary of your position and give reasons for your decision.

5. Write a paper comparing and contrasting the directive control and directive informational supervisory approaches. Include advantages and disadvantages of each.

Field

1. Assume the role of a supervisor using a directive informational approach, by either using the simulated activity in item B3 of Appendix B or conducting an actual postobservation conference with a teacher. Prepare a written report in which you (a) evaluate your success in displaying directive informational behaviors, (b) summarize the problems discussed and decisions made during the conference, (c) give your perceptions of the teacher's responses to your directive efforts, and (d) judge the conference in terms of overall success.

2. Interview teachers who prefer the directive informational approach. Write a summary of your findings.

3. Record times you or a supervisor at your school has used the directive informational approach. Describe the situation being dealt with and the results. Overall, how successful have you or your supervisor been with this approach? Explain your answer.

4. Tape-record a faculty meeting during which the supervisor uses the directive informational approach. Analyze the tape to determine whether the meeting was successful. Make a chart with a space for each of the directive informational supervisory behaviors. As you listen to the tape, record each time a behavior is used and in what sequence. Does a correlation exist between the overall success of the meeting and the frequency and sequence of the supervisory behaviors? Prepare a report of your findings.

5. Create a collage of pictures and/or words that shows when it is appropriate to use directive informational behaviors. Use the six examples given in this chapter to guide you. Provide a narrative explaining your collage.

Developmental

1. Tape-record a conference during which you, as the supervisor, attempt to use the directive informational approach. Review and analyze the tape. Note the sequence of behaviors. At a later date, record another conference during which you use the directive informational approach. Analyze the tape and note the sequence of behaviors. Was the sequence the same in both conferences? How did the sequences of behaviors affect the outcome?

2. Keep a log each time you use the directive informational approach. Record the problem discussed, the teacher(s) involved, and the decision made. After several months, study your log for any patterns. Do you use this approach with the same teachers? Are the problems similar? Consider the patterns, if any, to evaluate your behavior and effectiveness as a supervisor.

3. Begin a chart that delineates what you consider to be each teacher's expertise and experience level in your work situation. Ask four or five teachers to list those areas or topics about teaching in which they could use more information and specific suggestions. Do you find common areas where a directive informational group approach would be appropriate?

REFERENCE

Glickman, C. D., and Pajak, E. F. 1986. Supervisors' discrimination among three types of supervisory scripts. *Educational and Psychological Research,* 6(4), 279–289.

Grainer, L. E. 1967. Patterns of organizational change. *Harvard Business Review, 45,* 119–130. See the "decisions from alternatives approach."

Pajak, E. F., and Glickman, C. D. 1989. Informational and controlling language in simulated supervisory conferences. *American Educational Research Journal,* 26(1), 93–106.

Pajak, E. F., and Seyfarth, J. J. 1983. Authentic Supervision reconciles the irreconcilables. *Educational Leadership, 40*(8): 20–23.

SUGGESTED READINGS

Acheson, K. A., and Gall, M. D. 1992. *Techniques in the clinical supervision of teachers* (3rd ed.). New York: Longman.

Pajak, E. 1993. Madeline Hunter's decision making. In *Approaches to clinical supervision* (pp. 183–208). Norwood, MA: Christopher-Gordon Publishers.

chapter 10
Collaborative Behaviors

Teacher: I refuse to have Steve sent out of my class.

Supervisor: Don't you think being hit by him and being bruised is the last straw?

Teacher: No, I don't. It's my body and I don't think Steve meant it. He was angry and didn't know what he was doing.

Supervisor: Listen, he's been in fights with other students since the first day of school, and the latest episode of striking could have resulted in serious damage. He has to come out.

Teacher: I know that you're thinking about my own welfare, but that kid is making progress. He's beginning to do some assignments and has been behaving better. The hitting incident was an accident. He's not bothering the other students too much.

Supervisor: I think you're wrong. Let's put him into a special classroom.

Teacher: No, he stays with me.

Supervisor: You know that whatever is done, we will both agree to do. You don't want him to leave and I think, for his own good, he should be given special attention. Steve is dangerous to you and the other students.

Teacher: I don't have anything against special attention. It's just that we've come so far and I hate to see him cut off from me and the class. He has a better chance to make it in our class than to begin all over in another class.

Supervisor: Then you would be receptive to having him receive special attention as long as he stays in your class?

Teacher: Yeah, I think so. I have no problem with a qualified person working with him in my classroom or even for a small part of the day outside of the classroom.

Supervisor: That seems reasonable, I think that we are getting somewhere . . . .

Collaborative Continuum of Behaviors

The foregoing script, based on a real conference, highlights collaborative supervisory behaviors. The supervisor wishes to resolve a problem that is shared equally with the teacher. The supervisor encourages the teacher to present his or her own perceptions and ideas. Yet the supervisor also honestly gives his or her own views. The result is a frank exchange of ideas. Both participants know they will have to agree on any course of action. In fact, when the disagreement becomes obvious, the supervisor restates the disagreement and reassures the teacher that they will have to find a mutual solution. Disagreement is encouraged, not suppressed. As the conversation continues, some openings for possible agreements become apparent, and the supervisor steers the conversation toward those ends. Finally, they will either agree to an action or wind up stalemated. A stalemate will mean further negotiating, rethinking, and even the possible use of a third-party mediator or arbitrator.

Figure 10.1 shows a prototype of collaborative behaviors according to the supervisory behavior continuum. A conference between supervisor and teacher begins with an understanding of each other's identification of the problem and concludes with mutual agreement on the final plan. The reader should think of the supervisory behaviors as a piano keyboard, with the musician beginning by hitting the keys on the left, then playing the keys back and forth, and culminating by hitting the middle key—negotiating.

1. Clarifying: *Identifying the problem as seen by the teacher.* First, ask the teacher about the immediate problem or concern: "Please tell me what is bothering you." "Explain to me what you see as the greatest concern."

2. Listening: *Understanding the teacher's perception.* You (the supervisor) want to have as much information about the problem as possible before thinking about action. Therefore, when the teacher narrates his or her perceptions, the full range of nondirective behaviors should be used (eye contact, paraphrasing, asking probing questions, and being willing to allow the teacher to continue talking): "Tell me more." "Uh huh, I'm following you." "Do you mean . . . ?"

3. Reflecting: *Verifying the teacher's perception.* When the teacher has completed his or her description of the problem, check for accuracy by summarizing the teacher's statements and asking if the summary is accurate: "I understand that you see the problem as . . . . Is this accurate?"

4. Presenting: *Providing the supervisor's point of view.* Until this point, we have seen an abbreviated nondirective conference. Instead of asking the teacher to begin thinking of his or her own possible actions, however, you now move in and become part of the decision-making process. Give your own point of view about the current difficulty and fill in any information about the situation of which the teacher might be unaware: "I see the situation in this way." "The problem, as I see it, is . . . ." (To minimize influencing the teacher's position, it is better for you to give your perceptions only after the teacher has given his or hers.)

5. Clarifying: *Seeking the teacher's understanding of the supervisor's perception of the problem.* In the same way that you paraphrased the teacher's statement of the problem and asked for verification, you now ask the teacher to do likewise: "Could you repeat what you think I'm trying to say?" Once you feel confident that the teacher understands your views, problem solving can begin.

6. Problem solving: *Exchanging suggestions of options.* If you and the teacher are familiar with each other and have worked collaboratively before, you can simply ask for a list of suggestions: "Let's both think about what might be done to improve this situation." Then listen to each other's ideas. If the teacher is not familiar with you or with the collaborative process, however, he or she may feel apprehensive about suggesting an idea that is different from the supervisor's. It might be better to stop the conference for a few minutes and have both supervisor and teacher write down possible actions before speaking: "So that we don't influence each other on possible solutions, let's take the next few minutes and write down what actions might be taken and then read each other's list." Obviously, once actions are in writing, they will not change according to what the other person has written. You the supervisor, therefore, have promoted a spectrum of personal ideas that are ready to be shared and discussed.

7. Encouraging: *Accepting conflict.* To keep the conference from turning into a competitive struggle, you need to reassure the teacher that disagreement is acceptable and that there will be no winners or losers: "It appears that we have some different ideas on how to handle this situation. By disagreeing we will find the best solution. Remember our agreement—we both have to agree with the solution before it will take place." You must genuinely believe that conflict between two caring professionals is productive for finding the best solution.

8. Negotiating: *Finding an acceptable solution.* After sharing and discussing, ask if there are suggestions common to both—"Where do we agree?"—and if there are suggestions markedly different—"Where do we differ?" If you find agreement, then the conference proceeds. But if there is a vast difference in suggestions, then you can take four sequential actions. First, check to see whether the differences are as vast as they appear by having both yourself and the teacher explain thoroughly what is meant by your respective suggestions. Second, if the disagreement is still real, then find out how con-

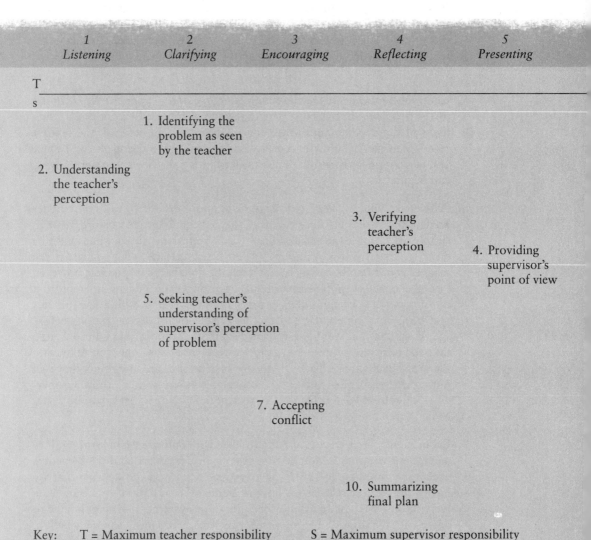

	1 Listening	2 Clarifying	3 Encouraging	4 Reflecting	5 Presenting
T					
s					

1. Identifying the problem as seen by the teacher

2. Understanding the teacher's perception

3. Verifying teacher's perception

4. Providing supervisor's point of view

5. Seeking teacher's understanding of supervisor's perception of problem

7. Accepting conflict

10. Summarizing final plan

Key: T = Maximum teacher responsibility   S = Maximum supervisor responsibility
      t = Minimum teacher responsibility   s = Minimum supervisor responsibility

FIGURE 10.1 *The Supervisory Behavior Continuum: Collaborative Behaviors* vinced each of you is that your suggestion be chosen: "How important is it to you that we do it your way?" If the importance of one person's suggestion is far greater than that of the other person's suggestion, then the question becomes whether one can give up his or her idea and live with the other's. Third, if grounds for agreement are not reached, you can consider a compromise: "How about if I give up this part of my suggestion and if you give up . . . ." Or see if a totally new idea can be found: "Since we can't agree, let's drop our top choices for solutions and see if we can find another one."

6	7	8	9	10
Problem Solving	*Negotiating*	*Directing*	*Standardizing*	*Reinforcing*

t

S

6. Exchanging
   suggestions
   of options

8. Finding an
   acceptable
   action

9. Agreeing on
   details of plan

9. Standardizing: *Agreeing on details of plan.* Once agreement on an acceptable action has been reached, the supervisor needs to attend to the details of time and place. When will the plan be implemented? Where will it take place? Who will help? What resources are needed? These details need to be discussed and agreed to so there will be a clarity and precision to the final plan.

10. Reflecting: *Summarizing the final plan.* The supervisor concludes the conference by checking that both parties agree to the action and details. The supervisor might do this verbally—"Could you repeat what you understand the plan to be and then I'll repeat my understanding"—or in writing—"Let's write this down together so that we are clear on what we've agreed to do."

Issues in Collaborative Supervision

Our work with collaboration has shown that it is a deceptively simple set of behaviors for supervisors to understand. The reason is that collaboration appears to be the democratic way of doing things. Most of us have been schooled in equality and democracy, and collaboration appears to be democracy in action. Therefore, it seems apparent that we should ask others for input and that decisions should be made by the majority. However, collaboration with an individual or a group involves more than the mechanical procedures of democracy.

One difficulty in working collaboratively occurs when the teacher (or group) believes a supervisor is manipulating the decision when in fact he or she is not. The teacher appears to concur with the supervisor's ideas and suggestions not because of their merit but because the teacher believes the supervisor is really giving a directive. The underlying message the teacher perceives is: "This is my supervisor telling me what she thinks I should do. Even though she says we are making a joint decision, I know I had better do what she says." How does the supervisor know whether a teacher's agreement is sincere or mere compliance? The supervisor might confront the issue by asking the teacher whether he or she is agreeing or only pretending to agree with the supervisor's idea. Acknowledging that the supervisor suspects something is amiss brings the issue out into the open. A teacher who responds, "I don't believe you really are going to let me have equal say" can be dealt with more easily than is possible when a supervisor guesses at the teacher's hidden feelings.

Teachers who refuse to disclose their feelings probably have a history of being mistreated by supervisors. Until the supervisor can demonstrate consistently that he or she really means to be collaborative, no progress will be made. The teacher is not going to believe the supervisor is being collaborative until there is proof. True intent can be demonstrated by refusing to allow decisions to be made without teacher feedback. With nonresponsive and readily acquiescing teachers, a supervisor might say: "I don't know if you're agreeing with me because you like the idea or because of some power I hold over you. We won't carry out any action unless we both agree with that action. I want to be collaborative because I believe you have as much expertise on this matter as I do. Together we can make a better decision than separately. I'm uncertain why you are agreeing with me. Please tell me what you think."

A supervisor cannot find out what a teacher thinks without asking. As they continue to meet, the supervisor should begin by encouraging teachers to offer their own thoughts about the problem and suggestions for action. The supervisor should try to withhold any ideas of his or her own. Once the teacher's ideas are forthcoming, the supervisor can offer his or her ideas. When negotiating a final decision, the supervisor should let teachers take the lead. If teachers continue to be unresponsive or overly compliant with the supervisor after he or she has confronted the issue of perception and encouraged teacher initiative, then, after several unsuccessful attempts, the supervisor might consider another approach.

When to Use Collaborative Behaviors

There are circumstances in which a supervisor definitely should use collaborative behaviors. We will leave more detailed instructions for Chapter 12, but, for now, collaboration should be used:

1. When teachers are functioning at moderate or mixed developmental levels.
2. When the teacher(s) and supervisor have approximately the same degree of expertise on the issue. If the supervisor knows part of the problem and teachers know the other part, the collaborative approach should be used.
3. When the teacher(s) and supervisor will both be involved in carrying out the decision. If the teacher(s) and supervisor will be held accountable for showing results to someone else (say, parents or the superintendent), then the collaborative approach should be used.
4. When the teacher(s) and supervisor are both committed to solving the problem. If teachers want to be involved, and if leaving them out will lead to low morale and distrust, then the collaborative approach should be used.

Item B4 in Appendix B provides a format for skill practice in collaborative behaviors. Since the collaborative approach involves extensive teacher as well as supervisor input, you will probably find that your collaborative practice session is more complex and longer in duration than your directive simulations.

Moving from Collaborative toward Nondirective Behaviors

The developmental supervisor attempts gradually to move from collaborative toward nondirective interpersonal behaviors. As the teacher or group increases expertise, problem-solving capacity, and motivation, the supervisor hands over more and more decision-making responsibility. An example of a transitional phase between the collaborative and nondirective approach would be to use collaborative behaviors while assisting a teacher or group to decide on an instructional improvement goal, then shift to nondirective behaviors as the teacher or group decides on actions to reach the goal. Nondirective behaviors are discussed in the following chapter.

Collaboration and Cooperation

The supervisor using collaborative interpersonal behaviors jointly shares decision-making responsibility with the teacher or group. Collaborative supervision should not be confused with supervisor-teacher cooperation. To *cooperate* is "to work or act together toward a common end or purpose" (*American Heritage Dictionary*, 2000, p. 404). The supervisor should strive for cooperation with the teacher or group regardless of his or her supervisory approach. Supervisors and teachers can maintain positive professional relationships and work together toward the common purpose of instructional improvement whether the supervisor uses controlling directive, informational directive, collaborative, or nondirective behaviors, provided the supervisor selects and effectively implements the correct approach.

Critical Reflection on Collaborative Supervision

Questions to foster the supervisor's critical reflection on collaborative behaviors include the following:

- Beyond my mechanical use of collaborative behaviors, have I really given the individual or group equal decision-making power regarding the problem to be solved?
- Have I verified that the teacher or group perceives the decision-making process to be collaborative?
- Have I accepted conflict and reassured the teacher or group that disagreement is part of the decision-making process?
- Have I continued the collaborative process toward a solution acceptable to both the teacher or group and me?

SUMMARY

Collaborative supervision is premised on participation by equals in making instructional decisions. Its outcome is a mutual plan of action. Collaborative behaviors consist of clarifying, listening, reflecting, presenting, problem solving, negotiating, and standardizing. Collaboration is appropriate when teachers and supervisors have similar levels of expertise, involvement, and concern with a problem. The key consideration for a supervisor is the fact that collaboration is both an attitude and a repertoire of behaviors. Unless teachers have the attitude that they are equal, collaborative behaviors can be used to undermine true equality.

PRACTITIONER REFLECTION

Going Beyond Collaborative Language

Jan Newby-Parham, *Special Education Instructional Coordinator,*
Austin Independent School District

My primary job is to supervise the special education programs on four high school campuses scattered across the district. Two years ago, I was provided a staff development opportunity that allowed me to work collaboratively with a dedicated special education teacher who works on one of the campuses that I supervise. Even though the opportunity was offered two weeks before school was to begin, in one of our busiest times of the year, the director of special education approved our attendance at the two-week workshop with one stipulation. She insisted that we bring back the information we learned and present it in districtwide staff development sessions that would enhance our current social behavioral programs and thus have a positive impact on instruction throughout the district.

The two-week training was invigorating, despite the early morning daily commutes in heavy traffic and the one hundred plus miles per day of driving. We carpooled together and a genuine collaborative relationship developed. I did all of the driving and my partner did all of the navigating. We shared stories of student success and failures, we discussed common problems in working in a large urban district, and we shared our thoughts and ideas regarding ways to improve district initiatives. On a personal level, we talked about our families, shared concerns, and told stories about our childhood experiences growing up in southeast Texas. By the end of the two-week training a bond between two educators working toward a shared goal was created. Unlike any other staff development opportunity I have encountered over the years, we met our professional goals with incredible collaboration.

Having just learned so many wonderful strategies to teach teachers, we set out to share these best practices with our colleagues. We believed we were well prepared to provide the professional development. After all, we had a combined total of 27 years of classroom teaching experience, over the years we had worked with students with some of the most severe behavioral challenges, and we had just attended 80 hours of intensive training in this particular subject. We worked together with an urgency to obtain staff development approval, following bureaucratic procedures set forth by the school district.

While we waited for formal approval from the professional development academy in our district, we prepared the framework for our presentation, which included a PowerPoint presentation, handouts, captivating music, posters, games, best teaching practices, and examples of successful ways to teach students on various academic levels. Once the structure of our presentation was established, we practiced the delivery of the workshop together in front of our families. We spent countless hours together, often meeting during our lunch hour to work through the details of the upcoming presentation. Cell phone and e-mail communication also were utilized in an effort to share information and ideas that could enhance our upcoming presentation. A great deal of emphasis was placed on modeling best teaching practices for teachers. We wanted to create the ideal learning environment for our participants.

We finally presented the staff development session to an audience of nearly 100 teachers, administrators, and instructional support staff. We provided the professional development to a smaller school district as well. The response to both sessions was overwhelmingly positive.

The stipulation had now been fulfilled, but it was just the beginning of a long, collaborative relationship between two colleagues, brought together with shared goals and a shared dedication to helping other educators help children succeed. Our journey took us through uncharted territory. It was a journey of storytelling, meaningful relationships, effective communication, prioritizing, trust, and fulfilling an obligation despite obstacles. As I reflect on this experience, I realize that our profession is rich in opportunities to collaborate with other educators. The staff development was the vehicle that brought us together, but it was our collaborative relationship that made the journey a success for us and for the teachers with whom we worked.

EXERCISES

Academic

1. Write an imaginary dialogue between a supervisor and a teacher during a conference in which the supervisor successfully makes use of a collaborative approach. Be sure to include examples of each of the 10 collaborative behaviors discussed in Chapter 10.

2. This chapter suggests that a sequence of 10 collaborative behaviors takes place during a collaborative conference. Think of a situation in which a successful collaborative conference would start with the first suggested behavior (identifying the problem as seen by the teacher) and end with the tenth (agreeing to final plan), but would have a *different sequence* of 8 intermediate behaviors. Describe the situation and modified sequence of collaborative behaviors in writing. Include a rationale for the suggested sequence.

3. Write an imaginary dialogue between a supervisor and a teacher in which the supervisor implements apparently collaborative procedures with mechanical precision but fails to be collaborative in an effective sense.

4. Prepare a report comparing the collaborative approach as described in this book with the version of collaboration espoused by an author cited in the Suggested Readings.

5. Listening, clarifying, presenting, problem solving, and standardizing are categories of behavior this chapter uses when describing the informational directive as well as the collaborative approach to supervision. Write a paper explaining how each of these five categories actually refers to different behaviors, depending on whether the informational directive or the collaborative approach is being

used. For each of the five behavior categories, give a specific behavior that might be displayed by an informational directive supervisor and a specific behavior that might be displayed by a collaborative supervisor.

Field

1. Assume the role of a supervisor using a collaborative approach by either using the simulation activity found in Appendix B (item B4) or conducting an actual postobservation conference with a teacher. Prepare a written report in which you (a) evaluate your success in displaying collaborative behaviors, (b) summarize the problems discussed and decisions made during the conference, (c) give your perceptions of the "teacher's" responses to your collaborative efforts, and (d) judge the conference in terms of overall success.

2. Participate in a group conference that results in a collaborative contract, with some type of instructional improvement as the anticipated result of contract fulfillment. Prepare a report on how the meeting was conducted, any problems that arose, and how the group reached decisions.

3. Observe an educational supervisor or other leader whom you know to have a collaborative orientation in dealing with individuals and/or groups. On the basis of your observations and/or an interview with the leader, prepare a report describing both successes and failures the selected leader has experienced while using collaborative behaviors. Include possible reasons that the collaborative leader was more successful in some situations than in others.

4. Prepare a photo album entitled "Collaboration for Instructional Improvement." Each photograph should be accompanied by a written explanation of how that entry relates to the album theme.

5. Videotape or audiotape a collaborative conference or professional development activity. As you review the tape, compare the recorded activities with the sequence of behaviors that, according to this chapter, exemplifies the collaborative decision-making process. Prepare a written report on your findings.

Developmental

1. Through interaction with various individuals in a variety of situations, begin to establish a set of personal guidelines that will indicate when the collaborative approach is most appropriate for your own use in carrying out present or anticipated leadership functions.

2. Initiate an in-depth study of Japanese-style management. As you proceed with your study, compare and contrast this style of management with the collaborative approach to supervision discussed in this chapter.

3. Record a simulated or actual supervisor-teacher conference in which you, as supervisor, attempt to display collaborative behaviors. Review the tape for analysis of your performance. Over the next four weeks, attempt to practice collaborative leadership whenever appropriate opportunities arise. Record another simulated or actual supervisor-teacher conference, and determine what changes you have made.

REFERENCES

American Heritage Dictionary (4th ed.). 2000. Boston: Houghton Mifflin.

SUGGESTED READINGS

Bryk, A. S., and Schneider, B. L. 2002. *Trust in schools: A core resource for improvement.* New York: Russell Sage Foundation.

Pajak, E. 1993. Morris Cogan's clinical supervision. In *Approaches to clinical supervision* (pp. 73–98). Norwood, MA: Christopher-Gordon Publishers.

Schön, D. A. 1988. Coaching reflective teaching. In P. P. Grimmett and G. L. Erickson (Eds.), *Reflection in teacher education.* New York: Teachers College Press.

Sparks, D. 1990. Cognitive coaching: An interview with Robert Garmston. *Journal of Staff Development, 11*(2), 12–15.

Nondirective Behaviors

Teacher: (barging into supervisor's office) This damn place is a zoo! I can't stand it any longer. These kids are a bunch of ingrates! I've had it.

Supervisor: (looking at the teacher) Wow, you are angry! Tell me what's going on. Have a seat.

Teacher: (refusing to sit) I get no help around here from you or the administration. The students know that they can act any way they damn please and get away with it. I'm not going to put up with it anymore.

Supervisor: What have they been doing?

Teacher: Just now, I went back into the class after being called out for a message and they were jumping all over the place, running around, throwing papers, and being totally obnoxious. I can't leave them for a minute.

Supervisor: What did you do?

Teacher: What do you think? I screamed my bloody head off at them and after it all, Terence had the nerve to laugh at me.

Supervisor: Terence laughed at you?

Teacher: Yeah, that little snot! He always has the last word. He's so defiant it drives me mad!

Supervisor: Is he always like that?

Teacher: He sure is. Terence is my number one problem; if I could get him to behave and learn, the rest of the class would be no problem.

Supervisor: So the main problem is Terence. What do you do when he misbehaves?

Teacher: I've been sending him out of the room but that doesn't work. He couldn't care less about school and will only work when forced to. He really gets to me.

Supervisor: He's a lot to handle.

Teacher: He sure is! That kid is a bundle of jumping nerves. He doesn't pay any attention to what goes on in class.

Supervisor: He must really keep you hopping! Does Terence do anything right in class?

Teacher: Hardly! He's just not excited about anything in school. If he could live in a world of rock videos and football games, he'd be just fine.

Supervisor: (joking) Well, maybe we need a flashing movie room of video and football highlights to keep him entertained!

Teacher: (laughing and calming down) Oh, I don't know. He just drives me nuts. He's not a bad kid.

Supervisor: Could we capitalize on his interests to improve his classroom behavior?

Teacher: I need to sit down with him and talk to him one on one. I really want to find something in class that would interest him and keep him out of my hair.

Supervisor: What might that be?

Teacher: Students get to do special history projects in class. Maybe I could tie his love for music or sports into a history project, or maybe make a contract with him about his good behavior so that he could earn time to listen to music? Let me talk to him.

Supervisor: Sorry about your class today. It sounds to me as if Terence is the key and you have some ideas. Are there ways that I could help?

Nondirective Continuum of Behaviors

Nondirective supervision is based on the assumption that an individual teacher knows best what instructional changes need to be made and has the ability to think and act on his or her own. The decision belongs to the teacher. The role of the supervisor is to assist the teacher in the process of thinking through his or her actions.

As the foregoing hypothetical script shows, the supervisor behaves in ways that keep the teacher's thinking focused on observation, interpretation, problem identification, and problem solutions. Notice how in the example the nondirective approach allowed the teacher to move from an angry outburst about the entire class to an analytical focus on Terence's behavior. Rarely will a teacher move this rapidly from anger to reflection, but the pattern of the supervisor helping the teacher to come to his or her own conclusions is characteristic of a nondirective approach. The supervisor does not interject his or her own ideas into the discussion unless specifically asked. All verbalizations by the supervisor are intended as feedback or to extend the teacher's thinking; they do not influence the actual design.

Refer to the supervisory behavior continuum to understand how nondirective behaviors are used. Read carefully, because the misuse of listening, clarifying, encouraging, reflecting, problem-solving, and presenting behaviors can result in a decision that is not really the teacher's.

Figure 11.1 shows a typical pattern of supervisory interpersonal behaviors used in a nondirective conference. They begin with listening and end with asking the teacher to present his or her decision. The sequence of behaviors between start and finish can vary, but the end should be the same—a noninfluenced teacher decision.

1. Listening: *Wait until the teacher's initial statement is made.* Face and look at the teacher; concentrate on what is being said. Avoid thinking about how you see the problem or what you think should be done. It is not easy to restrain your mind from galloping ahead, but your job is to understand what the teacher initially has said.

2. Reflecting: *Verbalize your understanding of the initial problem.* Include in your statement the teacher's feelings and perceived situation: "You're angry because students don't pay attention." Wait for an acknowledgment of accuracy from the teacher: "Yes, I am, but . . . ." Do not offer your own opinion; your job is to capture what the teacher is saying.

3. Clarifying: *Probe for the underlying problem and/or additional information.* You now ask the teacher to look at the problem in some different ways and to consider new information that might be contributing to the problem. Clarifying is done to help the teacher further identify, not solve, the problem. Questions such as "Do you mean that you are really fed up with school?" "Is it a particular student who is getting to you?" and "When has this happened before?" are appropriate information-seeking questions. Avoid questions that are really solutions in disguise. Such questions as "Have you thought about taking up yoga to relax?" and "Maybe you could suspend that student for a few days, what do you think?" are inappropriate. Such leading or suggestive questions are attempts to influence the teacher's final decision.

1	2	3	4	5
Listening	Clarifying	Encouraging	Reflecting	Presenting

T

s

1. Wait until the immediate message is finished

2. Verbalize initial problem—feeling and situation

3. Probe for under-lying problem and/or additional information

4. Show willingness to listen further

5. Constantly para-phrase understanding of teacher's message

8. Ask teacher for commitment to a decision

10. Restate the teacher's plan

Key: T = Maximum teacher responsibility   S = Maximum supervisor responsibility
        t = Minimum teacher responsibility   s = Minimum supervisor responsibility

FIGURE 11.1 *The Supervisory Behavior Continuum: Nondirective Behaviors*

6	7	8	9	10
Problem Solving	*Negotiating*	*Directing*	*Standardizing*	*Reinforcing*

t

S

6. Ask teacher to think
   of possible actions

7. Ask teacher to consider
   consequences of various
   actions

9. Ask teacher to set
   time and criteria
   for action

4. Encouraging: *Show willingness to listen further as the teacher begins to iden-tify the real problems.* Show that you will continue to assist and not leave the discussion incomplete. Statements such as "I'm following what you're say-ing, continue on," "Run that by me again," and "I'm following you" are cor-rect. Saying, "I like that idea," "Yes, that will work," "Ah, I agree with that," are, even unintentionally, influencing behaviors. A teacher, like any other person, cannot help but be influenced by the judgments a supervisor is making on what he or she says. Encouraging keeps the teacher thinking; praise, on the other hand, influences the final decision.

5. Reflecting: *Constantly paraphrase understanding of the teacher's message.* Throughout the discussion, check on the accuracy of what you understand the teacher to be saying. When the teacher adds more information to the per-ceived problem, or explains different sources of the problem, considers the possible actions, and finally makes a decision, the supervisor should para-phrase. First, whenever you are uncertain of what the teacher is saying, you should paraphrase with a statement such as: "I think you're saying . . ." or "I'm not sure but do you mean . . . ." Then you can sit back and allow the teacher to affirm or reject your understanding. Second, when the teacher has come to a halt in thinking about the problem, the paraphrase should be used to jog the teacher's mind to reflect on what has already been said and what more needs to be done. For example, after a considerable pause in the teacher's talk, the supervisor might say, "Well, let me see if I can summarize what has been said so far . . ." or "So this is where you are—you're angry because . . . ." Comprehensive summarizing allows the teacher to rest, men-tally stand off from himself or herself, and think about what has been said. Usually, such paraphrasing will stimulate the teacher to interject, add, and continue. Reflecting should not become mechanical or artificial, with the su-pervisor paraphrasing every teacher statement. Instead, it should be used ju-diciously when the supervisor is not completely clear about what has been said or when there is a long pause in the conversation. Incessant interjections of "I hear you saying . . . ," without aid or purpose, make teachers skeptical about the supervisor's concern.

6. Problem solving: *Ask the teacher to think of possible actions.* After the teacher has finished identifying the problem and you are clear about his or her perception of the problem, your responsibility shifts to helping the teacher generate possible solutions. You can do this by asking straightforward ques-tions: "What can you do about this?" "What else could be done?" "Think hard about actions that might help." "Let me see if you can come up with four to six possible solutions." It is helpful to allow the teacher to think for a minute or two about possible actions before verbalizing them. After actions have been proposed, you should reflect on the proposals, check on their ac-curacy, and probe for others. Regardless of whether the teacher proposes only a few or many possibilities, if further probing is not successful, then you should move the conference on.

7. Problem solving: *Ask the teacher to consider consequences of various actions.* The moment of truth is almost at hand. Your emphasis is on having the teacher move from possible to probable solutions. Taking each solution in order, ask: "What would happen if you did . . . ?" "Would it work?" "What problems would be associated with it?" Finally, after having the teacher explore the advantages and disadvantages of each action, he or she should be asked to compare the various actions: "Which would work best?" "Why do you think so?" "How would that be better than the others?"

8. Presenting: *Ask the teacher for a commitment to a decision.* After you have explored possible actions and the teacher has compared their likelihood of success, you must emphasize that the teacher should select actions that are within his or her resources *(do-able),* can be implemented in a short period of time *(feasible),* and are concrete *(accountable).* A simple question—"Well, what will you do now that is likely to improve the situation?"—should cut quickly to the heart of the matter.

9. Standardizing: *Ask the teacher to set time and criteria for action.* The teacher is assisted in monitoring his or her own decision about future improvement by specifying the time period during which the action will be implemented, when various parts of the plan will be done, what resources are needed, and how the teacher will know the decision is working. A further series of supervisor questions to accomplish this purpose would be: "Now tell me what you are going to do." "What will be done first, next, last?" "What do you need in order to do it?" "How will you know it's working?" "When will it be done?" When the teacher can answer these questions, the conference is near completion.

10. Reflecting: *Restate the teacher's plan.* Before leaving, repeat the teacher's entire plan with "So you're going to do . . . ." After the teacher verifies the restated plan, the session is over.

Initiating Nondirective Supervision

At a workshop facilitated by one of the authors, the author decided to illustrate the nondirective approach with an unstructured simulated conference, with the author taking the role of a supervisor and a volunteer participant assuming the role of a teacher. The focus of the conference was a real-world problem that the volunteer, a mentor-teacher, was experiencing. After a successful simulation in which the author used nondirective behaviors to facilitate the teacher's reflection on the problem, consideration of alternative solutions, and an action plan for solving the problem, the author congratulated the volunteer on a simulation well done. The teacher responded, "I don't feel as if I did a very good job. I didn't know what you were trying to get me to say. Was my solution the one you were looking for?" The author explained that there was no preconceived solution to the problem, that the "supervisor" in the role play was not trying to elicit any particular responses from the teacher. The teacher, who had been selected by his district as a mentor of other teachers because of his outstanding teaching and leadership, explained that he simply did not know how to respond to nondirective supervision because in his many years of teaching he had never been exposed to a nondirective approach.

This story illustrates the point that supervisors seldom use nondirective behaviors with teachers (indeed, the supervisory approach most often used is directive; Gordon, 1989). Moreover, supervisors sometimes create the illusion of using nondirective behaviors when in fact they are manipulating a supervisory conference or group meeting toward a predetermined decision. When this happens often enough, teachers realize that the supervisor is attempting to manipulate them. Without any experience with authentic nondirective supervision, then, it's no wonder that teachers are leery of the supervisor who is trying to use that approach with them for the first time.

What's the solution when a teacher is perfectly capable of solving his or her own instructional problems but who, because of past experience, is likely to become confused or suspicious of the supervisor's first use of nondirective supervision? One technique is simply to explain to the teacher or group what nondirective supervision is, what specific behaviors are involved, and why the supervisor believes the teacher or group can benefit from the nondirective approach. Even when the supervisor has provided a rationale for nondirective supervision, some teachers may still be reluctant to identify problems, consider actions, commit to decisions, or establish criteria for success. When this happens, the supervisor should not automatically assume that the nondirective approach is inappropriate for the teacher or group. Rather the supervisor should continue to build trust and rapport through active listening, probe for problems and related information, and encourage the teacher or group to describe situations and feelings. Eventually, the teacher or group should reach a stage of trust and self-confidence that will enable them to consider alternatives and generate an improvement plan. Supervisor commitment to teacher self-direction, along with the use of appropriate interpersonal behaviors, will ultimately lead to teacher-driven instructional improvement.

Nondirective, Not Laissez Faire, Supervision

Some educators have criticized nondirective supervision by arguing that supervisors who use nondirective behaviors are abdicating their responsibility to assist teachers to improve their instructional performance. This is a valid argument against laissez faire supervision, which advocates minimal supervisor involvement in the instructional improvement process. However, under our definition of nondirective supervision, the supervisor is actively involved in instructional improvement, clarifying, encouraging, reflecting, and facilitating teacher decision making at each stage of the improvement process. Also, in developmental supervision the nondirective approach is used only with those teachers who are operating at high levels of abstraction, motivation, and expertise. The developmental supervisor uses one of the other three supervisory approaches with teachers who are not ready to assume full decision-making responsibility.

Issues with Nondirective Supervision

Based on numerous skill-training sessions conducted with school leaders on employing nondirective behaviors, some common issues and practical questions have arisen:

1. Can a supervisor really remain nonjudgmental and not influence the teacher's or group's decision?
2. What happens if the teacher or group desires the supervisor's input?
3. What does a supervisor do with a teacher or group that is reluctant or not capable of generating solutions?
4. How exact or variable is the sequence of nondirective behaviors?
5. In what circumstances should nondirective behaviors be used?

Whether a supervisor can really remain nonjudgmental is a legitimate concern. Even when one is consciously avoiding praise, not interjecting one's own ideas, and not offering solutions in the guise of questions, some influencing probably will take place. Studies by Mears, Shannon, and Pepinsky (1979) analyzing the tapes of counseling sessions conducted by the most renowned expert on nondirectiveness, psychologist Carl Rogers, revealed a definite pattern to his interrupting the patient and to which statements he selected to paraphrase. It is apparent that any interaction between humans is bound to be influential. Frequency of eye contact, timing of questions, facial expressions, and ways of paraphrasing can always be interpreted by a teacher as approving or disapproving. There is no way to avoid influencing through unconscious supervisory responses. The best one can do is to minimize those behaviors that knowingly influence. One should not knowingly offer ideas, praise, or directions that will influence the teacher's decision.

What if the teacher or group asks for the supervisor's suggestions? The answer to this question centers on timing. If the suggestions are asked for and given in the initial stages of a conference or meeting before the teacher or group has been required to think through the issue, then such feedback will structure the stream of subsequent thought and heavily influence the decision. If the suggestions are given after the teacher or group has already narrowed its own choices of actions, however, a supervisor's answer will not be as influential. Ideally, it is better to refrain completely from giving one's own ideas. If asked, the supervisor might respond, "I'm sorry, but I don't want to answer that. Instead, I want you to think through what can be done. Only you know your own situation. Therefore, what *I* think is not as important as what *you* think."

Being nondirective with an individual or group that is reluctant or not capable of generating solutions is tricky. Reluctance and capability are not necessarily inversely related. If the teacher is reluctant but capable, the worst possible response would be for the supervisor to take over decision making for the teacher. Such a move might reinforce the teacher's reluctance to speak his or her own mind. Reluctance usually stems from a disbelief that one will be listened to or allowed to act on one's own initiative. The supervisor must be patient, give constant encouragement, and be persistent. Patience is shown by listening and waiting, encouragement by accepting what the teacher says, and persistence by not allowing the teacher to rest without making a decision. A supervisor can be persistent by asking questions, by taking breaks from the conference, and by giving the teacher time for further reflections.

Capability is a different matter. What if a teacher or group is incapable of making a decision? If they continually insist they do not know what the problem is or have no ideas about what could be done, and if every supervisory prompt is met by vacant stares and shrugs of shoulders, then patience, encouragement, and persistence on the part of the supervisor will create further frustration and perhaps antagonism. If they simply don't know, no matter how nondirective the supervisor is, no decisions will be forthcoming. Obviously, if lack of capability is the source of nonresponsiveness, then the nondirective approach is an unwise choice of supervisory behaviors.

Finally, there is the question of sequence of nondirective behaviors. How precise is the order? The description of nondirective behaviors presented a prototype of 10 steps within the supervisory behavior continuum (Figure 11.1). One might visualize these steps as analogous to playing the left-hand side of a piano keyboard. The supervisor-pianist begins the musical score with the furthest left-hand note (listening-waiting) and will end the score at note 10 (reflecting-restating). During the score (conference or meeting) the adept player will strike the notes (behaviors) back and forth between 1 and 10 pounding on some notes, lightly touching on others, returning, and swelling the underlying tone of the teacher or group voice. The score ends on note 10—reflecting and restating the teacher's or group's decision. The behaviors are not a prescription of fixed steps but rather a directionality of movements with a definite beginning and end.

When to Use Nondirective Behaviors

When and with whom should nondirective behaviors be used? A supervisor should consider using a nondirective approach:

1. When the teacher or group is functioning at high developmental levels.
2. When the teacher or group possesses most of the knowledge and expertise about the issue and the supervisor's knowledge and expertise are minimal: "If you don't know anything about it and they do, let them solve it."
3. When the teacher or group has full responsibility for carrying out the decision and the supervisor has little involvement: "If they are going to be accountable for it and you aren't, let them solve it."

4. When the teacher or group is committed to solving the problem but the problem doesn't matter to the supervisor: "If they want to act and you couldn't care less, let them decide."

There are special circumstances in which initial use of nondirective behaviors are appropriate even if the preceding criteria are not met. Regardless of teacher developmental level, expertise, responsibility, or commitment, when a teacher or group has become extremely emotional over a problem, rational problem solving using any of the four supervisory approaches may be unproductive. What may be more beneficial in such situations is the initial use of the nondirective behaviors of listening, clarifying, encouraging, and reflecting as the teacher or group describes the problem and expresses the anger, frustration, fear, resentment, or other feelings the problem has generated. Once the teacher or group has had the opportunity to vent emotions in the presence of an empathetic listener, the supervisor can then shift to a problem-solving mode, using the criteria of developmental level, expertise, responsibility, and commitment to select the appropriate supervisory approach for the problem-solving phase of the conference or meeting.

Nondirective Supervision, Teacher Collaboration

Although nondirective supervision can be a valuable means of assisting individual teacher development, we see its greatest potential in the supervisor facilitating expert teachers' collaborating with each other for classroom and schoolwide instructional improvement. An example of nondirective supervision of teacher collaboration at the classroom level would be the supervisor facilitating a teacher-driven peer-coaching program. An example of nondirective supervision for schoolwide instructional improvement would be the supervisor assisting a group of teachers as the group plans, implements, and evaluates a series of integrated instructional units cutting across several content areas. The ultimate goal of developmental supervision is for the supervisor to be facilitating a self-actualized teaching staff engaged in collaborative and continuous instructional improvement.

Item B5 in Appendix B allows you to practice nondirective behaviors. Practice in nondirective supervision is especially important, since research indicates that it is the most difficult supervisory approach to implement (Gordon, 1990).

Critical Reflection on Nondirective Supervision

The supervisor can consider the questions below when reflecting on the use of nondirective behaviors:

- Is the teacher or group reluctant to assume decision-making responsibility? If so, what might be the reason for that reluctance?

- In addition to using overt nondirective behaviors such as clarifying, encouraging, and reflecting, do I avoid influencing the teacher or group through subtle comments or nonverbal behaviors?
- If the teacher or group asks for my input, do I respond appropriately?
- Am I actively facilitating the teacher or group's decision making, or do I sometimes slip into laissez faire supervision?

SUMMARY

Supervisors can use nondirective behaviors in helping teachers determine their own plans. Such supervisory behaviors consist of listening, reflecting, clarifying, encouraging, and problem solving. When individuals and groups of teachers are functioning at high developmental levels and possess greater expertise, commitment, and responsibility for a particular decision than the supervisor does, then a nondirective approach is appropriate. Important considerations for a supervisor when using nondirectiveness are attempting to be nonjudgmental, hesitating in response to teachers' wishes for more supervisor input, and adjusting one's behavior when teachers demonstrate reluctance to generate solutions. The purpose of nondirective supervision is to provide an active sounding board for thoughtful professionals.

PRACTITIONER REFLECTION

A Nondirective Approach as I'm Developing

Lynn M. Rasmussen, *Principal, Breidablik Elementary School*

I never set out to be a school principal. I actually set out to be a great teacher. I had visions of changing the lives of children through teaching in public schools. As a teacher I wanted the children's learning to be authentic, to be related to the rest of their lives, to be developmentally appropriate for each child, and to actually mean something for them in 10 or 20 years. I didn't want to teach them stuff just because it had been taught to me. When I became a principal, I wanted to engage teachers in the evaluation process so that it was authentic, related to their daily lives in the classroom, appropriate to their developmental teaching stages, and something they would remember as helping them become a better teacher. Having been evaluated for numerous years as a teacher, I recall clearly the variety of models used.

One model was prescriptive and mandated by the district office. It expected all teachers to be able to strictly follow the Madeline Hunter lesson design within a 48-minute class period. Another model was also prescriptive, requiring completion of the district instructional model within a given lesson. The other two forms of supervision I was exposed to as a teacher consisted of showing me the written copy of my principal's script tape and signing off that those were all the words I had spoken within the classroom. For each of my observations, the level of my reflection consisted of wondering what the principal thought of my lesson and how it would be written up. I also reflected on the probability that the observation would forever be stored in the bottom of a personnel file never to be seen again.

These experiences with evaluation influenced me to utilize the nondirective approach in my role as principal. The nondirective approach assumes that the teacher is at a high level of abstraction and is willing to direct his or her own growth. It also assumes a positive working relationship between the supervisor and teacher with a willingness to improve. In the last few years I've asked a few teachers who have exhibited these characteristics if they would participate in team "preconferencing" and "postconferencing." The team time typically consisted of three to four teachers, of varying grade levels and experience, dialoguing about their lesson. I would facilitate the conferencing with dialogue-based questions to invite group conversation on teachers' lesson goals and student learning outcomes. The conversation quickly became multilayered with teachers talking to each other, instead of just me, about their lesson design and their goal for the observation.

Teachers would share copies of their lesson plans with each other and then discuss how they wanted me to target my observation skills. I was often asked to focus my attention on the lower or slower achievers to help the teachers determine what they might do to reach these students during their instruction. The observations then occurred that same day and we would all postconference right after school, so the lessons and teacher reflections were fresh on their minds. I sought to facilitate the team postconference with dialogue-based questions to initiate the teacher's conversation. It was always a very lively discussion with teachers reflecting aloud to each other about their instruction and then sharing possible ideas for their dilemmas. I would informally seek out each of the teachers after this experience to determine if they liked it more than the one-on-one conferencing. All indicated they much preferred the team conferencing to the individual conferencing.

On a few occasions I invited teachers to the team conferencing who weren't operating on a high level of abstraction. I naively thought it might encourage or pull them up to higher levels of thinking, reflection, and abstraction. The dialogue that ensued was usually beyond their capabilities. On one occasion a teacher was able to crudely articulate her inability to participate, "I just can't even begin to understand and talk about instruction like you guys are, I just have so much to learn." The group was very supportive of her, but some appeared a bit mystified by her inability to "get it."

That moment taught me that nondirective forms of supervision were best utilized with teachers who are functioning at a high level of abstraction and ready to direct their own professional growth. By being nondirective with a teacher who isn't quite ready, the supervisor might appear lazy or unsupportive to the teacher's needs. I'm still working with teachers to learn how we can engage in our team conferencing. It's still in the infancy as one tool for nondirective supervision.

As a continuously developing supervisor I always go back to the core of my teaching focus. I want teachers' learning to be authentic, related to the rest of their lives, developmentally appropriate for each teacher, and still meaningful for them in 10 or 20 years. Maintaining this focus, I believe, can greatly facilitate teacher and student success.

EXERCISES

Academic

1. Write an imaginary dialogue between a supervisor and a teacher during a conference in which the supervisor successfully uses a nondirective approach. Be sure to include examples of each of the 10 nondirective behaviors discussed in Chapter 11.

2. The chapter explains a sequence of 10 nondirective behaviors that take place during a nondirective conference. Think of a situation in which a successful nondirective conference would start with the first suggested behavior (listening-waiting) and end with the tenth (reflecting-restating the plan), but would have a *different sequence* of 8 intermediate behaviors. Describe the situation and modified sequence of nondirective behaviors in writing. Include a rationale for the suggested sequence.

3. Write an imaginary dialogue between a supervisor and a teacher in which the supervisor implements nondirective procedures with mechanical precision but still fails to be truly nondirective.

4. Write a paper comparing the nondirective approach as described in this book with the version of nondirective assistance espoused by an author cited in the References or Suggested Readings.

5. Assume you have just listened to a talk by a school administrator in which he or she argued against the use of nondirective behaviors by educational supervisors with *any* teacher. The thrust of the administrator's argument was that such an approach is essentially *laissez faire* and allows complete deference to teacher decisions, even when such decisions are clearly in error and are likely to result in harm to the teacher's instructional performance or to the students. The administrator further argued that for a supervisor to withhold his or her observations, perceptions, and suggestions, unless they are requested by the teacher, is counterproductive to the supervisory process. You have been asked to prepare a reply to the administrator to be presented at an upcoming seminar. Write a paper in which you argue for the use of nondirective behavior with certain teachers. Address the administrator's objections in your paper.

Field

1. Use a nondirective approach by either using the activity found in Item B5 of Appendix B or conducting an actual postobservation conference with a teacher. Prepare a written report in which you (a) evaluate your success in displaying nondirective behaviors, (b) summarize the problems discussed and decisions made during the conference, (c) give your perceptions of the "teacher's" responses to your nondirective efforts, and (d) judge the conference in terms of overall success.

2. Observe an educational supervisor or other leader whom you know to possess a nondirective orientation. Based on your observations and interview with the

leader, write a paper describing both successes and failures that he or she has experienced while using nondirective behaviors. Include possible reasons for the nondirective leader's greater success in some situations than in others.

3. Observe three teachers or staff members who clearly respond positively to nondirective supervision. Prepare a report examining personal and social characteristics of these individuals that may account for their positive response to a nondirective approach.

4. Prepare a picture album entitled "Self-Direction for Instructional Improvement." Each picture should be accompanied by a written explanation of how that entry relates to the album theme.

5. Videotape or audiotape a conference or professional development activity in which the supervisor is using a nondirective approach. As you review the tape, compare the recorded activities with the sequence of behaviors that, according to the authors, exemplifies the nondirective approach of a supervisor during a decision-making process. Prepare a report on your findings.

Developmental

1. Through interaction with various individuals in a variety of situations, begin to establish a set of personal guidelines that will indicate when the nondirective approach is most appropriate in carrying out present or anticipated leadership functions.

2. Begin an in-depth study of the writings of a prominent humanistic educator or psychologist. Relate that author's ideas to the concepts of nondirective supervision discussed in this chapter.

3. Record a simulated or actual supervisor-teacher conference in which you, as supervisor, attempt to display nondirective behaviors. Review the tape for analysis of your performance. Over the next four weeks, practice nondirective leadership whenever appropriate opportunities arise. Record another simulated or actual conference in four weeks. Review both tapes to discover any improvement in terms of successfully displaying nondirective behaviors.

REFERENCES

Gordon, S. P. 1989. *The theory of developmental supervision: An investigation of the critical aspects.* Unpublished Ed.D. dissertation, University of Georgia, Athens.

Gordon, S. P. 1990. Developmental supervision: An exploratory study of a promising model. *Journal of Curriculum and Supervision, 5,* 293–307.

Mears, N. M., Shannon, J. W, and Pepinsky, H. B. 1979. Comparison of the stylistic complexity of the language of counselor and client across three theoretical orientations. *Journal of Counseling Psychology, 26*(3), 181–189.

Rogers, C. R. 1951. *Client-centered therapy: Its current practice, implications, and theory.* Boston: Houghton Mifflin.

SUGGESTED READINGS

Gitlin, A., and Price, K. 1992. Teacher empowerment and the development of voice. In C. D. Glickman (Ed.), *Supervision in transition.* Alexandria, VA: Association for Supervision and Curriculum Development.

Pajak, E. 1993. *Approaches to clinical supervision.* Norwood, MA: Christopher-Gordon Publishers. See the following: (1) Robert Goldhammer's Clinical Supervision (pp. 25–50), (2) Ralph Mosher and David Purpel's Ego Counseling Model (pp. 51–72), (3) Arthur Blumberg's Interpersonnel Intervention (pp. 103–126), and (4) Noreen Garman's "Reflective Heart" of Clinical Supervision (pp. 296–298).

Retallick, J. A. 1990. *Clinical supervision and the structure of communication.* Paper presented at the annual meeting of the American Educational Research Association, Boston, April.

Symth, W. J. 1990. *Problemizing teaching through a "critical" approach to clinical supervision.* Paper presented at the annual meeting of the American Educational Research Association, Boston, April.

chapter 12

Developmental Supervision

Theory and Practice

Thus far in Part III we have introduced the supervisory behavior continuum, provided an overview of developmental supervision, and explained each of the four supervisory approaches (directive control, directive informational, collaborative, and nondirective). This chapter provides an in-depth discussion of developmental supervision as an integrated model. The first part of the chapter presents the underlying rationale for developmental supervision. The second part explains how the model can be applied in practice.

Rationale for Developmental Supervision

One aspect of developmental supervision is the match of initial supervisory approach with the teacher's or group's developmental levels, expertise, and commitment. In Chapter 4, we described characteristics of teachers functioning at various stages of adult and career development. Teachers functioning at generally low developmental levels were described as performing at the concrete operations stage of cognitive development, low conceptual levels, the preconventional level of moral reasoning, the fearful stage of ego development, the durable category level of consciousness, and the self-adequacy stage of concern. Teachers or groups of low developmental levels, expertise, and commitment seem well matched to directive supervision. They have difficulty defining problems, have few ways of responding to problems, and are unlikely to accept decision-making responsibility. They clearly are in need of the structure and intensive assistance provided by directive supervision. For most teachers in need of direction, an informational directive approach is appropriate. For teachers functioning at extremely low levels of development, expertise, and commitment, and with serious instructional problems, a controlling directive approach might be necessary.

Teachers of generally moderate developmental levels were described as functioning at the formal operations stage of cognitive development, moderate conceptual levels, the conventional level of moral reasoning, the conforming stage of ego development, the cross-categorical level of consciousness, and the teaching tasks stage of concern. Teachers or groups at moderate developmental levels, expertise, and commitment are usually best served by a collaborative supervisory approach. They can generate some possible solutions to an instructional problem, but still need some assistance in examining all options and developing a comprehensive plan for instructional improvement. The brainstorming inherent in collaborative supervision allows the teacher or group to share perceptions and offer some possible alternatives for future action, but also to receive the benefit of supervisor perceptions and proposals. Negotiated action plans made during collaborative supervision allow teachers to meet needs of emerging independence while receiving the moderate guidance needed to assure that the plan will lead to instructional improvement.

Teachers functioning at generally high developmental levels were described in Chapter 4 as being at the postformal operations stage of cognitive development, high conceptual levels, the postconventional level of moral reasoning, the autonomous stage of ego development, the systems or trans-systems level of consciousness, and the teaching impact stage of concern. Teachers or groups functioning at generally high developmental levels, expertise, and commitment are ready for the self-direction fostered by the nondirective supervisory approach. They are autonomous, explorative, and creative. They can think of a problem from many perspectives, generate a variety of alternative actions, think through each step of an action plan, and follow the plan through to completion.

The Problem of Variability

The fact that the criteria for selecting a supervisory approach may fluctuate means that choosing the best approach can become more complicated than the broad guidelines just discussed might suggest. The following possibilities must be kept in mind:

1. Individual or group levels of development, expertise, and commitment may vary. For example, a teacher might be functioning at high levels of consciousness as well as cognitive, conceptual, and moral development but at

only moderate levels of ego development, concern, and commitment. In addition, a group might include teachers of low, moderate, and high developmental levels. Some general guidelines are to use a controlling directive approach if most characteristics of an individual or group indicate an extremely low decision-making capacity, informational directive supervision if most attributes point to a fairly low capacity, a collaborative approach if most characteristics indicate a moderate capacity, and nondirective supervision if most attributes point to a high capacity for decision making. When working with an individual or group with widely fluctuating characteristics, a collaborative approach would probably be most effective.

2. Characteristics of teachers and groups might change in certain situations. For example, a teacher who has successfully taught general science to middle school students for 10 years might regress to lower levels of development, expertise, or commitment after being transferred to a senior high school to teach chemistry and physics. Similarly, a faculty at a former junior high school might regress to lower levels of group development, expertise, or commitment after the campus has been converted to a middle school. In short, the developmental supervisor sometimes must change supervisory behaviors in order to adapt to a change in the teacher or group's situation.

Research on adult and teacher development can suggest guidelines for determining the best supervisory approach. The tremendous variability of teacher characteristics, however, means that the supervisor must choose his or her approach on a case-by-case basis, relying on the knowledge base on teacher characteristics, recent observations of and interactions with the teacher or group, and analysis of the current situation.

One way to describe developmental supervision is to say that it provides teachers with as much initial choice as they are ready to assume, then fosters teachers' decision-making capacity and expanded choice over time. But why be so concerned with teacher choice? Why not simply train teachers in effective teaching methods, monitor classroom instruction, reinforce successful teaching, and remediate (or eliminate) ineffective teachers? In short, why not simply do one's best to control teachers and instruction for the sake of students and society, who, after all, are the real clients of the schools? This question will be answered through the following discussions of motivation, choice, and controlling versus informational environments.

SuperVision for Teacher Development

The long-term goal of developmental supervision is teacher development toward a point at which teachers, facilitated by supervisors, can assume full responsibility for instructional improvement. In addition to the motivational factors already discussed, there are several other reasons why we believe that teacher development should be a critical function of supervision. First, as described in Chapter 4, teachers functioning at higher developmental levels tend to use a wide variety of instructional behaviors associated with successful teaching. Second, teachers who have themselves reached high stages of cognitive, conceptual, moral, and ego development are more likely to foster their own students' growth in those areas. In a democratic society, it is vital that students learn to think reflectively, function at high stages of moral reasoning, and be autonomous decision makers. Finally, teachers at higher levels of adult development, expertise, and commitment are more likely to embrace "a cause beyond oneself" and participate in collective action toward schoolwide instructional improvement—a critical element found in the effective schools research. This section has focused on the *why* of developmental supervision. The remainder of the chapter is concerned with *how* developmental supervision can be applied in the real world of schools and teachers.

Applying Developmental Supervision

Chapter 7 introduced the three phases of developmental supervision. To review, they are (1) choosing the best entry-level supervisory approach, (2) applying the chosen approach, and (3) fostering teacher development while gradually increasing teacher choice and decision-making responsibility. Our discussion of applying developmental supervision addresses each of these three phases.

Phase 1: Choosing the Best Approach

There are two primary ways to assess a teacher's developmental levels, expertise, and commitment, all of which should be considered when choosing the supervisory approach to be used. One way is to observe the teacher teaching or working with other teachers. Another way is to discuss with the teacher his or her ideas about students, teaching, and instructional improvement. Below are excerpts from actual observation reports on behaviors of teachers diagnosed at various development levels (Gordon, 1989). First, let's review excerpts from reports on teachers who supervisors perceived to be in need of directive informational supervision:

- I found her rigid and uptight in her relationships with the students.
- He was inconsistent in applying rules of behavior. His directions for the lesson were unclear and confusing. As a result, the students became disruptive. Some students even became hostile, while others started telling him what to do. He gave up on an activity in social studies because he said the class was too noisy. Actually they were confused over the poor directions.
- In watching her in her classroom . . . half of the time was spent correcting, redirecting. "Sit in your seats . . . ," "How many times do I have to tell you to raise your hand?"
- He found out that games worked . . . his lectures, and workbooks, and games, and that was about it.

Here are excerpts from observation reports on teachers for whom supervisors chose a collaborative approach:

- In committee work, I have found him dependable and willing to cooperate but not an initiator of ideas.
- I've worked with this teacher for several years. . . . I've observed her growth. . . . She is becoming more independent and is willing to try some new ideas and methods.
- (The teacher) possesses several (instructional) strategies but has difficulty adopting strategies and individualizing (instruction).

Finally, some observations of teachers matched with a nondirective approach follow:

- She develops her own units of instruction with minimum guidance. She is able to start with an idea for an instructional unit and then pool available resources. If a resource is not available, she often makes it herself. She is very artistic and has a wealth of good ideas.
- He uses a variety of teaching methods.
- She is sensitive to her students' needs and is even thinking beyond (this year) to next year. They will be going to a new school, and her concerns now are to make the students more responsible, self-sufficient, etc., so they'll function (successfully) at the new school.
- Students are treated like individuals, and creativity and expression of feelings encouraged.
- This teacher sees the child in a holistic way: a growing, developing human being whose learning style is multifaceted and whose learning occurs in all areas—cognitive, social, emotional, and physical. She gears instruction not only to groups of learners but also to individuals.
- He has served as president of a statewide educational association. He has written several books and journal articles for teachers and parents, conducts workshops, and is very active in local organizations dedicated to the improvement of teaching.

The best way to determine teacher characteristics and supervisory approach is to combine observations of teachers in action with supervisor-teacher discussion. To assess teacher characteristics, the supervisor can use discussions with the teacher to find answers to the following questions:

1. Is the teacher aware of improvements that can be made in the classroom? Can the teacher identify those needs?
2. Has the teacher considered possible causes of the instructional needs? Does the teacher gather information from multiple sources about the instructional needs?

3. Can the teacher generate several possible solutions? How carefully does the teacher weigh the merits of each solution? Does the teacher consider what he or she can do to reach the goal without looking unrealistically for outside help?
4. Can the teacher be decisive in choosing a course of action? Does the teacher commit himself or herself to an implementation procedure?
5. Does the teacher do what he or she says?

Teacher responses to questions like these can provide clues to the appropriate supervisory approach.

The following quotes are excerpts from supervisor reports on discussions with teachers. The first set of excerpts describe teachers for whom supervisors selected a directive informational approach:

- At the end of the lesson I observed, he said, "I need help. Please tell me what to do."
- A student below grade level was transferred to her class. She wanted me to list appropriate materials to use with this child and asked me to come to her school and demonstrate appropriate techniques with this child. I did this, and I think she felt more relaxed about the situation, although she still seeks and receives much guidance in working with this child.
- He has (said) to me that "at this age, lecturing seems to be the only way to get ideas and materials across to students."
- In conferences, when I ask for goals or what types of things would she like to work on, she doesn't know. She says, "I just don't know."

Following are supervisor's reports on conferences with teachers who supervisors matched with a collaborative approach:

- He has come to me on many occasions asking me how to handle things and has been able, at the same time, to give me some of his ideas.
- In seeking assistance in her classroom she is seldom without ideas or suggestions. However, she does not feel totally secure in trying out new ideas without first discussing them with the principal or me.
- This teacher is open to ideas but does not like to be told what to do . . . he is starting to make some decisions on his own.

Last, some supervisor descriptions of conference behaviors of teachers matched with nondirective supervision follow:

- She often comes to me to talk about the things that she has going on in her classroom, not because she wants me to help make a decision, but because she simply wants to sound out what she plans to do.
- This teacher's performance at our meetings is impressive. He comes prepared and is really capable of handling the meetings himself. . . . He always manages to work out any problems himself.

Some cautions need to be made here concerning the organizational relationship between the individual providing supervision and the teacher or group receiving supervision. Generally, directive control supervision should be used only by supervisors in line relationships with teachers (supervisors who have been given formal authority by the school district over teachers they are supervising). Informational directive supervision should be used only by those who are acknowledged by the organization to have special expertise. Examples of individuals with acknowledged expertise include supervisors in line or staff relationships with teachers, lead teachers, mentors of beginning teachers, and so on. Collaborative and nondirective behaviors can be used by supervisors in line or staff relationships, teachers designated as instructional leaders, and teachers in reciprocal helping relationships, such as peer coaches. Table 12.1 provides a review of supervisory approaches normally appropriate for use by those carrying out some common supervisory roles. The task of the person in a particular supervisory role is to choose the best approach from those appropriate for his or her role.

Phase 2: Applying the Chosen Approach

Previous chapters provided scenarios of supervisors using each of the four supervisory approaches. But can a supervisor shift from one approach to another when working with teachers and groups at different developmental levels? Stated differently, can the same supervisor effectively use directive informational, directive control, collaborative, and nondirective behaviors? The question of *supervisor flexibility* was addressed by Gordon (1989, 1990) during a study in which he trained supervisors in developmental supervision, then asked each supervisor to work with separate teacher triads. The supervisors attempted informational directive supervision with one teacher, collaborative supervision with a second

| **TABLE 12.1** | Supervisory Roles and Approaches |

	Approaches Appropriate for Particular Supervisory Roles			
Supervisory Roles	*Directive Control*	*Directive Informational*	*Collaborative*	*Nondirective*
Line Supervisor	X	X	X	X
Staff Supervisor		X	X	X
Lead Teacher		X	X	X
Designated Mentor		X	X	X
Peer Coach			X	X

teacher, and nondirective supervision with a third teacher (supervisors based their decisions on supervisory approach on earlier observations of and conferences with teachers). When supervisors attempted the different approaches, their conferences with teachers were audiotaped. The taped conferences were analyzed to determine if attempted approaches were effectively used. The investigator found that 93 percent of the supervisors were able to implement informational directive supervision, 100 percent were able to engage in collaborative supervision, and 70 percent were able to use nondirective supervision. An implication of this study is that supervisors being trained to use developmental supervision must receive their most intensive training in nondirective supervision, which seems to be the most difficult approach for many to use.

What if a supervisor in the early stages of working with a teacher or group—even after preliminary observation and discussion—is not sure which supervisory approach to use? A good rule of thumb in such cases is to *prepare to use a collaborative approach, but be ready to shift to a nondirective or directive approach if necessary.* When preparing to use a collaborative approach a supervisor determines possible improvement goals, actions, and criteria to be considered and potentially integrated with goals, actions, and criteria suggested by the teacher or group. However, if during the early phases of the conference or meeting it becomes apparent that the teacher or group will be able to identify an appropriate goal and action plan on their own, then the supervisor can forget about his or her possible suggestions and shift to nondirective behaviors as a means of facilitating self-directed teacher planning. If, on the other hand, the teacher or group is unable to identify an obvious problem, any of its underlying causes, or any possible solutions, the supervisor can shift to a directive mode, mandating (directive control) or suggesting (directive informational) a goal, actions, and improvement criteria.

One type of *supervisor flexibility* is the ability to plan and implement different supervisory approaches with different teachers and groups. The ultimate supervisor flexibility, however, is the ability to "shift supervisory gears," so to speak, and effectively use an approach not originally planned because of new discoveries about teachers or the situation at hand. Like successful teachers, successful supervisors must be able to think on their feet, and flex accordingly (Zellermayer and Margolin, 2005).

Phase 3: Fostering Teacher Development

Simply matching the best supervisory approach to the teacher or group's current developmental levels can promote some degree of teacher development. For example, Siens and Ebmeier (1996) found that teachers assisted by supervisors trained to tailor their conference approaches to teachers' levels of motivation, analytical skill, and knowledge experienced significantly more growth on a measure of reflective thinking than did a control group of teachers receiving only the regular supervision provided at their schools. Previous chapters in this text have discussed facilitating teacher development by gradually decreasing supervisor control and increasing teacher control over the decision-making process. There are additional strategies that supervisors can use to stimulate teacher development. One method is to introduce teachers to new information about students and learning, innovative teaching strategies, and novel ways to frame and solve problems. Initially, new ways of thinking and acting that teachers are invited to explore should be linked to their existing knowledge, experience, and values. Gradually, teachers can be exposed to a broader spectrum of theory and practice.

Another method is to assign teachers to decision-making teams or learning groups in which most of the other members are functioning at slightly higher developmental levels. Significant, ongoing professional interaction with teachers of somewhat higher development will tend to pull the teacher of lower development toward the group's functioning level. Unfortunately, the reverse is also true. Teachers of higher developmental levels assigned to groups in which the majority of teachers are functioning at lower developmental levels tend to be "pulled down" to the group's level.

Lois Thies-Sprinthall (1984) has identified five conditions necessary to promote psychological/cognitive growth:

1. Role-taking experiences
2. Careful and continuous guided reflection
3. Balance . . . between real experience and discussion/reflection
4. Both personal support and challenge
5. Continuity (programs should be at least six months in length with meetings at regular intervals). (p. 54)

Phillips and Glickman (1991) studied a peer-coaching program that incorporated Thies-Sprinthall's five conditions for psychological/cognitive growth. The participants were 22 teachers who attended four professional development sessions in which they learned observation, problem solving, and collaborative and nondirective interpersonal skills. The workshops included lectures, demonstrations, practice observations, conference role playing, outside readings, and opportunities for discussion and reflection. A coaching cycle consisted of a preconference, classroom observation, postobservation conference, and follow-up session. Coaching partners engaged in four coaching cycles. Each teacher assumed the role of coach in two of the cycles and was coached by his or her partner in the other two cycles. The instructor and participants engaged in group debriefing sessions after each coaching cycle. Phillips and Glickman measured participants' conceptual levels before and after the program, and found that a significant increase in teachers' conceptual levels had occurred by the end of the program. Research on attempts to foster teacher development is still in its early stages. Exploratory research such as the study reported by Phillips and Glickman, however, indicates that stimulation of teacher growth toward higher developmental levels is possible.

Not Algorithms, But Guideposts for Decisions

Eventually, we must discuss, question, and ask each other (in a supervisor-supervisee relationship) which supervisory approach has been most helpful in the past, which will be most helpful in the present, and which approach we should be striving for in the future. With the exception of emergency situations, this is the responsibility of both parties.

Life in the school world is ragged and complex. This chapter has offered information to ponder about available behaviors, human motivation, types of environments, and characteristics of individuals and groups. There are no algorithms to provide exactly correct responses to human behavior. Such formulas as "If individual X exhibits characteristics A, B, and C, then supervisor Y should do D, F, and G" do not and should not exist. Such algorithms are useful only in mechanically and technically controlled systems (such as computer operations, assembly production, or chemical alterations). Algorithms work in technical but not human endeavors, and it would be misleading to suggest that such supervision formulas are available. Instead, what is available is information about ourselves and others that can serve as guideposts to suggest what *might* be of use. Such developmental guideposts can help reduce some of the infinite complexity of the school world so that supervision can be a purposeful and thoughtful function for improving instruction.

Scenario and Discussion: Inappropriate Use of Interpersonal Behaviors?

Megan Janson, a teacher at Lakeside High School, has come to instructional supervisor Jim Autry with a concern. Several female teachers have complained that Jim seems to be overly directive with them during conferences focused on instructional supervision. These same teachers have told Megan that they have heard from a number of male colleagues that Jim is nondirective when conferring with the male teachers.

Megan, a close friend of Jim, tells him she wanted him to know this so he could reflect on the situation and decide what, if anything, to do about it. Jim has been using different supervisory approaches with different teachers and groups lately, but has been trying to use collaborative supervision with most teachers and has been intentionally directive with only one female teacher and intentionally nondirective with only one male teacher. He is surprised and disturbed at the comments from female teachers reported by Megan.

What advice would you give Jim on each of the following issues:

1. How can Jim determine whether he is using directive behaviors with females better matched with a different approach, and/or being nondirective with males better matched with a different approach?

2. If Jim concludes that he really is using unintended interpersonal behaviors with some teachers, how can he explore possible reasons for such unintended behaviors?

3. If Jim eventually concludes that he has been engaging in unconscious gender bias in his supervisory conferences, what can he do to correct the situation? How can he verify improvement in this area?

SUMMARY

This chapter explored the theory and practice of developmental supervision in detail. We discussed the rationale for matching various supervisory approaches with different teacher characteristics, as well as the problem of variability of those characteristics. Human motivation, according to Maslow, Herzberg, deCharms, and Deci, explains why information environments that provide choice for teachers are more likely to sustain instructional improvements than are control environments that limit choice. We also argued that the long-term goal of supervision should be to foster teacher growth toward higher levels of development, expertise, and commitment.

In the second part of the chapter, we discussed the application of developmental supervision. We suggested observations of and discussions with teachers as ways to assess teacher characteristics, and shared supervisor descriptions of teachers matched with directive, collaborative, and nondirective supervision. Finally, we proposed that the supervisor needs to use his or her own decision-making abilities to determine the most appropriate interpersonal approaches to use with his or her staff.

PRACTITIONER REFLECTION

Using Developmental Supervision in the Curriculum Development Process

Denise Villa, *Assistant Principal and Dean of Curriculum and Instruction, Manor Middle School*

An assistant principal in the public school system holds many duties. These duties range from assistant janitor and glorified secretary, to counselor and instructional leader. Far too often we get caught up in our day-to-day agenda and forget the most relevant part of our job—being an instructional leader. This is the part of my job that I enjoy the most, even though I consider it to be the most challenging.

Presently, I work at a midsized rural middle school. The school is the educational house for 800 students and 63 teachers. Approximately half of the staff are veteran teachers with more than five years' experience. In the past school year our district has begun to pave a path for excellence. It is the mission of the school district to take our academically acceptable school to exemplary school status in three years. The school district has started this process by focusing on curriculum for grades K–12. The superintendent predicts that it will take 18 months to totally revamp the curriculum.

We began this process by forming a curriculum team. The leadership of our school's curriculum team consisted of staff from central administration and one assistant principal (myself). The team included two teachers from every subject area and every grade level. Selecting these teachers was to be the first task of the core curriculum team. Teachers with more than five years' experience make up 95 percent of the team. The supervisory environment for veteran teachers tends to be more collaborative to nondirective. For this project, there was a high need for a less controlling environment. We needed teachers who were abstract thinkers, were informed about their content area, were secure about instructional strategies, and preferred a collaborative to nondirective approach. With the selection of the teachers completed, a meeting was scheduled during the summer to begin the process of redesigning our curriculum.

Asking the teachers to make systemic changes for the entire school required commitment, expertise, and careful consideration. The discussion with teachers began by presenting foundational information on curriculum development. A curriculum guru was hired and spent two days with the teachers, providing professional development on designing curriculum. His presentation was geared to spark questions from the teachers rather than a typical "sit-and-get" lecture. The teachers began to see the areas in need of improvement and generated alternative solutions. As a group they were able to choose a course of action and begin an implementation procedure.

The implementation took place in many phases. As a supervisor, I knew I would have to be flexible in my leadership. In the early stages of the project, the teachers needed more direction as they were bombarded with much new information that they needed to reorganize and synthesize. Broad curriculum improvement goals, action steps, and criteria for success needed to be quickly established. However, as the project progressed, I shifted from an informational directive approach toward a collaborative to nondirective approach.

All of the phases of curriculum development involved discussions among the teachers of that subject. The discussions were intense but extremely productive. Trust and confidence were established, which fostered reflective thinking and critical analysis. The teachers took ownership of the curriculum and it quickly became their project. It was no longer my project to lead!

Being the supervisor of a large group of teachers working on a major project can be very challenging. Using a supervisory approach that facilitates teacher development is crucial. If I had been too directive with this decision-making team, the teachers would not have gained confidence, nor would they have bought into the project. Leading through a combination of supervisory styles led to empowering teachers, a successful project, and a satisfied supervisor.

EXERCISES

Academic

1. Prepare written composite profiles of (a) a teacher who would benefit most from nondirective supervision, (b) a teacher who would benefit most from collaborative supervision, (c) a teacher who would benefit most from directive informa-

tional supervision, and (d) a teacher who would benefit most from directive control supervision.

2. Write scenarios in which the same teacher or group requires different supervisory approaches in two different situations. Explain in your paper how the supervisor changes his or her interpersonal approach from the first to the second scenario.

3. Write a paper in which you discuss two or more alternative theories of motivation, and relate those theories to supervision and teachers. Use at least three outside references in your paper.

4. Describe a situation in which a supervisor would be required to use directive control, and explain what specific behaviors you as a supervisor would exhibit in that situation. Describe a second set of circumstances in which directive information would be more appropriate, and explain specific behaviors you would display if you were the supervisor in that second situation.

5. Design a program for stimulating teachers' cognitive, conceptual, moral reasoning, and/or ego development over a nine-month period.

Field

1. Observe and hold separate discussions about students, teaching, supervision, and instructional improvement with five different teachers. Write a paper describing each teacher's characteristics and identifying which of the four supervisory approaches discussed in this text would be most appropriate for each teacher.

2. Examine developmental characteristics of an individual for whom you have supervisory responsibility. Use the supervisory approach (nondirective, collaborative, directive informational) that you perceive as the best match for the selected individual. Summarize and evaluate your matched supervision.

3. Examine developmental characteristics of a group for which you have supervisory responsibility. Use the supervisory approach (nondirective, collaborative, or directive informational) that you perceive as the best match for the group. Summarize and evaluate your matched supervision.

Developmental

1. Begin an in-depth investigation of one of the following:
   a. Achievement motivation
   b. Organizational management
   c. Creative problem solving
   d. Job satisfaction

2. Continue to observe differing characteristics of beginning teachers, experienced teachers, and superior teachers. Hypothesize how supervision might be modified to accommodate such differences.

3. Begin to analyze ways in which your needs, concerns, and motivations change in relation to varying situations and changing circumstances.

REFERENCES

Gordon, S. P. 1989. *The theory of developmental supervision: An investigation of the critical aspects.* Unpublished Ed.D. dissertation, University of Georgia.

Gordon, S. P. 1990. Developmental supervision: An exploratory study of a promising model. *Journal of Curriculum and Supervision, 5,* 293–307.

Phillips, M. D., and Glickman, C. D. 1991. Peer coaching: Developmental approach to enhancing teacher thinking. *Journal of Staff Development, 12*(2), 20–25.

Siens, C. M., and Ebmeier, H. 1996. Developmental supervision and the reflective thinking of teach-ers. *Journal of Curriculum and Supervision, 11*(4), 299–319.

Thies-Sprinthall, L. 1984. Promoting the developmental growth of supervising teachers: Theory, research programs, and implications. *Journal of Teacher Education, 35*(3), 53–60.

Zellermayer, M., and Margolin, I. 2005. Teacher educators' professional learning described through the lens of complexity theory. *Teachers College Record, 107*(6), 1275–1304.

SUGGESTED READINGS

Boggiano, A. K., and Pittman, T. (Eds.). 1992. *Achievement and motivation.* Cambridge: Cambridge University Press.

Carr, J. F., Herman, N., and Harris, D. E. 2005. *Creating dynamic schools through mentoring, coaching and collaboration.* Alexandria, VA: Association for Supervision and Curriculum Development.

Ford, M. E. 1992. *Motivating humans.* Newbury Park, CA: Sage.

Gordon, S. P. 1990. Developmental supervision: An exploratory study of a promising model. *Journal of Curriculum and Supervision, 5,* 293–307.

Pajak, E. 2003. *Honoring diverse teaching styles: A guide for supervisors.* Alexandria, VA: Association for Supervision and Curriculum Development.

Phillips, M. D., and Glickman, C. D. 1991. Peer coaching: Developmental approach to enhancing teacher thinking. *Journal of Staff Development, 12*(2), 20–25.

part four
Technical Skills

The supervisor who knows about characteristics of successful schools, the norms that mediate against success, and the ways teacher development contrasts with optimal adult development can begin to formulate a supervisory belief system that becomes a reality when interpersonal and technical skills of supervision are applied in practice.

The previous section matched directive, collaborative, and nondirective interpersonal skills in working with developmental levels of individuals and groups of teachers. Part IV deals with the technical supervisory skills needed in working with teachers to assess, plan, observe, research, and evaluate. Understanding schools and relating well to teachers are necessary components, but technical skills are equally important for accomplishing the tasks of supervision.

chapter 3

Assessing and planning skills are useful to a supervisor in setting goals and activities for himself or herself as well as for others. The chapter begins with personal organization of time—assessing one's current use of professional time and then planning and managing the use of future time. It goes on to focus on techniques for organizational planning for the improvement of instruction.

Assessing and planning are two sides of the same coin. *Assessing* involves determining where you and your staff have been and where you and your staff currently are. *Planning* includes deciding where you want to go and choosing the path you and your staff hope to traverse in order to reach that destination. Until you are certain of the origination and destination of your travel, a map is useless. Once you are certain, a route can be created.

Personal Plans

One of the authors visited a school system to meet with several first-year principals. The purpose of the consultation was for the new principals to talk to the consultant privately about their beginning experiences and to discuss possible changes that might improve their situations.

One principal stated that she was averaging three hours a day observing and participating in classrooms. Her major concern was with the amount of waiting time students were experiencing. Most of her teachers had divided their heterogeneous classrooms into numerous small groups. The principal wondered whether, if certain classes were grouped homogeneously to begin with, there might be fewer groups and less waiting time. The principal and consultant discussed the possible consequences of such a major change and whether less radical changes within the existing instructional program might be better. She left the session with a plan to discuss with the faculty the issue of waiting time and student grouping at the next school meeting.

The second beginning principal said that his major problem was getting out of his office to visit teachers. He wanted to be with his staff but found that paperwork, phone calls, and student discipline referrals kept him trapped in the office. He could find barely an hour a day to talk with staff and visit classrooms. Furthermore, the one-hour time outside the office was often interrupted by the school secretary calling him back with urgent business. The consultant and principal discussed why he was trapped in his office and what changes might be made.

After hearing about the second principal's situation, the consultant realized that the second principal had no more constraints on his time than did the first principal, who was averaging three hours a day visiting classrooms. Both had schools of comparable size in the same neighborhood. They worked for the same superintendent and had identical job responsibilities. Yet one principal was functioning as a supervisor attending to instructional improvement, while the other one was functioning only minimally in the realm of supervision. It seemed that the real difference between the two principals was not their intentions to function as supervisors but their ability to assess and plan professional time to correspond with professional intentions. Let's look at the use of professional time.

Assessing Time

To organize future time, one must assess one's current use of time. This can be done by keeping a daily log for 5 to 10 consecutive schooldays. Those supervisors who keep detailed appointment books might need only to return to their books at midday and at the end of the day to add notations on what actually transpired. Those who do not operate with such planned schedules can keep a daily log to be filled out at midday and at the end of the day. The log should be simple and should require only a few minutes to fill out. It might look like this:

Monday

8:00–8:50	Walked halls, visited teachers and custodians
8:50–9:20	Conference with parent
9:20–9:35	Phone call from textbook salesperson

9:35–10:30	Emergency—covered for sick teacher
10:30–12:00	Worked on class schedules—made 3 phone calls, received 5 phone calls
12:00–12:30	Ate in cafeteria with teachers
12:30–12:35	Wrote morning log
12:35–12:55	Met with textbook salesperson
12:55–1:30	Classroom visitation of Mr. Tadich
1:30–2:30	Meeting at superintendent's office
2:30–3:00	Helped supervise school dismissal
3:00–3:15	Talked with parents
3:15–4:00	Faculty meeting
4:00–4:15	Talked with teachers informally
4:15–4:50	Answered mail
4:50–5:00	Wrote afternoon log

After at least 5 days (preferably 10), the supervisor can analyze his or her current use of time by subsuming daily events in the log under large categories of time consumption. Figure 13.1 shows a sample categorical scheme.

Before transferring the daily log entries onto the time consumption chart, the supervisor should look at his or her job description and determine how his or her time *should* be spent according to job priorities. Which categories of supervisory involvement ought to receive the most attention? The supervisor can indicate approximate percentages according to this ideal use of time. After making a list of ideal time use, he or she can then write in actual time on the consumption charts, add up total time for each category, and then find the actual percentage of time being consumed for each category. He or she then has a comparison between preferred and actual consumption of time. The comparison might look like this:

Preferred Time	*Actual Time*
Paperwork—10%	25%
Phone calls—5%	6%
Private conferences—25%	25%
Students—5%	10%
Parents—3%	5%
Faculty—10%	5%
Auxiliary—3%	1%
Central office—1%	1%
Others—3%	3%

Preferred Time	Actual Time
Group meetings—25%	28%
Students—2%	5%
Parents—5%	2%
Faculty—15%	7%
Auxiliary—1%	6%
Central office—1%	8%
Others—1%	0%

	Monday	Tuesday	Wednesday	Thursday	Friday	Total	%
Paperwork							
Phone calls							
Private conference							
Students							
Parents & community							
Faculty							
Auxiliary personnel							
Central office							
Others							
Group meetings							
Students							
Parents & community							
Faculty							
Auxiliary personnel							
Central office							
Others							
Classroom visits							
School hall and ground visits							
Private time for thinking							
Miscellaneous: emergencies							

FIGURE 13.1 *Supervisor Time Consumption Chart*

Preferred Time	*Actual Time*
Classroom visits—25%	10%
School hall and ground visits—5%	2%
Private time for thinking—3%	1%
Miscellaneous visits—2%	3%

This comparison of time was that of the second principal, who complained about the inability to get out of his office. The comparison showed that he was indeed spending much more time in the office (10 percent preferred, 25 percent actual) and much less time on classroom visits (25 percent preferred, 10 percent actual). Further discrepancies were noted in considerably more time spent in private conferences with students (5 percent preferred, 10 percent actual) and group meetings with central office (1 percent preferred, 8 percent actual).

Changing Time Allocations: Planning

With this information on preferred and actual time use in front of the supervisor, he or she can decide what changes realistically can be made to attain the goal of increasing visitation time with teachers. The supervisor can consider a range of options to increase teacher visitation time. Some possibilities might be:

Paperwork: Delegate more clerical work to secretary, aides, or assistants. Schedule paperwork for uninterrupted hours after school.

Private conferences: Spend less time disciplining students by setting more stringent procedures for teacher referrals of students to office.

Group meetings: See if central office meetings could be shortened or scheduled after school hours.

Classroom visits: Increase classroom visits from one to two periods a day. Set up backup system with secretary to cover all but real emergencies when in the classroom. Schedule visits for a set time each day.

Naturally, this supervisor cannot hope to achieve exact congruence between preferred and actual time use, but he can come closer to his preference. Some time constraints, such as the time of central office meetings, probably are not under the principal's control. There are other factors over which he does have direct control: when he will meet parents, accept phone calls, do paperwork, and accept student referrals. The key to future planning of time use is to accept the limitations that exist and work on those time periods that can be altered.

The first part of a plan to make actual use of time closer to preferred time use is to answer the question: What is the objective? A sample response might be: To double classroom visitation time. The second part of the plan is to answer the question: What actions need to be taken? A sample response might be: (a) Schedule set times each day for two classroom observations, (b) schedule uninterrupted paper-work in two two-hour blocks of time after school. The third part of the plan is to answer the question: When will these activities be done? Sample responses might be: (a) Classroom visits from 9 to 11 A.M. Monday and Wednesday and 1:00 to 2:30 P.M. Tuesday and Thursday, (b) paperwork scheduled for Monday and Friday 3:00 to 5:00 P.M. The fourth part of the plan is to answer the question: What resources will be needed to implement the activities? Sample responses might be: (a) Explain to secretary the need to protect uninterrupted times, (b) discuss with faculty the change and rationale behind my new schedule and arrange classroom visitation schedule. The fifth and final part of the plan is to answer the question: How will the success of the goal be evaluated? A sample response might be: Check whether the new schedule was followed and, after two weeks, review daily log to see if time in classrooms has doubled.

A supervisor could engage in more elaborate planning techniques by developing a flowchart (see Figure 13.2). Although flowcharts look impressive, they are not necessary for simple plans. When looking at more complex planning, however, keep flowcharts in mind. As long as we can answer the five questions dealing with (1) objective, (2) activities, (3) time deadlines, (4) resources, and (5) evaluation, then implementation can proceed. If we cannot answer any of the five questions, the plan is incomplete. For example, if we know our objective but don't know what activities, resources, or evaluation to use, then we are unsure of what to do. However, if we know our objective, activities, and resources but don't know how to evaluate our success, we will be acting without any knowledge of results.

As we move from assessment and planning of personal change to assessment and planning of faculty improvement, the elements to be considered become more complex and planning becomes more detailed. Other techniques for planning may be necessary. Let's use a "wild" analogy. When a naturalist is tracking a single large elephant, she can basically track the beast by herself. But when the naturalist's task expands to tracking three herds of 45 elephants each, then she needs other people, more equipment (radios, binoculars, cameras, jeeps, and helicopters), and an awareness of multiple potential obstacles (ill staff workers, malfunctioning equipment, rough terrain). This analogy can be extended only so far, as supervisors are not naturalists, nor are teaching faculties herds of elephants, but the point is that the larger the organizational effort, the more carefully one needs to account for the sequence and the relationships of activities, resources, and evaluation to overall objectives.

Assessing and Planning within the Organization

The five steps of assessing and planning are the same for both personal and organizational plans. Only the complexity and specificity differ. We might think of assessing and planning as a recipe (Bruce and Grimsley, 1979). A plan for direct

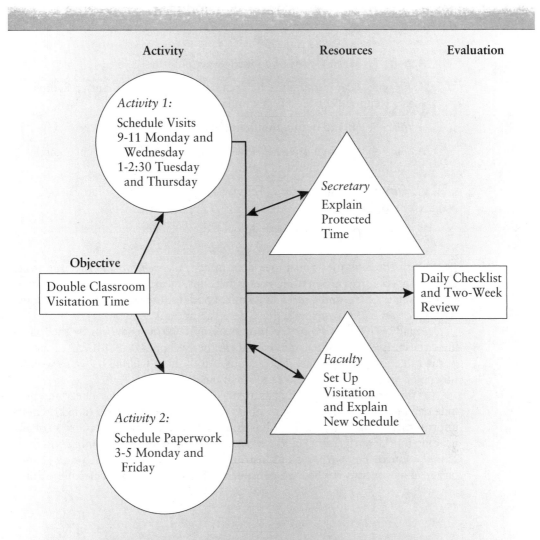

| Activity | Resources | Evaluation |

FIGURE 13.2 *Flowchart for Increasing Classroom Visits*

assistance, professional development, curriculum development, or group development has the same elements as a cooking recipe. *We decide our objective:* "to bake a sweet potato soufflé" (thanks to Ms. Donna Bell for providing this culinary example). Knowing our family's previous history of food preferences, we are confident that if we cook the soufflé correctly, they will enjoy it and we will be held in positive regard for at least 10 minutes. Next, *we determine the activities and when they will take place.*

> *Activity 1:* Mash 6 cups of cooked sweet potatoes.
>
> *Activity 2:* Beat into the mashed potatoes: 4 eggs, 1 cup butter, 2 cups sugar, 1 cup milk, 1 teaspoon vanilla.
>
> *Activity 3:* Spread out in unbuttered pan.
>
> *Activity 4:* Mix in a separate bowl: 1 cup brown sugar, 2/3 cup flour, 1 cup butter, 1 cup chopped pecans.
>
> *Activity 5:* Spread this mix (Activity 4) evenly over the potatoes (Activity 3).
>
> *Activity 6:* Bake at 350° for 1 hour.

With the activities and times determined, *we need to identify resources.* Equipment resources are an oven, measuring cups, measuring spoons, a large bowl, a pan, a mixing fork, and a spreading knife. Food resources are potatoes, eggs, butter, sugar, vanilla, brown sugar, flour, pecans, and milk.

Finally, *we will evaluate the success* of our cooking endeavor by the following criteria: Everyone in our family will eat the sweet potato soufflé. At least two of the three members will ask for seconds. All of them will tell us we're wonderful cooks, and they will volunteer to wash the dishes.

If the supervisor tries acting as a gourmet of instructional cookery and planning recipes for success, all staff members will delight in the soufflé of instructional improvement. The food analogy has run its course (by now, you are probably heading for the refrigerator), and we can turn to assessing and planning within the school context. For purposes of illustration, let's take an example of an elementary reading supervisor who is responsible for developing revised curriculum guides in reading.

Ways of Assessing Need

The first question for the reading supervisor is: What do we hope to accomplish with a new curriculum guide? To answer this question, we need to collect information about the past and present state of reading instruction. The supervisor can use multiple ways of assessing need: (1) eyes and ears, (2) systematic classroom and school observations, (3) official records, (4) review of teacher and student work products, (5) third-party review, (6) written open-ended survey, (7) check and ranking list surveys, (8) the Delphi technique, and (9) nominal group technique.

Eyes and Ears

Talk to teachers, administrators, aides, and anyone else who works directly with the task under consideration. In this case, the supervisor would want to ask teachers and aides individually and in small groups what they believe are the strengths and weaknesses of the curriculum guide. How is it being used? Is it helpful, and in what ways? Where does it break down? When is it not useful?

Systematic Classroom and School Observations

This type of assessment goes beyond informal discussions and observation. It consists of the systematic gathering of quantitative or qualitative observation data. Chapter 14 provides a variety of classroom observation instruments. Such instruments can be used to assist the individual teacher, but also can be used to gather data from many classrooms and identify schoolwide instructional needs. For example, in a schoolwide needs assessment one of the authors coordinated, observers used the same observation instrument to gather data on instructional methods used in classrooms throughout the school. The observers found that most of the teachers in the school relied on lecture and independent seatwork as their primary instructional methods. It was concluded that there was a need for teachers to develop a wider variety of instructional methods. Observations also can be carried out in common areas of the school. In one school experiencing disruptive student behavior during lunch periods, the teachers gathered a variety of observation data on student behaviors in the cafeteria, and based on that data identified needed changes in the school's lunch procedures.

Official Records

Look at any documents that indicate the current use and effect of the task under consideration. In this case, what do reading achievement test scores show? How about diagnostic reading tests? Are students mastering reading skills, or are there certain areas (comprehension, fluency, vocabulary) that are consistently out of line with others? What about the curriculum guide itself? When was it last revised? What recent knowledge about writing curriculum guides, instructional approaches to reading, and reading topics are not reflected in the current curriculum?

Review of Teacher and Student Work Products

Assessors can review teacher and student work products to assess need. Examples of teacher work products are unit and lesson plans, videos of teaching, and teacher portfolios. Examples of student work products include daily assignments, videos of student presentations, student projects, and student portfolios. Samples of work produced by several teachers or students can be reviewed to identify common instructional needs. In some schools, teachers build classroom and school portfolios that can be reviewed to analyze representative teacher and student work products.

Third-Party Review

Having a neutral outside person review the task area can be helpful. The supervisor might contact a university or central office consultant, a graduate doctoral student, or some other person with expertise to do an investigation and write a report. The third-party person should be given a clear description of the task (to look at the strengths and weaknesses of the reading curriculum guides), and care should be taken not to bias the third-party person's judgment. The report can then serve as an additional source of objective knowledge, not tied to any special interest in the forthcoming project.

Written Open-Ended Survey

To document and add to the information already received through eyes and ears and official records, a written survey can be administered. Send out a brief questionnaire that asks teachers, aides, administrators, and parents what they think about the current reading curriculum. Keep the survey brief, and word the questions simply, without education jargon. An example of a survey is found in Figure 13.3.

Explanation: As you may know, this year we are determining changes to be made in our reading curriculum. Would you please take a few minutes to respond to the following questions. Please be frank! We will use the information to rewrite our curriculum guides.

Question 1. What do you think about the current reading curriculum?

Question 2. What are the strengths of the current reading curriculum?

Question 3. What are the weaknesses of the current reading curriculum?

Question 4. What changes do you believe would improve the reading curriculum?

FIGURE 13.3 *Survey of Reading Curriculum*

Check and Ranking List

After gathering ideas of the strengths and weaknesses of the task at hand from many sources, the supervisor can ask staff to rank the ideas. The supervisor can then compile a group frequency and numerical priority for each idea previously mentioned. For example, if—through eyes and ears, official documents, and open-ended surveys—the supervisor has collected a list of ideas about perceived weaknesses of the current reading program, he or she then could disseminate the list back to teachers, aides, and others. The disseminated form might be as shown in Figure 13.4. The supervisor can meet with the staff and show the frequency of numbers assigned to each idea and the average score for each item. Those items receiving frequent low scores and/or with the lowest average scores would be the first to focus on when discussing curriculum revisions. The ranking list can be further refined by having the participants do two separate rankings—first, to see how all the ideas rank, and second, to rerank a shortened list of prioritized ideas.

Delphi Technique

Another written way to prioritize needs is the Delphi technique, developed by the Rand Corporation (Hostrop, 1975; Weaver, 1971; Wilhelm, 2001). The technique, originally intended to forecast future trends, is often used for needs assessment. It is a combination of open-ended survey and ranking. The supervisor sends around a problem statement to staff: "We are looking at revisions in the reading curriculum. Write down what you believe needs to be done." The supervisor retrieves the

Directions: The following are the ideas for possible changes that you have suggested. Please prioritize this list by placing the number 1 next to the idea needing the greatest attention, number 2 next to the item needing the next most attention, and so on, until all items are ranked.

____ Format of the guides.

____ Readability of the guides.

____ Activities to go with curriculum objectives.

____ Objectives and units dealing with reading newspapers.

____ Objectives and units dealing with reading in other subject areas.

____ More phonic and word recognition objectives.

____ Cross-reference units with materials in the classrooms.

____ Cross-reference objects with fourth-grade competency based reading test.

FIGURE 13.4 *Ranking Ideas for Improving Reading Curriculum*

written comments, reproduces everyone's comments, and returns all the comments to the participants. They read the comments and then individually write a synthesis of the various ideas. The supervisor then collects everyone's syntheses and makes a new list of all synthesized ideas. The new list goes back to the participants for ranking. The supervisor collects and computes average and frequency of ratings and then returns the tallies to participants to rerank. This procedure continues until clear priorities emerge.

Nominal Group Technique

The nominal group technique, made popular by Delbecq, Van de Ven, and Gustafson (1975), is an effective way to involve all individuals within large groups of stakeholders in needs assessment and goal setting. The process is outlined here in eight steps:

1. The large group is divided into small groups. Each small group is assigned a facilitator to explain and coordinate the process.
2. Each individual within a small group silently generates and writes perceived needs.
3. In round-robin manner, participants orally share with their small group one perceived need at a time. The facilitator records each idea on a flip chart. At this point, there is no discussion—only a listing of perceived needs.
4. Small-group discussions of each perceived need are led by the facilitators. The purpose of the discussion is clarification of the perceived needs, not debate on their validity.
5. Individuals within each small group rate all of the perceived needs that were listed in step 3. This step usually takes the form of participants assigning each perceived need a numerical value. For example, the facilitator might instruct group members to rate each need from 1 to 5, with an item assigned a value of 1 considered to be unimportant and an item rated a 5 perceived to be an extremely important need.
6. Each small-group facilitator collects all group members' ratings and calculates a mean for each perceived need. The facilitator rewrites the perceived needs in rank order by mean and shares the results with the small group.
7. Each small group submits its list of ranked needs (without the means) for large-group consideration. By preagreement, each small group might submit only its top-ranked needs (perhaps its top five needs) to the large group.
8. A lead facilitator then takes the large group through steps 4 through 6. In the large-group version of step 4, any participant can ask for clarification of any perceived need, with the appropriate small-group facilitator providing the requested clarification. In the whole-group version of step 5, each participant rates all perceived needs presented to the large group. The product of the large-group version of step 6 is a list of organizational needs in rank order.

Analyzing Organizational Needs

Some organizational needs are easily understood and addressed by supervisors and teachers. Others are more complicated. They require analysis to determine their underlying causes before a plan can be formulated. For decades, W. Edwards Deming argued for the use of data displays to examine factors that may contribute to organizational needs and problems. In this section we'll discuss a few types of charts suggested by Deming and his colleagues. We'll do this by applying each chart to a school situation. The words of Mary Walton (1986) should allay any anxiety concerning the use of such charts that the reader without expertise in complex data analysis might be experiencing:

> Some of the most useful statistical tools are neither difficult nor complicated to master. The level of mathematics necessary is no more than a seventh or eighth grader might learn. Several of the basic tools are merely ways of organizing and visually displaying data. In most cases, employees can collect the data and do much of the interpretation, and they are happy to do so because it gives them more responsibility. (p. 94)

Cause and Effect Diagrams

Figure 13.5 is an example of a cause and effect diagram, often referred to as a *fishbone diagram*. In our example, a newly formed staff-development committee has received feedback from teachers throughout the district that recent staff-development programs have been ineffective. Based on a series of interviews with representative groups of teachers, the committee constructed the cause and effect diagram in Figure 13.5.

Four general causes were identified for the ineffective professional development: (1) poor planning, (2) low-quality staff-development sessions, (3) inadequate support for the program, and (4) unsatisfactory program evaluation. Contributing causes within the poor planning category included failure to involve teachers in the planning process, the fact that the professional development plan was not based on teacher needs, and the absence of alternatives for staff from different grade levels, content areas, and specialty areas.

The poor quality of the staff-development sessions was ascribed to the fact that too many teachers were present, each session was a one-shot workshop unrelated to the other workshops in the program, and the workshop presentations were of poor quality. The workshops were perceived to be substandard because the outside presenters did not have a good understanding of the school culture or the purposes of the program, and their presentations were too abstract to evoke teacher interest.

Problems with support included a lack of funds to purchase instructional materials necessary to implement ideas introduced in the workshops and a failure to provide support for teachers attempting to transfer workshop concepts to the classroom. Finally, the committee found that the district's evaluation of the

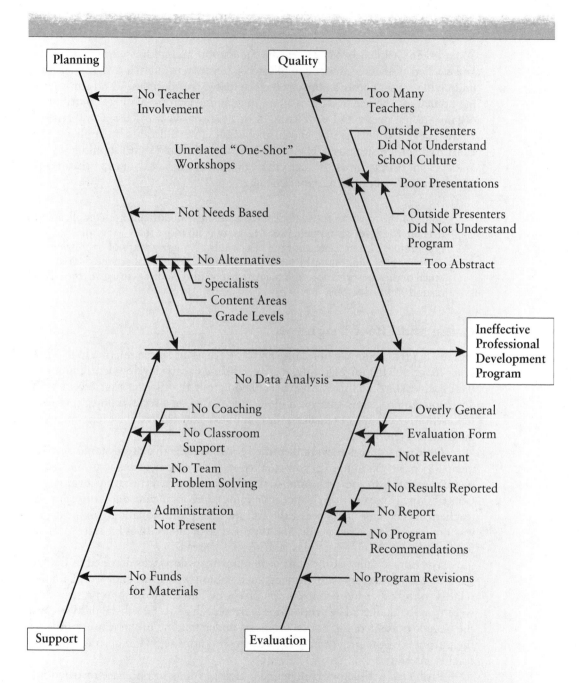

FIGURE 13.5 *Cause and Effect Diagram*

program had been inadequate. The evaluation forms used by the district were the same ones used for all staff-development workshops; they were not relevant to the specific content of the workshops being assessed. Additionally, the wording of the evaluation questions was so general that teachers were not sure what the questions were asking. Since no formal analysis of evaluation data took place, no information on program outcomes was available and no program revisions were made. The "anatomy of a failure" depicted in Figure 13.5 is not the most pleasant project the planning committee could have undertaken. Yet, the completed diagram was a valuable tool in planning future professional-development programs.

Flowcharts

A flowchart can be used to review a process when either the process or conflicting perceptions of the process are resulting in unmet needs. When different parties involved in a process draw their own flowcharts, the charts often are dissimilar. Figure 13.6 shows a flowchart tracking what happens from the time a student is sent to the office for misbehavior until the student returns to class. This chart was drawn by the principal's secretary. Flowcharts of the same process drawn by the principal, the teacher, and the student might be very different from the secretary's and each other!

Pareto Charts

A Pareto chart illustrates in descending frequency of size those factors that cause a need or problem. Displaying the relative impact of causal factors gives planners information to help them set priorities and allocate resources. Figure 13.7 illustrates a Pareto chart with bars showing the percentage of students dropping out of a senior high school for each of several reasons. Above the bars, a cumulative percentage line runs across the chart. This data would be valuable to a planning team designing a dropout prevention program.

Planning

After assessing and prioritizing needs and identifying causes, planning proceeds. Techniques of planning discussed in this section include affinity diagrams, impact analysis charts, and Gantt charts.

Affinity Diagrams

Let us assume that a needs assessment has identified a number of specific needs, with many of those needs appearing to be related to each other. An affinity diagram is a way of clustering needs, and identifying broad goals that address a set of related needs. One way to begin the building of an affinity diagram is to list each

FIGURE 13.6 *Flowchart*

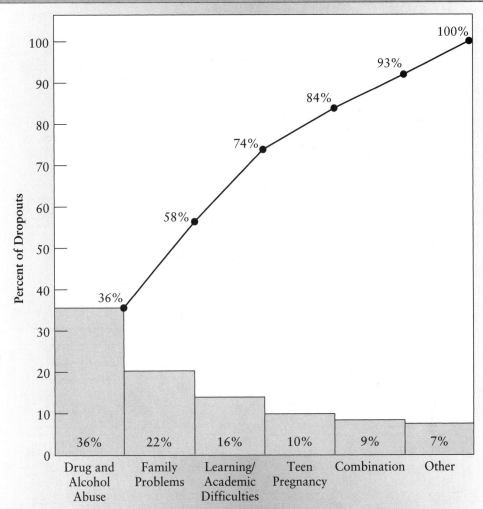

FIGURE 13.7 *Pareto Chart*

identified need on a separate card or post-it. Later in the chapter Figure 13.10 displays results of a curriculum needs assessment. In the assessment, teachers, parents, and community members stated that students should attain each of the outcomes in Figure 13.8. The affinity diagram in Figure 13.9 clusters the curriculum needs and identifies a broad goal common to each cluster. Enfolding specific needs

Ethical Values	Math Skills	Commitment to Democratic Principles	Problem-Solving Skills
Commitment to Wellness	Acceptance of Others' Cultures	Understanding of History's Effects on the Present	Positive Self-Concept
Creative Expression	Health Awareness	Understanding of Basic Scientific Concepts	Commitment to Community Service
Collaborative Skills	Self-Monitoring Skills	Writing Skills	Physical Fitness
Reading Skills	Critical Thinking Skills	Inquiry Skills	Persistence
Global Awareness	Work Ethic	Technological Literacy	Emotional Intelligence
Ability to Express Oneself Orally	Commitment to Social Justice	Interpersonal Skills	Geographic Literacy

FIGURE 13.8 *Curriculum Needs, to Be Clustered in Affinity Diagram*

INTRAPERSONAL DEVELOPMENT

Ethical Values

Positive Self-Concept

Self-Monitoring Skills

Persistence

Work Ethic

Emotional Intelligence

HEALTH AND FITNESS

Commitment to Wellness

Physical Fitness

Health Awareness

BASIC KNOWLEDGE AND SKILLS

Math Skills

Understanding of History's Effects on the Present

Understanding of Basic Scientific Concepts

Writing Skills

Reading Skills

Technological Literacy

Ability to Express Oneself Orally

Geographic Literacy

COGNITIVE DEVELOPMENT

Inquiry Skills

Creative Expression

Problem-Solving Skills

Critical Thinking Skills

SOCIAL DEVELOPMENT

Commitment to Democratic Principles

Commitment to Community Service

Interpersonal Skills

Acceptance of Others' Cultures

Commitment to Social Justice

Global Awareness

Collaborative Skills

FIGURE 13.9 *Affinity Diagram*

within larger categories enables the planning team to focus on a few broad goals, while retaining information on specific needs.

Impact Analysis Charts

Impact analysis charts are usually constructed early in the planning process. Their purpose is to assist planners in projecting who and what a potential program or change will affect and what the effects might be. In Figure 13.10, triangles represent people and things a revised reading curriculum would impact. Predicted effects are symbolized by rectangles. Impact analysis charts can become far more

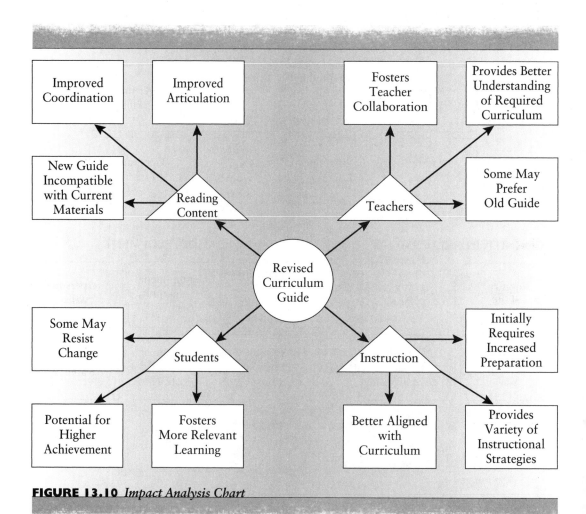

FIGURE 13.10 *Impact Analysis Chart*

complex than the example in Figure 13.10 (the more ambitious the goals, the more extensive the chart). Building and discussing impact analysis charts can help planners to create a "conceptual map" of areas they want to address during the planning process. They can also help planners to include objectives, activities, and evaluation procedures in their formal plan that they might otherwise neglect.

Gantt Charts

A Gantt chart is simply a graph that portrays the beginning and completion dates of each activity involved in completing the overall task (Bishop, 1976). As shown in Figure 13.11, the activities for revising the curriculum guides are placed on the left-hand side of the chart. The beginning and ending time for each activity is shown by a white bar across the time line. The supervisor can refer to the chart at any time to check on the progress of the project and be reminded of what groups and what subtasks should be receiving his or her attention.

Models Combining Assessment and Planning

Thus far we have considered assessment and planning as separate entities. Three models that combine these functions are force field analysis, the PDSA cycle, and strategic planning. All three models attempt to address the dynamic, unpredictable nature of complex organizations. In recent years these three models have been applied to education.

Force Field Analysis

This process can help educators define goals, analyze competing forces, and plan how to bring about needed change. A force field analysis consists of 10 phases.

1. Describe the desired state of affairs (what should be).
2. Describe the current state of affairs (what is).
3. Describe the gap between the desired and current state of affairs.
4. Describe the restraining forces: those forces that resist movement toward the desired state.
5. Describe the driving forces: those forces that can assist movement toward the desired state.
6. Select from the restraining forces those that will be addressed during change efforts. Restraining forces that both are important and capable of being weakened are chosen.
7. Select from the driving forces those that will be addressed during change efforts. Driving forces that both are important and capable of being strengthened are those chosen.

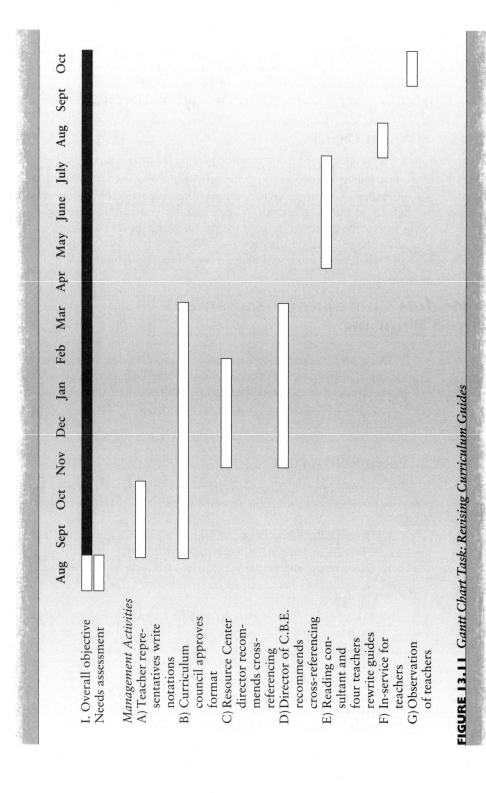

FIGURE 13.11 *Gantt Chart Task: Revising Curriculum Guides*

8. For each restraining force chosen in phase 6, identity actions that will weaken the restraining force.

9. For each driving force chosen in phase 7, identify actions that will strengthen the driving force.

10. Integrate and sequence the actions chosen in phases 8 and 9 to create a comprehensive action plan for moving from the current state of affairs to the desired state of affairs. Include a plan for evaluating the effects of the action plan, and a time line for implementing the action plan and evaluation.

A force field analysis is most effective if the descriptions of the desired and current state of affairs as well as restraining and driving forces are based on data gathered during the force field analysis, rather than the planners' perceptions alone.

PDSA Cycle

W. Edward Deming's (1986) popular "14 points for managers," "seven deadly sins," and data-based approach to quality control (see Walton, 1986) have had enormous impact in Japan and North America. Educators have jumped on the total quality management (TQM) bandwagon, adapting the ideas of Deming and others associated with TQM to teaching and school leadership (see Bonstingl, 1992a, 1992b; Brandt, 1992). Full discussions of Deming's management method and TQM are beyond the scope of this chapter. However, one process with its origins in the total quality movement is especially relevant to our discussion of assessment and planning. That process is the PDSA cycle (alternative versions of the process are referred to as the *Shewhart, Deming,* or *PDCA cycle*).

The PDSA cycle consists of *planning, doing, studying,* and *acting*. The cyclical relationship of these four stages is illustrated in Figure 13.12. In the *planning*

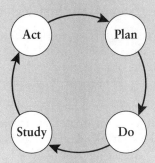

FIGURE 13.12 *PDSA Cycle*

stage, assessment and planning take place. In the *doing* stage, the plan is implemented, usually on a small scale. In the *studying* stage, data are collected on the implementation process and its effects. In the *acting* stage, the data are analyzed and conclusions about strengths and weaknesses of the plan and its implementation are drawn. A new cycle then begins with the formulation of a revised plan. The PDSA cycle is the heart and soul of "continuous quality improvement."

Strategic Planning

Strategic planning assumes that a plan's implementation and results will be affected by the organization's internal and external environments, and that it is impossible to completely predict and control the future in our rapidly changing world. There are many versions of strategic planning (see, for example, Dyson, 1990; Kaufman, 1991) as well as applications to education (Cook, 1990; Kaufman, 1992; Shapiro and Nunez, 2001; Moore, 2004). A nine-step strategic planning process is presented below:

1. *Identify common beliefs.* This first stage of strategic planning becomes the foundation of everything that follows. Cook (1990) discusses the statement of beliefs:

   It is a formal expression of the organization's fundamental values: its ethical code, its overriding convictions, its inviolate commitments. Essentially, it describes the moral character of the organization. That means that the statement of beliefs of an organization must represent a composite, a distillation, of the personal values of those who make up the organization. (p. 89)

2. *Identify the organization's vision.* The organization's vision is its scenario of what *should be* in the future. For a school district or school, this includes such things as the abilities and attitudes graduates should possess. A vision statement should focus on intended outcomes, not processes. One common visioning strategy the authors have found successful is to ask planners what characteristics they would like their next kindergarten class to possess when those students graduate from high school.

3. *Identify the organization's mission.* A mission statement is a summary (usually one sentence in length) of the organization's purpose. The mission is based on the organization's beliefs and vision. It becomes the focus of all remaining phases of the strategic planning process.

4. *Formulate policies.* In relationship to strategic planning, policies are ground rules that will apply to the remaining phases of the planning process, the content of the strategic plan, and its implementation. An example of a strategic policy is "All action plans will be based on the best interest of the school district's students." Another example is "No new curricula or instructional programs will be established without the agreement of at least three-fourths of

the teachers who will have responsibility for implementing the new curriculum or program." Strategic policies become the boundaries within which future planning and change take place.

5. *Conduct external analysis.* This phase consists of analysis of demographic, economic, political, social, and technological factors in the external environment. Current conditions and predicted futures concerning each of these five factors are analyzed. The purpose of external analysis is to identify external *threats* to the organization's mission as well as *opportunities* for external assistance or collaboration in carrying out the mission. Threats or opportunities within each of the five factors are identified.

6. *Conduct internal analysis.* The internal analysis consists of examination of such factors as school governance, culture, leadership, staff expertise and commitment, curriculum and instruction, student characteristics, and student achievement. As with external analysis, both current conditions and future predictions within each factor are examined. The purpose of internal analysis is to determine the organization's *strengths* and *weaknesses,* especially in respect to its mission.

7. *State objectives.* The objectives are tied directly to the organization's mission. In other words, if all of the organization's objectives are met, then in all probability the mission will be achieved. Like the vision statement, the objectives focus on outcomes, not processes. Strategic objectives should be student centered, few in number, specific, measurable, and clearly stated.

8. *Develop and analyze alternative strategies.* At this point in the strategic planning process, action teams can be formed for each objective. After reviewing decisions made during the first seven phases of the process, action teams develop and analyze alternative strategies for reaching their assigned objective. Alternative strategies are then compared. One type of comparison is carried out by testing each strategy for consistency with the organization's beliefs, vision, mission, and policies. Another type of comparison involves considering the feasibility of each strategy in light of external threats and opportunities as well as internal strengths and weaknesses. A third way to compare strategies is to create scenarios of each strategy being implemented, projecting the strategic effects on the organization and its mission.

9. *Design action plans.* Based on the analysis from phase 8, action teams choose the strategies most likely to achieve the objectives, and sequence those strategies into action plans. The action plans involve time lines for implementation as well as provisions for monitoring progress and outcomes. Since the effects of any plan are not completely predictable, strategic action plans have built-in contingencies—backup plans enabling adaptation to changing external or internal conditions. During implementation of action plans, periodic reviews are carried out to determine if alternative strategies are needed.

Strategic plans can be comprehensive district or school-based plans (macroplans) or specific programs (microplans). In school-based strategic planning, care must be taken to assure that the school and district's beliefs, visions, missions, and policies (phases 1–4) are consistent. Specific program planning begins with a review of the organization's existing beliefs, vision, mission, and policy, with actual program planning beginning in phase 5.

Cautions Concerning Planning

Postmodern theory warns us that the rational analyses, predictions, controls, and measurements that make up conventional planning often are inconsistent with the multiplicity of realities and competing interests that make up the real world. Chaos theory reminds us that, unlike traditional plans, complex systems such as schools do not consist of simple cause and effect relationships, are affected by seemingly unrelated variables inside and outside the system, and are subject to unpredictable events and changes (a full discussion of chaos theory and its implications for schools is presented in Chapter 21).

Do these cautions mean that we throw out the planning tools discussed in this chapter and simply "wing it" regarding instructional improvement? No, but they do mean that we change our traditional concept of planning to provide for the following:

- Planning that is centered on people—students, teachers, parents, and community members—not on planning tools and documents (the tools and documents should be used in the service of people)
- Decentralized planning in which the supervisor becomes the coordinator of stakeholder teams actively involved in the planning process
- Diversity, in terms of both the groups represented and the ideas considered in the planning process
- Regular interaction among planners, and between planners and those who will be affected by the plan
- A recognition by planners of the complexity, multiplicity, and nonlinearity inherent in the school organization
- The consideration of alternative futures for the school community
- Improvement plans with built-in flexibility, allowing a fair degree of spontaneity and exploration during implementation
- Provisions for continuous and critical assessment of the plan during implementation
- An understanding that the important thing is the goal the plan is intended to reach, not the plan itself; and a willingness to revise the plan when appropriate

SUMMARY

This chapter has explained the complementary nature of assessment and planning for realizing a vision about instructional improvement. It began with examining ways to assess and plan supervisory time. The next topic was assessing and planning organizational change. Assessment techniques discussed were: eyes and ears, systematic classroom and school observations, official records, review of teacher and student work products, third-party review, written open-ended surveys, check and ranking lists, the Delphi technique, and the nominal group technique. Ways of determining the underlying causes of needs discussed were: cause and effect diagrams, flowcharts, and Pareto charts. Planning techniques discussed were: affinity diagrams, impact analysis charts, and Gantt charts. Techniques described as combining assessment and planning were force field analysis, the PDSA cycle, and strategic planning. The last section discussed when to use extensive written and formalized plans. Assessing and planning skills are generic; they help us to organize our own professional life as well as organize instructional improvement programs that involve many people. Assessing and planning enable us to take stock of present conditions, analyze consequences, and choose events, activities, and resources.

PRACTITIONER REFLECTION

Creative Double Think—Holding Two Contradicting Ideas and Making It Work

Sherrie Gibney-Sherman, *Associate Superintendent for Instruction, Jefferson City Schools*

Never have educators had to be publicly accountable to so many audiences in so many ways. The pressure is on all of us to sharpen the focus until there is a shared vision on what is being taught, what is being learned, and if learning is not taking place, what measures need to be enacted. The cycle is clear. The beliefs, the pathways, and the commitment, however, often are not. The uncertainty we feel is rooted in this conflict: On the one hand, we want to work toward shared national goals and be successful in the eyes of the public; on the other hand, we want to be true to what we know and believe about students, teachers, and learning. Ideally these two strands align closely with each other but in reality individual teachers have their own thoughts of what it means to be successful in the classroom and these ideas do not always mesh neatly with externally imposed standards.

Everything we do now, it seems, lines up with the federal obligation of the No Child Left Behind Act (NCLB). The state of Georgia has made its mark in the sand regarding how local school districts must document that they are indeed making adequate yearly progress (AYP) with all 10 subgroups of students served: Black, White, Indian, Asian, Hispanic, multiracial, English Language Learners (ELL), students with disabilities (SWD), economically disadvantaged students, and of course all students.

Adequate yearly progress for Georgia school districts is measured by the *Criterion Referenced Competency Test (CRCT)* in grades 3 through 8 in the areas of reading, language arts, and mathematics, and in grade 11 by the *Georgia High School Graduation Test (GHSGT)* in the areas of language arts and mathematics. In addition, schools are held accountable for graduation rates, attendance (or other optional achievement areas), and participation rates in the AYP testing program. The formulas for computing success for all these variables are convoluted and arcane. They frequently lead to inconsistent results, where for example, a district with very high test scores might barely make AYP (or not make it at all) while another district with much lower scores is deemed adequate. This might be seen as a strength of the AYP program in that it recognizes that districts are starting from very different places. But, it can also lead to cynicism and frustration on the part of educators and the public as they try to understand exactly what is being measured.

In Jefferson City Schools, where I work, as in many school districts around the country, our first challenge was a change in mindset. We had to embrace standards and accountability and understand that we were going to have to do it in the terms laid out by NCLB. We could no longer rely purely on our home-grown standards and measures. In short, whether we liked it or not, we had to learn how to play the AYP game. That was not necessarily a bad thing. Certainly our district and districts everywhere had to acknowledge that schoolwide success meant more than overall averages. It meant that we had to look honestly at the achievement of all the subgroups that make up our school district.

One thing that the NCLB legislation has done is to bring national attention to who is making it and who is not. The clarity, however, is defined in legislative terms, and we have left the door open for this to happen. Although local improvement efforts were often inspired and effective, there was very little consistency in accountability from one classroom to the next, much less from school to school or from district to district. Maybe it was inevitable, because schools and teachers are so stubbornly autonomous and unique in their outlook, but it is also true that we have failed in the past to disaggregate student achievement data so that there is no question about who is making it, who needs help, who is getting help, and who isn't.

Developing a shared vision for accountability has taken our district several years and the process is continually being refined. The first task was to be clear about the target. Once our teachers began to move, in some cases begrudgingly, toward an acceptance that we had to meet outside measures of success, they had to turn their attention to the specific practices in their own classrooms. For years, in the absence of firm outside standards, teachers developed—and took great pride in—their own idiosyncratic ways of determining whether or not their students were "making it."

The state of Georgia has changed the rules of that game by creating the Georgia Performance Standards (GPS) in all disciplines, kindergarten through grade 12. This is an enormous undertaking that will take at least 10 years to develop and implement completely. Even so, teachers are expected to understand, teach, and be measured by these partially formed standards. Many teachers embrace the idea of teaching to performance standards even while they are frustrated by being held accountable for a target that is still being developed. Because these teachers find themselves aiming at a shifting target that is moving while they are shooting at it, there is a temptation to go back to the old tried and true way of teaching and assessing rather than to make the leap to the new standards. However, love these new standards or not, teachers do not have a choice.

In our own district, we had to begin by asking, "How can we take what we know about good teaching and learning, apply that to the new learning standards, and move forward?" First, conflicting issues had to be acknowledged. Once the issues were acknowledged, a path was cleared to understand the new learning task for all students. Next, we had to understand our student data and use the data to understand what learning was taking place on AYP terms. Shared district goals had to be established followed by school and grade-level goals for all sub-groups of students. No longer would anecdotal experience be sufficient; hard, honest data had to drive our practice.

Strategies had to be developed that would support the new targets. Formative and summative assessments were established and agreed upon by teachers. Plans for students who were not successful also had to be established as well as plans for those who exceeded expectations. Communication with all stakeholders was another key issue—there was (and still is) a lot of uncertainty about all of the implications of AYP. Thus, plans for sharing this information with students, parents, and educators had to be developed. New professional learning opportunities, ones that were better focused on student learning goals, were created. And, of course, more time for teachers to discuss and share student outcomes had to be created.

We are in the accountability game now. We have to play or lose trust in the ability of public education to succeed. That is the cycle, but the barrier of commitment, belief, and pathway is an on-going challenge. This district has enjoyed high test scores for many years. The challenges of growth (47 percent growth in the student body in the last four years), the closer examination of the achievement of subgroups of students, and the ultimate federal goal of having all students, regardless of their abilities, achieving on grade level by the year 2014 makes the task of staying the course harder if not unrealistic. We have many high-achieving students in our district, but, like everyone, we are asking, "How can anyone expect all students, regardless of their abilities, to be on grade level by 2014?" It feels like the emperor without any clothes marching right on through the parade holding a banner that all students will be on grade level—regardless of their innate abilities. Some folks, and not just the most cynical among our group, are openly asking these questions.

Communicating goals and outcomes to our board of education has taken on more importance—and pressure—than ever before. Our board of education is very interested in our school district staying off "the bad list." It is critical that all school employees understand what "the list" means and how close we are to being on the list, despite the high test scores.

We also must now understand that we are in this together. No longer can individual schools within a district rest easy because they are "making it." In the past, each school in our district did its own individual self-study and accreditation reporting. This left many schools isolated and worried only about their own program, rather than the success of the whole district. With our new awareness that the failure of a single school in a district renders the entire district as "not adequate," our district changed. In the past year we went from a school-by-school accreditation process to a districtwide application process for accreditation (through the Southern Association of Colleges and Schools—SACS). The district process forces district-level staff to align resources to support schools and it compels schools to communicate clearly who is succeeding, to explain why or why not, and to point to resources that are needed for success.

Where are we today? The tragic events surrounding Hurricane Katrina were a painful reminder that, within single schools, districts, or communities, there are wide disparities in access to education and other resources. The event was also a good metaphor and reminder that "doing OK" by most folks is not good enough anymore. Some pointed with pride to the fact that 80 percent of the city of New Orleans was evacuated and saved before the storm. What about the other 20 percent? Those are people who did not make it out. Would we want our families to be part of the 20 percent left behind? The same equation applies to schools: It is no longer all right if half or most of the students are succeeding; *all* students need to make it. Should we want any less, even if we know it just might not ever happen? Holding the balance of these two thoughts is the conundrum of planning and assessment in this day of NCLB.

EXERCISES

Academic

1. Prepare a written summary of the major suggestions of one writer on time management. Discuss how the suggestions can be applied to educational supervision.

2. Describe and compare two program assessment processes successfully used in a public school system and not discussed in this book.

3. Locate outside literature on the Deming management method (such discussions may be included in the literature under the topics "Total Quality Improvement," "Total Quality Control," or "Total Quality Management"). Write a paper reviewing Deming's ideas and discussing how they could be or have been applied to educational assessment and planning. Include at least three outside references in your paper.

Field

1. After using the methods suggested in this chapter for assessing your work time (daily log, time consumption chart, comparison of preferred priorities to actual time spent), write out a personal plan for making actual use of time closer to preferred use. Be sure each of the five questions in a personal improvement plan is answered. Implement your plan over a period of two weeks. At the end of the implementation period, prepare a written evaluation of your plan.

2. Write out a personal work improvement objective. Prepare a flowchart as an aid for reaching your objective. Carry out the activities outlined in your flowchart; then evaluate whether your objective has been met. Write a report analyzing your improvement plan and its implementation. Include a discussion of the utility of the flowchart as part of your improvement effort.

3. Use at least one of the six ways of assessing need within an organization (eyes and ears, official records, third-party review, written open-ended survey, Delphi

technique, nominal group technique) to determine needs within an educational program. Write a report on your assessment. Include a discussion of the assessment process and the needs that were discovered.

4. Participate in a group in which an educational improvement plan is created, using at least one of the following planning techniques: (a) Gantt charts; (b) flow-charting; (c) the PDSA cycle; (d) strategic planning. Prepare a written report on the experience.

5. Interview a leader in business, industry, government, or the military who has had extensive experience with one of the planning techniques listed in the previous exercise. Prepare a report on your interview, including a description of how the technique is used in the interviewee's field and a discussion of how it might be modified for use in an educational setting.

Developmental

1. Use a Gantt chart to plan a long-range personal project. Carry the project through to completion.

2. Volunteer for participation in an educational planning process.

3. Begin an in-depth exploration of what prominent authors in educational supervision have to say about educational assessment and planning.

REFERENCES

Bishop, L. J. 1976. *Staff development and instructional development: Plans and procedures.* Boston: Allyn and Bacon.

Bostingl, J. J. 1992a. The total quality classroom. *Educational Leadership, 49*(6), 67.

Bostingl, J. J. 1992b. *Schools of quality: An introduction to total quality management in education.* Alexandria, VA: Association for Supervision and Curriculum Development.

Brandt, R. (Ed.). 1992. *Educational Leadership, 50.* Theme issue on "Improving School Quality."

Bruce, R. E., and Grimsley, E. E. 1979. Course supplementary reading—Introduction to supervision. Unpublished manuscript, University of Georgia.

Cook W. J. 1990. *Bill Cook's strategic planning for America's schools* (rev. ed.). Arlington, VA: American Association of School Administrators.

Delbecq, A. L., Van de Ven, A. H., and Gustafson, D. H. 1975. *Group techniques for program planning.* Glenview, IL: Scott, Foresman.

Deming, W. E. 1986. *Out of the crisis.* Cambridge, MA: Massachusetts Institute of Technology.

Dyson, R. G. 1990. *Strategic planning: Models and analytical techniques.* Chichester, England: John Wiley and Sons.

Hostrop, R. W. 1975. *Managing education for results* (2nd ed.). Homewood, CA: ETC Publications.

Kaufman, R. 1991. *Strategic planning: An organizational guide.* Glenview, IL: Scott, Foresman.

Kaufman, R. 1992. *Mapping educational success: Strategic thinking and planning for school administrators.* Newbury Park, CA: Corwin.

Moore, E. A. 2004. Strategic planning during times of uncertainties and opportunities. *The Agricultural Education Magazine, 77*(3), 23–25.

Shapiro, L. T., and Nunez, W. J. 2001. Strategic planning synergy. *Planning for Higher Education, 30*(1), 27–34.

Walton, M. 1986. *The Deming management method.* New York: Putnam.

Weaver, W. T. 1971. The Delphi forecasting method. *Kappan, 52,* 267.

Wilhelm, W. J. 2001. Alchemy of the oracle: The Delphi technique. *Delta Pi Epsilon Journal, 43*(1), 6–26.

SUGGESTED READINGS

Bonstingl, J. J. 1992. *Schools of quality.* Alexandria, VA: Association for Supervision and Curriculum Development.

Cook, W. J. 1990. *Bill Cook's strategic planning for America's schools.* Arlington, VA: American Association of School Administrators.

Goodlad, J. I. 2000. Educational renewal and the arts. *Arts Education Policy Review, 101*(4), 11–14.

Holcomb, E. L. 1996. *Asking the right questions: Tools and techniques for teamwork.* Thousand Oaks, CA: Sage.

Kaufman, R. 1991. *Strategic planning plus.* Glenview, IL: Scott, Foresman.

Kaufman, R. 1995. *Mapping educational success.* Thousand Oaks, CA: Corwin.

Kaufman, R., and Zahn, D. 1993. *Quality management plus: The continuous improvement of education.* Newbury Park, CA: Corwin.

Marzano, R. J., Waters, T., and McNulty, B. A. 2005. *School leadership that works: From research to results.* Alexandria, VA: Association for Supervision and Curriculum Development.

Schmoker, M. J., and Wilson, R. B. 1993. *Total quality education: Profiles of schools that demonstrate the power of Deming's management principals.* Bloomington, IN: Phi Delta Kappa.

chapter 14

Observing Skills

Consider the classroom shown in Figure 14.1. If you were an observer of this classroom, what would you say is happening? Of course, one illustration is not enough basis for an observation, but pretend you are seeing this episode for an entire class period. Could you say that the students have behavior problems, discipline is lax, the teacher is not responding to the students' interests, or the teacher is lecturing too much?

If your observations are similar to those listed here, then you have fallen into the *interpretation trap,* which is the downfall of most attempts to help people improve their performance. How would you respond if your evaluator—say, the superintendent of schools—observed you conducting a faculty meeting and later told you that teachers lack respect for you? Your response probably would be a combination of defensiveness ("It isn't so"), confusion ("What do you mean?"), and quiet hostility ("Who are you to say that to me?"). The superintendent has inadvertently turned you against him or her, and compliance on your part will be grudging at best.

Observation is a two-part process—first *describing* what has been seen and then *interpreting* what it means. The mind almost simultaneously processes a visual image, integrates that image with previously stored images related to satisfactory and unsatisfactory experiences, and ascribes a value or meaning to that image. If a student yawns, our mind signals "boredom." If a teacher yells at students, our

FIGURE 14.1 *Classroom Picture*

mind registers "losing control." A judgment derives from an image or a description of events. We must be aware of splitting that almost simultaneous process, of separating description from interpretation. When we lose the description of the event and retain only the interpretation, we create communication difficulties and obstacles to improvement.

Let's return to the superintendent's interpretation that "teachers lack respect." How much different would your response have been if the description behind the interpretation had been shared with you: "I saw that 6 of the 15 teachers arrived late to your faculty meeting." You could agree that, indeed, 6 members did arrive late; however, you might disagree with the interpretation of lack of respect as arbitrary. You could not only accept that 6 members had been late but also do something about it. You cannot do anything about lack of respect because you don't know what needs to be changed. On the other hand, you can correct lateness and eventually improve the superintendent's interpretation of the teachers' respect.

Sharing the description of events is the forerunner of professional improvement. Interpretation leads to resistance. When both parties can agree on what events occurred, they are more likely to agree on what needs to be changed.

Remember that if the goal of supervision is to enhance teachers' thought and commitment about improving classroom (and school) practice, observations should be used as a base of information to create an instructional dialogue between supervisor and teacher. Using description first when talking to a teacher about his or her classroom creates an instructional dialogue. Providing interpretations and evaluative statements first ushers in defensiveness, combativeness, or resentment in the teacher and stifles discussion (see Glickman and Jones, 1986).

Differentiating description from interpretation in observation is so crucial for instructional improvement that we need to refer back to our original illustration of the classroom (Figure 14.1). Look at the picture again and tell what you now see going on. You might say that there are three students looking away from the teacher and talking to each other while the teacher stands in front of the room calling on a student in the front row. Can we agree that this is happening? Probably so, and thus we can *later* judge the rightness or wrongness of the event in regard to student learning. The teacher can more readily change the events of three students talking to each other and two others looking away than he or she can change being "a poor classroom manager."

Formative Observation Instruments Are Not Summative Evaluation Instruments

A formative observation instrument used to describe what is occurring in a classroom (consistent with what teacher and supervisor agreed to focus on and later discuss) is a means for professional growth and instructional improvement. Therefore, the use of a formative observation instrument is conditioned on prior agreement about what is most worthy of learning by that teacher in that classroom—whether the interest is derived from a desire to know more about himself or herself as a teacher, attempting a particular instructional model, experimenting with a new practice or strategy, or struggling with a problem or weakness. A summative evaluation instrument, on the other hand, is an externally imposed, uniformly applied measure, intended to judge all teachers on similar criteria to determine their worthiness, merit, and competence as employees. Distinctions between summative and formative evaluation are discussed in detail in Chapter 15.

Ways of Describing

There are many ways to record descriptions. At the end of this chapter, there are multiple references to various observation methods and instruments. An observation instrument is a tool for organizing and recording different categories of classroom life. It can be as simple as a single category or as complex as a matrix of dozens of possible coded combinations. For example, an instrument can be used to count the displays on a classroom wall or to record the hundreds of students' and teachers' verbal and nonverbal interactions.

We will first look at quantitative observations, including categorical instruments, performance indicator instruments, visual diagramming, and space utilization. The second section will deal with qualitative observations, including verbatim, detached open-ended narrative, participant open-ended observation, focused questionnaire observation, and educational criticism. Finally, we will discuss tailored observations—quantitative or qualitative observations designed to gather data on specific teacher concerns.

Quantitative Observations

Quantitative observations are ways of measuring classroom events, behaviors, and objects. Definitions and categories must be precise. Eventually, the observations can be used for statistical operations.

Categorical Frequency Instrument

A categorical instrument is a form that defines certain events or behaviors that can be checked off at frequency intervals and then counted. Figure 14.2 is a categorical instrument that measures the frequency of different types of questions asked by the teacher. The seven categories of teacher questions are based on Bloom's taxonomy (the taxonomy is explained in Chapter 19). By dividing the number of questions in each category by the total number of questions asked by the teacher

Question Category	Tally	Total	Percent
Evaluation		0	0
Synthesis	/	1	5
Analysis	/	1	5
Application	//	2	10
Interpretation	///	3	15
Translation	////	4	20
Memory	~~////~~ ////	9	45
Total of Questions Asked = 20			

FIGURE 14.2 *Teacher Questions*

during the lesson, the observer can calculate the percent of total questions each category represents.

Other classroom topics can be observed with categorical instruments. For example, one can focus on on-task and off-task behavior. To complete the instrument in Figure 14.3, the observer begins a sweep of the classroom every 5 minutes. During each sweep, the observer focuses on each student for approximately 20 seconds,

Student	Time When Sweep Began							
	9:00	9:05	9:10	9:15	9:20	9:25	9:30	9:35
Andrew	A	C	D	E	E	A	B	B
Shawn G.	A	A	D	E	E	A	C	B
Maria	A	A	D	E	E	C	B	B
Sam	I	F	F	E	F	A	B	C
Barbara	H	F	D	E	E	F	F	B
Angie	C	G	G	C	E	G	G	G
Jeff	A	A	C	E	E	A	B	B
Jessica	F	F	D	E	E	A	B	E
Shawn L.	A	A	D	E	H	H	B	B
Chris	F	F	D	E	E	A	B	C
Michele	A	A	D	E	H	H	B	B
Mark	A	I	I	F	I	I	I	F
Melissa	C	A	D	E	E	C	H	B
John	J	A	J	I	J	J	J	J
Rolanda	A	C	D	E	E	A	B	F

Key

A = on task, listening/watching

B = on task, writing

C = on task, speaking

D = on task, reading

E = on task, hands-on activity

F = off task, passive

G = off task, doing work for another class

H = off task, listening to others

I = off task, disturbing others

J = off task, playing

FIGURE 14.3 *Student On-Task and Off-Task Behavior*

then records that student's behavior. During a 40-minute lesson, 8 sweeps can be made. The instrument allows the observer to record specific on-task and off-task behaviors listed in the key at the bottom of the chart.

Performance Indicator Instruments

A performance indicator instrument records whether or not actions listed on the observation instrument have been observed. With some instruments, a third option—"not applicable" (N/A)—is included. Performance indicator instruments

Elements	Response	Comments
Anticipatory set	Yes ___ No ___ N/A ___	_____
		_____
		_____
Statement of objective and purpose	Yes ___ No ___ N/A ___	_____
		_____
		_____
Input	Yes ___ No ___ N/A ___	_____
		_____
		_____
Modeling	Yes ___ No ___ N/A ___	_____
		_____
		_____
Checking for understanding	Yes ___ No ___ N/A ___	_____
		_____
		_____
Guided practice	Yes ___ No ___ N/A ___	_____
		_____
		_____
Independent practice	Yes ___ No ___ N/A ___	_____
		_____
		_____

FIGURE 14.4 *Hunter Model Performance Indicators*

may also include space for the observer to add supplemental notes concerning the presence or absence of the action. Figure 14.4 is a performance indicator instrument used to record the presence or absence of the elements in Madeline Hunter's lesson design model, a model well suited for direct instruction. Figure 14.5 is an instrument to assess whether or not each of the basic elements of a cooperative learning lesson is present.

The instrument in Figure 14.6 lists indicators of an authentic constructivist lesson, and Figure 14.7 lists indicators of culturally sensitive teaching. Since the indicators in Figures 14.6 and 14.7 are more open to interpretation than indicators in many instruments of this type, it is especially important for the observer to describe in the comments column specific classroom behaviors that are the basis for the observer's responses.

Elements	Response	Comments
Explanation of academic and social objectives	Yes ___ No ___ N/A ___	_____ _____ _____
Teaching of necessary social skills	Yes ___ No ___ N/A ___	_____ _____ _____
Face-to-face interaction	Yes ___ No ___ N/A ___	_____ _____ _____
Positive interdependence	Yes ___ No ___ N/A ___	_____ _____ _____
Individual accountability	Yes ___ No ___ N/A ___	_____ _____ _____
Group processing	Yes ___ No ___ N/A ___	_____ _____ _____

FIGURE 14.5 *Cooperative Learning Performance Indicators*

Indicators	Response	Comments
Co-planned by teacher and students	Yes ___ No ___ N/A ___	_____
In-depth explanation of big idea	Yes ___ No ___ N/A ___	_____
Student initiated questions	Yes ___ No ___ N/A ___	_____
Problem-centered	Yes ___ No ___ N/A ___	_____
Use of primary material	Yes ___ No ___ N/A ___	_____
Students test own hypotheses	Yes ___ No ___ N/A ___	_____
Dialogue fostered	Yes ___ No ___ N/A ___	_____
Active learning	Yes ___ No ___ N/A ___	_____
Collaborative learning	Yes ___ No ___ N/A ___	_____
Students construct knowledge	Yes ___ No ___ N/A ___	_____
Self and group reflection on constructions	Yes ___ No ___ N/A ___	_____
Learning assessed by teachers and students	Yes ___ No ___ N/A ___ Yes ___ No ___ N/A ___	_____
Assessment of process and product	Yes ___ No ___ N/A ___	_____

FIGURE 14.6 *Indicators of a Constructivist Lesson*

Indicators	Response	Comments
The Teacher		
Displays understanding of diverse cultures	Yes ___ No ___	_____ _____
Displays personal regard for all students	Yes ___ No ___	_____ _____
Uses instructional materials free of cultural bias	Yes ___ No ___	_____ _____
Uses examples and materials that represent different cultures	Yes ___ No ___	_____ _____
Promotes examination of concepts and issues from different cultural perspectives	Yes ___ No ___	_____ _____
Facilitates higher-level learning for all students	Yes ___ No ___	_____ _____
Adopts materials and instruction to different student learning styles	Yes ___ No ___	_____ _____
Provides equitable opportunities for student participation	Yes ___ No ___	_____ _____
Provides individual assistance, when necessary, for all students	Yes ___ No ___ N/A ___	_____ _____
Intervenes to address acts of student intolerance	Yes ___ No ___ N/A ___	_____ _____
Uses "teachable moments" to address cultural issues	Yes ___ No ___ N/A ___	_____ _____
Reinforces student acts of respect for diverse cultures	Yes ___ No ___ N/A ___	_____ _____

FIGURE 14.7 *Indicators of Culturally Sensitive Teaching*

Remember that performance indicators used for observation purposes should not imply an absolute standard. The fact that a teacher does not perform all of the activities listed on the observation instrument may or may not be a cause of concern. Only after the supervisor and teacher have discussed the circumstances surrounding the teacher's instructional procedures can they be properly interpreted.

Visual Diagramming

Visual diagramming is another way to portray what is occurring in a classroom. Videotaping a classroom captures the closest representative picture of actual occurrences. Without videotapes, however, there are other ways to portray observations, such as verbal interactions among teachers and students and how a teacher uses space. After diagramming the occurrence, the supervisor and the teacher can view the picture and then analyze the events.

Classroom verbal interactions can be charted by drawing arrows symbolizing verbal statements between members in a classroom (see Figure 14.8). The observer can use six separate sheets of this diagram and fill out one sheet for each time sample of five minutes spaced throughout the hour. Each arrow drawn on the diagram would indicate a full statement directed to another person. The arrows are numbered in the sequence of statements. After diagramming, the observer would then have information on the frequency of individual student interaction, the amount of interaction with different areas of the room, which students triggered interactions among others, and which students were excluded. For illustration purposes, if the diagram was a sample consistent with the other five samples of the classroom period, the observer would be able to state some of the following conclusions:

1. Interaction is mainly directed toward the left aisle and front row.
2. There is almost no attention to the last two rows in the back of the room or the two rows on the right.
3. Of 14 interactions, 12 included the teacher and 2 were between students.

Such diagramming is easier to follow with small groups and when students are not moving around the classroom. Class activities such as teacher lecturing interspersed with questions and answers or classroom discussions would be instructional sessions appropriate for diagramming. Another type of diagramming is flowcharting teacher space utilization, which follows the teacher's movement throughout the classroom. A sketch of the physical classroom is done first; then the observer follows the teacher by using arrows on the sketch (see Figure 14.9).

Figure 14.9 illustrates a period of reading instruction. The arrow follows the teacher with each movement and is labeled with the time on the clock. After a class period, the observer and the teacher can see where the teacher has been and for

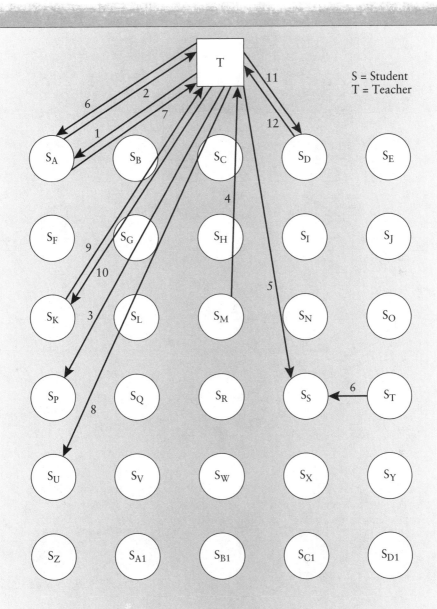

FIGURE 14.8 *Diagram of Verbal Interaction, 9:10–9:15*

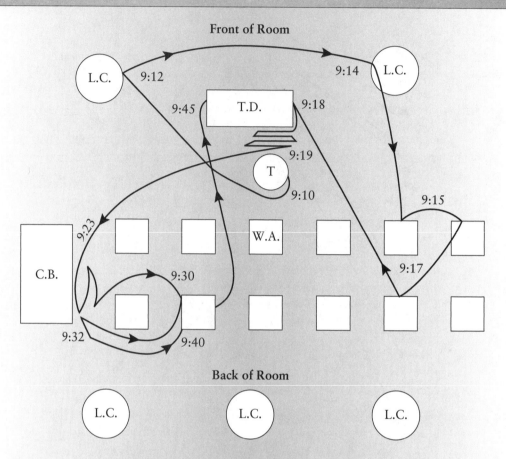

FIGURE 14.9 *Teacher Space Utilization*

how long. Such information might help make a teacher aware of the relationship of his or her space utilization to concerns of classroom management and instruction. For example, in Figure 14.9 there is much physical presence in the front and on the left side of the classroom, with no presence at the rear learning centers or the middle work area.

Qualitative Observations

There are alternative means of observing based on not knowing exactly what is to be recorded. These are called *qualitative or descriptive forms of observation.* The observer goes into the classroom with a general focus, or no focus at all, and records events as they occur. The events are not made to fit into a specific category, nor are they measured. Only after the recording of events does the observer rearrange his or her observations into themes. Such recording of observations defies the use of an instrument (an instrument is technically a measurement device). Instead, qualitative observations record the complexity of classroom life.

There are several types of qualitative observations. We will look at verbatim, detached open-ended narrative, participant open-ended observation, focused questionnaire observation, and educational criticism. These observations can be used by a supervisor to provide a broad and complex recording of classroom life.

Verbatim and Selected Verbatim

The observer taking verbatim notes (sometimes called *scripts*) records all verbal interaction taking place in the classroom. Verbatim notes allow the observer and teacher to identify patterns of interpersonal behavior during a lesson. Verbatim also provides specific examples of teacher-student or student-teacher interactions. For more efficient recording, the observer may abbreviate words and leave out words that add no meaning to the transcript. Despite these time-savers, verbatim can be an arduous process requiring the observer to spend every moment taking notes, with no time for attention to anything else going on during the lesson. One alternative to verbatim is *selected verbatim,* in which the observer records only those interactions that relate to a particular focus agreed to by the observer and teacher prior to the observation. Figure 14.10 provides an excerpt from selective verbatim notes focused on teacher responses to students who initially gave incorrect or partially correct answers to teacher questions.

Detached Open-Ended Narrative

Detached open-ended narrative occurs when the supervisor steps into a classroom and records every person, event, or thing that attracts his or her attention. At the start, the pages are empty, without questions, indicators, or categories. The heading might simply say:

Open-Ended Narrative

Observation Teacher: _____ Time: ____ Observer: _____

C = Chris D.   10:20
T = Teacher
T.   C, what are 3 branches of fed. Govt.?
C.   President, House, Senate
T.   What branch fed. Govt. is pres. head of?
C.   Ah, I don't know
T.   The president is Chief _____.
C.   Executive! Executive branch!
T.   The House and Senate are both part of what branch?
C.   Legislative
T.   Legislative branch, but both mean same thing. That's
      2 branches, exec. and leg. What is the third branch?
C.   The Courts.
T.   What branch is made of Sup. Ct and other fed. cts.
C.   Judicial
T.   Right!

FIGURE 14.10 *Excerpt from Selective Verbatim Notes*

Originally published in S. Gordon (1990). *Assisting the entry-year teacher: A leadership resource.*
Columbus, OH: Ohio Department of Education

The recorder then has the task of writing, writing, and more writing. A sample of such an observation might read:

> Students begin arriving at 10:13; the teacher is at his desk correcting papers. The bell rings at 10:15 to begin third period. Students keep arriving. Mr. X gets up from his desk to begin class at 10:25. In the meantime, students have put away their school bags and are awaiting instruction, except three girls in the back corner who are talking, combing their hair, and spreading the contents of their pocketbooks on their desks. Five minutes after Mr. X begins, he talks to them and they put away combs and pocketbooks. Mr. X describes the activities for the day but then cannot find his prepared handouts. After two minutes of looking, he finds the papers in his desk drawer.
>
> The intercom comes on at 10:30 with two announcements by the principal. Mr. X gives the assignments, and the class begins to read at 10:33. Two students are reprimanded for talking, and occasional student talk can be heard as Mr. X moves around and reviews yesterday's homework with students. He talks with 12 students before asking for class attention at 10:45. He then lec-

tures on the classification of insects. The overhead projection on the board is difficult for students in the back to read. One student asks if he can darken the lights. . . .

With practice, the observer can write in shorthand to keep up with the flow of events. It is impossible to record all that could possibly be seen and heard in a classroom. The observer must constantly scan the entire classroom and decide what is significant.

Participant Open-Ended Observation

Participant open-ended observation occurs when the supervisor becomes a functioning part of the classroom (Spradley, 1980). He or she assists in the instruction, helps students with questions, uses classroom materials, and talks with the teacher and students. Being involved in the classroom gives the supervisor an inside-out view of the classroom different from that of the detached observer who tries to be invisible and keep away from students and teachers. Obviously, events cannot be written down as they occur if the supervisor is engaged in talking, moving, and assisting. Instead, he or she must write between pauses in the action. The observation form can be carried on a clipboard so that notes can be taken on the run.

The participant observer takes sketchy notes (catch phrases and words) during classroom time so that afterward he or she can write in greater detail. These quick notes serve to remind the observer of the situation that will be described more fully after the observation period is over. The following is an example of such short notes.

Teacher X directs students into study groups.

John B. does not understand the assignment. I work with him on organizing the theme of a play.

Sally T. and Ramona B. are wandering around. I ask them if they need help; they say no and leave the room (ask teacher about this).

Sondra and her group are ready to role play their theme. I listen as they read through their parts.

Steven's group is stuck; he doesn't know how to find materials on historic buildings. I suggest calling the town historic society.

Susan is not participating at all—looking at *Teen Magazine*. The rest of the group just leaves her alone. (I wonder why?)

The filmstrip shown has everyone's attention.

Teacher B dismisses the class. I overhear a student say, "This class goes so quickly. I wish other classes were as much fun."

These are some notes from a 50-minute classroom period. Much more happened in the classroom than is noted, but the observer picks up insights from his or her involvement. The supervisor can later fill in details—the two girls leaving the classroom, the specifics of John's confusion about the theme, Susan's absorption in *Teen Magazine,* and so on.

Focused Questionnaire Observation

Qualitative observation can be done in a more focused manner by having general topics to use in recording events. An observer seeks information about specific questions.

Particular instructional models and learning goals can be used in a focused questionnaire. For example, if a teacher were attempting to use a student-centered approach aimed at increasing critical and creative thinking about a current world concern, the observer might be able to focus descriptions according to the following questions (Marzano et al., 1988).

What Does the Teacher Do to Assist Students to Acquire Core Thinking Skills for

1. *Focusing:* Defining problems and setting goals?
2. *Information gathering:* Observing to obtain information and formulate questions to seek new information?
3. *Remembering:* Storing and retrieving information?
4. *Organizing:* Comparing, classifying, observing, and representing?
5. *Analyzing:* Identifying attributes and components, relationships and patterns, main ideas, and errors?
6. *Generating:* Inferring, predicting, and elaborating?
7. *Integrating:* Summarizing and restructuring?
8. *Evaluating:* Assessing the reasonableness and quality of ideas?

A focused questionnaire can revolve around a particular instructional model, such as direct instruction, cooperative learning, jurisprudence, advanced organizers, or indirect learning. It can be as narrow as looking at one or two questions within a particular model or be as extensive as to include numerous questions about a model, or be generic in posing questions that would cross different teaching practices.

In order to answer the questions, the observer writes pertinent evidence. For example, Harris (1975, pp. 364–376) has developed a detached observation questionnaire that has as its topics: (1) classroom, (2) teacher, (3) pupil, and (4) lesson. Figure 14.11 shows sample questions taken from each category.

An observer enters the classroom with questions in hand and looks for the answers. Some questions lend themselves to detached observations; others demand participant observations. For example, the question "What shows that the teacher has a warm, friendly relationship with pupils?" could be answered by participant observation, such as: "Overheard three students saying how nice Ms. Y is. Noticed

Topic 1: Classroom
How is the classroom made attractive?

Topic 2: Teacher
What shows that the teacher has a warm, friendly relationship with the pupils?

Topic 3: Pupil
What indicates that pupils know what they are doing and why they are doing it?

Topic 4: Lesson
How do classroom and homework assignments indicate that consideration is given to, and use made of, resources of the community and real-life situations of pupils?

FIGURE 14.11 *Focused Questionnaire*

how Ms. Y put her hand on the shoulders of five different students when speaking to them." The question "How is the classroom made attractive?" could be answered by detached observation: "Classroom freshly painted, bulletin boards have recent work. Student artwork is framed and evenly spaced." It is the task of the observer to respond to these questions with descriptions of the evidence.

Educational Criticism

Elliott Eisner (1985) has developed an approach to observation that merges detached and participant observation with description and interpretation. Observers are trained to look at the classroom as an art critic might look at a painting. Just as a person would have to accumulate the experience of viewing numerous paintings and become knowledgeable in the history and variations of particular art forms to be a critic, so must an educator become familiar with many types of classrooms and forms of instruction to be an education critic.

Eisner has stated classroom observations can be done via the same procedures of criticism. He calls the needed educational expertise "connoisseurship." Just as a wine connoisseur can look at the color, viscosity, smell, and taste of a wine to form specific judgments about its overall quality, so can an educational connoisseur make judgments about the specifics of classroom events and the overall quality of classroom life.

Eisner argued that supervisors can develop educational connoisseurship by finding what the classroom *means* to the participants. The education critic attempts to take the perspective of students and teachers in viewing the influence of the classroom environment, events, and interactions and then makes the hidden meaning of the classroom known to the participants to see whether they agree. Teachers and students may be so involved in the classroom that they are unaware of the meaning of what they do. The participant observer attempts to describe and interpret events through their eyes.

The following are excerpts from observations and interpretations of a college composition class made by Sugie Goen,* one of Eisner's students. In the first excerpt, Goen provides a vivid description of "Life in Room 132":

> A few minutes after six, the teacher Helen Deakin, enters the room—streams in is more like it. Her movements are liquid, from the way her loose fitting clothing flows around her as she moves into the room, to the way she repeatedly gathers full handfuls of long thick hair that, in one sweeping gesture, she lifts from her forehead, releasing great locks that spill languidly down her back. She flows into the room slowly, in no apparent hurry even though it is now several minutes past six o'clock. Her students are in no apparent hurry either. Right at six o'clock, the scheduled start time for class to begin, only six of the seventeen students are present. Students continue to arrive until half past the hour, an arrival pattern that I was to witness during each of my visits. This is clearly a class where no one rushes. Life in Room 132 doesn't gush, torrent or swell. It flows; it spreads out thickly and slowly; maybe even, I would soon suspect, deliberately.
>
> While students are arriving, Helen stands in front of the class, gazing out at the students sitting at the even rows of tables. "Do you want to sit this way? Or in a circle like before?" No rhetorical question here, for she stands patiently still, waiting for a response. When none comes, she poses the question again, and again she waits.

The next excerpt from Goen's narrative illustrates the interpretive dimension of educational criticism:

> Helen dares to design a course that explores the contours of choice and one that wonders aloud how selection determines what can and cannot be known. And, the question of choice in Room 132 is not mere intellectual calisthenics. At every turn, Helen provides opportunities for her students to practice choosing: how to arrange their seats, what writing prompt to use, from what vantage point to view their classmate's clothing, to what time class should adjourn.
>
> Yet, choice comes with a lot of baggage. For instance, Helen deliberately allows much more time for the flow of classroom management than I could ever imagine being comfortable with. And though she comments more than once about "the luxury of time" afforded by the three hour and twenty minute class sessions, the time required to decide the seating arrangement, or to discuss and vote on whether to proceed with or without a scheduled break, eats up enormous chunks of class time. And at times, I get the distinct impression that students are frustrated by all the choices, for instance, when Thanh blurts out "who cares" when faced with yet another decision. Furthermore, I could not help but notice that only a few students make the vast majority of decisions. Of the seventeen

---

*Excerpts are from "School Choice and the Teaching of First-Year Composition: The Story of Room 132," Sugie Goen, Stanford University. Reprinted with permission.

students, I estimate that nearly half rarely speak at all. Moreover, in matters of classroom management, the "policymakers" tend to be the same three of four men (with the exception of Keesha, by far the most vocal student, either male or female). In short, practicing student choice is enormously time consuming and I wonder if such choice is possible, or even desirable, in the fifty or ninety minute class formats of the regular academic school year. Moreover, it strikes me as necessarily labor intensive to properly monitor participation in decision making to safeguard against this "tyranny" of the vocal minority.

Of more concern to me, however, are the tensions that manifest around the idea of language choice. A number of students express discomfort with the idea of deliberately choosing language to convey a point of view. Miguel, in particular, voices his concern that to deliberate over word choice in order to persuade for a particular point of view renders writing biased when it is supposed to be "objective." Even in a writing assignment that asks them to examine the particular language choices of newspaper journalists, Miguel worries about how he can "write an unbiased paper about an article that is biased?" Besides, another student adds "if you have no opinion about affirmative action before, when you read all the articles you will form an opinion by the time you finish, so how can you be objective?" And yet another student chimes in that examining these articles is like looking for strategies writers use "to get something over on you."

It both interests me and concerns me that by focusing attention on the choices that writers use to express a point of view, the students in Room 132 may be deciding that choice is a negative thing, that it somehow suggests bias, prejudice, and manipulation at the cost of objectivity, whatever that is. But then again, their experiences in the world outside of school may be inadvertently reinforced each night in Room 132. After all, the students who command a facile use of language are more able (or willing) to vie for their position in class decision making. Perhaps the feelings of Miguel and others suggest that they occasionally feel manipulated by their more verbally powerful classmates. Perhaps they feel that something has been "gotten over on them." Perhaps too, they cling tenaciously to notions of objectivity as the promise of a world where everyone is equal, where no single perspective can persuade over another, where bias and prejudice don't exist at all. For these students, maybe college is supposed to be just such an "objective" place. Viewed this way, what does it mean for these students to be encouraged to choose when the playing field isn't level? Are we inviting them to play in a game where only the fittest survive?

Tailored Observation Systems

Supervisors often observe lessons to collect data on unique instructional concerns or improvement efforts. If no observation system exists that is capable of gathering the desired data, the supervisor can design a tailored observation system. Tailored observation systems can be quantitative, qualitative, or a combination of both. Figure 14.12 is a system designed to collect four specific types of data. The teacher in this example requested that the observer collect data on (1) how often the teacher called on each student; (2) whether each student's response was correct or incorrect; (3) whether the teacher drew out correct student responses

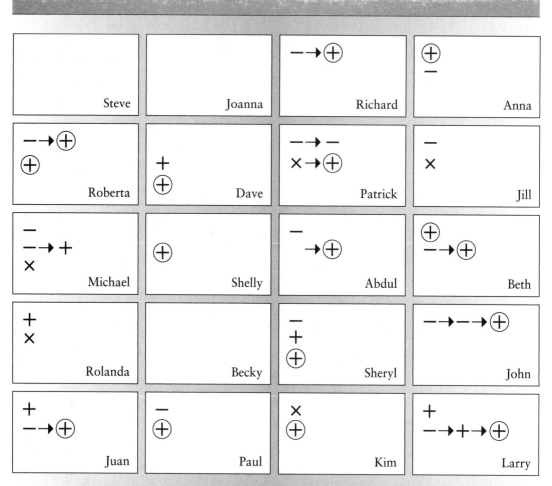

FIGURE 14.12 *Tailored Question-Response Instrument*

Key

— Incorrect response

→ Teacher prompt or encouragement

+ Correct response

✕ Response cannot be classified as correct or incorrect

◯ Positive teacher feedback following student response

through encouragement or prompting, especially after a student's initial response was incorrect; and (4) how often the teacher provided positive feedback to students making correct responses. In Figure 14.12, codes symbolize both student responses (–, +, ×) to teacher questions, and teacher reactions (→, o) to student responses. Several codes on the same line indicate verbal behaviors that were part of the same series of interactions. Codes on different lines indicate separate series of interactions.

In another example, teacher Simmons was concerned about the conduct of one of his students and asked the supervisor to collect data on the student's behaviors, Simmons's responses, and the effects of those responses on the student. Figure 14.13 is the observation chart completed by the supervisor. Arrows point to immediate responses of the teacher to selected student behaviors and immediate responses

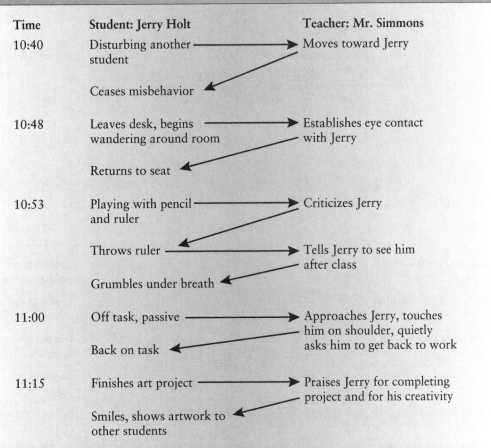

Time	Student: Jerry Holt	Teacher: Mr. Simmons
10:40	Disturbing another student	Moves toward Jerry
	Ceases misbehavior	
10:48	Leaves desk, begins wandering around room	Establishes eye contact with Jerry
	Returns to seat	
10:53	Playing with pencil and ruler	Criticizes Jerry
	Throws ruler	Tells Jerry to see him after class
	Grumbles under breath	
11:00	Off task, passive	Approaches Jerry, touches him on shoulder, quietly asks him to get back to work
	Back on task	
11:15	Finishes art project	Praises Jerry for completing project and for his creativity
	Smiles, shows artwork to other students	

FIGURE 14.13 *Tailored Behavior-Response Observation*

of the student to relevant teacher behaviors. Some of the most meaningful and helpful classroom observation data we have viewed has been collected with instruments designed by supervisors and teachers focused on specific teacher concerns.

Types and Purposes of Observation

Figure 14.14 illustrates the types of observation available to a supervisor. The purpose of the observation should determine the type, method, and role of observation. The categorical-frequency observation is a quantitative method used by a detached observer for the purpose of counting, totaling, and statistically analyzing behaviors. The performance-indicator observation is quantitatively used by a detached observer to record evidence of human behavior. Visual diagramming is a quantitative observation used by a detached observer for the purpose of depicting verbal interaction. Human space utilization observation is a quantitative

	Method		Role of Observer		
Type	*Quantitive*	*Qualitative*	*Detached*	*Participant*	*Purpose*
Categorical frequency	x		x		Count behaviors
Performance indicator	x		x		Evident or not
Visual diagramming	x		x		Picture verbal interaction
Space utilization	x		x		Picture movement
Verbatim		x			Script of verbal interaction
Detached open-ended narrative		x	x		Attention to unfolding event
Participant open-ended observation		x		x	Inside-out view
Focused questionnaire		x	x or	x	Focus on particular events
Educational criticism		x	x or	x	Meaning to participants
Tailored	x or	x	x or	x	Address unique concerns

FIGURE 14.14 *Observation Alternatives*

measure used by a detached observer for the purpose of depicting the length and pattern of physical movement. Verbatim is a qualitative method in which the observer records all verbal interaction. The detached open-ended narrative is a qualitative observation used by a detached observer for recording events as they unfold. Participant open-ended observation is a qualitative technique used to record how people and events unfold to one involved in the classroom. The focused questionnaire is another qualitative method that can be used by a detached or participant observer for the purpose of gathering evidence according to general questions about classroom topics. Educational criticism is a qualitative observation conducted by a combination of detached and participant observation for the purpose of capturing the meaning of classroom life from the teacher's and students' perspective.

Finally, tailored observation systems cut across the different categories previously discussed. They are designed by the supervisor (or supervisor and teacher) to collect data on specific teacher concerns when there is no existing observation system for collecting such data. They may be quantitative or qualitative and may be used by a detached or participant observer.

Cautions Concerning Observations

Quantum physics informs us that a phenomenon cannot be measured without the measurement process interacting with the phenomenon and thus affecting the measurement (Greene, 2004). Closer to home for those of us who are educators, the constructivist epistemology holds that, rather than identifying a fixed reality through objective observation, we construct knowledge by interacting with our environment and with others. One implication for classroom observation is our need to realize that our observations are affected by our personal experiences and values, our presence in the classroom during the observation, the observation instrument we use, our skill at recording data, and so on. Another implication is that the interpretation of what the observation data means is a construction, and in most cases is best co-constructed with the teacher. Observation data, thus, should be an entry point for teacher-supervisor dialogue and co-interpretation during a post-observation conference. Clinical supervision, discussed in Chapter 16, provides a structure for teacher-supervisor dialogue on classroom observation.

SUMMARY

There are many ways to observe classrooms. The choice of a particular type of observation depends on the purpose and focus of the observation. Observation enables a supervisor to put a mirror of the classroom up to the teacher, who can then attend to matters previously unknown. Several studies (Brophy and Good, 1974) have shown that teachers often change instructional behaviors on their own after their classrooms have been described to them by an observer. The mirror can often be the stimulus for change. The observer must be careful in using interpretations, because such value judgments can actually cloud the mirror and prevent the teacher from seeing his or her own image. At all times, the observer needs to distinguish description from interpretation when recording and explaining events to the teacher.

PRACTITIONER REFLECTION

Observations

Cathryn Mitchell, *Principal, J. Houston Elementary*

As the principal of a large urban elementary school, my primary responsibility is to ensure that each student's instructional needs are met through a safe and nurturing environment. I must be well versed in the curriculum and expectations for each grade level, identify the best instructional models for teachers to use, and then be able to communicate this information to the teachers and parents. Being the instructional leader on my campus is one of my most important responsibilities, because encouraging the growth of teachers is essential for student improvement.

Conducting effective and efficient observations is a necessity for any administrator and something I am continuing to learn how to do. During my five years as an administrator, I have used different tools for observing teachers. The tools have been formal and informal, mandated and optional, formative and summative. All parties should agree on the purposes of different types of observations. Part of the process is helping teachers understand the difference between summative and formative observation and when each will be used.

Observations can be an effective way to change instructional behaviors, if trusting relationships are first established. Knowing each teacher and the growth that needs to occur and/or areas the teacher would like to improve in is essential. On a large campus such as mine, knowing the current needs of all teachers is a daunting task. This is what makes a preconference for any observation a necessity. During the preconference, the teacher and administrator can identify areas of strength and concern. Once these areas are identified, discussion can begin on the specific purpose of the observation and the observation data to be gathered. This process helps to enhance the trusting relationship between the supervisor and teacher that is essential for growth to occur.

Recently the use of a different type of observation tool was needed to address a common concern on my campus about the amounts of time teachers spend in front of the class in didactic instruction to the whole class. To address this area of concern as a school, we created a quantitative checklist that identifies different instructional models: whole group, small group, individual work, teacher side-by-side, and so on. Over the span of several weeks, my administrative team conducted informal classroom observations using this form. The information gathered was used to help teachers recognize the amount of time used on didactic instruction and begin the process of developing additional instructional strategies with the aim of improved student learning.

When used appropriately, individualized or common observations can promote growth and learning for teachers, therefore enhancing academic success for all students.

EXERCISES

Academic

1. Write a paper contrasting observation systems used purely for assisting teachers to improve their instruction with summative teacher evaluation systems. Cite at least three outside references in your paper.

2. Locate three formative observation instruments in the literature on instructional supervision. Describe the instruments and discuss the specific purpose and procedures for the use of each.

3. Write a paper comparing and contrasting quantitative classroom observation with qualitative classroom observation. Cite relevant works found in the references for Chapter 14 in your writing.

4. Write a paper summarizing Eisner's ideas on educational connoisseurship.

5. Write an essay giving your position on each of the three issues presented at the beginning of this chapter. Support your position with citations from relevant readings listed in the references for Chapter 14.

Field

1. Use a categorical-frequency instrument. Arrange to observe a class and try out the instrument.

2. Use a performance-indicator instrument. Use the instrument during a classroom observation.

3. Write a detached open-ended narrative during a visit to a classroom.

4. Visit a classroom. Write a description of the classroom, learning activities, and teacher-student interactions from the teacher's perspective. Next, write descriptions of the classroom, learning activities, and teacher-supervisor interactions from the students' perspective.

5. Review an instrument used by supervisors in a selected school district during classroom observations. Prepare a written evaluation of the instrument. Include your opinion on whether the instrument fulfills its stated purpose.

Developmental

1. Continue to differentiate between descriptions and interpretations of observed events by listening to others discuss observations they have made and by reviewing your own comments regarding your observations.

2. Continue to review systems and instruments designed for use as tools for quantitative observations. Attempt to match different systems and instruments with different observation purposes and goals.

3. Through continued readings and practice in classroom observation, especially in listening to teachers and students, begin to develop the skills of Eisner's educational critic.

REFERENCES

Brophy, J. E., and Good, T. L. 1974. *Teacher-student relationships: Causes and consequences.* New York: Holt, Rinehart and Winston.

Eisner, E. W. 1985. *The educational imagination: On the design and evaluation of school programs* (2nd ed.). New York: Macmillan.

Glickman, C. D., and Jones, J. W. 1986. Research in supervision: Creating the dialogue. *Educational Leadership, 44*(3), 83.

Gordon, S. P. 1990. *Assisting the entry-year teacher: A leadership resource.* Columbus: Ohio Department of Education.

Greene, B. 2004. *The fabric of the cosmos: Space, time and the texture of reality.* New York: Vintage Books.

Harris, B. M. 1975. *Supervisory behavior in education* (2nd ed.). Englewood Cliffs, NJ: Prentice Hall.

Marzano, R. J., Brandt, R., Hughes, C. S., Jones, B. F., Presseisen, B. Z., Rankin, S. C., and Suhor, C. 1988. *Dimensions of thinking: A framework for curriculum and instruction.* Alexandria, VA: Association for Supervision and Curriculum Development.

Spradley, J. P. 1980. *Participant observation.* New York: Holt, Rinehart and Winston.

SUGGESTED READINGS

Acheson, A. A., and Gall, M. D. 1992. *Techniques in the clinical supervision of teachers* (3rd ed.). New York: Longman.

Croll, P. 2005. *Systematic classroom observation* (2nd ed.). London: Falmer Press.

Goldhammer, R., Anderson, R. H., and Krajewski, R., J. 1993. *Clinical supervision: Special methods for the supervision of teachers* (3rd ed.). Fort Worth: Harcourt Brace Jovanovich.

Pajak, E. 2003. *Honoring diverse teaching styles: A guide for supervisors.* Alexandria, VA: Association for Supervision and Curriculum Development.

Research and Evaluation Skills

Perhaps no area in education has gone through such a dramatic expansion in knowledge, techniques, and attention than the field of educational research and evaluation. What once seemed the province of experts, consultants, and "university types" doing laboratory experiments has now become a part of day-to-day operations in schools. The national accountability and testing movement has certainly been a contributing cause. More important has been the role of the literature on successful schools, which has made clear that decisions about instructional changes should be made from a base of comprehensive and credible data about students and that those affected most directly by instructional change (i.e., teachers) should be involved in defining, implementing, and interpreting the research and evaluation agenda.

For example, in a study of 15 exemplary elementary and middle schools in three school districts that had improved instruction in reading and mathematics over a three-year period, a common characteristic of these schools was found to be the deliberate collection of information about student progress and the use of that information to decide on schoolwide actions for changing curriculum, lesson planning, professional development, and individual assistance to teachers. The schools continuously collected and used data about student achievement to determine whether positive changes had resulted and what further revisions in practice needed to be implemented (Glickman and Pajak, 1987).

In schools and districts that do improve instruction, evaluation and research are not perfunctory paper assignments done by a particular person or division to fulfill district or state requirements. Rather, evaluation and research are seen as the basis for determining professional actions as to the what and the how of improving learning for students. Knowledgeable decision making about instruction comes from intense and critical study of the consequences of the common work of teachers: teaching. Including teachers in determining the criteria, procedures, and use of evaluative data in schools is not simply a nice thing to do—*it is essential to do*. If teachers are to extend their own thinking and commitment about collective instruction, they have to be part of the research and evaluation process. Without their involvement, policy makers have denied teachers the intellectual engagement of viewing teaching as a collective activity—"a cause beyond oneself."

Such engagement, in itself, enhances thinking and decisions about individual practice. In a high school in the Southeast, during the year when teachers and administrators in the school began to collect data on profiles of high school dropouts, the dropout rate decreased by more than 12 percent (Glickman, 1989). This was *before* the school had determined what interventions to make. One teacher said, "It simply never occurred to me, until we researched and evaluated our school, that we had a problem with dropouts. I and most of my peers have certainly changed our attitudes towards average students. The dropout rate is coming down right now because of our awareness. I can't wait until next year when we implement new programs!"

Alternative Approaches to Research and Evaluation

Research on and evaluation of instructional programs is based on methodology derived from one of two broad approaches to research, or in some cases a combination of both approaches. These two approaches are *quantitative* and *qualitative*. The difference between quantitative and qualitative research goes way beyond the fact that quantitative results are reported numerically and qualitative results are reported through narrative. The two approaches are based on different conceptions of reality, the purpose of research, the researcher's role, the role of values in research, the relationship between researcher and subject, and appropriate research methodology. Let's begin this discussion by outlining the major differences between these two alternatives.

Quantitative and Qualitative Research Compared

A number of scholars have compared quantitative and qualitative research in relation to critical research issues (Bogdan and Biklen, 1992; Borg and Gall, 1989; Fang, 1995; Hathaway, 1995; Lincoln and Guba, 1985; Shank, 1994; Anfara,

Brown, and Mangione, 2002; Creswell, 2001; Nastasia and Schensul, 2005). The assumptions of quantitative and qualitative researchers regarding seven such issues are discussed below.

What Is the Nature of Reality and Knowledge? Quantitative research is based on the assumption that there is a single, external reality. Knowledge consists of objective measurements of phenomena which are part of that reality. Complex phenomena can be broken down into simple variables that can be studied independently. Eventually, the study of component variables leads to an overall understanding of a phenomenon, which in turn can lead to prediction and control of the phenomenon.

Qualitative research is based on the assumption that the world consists of multiple realities that are constructed by individuals or groups. Knowledge comes with understanding of an individual's or group's assumptions, relationships, intentions, actions, perceptions, and feelings within a given context. A phenomenon can only be studied holistically. Since each phenomenon is unique, prediction and control of future phenomena are unlikely.

What Are the Goals of Research? The goals of quantitative research are to identify relationships between variables, explain causes, predict and control phenomena, and develop knowledge that is *generalizable* to other contexts. The goals of qualitative research are to describe phenomena from the perspective of participants, discover multiple realities, and develop a holistic understanding of individual phenomena within particular contexts. This is done through a continuous cycle of intense observation and in-depth description, formation of working hypotheses, more observation and description, and so on.

What Is the Researcher's Role? In quantitative research the researcher assumes the role of the detached observer. The purpose of detachment is to avoid bias. This detachment extends to the researcher's relationship with the *subjects* of the study. The researcher is to have as little interaction with the subjects as possible. Quantitative research methods are designed to minimize the effects of any unavoidable interaction between the researcher and the study or subjects.

Qualitative research assumes that the researcher and the study will interact and affect each other. In fact, the qualitative researcher intentionally becomes deeply involved with the phenomenon being studied. The researcher attempts to develop empathy, trust, and even friendship with the study's *participants*. The researcher documents interactions with the study and its participants, and critically examines his or her effects on the research and results.

What Is the Importance of Context in Research? Context is the setting or framework within which the phenomenon being studied exists. The quantitative view is that a phenomenon can be studied independently of its context. Indeed, quantitative research attempts to develop context-free generalizations. Qualitative research assumes that a phenomenon is greatly influenced by its particular context. The whole is greater than the sum of its parts. This is why a qualitative study places so much emphasis on describing context, and usually will not attempt to generalize results to other contexts.

What Place Do Values Have in Research? Both quantitative and qualitative research admit that values can affect research. Quantitative research responds to the values issue by attempting to make the research as value free as possible through the use of objective research methods. Qualitative research is based on the assumption that the researcher, participants, context, and research methodology all possess values that will inevitably influence the study, and so it is best to describe those values and their effects as part of the study.

What Is the Relationship of Cause and Effect? Quantitative research assumes that every *effect* can be explained by a preceding *cause* or combination of causes. It attempts to identify cause-effect relationships. Qualitative research assumes that variables which are part of a phenomenon are mutually and simultaneously affecting each other. Thus it is impossible to separate causes from effects.

How Should Research Studies Be Designed? Shank (1994) compares the quantitative approach to manufacturing: A blueprint for the study is created, then quality control ensures that production takes place according to the blueprint. A hypothesis is stated. A research design, such as correlational, experimental, or quasi-experimental, is chosen. Formal data collection instruments such as inventories, questionnaires, or tests are selected or developed. Subjects are identified and grouped according to precise procedures (random selection, stratified samples, experimental and control groups, and so on). Only after all of the above have been completed does data collection begin; and after data collection is complete, data analysis begins. Analysis involves the use of statistical techniques intended to reduce bias and error, control for extraneous variables, determine whether or not the hypothesis is correct, and indicate to what extent results can be generalized.

Shank (1994) compared qualitative research to *hunting and gathering*—the qualitative researcher is not trying to test a predetermined hypothesis, but is searching for evidence and understanding of processes and relations. The qualitative research design is broad, emergent, and flexible. The research sample is small and hand picked to meet the purpose of the study. Data collection methods include long-term observation, participation, open-ended interviews, gathering of documents and artifacts, videotaping, and photography, to name a few. The most important data collection instrument is the *researcher*. Data analysis consists of: reviewing; inductive coding; comparing; integrating; and constructing themes, concepts, hypotheses, and models. Data collection and data analysis are cyclical and interactive; initial data collection and data analysis may lead to the formulation of a working hypothesis which then calls for a new round of data collection and analysis. The aim of this continuously evolving research design is to develop a body of in-depth knowledge concerning the particular phenomena being studied.

TABLE 15.1	Comparison of Quantitative and Qualitative Research

Research/Issue	Quantitative Research	Qualitative Research
Nature of Reality and Knowledge	A single, external reality; Knowledge consists of objective measures	Multiple realities; Knowledge comes with understanding of these realities
Goals of Research	Explain causes; Predict and control; Develop generalizable knowledge	Describe phenomena; Discover multiple realities; Holistic understanding
Researcher's Role	Detached observer	Interact and become involved with phenomenon being studied
Importance of Context	Phenomenon can and should be studied separate from context	Phenomenon is greatly influenced by its context; they must be studied together
Values in Research	Make research objective (value free)	Describe values and their inevitable effects
Cause and Effect	Each effect has preceding cause; Identify cause-effect relationships	Variables mutually and simultaneously affect each other
Research Design	Correlational, experimental, or quasi-experimental; formal instruments; precise procedures; statistical techniques; Determine if predetermined hypothesis is correct, if results are generalizable	Broad, emergent, and flexible; long-term observation, participation; Data collection and analysis are cyclical and interactive; Formulate working hypothesis, developing in-depth knowledge of particular phenomena

Table 15.1 summarizes our comparison of quantitative and qualitative research.

Can Quantitative and Qualitative Methods Be Used in the Same Study?

Is it desirable or even possible to effectively use both quantitative and qualitative methods in the same research or evaluation study? There are a number of positions on this issue taken by different experts. One position, taken by some quantitative and some qualitative proponents, is that the approach they embrace is not only incompatible with the other approach, but is so superior to it that the approach they favor should be the only one used in any serious study. A second group of experts agrees with the first group's contention that quantitative and qualitative research are incompatible, but does not endorse one approach as superior to the other. This group takes the position that quantitative research is the more appropriate methodology for some studies, but that qualitative research is more appropriate for others.

A third group of experts believes that quantitative and qualitative research are compatible and that the best studies combine the two approaches. This view may seem curious in light of the comparison of quantitative and qualitative research provided above. But proponents of mixing the two approaches point out that each approach can generate types of information that the other cannot, that only quantitative and qualitative perspectives used together can form a complete picture of the phenomenon being studied, and that the results of one method can help to explain and validate the results of the other (Piontek, 1992; Chatterji, 2005).

As the reader of previous chapters in this text may have already predicted, the authors adhere to a fourth, eclectic view concerning the quantitative-qualitative debate. First, we do not agree that quantitative and qualitative research are in all cases incompatible, or that either approach is inherently superior to the other. Based on our own experience as researchers and evaluators, we believe that:

- For *some* studies, using quantitative methods is the best approach.
- For *some* studies, using qualitative methods is the best approach.
- For *many* studies, a combination of quantitative and qualitative methods is the best approach.

The following criteria are recommended for determining whether a quantitative, qualitative, or combined approach is the most appropriate methodology for a research or evaluation study:

1. The context of the study (school history, demographics, culture, climate, and so on)
2. The goals of the study
3. The values and skills of the person or group conducting the study
4. The resources available for the study
5. The values of those who will participate in the study (principals, teachers, students, parents), as well as the time and effort participants are able and willing to contribute (Qualitative studies often require more participant time and effort than quantitative studies.)
6. The values and needs of the audience to whom the study will be reported

In the remainder of this chapter we'll examine individual program evaluation and evaluation of the overall instructional program. The following pages will provide examples of how quantitative and qualitative methods can be applied to each of these types of evaluation.

Judgments

How do we know our instructional programs are successful? Should we continue with the same curriculum, instructional methods, scheduling, and grouping practices, or should changes be made? Evaluating is the act of making such a judgment.

How do we decide whether something is good or bad? Frequently, we make judgments with statements such as, "What a great reading program," "What a lousy classroom," or "What wonderful students." How do we really know if something is great, lousy, or wonderful? Wolfe (1969) has offered a tongue-in-cheek classification of five typical methods by which we make such judgments:

Cosmetic method: You examine the program, and if it looks good it is good. Does everybody look busy? The key is attractive and full bulletin boards covered with projects emanating from the project.

Cardiac method: No matter what the data say, you know in your heart that the program was a success. This is similar to the use in medical research of subclinical findings.

Colloquial method: After a brief meeting, preferably at a local watering hole, a group of project staff members conclude that success was achieved. No one can refute a group decision.

Curricular method: A successful program is one that can be installed with the least disruption of the ongoing school program. Programs that are truly different are to be eschewed at all costs.

Computational method: If you have to have data, analyze it to death. Whatever the nature of the statistics, use the most sophisticated multivariate regression discontinuity procedures known to humans.

Wolfe's humor aside, let's look at reasonable, valid ways of evaluating. In the turbulence of instructional change, it is useful to know whether the new practice is going to be any better than the old. If not, then we may be investing large amounts of energy without a justifiable increase in instructional benefits to students. As discussed in Chapter 13 (assessing and planning), if we are to make a commitment to instructional change, we must also make a commitment to evaluating that instructional change. If not, then we truly do not know what we are doing.

Evaluating Specific Instructional Programs

How does one make a judgment of worth? When assessing specific instructional programs, there are six components of a comprehensive program evaluation:

1. *Evaluation of needs assessment:* The most basic question that program evaluators can ask is: Was there a need for the program? At first glance, this might seem like an unnecessary evaluation component. Why would a school expend resources to adopt a program unless there is clear evidence of need? Yet, after studying innovations in urban secondary schools, Nelson and Sieber (1976) concluded that schools often adopted innovations because of good

salesmanship, the innovation's transportability, or the publicity value of the innovation rather than a desire for educational reform. Also, Berman and McLaughlin (1976) found that schools often adopted innovations in order to receive external funding rather than to respond to locally identified needs. Many new programs, of course, are adopted as a result of genuine needs assessments. In these cases, the needs assessment process (data gathering, data analysis, conclusion drawing) should be reviewed to determine if the assessment was valid—if it identified actual educational needs.

2. *Evaluation of program design:* In Chapter 13 we saw that program planning can take a variety of different forms. For educational programs, some type of coherent, written plan should be made. A second component of program evaluation is to review the written plan. Evaluations should determine whether program goals and objectives are consistent with the needs the program was created to meet (if the goals and objectives are met, will the needs be met?) and whether program activities are consistent with program goals and objectives (if the activities are effectively carried out, will the objectives and goals be met?). Finally, evaluators need to determine if adequate human and material resources have been committed to the program.

3. *Evaluation of readiness:* No matter how critical a need or how logical a plan, programs often fail because some stakeholders (principals, teachers, students, parents, other community members) are not prepared to support implementation. For instance, a sex education program that has been extremely successful in other school districts might be a complete failure in a conservative district if stakeholders are not provided with extensive information about the program and opportunities to have their concerns addressed. Likewise, a peer-coaching program, by itself, is not likely to be successful in a school with a history of teachers exhibiting distrust and animosity toward each other. Extensive communication and trust-building activities would have to precede the peer-coaching program. To carry out this component, evaluators determine if stakeholders were ready for the program, and, if not, whether effective readiness activities were carried out prior to program implementation.

4. *Implementation evaluation:* Key questions evaluators need to answer in this component are: Was the program implemented as planned? If not, why not? and if not, how did the program's implementation differ from the original plan? Three phases of implementation need to be examined: (1) program initiation, (2) program continuation over time, and (3) program integration with the school culture. Implementation evaluation is important because many programs have "failed" because they were never actually implemented as intended, or because initial implementation was followed by a gradual loss of program fidelity. One aspect of implementation that evaluators are wise to examine is the level of administrative support for the program. (In our own

work as program evaluators, we have found that a key aspect of effective implementation is continued, coordinated support by central office administrators, supervisors, and principals.)

5. *Evaluation of outcomes:* There are two types of outcomes or products that evaluators can measure. *Intended outcomes* are the program goals and objectives. *Unintended outcomes* are unforeseen results of the program. Unintended outcomes can be positive or negative.

6. *Cost-benefit analysis:* In cost-benefit analysis, evaluators compare the costs of the program (human and material resources expended, unintended negative outcomes) to its benefits (intended and unintended positive outcomes). This component, used infrequently in educational program evaluations, takes us beyond whether or not program goals were met, to judgments about the relative worth of the program.

The authors' observation and review of program evaluations in education have caused us to conclude that most schools do not engage in comprehensive evaluations involving these six components. Rather, typical evaluations tend to include only Component 5: Evaluation of outcomes. The number of components included in an evaluation will depend on the school's resources, the size of the program to be evaluated, and the purpose of the evaluation. However, a study including all six components will provide those with program decision responsibilities (school committees, curriculum councils, superintendents, school boards, state and federal agencies) the most thorough and informative evaluation results.

Key Decisions in the Program Evaluation Process

Regardless of how many of the six components are included in a program evaluation, a number of key decisions must be made. We will examine each of these decisions.

What Is the Purpose of the Evaluation?

There are two broad purposes of educational evaluation. *Formative evaluation* is intended to improve a program. It is carried out while the program is in progress and can be ongoing throughout the life of the program. *Summative evaluation* results in a definitive judgment about the value of a program. It is carried out after a program has been in existence for a period of time. A summative evaluation is usually the basis for a decision about whether the program will continue, undergo major revisions, or be terminated. Formative and summative program evaluations are not always mutually exclusive. For instance, data gathered for formative evaluations might be reanalyzed later as part of a summative evaluation.

Who Will Evaluate?

Whether the supervisor, a team of faculty members, central office personnel, or private consultants should have major control over evaluation depends on the particular school's resources and the purpose of the evaluation. However, it is critical that teachers be involved in evaluation of instructional programs and the overall instructional effectiveness of their schools and district. All stakeholders (those affected by the decisions from the evaluation) should be not only subjects of study but co-investigators of the study as well. As Greene (1986) has noted, there exists a "consensus on the need for stakeholder participation" (p. 1), and such participation is defined as "shared decision making, rather than just advising or providing input" (p. 9).

What Questions Need to Be Answered?

Specific questions can be formulated for each of the six components of a comprehensive evaluation discussed earlier in this chapter. Evaluation questions will depend on the nature of the program and what members of the evaluation's audience wish to learn about the program. Let's say that a new social studies curriculum is to be evaluated. An *implementation* question might be: To what extent has the new curriculum been implemented at the classroom level? An *outcomes* question might be: What changes in students' knowledge, skills, and attitudes have resulted from the new curriculum? Once the evaluation questions have been formulated, they become the basis for the remainder of the evaluation.

What Data Will Be Gathered and How?

Data sources are persons, places, things, events, or processes from which data needed to answer evaluation questions can be gathered. Examples of data sources are students, teachers, principals, parents, teaching episodes, student products, and school records. *Data-gathering methods* are ways to collect data from sources. Examples include testing, observations, content analysis, case studies, review of records, administration of rating scales and surveys, and interviewing. Our bias is toward using multiple sources of data and multiple data collection methods for each evaluation question. Later in this chapter, we will provide examples of program and school evaluations using multiple sources and methods.

How Will the Data Be Analyzed?

Data analysis is largely determined by the evaluation questions and types of data. Decisions to be made include how to organize, summarize, and display data, and how to reach conclusions based on the data. Central office, university, or private experts may be necessary to assist with complex quantitative or qualitative analysis. Stakeholders, however, can make valuable contributions to data analysis, especially by reviewing results and suggesting explanations, implications, and conclusions.

How Will the Evaluation Be Reported?

After collecting and analyzing the results of tests, observations, surveys, interviews, and testimonials, how should the evaluation be reported? The answer is largely determined by the audience. Most school board members and superintendents will not read a 200-page technical report on the raw data, statistical treatments, and evaluation methodologies. They are interested in the results and conclusions. The technical report should be available to decision makers as a reference to the summarized paper. Any reader of the condensed paper who is confused or desires more information about certain parts of the paper can check the complete technical report.

On the other hand, if the audience for the evaluation report consists of people with sophisticated evaluation skills, a complete technical report would be in order. In a study of violations of evaluation standards (Newman and Brown, 1987, p. 9), among the most frequent violations were "those concerning the evaluator's lack of knowledge of the audience."

Regardless of the audience, there are certain types of information included in most evaluation reports (again, these components will vary in length and technical sophistication depending on the audience). Typical evaluation reports include discussions of

1. The purpose of the evaluation
2. A description of the program being evaluated
3. Evaluation questions or objectives
4. Methodology: data sources, data-gathering methods, and data analysis methods
5. Results and conclusions, including strengths and weaknesses of the program
6. Recommendations for the future

Multiple Sources and Methods

Now that we've taken a close look at the components and key decisions in program evaluation, let's explore the idea of using multiple data sources and multiple data-gathering methods to a comprehensive evaluation of a science program that has been in place for two years. In the first evaluation component, *evaluation of needs assessment,* data sources might be school records of student achievement in science prior to the new program, teachers who used the old science program, and data from the needs assessment administered to science teachers prior to the school's decision to adopt the new program. Data-gathering methods could include interviews of teachers and review of student achievement and needs assessment data.

For the second component, *evaluation of program design,* data sources might be the new science curriculum (goals, objectives, activities, resources and materials, assessment) and the original needs assessment (for comparison with the curriculum). Data would be collected during comparison of these two sources.

The third component, *evaluation of readiness,* could include as sources the science supervisor, teachers, and records of professional-development activities intended to prepare teachers to implement the new program. Data-gathering methods might be interviews, rating scales asking the supervisor and teachers to rate teacher readiness for the new program, and document review.

In the fourth component, *evaluation of implementation,* we would determine whether the new science curriculum was being used as intended. Data sources could be teachers, science lessons, and reports on material utilization. Corresponding data-gathering methods might be teacher self-reports and surveys, classroom observations, and document review.

For the fifth component, *evaluation of outcomes,* data sources could be test scores, grades, exhibits, awards, extracurricular science activities, students, teachers, and parents. Data-collection methods might include review of school records and student products, classroom observations, interviews, and surveys.

Finally, the sixth component, *cost-benefit analysis,* would involve reviewing the data from Component 5 as well as the human and material resources expended on the program, and listing program costs and benefits for review by decision makers.

Overall Instructional Program Evaluation

Evaluating a school's overall instructional program is different from evaluating specific programs. In this section we'll outline an evaluation model that we have used when serving as consultants to schools wishing to evaluate the quality of their instruction with an eye toward comprehensive, schoolwide instructional improvement. We always recommend extensive participation by the school community in planning the evaluation, developing data collection methods, analyzing data, and drawing conclusions about current quality and needed change.

Phase One: Selecting Areas to Be Examined

The evaluation process begins with a meeting with the school's administration and an evaluation steering committee representing key stakeholders from the school community. At that meeting we recommend the following broad areas for evaluation, based on the rationale that each of these areas is significantly related to the success of the school's overall instructional program:

1. Community characteristics
2. School culture and climate
3. School governance
4. Student characteristics
5. Teacher characteristics
6. Parent characteristics

7. Instructional supervision
8. Curriculum and curriculum development process
9. Classroom teaching practices
10. Student assessment methods
11. Student achievement
12. Professional development programs
13. Parent and community involvement programs
14. Relationships with other schools, central office, and external organizations

Of course it's up to the school district or school to decide which areas to evaluate, and the steering committee may wish to delete or add evaluation areas. However, most steering committees agree that a comprehensive evaluation needs to examine all of the preceding areas. At this initial meeting we also propose the remainder of the evaluation process outlined here, with the understanding that the actual evaluation plan will result from a collaborative effort of the consultants and steering committee with input from all of those who will be affected by the evaluation.

Phase Two: Identifying Specific Evaluation Questions

The second phase of the process begins with a large group session attended by administrators, teachers, other staff members, parents, and other community members. After a general session to review the areas to be examined in the evaluation, the group splits up into small planning teams. The number of planning teams is equal to the number of areas to be examined. To the extent possible, each of the stakeholder groups listed earlier is represented within each planning team. Each team is assigned one of the areas for evaluation decided on in phase one and the task of recommending specific evaluation questions for their area. For example, the *community characteristics* planning team agrees on a set of evaluation questions about the community that it believes should be answered by the evaluation, the *school culture and climate* team proposes a set of evaluation questions concerning their assigned area, and so on. A *community characteristics* evaluation question might be "To what extent are community resources used to enhance teaching and learning in our school?" A *school culture and climate* question might be "Is our school culture consistent with the research on successful schools?"

After all planning teams agree on proposed evaluation questions for their broad area, each team presents and explains its recommendations to a general session. Suggestions for deleting, adding, or revising questions are made by general session participants, then considered by the appropriate teams. After each planning team has had the opportunity to revise proposed questions, each team presents its final recommendations to another general session. At this final general session, the entire body of participants votes on whether to include each proposed evaluation question in the evaluation. After the large group session is completed, the consultants and steering committee rewrite the evaluation questions for each area, so that the questions can be presented in a common format. Although the language of a question may be revised, the basic content of the question must remain as it was approved at the general session.

Phase Three: Designing the Evaluation

Phase three consists of consultants, the steering committee, and planning teams collaborating to design the evaluation proper. Teams propose sources (persons, places, things, events, processes) from which data necessary to answer each of their evaluation questions can be gathered, as well as data-gathering methods (testing, observations, content analysis, case studies, record review, rating scales, surveys, interviews, and so on). For reasons of coordination and efficiency, however, it is the evaluation steering committee that makes the final decisions on data sources and data-gathering methods.

After identifying sources and methods, it is time to select or design data-gathering instruments such as tests, classroom observation systems, written surveys, interview guides, and so on. Planning teams make suggestions for specific test items, survey and interview questions, classroom behaviors to be observed, and so on, then the consultants and steering committee construct the instruments. With the wide variety of areas to be assessed, efficiency becomes critical. For example, let's assume that six planning teams each propose several teacher survey questions aimed at gathering data for their assigned areas and research questions. Rather than constructing six different surveys, the consultants and evaluation committee might design a single survey divided into six sections, with the questions within each section designed to gather data sought by a different evaluation team. Figure 15.1 provides a matrix for planning an evaluation of a school's overall instructional program. The grid is used to develop an overview of data sources and data-gathering methods relative to each area to be assessed.

Phase Four: Gathering and Analyzing Data

Teachers, supervisors, and consultants can all assist in gathering data needed to answer evaluation questions. For example, teachers can interview or survey students, gather representative student work, or videotape sample lessons. Supervisors can conduct classroom observations, interview or survey parents, or gather schoolwide student-achievement data. Consultants can provide technical assistance, interview or survey teachers, or conduct qualitative case studies. The best matches of personnel with data-gathering assignments will depend on the nature of the data to be collected and the skills and interests of participants, and thus will vary from school to school. In any evaluation, however, it is essential to clearly define (1) who will be responsible for collecting each type of data and (2) the data-gathering procedures they will follow. Teachers and other staff who will collect data may need staff development to acquire necessary data-gathering skills.

Teachers can also work with supervisors and consultants to analyze evaluation data. Although it may be necessary for consultants to perform more complex

	Data Sources and Data-Gathering Methods																															
Areas to Be Assessed	Students				Teachers				School Leadership				Parents				Community				Central Office				Written Curriculum				School Records			
	R	O	S	I	R	O	S	I	R	O	S	I	R	O	S	I	R	O	S	I	R	O	S	I	R	O	S	I	R	O	S	I
Community Characteristics																																
School Culture & Climate																																
School Governance																																
Student Characteristics																																
Teacher Characteristics																																
Parent Characteristics																																
Instructional Supervision																																
Curriculum																																
Classroom Teaching																																
Student Assessment																																
Student Achievement																																
Professional Development																																
Parent-Community Involvement																																
External Relations																																

Key: R = Review of existing data (demographic data, student achievement data, etc.)
　　　O = Observation or videotaping
　　　S = Written survey, rating scale, etc.
　　　I = Interview

Checks (✓) are placed in appropriate cells to indicate the relationship of areas to be assessed, data sources, and data gathering methods.

FIGURE 15.1 *Planning Grid for Evaluating Overall Instructional Program* statistical or qualitative analysis, teachers can engage in a variety of data analysis activities. They can assist in organizing, reviewing, comparing, and interpreting most types of data, and can participate in data-based decisions concerning needed improvements in the school's instructional program.

Data gathering and data analysis need not be treated as discreet activities. Analysis of data gathered early in the evaluation process may indicate the need to collect additional data in order to adequately answer an evaluation question. Data gathering and analysis thus can be viewed as an interactive cycle rather than a linear process. The data-gathering and analysis process is coordinated by the consultants and steering committee. Figure 15.2 contains an example of a chart that can be used to coordinate gathering and analysis of data for each evaluation question.

Phase Five: Preparing and Presenting the Evaluation Report

Due to the variety of areas addressed in an evaluation of the overall instructional program, this type of evaluation report will be more extensive than an evaluation report on a specific program. The report should address not only each area that was assessed, but also *relationships* between those areas. For example, if most teachers report that the school culture (one area assessed) affects their classroom teaching (another area), observed effects should be discussed in the report. Conclusions made in the report should be based on data gathered during the study and collaborative interpretation of that data.

Recommendations for improving the school's overall instructional program should be directly related to the study's results and conclusions. Some recommendations for improvement will be for specific areas (school governance, curriculum, classroom teaching, and so on), but others will be comprehensive, involving suggested changes that will impact several or all of the areas that have been assessed. Since implementation of all recommendations may not be feasible, they should be prioritized. Like reports on specific programs discussed earlier, the depth and length of the report on an evaluation of the overall instructional program should be tailored to the intended audience, with different audiences receiving different types of reports. Finally, just as we have argued that teachers and other stakeholders should be involved in planning and carrying out the evaluation, we also recommend that representatives of these various groups participate in scheduled presentations of results to the central office, school board, and community groups.

Program Evaluation and Teacher Empowerment

Fetterman (1996) uses the term *empowerment evaluation* to describe program participants evaluating their own program. Empowerment evaluation has two purposes: improving the program and fostering self-determination. Fetterman

Evaluation Question	Coordinator	Evaluation Team Members	Data Sources	Data Gathering Methods	Data Analysis Methods	Evaluation Timeline	Resources Needed
1)							
2)							
3)							
4)							
5)							
6)							

FIGURE 15.2 *Chart for Planning Data Gathering and Analysis*

describes five stages of empowerment evaluation that can be applied to supervisors working with teachers to evaluate instructional programs.

- *Training:* The supervisor teaches teachers how to conduct program evaluations.
- *Facilitation:* The supervisor coaches teachers as they plan and implement the program evaluation.
- *Advocacy:* The supervisor seeks support for the self-evaluation from the administration, parents, and community. If the evaluation results show the need for program changes, the supervisor advocates that teachers be allowed to change the program accordingly.
- *Illumination:* As a result of the evaluation, teachers tend to develop new understanding of the program, their roles, and their relationships with others.
- *Liberation:* Empowerment evaluation often serves to free teachers from previous constraints and roles and enables teachers to become more self-directed.

Empowerment evaluation does not replace program evaluation by external evaluators, but can compliment traditional evaluation by providing rich data to outside evaluators. Since most external evaluations are one-time snapshots of instructional programs, self-evaluations have benefits not typically provided by external evaluations, such as ongoing program improvement and teacher development.

What Is the Supervisor's Role in Program Evaluation?

A supervisor cannot be personally involved in every evaluation but should be responsible for seeing that evaluation of special projects and of the overall instructional programs is ongoing. The supervisor—whether school principal, department head, lead or master teacher, district director, or assistant superintendent—should constantly remind himself or herself of the standards for evaluation of educational programs (Stufflebeam, 1981).

1. *Utility:* Ensure that an evaluation will serve the practical information needs of the audiences.
2. *Feasibility:* Ensure that an evaluation will be realistic, prudent, diplomatic, and frugal.
3. *Propriety:* Ensure that an evaluation will be conducted legally, ethically, and with due regard for the welfare of those involved in the evaluation, as well as those affected by its results.
4. *Accuracy:* Ensure the conveyance of technically adequate information.

With these standards in mind, there are two questions that serve as the core to a purposeful school (Hamilton, 1980):

1. Is what we are doing working?
2. How does it work?

Teacher Evaluation

Although teacher evaluation involves some of the same skills as program evaluation (e.g., data gathering, data analysis), it is essentially a separate process requiring different strategies and techniques. In this section we will compare summative and formative teacher evaluation, propose that these two types of evaluation be carried out separately, discuss self-evaluation, and consider team evaluation.

Comparing Summative and Formative Teacher Evaluation

Summative and Formative are two broad categories of teacher evaluation. **Summative Teacher Evaluation** is an administrative function intended to meet the organizational need for teacher accountability. It involves decisions about the level of a teacher's performance. Summative evaluation always seeks to determine if the teacher has met minimum expectations. If the teacher has not met his or her professional responsibilities, the summative process documents inadequate performance for the purpose of remediation and, if necessary, termination. Sometimes summative evaluation also gathers data to determine if a teacher is eligible for rewards provided by the district for outstanding performance.

Summative evaluation is based on policies that mandate its purpose, frequency, and procedures. Teacher performance is usually documented on an evaluation form. On the form, an administrator completes check lists, rating scales, or narratives indicating the extent to which the teacher has met performance criteria. Evaluation forms usually are standard (same criteria for all teachers) and global (general enough to apply to teachers with different responsibilities). Evaluation forms judge teachers on the quality of their instruction, including such areas as classroom climate, planning, the teaching act, and classroom management (Danielson and McGreal, 2000). But evaluation criteria usually include non-instructional areas as well, such as compliance with school regulations, cooperation with colleagues, completion of extra-curricular assignments, and so on.

Evaluation instruments must be valid (accurate) and reliable (consistent). Valid instruments are those that include all criteria considered essential for effective performance, exclude criteria considered extraneous to effective performance, and weight-relevant criteria in proportion to their importance (Haefele, 1993; Danielson and McGreal, 2000). Reliable instruments include low inference (as nearly objective as possible) rather than high inference (requiring a high level of evaluator subjectivity) indicators. For example, *"teacher clarity"* is an example of a high inference indicator, and *"uses examples when explaining"* is an example of a low inference indicator (Haefele 1993, p. 25). Reliability also requires that administrators be properly trained in the use of the evaluation instrument, so that they become aware of rating errors to avoid and develop a high level of intereval-uator reliability (agreement with experts and other administrators in their ratings of the same teacher).

In addition to validity and reliability of individual evaluations, experts suggest that evaluations be done several different times during the evaluation period rather than relying on a one-shot visit to a teacher's classroom. Also recommended are a preevaluation conference in which the administrator and teacher discuss the evaluation process, and a postevaluation conference in which the administrator reviews the results of the evaluation. Finally, legal and ethical considerations require that when a teacher's performance has been judged to be inadequate, the teacher be notified of deficiencies, given an opportunity to respond, provided a remediation plan and support for implementing the plan, and be reevaluated (Sutton, 1989).

Formative teacher evaluation is a supervisory function intended to assist and support teachers in professional growth and the improvement of teaching. It is focused on the needs of teachers rather than on the organization's need for accountability. Unlike summative evaluation, which usually considers teacher behavior inside and outside the classroom, formative evaluation is focused only on teaching and learning. Summative evaluation is concerned with a summary of performance over a specific time period, whereas formative evaluation is ongoing and concerned with continuous improvement. Rather than relying on standardized evaluation instruments that gather data on all essential performance criteria, formative evaluation is usually based on *systematic observation,* which is limited to a single aspect of classroom process (e.g., questioning techniques, student participation, classroom movement, and so on). Thus, the observation systems described in Chapter 14 are well suited for formative evaluation.

McGreal (1989) has recommended that, in addition to classroom observation data, classroom artifacts be analyzed to evaluate teaching. Artifacts include such things as assignments, experiments, practice activities, projects, quizzes, and tests. Although artifacts could be used as summative evaluation data, their variety and idiosyncrasy mean that comparing many of them to standardized criteria is difficult if not impossible. Artifacts are more useful for formative evaluation. Analysis of artifacts can help supervisors and teachers identify specific areas for instructional improvement as well as plan and monitor improvement efforts. Analysis of systematic observation data and artifacts together increases the value of formative evaluation.

Because it is not concerned with standardized, global criteria, formative evaluation can concentrate on particular contexts and needs of individual teachers. Since its purpose is helping teachers, not judging them, formative evaluation is not concerned with legal issues like due process. Rather, it is concerned with building trust and rapport, developing a collegial relationship between evaluator and teacher, and addressing teacher needs and concerns. Although some have recommended that students, peers, and parents participate in summative evaluation, administrators and teachers have resisted such involvement. However, student, peer, and parent feedback is much more likely to be offered and accepted if done as part of formative evaluation, purely for the purpose of helping the teacher to improve his or her instruction.

Table 15.2 summarizes our comparison of summative and formative teacher evaluation.

Why Summative and Formative Evaluation Should Be Separate

Most school districts have a single evaluation system, and maintain that their system meets both summative and formative needs. However, when schools attempt to carry out summative and formative evaluation simultaneously, they tend to place primary emphasis on summative goals, and formative evaluation is reduced to secondary status. "Too often school districts espouse a strong growth-oriented

TABLE 15.2	Comparison of Summative and Formative Teacher Evaluation	
	Summative	**Formative**
Function	Administrative	Supervisory
Purpose	Accountability; Judgment on teacher performance; Employment decisions	Assistance; Professional development; Improvement of teaching
Scope	Instruction; Compliance with regulations; Extracurricular responsibilities; Personal qualities	Instruction
Focus	Evaluation form	Any classroom data (observation, artifacts, etc.) relevant to the teacher's instructional concerns and needs
Duration	Set period (usually one academic year)	Ongoing (aimed at continuous improvement)
Concerns	Standardization, validity, reliability, due process	Building trust, rapport, collegiality; Understanding context; Understanding and addressing teacher concerns and needs
Evaluator	Usually an administrator; Final decision by administrator	Administrator, supervisor, self, peers, students, sometimes parents

position but the evaluation system constructed does not reflect that stance" (Mc-Greal, 1989, p. 38).

Evaluation systems that purport to combine summative and formative evaluation while relying on rating scales alone are particularly suspect. "A school system that relies solely on periodic evaluations of teacher performance through rating scales *may* capture data suited for in-system summative purposes but will be handicapped in pursuing formative/developmental objectives . . ." (Allison, 1981, p. 15; emphasis in original). One reason for this is that summative rating scales are designed to be standardized, global, legally defensible, efficiently completed and processed, and include many noninstructional criteria. This means not only that the ratings have little value for formative evaluation, but also that the richest, most meaningful data for formative assessment is precluded (Allison, 1981; Stiggins and Bridgeford, 1984).

It is widely recognized that summative evaluation, while necessary to make employment decisions, does not lead to instructional improvement for most teachers (Stiggins and Bridgeford, 1984). In fact, summative evaluation can actually discourage improvement by promoting "negative feelings about evaluation which, in turn, lead to a lack of participation and a lower likelihood of teachers being willing to alter classroom behavior" (McGreal, 1982, p. 303). Successful formative evaluation depends on trust and open communication between the teacher and evaluator. Yet summative evaluation is potentially punitive (Sutton, 1989). The possibility of a bad performance rating is always lurking in the background. It's no wonder that the two types of evaluation don't mix!

We're not arguing that summative evaluation should be eliminated in favor of formative evaluation. Both types of evaluation are necessary. Like Popham (1988), we maintain that since they have entirely different purposes, they need to be kept separate. With McGreal (1982), we argue that the likelihood that either type of evaluation system will succeed is greater if both systems are internally consistent, which can only be accomplished by the two systems being kept separate. If separated, can the two systems coexist? Yes, but only if the purpose of each is clearly defined, they are perceived by teachers as distinct, and the integrity of each is protected (Allison, 1981).

How to Separate Summative and Formative Evaluation

One way to separate the two types of evaluation is to use different evaluators. For example, first-year teachers (who clearly need to have both types of evaluation) could have their summative evaluation carried out by an administrator and formative evaluation by an experienced teacher assigned as their mentor. Experienced teachers could receive summative evaluation from the principal and formative evaluation from an assistant principal for instruction, lead teacher, or peer coach. There are many different combinations of summative and formative evaluators. The important thing is to make clear to everyone who is responsible of each type of evaluation, and to have each evaluator carry out their assessment separately from the other.

Another way to separate summative and formative evaluation relates to the time period when each is carried out. For example, all summative evaluations could be carried out in the fall of each school year, leaving the remainder of the year for formative assessment. When this strategy is used, the same person or persons can perform both types of evaluation. This strategy does not work as well if formative evaluation is carried out in the fall and summative evaluation takes place throughout the rest of the year. This is because the teacher involved in formative evaluation during the fall realizes that summative evaluation is looming on the horizon. That knowledge may affect the willingness of the teacher to engage in open and honest communication about his or her need for instructional improvement. Better to get the summative evaluation out of the way early in the year, give the teacher his or her "seal of approval," and then allow the teacher and supervisor to engage in nonjudgmental assessment for the remainder of the school year. A long-term variation of the "separate time periods" strategy is to conduct summative evaluation throughout the first year of a multiyear cycle, and then focus on formative evaluation for the next two to three years, returning to a summative year at the beginning of the next three- to four-year cycle. Should serious problems with a teacher's performance develop during a formative assessment year, that teacher could be shifted back to a summative evaluation-remediation track until the problem is resolved.

A third way of separating summative and formative evaluation has been suggested by Thomas McGreal (1983). Under McGreal's model, a clear and visible set of minimum performance expectations would be developed, including administrative, personal, and instructional expectations. Teacher performance regarding these minimal expectations would be continuously, informally monitored, but no special procedures or evaluation instruments would be established. If a problem occurred with a teacher's performance, the administrator would remind the teacher of minimum expectations. If the problem continued to occur, the administrator would issue to the teacher a written notice of the teacher's deficiency, with a copy placed in the teacher's file. If serious violations continued even after the formal notice, the administrator would recommend more serious administrative action. Beyond these contingencies, there would be no standard summative evaluation process or annual write-up. This would take care of summative evaluation. Most of the time and energy spent on evaluation would be for formative assessment, including goal setting, a focus on teaching, systematic classroom observation, and collecting and analyzing additional classroom data. This additional data could include peer, parent, student, and self-evaluation, as well as student performance and classroom artifacts (McGreal, 1983).

Which strategy for separating summative and formative evaluation is the best for a district or school will depend on the level of administrative and supervisory expertise, the size of the staff, teacher preference, and available resources. The important thing is that they be kept separate. Doing so will mean that both summative and formative evaluation are carried out more effectively.

Self-Evaluation

Self-evaluation can be an important part of the formative evaluation process for teachers functioning at moderate or high levels of development, expertise, and commitment. Self-assessment can take a variety of forms, including any of the following:

- Visits to the classrooms of several expert teachers for the purpose of comparing expert teaching to one's own teaching, and identifying self-improvement goals based on such comparison
- Videotaping one's own teaching across several lessons, then analyzing teaching performance while reviewing the videotape
- Designing or selecting and analyzing results of surveys or questionnaires administered to students or parents
- Interviewing supervisors, peers, students, or parents about effective teaching and learning or about one's own instructional performance
- Keeping a journal of teaching experiences, problems, and successes, accompanied by critical reflection for the purpose of instructional improvement
- A comprehensive review of student achievement on traditional tests as well as student projects, presentations, portfolios, social behavior, and so on
- The development of a teaching portfolio for the purpose of self-reflection and analysis. Danielson (1996) has recommended a variety of items for possible inclusion in a portfolio, including unit and lesson plans, knowledge of students and resources, videotapes of teaching, examples of student work, written reflections on lessons taught, and logs on professional service, growth, and research. Langer (Teaching for Performance, 1996) has argued for a more focused approach, in which the teacher's portfolio documents a process in which the teacher defines a problem, sets an improvement goal, designs a plan to reach the goal, implements the plan, collects data on professional growth, and reflects upon results. Both Danielson's broad approach and Langer's focused approach go beyond the documentation of teaching accomplishments (the purpose of portfolios used in summative teacher evaluation) by providing teachers with opportunities for self-assessment as the basis for instructional improvement.

It's important to note that self-evaluation of teaching need not be done in isolation. Videotapes, survey or interview results, journals, student achievement data, and teacher portfolios can be analyzed and discussed collaboratively with a supervisor or peers, and in some cases with students or parents. The process is called self-evaluation because the teacher assumes full responsibility for decision making regarding planning and implementing the evaluation as well as the instructional improvement plan which results (Keller and Duffy, 2005). Once the teacher has completed the self-evaluation, she or he may select from a number of vehicles for meeting instructional improvement goals. The teacher might request clinical supervision from a formally designated supervisor, become part of a peer coaching program (see Chapter 16), or begin an individualized professional development program (see Chapter 18).

SUMMARY

Educational program evaluation has been influenced heavily by educational research design. The attention to school performance has stimulated multiple data sources, research designs, and compositions of evaluation teams. A consensus on the need for involving stakeholders in program evaluation has occurred. We must be cautious in selecting instruments that measure what we truly wish to find out about a program. Various types of educational evaluations are used for specific programs and for the overall instructional program. It is not sufficient to know intuitively that a program is good or bad. Rather, decisions about revising, improving, or discarding need to be made with multiple sources of information. The school as a collective enterprise must center its work on questions of educational value and use answers to those questions as guidance for instructional change. Finally, summative and formative teacher evaluation are both necessary but need to be separate. Formative evaluation is more likely to lead to the improvement of instruction.

PRACTITIONER REFLECTION

Real Evaluation

Rebecca B. McCoy, *Assessment Director,*
Georgetown Independent School District

I once thought of evaluation as a very formal process conducted by outside experts confirming what we basically already knew for the sake of justifying a program whenever funding for that program was in jeopardy. Similarly, research was something conducted at the university level and had little practical application to what was happening in my classroom. At least that was my viewpoint early on in my career, which began in the mid-1980s. Research and evaluation seemed far removed from the classroom, like afterthoughts or add-ons in the already hectic and busy world of teaching. A lot has changed since then, including my view of research and evaluation.

Today, research and evaluation are common topics of conversation among teachers, parents, and administrators alike. Our teachers want to read and understand the research behind the state's early childhood reading inventory. Administrators want to see the evaluation data associated with a new program under consideration. Parents want reassurance that their children will benefit from the instructional methods and materials being used. We all want proof that what we are doing is effective. Research and evaluation are seen as ways to help us work smarter and improve schools.

I am very fortunate to be working in a school district that is truly dedicated to improving the quality of instruction through careful analysis of data to evaluate student progress and help guide program decisions. As the assessment director, I work with other program directors and subject area coordinators to design evaluation methods that will provide us with the information we need to make good instructional decisions.

We have a new math coordinator this year who is in the process of learning about the district's math program and making judgments about the program. In a sense, she is conducting an informal evaluation of the district mathematics program. Not only is she studying state and local test results for math, she is also observing in classrooms, talking with teachers and principals, examining student work, and reviewing curriculum materials. She is also working with a district vertical team for mathematics and conversing with program directors and the other subject area coordinators to assist her in collecting and analyzing data. Her assessment of the mathematics program will be much more comprehensive because of the multiple data sources she is using.

Although her evaluation is based on a variety of data-gathering methods and data sources, many evaluations are not so well balanced. I spent the first part of the school year pulling together data for a state evaluation in reading and math. It would have been almost impossible or certainly more time consuming if it had not been for our district's use of technology to enter and store the data. Our teachers entered the reading data in computerized databases so that data retrieval was fairly efficient. Likewise, math data were available in computerized format, which worked well for the state program evaluation. The only data requested were purely quantitative: number of students identified, number of students served, number of teachers trained, amount of money spent, and type of funding used. There were no open-ended questions allowing feedback about teachers' perceptions, attitudes, or behaviors. There were no opportunities to record comments about students' attitudes or behaviors or what strategies worked well and which ones did not fair as well. The narrow focus of the data requested makes me wonder about the true purpose of the state evaluation and how or even if that information can be used to help improve math and reading programs.

One of the projects I have been involved with in our district is making data more accessible to teachers and administrators. I utilized the data that was entered by our teachers into computerized databases for the state evaluation. This database allows teachers and administrators easy access to the data. We have developed training documents to help teachers and administrators understand both how to access the data and use the data to plan for instruction. We have a strong belief in our district that the purpose of evaluation data is to improve the instructional program, thus improving student learning. Data are displayed in computerized spreadsheets and formatted to help teachers identify the specific strengths and weaknesses of their students. This allows teachers to group students more easily for targeted instruction of similar concepts. Teachers can sort and filter the data in a variety of ways to help guide their instructional interventions.

Of course, our ultimate goal is to use evaluation data not only to make good decisions about appropriate interventions but also to improve our instructional programs so that fewer students are in need of intervention. Our professional conversations and practices are taking us in that direction. I have seen a transformation over the past few years as principals and teachers engage in dialogue that is truly focused on improving programs so that all students can be successful. I look forward to working with my colleagues to expand our evaluation methods, gathering a wider variety of data and engaging in increasingly more sophisticated data analysis for program improvement.

EXERCISES

Academic

1. Locate one qualitative study and one quantitative study in educational research. Write a summary of each study. Include in each summary a description of the study's purpose, participants, methodology, results, and conclusions.

2. Locate and summarize evaluations (not descriptions) of three instructional programs. Include in each summary a description of the evaluation participants, methodology, results, and conclusions. Discuss your perceptions of the quality of each evaluation.

3. Locate and review a program evaluation model not discussed in Chapter 15. Write a description and critique of the model.

4. Compare and contrast quantitative research with qualitative research. Refer to at least four outside sources in the paper.

5. A traditional debate in supervision is whether summative and formative teacher evaluation should be integrated within the same evaluation system or kept separate. Find authors (other than the authors of this book) on both sides of this issue. Write a paper summarizing the arguments of the authors.

Field

1. Interview the individual in a school district who is ultimately responsible for evaluating specific and overall instructional programs about procedures for carrying out such evaluations. Write a report summarizing the interview and evaluating the school district program's specific and overall instructional evaluation methods.

2. Interview a person who has served on a self-study team as part of a school evaluation. Include questions on the interviewee's role and function as a team member, self-study methods used by the team, team conclusions and recommendations, changes ultimately made as a result of the self-study, and the interviewee's reactions to his or her participation. Prepare a report on the interview.

3. Develop a written plan for evaluating a specific instructional program with which you are familiar (for example, a K–6 math program, a senior high school Spanish program, or a remedial reading program).

4. Interview a supervisor to determine his or her views on three universal concerns about program evaluation addressed in the chapter: Who should evaluate? How should an evaluation be reported? What is the supervisor's role in evaluation? Prepare a written or verbal report on the interview.

5. Interview a school administrator who has primary responsibility for both summative and formative evaluation of teachers. Ascertain whether the administrator attempts to separate these two functions, and if so, how he or she attempts to maintain such separation. Question the administration on the advantages and disadvantages of such dual responsibility. Prepare a report on your interview.

Developmental

1. Begin to analyze judgments made by educational leaders and others regarding instructional programs to determine which decisions are based on comprehensive evaluation and which are based on cosmetic, cardiac, colloquial, curricular, or computational methods.

2. Begin an in-depth investigation of alternative models for instructional program evaluation.

3. If the opportunity presents itself, volunteer for membership on a school self-study team or a visiting school evaluation team.

REFERENCES

Allison, D. J. 1981. *Process evaluation: Some summarizing and integrating notes on the organizational implications of this form of teacher evaluation.* (ERIC ED 235 580)

Anfara, V. A., Brown, K. M., and Mangione, T. L. 2002. Qualitative analysis on stage: Making the research process more public. *Educational Researcher, 31*(7), 28–38.

Berman, P., and McLaughlin, M. 1976. Implementation of educational innovation. *Educational Forum, 40*(31), 345–370.

Behuniak, P. 2002. Consumer-referenced testing. *Phi Delta Kappan, 84*(3), 199–207.

Bogdan, R. C., and Biklen, S. K. 1992. *Qualitative research for education: An introduction to theory and methods* (2nd ed.). Boston: Allyn and Bacon.

Borg, W. R., and Gall, M. D. 1989. *Educational research: An introduction* (5th ed.). New York: Longman.

Chatterji, M. 2005. Evidence on "what works": An argument for extended-term mixed-method (ETMM) evaluation designs. *Educational Researcher, 34*(5), 14–24.

Creswell, J. 2001. *Educational research: Planning, conducting, and evaluating quantitative and qualitative research.* Upper Saddle River, NJ: Prentice Hall.

Danielson, C. 1996. *Enhancing professional practice: A framework for teaching.* Alexandria, VA:

Association for Supervision and Curriculum Development.

Danielson, C., and McGreal, T. L. 2000. *Teacher evaluation: To enhance teacher professional practice.* Alexandria, VA: Association for Supervision and Curriculum Development.

Fang, Z. 1995. On paradigm shift in reading/literacy research. *Research Psychology, 16,* 215–260.

Fetterman, D. M. (1996). Empowerment evaluation: An introduction to theory and practice. In D. M. Fetterman, S. J. Kaftarian, and A. Wandersman (Eds.), *Empowerment evaluation: Knowledge and tools for self-assessment and accountability* (pp. 3–46). Thousand Oaks, CA: Sage.

Glickman, C. D. 1989. *The story of Ogelthorpe County High School: Five years of shared decision making.* Athens, GA: Monographs in Education.

Glickman, C. D., and Pajak, E. F. 1987. *Concepts of change in school systems improving criterion referenced test scores.* Presentation to the American Educational Research Association, Washington, DC, April.

Greene, J. C. 1986. *Participatory evaluation and the evaluation of social programs: Lessons learned from the field.* Paper presented to the annual meeting of the American Educational Research Association, San Francisco, April.

Haefele, D. L. 1993. Evaluating teachers: A call for change. *Journal of Personnel Evaluation in Education,* 7(1), 21–31.

Hamilton, S. F. 1980. Evaluating your own program. *Educational Leadership, 37*(6), 545–551.

Hathaway, R. S. 1995. Assumptions underlying quantitative and qualitative research: Implications for institutional research. *Research in Higher Education, 36*(5), 535–562.

Keller, C. L., and Duffy, M. L. 2005. "I said that?" How to improve your instructional behavior in just 5 minutes per day through data-based self-evaluation. *Teaching Exceptional Children, 37*(4), 36–39.

Lincoln, Y. S., and Guba, E. G. 1985. *Naturalistic inquiry.* Beverly Hills: Sage.

McGreal, T. L. 1982. Effective teacher evaluation systems. *Educational Leadership, 39*(4), 303–305.

McGreal, T. L. 1983. *Successful teacher evaluation.* Alexandria, VA: Association for Supervision and Curriculum Development.

McGreal, T. L. 1989. Necessary ingredients for successful instructional improvement initiatives. *Journal of Staff Development, 10*(1), 35–41.

Nastasia, B., and Schensul, S. 2005. Contributions of qualitative research to the validity of intervention research. *Journal of School Psychology, 43*(3), 177–195.

Nelson, M., and Sieber, S. 1976. Innovations in urban secondary schools. *School Review, 84,* 213–231.

Newman, D. C., and Brown, R. D. 1987. *Violations of evaluation standards: Frequency and seriousness of occurrence.* Paper presented at the annual meeting of the American Educational Research Association, Washington, DC, April.

Piontek, M. E. 1992. *Synthesized approaches: Expanding the perspectives and impact of qualitative and quantitative evaluation.* Paper presented at the annual meeting of the American Evaluation Association, Seattle, November.

Popham, J. 1988. The dysfunctional marriage of formative and summative evaluation. *Journal of Personnel Evaluation in Education, 1,* 269–273.

Shank, G. 1994. Shaping research in educational psychology. *Contemporary Educational Psychology, 19,* 340–359.

Stiggins, R. J., and Bridgeford, N. J. 1984. *Performance assessment for teacher development.* Portland, OR: Northwest Regional Educational Lab Center for Performance Assessment.

Stufflebeam, D. 1981. *Standards for evaluations of educational programs, projects, and materials.* New York: McGraw-Hill.

Sutton, J. H. 1989. *Evaluation: A primer for teachers.* (ERIC ED 310 146)

Teaching for performance: New assessments help reshape classroom practice (1996, December). *Education Update, 38*(8), 1, 6.

Wolfe, R. 1969. A model for curriculum evaluation. *Psychology in the Schools, 6,* 107–108.

SUGGESTED READINGS

Borg, W., and Gall, M. D. 1989. *Educational research: An introduction* (5th ed.). White Plains, NY: Longman.

Costa, A. L., and Kallick, B. 1995. *Assessment in the learning organization: Shifting the paradigm.* Alexandria, VA: Association for Supervision and Curriculum Development.

Danielson, C. 1996. *Enhancing professional practice: A framework for teaching.* Alexandria, VA: Association for Supervision and Curriculum Development.

Danielson, C., and McGreal, T. L. 2000. *Teacher evaluation: To enhance teacher professional practice.* Alexandria, VA: Association for Supervision and Curriculum Development.

Duke, D. L. (Ed.). 1995. *Teacher evaluation policy: From accountability to professional development.* Albany: State University of New York Press.

Eisner, E. W., and Peshkin, A. 1990. *Qualitative inquiry in education.* New York: Teachers College.

Gredler, M. E. 1996. *School-based evaluation: A dialogue for school improvement.* Oxford, UK: Elsevier Science.

Kremer-Hayon, L. 1993. *Teacher self-evaluation: Teachers in their own mirror.* Boston: Kluwer.

McColskey, W., and Egelson, P. 1993. *Designing teacher evaluation systems that support professional growth.* Greensboro, NC: Southeastern Regional Vision for Education, School of Education, University of North Carolina at Greensboro. (ERIC ED 367 662)

McGreal, T. L. 1983. *Successful teacher evaluation.* Alexandria, VA: Association for Supervision and Curriculum Development.

Nevo, D. 1995. *School-based evaluation: A dialogue for school improvement.* Oxford, UK: Elsevier Science.

Patton, M. Q. 1990. *Qualitative evaluation and research methods.* Newbury Park, CA: Sage.

Peterson, K. D., and Peterson, C. A. 2005. *Effective teacher evaluation: A guide for principals.* Thousand Oaks, CA: Corwin.

Shrinkfield, A. J., and Stufflebeam, D. 1995. *Teacher evaluation: Guide to effective practice.* Boston: Kluwer.

Spray, M. 1993. State assessment programs. Images of state reform. *R and D Preview,* 8(6), 4–5.

Strong, R. W., Silver, H. F., and Perini, M. J. 2001. *Teaching what matters most: Standards and strategies for raising student achievement.* Alexandria, VA: Association for Supervision and Curriculum Development.

Stuffelbeam, D. L. 1991. *The personnel evaluation standards: How to assess systems for evaluating educators.* Newbury Park, CA: Sage.

Tucker, P. D., and Stronge, J. H. 2005. *Linking teacher evaluation and student learning.* Alexandria, VA: Association for Supervision and Curriculum Development.

part five
Tasks of
SuperVision

If one has responsibility for the improvement of instruction, what does one do? We've accounted for what the supervisor needs to possess in terms of knowledge, interpersonal skills, and technical skills. What are the tasks of supervision that can bring about improved instruction? They are direct assistance to teachers, group development, professional development, curriculum development, and action research. How does instruction improve?

Direct assistance: The supervisor can provide or facilitate one-to-one feedback with teachers to improve instruction.

Group development: The supervisor can provide for instructional problem-solving meetings among teachers to improve instruction.

Professional development: The supervisor can provide learning opportunities with teachers to improve instruction.

Curriculum development: The supervisor can provide for changes in teaching content and instructional materials to improve instruction.

Action research: The supervisor can provide teachers with ways to evaluate their own teaching to improve instruction.

Each of these tasks is directly related to improved instruction. A supervisor needs to take responsibility for these tasks if a school is to become increasingly effective. Part V will detail how these tasks can be performed so that teachers take individual and collective responsibility for instructional improvement.

chapter 6

Direct Assistance to Teachers

Direct assistance to help teachers improve instruction can come from different sources. This book has contended that someone needs to take responsibility for the supervisory function of direct assistance to ensure that teachers receive feedback, are not left alone, and are involved as part of a collective staff. Research by Dornbush and Scott (1975) and Natriello (1982) has shown that teachers who receive the most classroom feedback are also most satisfied with teaching. Other research studies have shown that teachers in need of assistance tend to seek out first fellow teachers and second supervisory or administrative personnel (Lortie, 1975). Direct assistance to teachers is one of the crucial elements of a successful school (Little, 1982; Rosenholtz, 1985; DuFour, 2002; Glickman, 2002; Davenport and Smetana, 2004). Keeping the frequency and source of direct assistance in mind, we will look at an established structure for assisting teachers and then at some alternative ways of implementing the structure.

Clinical Supervision

Although there are multiple ways of observing, the model for conducting observations with teachers is relatively standard and accepted, and has a respectable research base (Sullivan; 1980; Adams and Glickman, 1984; Pavan, 1985; Nolan,

Hawkes, and Francis, 1993; Glickman, 2002). In fact, over 90 percent of school administrators in a southern and a midwestern state have cited their knowledge of the use of this structure with teachers (Bruce and Hoehn, 1980). The model, commonly referred to as *clinical supervision,* is derived from the pioneering work of Morris Cogan with supervisors of intern teachers at Harvard University. Cogan's *Clinical Supervision* (1973) and Robert Goldhammer's book, also entitled *Clinical Supervision* (1969), are publications resulting from this pioneer work. Since then, numerous refinements and alterations of clinical supervision have been made (Goldhammer, Anderson, and Krajewski, 1993; Acheson and Gall, 1992; Costa and Garmston, 1985; Anderson and Snyder, 1993; Pajak, 1993, 2002). Those desiring an in-depth study of the research and development of clinical supervision can find references at the end of this chapter.

Clinical supervision is both a concept and a structure. Goldhammer, Anderson, and Krajewski (1993) reviewed nine characteristics of clinical supervision as a concept:

1. It is a technology for improving instruction.
2. It is a deliberate intervention into the instructional process.
3. It is goal-oriented, combining the school needs with the personal growth needs of those who work within the school.
4. It assumes a professional working relationship between teacher(s) and supervisor(s).
5. It requires a high degree of mutual trust, as reflected in understanding, support, and commitment to growth.
6. It is systematic, although it requires a flexible and continuously changing methodology.
7. It creates a productive (i.e., healthy) tension for bridging the gap between the real and the ideal.
8. It assumes that the supervisor knows a great deal about the analysis of instruction and learning and also about productive human interaction.
9. It requires both preservice training (for supervisors), especially in observation techniques, and continuous in-service reflection on effective approaches. (pp. 52–53) (parenthetical explanation provided)

The structure of clinical supervision can be simplified into five sequential steps:

1. Preconference with teacher
2. Observation of classroom
3. Analyzing and interpreting observation and determining conference approach
4. Postconference with teacher
5. Critique of previous four steps

Step 1. At the *preconference,* the supervisor sits with the teacher and determines (1) the reason and purpose for the observation, (2) the focus of the observation, (3) the method and form of observation to be used, (4) the time of observation, and (5) the time for postconference. These determinations are made before the actual observation, so that both supervisor and teacher are clear about what will transpire. The purpose of the observation, as mentioned in Chapter 14, should provide the criteria for making the remaining decisions on focus, method, and time of observation.

Step 2. The next step, *observation,* is the time to follow through with the understandings of the preconference. The observer might use any one observation or combinations of observations. Methods include categorical frequencies, performance indicators, visual diagramming, space utilization, verbatim, detached open-ended narratives, participant observation, focused questionnaire, and tailored observation systems. The observer should keep in mind the difference between *descriptions* of events and *interpretations.* Interpretation should follow description.

Step 3. The *analysis* and *interpretations* of the observation and determination of approach are now possible. The supervisor leaves the classroom with his or her observations and seeks solitude in an office or corner. He or she lays out the recorded pages of observations and studies the information. The task might be counting up frequencies, looking for recurring patterns, isolating a major occurrence, or discovering which performance indicators were present and which were not. Regardless of the instrument, questionnaire, or open-ended form used, the supervisor must make sense out of a large mass of information. Then the supervisor can make interpretations based on the analysis of the description. Figure 16.1 is a form that can be used to organize this task.

A case study might help to clarify this worksheet. Supervisor A has completed a verbal interaction instrument for students and teacher. She reviews the 10 sheets, tallies the columns, and writes in the worksheet under analysis:

1. The teacher asked 27 questions and received 42 answers.
2. Out of 276 total verbal moves, 6 were student to student; the other 270 were teacher to student or student to teacher.
3. . . .

The supervisor, knowing that the purpose of the lesson was to encourage student involvement, now makes interpretations on the worksheet *corresponding* to the analysis:

1. The teacher encouraged students to answer questions.
2. There was little interaction among students.
3. . . .

A. Analysis: Write the major findings of your observation. Write down only what has been taken directly from your observation.

1.

2.

3.

4.

5.

B. Interpretations: Write below what you believe is desirable or not desirable about the major findings.

1.

2.

3.

4.

5.

FIGURE 16.1 *Worksheet for Analysis and Interpretation of Data*

Note the relationship between analysis 1 and interpretation 1. There is clear documentation of evidence leading to the supervisor's judgment.

Let's examine one more case, this time of supervisor B doing a participant observation. The supervisor reads through his brief classroom notes, picks out the most significant events, and writes under "Analysis":

1. James, Tyrone, Felix, and Sondra asked me about the assignment they were supposed to be doing.
2. Kirk and Felipe were talking with each other about sports the three times I overheard them.
3. . . .

From this analysis, the supervisor makes the following interpretation:

1. The teacher was not clearly communicating the directions to some students.
2. At least a couple of students were not interested in the classwork.
3. . . .

Although one could argue with the supervisor's interpretation, it is readily apparent how it was logically derived from the recorded descriptions.

The last determination for the supervisor to make in step 3 of the clinical structure is to choose what interpersonal approach to use with the teacher in the postconference. The directive control, directive informational, collaborative, and nondirective approaches to supervision were explained in Chapters 8, 9, 10, and 11, respectively. Should the supervisor use a directive approach by presenting his or her observations and interpretations, asking for teacher input, setting a goal, and either telling the teacher what actions to take (directive control) or providing teachers with alternative actions to choose from (directive informational)? Should the supervisor be collaborative by sharing the observation, allowing the teacher to present his or her own interpretations, and negotiating a mutual contract for future improvement? Should the supervisor be nondirective by explaining his or her observations and encouraging the teacher to analyze, interpret, and make his or her own plan? The supervisor must consider the individual teacher's level of development, expertise, and commitment as explained in Chapter 12. When working with a teacher who is best matched with a collaborative or nondirective approach and who has experience with clinical supervision, some supervisors provide the teacher with the observation data prior to the postconference. This allows the teacher to review the data in advance and bring his or her preliminary interpretations to the postconference.

Step 4. With the completed observation form, completed analysis, and interpretation form, and with the chosen interpersonal approach, the supervisor is ready to meet with the teacher in a *postconference*. The postconference is held to discuss the analysis of the observation and, finally, to produce a plan for instructional improvement.

The first order of business is to let the teacher in on the observation—to reflect back to the teacher what was seen. Then the supervisor can follow the chosen approach—directive controlling, directive informational, collaborative, or nondirective. The responsibility for developing a future plan may reside with the supervisor, be equally shared, or belong to the teacher. The conference ends with a plan for further improvement. Figure 16.2 can be used to develop such a plan.

The *objective* is a statement of what the teacher will attain for the next observation: "I will improve student-to-student interaction by 50 percent in group discussions." *Activities* are the listed preparation points to accomplish the objective: (1) Practice pausing at least three seconds before answering a student response. (2) Practice using open-ended questions. (3) Set up ongoing mini-debates. *Resources* are the materials and/or people needed to do the activities: (1) Read a book on *Leading Discussion Groups*. (2) Attend a workshop on "Involving Students." (3) Observe Mr. Filler when he holds a science discussion. *Date* and *time* specify when the teacher will be ready to display his or her improvement. Such a

Postconference Date _____ Observed Teacher _____

Time _____ Peer Supervisor _____

Objective to be worked on:

Activities to be undertaken to achieve objectives:

Resources needed:

Time and date for next preconference:

FIGURE 16.2 *Plan for Instructional Improvement*

plan—whether designed by the teacher, the supervisor, or both—should be clearly understood by both parties before they leave the postconference.

Step 5. The *critique* of the previous four steps is a time for reviewing whether the format and procedures from preconference through postconference were satisfactory and whether revisions might be needed before repeating the sequence. The critique can be held at the end of the postconference. It need not be a formal session but can be a brief discussion, consisting of questions such as: What was valuable in what we have been doing? What was of little value? What changes could be suggested? The critique has both symbolic and functional value. It indicates that the supervisor is involved in an improvement effort in the same way as the supervisee. Furthermore, the feedback from the teacher gives the supervisor a chance to decide on what practices to continue, revise, or change when working with the teacher in the future.

The five steps are now complete, and a tangible plan of future action is in the hands of the teacher. The supervisor is prepared to review the plan in the next preconference and reestablish focus and method of observation.

Comparing Clinical Supervision with Teacher Evaluation

In Chapter 15 we discovered the differences between summative and formative evaluation. Clinical supervision is consistent with formative evaluation; it provides nonjudgmental assistance aimed at improving the teacher's instruction. Indeed, it has been equated by some with formative evaluation. Clinical supervision actually includes but goes beyond formative evaluation by helping the teacher to design and implement an action plan to meet instructional improvement goals.

Clinical supervision is *not* consistent with summative evaluation; it is not intended to gather data to make judgments about whether teachers are meeting performance criteria for continued employment. Some school districts have confused the two processes by calling their summative evaluation cycle clinical supervision. At one level this is understandable. Both clinical supervision and summative evaluation can take place within similar structures, including a preconference, classroom visit, and postconference. To understand the difference between the two concepts we must look beyond the structure to the purpose and principles of clinical supervision, which clearly are not consistent with summative evaluation. The two processes need to be separate, for the same reasons that summative and formative evaluation should be separate (see Chapter 15).

Integrating Clinical Supervision and Developmental Supervision

As discovered in Part III, developmental supervision calls for the supervisor to match one of four interpersonal approaches—directive control, directive informational, collaborative, or nondirective—with teachers' developmental levels, expertise, and commitment. Are all four of these interpersonal approaches consistent with clinical supervision? The answer to this question depends to some extent on the model of clinical supervision being considered. Goldhammer's (1969) text on clinical supervision emphasizes a nondirective interpersonal approach. Cogan's (1973) clinical cycle reflects a collaborative orientation. Hunter's (1980, 1983, 1984, 1986) clinical model supports a directive approach. Our own view is that directive informational, collaborative, and nondirective supervisory approaches are all consistent with the clinical model.

Using a directive informational approach, the supervisor can suggest and explain two or three alternative observation foci and data collection methods in the preconference, and ask the teacher to select from the options provided. In the postconference, the supervisor can help the teacher to interpret observation data, and ask the teacher to choose from a limited range of possible improvement objectives, activities, and follow-ups. The supervisor and teacher engaged in a collaborative preconference can consider observation alternatives and select a mutually agreeable observation focus and data-collection method. In the collaborative postconference, the supervisor and teacher can share decision-making responsibility as they build an action plan for instructional improvement. The supervisor using nondirective behaviors in a preconference can ask the teacher to choose the focus of the observation, and facilitate the teacher as he or she chooses or creates an observation system that the supervisor would feel comfortable using. In the postconference, the supervisor would clarify, encourage, and reflect as the teacher designed his or her own improvement plan.

Although directive control behaviors are necessary in rare situations, we do not consider those behaviors to be consistent with the purpose and principles of clinical supervision. Directive control should be used only in short-term, crisis situations, not as part of a normal clinical cycle.

Peer Coaching

Since teachers naturally turn to each other for help more often than to a supervisor, and since supervision is concerned primarily with improving instruction rather than with summative evaluation (renewal of contracts), teachers helping teachers has become a formalized and well-received way of assuring direct assistance to every staff member. With the advent of extended responsibilities for career-ladder teachers, mentor teachers, master teachers, grade-level chairpersons, team leaders, and department heads, the time and resources for peer assistance have increased (see the theme issues of *Educational Leadership*, 1987a, 1987b; and *Journal of Staff Development*, 1987). Keedy (1987) recommended that principals and supervisors provide instructional leadership through the coordination of instructional specialists, rather than by attempting on their own to provide direct assistance to all teachers in the school. If teachers become proficient in observation skills and the format of clinical supervision, the supervisor can take on the role of clarifier, trainer, scheduler, and troubleshooter—clarifier by determining the purpose; trainer by preparing the teachers for the task; scheduler by forming teams or trios of teachers who take responsibility for preconferencing, observing, and postconferencing with each other; and troubleshooter by consulting with teams of teachers who are experiencing difficulties and with individual teachers who need more specialized attention. The use of teachers helping teachers through clinical supervision has been labeled *peer supervision* or *peer coaching*.

Obviously, the way to begin such a program is not to call a staff meeting and announce, "Since I can't see each of you as much as I would like, why don't you start to visit each other? Go to it!" Without planning and resources, disaster is inevitable. To be successful, peer coaching needs components addressing purpose, preparation, scheduling, and troubleshooting. Let's take each in turn.

Purpose

Before beginning a peer-coaching program, clarity of purpose and goals are necessary (Garmston, 1987; Barbknecht and Kieffer, 2001). First, is it really a question of peer assistance (reciprocal interactions of equals) or is it a matter of hierarchical, one-way assistance (a better trained or more experienced teacher helping less well-trained or less experienced teachers)? Second, in a peer program, who is to be the recipient of assistance? Should a teacher who is the observer take from the observation some ideas to use, or should the teacher who is the observed take from the observation some actions to use? Third, will the observations and feedback focus on common instructional skills that each teacher is attempting to learn and implement, or will the observations and feedback focus on the teacher's own idiosyncratic concern with his or her teaching? Fourth, should the observations and feedback focus on the teacher's teaching or on individual students' behaviors? Fifth, is the goal of coaching to be greater awareness and more reflective decision making, or is it to implement particular teaching skills? Ultimately, how does the coaching goal fit into the larger school goal of improving instruction for students?

These are not idle questions. A peer-coaching program void of articulated definition and purpose has no rudder for steering and selecting the training, scheduling, and troubleshooting essential for success. Instead, it becomes another fad, exciting in that it's on the "cutting edge" of school change, but lacking substance in terms of what is to be accomplished. If there is a lack of direction in peer-coaching programs, well-intentioned teachers will have a vague sense of having done something pleasant but little sense of accomplishment (see Little, Galagaran, and O'Neal, 1984). Therefore, the first step is to meet with teachers to discuss how a proposed peer-coaching program would fit into a school's or district's instructional goals and then to decide on the specific purposes of the program. For example, if the purpose is simply to acquaint teachers with each other's teaching strategies, less preparation is needed than if the purpose is to provide teachers with feedback on their teaching and assist them to develop action plans for instructional improvement. The next subsection provides some training guidelines for proceeding with a peer-coaching program that is focused on the purpose of reflective decision making.

Preparation

Before implementation, preparation of teachers would include training on (1) understanding the purpose and procedures of peer coaching, (2) conducting a preconference for determining the focus of observations, (3) conducting and analyzing an observation to distinguish between observing and interpreting classroom events, and (4) conducting two postconferences with different approaches for developing action plans—one using a nondirective approach, the other using a collaborative approach.

A standard form for writing instructional improvement plans in the post-conference should be reviewed. The form should be simple and easy to fill out. Each peer member should understand that a completed plan is the object of the first four clinical steps and the basis for beginning the next round of supervision. For purposes of training, you may use the forms found in this chapter and in Chapter 14.

Training sessions of about six hours should provide the minimum knowledge and skills to begin peer coaching. After peers have gained some familiarity with the process through demonstrations, modeling, and practice in the workshop setting, they will be anxious but ready to begin a coaching cycle. For the initial attempts, perfection is not expected, of course. After the first cycle of implementation, a follow-up meeting should be held to discuss what has occurred and what revisions need to be made before beginning the second cycle. It is often convenient to review the past cycle and conduct the preconference for the next cycle during the same meeting. This gives participants a sense of sharing and learning from each other, enables the trainer to answer questions, allows for observation schedules to be arranged, and eliminates the need to meet another time to hold the preconference. From this point on, follow-up meetings concluding and beginning further cycles can be held every two to three weeks until the agreed-upon number of peer cycles have been finished. For the first year, it is recommended that at least four cycles be conducted—two times being the coach and two times being coached.

Toward the end of the year, a culminating meeting should be held to summarize the advantages and disadvantages of using peer coaching and to make a recommendation on whether to continue the program for the following year.

Let's emphasize that the program should be based on *agreement* and *volunteerism*. If an entire staff is willing to be involved, that's fine, but if only three teachers are willing, it is still a beginning and a previously unavailable source of help for those three teachers.

Scheduling

A teacher will have a more difficult time becoming enthusiastic about a project if it means increasing the amount of personal time and energy expended beyond an already full day. Because peer coaching will require additional time, the program should be voluntary, at least in the beginning. Greater participation of teachers is likely if the supervisor can schedule time for peer coaching during the schoolday. For example, placing teachers together in teams that share the same planning or lunch periods would allow for pre- and postconferences during the schoolday. Hiring a few substitutes for two days, twice a year, would allow teachers to be relieved of class duties so that they can observe their peers. One substitute could relieve six classroom teachers for one period at a time. Relief could also be found by having the supervisor (we mean you!) occasionally substitute for a teacher for one class period. This would enable the teacher to observe and would also give the supervisor a glimpse into the operating world of the classroom. Another way of freeing time for peer observations is for teachers to release each other by periodically scheduling a video, lecture, or some other large-group instruction so that two classes can be taught by one teacher. Whatever the actual schedule used to release teachers for peer coaching, preplanning by supervisor and teachers is needed to ensure that teachers can participate without extreme personal sacrifice. Research on lasting classroom change has shown that scheduling released time for teachers during the schoolday is critical (Humphries, 1981; Ballinger, 2000).

Another issue is arranging teams of teachers. As in most issues in education, there are no hard and fast rules. Generally, teachers should be grouped with each other so that they are comfortable together but not necessarily at identical levels of experience and/or competence. It may be useful to put experienced teachers with new ones, superior teachers with adequate ones, or adequate teachers with struggling ones.

Troubleshooting

The third component of establishing a peer-coaching program is the close monitoring of peer progress. The supervisor should be available to peer teams as a resource person. For example, what happens when the preconference concludes with an agreement to observe a teacher's verbal interaction in the classroom, and the peer coach is at a loss about where to find such an observation instrument? The training program should answer such questions, but orientation meetings cannot cover all possible needs. The supervisor must therefore monitor the needs of peer teams and be able to step in to help.

An elaborate monitoring device is not necessary. The supervisor might simply wander around the halls and check with peer coaches every few weeks. At periodic faculty meetings, he or she might ask peer coaches to write a note on their team progress. The supervisor should be sure that books, videos, and methods/instruments for observations are catalogued and available to teachers in the professional library.

Now that the supervisor can attend to *purpose, training, scheduling,* and *troubleshooting,* a peer-coaching supervision program can be implemented. The initial implementation of such a program undoubtedly will create more work for the supervisor. However, the initial work is less than would be necessary for providing clinical supervision to every teacher two or three times a year. If it is important enough to supervisor and staff, the time spent at the start in preparing for the program will pay off with ongoing instructional improvement of teachers.

Other Forms of Direct Assistance

Clinical supervision and peer coaching are currently two of the most popular forms of direct assistance in schools, but a variety of other forms are available. A few additional examples of direct assistance follow:

- *Demonstration teaching:* The supervisor or expert peer can be a guest teacher, demonstrating a new teaching model or method for the teacher requesting assistance. Alternatively, the teacher seeking to learn new skills can visit an expert peer's classroom for a demonstration lesson. A demonstration teaching cycle can include a preconference in which the demonstrator previews the lesson, and a postconference in which the demonstrator and observer analyze the completed lesson and discuss how the model or methods can be adapted to the observer's teaching.

- *Co-teaching:* The supervisor or expert peer and the teacher seeking assistance together can plan, teach, and evaluate a lesson. Co-teaching establishes trust and rapport, and fosters the collegiality, dialogue, and mutual reflection that foster teacher growth.

- *Assistance with resources and materials:* An unglamorous but vital supervisory activity is providing, explaining, and demonstrating instructional resources and materials. All of us in education are aware of teachers who make little or no use of particular instructional resources and materials (from manipulatives to technology) because of a lack of awareness or expertise. Many teachers would benefit greatly from the effective use of such resources and materials, but they need individualized assistance for technical mastery and adaptation to teaching content and students.

- *Assistance with student assessment:* There is a clear trend within the educational reform movement toward alternative forms of student assessment, especially authentic assessment (Clark and Clark, 2000; Coladarci, 2002; Stiggins, 2002). In the coming years, teachers will likely need considerable direct assistance from supervisors in developing criteria and skills for assessing such things as student portfolios, "real-world" performances, and integrative projects. No doubt, authentic assessment techniques will be introduced to teachers through professional development sessions. However, adapting new assessment techniques to particular content areas, grade levels, and individual students will, we believe, require individualized assistance.

- *Problem solving:* Teachers experience a variety of professional problems that can be solved in one-to-one conferences and without classroom observation. Once a relationship of openness, trust, and rapport has been established, a supervisor can assist a teacher through a problem-solving process involving (1) identification of the problem, (2) generation and weighing of alternative actions, (3) selection of the most appropriate actions, and (4) planning follow-up to assess the results of chosen actions.

- *Mentoring:* In schools, mentoring typically is direct assistance provided by an experienced teacher to a beginning teacher. The mentor might provide any of the forms of direct assistance discussed previously—expert coaching, demonstration teaching, co-teaching, and so on. The heart of mentoring, however, goes beyond any specific form of direct assistance to the ongoing relationship of mentor and beginner. This trusting, helping relationship can make the difference between a successful and a failed entrance to the profession. The formal supervisor has a significant role to play in mentoring programs, helping to select and prepare mentors, assisting with the matching of mentors with beginners, and providing ongoing support for mentors.

Beyond Technical Assistance: Improving Classroom Culture

A great deal of direct assistance is for the purpose of improving teachers' instructional skills or solving immediate instructional problems. As important as these goals are, direct assistance can help teachers reach deeper goals based on democratic and moral purposes. The classroom can be viewed as both a microcosm of the larger culture and as a vehicle for transforming that culture. By modeling and encouraging adherence to democratic and moral values in the classroom, the teacher fosters a democratic and moral society.

The teacher and supervisor can begin the process of improving classroom culture by asking questions like the following:

1. Are students treated equitably by the teacher and by each other?
2. Do the teacher and students follow democratic principles appropriate to the students' ages and maturity levels?
3. Do the teacher and students demonstrate compassion to those in need?
4. Do students feel physically and emotionally safe?
5. Are all cultures respected, valued, and celebrated?

Processes such as clinical supervision and peer coaching can be used to answer questions such as these. Quantitative observation data can be gathered in this arena (for example, data can be gathered on whether the teacher gives students response opportunities, assistance, or praise in an equitable manner), but often rich narrative is needed to adequately describe classroom culture. The teacher and supervisor can work together to interpret the meaning of data on classroom culture, and to develop action plans for cultural improvement. Because classroom culture is so complex, teacher-supervisor conferral and action planning for cultural improvement will be more complicated than conferral and planning for technical improvement, and cultural improvement will take much longer than implementing a new teaching skill. However, if a critical goal of education is a more democratic society, then the increased complexity and longer duration of cultural improvement efforts are well justified.

SUMMARY

Regardless of how or where the responsibilities reside, no school or school system can hope to improve instruction if direct assistance is not provided to teachers. To leave classroom teachers alone and unobserved in their classrooms, without professional consultation and without school resources tailored to their unique needs, is a statement (intended or not) that teaching is unimportant. The message to teachers is that what is important is keeping your class quiet, your doors shut, and your problems to yourself. Assuredly, this is not the message we want to give.

A different message can be given by arranging for observation, feedback, and discussion of classroom improvement. Within the structure of clinical supervision, peer coaching is a recognizable structure for assistance that teachers can use to help each other. Furthermore, supervisors can be accessible, facilitate self- and group evaluation, arrange contact times, and refer specialists to teachers. Direct assistance, separated from summative evaluation, will help teachers confide, improve, and move with each other toward collective action.

PRACTITIONER REFLECTION

A Springboard to Professional Learning Communities

Pam Johnson, *Math Science Coordinator, Hays Consolidated Independent School District*

Serving a district with just over 10,500 students, my position was created to coordinate direct instructional support to teachers. In addition to coordinating ongoing professional development, I lead K–12 vertical teams for instructional improvement in mathematics and science. A primary focus of my position is to facilitate teacher leadership for sustained change and school improvement. I provide feedback to teachers as they implement best practice strategies such as constructivist mathematics and inquiry-based science instruction. More importantly, I consistently utilize opportunities to support the development of professional learning communities at each of the campuses I serve.

Clinical supervision provides an authentic tool for educators to assist one another by examining data gathered in the classroom. This reflection will share a recent experience and explain the steps we are currently taking in our district to bring about a wide-scale use of the clinical supervision cycle as a process for encouraging the development of professional learning communities.

Catherine Rogers, a second-grade teacher and past recipient of the "Teacher of the Year" award for her campus, was teaching a fourth-grade class during summer school. We met on a Monday afternoon in her classroom to conduct our preobservation conference. Miss Rogers explained that she enjoyed summer school because she had the opportunity to work with a diverse group of students with a wide array of instructional challenges. All but one of the 14 students in her summer school class participated in the free lunch program, in comparison to none of her second-grade students at the school where she teaches during the school year. "Poverty," she commented to me, "is indeed a very real challenge in the learning process."

Prior to our preconference, Miss Rogers had given some thought to the data that she would like me to collect during the observation on the following day. She was specifically interested in receiving feedback on the number of open-ended questions she asked in comparison to the number of closed questions asked. Her curiosity was fueled by wondering if her varied expectations of the summer school students affected the level of questioning she applied in the classroom. Would the data collected be evidence that her expectations varied for low socioeconomic students? Or would the data confirm that she applied the same critical thinking expectations for the students enrolled in summer school?

During the preconference, to clarify expectations, we discussed what constituted a closed question as opposed to an open-ended question. Together we designed a chart to denote whether the questions were directed to the whole class, groups, or individuals. The simple, handwritten chart would allow for me to tally the types of questions, and it provided a space for me to script examples of open-ended and closed questions I observed.

The next morning, during the observation, Miss Rogers read a chapter from *Charlie and the Chocolate Factory*. As she asked questions, I sat in the back of the classroom and quietly gathered the data, tallying and scripting. As the observer, the most difficult challenge is remaining focused during the data-gathering process. I concentrate on gathering the data by seeing myself as "the instrument," recording accurate data as it occurs, and resisting the urge to crawl on the floor with the students and be led away by the delightful lesson. The more entertaining the lesson, the more difficult the task of focusing can become for the observer! I collected over four pages of data to share.

The next step in the process led me to "clean up my notes." During this time I began to analyze the data as I looked for patterns and relationships between the tally marks and the types of questions. Appreciating that I am the outside observer, I made note of questions that I would ask to clarify the data I gathered during the observation. During the analysis process, I planned questions to ask Miss Rogers such as, "When you asked this student a follow-up question, were you seeking clarification by the student to check for understanding or were you purposefully asking the question to prompt additional thought and to extend the student's thinking past the immediate response?" When examining the direct assistance I provided to teachers, the same might be asked of my follow-up questions. During the postconference session, as the supervisor, I intentionally asked questions to springboard conversation about the learning process.

During our postobservation discussion, Miss Rogers noticed that some of the closed questions that I recorded could have been asked differently to create open-ended questions by simply adding a phrase of "why" or "explain your thinking." As we discussed the data, we debated different questions and further discussed what constituted closed versus open-ended questions. As the observer and supervisor, I was learning too. We were on common ground and having a rich conversation about student participation.

When we met for the postprocess critique, Miss Rogers had some interesting observations to share regarding the clinical supervision process. She described enjoying the process because, unlike other observations, she did not feel she was being evaluated, but rather that this was a collaborative exploration of student learning. She suggested that the process made her more consciously skilled at asking open-ended questions and therefore she would look to extend the skill. We agreed that to determine if her questioning really did vary in the summer school setting, I would need to gather the same type of data in Miss Rogers's second-grade class during the school year.

Offering to return the favor of the data-gathering experience, Miss Rogers agreed to work with me during a teacher in-service in August, using the same chart to gather data on the types of questions I ask teachers during a 45-minute period of professional development. We agreed that this could be the beginning of a practice across our district that offered objective feedback to teachers that was less apt to encourage judgment and criticism, which is frequently feared in any type of peer observation. To achieve this district approach, Miss Rogers, a member of the district math vertical team, would share the clinical supervision process with our vertical teams with the intention of sending our district math and science leaders back to their campus with a new strategy for providing direct assistance.

As we planned, the practice of clinical supervision is growing in our district. Clinical supervision allows for instructional leaders to focus their classroom observations on specific aspects of teaching and learning as determined by the teacher being observed. The power behind the process is the reflection, conversation, and action for improving our practice that is generated through the collaborative look at teaching and learning. In a district position, this process enables me to coordinate direct assistance to teachers in a way that strengthens professional relationships. Strong collaborative relationships are the heart of building professional learning communities.

EXERCISES

Academic

1. Locate three research studies on clinical supervision. Write a summary of each study, including purpose, participants, methodology, results, and conclusions.

2. Write a paper (a) giving advantages and disadvantages of having clinical supervision done by a formally designated supervisor and (b) giving advantages and disadvantages of having clinical supervision performed by other teachers (peer coaching). Refer to at least three outside sources in your paper.

3. Locate three research studies on peer coaching. Write a summary of each study, including purpose, participants, methodology, results, and conclusions.

4. Assume you are a supervisor who has been asked by the superintendent to begin a peer-coaching program in one of the district's medium-sized schools. Prepare a written plan for introducing peer coaching to all the school's teachers, training a volunteer group of teachers in the clinical process, selecting teams (matching teachers), scheduling an initial round of clinical cycles, and monitoring the peer-coaching program.

Field

1. Interview a supervisor who follows the clinical model in supervision of teachers on the practical advantages and disadvantages of clinical supervision. Prepare a report on your interview.

2. Arrange to supervise a teacher using the clinical model (preconference, observation, analysis and interpretation, postconference, critique). Record the preconference, postconference, and critique on audiotape, and write a summary of the clinical cycle.

3. Conduct a group interview with a team of teachers involved in peer coaching on the specifics of the program, problems encountered, and perceived value of peer coaching for instructional improvement. Prepare a report on the interview.

4. Prepare a survey instrument to be completed by teachers that (a) defines direct assistance, (b) asks teachers to list the types of direct assistance they desire from supervisors, and (c) asks teachers to list the types of direct assistance they desire from other teachers. Distribute the survey to at least 10 teachers, and request that they respond anonymously, in writing, to the 2 survey questions. Collect the surveys and process and analyze response data. Prepare a report on which types of direct assistance the respondents desire from supervisors and from fellow teachers.

Developmental

1. Begin an in-depth study of the development of clinical supervision by comparing three major works in clinical supervision, such as Goldhammer (1969); Cogan (1973); and Goldhammer, Anderson, and Krajewski (1993).

2. Begin an in-depth study of peer coaching.

3. As you continue your readings on the tasks of supervision, note the interrelationship of direct assistance with the other tasks of supervision and how previously discussed knowledge and skills of supervisors are common prerequisites for each task.

REFERENCES

Acheson, A. A., and Gall, M. D. 1992. *Techniques in the clinical supervision of teachers* (3rd ed.). New York: Longman.

Adams, A., and Glickman, C. D. 1984. Does clinical supervision work? A review of research. *Tennessee Educational Leadership, 11*(11), 38–40.

Anderson, R. H., and Snyder, K. J. (Eds.). 1993. *Clinical supervision: Coaching for higher performance.* Lancaster, PA: Technomic Publishing.

Ballinger, J. 2000. Programs aim to stop teacher washout. *Journal of Staff Development, 21*(2), 28–33.

Barbknecht, A., and Kieffer, C. W. 2001. *Peer coaching: The learning team approach.* Arlington Heights, IL: Skylight.

Bruce, R. E., and Hoehn, L. 1980. *Supervisory practice in Georgia and Ohio.* Paper presented at the annual meeting of the Council of Professors of Instructional Supervision, Hollywood, FL, December.

Clark, D. C., and Clark, S. N. 2000. Appropriate assessment strategies for young adolescents in an era of standards-based reform. *The Clearing House, 73*(4), 201–204.

Cogan, M. 1973. *Clinical supervision.* Boston: Houghton Mifflin.

Coladarci, R. 2002. Is it a house or a pile of bricks? Important features of a local assessment system. *Phi Delta Kappan, 83*(10), 772–774.

Costa, A. L., and Garmston, R. 1985. Supervision for intelligent teaching. *Educational Leadership, 42*(5), 70–80.

Davenport, J., and Smetana, L. 2004. Helping new teachers achieve excellence. *The Delta Kappa Gamma Bulletin, 70*(2), 18–22.

Dornbush, S. M., and Scott, W. R. 1975. *Evaluation and the exercise of authority.* San Francisco: Jossey-Bass.

DuFour, R. 2002. How deep is your support system? *Journal of Staff Development, 23*(4), 72–73.

Educational Leadership. 1987a. Theme issue: Staff development through coaching, *44*(5).

Educational Leadership. 1987b. Theme issue: Collegial learning, *45*(3).

Garmston, R. J. 1987. How administrators support peer coaching. *Educational Leadership, 44*(5), 71–78.

Glickman, C. D. 2002. *Leadership for learning: How to help teachers succeed.* Alexandria, VA: Association for Supervision and Curriculum development.

Goldhammer, R. 1969. *Clinical supervision: Special methods for the supervision of teachers.* New York: Holt, Rinehart and Winston.

Goldhammer, R., Anderson, R. H. and Krajewski, R. J. 1993. *Clinical supervision: Special methods for the supervision of teachers* (3rd ed.). Fort Worth: Harcourt Brace Jovanovich.

Humphries, J. D. 1981. *Factors affecting the impact of curriculum innovations on classroom practice: Project complexity, characteristics of local leadership and supervisory strategies.* Unpublished Ed.D. dissertation, University of Georgia.

Hunter, M. 1980. Six types of supervisory conferences. *Educational Leadership, 37,* 408–412.

Hunter, M. 1983. Script-taping: An essential supervisory tool. *Educational Leadership, 41*(3), 3.

Hunter, M. 1984. Knowing, teaching, and supervising. In P. L. Hosford (Ed.), *Using what we know about teaching.* Alexandria, VA: Association for Supervision and Curriculum Development.

Hunter, M. 1986. Let's eliminate the preobservation conference. *Educational Leadership, 43*(6), 69–70.

Journal of Staff Development. 1987. Theme issue: Peer coaching, *8*(1).

Keedy, J. L. 1987. Principals as instructional leaders: A realistic definition. *ERS Spectrum: Journal of School Research and Information, 5*(1), 3–7.

Little, J. W. 1982. Norms of collegiality and experimentation: Work place conditions of school success. *American Educational Research Journal, 19*(3), 325–340.

Little, J. W., Galagaran, P., and O'Neal, R. 1984. *Professional development roles and relationships: Principles and skills of "advising."* (Contract 400–83–003.) San Francisco: Far West Laboratory for Educational Research and Development.

Lortie, D. C. 1975. *School teacher: A sociological study.* Chicago: University of Chicago Press.

Natriello, G. 1982. *The impact of the evaluation of teaching on teacher effect and effectiveness.* Paper presented at the annual meeting of American Educational Research Association, New York, March.

Nolan, J., Hawkes, B., and Francis, P. 1993. Case studies: Windows into Clinical Supervision. *Educational Leadership, 51*(2), 52–56.

Pajak, E. 1993. *Approaches to clinical supervision: Alternatives for improving instruction.* Norwood, MA: Christopher-Gordon.

Pajak, E. 2002. Clinical supervision and psychological functions: A new direction for theory and practice. *Journal of Curriculum and Supervision, 17*(3), 189–205.

Pavan, B. N. 1985. *Clinical supervision: Research in schools utilizing comparative measures.* Paper presented at the annual meeting of the American Educational Research Association, Chicago, April.

Rosenholtz, S. J. 1985. Effective schools: Interpreting the evidence. *American Journal of Education, 93,* 352–388.

Stiggins, R. J. 2002. Assessment crisis: The absence of assessment for learning. *Phi Delta Kappan, 83*(10), 758–765.

Sullivan, C. G. 1980. *Clinical supervision: A state of the art review.* Alexandria, VA: Association for Supervision and Curriculum Development.

SUGGESTED READINGS

Acheson, A. A., and Gall, M. D. 1992. *Techniques in the clinical supervision of teachers* (3rd ed.). New York: Longman.

Anderson, R. H., and Snyder, K. J. 1993. *Clinical supervision: Coaching for higher performance.* Lancaster, PA: Technomic.

Coe, P. E. 1990. *Toward collegial inquiry: Is there more to clinical supervision than the improvement of practice?* Paper presented at the annual meeting of the American Education Research Association, Boston, April.

Goldhammer, R., Anderson, R. H., and Krajewski, R. J. 1993. *Clinical supervision: Special methods for the supervision of teachers* (3rd ed.). Fort Worth: Harcourt Brace Jovanovich.

Neufeld, B., and Roper, D. 2003. *Coaching: A strategy for developing instructional capacity.* Cambridge, MA: Education Matters.

Pajak, E. 1993. *Approaches to clinical supervision.* Norwood, MA: Christopher Gordon.

Richard, A. 2003. *Making our own road: The emergence of school-based staff developers in America's public schools.* New York: Edna McConnell Clark Foundation.

Willerman, M., McNeely, S. L., and Koffman, E. C. 1991. *Teachers helping teachers.* New York: Praeger.

Group Development

Avertical team at Highlands Elementary School is using action research to improve student literacy. The Level Six team at M. L. King Middle School is developing a new interdisciplinary curriculum. A teacher task force at Edwards High School is examining strategies for assisting at-risk students.

The teams described above are different in terms of school level and purpose, but they also have much in common. Each of the groups has a task it is expected to complete that will involve making a number of decisions along the way. Each group needs to be concerned about maintaining positive interpersonal relationships. And each group is almost certain to face some level of conflict and some types of dysfunctional behavior along the way. There are myriad teams with myriad purposes operating at schools across the nation, but they all possess some common roles, developmental phases, and challenges. This chapter discusses task and personal roles needed by all groups, dysfunctional roles that can impede any group, and general approaches to conflict management and decision making. There are, of course, differences among groups, including differences in group purposes, ability, and commitment. This chapter also addresses changing group leadership style to match group readiness for the situation at hand.

Learning the skills of working with groups to solve instructional problems is a critical task of supervision. Just as cooperative learning with students has been found to produce significant gains in academic and social outcomes (Cooper, 2002; King, 2002; Slavin, 1987; Wheelan and Kesselring, 2005), so have collegial adult groups been shown to produce higher adult achievement and performance than individualistic or competitive learning (Johnson and Johnson, 1987b; Yorks and Kasl, 2002; Kasl and Yorks, 2002). This chapter covers knowledge, skills, and procedures for developing productive instructional improvement groups: using group observations, changing group leadership styles, dealing with dysfunctional members, resolving conflict, preparing for meetings, and facilitating large-group involvement.

Professional people who are brought together to deal with pressing mutual problems have the right to expect results. Meetings that drag on, with seemingly endless and unfocused discussion, are morale breakers. Participants become reluctant, apathetic, and sometimes hostile toward future meetings. They might even suspect that the group leader is deliberately leading them astray, so that the group's inability to decide can be used as an excuse for the leader to do whatever he or she wishes. Regardless of whether the leader is actually trying to create confusion or truly desires a group decision, the lack of clear results erodes unity and common purpose. We already know how important unity, common purpose, and involvement are in developing a cause beyond oneself related to school success.

Groups that work productively, efficiently, and harmoniously generally have a skillful leader. Unfortunately, since being part of a group is such an everyday occurrence in professional, personal, and social life, we seldom stop to think about what makes some groups work well and others fail. It is unrealistic for the leader of a new group to expect the group to proceed naturally in a professional manner. A leader needs to be conscious of the elements of a successful group, select clear procedures for group decision making, be able to deal with dysfunctional behavior, use conflict to generate helpful information, and determine appropriate leadership style.

Dimensions of an Effective Group

There are two dimensions of an effective professional group (Bales, 1953): the task dimension and the person dimension. The *task* dimension represents the content and purpose of the group meeting. The task is what is to be accomplished by the end of the meetings. Typical tasks of professional groups might be deciding on a new textbook, writing a new instructional schedule, coordinating a particular curriculum, or preparing a professional development plan. An effective group, obviously, accomplishes what it sets out to do. The *person* dimension of an effective group comprises the interpersonal process and the satisfaction participants derive from working with each other. Concern and sensitivity to participants' feelings create a climate of desiring to meet with each other from week to week to accomplish and implement the group task.

Let's explain these two dimensions in a different way. Specific task behaviors are clarifying the group's purpose, keeping discussions focused, setting time limits, and appraising group progress toward the goal. A leader who says, "We're getting off the track; let's get back to discussing textbooks," is exhibiting a task behavior. Specific person behaviors seen in a group include recognizing people for their contributions, smiling, injecting humor, and listening attentively. A leader who says, "Fred, I'm following what you've been saying; it's a point worth considering," would be demonstrating a person behavior. Imagine a group that exhibits only task behaviors. The meeting would be formal, cold, and tense. People would not receive feedback, would not be encouraged, and probably would swallow hard before addressing the unsmiling, staring faces. Such a group would accomplish its task quickly, with little mutual support. The decision would be quick because participants would wish to remove themselves from the tense environment as soon as possible. The formality of the sessions would prevent in-depth discussions of feelings, attitudes, and differences of opinion. Decisions would be made on the basis of incomplete information and commitment from group members. The implementation of the decision would be problematic at best.

Next, imagine a group that exhibits only person behaviors. There would be much personal chatter, humorous storytelling, and frequent back slapping and touching. People would be smiling and laughing. The image of a raucous cocktail party might characterize a group with all person behaviors and no task behaviors, and the morning-after hangover is also analogous to the sense of accomplishment after a meeting devoid of task behaviors. People would enjoy each other's company for its own sake; everyone would have a wonderful time, but little would be done.

Group Member Roles

First, the leader needs to determine what behaviors are indicative of roles already in existence. Are some members displaying task roles and/or person roles? What roles are ongoing? Are certain roles lacking? Remember that both task and person roles are functional to group performance. Another set of roles and behaviors, called *dysfunctional,* distract a group from task and person relations. Dysfunctional roles, unlike functional roles, are a concern when present. After listing and briefly describing the most common functional member roles, we will examine dysfunctional roles.

Task Roles

The following descriptions are adapted from those listed by Benne and Sheats (1948):

Initiator-contributor: Proposes original ideas or changed ways of regarding group problem, goal, or procedure. Launches discussion, moves group into new areas of discussion.

Information seeker: Asks for clarification in terms of factual adequacy. Seeks expert information and relevant facts.

Opinion seeker: Asks for clarification of values pertinent to the group undertaking or to proposed suggestions. Checks on others' attitudes and feelings toward particular issues.

Information giver: Provides factual, authoritative information or gives own experience relevant to the issue.

Opinion giver: Verbalizes his or her own values and opinions on the group problem; emphasizes what the group should do.

Elaborator: Picks up on others' suggestions and amplifies with examples, pertinent facts, and probable consequences.

Coordinator: Shows the link between ideas and suggestions, attempts to pull diverse proposals together.

Orienter: Clarifies the group's position, gives a state-of-the-scene review. Summarizes what has been discussed, points out where discussion has departed from the goal, and reminds the group of their ultimate goal.

Evaluator-critic: Evaluates the proposals of the group against a criteria of effectiveness. Assesses whether proposals are "reasonable," "manageable," "based on facts," and derived through fair procedures.

Energizer: Focuses the group to move toward decisions. Challenges and prods group into further action.

Procedural technician: Facilitates group discussion by taking care of logistics. Sees that the group has the necessary materials for the task (paper, pencils, chalk, and so on).

Recorder: Writes down the group's suggestions and decisions. Keeps an ongoing record of what transpires in the group.

A group needs these member roles to keep moving toward accomplishing its task. A leader can use these descriptions to figure out what roles are missing. Additional roles might need to be assigned to group members or incorporated by the leader. For example, a group might contain most of the task roles except for a procedural technician or recorder. Such a group probably would converse easily but would bog down on recalling what has been said. The leader who knows what roles are needed can ask for a volunteer to be a recorder and summarizer. Knowledge of task roles and behaviors enables a leader to assess what roles are evident and what further roles need to be assigned. The leader might take on some of the missing roles, assign them to others, or add particular persons to a group.

Person Roles

The knowledge of person roles and behaviors provides a guide to the group leader. Consider the following descriptions:

Encourager: Affirms, supports, and accepts the contribution of other members. Shows warmth and a positive attitude toward others.

Harmonizer: Conciliates differences between individuals. Looks for ways to reduce tension between members through nonthreatening explanations and humor.

Compromiser: Offers to change his or her proposals for the good of the group. Willing to yield position or to acknowledge own errors by meeting other opposing ideas halfway.

Gatekeeper or expediter: Regulates flow of communication by seeing that all members have a chance to talk. Encourages quiet persons to speak and puts limits on those who dominate the conversation. Proposes new regulations for discussions when participation becomes unbalanced.

Standard setter: ego ideal: Appeals to group's pride by not letting group members give up when trouble occurs. Exudes confidence that the group is a good one and can make sound decisions.

Observer and commentator: Monitors the working of the group. Records who speaks to whom, where and when most roadblocks occur, and the frequency and length of individual members' participation. Provides feedback when the group wishes to evaluate its procedures and processes.

Follower: Is willing to accept the decisions of the group and follow them even though he or she has not been active or influential in those decisions. Serves as a listener to group discussion.

The seven person roles provide human satisfaction and group cohesiveness. People feel positive about meeting and talking with each other and comfortable enough to express their ideas. As a result, meetings are seen as pleasant times to continue the group's work. When person roles are missing, a group may face severe difficulties in making acceptable and committed decisions. Without person behaviors and roles, only the strongest, most assured, and vocal members will speak. Decisions might be made that more timid persons strongly reject but the group may not know that such strong disapproval exists. Again, it is the group leader's responsibility to see if people roles are evident. If roles are missing, then he or she can confront the group with their absence, pick up the role(s) himself or herself, quietly suggest particular roles to existing members, or add to the group other individuals who more naturally play such roles. *Both task and person roles, when not already in existence, need to be added.*

Dysfunctional Roles

Dysfunctional roles and behaviors are those that are conspicuous in their presence. Such roles and behaviors disrupt the progress toward a group goal and weaken group cohesiveness. Consider the following:

Aggressor: Personally attacks the worth of other members. Belittles and deflates the status, wisdom, and motivation of others. Examples of such verbal attacks are: "That's the most ridiculous thing I've ever heard," "You must be crazy to suggest . . . ."

Blocker: Sees all opinions and suggestions by group members as negative. Opposes any decision being made and stubbornly refuses to propose alternatives. Examples of such blocking statements are: "That's a terrible idea," "I don't want to do that," "It's futile to do anything."

Recognition-seeker: Uses the group setting to receive personal attention. Examples of such behaviors are dropping books, scattering papers, coughing incessantly, pretending to be asleep, raising hand and then forgetting what one was going to say.

Self-confessor: Uses the group to ventilate personal feelings not related to the group's tasks. Talks about personal problems or feelings of inadequacy whenever he or she can see ways to slip such confessions into the group discussion. Examples of self-confessing statements are: "This discussion reminds me of when I was a little child and the weight problem I had," or when the group is talking about differences of opinion, "You should hear my son and me fight; I don't know what to do about him."

Playboy or playgirl: Lacks interest and involvement by using the group setting to have a merry time. Distracts other members from the group's purpose. Tells private jokes, passes notes, makes faces at others, plays cards, and so on.

Dominator: Asserts superiority in controlling group discussion and dictates what certain members should do. Claims to know more about the issue under discussion and have better solutions than anyone else. Has elaborate answers to almost every question and monopolizes the discussion.

Help-seeker: Tries to gain group's sympathy by expressing feelings of inadequacy or personal confusion. Uses such self-derogation as reason for not contributing: "This is all too confusing for me," "I can't make a decision on my own," "Why ask me? I can't help."

Special-interest pleader: Has no opinion or suggestions of his or her own but instead speaks for what others would say or do. Cloaks own bias by using an outside group: "We couldn't do that. Do you know what the school board would think?" "If those parents down in the local restaurant ever heard that we were going to change . . . ."

Dysfunctional roles are fairly self-evident in a group. The leader's responsibility is to reduce or eliminate such dysfunctional roles before they severely harm the morale and efficiency of the group. He or she might try to understand the dysfunctional member's reason for acting as an aggressor, playboy, special interest pleader, and so on, and then might either confront the person privately or provide changes within the group to satisfy the unmet needs that are leading to the dysfunctional behavior. Methods for dealing with dysfunctional behaviors will be discussed shortly, but first let's focus on leadership styles matched with maturity levels of groups.

Changing Group Leadership Style

If a group lacks either task or person behaviors, the leader can choose a style that will fill the void. A group that exhibits much initiative, information, and competitiveness (high task) as well as hostility, aggression, and bitterness (low person) could benefit from a leadership style that is encouraging, praising, harmonizing, and humorous (high person). A group that exhibits much positive camaraderie (high person) but is being uninterested, apathetic, or uninformed (low task) could benefit from a leadership style that presses for information, sets goals, and enforces procedures (high task).

The work of Hersey and Blanchard (1969, 1988) on what they call the "life-cycle theory of leadership," also known as *situational leadership,* is a comprehensive theory of leadership style in response to group characteristics. Hersey and Blanchard identified four styles of leadership based on the relative emphasis on task and relationship (person) behavior:

Style 1 (S1): High task, low relationship. This is an autocratic style, whereby the leader tells the group members what is to be done, when, and by whom. The leader makes decisions for the group. This style is similar to directive supervision, discussed in Chapters 8 and 9. One word that describes this style is *telling.* The leader determines both the process and the content of decision making.

Style 2 (S2): High task, high relationship. This is a democratic style whereby the leader actively participates with the group both as a facilitator of the decision-making process and an equal member contributing his or her own ideas, opinions, and information. This style is similar to collaborative supervision, explained in Chapter 10. One word that describes this influencing style is *selling.* The leader attempts to influence both the processes and the content of decision making by being a persuasive equal.

Style 3 (S3): High relationship, low task. This is an encouraging and socializing style whereby the leader promotes cohesion, open expression, and positive feelings among the members but does not influence or interfere with the actual decision. (The leader's role is one of clarification, encouragement, and reflection.) The style is similar to nondirective supervision, described in Chapter 11. Note that the leader participates by helping members express their ideas, opinions, and needs but does not participate in the sense of offering his or her own ideas, opinions, and needs. The leader participates in the process but not in the content of decision making.

Style 4 (S4): Low relationship, low task. This is a hands-off or laissez-faire style whereby the leader turns the task over to the group and does not participate in any manner. The leader tells the group what the task is and then physically or mentally removes himself or herself from any further involvement. One word that describes this style is *delegating*. The leader is involved in neither the process nor the content of decision making.

Hersey and Blanchard (1988) stated that effective leadership is based on matching leadership style to the readiness of the group. The readiness of a group depends on the particular task; the same group could be of high readiness for one task and low readiness for another. Readiness can be assessed according to the characteristics of ability and willingness.

Ability is the knowledge, skills, and experience to achieve without the need for outside assistance.

Willingness is the degree of motivation, confidence, and interest in accomplishing certain tasks.

The leader can assess the readiness of individuals and a group according to these levels (Hersey and Blanchard 1988, pp. 176–177):

- *Readiness Level One (R1)*
  Unable and unwilling
  Unable and insecure

- *Readiness Level Two (R2)*
  Unable but willing
  Unable but confident

- *Readiness Level Three (R3)*
  Able but unwilling
  Able but insecure

- *Readiness Level Four (R4)*
  Able and willing
  Able and confident

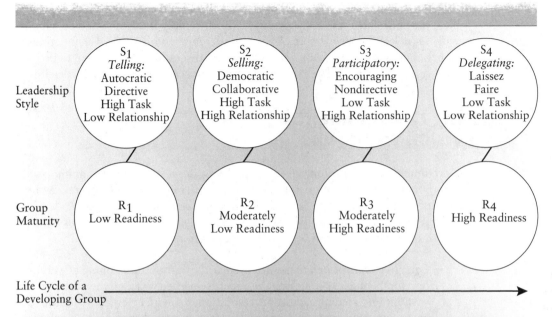

FIGURE 17.1 *Matching and Directionality of a Developing Group*

Situational leadership matches leadership style to the readiness level of the group (see Figure 17.1 on matching and directionality of a developing group). An R1 group is best matched with a *telling* autocratic style (S1). An R2 group is best matched with a *selling,* democratic style (S2). An R3 group is best matched with a *participating,* encouraging style (S3). An R4 group is best matched with a *delegating,* laissez-faire style (S4).

Hersey and Blanchard's theory was originally called *life-cycle leadership* but is now more commonly referred to as *situational leadership.* This is an unfortunate change in terminology, because *life cycle* connotes development or growth in both leader and group behaviors, an implication that is missing from the term *situational.* Groups are complex human entities that respond to the gradual shifting of a group leader's external control in the same manner that an individual teacher will respond to gradual shifting of supervisory control. In other words, an R1 (low readiness) group with an S1 (telling and autocratic) leadership style will not develop until the leader gradually allows them to gain greater internal control. An unmotivated group might work most efficiently with S1 leadership at first. As the group gains experience, as members become acquainted with each other, and as the group acquires expertise, the leader should be alert to those signals of increasing readiness and provide for greater group involvement by shifting to an S2 leadership style. It is conceivable that a group working on a long project might complete the entire life cycle by beginning with S1 (telling) leadership and concluding with S4 (delegating) leadership. A group leader might work toward eliminating his or her control over the group. The ultimate goal should be for a group to provide its own task and person behaviors and not be dependent on formal leadership.

Applying Developmental Supervision to Groups

Developmental supervision, when applied to groups, has much in common with situational leadership but also has some key differences. Let us first review how developmental supervision is used with groups, and then compare the developmental model with situational leadership. The developmental supervisor matches one of the four supervisory approaches to the group's characteristics:

- *Directive control behaviors* are used with a group functioning at very low developmental levels, lacking the expertise needed to act on the problem, and without any commitment to its resolution, or in an emergency situation. In group meetings, a supervisor uses directive control behaviors to give a clear message about what changes are expected. The supervisor *presents* by stating his or her understanding of the problem, *clarifies* by asking group members if they have any perceptions to add, *listens* to input, and then *problem solves* by reassessing the problem and possible solutions. She or he then *directs* by stating what is to be done, *clarifies* by asking for additional input, *standardizes* by laying out a specific timeline and expectations, and *reinforces* by monitoring the expected group performance. The supervisor moves away from directive control and toward directive informational behaviors as soon as possible.

- *Directive informational behaviors* are used with a group functioning at fairly low developmental levels, with little expertise, and little commitment. The supervisor *presents* by stating his or her understanding of the problem, *clarifies* by asking group members for input, *listens* to their perceptions of the problem, and *problem solves* by formulating two or three alternative solutions. He or she *directs* by stating the alternatives, *listens* after asking the group for input, and *directs* by reformulating and stating final choices. The supervisor *clarifies* by asking the group to choose from alternatives, *standardizes* by suggesting a timeline and criteria for success, and *reinforces* by suggesting ways to follow-up.

- *Collaborative behaviors* are used when the group is functioning at moderate or mixed levels of development, the supervisor and group have the same degree of expertise concerning the problem, and both the supervisor and group are committed to solving the problem. The supervisor *clarifies* by asking group members for their perceptions of the problem, *listens* to group perceptions, and *reflects* by verifying group perceptions. The supervisor *presents* by adding his or her perceptions, *clarifies* by determining if the group understands supervisor perceptions, *problem solves* by exchanging suggested solutions, *encourages* by accepting conflict, and *negotiates* a mutually acceptable solution. Finally, the supervisor *reflects* by summarizing the collaborative plan.

- *Nondirective behaviors* are used when the group is functioning at high developmental levels, possesses extensive expertise, and is highly committed to solving the problem. The supervisor *listens* as group members provide their perceptions of the problem, *reflects* by paraphrasing group members' perceptions and feelings, *probes* the group for additional information on the problem's underlying causes, *listens* further to teacher perceptions, and *reflects* further by continuing to paraphrase group members' comments. The supervisor *problem solves* by asking the group to think of possible actions and to consider the consequences of potential actions, *presents* by asking the group to commit to a plan of action, *standardizes* by asking the group to establish a timeline and criteria for success, and *reflects* by restating the group's plan.

The long-term goal of the developmental supervisor is to foster the group toward higher levels of development, expertise, and commitment. This can be accomplished through training in collaborative skills (communication, decision making, problem solving, and so on), providing observer feedback on group behaviors, facilitating self-study, facilitating reflection on group process, and a variety of other strategies for group development. As the group develops, the supervisor gradually shifts from directive to collaborative or from collaborative to nondirective behaviors.

Comparing Developmental Supervision with Situational Leadership

Situational leadership and developmental supervision with groups have several commonalities. Both begin with the leader assessing group characteristics. In situational leadership, ability and willingness are assessed; and in developmental supervision, adult development levels, expertise, and commitment are assessed. Both models match alternative leadership approaches with group characteristics. The situational leader matches a telling approach (high task, low relationship) to groups of low readiness, and a developmental supervisor matches directive control or directive informational behaviors to low readiness groups. Unlike developmental supervision, situational leadership does not distinguish between controlling and informational "telling."

Both the developmental and situational models call for using high-task, high-relationship leadership with groups of emerging readiness. In developmental supervision this approach is referred to as *collaborative*, and in situational leadership it is called *selling*. Developmental supervision's nondirective approach is similar to situational leadership's participatory style: both involve low-task, high-relationship leadership. A major difference between the two leadership models is that, unlike situational leadership, developmental supervision does not include a "delegating" (laissez-faire) approach. The developmental model holds that laissez-faire supervision is inappropriate even when working with groups functioning at the highest readiness levels. For the developmental supervisor, nondirective supervision of highly developed groups still includes forming or maintaining a strong relationship with the group, and active group facilitation through listening, clarifying, encouraging, and reflecting.

Critical to both developmental supervision and situational leadership is leadership to assist the group toward higher levels of readiness and performance, with increasing decision-making responsibility handed over to the group as it grows in its capacity to assume responsibility.

Dealing with Dysfunctional Members

The fact that a group is made up of individuals with varying temperaments and motivations is important when thinking about ways to work with groups. Dealing with individuals, particularly those who display dysfunctional behaviors, is an additional responsibility of a group leader.

If the leader has observed the group at work and has determined that his or her own leader behaviors are appropriate for most members of the group, yet there continue to be a few dysfunctional members, then individual treatment might be in order. The procedure for treating a dysfunctional member is (1) observe the member, (2) try to understand why the member is acting unproductively, (3) communicate with the member about the behavior, (4) establish some rules for future behavior, and (5) redirect the unfavorable behavior (Corey and Corey, 1982; Kemp, 1970). Each step of this procedure will be amplified.

1. *Observe the member:* When and with whom does the dysfunctional behavior occur? What does the group member do, and how do others respond? For example, a dominator might start monopolizing the conversation as soon as he or she walks into the meeting. Other people might be interested in the dominator's talk for the first few minutes of the meeting but become increasingly annoyed as the dominator continues. They might roll their eyes, yawn, fidget, or make comments to each other.

2. *Try to understand the member:* Why does the member persist with dysfunctional behavior? Does he or she know the behavior is unproductive? Is the behavior being used to mask some underlying emotion? For example, a playboy might be insecure about his own worth and pretend not to care rather than exposing inner thoughts to the scrutiny of the group.

3. *Communicate with the member:* What can you communicate about the group member's behavior and the situation? Describe the situation and the behavior to the member without denigration. Instead of saying, "You're being an aggressive son of a gun," say, "I've noticed that you speak loudly and angrily to Sara. At the last meeting, you told her to keep her mouth shut." Tell the dysfunctional member the effect of the behavior on you as group leader: "When you tell Sara to shut up and tell Bob that he's stupid, it starts an argument that takes time away from the meeting. I can't complete the agenda on time when those arguments take place" (see Gordon, 1980).

4. *Establish some rules for future behaviors:* Either ask the member to suggest some rules that he or she can abide by in the future, or tell the member your future rules, or establish them jointly. Regardless of which tactic is chosen, the leader should think of rules that would minimize further disruptions to the group. For example, the leader might say to a self-confessor, "The next time you have a personal problem, come speak to me privately about it," or to a dominator, "I'm going to enforce a two-minute limit on every member's participation," or to a blocker, "If you don't think we're on the right course, tell us your objection once and only once."

5. *Redirect the unfavorable behavior:* Pick up on the group member's dysfunctional behavior, and try to make it functional. A dominator can be assigned the role of recorder, summarizer, or time keeper. A playboy can be given an opening time for sharing a funny story to relax the group before starting official business. An aggressor can be asked to play devil's advocate and argue the position of an adversary.

The five steps outlined here will help the meeting leader understand and deal with individual dysfunctional behavior. The steps are predicated on the leader confronting the dysfunctional member in private. Dysfunctional behaviors that occur infrequently and in isolated situations might simply be ignored. The leader can respond to infrequent misbehaviors or make light of them: "Sara, I guess you really got wound up today; perhaps we might hear from someone else now." Only incessant behaviors that distract the entire group need to be dealt with via direct confrontation. Confrontation is not easy but is necessary at times for the sake of the group. Role play 17.1 provides for a demonstration of how to deal with a dysfunctional group member.

ROLE PLAY 17.1 Dealing with a Dysfunctional Group Member

Context. The purpose of this role play is for a subgroup of four to provide a demonstration to the remainder of the group on how to effectively deal with a dysfunctional group member. Participants will need approximately 20 minutes of preparation time away from the rest of the group. In the role play, a "supervisor" and three "teachers" are members of a committee meeting to discuss a schoolwide instructional issue. In their preparation for the role play, the role players may choose the school level (elementary, middle, or high school), the issue to be discussed, and any other details of the fictional situation that they need to agree on to perform an effective role play. The group is assigned or chooses a dysfunctional role that one member of the group will assume during the role play. The role play is presented in three scenes.

Scene 1 (10 minutes). The supervisor and three teachers begin the meeting. Throughout the scene, one of the teachers assumes a dysfunctional role that is clearly impeding the rest of the group's efforts to resolve the issue. The supervisor observes the teacher's dysfunctional behaviors. This scene ends with a break in the meeting, with the issue unresolved. During the break the other two teachers leave to get a cup of coffee, and the supervisor and the dysfunctional teacher are left alone.

Scene 2 (10 minutes). In a private discussion with the dysfunctional teacher during the break, the supervisor uses techniques suggested under this chapter's heading "Dealing with Dysfunctional Members" to address the teacher's behaviors. The specific discussion will depend on the dysfunctional role that the teacher has been playing. The discussion culminates with an agreed-upon plan for minimizing future disruptions.

Scene 3 (10 minutes). The other teachers return and the meeting resumes. Due to the agreements worked out during the break and the supervisor's support during the second part of the group meeting, the teacher's dysfunctional behaviors are greatly reduced. The group is able to resolve the issue under discussion.

Whole Group Processing (10 minutes). The entire group discusses what the dysfunctional role was, specific behaviors that indicated the dysfunctional role, and effects of the dysfunctional role on the group in Scene One. Next, the group discusses the techniques used by the supervisor in Scenes Two and Three to deal with the dysfunctional role, and the effects of those techniques on the teacher and group.

Resolving Conflict

The key to a productive group is the way ongoing conflict is resolved. Conflicts are particular disagreements that occur between two or more members at a particular time. *Conflict is not necessarily dysfunctional.* In fact, research has shown that successful groups exhibit much conflict (Johnson and Johnson, 1987a; Fullan, 2000). As Roger Johnson stated, "A critical moment of truth in a . . . group is when two teachers disagree strongly with each other and argue . . ." (Brandt, 1987). A group can make wise decisions only when there is a wealth of information and ideas to consider. Information and ideas are generated through conflict. To suppress conflict is to limit the group's decision-making capacity. Therefore, the leader should encourage conflict, not stifle it. Of course, conflict, if not handled correctly, can degenerate into adversarial and harmful relations. It is not conflict that is bad; it is the way the leader deals with it that determines its value.

Conflict occurs when there is a disagreement over ideas. The leader should keep the disagreement focused on the ideas rather than on the personalities of the members. The following procedure for handling conflict serves as a ready reference for the group leader:

1. Ask each member to state his or her conflicting position.
2. Ask each member to restate the other's position.
3. Ask each member if conflict still exists.
4. Ask for underlying value positions: Why do they still stick to their positions?
5. Ask other members of the group if there is a third position that synthesizes, compromises, or transcends the conflict. If not, reclarify the various positions. Acknowledge that there exists no apparent reconciliation, and move the discussion to other matters.

The following is an application of conflict-resolution procedures to a high school meeting:

> The supervisor from the central office has called a meeting of the English high school department heads to discuss possible changes in the tenth-grade English curriculum. The topic of composition writing comes up, and two department heads begin to argue. Mrs. Strick of Toofarback High School says, "We need to require three formal compositions each semester from each tenth-grader. Each composition should be graded according to spelling, punctuation, and format. I'm sick and tired of seeing kids coming into the eleventh grade without being able to put a sentence together!"
>
> Mr. Ease of Space High School objects: "Are you serious? Six technical compositions a year should just about kill any remaining interest that tenth-graders have in writing. That is a ridiculous idea!"

The language supervisor, Mr. Cool, is now aware of a conflict and wants to capitalize on these varying points of view in providing information to the group. At the same time, he is aware of emotional intensity in this conflict (words such as *sick and tired* and *ridiculous*) and wishes to soften the emotion and promote the ideas. So he uses step 1 and asks the two members to state their conflicting positions.

> "Mrs. Strick and Mr. Ease, you both have definite ideas about the requirements of technical compositions. We are interested in fully understanding what you think. Would you each take a few minutes and further explain your positions?"

After Mrs. Strick and Mr. Ease have stated their positions, the supervisor moves to step 2 by asking each member to restate the other's position.

"Now that you have stated your position, I want to make sure that you fully understand each other. Mrs. Strick, would you please paraphrase Mr. Ease's position, and Mr. Ease, would you repeat Mrs. Strick's position." Mrs. Strick says, "Mr. Ease thinks that technical writing assignments are a waste of time and students lose interest." Mr. Ease replies, "No, I didn't say they are a waste of time; but if such assignments are frequent, students learn to hate English class." Mr. Ease then restates Mrs. Strick's position: "You're saying that tenth-graders need skills in the basics of writing. Required compositions would ensure proper spelling, grammar, and format." Mrs. Strick replies, "Yes, that's what I'm saying."

Now that both positions have been made and paraphrased, Supervisor Cool goes to step 3 and asks if conflict still exists.

He asks Mrs. Strick and Mr. Ease: "Are you both still far apart about composition requirements for tenth-grade English?" Mrs. Strick nods, but Mr. Ease says, "Well, not as far apart as at the beginning. I'm not against some technical writing requirements. It's the number, three for each semester, that hangs me up. I could accept one per semester." Mrs. Strick replies, "Well, I can't. If they are going to write correctly, they must do it frequently. Three compositions a semester is just the minimum!"

Mr. Cool, knowing that Mrs. Strick is adamant about her position, goes to step 4, asking for the underlying value:

Mr. Cool asks Mrs. Strick: "Could you explain why technical composition writing is important to you?" Mrs. Strick says, "Kids today don't get any basics in writing. Everything is creativity, expression, write it like you speak it in the streets! I was taught standards of good manners and proper English. If these kids are to succeed in later life, they have to know how to write according to accepted business and professional standards. I'm not being hardnosed for my own sake. It's them I'm concerned about!" Mr. Cool turns to Mr. Ease and says, "What about you? Why do you disagree?" Mr. Ease replies, "I don't completely disagree, but I'm against making tenth-grade English class a technical writing drill. Writing should be a vehicle for expression and students should love, not dread, it. They should be able to write personal thoughts, juggle words and formats, and not worry about every comma and dotted *i*. Let them play with words before pushing standards at them. I don't write letters with one-and-a-half-inch margins to my friends or in my diary—why should kids have to? Sure, there is a need for them to learn to write formally, but not at the expense of hating to write!"

Mr. Cool restates the conflict to the group: "We have an obvious disagreement between Mrs. Strick and Mr. Ease. Mrs. Strick believes there should be at least three technical compositions per semester in the tenth grade. Mr. Ease believes there should be less emphasis on technical writing and more on expressive writing."

Supervisor Cool goes to step 5: *Asking other members of the group if there is a third position that can be taken.* Some members might side with one over the other, suggest a compromise (one technical composition in the first semester, two in the second semester), or offer a new alternative (let's require a three-week mini-course of technical writing and let each school decide the type of work and assignments). If the conflict between Mrs. Strick and Mr. Ease does not resolve itself, the supervisor acknowledges that the conflict remains: "We understand the difference of opinion that you both have, and we can't find a ready solution." Then he moves to other matters: "Eventually the committee will have to decide or vote on what to do about required assignments. For now, we'll leave this particular issue and discuss the tenth-grade testing program."

Conflict cannot and should not be avoided. Conflict, if encouraged and supported, will enable a group to make better decisions. It is the group leader's handling of conflict that makes the difference. The group should have the feeling that it is all right to disagree and that anyone who does disagree will be able to make his or her full position known. Role play 17.2 provides for demonstrations of the right way and the wrong way to deal with conflict within a group.

ROLE PLAY 17.2 Resolving Conflict

Context. The purpose of this role play is for a sub-group of five to provide a demonstration to the remainder of the group on how to effectively resolve conflict within a group. Participants will need approximately 20 minutes of preparation time away from the rest of the group. In the role play, a "supervisor" and four "teachers" are members of a committee meeting to discuss a schoolwide instructional issue. In their preparation for the role play, the role players may choose the school level, the issue to be discussed, and any other details of the fictional situation that they need to agree on to perform an effective role play. The group is assigned or chooses a conflict to be played out between two members of the group during the meeting. The role play is presented in two scenes.

Scene 1: Wrong Way (10 minutes). Soon after the beginning of the meeting, a conflict breaks out between two of the "teachers." The supervisor and the other teachers in the group deal with the conflict poorly, and the meeting deteriorates rapidly. The meeting breaks up with neither the interpersonal conflict nor the original issue resolved.

Scene 2: Right Way (10 minutes). This scene involves the same group, the same setting, and the same issue. The same conflict breaks out between the same two teachers. This time, however, the supervisor and teachers in the group use procedures discussed under this chapter's topic "Resolving Conflict" to facilitate a resolution of the conflict and the original issue by the end of the meeting.

Whole Group Processing (10 minutes). The entire group discusses the nature of the conflict, the failed efforts to resolve it, and effects of the conflict on the group in Scene One. Also discussed are the techniques used to resolve the conflict, and the effects of the conflict resolution process in Scene Two.

Preparing for Group Meetings

A group can proceed more easily with its task if the leader has made certain preparations. Shelton and Bauer (1994) suggested that premeeting planning should involve decisions about whether a meeting is necessary, who should attend the meeting, setting, agenda, and preparation. Figure 17.2 includes specific questions that Shelton and Bauer recommend planners consider when preparing for a meeting. Some especially important aspects of preparing for a meeting include planning an agenda, establishing ground rules, and writing guided discussion questions.

Should We Meet?

1. Can a memo be used instead of holding a meeting?
2. Is there a goal for the meeting?

Who Should Attend the Meeting?

3. Who needs to come to the meeting?
4. Will there be less than 15 participants?

The Setting

5. Where will the meeting be held?
6. Is the site convenient to participants?
7. Will a circular table arrangement be used?
8. Is the room temperature comfortable?
9. Have refreshments been arranged?

The Agenda

10. Have all participants been asked for agenda input?
11. Are the "For Information" items stated in sentence format?
12. Are the "For Discussion" items stated in question format?
13. Has the draft agenda been proofed?
14. Has the agenda been distributed, with at least two days lead time?

The Preparation

15. Have possible "troublesome items" been thought through?
16. If problem solving is a goal of the meeting, has the problem been adequately explained to meeting participants?
17. Has someone been asked to take minutes?
18. Has a follow-up on the previous evaluations been done?
19. Have evaluation forms (Blips) been distributed?

FIGURE 17.2 *Shelton and Bauer's Pre-Meeting Planner*

Source: Maria M. Shelton and Laurie K. Bauer, *Secrets of Highly Effective Meetings*, p. 43. Copyright © 1994 by Corwin Press. Reprinted by Permission of Sage Publications, Inc.

Agendas

A group has to be clear on its task and purpose. Why are they meeting? What are they to accomplish? Is there to be a product? An agenda distributed several days before the actual meeting will inform members of the reasons for the meeting and what will be accomplished. The agenda need not be elaborate. See Figure 17.3 as a sample agenda. Notice how the agenda includes a brief explanation and a break-down of items. Time limits for each item provide members with a sense of prior-ities as well as the assurance that the leader plans to end on time. Keeping to starting and ending times displays respect for group members' personal schedules.

Establishing Ground Rules

Participants will need to know not only agenda items like the meeting's purpose, place, time, and topics, but also behaviors that are expected of them at the meet-ing. Ground rules can be established in advance concerning any of the following:

- Type of participation expected (sharing of information, professional dia-logue, choosing from established alternatives, brainstorming, problem solv-ing, conflict resolution, and so on)
- Roles to be assigned (coordinator, time keeper, information giver, recorder, etc.)

To: All physical education teachers
From: Morris Bailey, athletic director
Subject: Agenda for the meeting of February 23 in Room 253, 3:30–5:00

Next Thursday will be the last meeting before voting on the revisions of our student progress forms. Remember, bring any progress forms you have collected from other school systems. Sally and Bruce are to report on the forms provided by the State Department. At the conclusion of the meeting, we are to make specific recommendations of changes.

Agenda

I. Review purpose of meeting	3:30–3:40
II. Report from Sally and Bruce on State Department forms	3:40–4:00
III. Report on other school system forms	4:00–4:20
IV. Discussion of possible revisions	4:20–4:40
V. Recommendations	4:40–5:00

See you Thursday. Please be on time!

FIGURE 17.3 *Sample Agenda*

- Interpersonal expectations (everyone contributes, use active listening, criticize ideas but not people, consider each person's views, use agreed upon conflict management strategies, and so on)
- Decision-making method (decision by averaging individuals' opinions, majority vote, consensus, etc.)
- Type of follow-up expected (assigned tasks, continued dialogue, classroom implementation, follow-up meeting, and so on)

Guided Discussion

When meeting with a small group to discuss an issue, it is helpful to have in mind the type of questions to ask. Typically, questions to be asked will shift during a meeting. At the beginning of the meeting, the leader usually spends time clarifying the topic for discussion. During the meeting, the leader uses open-ended questions that allow for seeking, elaborating, and coordinating of ideas, opinions, and information. At the conclusion of the meeting, the leader asks questions that summarize what has been accomplished and what remains to be done.

Some discussion questions that might help as a reference are presented in Figure 17.4. Prior to a meeting, the leader might review the questions in Figure 17.4 and write down specific questions concerning the topic to have in front of him or her. When the discussion stalls, the leader can look at his or her notes and ask one of the preselected questions. A discussion guide helps the leader ensure that the topic will be thoroughly examined.

Procedures for Large-Group Involvement

With small groups of up to 10 members, all members have a chance to participate actively throughout the decision-making process (Hare, 1976, pp. 230–231). When the number of group members is large, however, it becomes difficult for everyone to participate actively. For example, what does a curriculum director do when there is an important curriculum decision to make involving over 100 teachers? What does a school principal do when there is an important rescheduling decision to make that involves a faculty of 70 persons? From 75 to 100 teachers sitting in a cafeteria to discuss an issue would be an exercise in folly. At best, only a few brave souls would speak up, and the leader would have no sense of what others thought. If the leader truly wants the involvement of all members in making a decision, then tightly planned procedures are necessary. With all the procedures about to be described, faculty should clearly understand the decision-making method to be used for the final decision (majority vote, consensus, frequencies, and so on).

Three different procedures will be explained. An example involving a staff of 75 teachers brought together for the purpose of deciding how to allocate the

Questions Designed to Open Up Discussion

1. What do you think about the problem as stated?
2. What has been your experience in dealing with this problem?
3. Would anyone care to offer suggestions on facts we need to better our understanding of the problem?

Questions Designed to Broaden Participation

1. Now that we have heard from a number of our members, would others who have not spoken like to add their ideas?
2. How do the ideas presented so far sound to those of you who have been thinking about them?
3. What other phases of the problem should be explored?

Questions Designed to Limit Participation

1. To the overactive participant: We appreciate your contributions. However, it might be well to hear from some of the others. Would some of you who have not spoken care to add your ideas to those already expressed?
2. You have made several good statements, and I am wondering if someone else might like to make some remarks?
3. Since all our group members have not yet had an opportunity to speak, I wonder if you would hold your comments until a little later?

Questions Designed to Focus Discussion

1. Where are we now in relation to our goal for this discussion?
2. Would you like to have me review my understanding of the things we have said and the progress we have made in this direction?
3. Your comment is interesting, but I wonder if it is germane to the chief problem that is before us.

Questions Designed to Help the Group Move Along

1. I wonder if we have spent enough time on this phase of the problem. Should we move to another aspect of it?
2. Have we gone into this part of the problem far enough so that we might now shift our attention and consider this additional area?
3. In view of the time we have set for ourselves, would it be appropriate to look at the next question before us?

Questions Designed to Help the Group Evaluate Itself

1. I wonder if any of you have a feeling that we are blocked on this particular question? Why are we tending to slow down?
2. Should we take a look at our original objective for this discussion and see where we are in relation to it?
3. Now that we are nearing the conclusion of our meeting, would anyone like to offer suggestions on how we might improve our next meeting?

Questions Designed to Help the Group Reach a Decision

1. Am I right in sensing agreement at these points? (Leader then gives brief summary.)
2. Since we seem to be tending to move in the direction of a decision, should we consider what it will mean for our group if we decide the matter this way?
3. What have we accomplished in our discussion up to this point?

Questions Designed to Lend Continuity to the Discussion

1. Since we had time for partial consideration of the problem at the last meeting, would someone care to review what we covered then?
2. Since we cannot reach a decision at this meeting, what are some of the points we should take up at the next one?
3. Would someone care to suggest points on which we need further preparation before we convene again?

FIGURE 17.4 *Questions for Use in Leadership Discussion*

Source: Produced in group development course at the University of Georgia.

use of six new computers in the high school resource center will be used. All three methods are based on breaking the entire group into subgroups of 7 to 12 and having a representative committee of one member from each subgroup. Please refer to Figure 17.5 as the three procedures are explained.

Procedure A, postrepresentational, begins with step 1. The leader convenes the entire group and explains the task and procedures to be used and the method of decision making. Step 2 is assigning the 75 faculty members to seven subgroups of 10 to 11 members each. The leader should have decided on assignments of subgroups according to logical criteria (grade level, content field, or years of teaching experience). Grouping can be made horizontally (teachers of the same grade, content field, or teaching experience) or vertically (teachers from different grade levels, content fields, or years of teaching experience). The subgroups are assigned to discuss the topic, make recommendations, and select a representative both to report the group's position and to be a member of the representative committee. After the subgroup meeting, the representatives report orally on their subgroup's position to the entire faculty. After each subgroup has reported, the entire faculty recesses. In step 3, the representative committee, consisting of the seven representative members, meet on their own to recommend or decide the use of the computers. In step 4, the entire faculty reconvenes to hear the representative committee's recommendation or decision. Again, the leader should have made clear at the beginning whether the representative group would come to the faculty with a recommendation or a decision. If it was to be a recommendation, the entire faculty would vote on the proposal; if it was to be a decision, the entire faculty would listen to the decision.

The advantages of the postrepresentative procedure is that a decision can be made after only a few meetings. The disadvantage is that subgroup members might feel that hidden influences are affecting the representative committee. Since most faculty members (in the example, 68 out of 75) are omitted from the representative committee meeting, speculation might abound about what transpires in the representative group. However, since each faculty member helped to choose the representatives, trust in their work should prevail.

Procedure B, open representation, is similar to procedure A except that an open chair or open forum is added to the representative committee. This procedure provides an opportunity for every faculty member to have input throughout the decision-making process. Step 1 is an explanation to the entire faculty of the task. Step 2 involves subgroup meetings with the election of a representative and a report of the subgroup's position to all faculty. Step 3 is a meeting of the representative committee with an invitation for any other faculty member to attend and participate. The representative committee deliberates in an open meeting. Times are built into the meeting for the use of an open chair or open forum where outside faculty might make comments. The open chair is at the table of the representative committee. An outside member can take the seat and speak for a certain length of time (usually two minutes), and then must relinquish the seat. Outside members are limited to a certain number of appearances. An open forum is similar except that an outside member does not physically have to move to a chair. He

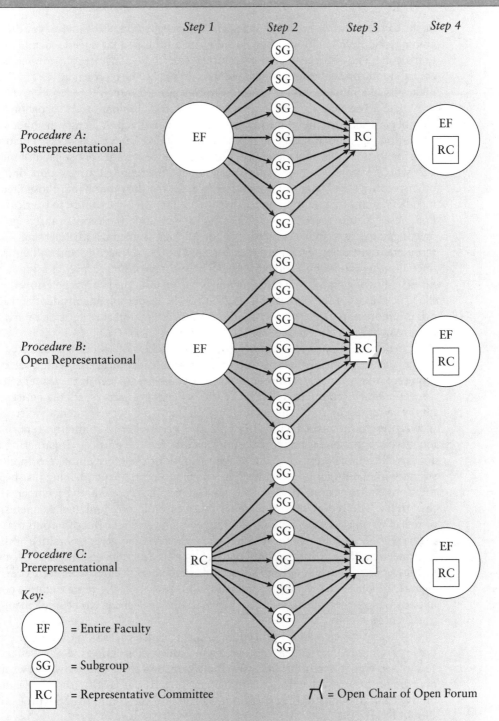

Step 1 Step 2 Step 3 Step 4

Procedure A:
Postrepresentational

Procedure B:
Open Representational

Procedure C:
Prerepresentational

Key:

EF = Entire Faculty

SG = Subgroup

RC = Representative Committee

⌐| = Open Chair of Open Forum

FIGURE 17.5 *Three Procedures for Large-Group Decision Making* or she can raise his or her hand and speak when called on. Certain times at the beginning, middle, and closing of the meeting are established for outside-member participation. The representative committee can then consider outside-member contributions throughout their deliberations. In step 4, the representative committee makes its recommendation or decision to the entire group.

The advantage of open representation is the elimination of suspicion. All members, whether representatives or not, can be involved. A faculty member cannot rationally complain that he or she was excluded from the process. The open chair or forum invites participation but does not require it. Those faculty members who are indifferent about the decision, trust the representative group, or have other priorities are under no pressure to attend. On the other hand, those faculty members who care intensely or are distrustful have an opportunity to participate. For these various reasons, it is important to schedule the representative group meetings at a time that is convenient for all faculty members. (Releasing seven representatives from teaching duties for an 11:00 A.M. meeting and calling it an open meeting is not good enough.) The disadvantage of open representation is duration. Allowing input from other members throughout the process will slow down the proceedings of the representative groups. The leader might consider the trade-off. Is it more important to have some involvement for a quicker decision or greater involvement for a slower decision?

Procedure C, prerepresentational, is the quickest of all but is predicated on the greatest amount of trust between faculty and leader. It begins with a selected representative group *before* the entire faculty convenes. In step 1, the leader selects a seven-member committee that he or she believes best represents the entire faculty. The representative committee meets on its own to develop tentative recommendations to the entire faculty. In step 2, the representative committee reports its tentative recommendations to the entire faculty for the purpose of gathering reactions. Reactions are gathered by each member of the representative committee sitting with a subgroup of faculty. The subgroup participants, having just heard the representative committee's report, can now tell the representative member what they think. The representative member takes careful notes and at the conclusion of the subgroup meeting summarizes the reactions and tells the subgroup that he or she will personally give those reactions to the representative committee at their next meeting. In step 3, the representative committee reconvenes privately, listens to the report of each subgroup's reactions, and then decides whether to revise, change, or keep the original recommendation. In step 4, the representative committee gives its recommendation (to be voted on) or decision (to be implemented) to the entire faculty.

The critical element in procedure C is the leader's selection of the representative committee. The leader might be open to the criticism that the representative committee was selected on the basis of allegiance to the leader's own views and that the process was therefore manipulated. However, if faculty trust the leader's motives and understand the criteria for selection of the committee, the procedure should be effective.

The three procedures are alternative ways to have large-group involvement on important decisions. The task has to be important, of concern, and affect each person in order to justify such involvement. If the task is not important, if persons are indifferent and the effect will be minimal, the leader should not subject the faculty to such procedures. Decisions of lesser importance should be made in less involving ways. As a rule of thumb, decisions no one cares about should be made by the leader, decisions that already have been made by superordinates should simply be reported, and decisions that concern and affect some and not others should be made by those concerned and affected. The use of any of these large-group procedures should be reserved for only the most crucial decisions of broad impact.

SUMMARY

This chapter examined the knowledge and skills needed to help professional groups develop. Particular emphasis was put on the supervisor's role in terms of behaving, confronting dysfunctional members, resolving conflict, and preparing for meetings.

The theme of looking at professional groups in a developmental manner should be familiar by now. As a group works together, the leader needs to practice skills that enable the group to become more cohesive, responsible, and autonomous. Eventually the leader would hope to lessen his or her own control and influence so that the group becomes a wise and autonomous body.

PRACTITIONER REFLECTION

Working toward the Big Picture

Susan Maxey, *Advanced Academics Specialist,*
Region XIII Education Service Center

My first experience with group development in a school came in my beginning year of teaching. The administration of the middle school at which I had been hired asked the sixth-grade staff to form an interdisciplinary team. At the time, the idea of teachers who shared students but taught different subject areas at a particular grade level coming together to meet was very new. The high school model of organizing school by subject-area departments was more the norm. This interdisciplinary team arrangement was so new, in fact, that few models existed. Our principal was not even sure what exactly he expected us to do. The one thing he did make clear was that our purpose as a team of sixth-grade teachers was to support our students' transition to the middle school milieu. As is so often true of education initiatives, this forming of the academic team was poorly planned. It fell to my colleagues and me to determine whether it would be poorly executed.

I learned the ins and outs of group development at the grass-roots level. In the beginning, it seemed that there were far more outs. There was no official leader for our group. We functioned with the role of facilitator rotating among the members. We took turns taking notes; our administrator required that we turn in our notes weekly. For a while, these notes were the only tangible outcomes of our meetings. Since the only change we'd been given by our administrator was to ease the transition of our incoming middle schoolers, that is where we started. We worked together to discuss what the transition challenges were, and how we could make them better.

The entire first year of our interdisciplinary team was spent examining this one aspect of middle school life from myriad angles. We spent a great deal of time establishing activities early in the school year to make the new sixth-graders feel valued and cared for. We established advisory and tutoring networks that became models for the other grade-level teachers on our campus. Working together daily, we were able to pinpoint students who were beginning to stumble through the more rigorous middle school work; we caught them before they fell.

Although this work was productive and worthwhile, we spent some time that can only be described as spinning our wheels. We had days on which we discussed our lives outside of school—our hobbies, our kids, our weekends. We had a day or two when we argued politics and debated the relative merits of education funding initiatives. We even had days on which we simply sat together and graded papers. The wheel spinning was sometimes unusual and might be considered wasteful. All I can say is that it added to the work we did, in that we came to know each other as people as well as professionals.

As a teacher, I have received a great deal of training in cooperative learning and other ways of teaching that involve students working with their peers to accomplish a goal. I strongly believe in the value of group work; however, I contend that we should not ask students to work in groups unless the work they are doing is worthwhile and group work is necessary to accomplish the learning goal. What I learned from the work that I did with a group of my colleagues during my first year of teaching was that I could not do my job alone. Certainly I could teach my subject and work with my students in my classroom. However, to truly see the big picture of my work as an educator, I needed to work on a daily basis with colleagues who had the same investment in the kids and in the process of the group.

EXERCISES

Academic

1. Assume you are the leader of a group that is very person oriented but is routinely failing to attend to tasks for which it is responsible. Assume further that you have determined that the roles of initiator-contributor, coordinator, orienter, and energizer are missing and that their absence is largely responsible for the group's failure to attend to assigned tasks. Write a paper explaining what steps you can take to make sure these task roles become present.

2. Assume you are the leader of a group that is generally functioning well but contains a blocker and a recognition seeker, each of whom is reducing the effectiveness of the group. Write a paper discussing plans for dealing individually with each of these group members to eliminate or reduce their dysfunctional behaviors.

3. Summarize three small-group research studies. Include a discussion of the purpose, participants, methodology, results, and conclusions of each study. Analyze the findings in terms of whether they are congruent with information presented in this chapter.

4. Assume you have been charged with leadership of a meeting at which a department/team of nine teachers will decide on a new textbook series to be used by those teachers. (You may decide the subject area and grade or age levels for which the text is to be used.) Prepare a written plan for leading the group meeting. Include a general format, an agenda, your plan for opening the meeting, and a discussion guide with preselected questions.

5. Assume you have been assigned to organize a meeting of 130 teachers who are to decide on a proposal to adopt a buildingwide system of discipline. Write a paper discussing the procedure and specific strategies you will use in facilitating a group decision on the proposal.

Field

1. Record and analyze an audiotape of yourself leading a group decision-making process. Determine any leadership deficiencies you exhibited during the discussion. Was there a lack of preplanning for the meeting? Was your leadership lacking in facilitation of task or person behaviors? Did you fail to deal effectively with a dysfunctional member? Did you fail to handle conflict properly? Based on your analysis, prepare a self-improvement plan to be followed in a second group session. If possible, analyze an audiotape of a second meeting to see if you improved your leadership in the selected areas.

2. Assign task, personal, and dysfunctional roles to various members of a simulated group decision-making meeting. After the simulation, allow each member of the group to express personal reactions to the behaviors of the various role players. Hold a group discussion on how each member affected the group's effectiveness.

3. Hold a one-to-one meeting with a dysfunctional group member of a real group that you lead. The conference should aim to improve that individual's in-group behavior. Write a summary of the conference and its results.

4. Prepare for and lead a real-life small-group meeting. Prepare a written evaluation of your small-group leadership.

5. Prepare for and lead a large-group decision-making process, using one of the procedures for large-group involvement discussed in this chapter. Write a report on the success of the process.

Developmental

1. Using knowledge and skills you have acquired in group development, continue to facilitate long-range development of a group of which you are a leader or member.

2. Begin an in-depth study of one of the following areas:

   a. Small-group research

   b. Group counseling skills

   c. Leadership style

   d. Organizational management

   e. Group discussion/interaction

3. Begin a file of group development activities. Each group activity can be summarized electronically or on an index card and classified according to categories that are useful for you.

REFERENCES

Bales, R. F. 1953. The equilibrium problem in small groups. In T. Parsons, R. F. Bales, and E. A. Shils (Eds.), *Working papers in the theory of action* (pp. 111–161). Glencoe, IL: Free Press.

Benne, D. D., and Sheats, P. 1948. Functional roles of group members. *Journal of Social Issues, 4*(2), 41–49.

Brandt, R. 1987. On cooperation in schools: A conversation with David and Roger Johnson. *Educational Leadership, 45*(3), 14–19.

Cooper, S. M. 2002. Classroom choices for enabling peer learning. *Theory into Practice, 41*(1), 53–57.

Corey, G., and Corey, M. 1982. *Groups: Process and practice.* Monterey, CA: Brooks/Cole.

Fullan, M. 2000. *Change forces: The sequel.* Philadelphia, PA: George H. Buchanan.

Gordon, T. 1980. *Leadership effectiveness training—L. E. T.* New York: Bantam Books.

Hare, A. P. 1976. *Handbook of small group research* (2nd ed.). New York: Free Press.

Hersey, P., and Blanchard, K. H. 1969. Life-cycle theory of leadership. *Training and Development Journal, 23*(5), 26–34.

Hersey, P., and Blanchard, K. H. 1988. *Management of organizational behavior: Utilizing human resources* (5th ed.). Englewood Cliffs, NJ: Prentice Hall.

Johnson, D. W., and Johnson, R. T. 1987a. *Joining together: Group theory and group skills* (3rd ed.). Englewood Cliffs, NJ: Prentice Hall.

Johnson, D. W., and Johnson, R. T. 1987b. Research shows the benefits of adult cooperation. *Educational Leadership, 45*(3), 27–30.

Kasl, E., and Yorks, L. 2002. Collaborative inquiry for adult learning. *New Directions for Adult and Continuing Education, 94,* 3–11.

Kemp, C. G. 1970. *Perspectives on the group process: A foundation for counseling with groups* (2nd ed.). Boston: Houghton Mifflin.

King, A. 2002. Structuring peer interaction to promote high-level cognitive processing. *Theory into Practice, 41*(1), 33–39.

Shelton, M. M., and Bauer, L. K. 1994. *Secrets of highly effective meetings.* Thousand Oaks, CA: Corwin Press.

Slavin, R. E. 1987. Cooperative learning and the cooperative schools. *Educational Leadership, 45*(3), 7–13.

Wheelan, S. A., and Kesselring, J. 2005. Link between faculty group development and elementary student performance on standardized tests. *The Journal of Educational Research, 98*(6), 323–330.

Yorks, L., and Kasl, E. 2002. Learning from the inquiries: Lessons for using collaborative inquiry as an adult learning strategy. *New Directions for Adult and Continuing Education, 94,* 93–104.

SUGGESTED READINGS

Cherney, J., Whitney, D., Trosten-Bloom, A. and Fry, R. 2004. *Appreciative team building: Positive questions to bring out the best of your team.* New York: iUniverse, Inc.

Chivers, J. 1995. *Team building with teachers.* London: Kogan Page.

Folger, J. P., Poole, M. S., and Stutman, R. K. 1993. *Working through conflict.* New York: Harper-Collins.

Harrington-Mackin, D. 1994. *The team building tool kit: Tips, tactics, and rules for effective workplace teams.* New York: AMACOM.

Harvey, T. R., and Drolet, B. 2004. *Building teams, building people: Expanding the fifth resource.* Lanham, MD: Rowman & Littlefield Education.

Katzenback, J. R., and Smith, D. K. 1994. *The wisdom of teams: Creating the high-performance organization.* New York: HarperCollins.

Kayser, T. A. 1990. *Mining group gold.* El Segundo, CA: Serif.

Maeroff, G. I. 1993. *Team building for school change.* New York: Teachers College Press.

Moran, L., Musselwhite, E., and Zenger, J. H. 1996. *Keeping teams on track: What to do when the going gets rough.* Chicago: Irwin.

Morley, C. L. 1994. *How to get the most out of meetings.* Alexandria, VA: Association for Supervision and Curriculum Development.

Orsburn, J. D., Moran, L., Musselwhite, E., and Zenger, J. H. 1990. *Self-directed work teams: The new American challenge.* Chicago: Irwin.

Parker, G. M. 1994. *Cross-functional teams: Working with allies, enemies and other strangers.* San Francisco: Jossey-Bass.

Phillips, G. M. (Ed.). 1990. *Teaching how to work in groups.* Norwood, NJ: Ablex.

Prior, D. W., Thompson, J. W., and Miller, M. J. 1991. Teaching decision making using situational leadership. *Journal of Creative Behavior, 25*(1), 34–42.

Shelton, M. M., and Bauer, L. K. 1994. *Secrets of highly effective meetings.* Thousand Oaks, CA: Sage.

Tjosvold, D. 1993. *Learning to manage conflict.* New York: Lexington.

Zenger, J. H., Musselwhite, E., Hurson, K., and Perrin, C. 1994. *Leading teams: Mastering the new role.* Burr Ridge, IL: Irwin.

Professional Development

Bob Jeffries, director of professional development, calls six school principals into his office to plan for the upcoming in-service day. He begins by explaining that the in-service program will start with a morning session, attended by the entire school system faculty, in the high school auditorium. The afternoon will consist of individual school activities, with the principal being responsible for whatever transpires. Mr. Jeffries asks the principals, "What might we do for the morning session?" One principal suggests that at this time of year teachers could use an emotional lift, and that an inspirational speaker would be good. Another principal adds that she had heard a Dr. Zweibach give a great talk entitled "The Thrill of Teaching" at a national principals' conference last summer. She thinks he would be a terrific speaker. Bob Jeffries likes these suggestions and tells the principals he will call Dr. Zweibach and make arrangements for his appearance.

On the in-service day, 238 teachers file into the auditorium and fill all but the first 8 rows of seats. Mr. Jeffries makes a few introductory remarks about how fortunate "we" are to have Dr. Zweibach with "us" and then turns the session over to Dr. Zweibach. A rumpled, middle-aged university professor walks to the microphone and launches into his talk on the thrill of teaching. Within 10 minutes, signs of restlessness, boredom, and bitterness are evident throughout the audience.

It seems that 12 of the teachers are sitting through a talk they had heard Dr. Zweibach deliver verbatim two years earlier at a teacher convention; 15 others are thinking about the classroom work they could be doing to prepare for next semester and wondering, "Why in the world are we sitting through this talk?" Another 22 teachers have become impatient with Dr. Zweibach's continual reference to the academic high school settings where he found teaching thrills. Their own work settings are vocational, special education, and elementary; they can't relate what he is saying about high schools to their world. Eventually, some teachers begin to correct papers, read, or knit; a few appear to fall asleep. On the other hand, nearly half the members of the audience remain attentive and give Dr. Zweibach a rousing ovation when he concludes. The other half appear relieved that the talk is finally over and they can return to their own schools. Upon leaving the auditorium, one can overhear such remarks as "What a great talk!" and "Why do we have to put up with all this staff-development crap?"

This depiction of an in-service day is typical of many school systems. Some teachers find it valuable, but many do not. Staff development has been referred to as "the slum of American education, neglected and of little effect" (Wood and Thompson, 1980). Professional development is often viewed by supervisors, administrators, and teachers as a number of days contracted for in the school calendar that simply need to be endured. Three crucial questions will shape this chapter: (1) Why is professional development needed? (2) How should it be planned and conducted? (3) Are teachers to be the objects or the agents of professional development?

Why the Need for Professional Development?

Over 85 percent of a total school budget is used to pay employee salaries. Education is a human enterprise. The essence of successful instruction and good schools comes from the thoughts and actions of the professionals in the schools. So, if one is to look for a place to improve the quality of education in a school, a sensible place to look is the continuous education of educators—that is, professional development. Virtually any experience that enlarges a teacher's knowledge, appreciation, skills, and understandings of his or her work falls under the domain of professional development.

When one of the authors gave a presentation to a Michigan school board to explain the need to allocate more money for professional development, he used an analogy to the automobiles made in Detroit. When a customer purchases a new car costing upwards of $30,000, he or she brings it in every 5,000 miles for preventive maintenance and fine-tuning. The customer continues to put additional money into the car to prolong its life and performance. Simply to run the car into the ground would be a dumb way to protect such an investment! In education, the school board is the customer, who purchases more than a new car with its $30,000 initial investment—it purchases a living and breathing professional! Without resources for maintaining, fine-tuning, and reinvigorating the investment, the district will run teachers into the ground. This is far more consequential than a neglected car. The district will lose teachers, physically and/or mentally. The real losers will be the students of these teachers.

Professional development has gathered increased attention in both research and resource allocation across the nation. States have dramatically increased their expenditures for professional development in local districts and schools since the series of national reports issued in the mid-1980s. The National Staff Development Council has become the fastest-growing educational organization in the United States. Until 1957, only about 50 studies had been conducted on professional development in schools (Showers, Joyce, and Bennett, 1987). Now several times that number of studies are being conducted every year.

Since professional development should be a responsibility of those who supervise, the research and application discussed here will focus on the use of successful professional development to improve instruction. According to a study of teachers and administrators in New York state (Tetenbaum and Mulkeen, 1987, p. 11), the primary criticisms of professional development programs are that the activities are "one-shot deals" and that there is "no integration with a comprehensive plan to achieve school goals." Let's see how these criticisms can be avoided.

Characteristics of Successful Professional Development Programs

A considerable knowledge base exists on successful professional development, including original research and reviews of research and best practice (Loucks-Horsley et al., 1987; Orlich, 1989; Wood and Thompson, 1993; Guskey, 1994; Corcoran, 1995; U.S. Department of Education, 1996; Hawley and Valli, 1996; Joyce, Calhoun, and Hopkins, 1999; Fullan, 2000; Gordon, 2000; Zech, Gause-Vega, and Bray, 2000; Bernauer, 2002; Harris, 2002). Although these reports do not agree on all factors, there are a number of common characteristics of successful programs:

1. Involvement of participants in planning, implementing, and evaluating programs
2. Programs that are based on schoolwide goals, but that integrate individual and group goals with school goals
3. Long-range planning and development
4. Programs that incorporate research and best practice on school improvement and instructional improvement
5. Administrative support, including provision of time and other resources as well as involvement in program planning and delivery
6. Adherence to the principles of adult learning (see Chapter 4)

7. Attention to the research on change, including the need to address individual concerns throughout the change process (see Chapter 21)
8. Follow-up and support for transfer of learning to the school or classroom
9. Ongoing assessment and feedback
10. Continuous professional development that becomes part of the school culture

As you review these characteristics, think of a professional development program with which you are familiar. How many of the 10 characteristics are present in that program?

Integrating Schoolwide, Group, and Individual Professional Development

One characteristic of effective professional development is the integration of schoolwide, group, and individual goals. How does a school go about doing this? To begin, it is critical that all members of the school community provide input into schoolwide professional development goals. The schoolwide goals should be broad enough to allow groups and individuals to set their own goals, consistent with school goals.

For an example of integrating schoolwide and group professional development, let us assume that a middle school has identified improved student discipline as a schoolwide professional development goal. Different grade-level or instructional teams, all committed to improved discipline, might identify different group goals relative to the school goal. One group might decide that they need to focus their professional development on improving students' respect for others. Another group might determine that their primary need is to improve students' on-task behavior during class. A third group may wish to focus on finding ways to encourage self-discipline so that students take more responsibility for their homework, studying for tests, and asking for assistance.

Different groups also may decide that they prefer different professional development formats. One group may decide that they prefer to form a study group that will share readings, visit other schools to see how they address student discipline, and discuss how exemplary practices can be adapted to their students. The second group may decide that they wish to attend a training program on effective discipline, followed up by peer coaching at the classroom level. The third group might prefer to follow an action research format, gathering classroom data to find out more about the problem, designing an action plan, implementing the plan, and gathering evaluation data to determine effects. Although it is important that various groups within the school be allowed to adapt schoolwide goals to group needs, it also is important that each group show how its particular goals relate to and support the schoolwide goals.

A faculty is made up of individuals, and schoolwide professional development cannot take place without individual development. Thus, it is important to integrate individual professional development goals with group and schoolwide goals. Let us return to our example of the schoolwide goal of improved student discipline. You will recall that one possible group goal was improving students' respect for others. Even this more focused goal would have different meanings to different teachers within the group that chose the goal. For one teacher it might mean helping students work together in cooperative groups. For another teacher it could mean students respecting other students from different cultures. For a third teacher it might mean working with students who are disrespectful to authority figures. Thus, even within the group goal of increased respect for others there should be opportunities for teachers to identify individual goals consistent with group and school goals. Since adults, like students, have different experiences and learning styles, teachers within the study group might pursue different learning activities and make different contributions to the group. One teacher might bring to the group reports from visits to other schools, another teacher might share journal articles related to the topic of student respect for others, and so forth. The individual teacher can connect individual goals to group and schoolwide goals in a manner that allows the same professional development activities to serve all three types of goals.

Alternative Professional Development Formats

We are rapidly moving away from the era when professional development usually means either a 60-minute speech by an outside consultant or a "one-shot" workshop. A variety of new formats for professional development have emerged over the last several years. Some examples follow:

- *Beginning teacher assistance programs:* The new teacher is provided ongoing, intensive assistance throughout at least the first year of teaching. This support includes such things as an assigned mentor; an orientation to the school and community; assistance from a support team including the mentor, other teachers, and a supervisor; training in classroom management and effective teaching; and support seminars focused on beginning teachers' concerns.

- *Skill development programs:* This consists of several workshops over a period of months, and classroom coaching between workshops to assist teachers to transfer new skills to their daily teaching.

- *Teacher centers:* Teachers can meet at a central location to engage in professional dialogue, develop skills, plan innovations, and gather or create instructional materials.

- *Teacher institutes:* Teachers participate in intensive learning experiences on single, complex topics over a period of consecutive days or weeks.

- *Collegial support groups:* Teachers within the same school engage in group inquiry, address common problems, jointly implement instructional innovations, and provide mutual support.

- *Networks:* Teachers from different schools share information, concerns, and accomplishments and engage in common learning through computer links, newsletters, fax machines, and occasional seminars and conferences.

- *Teacher leadership:* Teachers participate in leadership preparation programs and assist other teachers by assuming one or more leadership roles (workshop presenter, cooperating teacher, mentor, expert coach, instructional team leader, curriculum developer). The teacher-leader not only assists other teachers but also experiences professional growth as a result of being involved in leadership activities.

- *Teacher as writer:* This increasingly popular format has teachers reflect on and write about their students, teaching, and professional growth. Such writing can be in the form of private journals, essays, or reaction papers to share with colleagues, or formal articles for publication in educational journals.

- *Individually planned professional development:* Teachers set individual goals and objectives, plan and carry out activities, and assess results.

- *Partnerships:* Partnerships between schools and universities or businesses, in which both partners are considered equal, have mutual rights and responsibilities, make contributions, and receive benefits. Such partnerships could involve one or more of the previously described formats (Moore and Seeger, 2004).

There can be considerable overlap between various professional development formats (not to mention between professional development and the other four tasks of supervision!). Our own experience as staff developers and researchers has led us to conclude that many of the most successful professional development programs combine multiple formats. Next, we will describe several professional development programs, each including a combination of formats.

Examples of Effective Professional Development Programs

We will describe several model professional development programs, including two districtwide programs, two site-based programs, and two individualized programs. Each of the examples is either an actual program or a composite based on several actual programs.

Districtwide Professional Development Programs

The *St. Mary's Achievement Related Teaching program (SMART)* was based on a written needs assessment of all district teachers conducted by the district's professional development planning committee, comprised of a majority of teachers. During the first year of the program, a group of 18 volunteer instructional leaders (14 teachers, 3 building administrators, and 1 central office supervisor) chosen by the committee participated in professional development leadership preparation. The leadership preparation was conducted by a team of professors from a nearby university that had entered into a formal partnership with the district. Leadership preparation addressed the following areas:

I. Generic Instructional Skills
   A. Classroom Management
   B. Lesson Design
   C. Student Assessment
   D. Teacher Expectations
   E. Questioning Skills
   F. Student Motivation

II. Instructional Models
   A. Concept Attainment
   B. Compare and Contrast
   C. Cooperative Learning
   D. Concept Mapping

III. Coaching and Leadership
   A. An Overview of Peer Coaching
   B. Systematic Observation of Instruction
   C. Conferencing Skills
   D. Professional Relationships
   E. Matching Coaching to Teacher Concerns

Leadership training consisted of 12 workshops over the course of a year. Between workshops, doctoral students from the university visited the school district and provided coaching to the staff developers as they implemented new instructional strategies and models in actual classroom lessons. This expert coaching was intended to (1) assist the staff developers to master strategies and models they would be conducting workshops on in the following year and (2) allow the staff developers to observe effective coaches in action.

During subsequent years, the staff developers became workshop presenters as small groups of regular teachers (groups of approximately 15) were cycled through the instructional strategies and models components of the program. Just as they had been coached by doctoral students in their leadership preparation, the district's staff developers provided coaching between workshops to assist new participants to transfer skills to their classrooms.

Buckeye School District's efforts to support beginning teachers began with the design of a beginning teacher assistance program by a planning committee made up of administrators, supervisors, and teachers. A key component of the program is a pool of experienced mentor teachers. Volunteer mentors are selected by a screening committee. Selection criteria include years of experience in the school system, effective teaching performance, interpersonal skills, past commitment to the profession, flexibility, and willingness to spend time helping beginning teachers. The selected teachers take part in an intensive mentor-preparation program, including the following elements:

- Introduction to the knowledge base on problems of beginning teachers, beginning teacher assistance programs, and mentoring
- Overview of the district's beginning teacher assistance program
- Research on effective classroom management
- Research on effective teaching
- Principles of adult learning
- Adult and teacher development
- Goal setting and action planning
- The coaching of teaching, including conferencing skills and observation skills
- Action research

A number of variables are considered when assigning mentors to beginning teachers, including grade level and content area, classroom location, and philosophical and personal compatibility of mentor and beginner. An attempt is made to make an overall "best match" of mentor and beginner.

Prior to the beginning of the school year, a special orientation for beginners is attended by novices and their mentors. During this orientation, new teachers are walked through key information about the community, district policies and procedures, and the curriculum they will be responsible for teaching. Later in the orientation, they are given tours of their schools and meet with building administrators and instructional leaders. Their mentors review building policies and procedures and provide them with a profile of the school, its staff, students, and parents.

The orientation is only the beginning of assistance for the beginning teacher in Buckeye School District. Ongoing support is provided throughout the school year. For each beginner, a support team is formed, consisting of a building administrator, department chairperson or instructional team leader, and mentor. The team meets on a regular basis. Continuous assistance is based on written needs assessments and discussions with support teams. Workshops are provided for beginners on such topics as classroom management, effective teaching, and working with parents. Mentors visit beginners' classrooms on a regular basis to provide nonevaluative assistance, including expert coaching following the five-step model presented in Chapter 16. Beginners visit the classrooms of mentors and other effective teachers to observe best practice. Mentors are available on a daily basis to provide beginners with psychological support, information, and instructional assistance.

Mentors, too, are given support by the district in the form of follow-up workshops, support seminars, tuition reimbursement for relevant university coursework, released time, and stipends. Their contributions to beginners and the district are recognized during faculty meetings, in district publications, and at an annual recognition dinner.

Buckeye School District's support program includes a partnership with a nearby university. Professors from the university collaborated with Buckeye School District in the design of its support program. The same professors assist with mentor preparation and offer course credit for mentors willing to do outside work beyond the mentor workshops. Finally, the professors assist in the delivery of several of the workshops for beginning teachers. To summarize, although mentoring is the heart and soul of Buckeye School District's beginning teacher assistance program, other formats—such as skill development programs, collegial support groups, and partnerships—are part of the overall program.

Site-Based Initiatives

There are numerous recent examples of staff development planned and implemented by school councils and school task forces as part of site-based initiatives to address the educational priorities of the particular school. Faculty and parents assess their current instructional programs, establish learning goals for students, and then decide whether the expertise to conduct staff-development programs lies within or outside the school. The various school renewal networks—such as the League of Professional Schools, the Coalition of Essential Schools, the Accelerated Schools, and the Comer Schools—have many powerful examples of decentralized, staff-development plans derived by faculty interested in learning new methods of instruction (such as models of teaching, cooperative learning, conflict mediation, service learning, Socratic discussions, interdisciplinary curriculum, higher-order thinking, nongraded schedules, team teaching, and technology integration). The schools plan their own retreats, staff-development days, and summer institutes. The results of many of these efforts have been major improvements in student achievement and attitudes, higher attendance, and lower incidents of discipline and vandalism (see Levin, 1994; Glickman, 1992, 2002; and Gursky, 1990).

Ponticell (1995) provided a description of a site-based professional development program in an *inner-city Chicago high school.* The aim of the program was instructional improvement based on collegial learning and support. The program was supported by a grant from a nearby university and facilitated by a professor from the university. The program began with a professional retreat where teachers engaged in reflective dialogue about teaching and began to build collaborative relationships.

Following the retreat, the teachers began to read and discuss research on effective teaching and professional development alternatives. Next, the teachers developed a cycle of monthly professional development activities including the following phases:

1. Teachers identified an instructional concern, read current research addressing that concern, selected ideas that made sense, developed a strategy for classroom implementation, and created a checklist of planned teacher behaviors.
2. Teachers videotaped themselves implementing improvement strategies, analyzed their own videotapes, and compared their actual behaviors to the checklist of anticipated behaviors.
3. Peer coaching, focused on the month's strategy, with a coaching cycle consisting of a preconference, observation, and postconference.
4. End-of-month group meetings in which teachers met to share video clips, discussed what aspects of the month's strategy had worked and not worked, reflected on what they had learned, and determined the topic of study for the following month.

Based on pre- and postinventories, direct observation, analysis of audiotapes of group discussions, and interviews with participants, Ponticell (1995) found that the site-based program had increased collegiality, improved self-analysis of teaching, enabled teachers to learn new ways of collaboratively observing and discussing each other's teaching, and fostered learning and experimenting with new teaching strategies.

A less formal model for site-based professional development is the Teachers Helping Teachers collegial problem-solving groups at *Tom Green Elementary* in Buda, Texas. At the Green school, small vertical teams help members solve immediate classroom problems. In a typical team meeting, a teacher will share an instructional problem she or he is experiencing. The teacher may present the group with data on the problem such as samples of student work, test results, or historical records on student performance. The initial tasks of the group are to listen to the teacher's presentation, review the artifacts, and ask clarifying questions. Next the group brainstorms possible solutions to the problem. The teacher selects a problem-solving strategy, and the group then assists the teacher in creating a specific action plan. Part of the action plan may involve group members agreeing to demonstrate teaching methods, share instructional materials, or observe the teacher's classroom to gather data on improvement efforts. A supervisor facilitates the problem-solving group, usually using nondirective behaviors. The supervisor may agree to assist the teacher to implement the action plan by sharing resources, observing the teacher, and so on. The teacher shares the results of the improvement plan at the next group meeting. A teacher who receives assistance from the group for one week more than likely will provide assistance to another group member the following week.

Individually Planned Professional Development

An individually planned professional development program at *Holidaysburg Area School District* (Wilshire, 1991) consisted of five phases:

1. *Invitation:* Interested teachers were invited to a meeting to discuss the program. After an overview of the program was provided, teachers who wished to participate completed biographical data sheets. The biographical information was used to match the volunteer teachers to facilitators from a nearby university. The role of the facilitators was to aid professional planning.

2. *Assessment:* Facilitators audiotaped individual interviews with participating teachers. Interview questions were designed to determine individual teachers' needs, interests, and preferred professional development formats. Facilitators reviewed interview transcripts and generated potential professional development projects or learning activities in which individual teachers might be interested.

3. *Validation-Negation:* In a second meeting with individual teachers, facilitators shared interview data and data-based professional development options. Teachers could select from options presented by their facilitators, propose their own options, or decide to reflect further on various options. Eventually, teachers, assisted by facilitators, developed their own written professional-development plans, including goals, objectives, activities, assessment, and needed resources and materials.

4. *Disclosure:* During a group meeting of facilitators and participants, the teachers shared their individual plans with each other. Collaboration was encouraged when two or more plans were similar.

5. *Implementation:* After a meeting with a district administrator to approve the individual plans, implementation began. Teachers had two years to complete their self-directed programs. Facilitators remained available to assist the participants as they carried out their plans. Participants were required to provide the district with products developed during their self-directed programs, which became resources for the district and its teachers.

Individual plans in the Holidaysburg program included developing new curricula, learning and using new instructional strategies, engaging in interdisciplinary team teaching, and collecting information about successful educational practices to share with school personnel. The Holidaysburg model and other individually planned programs open the door for individual teachers to become involved in any of the staff-development formats discussed earlier in this chapter, including *group* staff development to help them to reach their individual goals.

A second example of individually planned professional development can be found at *Leander (Texas) Middle School.* Individual improvement plans are tied to the school's annual improvement plan. Individual projects follow the PDSA cycle (Plan, Do, Study, Act) and are documented in teacher portfolios. In the *planning phase,* teachers gather a variety of self-assessment data (videotapes of lessons, student achievement data, peer observations, and so on), analyze the data, and design individualized professional development plans. The individual plans include objectives, learning activities, needed resources, and plans for self-evaluation.

The teacher implements the improvement plan during the *doing* phase. Professional development activities might include attending workshops or conferences, observing other teachers, peer coaching, participation in study groups, and so on. The teacher's portfolio documents learning activities, support received from colleagues, and changes in practice.

The *studying* phase involves gathering data to evaluate the plan's effectiveness. Data is gathered on the teacher's professional growth as well as changes in student learning. Evaluation data might include the teacher's reflective writing, classroom observation data, student achievement data, or artifacts of student work.

The *acting* phase consists of a portfolio conference with the teacher's supervisor. During the conference, the teacher reflects on activities completed, learning that has taken place, and future directions for professional growth. In Leander, all adults—teachers, supervisors, and staff—implement individual development plans and construct portfolios. Each spring, all members of the school community share their individual projects at a "portfolio fair."

In this section, we have presented examples of various levels (district, school, individual) and formats for professional development. In the next section, we will discuss stages of professional development that apply to any long-term professional development program.

Stages of Professional Development

Professional development typically involves three stages of learning: (1) orientation, (2) integration, and (3) refinement. To illustrate these three stages, we will relate them to staff development on the cooperative learning instructional model.

In the *orientation stage,* benefits, responsibilities, and personal concerns about involvement in staff development are addressed. Next, participants engage in learning necessary for initial "real-world" application. In our cooperative learning example, orientation topics might include the following:[1]

- Differences between cooperative, competitive, and individual learning
- Differences between cooperative learning and traditional group work
- Research on cooperative learning
- Basic elements of cooperative learning (teaching social skills, positive interdependence, face-to-face interaction, individual accountability, group processing)

- Forming cooperative groups
- Standard cooperative learning structures (think-pair-share, jigsaw, student teams achievement divisions [STAD], teams-games-tournaments [TGT], group investigation, and so on)
- Planning cooperative lessons

Failure to take teachers beyond the orientation stage is one reason why many staff-development programs are ineffective: Teachers are given rudimentary knowledge or skills and then are left to fend for themselves.

In the *integration stage,* teachers are assisted as they apply previous learning in their classrooms and schools. One aspect of integration is learning to adapt general learning to specific situations. In the cooperative learning example, this would mean learning to alter cooperative teaching strategies to make them appropriate for different learning content and students. A related aspect of integration is regular and effective use of the new learning. This would mean, for example, the teacher develops enough competence and confidence in cooperative learning methods to make them part of his or her standard repertoire of instructional strategies.

In the *refinement stage,* teachers move from basic competence to expertness through continuous experimentation and reflection. In the refinement stage of staff development on cooperative learning, teachers would become expert at a wide range of cooperative learning strategies and at mixing and matching those strategies for optimal student learning. Teachers in the refinement stage synthesize different types of previous learning in order to create new learning. In our cooperative learning example, a teacher at this stage might combine aspects of two or more standard cooperative learning structures to create a more complex structure. For another example, a teacher at the refinement stage might synthesize whole language and cooperative learning strategies to create an entirely new teaching strategy. Perhaps the best thing that a supervisor can do when teachers have reached this stage is to sign them up as teacher-staff developers!

The Nuts and Bolts

Professional development does not always need to take place in group sessions, but groups remain a major component of the majority of staff development formats and programs. The best planning for a group session is useless if the supervisor forgets the nuts and bolts. What value is an excellent speaker who lectures in a room where the acoustics garble every word? What good is a fast-paced microteaching demonstration if it conflicts with other teacher meetings so that few can attend? What good is an exciting role-playing activity whose participants have had no chance to eat, unwind, or use the restroom during the previous two hours? If one is going to the trouble to plan professional development, then one should go the extra step to ensure an environment that enables participants to be responsive and comfortable. Here are six important considerations:

1. *Prepare speakers by telling them exactly what they are expected to do.* If a speaker is invited to conduct an activity, make sure he or she understands the assignment. Speakers will do whatever they normally do unless someone tells them otherwise. Most speakers have their own topics, their own rehearsed presentations, and their own formats. If a speaker is expected to demonstrate a particular skill (for example, asking higher-order questions) or to include role-playing (scripts of classroom discussions), *tell him or her so.* Speaker and participants are both in an embarrassing situation when the speaker, through no fault of either party, is not doing what the participants have been led to expect.

2. *Check the facility beforehand for seating arrangements, media, and acoustics.* Make sure the facility is appropriate to the activity. For example, small-group discussions in an auditorium give teachers stiff necks and a stiffer attitude toward the next in-service. See that all equipment is operating correctly. Check microphones, cassettes, and overheads. Move around the room to see if displays on screen or walls can be viewed clearly by everyone. Have at hand spare bulbs and replacement equipment in case of an equipment failure.

3. *Provide refreshments and transition time at the beginning.* Tell participants where the restrooms are. Provide drinks and snacks. Informally greet the participants at the door and tell them when the session will begin. When formally beginning, inform participants when other breaks are scheduled.

4. *Check the comfort of the room.* Beforehand, check whether the room will maintain a comfortable temperature. Find out if the heating or cooling system is turned off at the time of the meeting and, if so, arrange to have the system operating. Estimate the temperature of the room when it is full. A room that feels comfortable when only a few people are present can become oppressively hot when full to capacity.

5. *Have materials run off and a plan for easy dissemination to participants.* Prior to the session, check with the leader of the activity to make sure all desired materials will be prepared. Also before the session, figure out a distribution system for materials. Often it is sufficient to place a table next to the entrance with collected materials and make one person responsible for telling entrants to pick up the materials.

6. *Have evaluation forms for participants to fill out after the session.* Asking participants to evaluate the session allows existing problems to be corrected before the next session. A simple form to be filled out anonymously by participants can be seen in Figure 18.1.

We would like your feedback to plan future professional development sessions. Please circle the number closest to your feelings and provide comments in the space provided on the form. If you need more space, feel free to use the back of the sheet. As you leave, please drop this form in the box on the back table.

Professional Development Topic _____

Date _____

	Poor	*Satisfactory*	*Good*	*Excellent*
1. The session today was	1	2	3	4

Comments _____

_____

_____

_____

2. The organization of the session was	1	2	3	4

Comments _____

_____

_____

_____

3. The meeting room was	1	2	3	4

Comments _____

_____

_____

_____

4. The materials were	1	2	3	4

Comments _____

_____

_____

_____

Suggestions for future meetings: _____

_____

_____

FIGURE 18.1 *Professional Development Evaluation*

Extending the Concept of
Professional Development

Professional development for much of its history focused primarily on the development of pedagogical skills. Pedagogical development remains a critical purpose of professional development, but in recent years the field has expanded to include a variety of other purposes.

Personal development entails helping teachers to move toward better understanding of their own adult life cycle, transition events, and roles, as well as improving teachers' self-concepts and self-efficacies.

Career development supports teachers as they move through phases of the teaching career from induction to retirement, helping teachers to address concerns as well as providing new professional opportunities and rewards during each career phase. Career development includes assisting teachers to assume various types of teacher-leadership roles as their careers progress.

Moral development enables teachers to model the principles of compassion, equality, and justice that they hope to instill in their students. Every word a teacher speaks and every action a teacher takes during the schoolday has moral implications, and professional development can enhance teachers' moral insight and decision making in ways that foster students' overall well-being.

School improvement is largely dependent on professional development. Almost any significant change in the school organization, curriculum, or instructional program is dependent on professional development to provide teachers with the capacity to implement the change. It is difficult to imagine *any* school improvement effort succeeding without professional development.

Improvement of the teaching profession has become a national goal in recent years, and professional development is the engine driving this movement. Although much of the impetus for improving the profession has come from national certification boards, associations, and networks, professional development for meeting and applying new standards often takes place at the local level.

Teachers as Objects or Agents
in Professional Development

A superintendent remarked that he had been at a national conference and attended a presentation on "Elements of Effective Instruction." He decided that this was exactly what the teachers needed. As a result, the district was off and running with a three-year commitment to training all principals and teachers in "elements." Highly paid national consultants were brought in; personnel were identified for advanced training and traveled during the summer to faraway sites; and virtually all contracted in-service time and school supervision was devoted to "elements." It was not long before a new evaluation instrument was established to check that every teacher was using the training in effective instruction in the same prescribed manner. Over the three years, expenditures by the school district exceeded $300,000, not including the cost of human time. What have been the results? No appreciable gain in student achievement, considerable grumbling by a core of "malcontent" teachers, enthusiasm by the chosen core of teachers who received special training and compensation, and a firm claim by the superintendent that "we now have focused long-term professional development on scientifically derived principles, and our teaching is more effective."

In recent years, education has been bombarded by packaged programs on "effective teaching," "effective schools," "effective supervision," and "effective discipline." All claim to be derived from research and to have documented success, and all use the components and sequence of transfer of training that have been sorely lacking in traditional professional development programs. The programs provide for explanation, demonstration, modeling, role-playing, practice, and coaching. They are not one-shot programs—they are focused and they are classroom based. The only problem is that the people who think these programs are worth the cost and effort are the same people who have a personal investment and commitment to use them (see Garman and Hazley, 1988; DiBernardo and Stiles, 1988). If the programs are not as successful as predicted, the decision makers do not blame the program but rather the lack of enough training to ensure that teachers "do it right" (Lambert, 1988). Schools, districts, and states that have committed themselves to such programs come to the ludicrous conclusion that they need more training, more money, and greater enforcement to see that all teachers will finally learn to teach as prescribed more frequently and correctly. This is an incredible rationalization by policymakers that their initial decision was right, regardless of the effect that the program is having on teachers.

This rationale underscores the point that was made about adult development earlier in the book. Commitment is premised on two dimensions: one is choice and the other is responsibility to make knowledgeable decisions about one's work. That's why the superintendent wants so badly to see this program on "effective elements" work. The superintendent had the choice and took responsibility for making the decision. The selected core of teachers also want to see this program work, because they were given choice and responsibility in making decisions on how to train others. Yet most teachers and principals were not given any choice or responsibility in these decisions about the needs of their students and themselves. Instead, they were treated as objects rather than as agents of professional development, without due regard for their capacity to make wise decisions in the interest of students and teaching. Without choice or responsibility to make knowledgeable decisions about their work, they have little motivation or commitment to somebody else's program.

To use knowledge about characteristics, formats, and stages of professional development, without an awareness of the need truly to involve teachers as decision makers in professional development, will leave us where we currently are. We will be more sophisticated in teaching teachers how to follow someone else's program, but we will find little commitment on the part of teachers or little stimulation to increase teachers' own collective and critical capacities to make lasting changes.

SUMMARY

For professional development to be meaningful to teachers and to lead to teacher renewal and instructional improvement, it must operate at two levels. First, teachers as individuals should have a variety of learning opportunities to support their pursuit of their own personal and professional career goals. Second, teachers as part of a school and district organization should together define, learn, and implement skills, knowledge, and programs that achieve common goals of the organization. Professional development must be geared to teachers' needs and concerns. Research on successful professional development programs has shown an emphasis on involvement, long-term planning, problem-solving meetings, released time, experimentation and risk-taking, administrative support, small-group activities, peer feedback, demonstration and trials, coaching, and leader participation in activities (Farmer, Hauk, and Neumann, 2005). Consideration for individual and group characteristics can help make professional development more relevant to the participant. Teachers move through three stages of professional development: orientation, integration, and refinement. Nuts-and-bolts considerations—informing speakers, checking facilities, and providing refreshments, materials, and evaluation—can increase the comfort and attentiveness of teachers. It is time to change the perception that professional development is a waste of teachers' time to the perception of professional development as time well spent. Viewing teachers as the agents rather than the objects of professional development will be the impetus for such change.

PRACTITIONER REFLECTION

Professional Development as Time Well Spent

Cheryl Granade Sullivan, *Educational Consultant*

At Kykuit, the Rockefeller mansion in Tarrytown, New York, one can stand on the hill overlooking the beautiful Hudson River or turn toward a carefully placed statuary in a massive entry way. One view rarely changes; the other is ever changing.

Inside the wonderful old structure, there is evidence of generations of inhabitants. Among the rarest treasures are ancient Chinese ceramics. Those ceramics are now housed in museum-type cases, which were added because the last family to live in the mansion included the little boys of Nelson and Happy Rockefeller. These active children brought baseball bats and other athletic gear into the house filled with priceless antiques. What harmony came from a seeming dichotomy! The art collection follows in a similar vein. A Gilbert Stuart portrait hangs on the wall as do major pieces of modern art. Their choice and placement create a remarkable environment.

What does Kykuit with its interesting vistas, dichotomies, and harmonies have to do with professional development in today's schools? I find it an effective metaphor. For years, schools have adopted a hierarchical way of operating. The chain-of-command puts central office staff developers above principals to whom teachers are subordinate. Even within a building, veteran teachers who have "earned their stripes" often get the plum opportunities for leadership and growth. The established tradition functions as an heirloom. Such had been the case for middle school teacher June Tribble in Forsyth County, Georgia. June was known as a good teacher and a fine mathematician. Her students liked her. Her test scores were admirable. With a leadership certificate in hand, June requested a transfer to the new middle school, Liberty, where she expected to be grade chair for the eighth grade and math department chair. She had followed the rules, served her time, and jumped all of the hurdles. And, indeed, June was chosen to be part of Liberty's founding leadership team.

June was not even allowed to settle in before she realized that her ordered expectations were being torn asunder by new models. Liberty Middle School's leadership team did not begin by defining a chain of command, assigning rooms in the new building, or creating agendas for orientation. June was amazed to find that the group spent time deciding on the most important aspects of Liberty's mission and culture. She kept asking about what the department chair would do and when the grade levels would meet.

Then, the group spent time in professional development activities focused on teamwork, problem solving, risk-taking, and communication skills. Some of the materials used had been published only the week before. The group created its own leadership plan using a grid and adopted the phrase "Break the Mold!" as its vision. All of this was labeled "leadership" and "professional development." That leadership team might as well have been rowdy players swinging their bats at June's precious, time-honored beliefs.

Although a veteran in years, June was by no means operating at the highest levels of development. Her steadfast loyalty to the one governance model that she knew well, her preference for professional development that has immediate classroom applications (especially "make and take"), and her desire for her own well-earned chance to be in the spotlight showed the need for growth.

What happened? June's principal, Dr. Cindy Styles, and the school's consultant recognized June's resistance. They also saw her great gifts. By positioning the work in leadership so it linked to and acknowledged June's stance and also pushed ahead for a more global vision and greater flexibility, they were able to engage June and also to challenge her. Activities and exchanges in the professional learning sequence were built from where June had been and used as a launching pad for new possibilities. In essence, the fine antiques were kept available and positioned to be compatible with some new things as well.

There were rocky moments. At times, June's greatest professional development came as she reflected ("vented") on the day in the parking lot. She had numerous private conversations with other members of the leadership team. So, how did the fragile and tough, the stable and changing, the old and new come to exist in meaningful harmony for June's development just as it did in Kykuit's design?

The turning point was a complex problem revolving around a faculty member who was one of June's close friends. As the leadership team explored strategies and professional development plans to remedy hostile attitudes and actions regarding a schoolwide sports event, June spoke up. In the moment, she seemed to synthesize the best of her prior learning and her new knowledge and skills. She presented a clear analysis of the situation as well as several options that would put the fellow teacher's talents to work and provide her an opportunity for growth. She broke her suggestions into segments that would provide security for the teacher and yet also include space for her creativity to shine. June offered to shepherd the entire process and participate in the final event.

Everyone was appreciative. When asked about her behavior, June said, "I've learned a lot. I was really entrenched, but this is a better way for the school." June's assessment of her own change led to expanded professional development and new goals. June is now in a doctoral program in leadership. She has presented at a variety of conferences. And, she is a recognized leader of leaders and learning. As she says, "I've grown so much, and I know that."

The balance in professional development for June Tribble, like that achieved at Kykuit, was the result of time well spent. Embedded in the entire scenario are careful respect for June and thoughtful attention to what would foster growth. The vignette points to some central questions for individuals, schools, and districts striving to make professional development a task of those with SuperVision.

- How can professional development be comfortable enough to be attractive and challenging enough to be meaningful? (How can levels of professional maturity be both accommodated and expanded?)
- Where should power reside? Who decides the *when, where,* and *what* of professional development?
- When does the design of professional development become its own professional learning?
- How is the tension that often exists between local, immediate needs ("me and my kids" or "district and standards") and global, altruistic qualities best addressed?
- How can the desires of the hearts of participants be included in professional development?
- How can educators devise professional development in which the "push" comes from within?
- When must true professional development be a set of questions rather than a list of answers?
- What are the real goals of professional development?

EXERCISES

Academic

1. Write a paper defining and discussing the concept of mentoring teachers. Include descriptions of successful mentoring found in the professional literature.

2. A small group of senior high teachers has requested a professional development program on making better use of open-ended questions during class discussions. The teachers are at moderate levels of development, expertise, and commitment,

and at the integration stage. Outline a plan for a professional development program for these teachers on the requested topic.

3. A small group of elementary teachers from the same school district has requested a professional development program on strategies for more effective team teaching. All these teachers have had considerable experience in team teaching, but they wish to improve their skills in this area. The teachers are at high levels of development, expertise, and commitment, and in the refinement stage of professional development. Outline a plan for a professional development program on team teaching for these teachers.

4. A general needs assessment, administered districtwide, has revealed that the number one perceived need of teachers in the district is for increased communication skills. Prepare a plan for assessing *specific* needs of various groups of teachers within this general topic and for including teachers in planning a professional development program that will meet their group and individual needs.

5. Write a paper summarizing three recent research studies on professional development not discussed in this chapter. Include the purpose, participants, methodology, results, and conclusions of each study. Analyze the findings in terms of whether they are congruent with research findings cited in this chapter.

Field

1. Evaluate the needs assessment process a school district employs in planning professional development programs. As part of your evaluation, interview teachers to determine whether decisions on professional development activities reflect actual teacher needs. Include recommendations for improvement of the needs assessment process.

2. Attend a professional development session for teachers. Evaluate the session in terms of (a) the extent to which the session reflects the major research findings on effective professional development; (b) whether varying levels of teacher development, expertise, and commitment are taken into consideration; (c) organization; (d) facilities; and (e) materials. Note informal reactions of teachers attending the session. Include suggestions for improving future professional development sessions.

3. Interview five teachers concerning a professional development program that is being proposed or introduced in their school. On the basis of interviews, attempt to classify each teacher according to his or her stage of professional development (orientation, integration, or refinement).

4. Interview an individual who has considerable experience at planning professional development sessions on the practical aspects of preparing for such sessions. Ask him or her to relate past experiences that illustrate potential problems to avoid, eventualities to consider, and areas in which special preparation is necessary. Prepare a report on your interview.

5. Interview the individual in charge of professional development on a school system's long-range professional development program. (Be sure the school system *has* a long-range professional development program before arranging the interview!) Prepare a report describing and evaluating the program.

Developmental

1. As you attend professional development activities over a period of time, observe the experience impact of different activities on various groups of teachers (the effects of high- and low-impact activities on teachers of various levels of development, expertise, and commitment).

2. Develop a file of ideas for professional development activities. Research on successful professional development programs can serve as a planning source. Activities can be developed for individuals and groups at various levels of development, expertise, and commitment, and at various stages of professional development (orientation, integration, refinement). Experience impact can be considered when designing activities for teachers with different characteristics.

3. Volunteer to help plan and implement professional development activities in your school or school system. Try to incorporate the research on effective professional development into the plans.

ENDNOTE

1. Outlining a complete professional-development program on cooperative learning is beyond the scope of this text. Some critical topics are listed to provide examples of the types of learning in each stage of professional development. Sources of cooperative learning professional development topics are Johnson, Johnson, and Holubec (1991) and Kagan (1992).

REFERENCES

Bernauer, F. 2002. Five keys to unlock continuous school improvement. *Kappa Delta Pi Record,* 38(2), 89–92.

Corcoran, T. B. 1995. *Helping teachers teach well: Transforming professional development.* CPRE Policy Briefs, RB-16-June. New Brunswick, NJ: Rutgers University, Consortium for Policy Research in Education.

DiBernardo, G., and Stiles, D. 1988. The Madeline Hunter and Lee Canter teacher improvement packages: What every school needs? *Democratic Schools,* 3(2), 1–9.

Farmer, J., Hauk, S., and Neumann, A. M. 2005. Negotiating reform: Implementing process standards in culturally responsive professional development. *The High School Journal,* 88(4), 59–71.

Fullan, M. 2000. *Change forces: The sequel.* Philadelphia, PA: George H. Buchanan.

Garman, N. B., and Hazley, H. M. 1988. Teachers ask: Is there life after Madeline Hunter? *Kappan,* 69(9), 669–672.

Glickman, C. D. 1992. The essence of school renewal. *Educational Leadership,* 50(1), 87–97.

Glickman, C. D. 2002. The courage to lead. *Educational Leadership,* 59(8), 41–44.

Gordon, S. P. 2000. *Professional development for teacher and school renewal: Alternative pathways, common characteristics.* Paper presented at the University Council for Educational Administration Annual Convention, Albuquerque, NM, November.

Gursky, D. 1990. A plan that works. *Teacher* (June/July), 46–54.

Guskey, T. R. 1994. *Professional development in education: In search of the optimal mix.* Paper presented at the annual meeting of the American Educational Research Association, New Orleans, April. (ERIC 369 181)

Harris, A. 2002. *School improvement: What's in it for schools?* New York: Routledge Falmer.

Hawley, W. D., and Valli, L. 1996. *The essentials of effective professional development: A new consensus.* Paper presented at the AERA Invitational Conference on Teacher Development and School Reform, Washington, DC.

Johnson, D. W., Johnson, R. T., and Holubec, E. J. 1991. *Cooperation in the classroom.* Edina, MN: Interaction Book Company.

Joyce, B., Calhoun, E., and Hopkins, D. 1999. *The new structure of school improvement: Inquiring schools and achieving students.* Philadelphia: Open University Press.

Kagan, S. 1992. *Cooperative learning.* San Juan Capistrano: Kagan Cooperative Learning.

Lambert, L. 1988. Staff development redesigned. *Kappa, 69*(9), 665–668.

Levin, H. M. 1994. Learning from accelerated schools. In S. H. Block, S. T. Evertson, and T. R. Guskey (Eds.), *Selecting and integrating school improvement programs.* New York: Scholastic Books.

Loucks-Horsley, S., Harding, C. K., Arbuckle, M. A., Murray, L. B., Dubea, C., and Williams, M. K. 1987. *Continuing to learn: A guidebook for teacher development.* Andover, ME: The Regional Laboratory for Educational Improvement of the Northeast and Islands.

Moore, R., and Seeger, V. 2004. Validating teaching and learning communities for teacher education reform. *The Teacher Educator, 40*(2), 116–132.

Orlich, D. C. 1989. *Staff development: Enhancing human potential.* Boston: Allyn and Bacon.

Ponticell, J. A. 1995. Promoting teacher professionalism through collegiality. *Journal of Staff Development, 16*(3), 13–18.

Showers, B., Joyce, B. R., and Bennett, B. 1987. Synthesis of research on staff development: A framework for future study and a state-of-the-art analysis. *Educational Leadership, 45*(3), 77–80.

Tetenbaum, T. J., and Mulkeen, T. A. 1987. *Prelude to school improvement: Understanding perceptions of staff development.* Presentation to the annual meeting of the American Educational Research Association, Washington, DC, April.

U.S. Department of Education. 1996. National Center for Education Statistics. *Measures of in-service professional development: Suggested items for the 1998–1999 Schools and Staffing Survey.* Working Paper No. 96-25, Washington, DC: Author.

Wilshire, D. K. 1991. *Teachers in transition: An exploratory study of self-selected change and educational planning in professional development.* Unpublished doctoral dissertation, Pennsylvania State University.

Wood, F. W., and Thompson, S. R. 1980. Guidelines for better staff development. *Educational Leadership, 37*(5), 374–378.

Wood, F. W., and Thompson, S. R. 1993. Assumptions about staff development based on research and best practice. *Journal of Staff Development, 14*(4), 52–57.

Zech, L. K., Gause-Vega, C. L., and Bray, M. H. 2000. Content-based collaborative inquiry: A professional development model for sustaining educational reform. *Educational Psychologist, 35*(3), 207–217.

SUGGESTED READINGS

American Federation of Teachers. 1995. *Principles for professional development: AFT's guidelines for creating professional development programs that make a difference.* Washington, DC: Author.

Barbknecht, A., and Kieffer, C. W. 2001. *Peer coaching: The learning team approach.* Arlington Heights, IL: Skylight.

Bell, L., and Day, C. 1991. *Managing the professional development of teachers.* Philadelphia: Open University.

Burke, P., Heideman, R., and Heideman, C. (Eds.). 1990. *Programming for staff development.* London: Falmer.

Caldwell, S. D. (Ed.). 1989. *Staff development: A handbook of effective practices.* Oxford, OH: National Staff Development Council.

DeBolt, G. P. 1992. *Teacher induction and mentoring.* Albany: State University of New York.

Glickman, C. D. 2002. The courage to lead. *Educational Leadership, 59*(8), 41–44.

Glickman, C. D. 2002. *Leadership for learning: How to help teachers succeed.* Alexandria, VA: Association for Supervision and Curriculum development.

Gordon, S. P. 1991. *How to help beginning teachers succeed.* Alexandria, VA: Association for Supervision and Curriculum Development.

Grimmett, P. P., and Neufeld, U. (Eds.). 1994. *Teacher development and the struggle for authenticity.* New York: Teachers College Press.

Guskey, T. R., and Huberman, M. (Eds.). 1995. *Professional development in education: New paradigms and practices.* New York: Teachers College Press.

Harris, A. 2002. *School improvement: What's in it for schools?* New York: Routledge Falmer.

Joyce, B. (Ed.). 1990. *Changing school culture through staff development.* Alexandria, VA: Association for Supervision and Curriculum and Development.

Levine, S. L. 1989. *Promoting adult growth in schools.* Boston: Allyn and Bacon.

National Staff Development Council. 1994. *Standards for staff development: Middle level edition.* Oxford, OH: Authors.

National Staff Development Council and National Association of Elementary School Principals. 1995. *Standards for staff development: Elementary school edition.* Oxford, OH: Authors.

National Staff Development Council and National Association of Secondary Schools Principals. 1995. *Standards for staff development: High school edition.* Oxford, OH: Authors.

Olsen, W. R., and Sommers, W. A. 2005. *Energizing staff development using film clips: Memorable movie moments that promote reflection, conversation, and action.* Thousand Oaks, CA: Corwin.

Orlich, D. C. 1989. *Staff development: Enhancing human potential.* Boston: Allyn and Bacon.

Pink, W. T., and Hyde, A. H. 1992. *Effective staff development for school change.* Norwood, NJ: Ablex.

Sparks, D., and Hirsh, S. 2000. *A national plan for improving professional development.* Oxford, OH: National Staff Development Council.

Sparks, D., and Hirsh, S. 1997. *A new vision for the staff development.* Alexandria, VA: Association for Supervision and Curriculum Development (and Oxford, OH: National Staff Development Council).

Stiggins, R. J. 2002. Assessment crisis: The absence of assessment FOR learning. *Phi Delta Kappan, 83*(10), 758–765.

Tate, M. L. 2004. *"Sit and get" won't grow dendrites: Twenty professional learning strategies that engage the adult brain.* Thousand Oaks, CA: Corwin.

"Teaching is a moral activity that implies thoughts about ends, means, and their consequences" (Zeuli and Buchmann, 1987). Moral activity is explicitly expressed in a school's curriculum. To be an effective school is of little matter unless the personnel within an organization first have defined what is meant by a good school—what should students learn in order to be well educated? The institutional job then becomes one of effectively achieving that definition of goodness. As Sergiovanni (1987) remarked, "It's not important to do things right, unless we are doing the right things!" Curriculum is the moral deliberation on what is "right" for students to be taught.

Hirsch, in *Cultural Literacy: What Every American Needs to Know* (1987), attacked American education as abandoning the essential literature, ideas, and facts of the national culture. Bloom, in *The Closing of the American Mind* (1987), likewise indicted schools for abandoning the core programs of traditional liberal arts education. In *What Do Our 17-Year-Olds Know?* (1987), educators Ravitch and Finn wrote that a large proportion of high school students don't know such basic facts as in what half-century the Civil War took place. Hirsch, Bloom, Ravitch, and Finn believe it is both necessary and right to reduce the school curriculum to a focus on predetermined, essential knowledge.

Yet the National Assessment of Educational Progress (NAEP), in its report card on high school students' knowledge of literature and U.S. history, suggests that students' inadequate knowledge may be because "the typical course relies heavily on a textbook . . . students regularly are expected to memorize important information, and are tested frequently . . . class time is spent listening to the teacher lecture" (Applebee, Langer, and Mullis, 1987). Indeed, what is taught and how it is taught, according to the NAEP study of literature and history, is no different from what Goodlad found in his national study of schooling. Goodlad (1984) found that nearly 90 percent of teaching across all subjects and grade levels is up-front teaching—lecturing, with students passively listening except for an occasional opportunity to answer questions. On one side, academic essentialists argue that the problem with curriculum is that too much stress is placed on process skills (problem solving, inquiry, and critical thinking) to the detriment of straight, old-fashioned teaching of content and basic skills. Social activists and experimentalists such as Goodlad reply that such teaching is what already exists and is to blame for inadequate student comprehension. Their argument is that there should be less facts and memorization and more active problem solving and conceptual understanding.

Sizer (1984) reasoned that schools are too concerned with teaching all subjects superficially. Instead, schools should teach fewer subjects, topics, and skills more thoroughly—"teach less, better" rather than "teach more, quicker." Others argued that curriculum should expose students to a vast array of educational experiences. Howard Gardner, a noted cognitive psychologist, stated (in Brandt, 1988b) that his research on human intelligence indicates that elementary and middle schools should not be concerned with subjects; instead, curriculum should focus on long-term core projects that integrate rather than separate learning of language, mathematics, science, reading, art, and physical education.

How does one make sense of these topsy-turvy controversies about curriculum? How can so many esteemed experts have so many contradictory ideas? It comes down to a matter of educational philosophy (as discussed in Chapter 5). Curriculum experts are humans too! They possess the same ideological, philosophical, and political biases as the rest of us. They may argue more eloquently and have better support for their claims than we do, but at the bottom of their discourse are philosophical premises and assumptions about education no different from ours. Ultimately, decisions about a good school, appropriate curriculum, and needs of students should be made by those closest to students. After considering the available experts, research, readings, and articulated conflicts, people in the schools, districts, and local communities should ultimately decide what is worthy to teach. However, by default, pressure, and abdication, curriculum decisions have generally been made by those farthest from the classroom action.

Sources of Curriculum Development

Curricula can be developed at many levels—by outside specialists, school district specialists, school curriculum teams, and teachers alone. At the national level, commercial materials such as textbooks, learning kits, and audiovisual materials are developed mainly by outside specialists. The No Child Left Behind Act of 2001 (Public Law 107-110) introduced unprecedented federal controls over K–12 school curriculum in the 50 states. At the state level, departments of education have become increasingly active in curriculum development. Many states have legislated statewide competency tests for student promotion and graduation and have developed curriculum guides for local schools to ensure the teaching of those competencies. At the local level, many school systems have written their own curriculum guides for coordinating instruction across grade levels. This is done either by having curriculum specialists at the district level write the guides themselves, or by having such specialists work with representative teams of teachers (perhaps with community and student representation). Rarely do local schools turn curriculum development entirely over to teachers.

We can think about sources of curriculum development according to Figure 19.1 (see Oliva, 1992). Much curriculum is developed at the state, federal, and commercial levels. In other words, most curricula are produced far away from the local teacher and the local schools.

Legislated Learning

It is a shame that most educators experience curriculum as something given, which they must follow. Why is it that curriculum is no longer a province for school inquiry and action, but rather a matter of complying with external mandates? The reason is that in the era of legislated learning, teachers and school leaders are seen as incapable of knowing what their students should be taught (Fitzharris, 2005).

State-Mandated Curriculum

In many states, legislatures are now mandating the curriculum to be taught in all public PK–12 schools. The purpose of the mandated curriculum is to transmit knowledge and skills deemed essential by the state legislature or educational bureaucracy. The required curriculum is often presented as a laundry list of required objectives in each subject area (or at least each "basic" subject area) at each grade

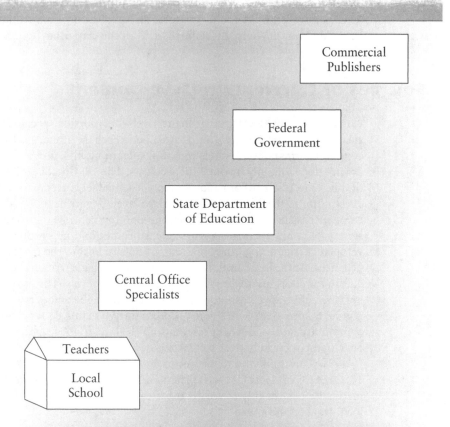

FIGURE 19.1 *Illustration of Sources of Curriculum Development*

level. Objectives tend to be within the lower categories of Bloom's taxonomy, at the memory or translation level. There are seldom any connections made between the objectives in different content areas. Even the objectives within a given content area are usually discreet from one another. In short, in terms of purpose, content, organization, and format, state-mandated curriculum tends to be at the lowest level of curriculum development. It is therefore very difficult for teachers in states with mandated curricula to function beyond the imitative maintenance level of involvement in curriculum development.

One argument often made by state officials discussing this reality is that teachers don't need to have a say in the curriculum because they can use their professional expertise and creativity when they plan how to teach the curriculum in their classrooms. These policy makers fail to understand that *the curriculum, if rigidly enforced, has a significant impact on how teachers teach*. For example, teachers working under a highly prescribed curriculum with long lists of required objectives will approach instruction quite differently than teachers with a webbed curriculum that they have designed themselves. In short, *what* gets taught (curriculum) has a strong impact on *how* it gets taught (instruction).

High-Stakes Tests and the Curriculum

One way the federal government and states have attempted to control curriculum in schools is through the use of high-stakes tests (discussed in detail in Chapter 15). When aligned with the state-mandated curriculum, state test scores are used as a measure of whether teachers are effectively implementing the curriculum. In states without a mandated curriculum but with high-stakes tests, the test itself becomes the curriculum. In these states the original notion of alignment (start with the curriculum and align instruction and assessment with the curriculum) is turned on its head, with local schools aligning their curricula with the state test.

> A standardized test would set the educational objectives for the teacher. Curriculum alignment would insure that the teacher would cover the material to be tested. The teacher would prepare plans and write reports to inform supervisors in the bureaucracy that the material was being covered. Evaluators would observe and inspect to make sure that teachers were using the proper methods. And, finally, the external test would demonstrate whether the teacher had properly executed his or her duties. (Wise, 1988, p. 330)

We don't want to imply that learning standards and assessment are by their very nature bad. Standards and assessment that have been constructed with wide participation and are thoughtful and reasonable for students to achieve can be a way to address class, race, and gender inequities of expectations, resources, and targeted assistance. The issue here is one of who should define such standards, what should be multiple ways of assessing such learning, what should be the consequences for students, teachers, and schools, and as importantly, what flexibility, freedom, and authority should be given to classrooms and schools to be accountable? After all, it is hard to be accountable for what one has no control over (Elmore and Rothman, 1999; Darling-Hammond, 1997; Glickman, 1999, 2000/2001).

Curriculum Development as a Vehicle for Enhancing Collective Thinking about Instruction

The tragedy of curriculum being simply a response to state tests is the loss of a powerful vehicle for creating a broader instructional dialogue in a school or district, which could enhance teachers' individual and collective thinking about these questions: What is worth teaching, how shall we teach, and how shall we assess? Most teachers—when trusted, when given time and money, and when given the assistance, choice, and responsibility to develop curricula—will make extraordinarily sound decisions about what students should be taught. Often, their decisions will be far superior to those made in central offices, state departments, or commercial publishing firms (McEvoy, 1986; McNeil, 1988).

Teachers who are involved in making decisions about school curriculum go through changes in their own thinking about teaching. To discuss, debate, and finally come to an agreement with peers about what is important for students to know is an intellectually challenging experience.

It is clear that in order for schools to be successful, teachers need to be involved in curriculum development. The issues that remain are:

1. What should be the purpose of the curriculum?
2. What should be the content of the curriculum?
3. How should the curriculum be organized?
4. In what format should the curriculum be written?
5. At what level of curriculum development should teachers be involved?

Forthcoming sections will discuss each of these issues.

What Should Be the Purpose of the Curriculum?

Alternative beliefs about the purpose of the curriculum are described by Miller and Seller (1985) as orientations to curriculum. They describe three "metaorientations" or positions:

- In the *transmission position* the function of education is to transmit facts, skills, and values to students. Specifically, this orientation stresses mastery of traditional school subjects through traditional teaching methodologies. (pp. 5 and 6) (emphasis supplied)
- In the *transaction position* the individual is seen as rational and capable of intelligent problem solving. Education is viewed as a dialogue between the student and the curriculum in which the student reconstructs knowledge through the dialogue process. The central elements in the transaction position are an emphasis on curriculum strategies that promote problem solving . . . application of problem solving skills within social contexts in general and within the context of the democratic process . . . and development of cognitive skills within the academic disciplines. (pp. 6 and 7) (emphasis supplied)
- The *transformation position* focuses on personal and social change. It encompasses . . . teaching students skills that promote personal and social transformation . . . (and) a vision of social change as movement toward harmony with the environment rather than an effort to exert control over it. (p. 8) (emphasis supplied)

If Miller and Seller's three orientations to curriculum sound vaguely familiar, it may be due to your review of educational philosophies in Chapter 5. The transmission curriculum orientation is related to the educational philosophy of essentialism. The transactional curriculum orientation is based largely on the philosophy of experimentalism. Finally, aspects of the transformation orientation are related to the philosophy of existentialism. In Chapter 5, we found that our educational beliefs help to shape our definition of effective teaching and instructional improvement. Similarly, curriculum orientations drive the curriculum development process and affect curriculum purpose, content, organization, and format. Therefore, it is important that early in the curriculum design process the curriculum development team examines alternative curriculum orientations and clarifies its own orientation. The most basic decision the team needs to make (with input from all stakeholders) is whether the purpose of the curriculum will be to transmit, transact, transform, or accomplish some combination thereof.

What Should Be the Content of the Curriculum?

Curriculum, for purposes of this book, is the *what* of instruction—what is intentionally taught to students in a district, school, or classroom. The elements of curriculum are sequence and continuity, scope, and balance (Doll, 1989). *Sequence* is the ordering of learning experiences, and *continuity* is the length or duration of such experiences. *Scope* is the range of learning experiences to be offered. *Balance* is the degree and amount of topics, subjects, and learning experiences that adequately prepare students. A curriculum is developed by deciding: (1) What should students learn? (2) What is the order of content for the student to follow? (3) How is the learning to be evaluated? (see Firth and Newfield, 1984; Glatthorn, 1987; Brandt, 1988a; Clark and Clark, 2000; Gandal and Vranek, 2001).

Decisions about curriculum content are influenced by priorities of state and federal governments, values of professional educators and the local community, knowledge of student development, current economics, and future societal conditions. Underlying all decisions about curriculum content are curriculum orientations (transmission, transaction, or transformation), which ultimately are derived from educational philosophies (essentialism, experimentalism, or existentialism).

Benjamin Bloom's taxonomy of learning might serve as a guide for determining types of learning within or across content areas (see Table 19.1). His lower-level learnings—(1) memory and (2) translation—are based on students recalling and demonstrating known answers. Curriculum objectives calling for memory and translation tend to dominate a curriculum with the purpose of transmission. Bloom's intermediate levels of learning—(3) interpretation, (4) application, and (5) analysis—are based on students using logic to discover relationships, solve problems, and reflect on their own thought process. Curriculum objectives at the

TABLE 19.1	Bloom's Taxonomy

Category Name	Description
1. Memory	Student recalls or recognizes information.
2. Translation	Student changes information into a different symbolic form or language.
3. Interpretation	Student discovers relationships among facts, generalizations, definitions, values, and skills.
4. Application	Student solves a life problem that requires the identification of the issue and the selection and use of appropriate generalizations and skills.
5. Analysis	Student solves a problem in the light of conscious knowledge of the parts and forms of thinking.
6. Synthesis	Student solves a problem that requires original creative thinking.
7. Evaluation	Student makes a judgment of good or bad, right or wrong, according to standards designated by student.

Source: G. Manson and A. A. Clegg, Jr., "Classroom Questions: Keys to Children's Thinking?" *Peabody Journal of Education, 47,* No. 5 (March 1970): 304–305. Reprinted by permission of Peabody Journal of Education.

interpretation, application, and analysis levels are emphasized in a curriculum with the purpose of transaction. Finally, Bloom's higher levels of learning—(6) synthesis and (7) evaluation—are based on combining various knowledge, facts, skills, and logic to make unique personal judgments. Curriculum objectives at the synthesis and evaluation levels are prevalent in a curriculum with the purpose of transformation. By examining a written curriculum, then, we can ascertain whether its purpose (and the curriculum developers' underlying orientation) is transmission, transaction, or transformation.

How Should the Curriculum Be Organized?

Three broad approaches to organizing curriculum content are discipline based, interdisciplinary, and transdisciplinary. A *discipline-based curriculum* is described by Jacobs (1989):

> The discipline-based content design option focuses on a strict interpretation of the disciplines with separate subjects in separate time blocks during the school day. No attempt for integration is made, in fact, it is avoided. Traditional approaches to subjects such as language arts, mathematics, science, social studies,

music, art, and physical education are the usual fare. In secondary programs, these general academic and arts areas break down into more specific fields, such as algebra under mathematics or American history under social studies. There are some variations of block scheduling and the way the week or cycle is programmed. Nevertheless, knowledge is presented in separate fields without a deliberate attempt to show the relationships among them. (p. 14)

Because of its emphasis on breaking learning down into discreet segments of traditional content to be learned in specified blocks of time, the discipline-based approach is best suited to a curriculum with the purpose of transmission. This approach clearly has been the dominant curriculum organization pattern in the United States.

In an *interdisciplinary curriculum,* common themes connect traditional content areas. For instance, different aspects of an instructional unit on transportation might be taught in science, math, social studies, language arts, art, music, and physical education. Or, a set of common concepts or skills (for example, technology or problem-solving skills) might connect different subject areas throughout the year. Figure 19.2 illustrates an interdisciplinary curriculum. A curriculum organization of this type requires extensive team planning. Since the interdisciplinary approach encourages students to discover relationships and make applications across existing content areas, it is most appropriate for a curriculum with the purpose of transactional learning (Jenkins, 2005).

FIGURE 19.2 *Illustration of an Interdisciplinary Curriculum*

Source: From Drake, S. M., Bebbington, J., Laksman, S., Mackie, P., Maynes, N., & Wayne, L. (1992). *Developing an Integrated Curriculum Using the Story Model*, p. 4. Ontario: The Ontario Institute for Studies in Education Press. Reprinted with permission of University of Toronto Press.

In a *transdisciplinary curriculum,* traditional disciplines do not exist. The entire curriculum is organized around common themes, skills, or problems. Daily learning activities are built around the topic being studied rather than conforming to academic disciplines or class schedules. For example, while studying the concept of commerce, students could spend all of their school time developing, managing, and analyzing their own in-school "marketplace." Students might study selected content from economics, math, sociology, communication, politics, ethics, history, and other academic disciplines, but only as such content became relevant to the commercial community they were developing. Transdisciplinary curricula usually begin with very broad intended learning outcomes. The integration into the curriculum of contemporary problems from the real world and students' interests and concerns become part of an ongoing curriculum development process. This type of curriculum organization can be successful only if teachers are willing to totally reconceptualize their concept of the school curriculum. A transdisciplinary curriculum organization requires students to synthesize knowledge and skills from various content areas and encourages student creativity and self-direction. Such an organizational pattern is most consistent with a curriculum with the purpose of transforming teaching and learning.

In What Format Should the Curriculum Be Written?

This section will discuss various formats used in writing curriculum. Behavioral objective, webbing, conceptual mapping, and results-only formats will be described. Like the content and organization of curriculum, the format it is written in reflects a curriculum orientation. Behavioral-objective formats reflect a transmission orientation. Webbing or conceptual mapping formats reflect a transaction orientation. Results-only formats reflect a transformation orientation.

Behavioral-Objective Format

Predetermined knowledge, facts, and skills are written in curriculum guides in a linear cause-and-effect format. The curriculum developers determine what is to be learned, state the learning as a behavioral objective, specify the teaching/learning activities, and conclude with a posttest to see if the objective has been achieved. The progression is

Objective   Activity   Evaluation

Figure 19.3 is an example of a behavioral-objective guide written for a fifth-grade social studies class. Curriculum developers break their unit into the most

Behavioral objective: At the end of the week, students will recall and spell the original 13 colonies at a 100 percent level of mastery.

Activities:

1. Lecture on 13 colonies.
2. Students fill in map of 13 colonies.
3. Students read pp. 113–118 of text and do assignments on p. 119 as homework.
4. Call on students at random to spell the various colonies.

Evaluation: Ask students to recall the names and spell correctly each of the 13 original colonies on a sheet of paper.

FIGURE 19.3 *Behavioral-Objective Format*

important facts or skills that cover the subject. They write behavioral objectives for each fact or skill. Each behavioral objective is the basis for a sequence of activities and evaluation. The teacher who uses such a curriculum guide is expected to follow the sequence of activities and administer the evaluation. Recycling activities might be included in the guide for those students who do not pass the evaluation. Each behavioral-objective plan is tightly sequenced so that one objective is mastered before a student moves to the next (for example, after identifying and spelling the original 13 American colonies, the next objective might be identifying and spelling those states that came into the Union from 1776 to 1810).

Most school curricula that have been written in the last two decades follow a behavioral-objective format. It is particularly easy to use in subjects such as mathematics and physical sciences, where skills are obvious and facts are clear (2 plus 2 is always 4, for example, but is war always justifiable?). So prevalent has been the behavioral-objective format in curriculum writing in the last few years that many educators know of no other way to write curricula.

Webbing

Curriculum can be written in a format that shows relationships of activities around a central theme. William Kilpatrick popularized this type of curriculum in writing about the work unit (Kilpatrick, 1925). Instead of predetermining the knowledge or skills, the curriculum developer determines the major theme, related themes, and then possible student activities.

The webbing format can be conceived of in this way:

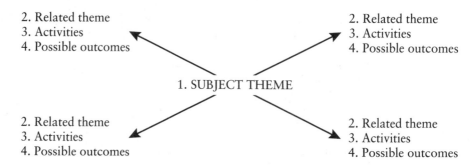

2. Related theme
3. Activities
4. Possible outcomes

2. Related theme
3. Activities
4. Possible outcomes

1. SUBJECT THEME

2. Related theme
3. Activities
4. Possible outcomes

2. Related theme
3. Activities
4. Possible outcomes

After the activities have been written, the curriculum developers write possible learning outcomes: "Students will be able to identify four major environmental issues," "Students will be able to argue and give evidence for both the pro and con sides of each issue," "Students will take a personal stance on each issue." In planning activities, developers consider multimodes of learning via reading, writing, listening, and constructing, and then integrate many fields of knowledge around a central theme. Notice how the theme of environmental issues integrates activities in sociology, mathematics, economics, history, journalism, physics, and biology.

A webbing curriculum guide would contain a blueprint of the web followed by sections for each related theme with activities, possible outcomes, and resources needed (see Figure 19.4). Notice that the webbed curriculum includes possible outcomes and allows for the possibility of others. In a behavioral-objective curriculum, activities are controlled toward predetermined ends. In a webbed curriculum, activities lead to possible and unanticipated learning.

Results-Only Format

A results-only format for curriculum provides teachers with the widest latitude for using materials, activities, and methods. Such a curriculum specifies the goals and general learning about a subject, theme unit, or course. The guide might include ways to evaluate the learning. For example, a results-only guide in elementary reading might specify the following skills to be learned:

Comprehension

1. Develops powers of observation
2. Classifies by name, color, shape, size, positions, use
3. Anticipates endings to stories
4. Discriminates between fact and fantasy
5. Understands who, what, when, where, how, and why phrases
6. Recalls a story sequence

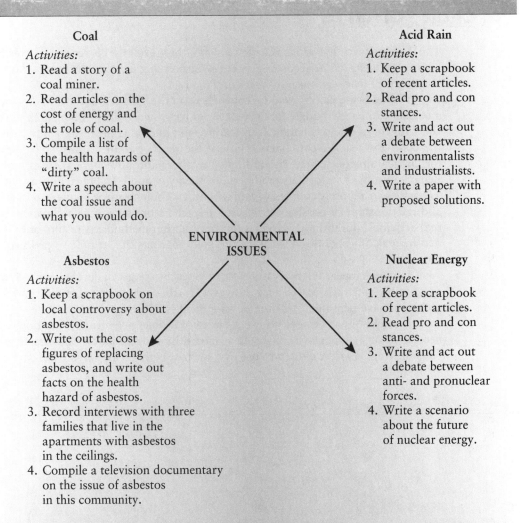

Coal

Activities:
1. Read a story of a coal miner.
2. Read articles on the cost of energy and the role of coal.
3. Compile a list of the health hazards of "dirty" coal.
4. Write a speech about the coal issue and what you would do.

Acid Rain

Activities:
1. Keep a scrapbook of recent articles.
2. Read pro and con stances.
3. Write and act out a debate between environmentalists and industrialists.
4. Write a paper with proposed solutions.

ENVIRONMENTAL
ISSUES

Asbestos

Activities:
1. Keep a scrapbook on local controversy about asbestos.
2. Write out the cost figures of replacing asbestos, and write out facts on the health hazard of asbestos.
3. Record interviews with three families that live in the apartments with asbestos in the ceilings.
4. Compile a television documentary on the issue of asbestos in this community.

Nuclear Energy

Activities:
1. Keep a scrapbook of recent articles.
2. Read pro and con stances.
3. Write and act out a debate between anti- and pronuclear forces.
4. Write a scenario about the future of nuclear energy.

FIGURE 19.4 *Webbing Format*

7. Reads to find the main ideas of a story
8. Reads to draw a conclusion
9. Compares and contrasts stories

It is then left to the teacher to determine when and how to teach these skills. The teacher is held accountable only for the results, not for the procedures used.

Curriculum Format as Reflective of Choice Given to Teachers

The less specificity and detail a curriculum has, the greater the choice given to teachers to vary instruction according to the situation. Figure 19.5 illustrates the enlargement of teacher choice by curriculum.

Picture being in a curriculum cone where, at the behavioral-objective bottom, a teacher can barely budge. As the teacher moves toward the webbing area, he or she finds room to move hands, feet, elbows, and knees. At the results-only end of the cone, the teacher can extend fully. If the teacher is allowed to step out of the curriculum cone, there are no limits on where and how he or she can move. Behavioral-objective formats predetermine the *what* and *how* of teaching as much as possible in a loosely coupled organization. A webbing format focuses on themes and relationships of possible activities for teachers but give them a choice of actual activities, duration of activities, and evaluation methods. A results-only format focuses on generalized learning and gives teachers the latitude to proceed as they wish.

It would appear relatively easy to match teacher stages of development to curriculum formats. It is not so easy, however; further examination of type and degree of involvement in curriculum development is necessary.

If a school has decided to use a behavioral-objective format, that does not necessarily mean that classroom teachers have little choice about how to teach. Perhaps the teachers have chosen to use that format; perhaps they wrote the curricu-

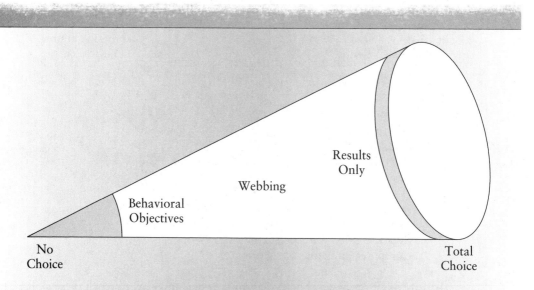

FIGURE 19.5 *Curriculum Format as a Reflection of Teacher-Choice: The Curriculum Cone*

lum themselves. Also, an elaborately detailed behavioral-objective curriculum could be presented to teachers as a reference guide to use as they wish. Simply knowing the format of the curriculum would not tell us how much choice was given to teachers. Although behavioral curricula usually are used as prescriptive teaching and can be equated with limiting choice, this is not always so. Therefore, before completing the picture of curriculum and teacher choice, it is necessary to consider how curricula are developed, interpreted, and implemented.

Relationship of Curriculum Purpose, Content, Organization, and Format

In previous sections we have proposed logical links between curriculum purpose, content, organization, and format. To review, a curriculum with the purpose of transmission is logically matched with memory and translation learning content, discipline-based curriculum organization, and behavioral-objective format. A curriculum with the purpose of transaction is well matched with interpretation, application, and analysis learning content; interdisciplinary curriculum organization; and webbing format. A curriculum with the purpose of transformation is consistent with synthesis and evaluation learning content, a transdisciplinary curriculum organization, and a results-only format. Table 19.2 illustrates logical relationships of curriculum purpose, content, organization, and format.

The "natural matches" we've outlined, of course, don't occur in all curricula. For instance, not all webbing formats are found within interdisciplinary curricula. The webbing format in Figure 19.4, for example, could be part of a science course within a discipline-based curriculum. For another instance, a results-only curriculum format could focus on learning content at the lower and intermediate as well as the higher levels of Bloom's taxonomy, or could be part of a discipline-based or interdisciplinary rather than a transdisciplinary curriculum. In general, however, our own review of K–12 curricula indicate that the logical matches in Table 19.2 tend to hold true in most schools.

TABLE 19.2	Logical Relationships of Curriculum Purpose, Content, Organization, and Format		
Curriculum Purpose:	Transmission	Transaction	Transformation
Curriculum Content:	Memory Translation	Interpretation Application Analysis	Synthesis Evaluation
Curriculum Organization:	Discipline Based	Interdisciplinary	Transdisciplinary
Curriculum Format:	Behavioral Objective	Webbing	Results Only

Levels of Teacher Involvement in Curriculum Development

Tanner and Tanner (1980) wrote of teachers and local schools functioning in curriculum development at one of three levels: (1) imitative maintenance, (2) mediative, or (3) generative. Teachers at level 1 are concerned with maintaining and following the existing curriculum. Teachers at level 2 look at development as refining the existing curriculum. Teachers at level 3 are concerned with improving and changing the curriculum according to the most current knowledge about learning and societal conditions. Tanner and Tanner explained these three levels.

Level I: Imitative Maintenance

Teachers operating at Level I rely on textbooks, workbooks, and routine activities, subject by subject. Skills are treated as dead ends rather than as means of generating further learning. Readymade materials are used without critical evaluation, resulting in a multiplicity of isolated skill-development activities. (The already segmental curriculum is further fragmented.) The imagination of the teacher does not go beyond maintaining the status quo. This teacher would like to think that he or she has less freedom than he or she may actually have for curriculum improvement. In the secondary school, concern for curriculum development is largely confined to each departmental domain.

When change is made, it is made on the adoption level, without adaptation to local needs. Curriculum development at this level is plugging in the package to the existing situation without attention to the resulting interactions. Teachers at this level tend to be left alone to struggle with innovations that are handed to them from above. Schools are turned inward, with the principal as the sole resource for classroom assistance.

Level II: Mediative

Teachers at Level II are aware of the need to integrate curriculum content and deal with emergent conditions. (Societal problems such as the energy crisis and children's questions about things that interest and concern them are examples of emergent conditions.) Although teachers at this level may have an aggregate conception of curriculum, implementation does not go beyond the occasional correlation of certain subjects. The focus of curriculum remains segmental; theory remains divorced from practice; curriculum improvement remains at the level of refining existing practice.

Yet teachers at the second level of curriculum development do not blindly plug in an innovation or curriculum package to the existing situation. The necessary adaptations, accommodations, and adjustments are made and capitalize on a range of resources for curriculum improvement, including pupils, parents, and peers; and they utilize resources beyond the local school. Teachers are consumers of professional literature on approved practices and tap the resources of the university through in-service courses. The mediative level is a level of awareness and accommodation. Teachers are attracted to, and can articulate, new ideas but their efforts to improve the curriculum fall short of the necessary reconstruction for substantive problem solving.

Level III: Creative-Generative

Teachers at Level III take an aggregate approach to curriculum development. Ideally, the curriculum is examined in its entirety by the teacher and the whole school staff, and questions of priority and relationship are asked. While individual teachers can and should be at the generative-creative level, a macrocurricular approach requires cooperative planning for vertical and horizontal articulation.

Granted that teachers as individuals usually cannot create new schoolwide curricula, an individual teacher can establish continuities and relationships in his or her own teaching and with other teachers. Teachers at Level III use generalizations and problems as centers of curriculum organization. They stress the broad concepts that specialized subjects share in common, and they use and develop courses of study that cross subject fields. These are aggregate treatments.

Teachers at the third level of curriculum development think about what they are doing and try to find more effective ways of working. They are able to diagnose their problems and formulate hypotheses for solutions. They experiment in their classrooms and communicate their insights to other teachers.

Teachers at this level are consumers of research and seek greater responsibility for curriculum decisions at the school and classroom levels. They exercise independent judgment in selecting curriculum materials and adapt them to local needs. They regard themselves as professionals and, as such, are continually involved in the problems of making decisions regarding learning experiences. To this end, their antennae are turned outward to a wide range of resources. (Daniel Tanner and Laurel N. Tanner, *Curriculum Development: Theory into Practice,* 2nd ed., pp. 636, 638–639. Copyright © 1980 by Macmillan Publishing Co., Inc., New York. Reprinted by permission.)

Integrating Curriculum Format with Developers and Levels of Development

To integrate what has been said about curriculum format, developers, and development, refer to Figure 19.6. When the developers are either outside the school system or from the district level and the curriculum is in a tightly prescribed format, development will be primarily *imitative,* characterized by teachers following the course of study. When the developers are intermediate teams of teachers led by district specialists and the curriculum is written with objectives and suggested activities, development will be primarily *mediative,* characterized by teachers revising and adapting the course of study to their immediate situation. When curriculum developers are teams of teachers using specialists as resource persons or

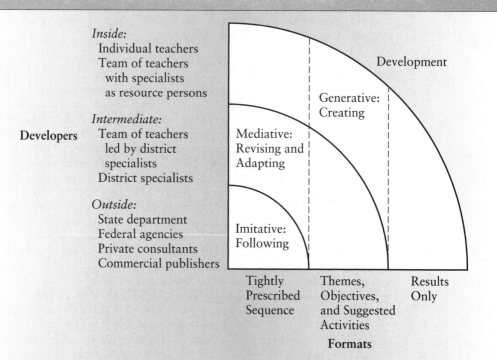

FIGURE 19.6 *Integrating Curriculum Format with Developers and Levels of Development*

individual teachers with a results-only curriculum format that identifies what students should learn and leaves activities to the teacher, then development is *generative,* characterized by ongoing creativity.

Matching Curriculum Development with Teacher Development

A progression of curriculum development matched with teacher development might look like Table 19.3. The supervisor might think of his or her staff in terms of the commitment, thinking, and expertise they currently bring to curriculum and then determine whether the current curriculum is appropriately matched with the teachers' level of curriculum functioning. If the present curriculum is inappropriate to teachers' development, readjustments to the curriculum would be in order.

A staff that has a low level of curriculum functioning—as displayed by little commitment to change, little ability to suggest possible changes, and little curriculum expertise—initially would be matched with an outside-developed, behavioral-objective, and imitative curriculum. They should be allowed to make minor revisions in adapting the curriculum to their classrooms. On the other hand, a staff that has a moderate level of curriculum functioning (as displayed by a desire to change, ability to think of possible changes, but a lack of expertise in writing curriculum) would be appropriately matched with a curriculum originally developed by outside experts but substantially revised by an internal team of teachers led by a curriculum specialist. The format of the curriculum might be eclectic in its use of behavioral objectives and webbing. Throughout the development and implementation, teachers should have problem-solving meetings for purposes of curriculum adaptation. Finally, a staff that is at a high level of curriculum functioning (as displayed by initiating and suggesting ways to change and knowing how to proceed in creating curriculum) would be appropriately matched with an internally developed curriculum. The format should emphasize "results only" with *suggested* activities, and should be continuously open to revision.

The supervisor should keep in mind the question: How does one increase teacher control over curriculum making? If a staff has been appropriately matched—for example, low-functioning staff with an imitative curriculum—and successful implementation is occurring, then the supervisor should plan for the next

TABLE 19.3 | **Progression of Curriculum Matched with Characteristics of Staff**

Staff Characteristics	Low	Moderate	High
Commitment to curriculum change	Low commitment to change	Would like to make change	Eager to make change
Level of thinking about curriculum	Low ability to think about possible changes	Can think of some possible changes	Has many suggestions
Expertise in curriculum procedures	Low expertise in how to proceed	Does not know how to write curriculum	Knows how to proceed

Curriculum Characteristics			
Developers	Outside developers	Outside developed but substantially revised by team of teachers led by specialists	Internally developed by team of teachers with specialists as resource
Format	Behavioral-objective, highly structured	Eclectic format using behavior objectives, webbing	Results-only, with suggested activities
Development	Imitative, with allowance for minor revisions	To be mutually adapted	To be discussed and changed continually

cycle of curriculum development to give teachers additional responsibilities by serving on decision-making teams under the leadership of a curriculum specialist. This would lead to more mutually adaptive curriculum and at the same time continue to stimulate and increase teacher commitment, development, and expertise.

The supervisor wishing to facilitate changes in curriculum purpose, content, organization, and format must remember that successful change will be based on teachers changing their conceptions of curriculum and their level of involvement in curriculum development. Change in teachers *and* curriculum is more likely to be successful if done in an incremental manner. For example, rather than announcing that the school will be moving from a discipline-based to interdisciplinary curriculum organization, the supervisor could initially encourage small teams of teachers functioning at moderate to high levels of development, expertise, and commitment to plan and teach a few interdisciplinary units of instruction throughout the school year. In another school already operating at an interdisciplinary level, movement toward a transdisciplinary curriculum could begin with a group of teachers operating at high levels of development, expertise, and commitment forming a "broad field." A *broad field* results from the fusion of two or more separate disciplines. Courses or subjects (rather than departments) with titles like "humanities," "social science," and "natural science" usually reflect a broad-field approach. The formation of one or more broad fields involving a subset of faculty and curricula would not represent a fully transdisciplinary curriculum, but would be a major step in that direction.

Large-scale teacher-driven changes in curriculum content, organization, and format will not take place unless teachers change their curriculum orientations or beliefs about the purpose of curriculum. Yet, teachers are not likely to change their orientations unless their levels of understanding of and involvement in curriculum development gradually increase. Supervisor openness and trust building, staff development in curriculum design, and time, support, and rewards for teacher involvement can all foster teacher *and* curriculum development. Throughout the curriculum development process, the supervisor must remember that if he or she has a curriculum orientation or favors a curriculum content, organization, or format different from teachers, he or she is not necessarily right and the teachers wrong. Government mandates, the community, the school's mission and culture, parents, teachers, and students must all be considered when deciding which direction curriculum development should take and at what rate it should proceed.

The Curriculum and Cultural Diversity

There are a variety of reasons why the curriculum should be culturally diverse. First, students from nondominant cultures are not likely to reach their learning potential if the curriculum ignores their culture. Second, a society cannot offer democracy, equal opportunity, and justice for all unless it experiences, understands, and respects the variety of cultures that make up the society. Third, communities and societies that recognize the value of diversity and invite citizens from different cultures to participate in their development experience more educational, economic, and social success: The quality of life for all citizens improves. A culturally diverse curriculum, then, benefits all students, as well as the community and society.

How do schools integrate multicultural and ethnic content into their curriculum? James Banks (2005) has described four approaches to integration. Banks presented the approaches as four levels of integration, with Level 1 the least effective and Level 4 the most effective. Level 1, the *contributions approach,* calls for inserting minority culture heroes, holidays, and elements (food, dances, music, art) into the curriculum alongside mainstream content. This is the easiest approach to implement, but it leaves the curriculum virtually unchanged. Level 2, the *additive approach,* adds concepts and perspectives from other cultures to the mainstream curriculum without changing the curriculum's basic structure. This approach might include adding books by minority authors, a few units of instruction, or a single course to the curriculum. Level 3, the *transformation approach,* changes the fundamental structure of the curriculum by enabling students to consider concepts, issues, and problems from several different cultural perspectives rather than from only the dominant culture's perspective. Finally, Level 4, the *social action approach,* includes all aspects of the transformation approach but also requires students to engage in critical inquiry about cultural issues and problems and to take action for social change. Figure 19.7 summarizes the four approaches.

Other scholars support Banks's assertion that transformative and social action approaches are more effective at integrating multicultural content into the curriculum than the contributions or additive approaches (Bennett, 2003; Gay, 1995; Nieto, 2000). Unfortunately, many school curricula have not gone beyond the contributions approach. Why the gap between scholarship on multicultural curriculum and practice? Geneva Gay (2005) has offered an explanation:

> Most school teachers and administrators have good intentions about implementing the ideas and proposals suggested in the scholarship on multicultural education. Unfortunately, many do not have the knowledge base and pedagogical skills needed. Others are still struggling with how to resolve what they see as inherent tensions between the national ideals of the United States embedded in the motto *E Pluribus Unum* and recognizing, accepting, and promoting diversity in schools and society. Confusion is still rampant over calls for diversity, equity, and excellence in education. Too many educators continue to believe that to treat students differently based on their cultural heritages, ethnic identities, and background experiences is synonymous to discrimination, and to promote diversity is to compromise high-quality performance and standards of excellence. This confusion drives some educators to question the merits of education for diversity, to judge it divisive and counterproductive, and to redefine it in ways that reaffirm their comfort levels and serve their own purposes. These reactions have different consequences on efforts to implement multicultural education, but in general they produce distortions, inaccuracies, and misconceptions that are not consistent with the thinking, research, and writing of multicultural education scholars. (pp. 109–110)

Level 4

The Social Action Approach

Students make decisions on important social issues and take actions to help solve them.

Level 3

The Transformation Approach

The structure of the curriculum is changed to enable students to view concepts, issues, events, and themes from the perspectives of diverse ethnic and cultural groups.

Level 2

The Additive Approach

Content, concepts, themes, and perspectives are added to the curriculum without changing its structure.

Level 1

The Contributions Approach

Focuses on heroes, holidays, and discrete cultural elements.

FIGURE 19.7 *Banks's Approaches to Multicultural Curriculum Reform*

Source: Reprinted with permission from (1988) James A. Banks, "Approaches to multicultural curriculum reform." *Multicultural Leader 1*(2), 1–3, 1988. Copyright © 1988 by James A. Banks.

Gay (2005) has proposed that we begin to close the gap between scholarship and practice by developing well-articulated guidelines for translating theoretical principles into practice, establishing performance standards for educators, and providing professional development to help educators meet those standards. The professional development Gay has proposed would be long-term, assisting educators to develop self-understanding, cultural knowledge, and multicultural education skills.

SUMMARY

Teachers will implement curriculum successfully if they have been involved in its development and can adapt it to their specific classroom and school situation. The failure of the teacher-proof curriculum movement should remind us that imposing curriculum from outside is useless. Instead, the questions for supervisors to consider have to do with type and degree of curriculum development. The supervisor can pick from six arenas. The first arena includes sources of development, ranging from teachers to district-level personnel, state and federal experts, and commercial writers. The second arena involves the purpose of the curriculum, based on one of three curriculum orientations: transmission, transaction, or transformation. The third arena consists of the content emphasis of curriculum: the lower, middle, or higher levels of Bloom's taxonomy. The fourth arena involves curriculum organization, including discipline-based, interdisciplinary, and transdisciplinary curricula. The fifth arena is curriculum format, including behavioral-objective, webbing, and results-only formats. Finally, the sixth arena consists of levels of teacher involvement, including imitative-maintenance, mediative, and creative-generative levels. The supervisor and teachers should work together to select curriculum purpose, content, organization, and format that (1) are most appropriate for the students and (2) increase teachers' choice and commitment to curriculum implementation. Curriculum, when treated as a task for school action, is a powerful, relatively nonthreatening intervention for enhancing collective thought and action about instruction.

PRACTITIONER REFLECTION

We Own Our Results—A Reflection on Context and Accountability

Kevin Tashlein, *Principal, Phoenix High School*

If you were to inform me 9 years ago that I would be in the midst of personally sharing a heightened sense of urgency with each of our teachers for developing accelerated academic interventions to aid students in passing state graduation tests, I would have reconsidered the assistant principal position I had just accepted. If I were informed of the same 15 years ago, I may not have pursued an education career in the first place. Such was my ignorance. At that point, or so I believed, my passion, educational background, and curriculum strengths were exclusively suited to working in a Coalition of Essential School (CES) environment. CES schools are variously characterized by student personalization, exhibition of learning, and uniquely guided by the Ten Common Principles (www.essentialschools.org).

Over the past six years, however, from a combination of both internal and external accountability requirements, we have rapidly shifted toward a results-driven curriculum. Simultaneously, we have enhanced both the rigor and richness of a largely college preparatory curriculum for our approximately 850 high school students. From my vantage point as a building-level administrator in a nontraditional public high school, current No Child Left Behind (NCLB) legislated requirements have had a significant impact on how we implement our curriculum and assess student learning. As I have grown professionally, the role of context in meeting accountability requirements has become exponentially more crucial and clear. In our local school context, the stakes have never been higher for our staff and especially for our students.

Our challenge: Recent 5-year trend data indicate that 60 to 65 percent of Phoenix High School students attended our school for 1 year or less prior to graduating, greater than 80 percent needed more than 4 years to graduate, and roughly 150 new students transferred into our school of choice, each 9 weeks, largely disillusioned about their educational prospects. Accountability fairness concerns aside, we have long embraced the fact that we own our results with each of our students.

Our opportunity: In order to effectively meet our student population's academic needs, we must build on 18 years of prior success by developing an accelerated academic model that addresses both internal (curricular richness, earning a diploma, and creating a viable postsecondary plan) and external accountability concerns (NCLB mandates, which include graduation rates and rising performance levels on state graduation tests). Our goal has always been and will remain to ensure that each student who chooses to enroll in our school earns a diploma upon graduation. Since we have no upper age limits to attend our school, if a student stays with us long enough, we know we will be successful.

Our bottom line: No student diploma may be awarded until all state-level graduation tests are passed and required coursework is successfully completed (whether a student is enrolled in nine weeks or nine mini-semesters). If our students do not earn their high school diploma with us, they will most likely not earn one—period. If we cannot successfully engage students with our enacted curriculum—what is actually taught by staff—then we will lose them. I wasn't always so concerned about or aware of our professional ability to impact student learning.

This is a far cry from my perspective and experiences as a beginning educator. My initial perspective on curriculum development was centered on student choice and empowerment. I argued that the required curriculum was neither relevant nor workable for the eighth-grade students I taught for one year in Central Harlem, New York City. This particular school was ranked 179 of 180 I. S. schools (grades 7 and 8) on citywide reading and math scores. Of over 800 students in this school, only 13 to 15 percent of students were determined to be on grade level the prior school year—hence the horribly poor ranking. I would certainly not have talked at length about personal and academic responsibility or meeting managed graduation requirements (crucial for our school in 2005–2006). Rather, from the midpoint of this year on, I would describe a system of curriculum development purely generative and founded on student-created essential questions.

What began as a curriculum of necessity and survival for me in Central Harlem became a key turning point in my conception of curriculum design and implementation. Note that throughout my master's program and first year of teaching, there was no concerted focus or expectation that students would actually learn the required content; rather, there was an expectation that there would be effective teaching through use of appropriate pedagogical methods. Systematically incorporating an array of student achievement data to improve the teaching and learning process was not addressed in my teacher education program. Quite frankly, once I began my teaching career the implicit message was to "keep the lid on" through managing my own teaching and classroom discipline challenges. In my context, that meant I was a successful beginning teacher. The reality was that I did not possess the skills nor have access to school-based data tools to ensure improvement in student learning over time. Beyond my own fuzzy classroom-based notions, there was simply no infrastructure in place to learn from colleagues or on how to measure my success.

Over time, and in a variety of other professional contexts, both individual and collegial opportunities to analyze student achievement data from a range of sources (student work collected in portfolios, teacher-developed assessments, and standardized measures) began to serve as important curriculum planning and reelection tools. Such opportunities to focus on results always helped prepare educators and schools to better plan for more powerful and focused improvement efforts.

Now, after nine years at my present school, three as assistant principal and six as principal, I can more clearly see the role of curriculum development from a school-based, schoolwide, NCLB perspective. Although I take issue with a variety of the measurement methods required by the NCLB in order to earn Adequate Yearly Progress, we appear to be finally at a point where we are required to look at student achievement across and within all student groups. Systematic review of required student data alongside other pertinent school data needs to be turned into information for planning school improvement.

Ultimately, data-driven decision making around student learning becomes a crucial tool in removing emotion and personality from school improvement efforts. Teaching the curriculum is ultimately for naught if a student has not engaged and mastered required learning objectives. Since our standards-based curriculum is already in place, our teaching staff routinely uses student performance data to adapt what we are required to teach in ways that both connect with our nontraditional students upon initial enrollment and ensure they learn through and beyond graduation.

Nationally, we are required to have *all* students performing at appropriate levels of proficiency by the 2013–2014 school year. *All* means all K–12 public school students in the United States. There is a historical educational landscape littered with such prior initiatives to improve the level of schooling for our students. Although the challenge in our nontraditional context is daunting, we will continue to use student achievement data to plan for more effective intervention and enrichment opportunities. In essence, our teachers continue to creatively adapt the little "whats" of the curriculum so that students can successfully develop the academic skills necessary to effectively engage and learn the big "whats" of our largely college preparatory curriculum. This evolving balancing act plays out in each of our classrooms every day. Our commitment will stay the same: graduating each student with a diploma and viable postsecondary plan in hand.

Throughout my career, I've heard a wide range of educators express concerns about high-stakes testing—I also have them. What tends to get lost in this debate, unfortunately, is that the stakes are also very high for students who do not earn their high school diploma and who are not prepared for postsecondary training. NCLB will remain imperfect, yet, from my perspective, it has in a very short time generated tremendous momentum for improving the education of our nation's students.

EXERCISES

Academic

1. Review a report on the results of federally supported curriculum development. Prepare a written summary and discussion of the highlights of the chosen report.

2. Summarize the recommendations of two curriculum textbook authors for providing each of the following in a school curriculum:
   a. Sequence and continuity
   b. Scope
   c. Balance

3. Create one or two sample pages of curriculum guides that reflect each of the following formats for curriculum development:
   a. Behavioral-objective format
   b. Webbing format
   c. Results-only format

4. Summarize, analyze, and evaluate the concept of an interdisciplinary curriculum.

Field

1. Examine the curriculum guide of a school with which you are *not* familiar. What orientation to curriculum is reflected by the curriculum guide? What national, regional, and local priorities are reflected? What examples of knowledge of student development, current economics, and predicted future societal conditions can be derived from the guide? What format was used in developing the curriculum? What categories from Bloom's taxonomy are evident in the curriculum objectives? What parental, central office, teacher, and student influences are recognizable? What commercial publishing influences can be discerned? Does the guide reflect an imitative-maintenance, mediative, or generative level of curriculum development? Was the guide most likely developed by outside developers with minimal revision, by outside developers with substantial revision, by a team of teachers led by a specialist, or internally by a team of teachers with specialists as resource people?

   Write a paper answering each question and provide examples from the guide to support your answers.

2. Examine the living curriculum of a school (what is actually taught) to determine how the development of that curriculum has been significantly affected by one of the following:
   a. The federal government
   b. The state department of education
   c. The local community
   d. Parents of students attending the school
   e. Central office personnel

   f. Teachers

   g. Students

   Write a paper discussing the effects of the chosen entity on the development of the school's living curriculum.

3. Examine a so-called canned curriculum, including the teacher's guide, teacher-proof texts and/or materials, programmed methods of measuring student progress, and all other major components of the program. Prepare a report describing and evaluating the selected curriculum. If your report is a verbal one, display and discuss physical components of the curriculum as part of your presentation.

4. Interview a teacher to determine to what extent the school's curriculum guide determines what he or she teaches. Probe for other influences on what is taught (for example, what the teacher was taught when he or she was a student, the text being used, other teachers, administrators, nationally normed achievement tests, and so on). Prepare a report summarizing and analyzing the interview.

5. Observe a working meeting of a curriculum development or curriculum review committee. What is the prevailing educational philosophy of the group? What influences (government, community, parental, administrative, commercial publishers) are influencing the group's decision making? What are some characteristics of individual members of the group (levels of commitment, development, expertise)? Is the curriculum development taking place at an imitative, mediative, or generative level? What curriculum development format (behavioral-objective, webbing, conceptual mapping, or results-only) is in evidence? Prepare a report on your observation, including answers to each of these questions. Support your answers with descriptions of behaviors or artifacts observed at the meeting.

Developmental

1. Volunteer for membership on a curriculum development or review committee.

2. Examine the writings of authors on educational supervision to compare their positions on the role and function of the supervisor in curriculum development.

3. Over a period of time, compare a school's written curriculum with its living curriculum (what is actually taught from day to day). How much congruence is there between the formal curriculum and what is actually taught?

REFERENCES

Applebee, A. N., Langer, S. A., and Mullis, V. S. 1987. *Literature and U.S. History: The instructional experience and factual knowledge of high school juniors. The nation's report card.* Princeton, NJ: Educational Testing Service.

Banks, J. A. 2005. Approaches to multicultural curriculum reform. In J. A. Banks and C. A. McGhee Banks (Eds.), *Multicultural education: Issues and perspectives* (5th ed., pp. 242–264). Hoboken, NJ: John Wiley & Sons.

Bennett, C. I. 2003. *Comprehensive multicultural education: Theory and Practice* (5th ed.). Boston: Allyn and Bacon.

Bloom, A. 1987. *The closing of the American mind.* New York: Simon and Schuster.

Brandt, R. S. (Ed.). 1988a. Content of the curriculum, 1988. In *ASCD Yearbook.* Alexandria, VA: Association for Supervision and Curriculum Development.

Brandt, R. S. 1988b. On assessment in the arts: A conversation with Howard Gardner. *Educational Leadership, 45*(4), 30–34.

Clark, D.C., and Clark, S. N. 2000. Appropriate assessment strategies for young adolescents in an era of standards-based reform. *The Clearing House, 73*(4), 201–204.

Darling-Hammond, L. 1997. *The right to learn: A blueprint for creating schools that work.* San Francisco: Jossey-Bass.

Doll, R. C. 1989. *Curriculum improvement: Decision making and process* (6th ed.). Boston: Allyn and Bacon.

Drake, S. M., Bebbington, J., Laksman, S., Mackie, P., Marnes, N., and Wayne, L. 1992. *Developing an integrated curriculum using the story model.* Toronto: The Ontario Institute for Studies in Education.

Elmore, R. F., and Rothman, R. (Eds.). 1999. *Testing, teaching, and learning; A guide for states and school districts.* Washington, DC: National Academy Press.

Firth, G. R., and Newfield, J. W. 1984. Curriculum development and selection. In J. M. Cooper (Ed.), *Developing skills for instructional supervision.* New York: Longman.

Fitzharris, L. H. 2005. Making all the right connections. *Journal of Staff Development, 26*(1), 24–28.

Gandal, M., and Vranek, J. 2001. Standards: Here today, here tomorrow. *Educational Leadership, 59*(1), 6–13.

Gay, G. (1995). Bridging multicultural theory and practice. *Multicultural Education, 3,* 4–9.

Gay, G. (2005). Standards for diversity. In S. P. Gordon (Ed.), *Standards for instructional supervision: Enhancing teaching and learning.* Larchmont NY: Eye on Education.

Glatthorn, A. A. 1987. *Curriculum renewal.* Alexandria, VA: Association for Supervision and Curriculum Development.

Glickman, C. D. 1999. *School based authority and responsibility.* Unpublished invited report to the Georgia Governor's Education Reform Study Commission. Atlanta, GA: The Office of the Governor of Georgia.

Glickman, C. D. 2000/2001. Holding sacred ground: The impact of standardization. *Educational Leadership, 58*(4), 46–51.

Goodlad, J. 1984. *A place called school.* New York: McGraw-Hill.

Hirsch, E. D., Jr. 1987. *Cultural literacy: What every American needs to know.* Boston: Houghton Mifflin.

Jacobs, H. H. 1989. *Interdisciplinary curriculum: Design and implementation.* Alexandria, VA: Association for Supervision and Curriculum Development.

Jenkins, R. A. 2005. Interdisciplinary instruction in the inclusion classroom. *Teaching Exceptional Children, 37*(5), 42–48.

Kilpatrick, W. H. 1925. *Foundations of method.* New York: Macmillan.

Manson, G., and Clegg, A. A., Jr. 1970. Classroom questions: Keys to children's thinking? *Peabody Journal of Education, 47*(5), 304–305.

McEvoy, B. 1986. *"Against our better judgements." Three teachers' enactment of mandated curriculum.* Paper presented at the annual meeting of the American Educational Research Association, San Francisco.

McNeil, L. N. 1988. Contradictions of control, Part 2. Teachers, students and curriculum. *Kappan, 69*(6), 432–438.

Miller, J. P., and Seller, W. 1985. *Curriculum: Perspectives and practice.* New York: Longman.

Nieto, S. (2000). *Affirming diversity: The sociopolitical context of multicultural education.* New York: Longman.

Oliva, P. F. 1992. *Developing the curriculum* (3rd ed.). New York: HarperCollins.

Ravitch, D., and Finn, L. E., Jr. 1987. *What do our 17-year-olds know? A report of the First National Assessment of History and Literature.* New York: Harper and Row.

Sergiovanni, T. 1987. *Introduction to the Breckinridge Conference on restructuring schools.* San Antonio, August.

Sizer, T. R. 1984. *Horace's compromise: The dilemma of the American high school.* Boston: Houghton Mifflin.

Tanner, D., and Tanner, L. W. 1980. *Curriculum development: Theory into practice* (2nd ed.). New York: Macmillan.

Wise, A. 1988. Legislated learning revisited. *Kappan, 69*(5), 328–333.

Zeuli, J. S., and Buchmann, M. 1987. *Implementation of teacher thinking research as curriculum deliberation.* Presentation to the annual meeting of the American Educational Research Association, Washington, DC, April.

SUGGESTED READINGS

Connelly, F. M., and Clandinin, D. J. 1988. *Teachers as curriculum planners*. New York: Teachers College Press.

Darling-Hammond, L. 1997. *The right to learn: A blueprint for creating schools that work*. San Francisco: Jossey-Bass.

Drake, S. M., Bebbington, J., Laksman, S., Machie, P., Maynes, N., and Wayne, L. 1992. *Developing an integrated curriculum using the story model*. Toronto: The Ontario Institute for Studies in Education.

Elmore, R. F., and Rothman, R. (Eds.). 1999. *Testing, teaching, and learning; A guide for states and school districts*. Washington, DC: National Academy Press.

Glickman, C. D. 2000/2001. Holding sacred ground: The impact of standardization. *Educational Leadership, 58*(4), 46–51.

Grandal, M., and Vranek, J. 2001. Standards: Here today, here tomorrow. *Educational Leadership, 59*(1), 6–13.

Guskey, T. R. 2005. Five key concepts kick off the process. *Journal of Staff Development, 26*(1), 36–40.

Hass, G., and Parkay, F. W. 1993. *Curriculum planning: A new approach* (6th ed.). Boston: Allyn and Bacon.

Jacobs, H. H. (Ed.). 1989. *Interdisciplinary curriculum: Design and implementation*. Alexandria, VA: Association for Supervision and Curriculum Development.

Jacobs, H. H. 1997. *Mapping the big picture: Integrating curriculum and assessment K–12*. Alexandria, VA: Association for Supervision and Curriculum Development.

Jacobs, H. H. (Ed.). 2004. *Getting results with curriculum mapping*. Alexandria, VA: Association for Supervision and Curriculum Development.

Kohn, A. 1999. *The schools our children deserve*. Boston: Houghton Mifflin.

Kovalik, S., and Olsen, K. 1994. *ITI: The model integrated thematic instruction* (3rd ed.). Kent, WA: Books for Educators.

Oliva, P. F. 1992. *Developing the curriculum* (3rd ed.). New York: HarperCollins.

O'Shea, M. R. 2005. *From standards to success: A guide for school leaders*. Alexandria, VA: Association for Supervision and Curriculum Development.

Wiggins, G., and McTighe, J. 2005. *Understanding by design* (2nd ed.). Alexandria, VA: Association for Supervision and Curriculum Development.

chapter 20

Action Research

The School as the Center of Inquiry

Why should our schools not be staffed, gradually if you will, by scholar-teachers in command of the conceptual tools and methods of inquiry requisite to investigating the learning process as it operates in their own classrooms? Why should our schools not nurture the continuing wisdom and power of such scholar-teachers? (Schaefer, 1967, p. 5)

The famous social scientist, Kurt Lewin, devoted his career to studying democracy and the relationships of individuals within groups. His contributions ushered in the school of gestalt psychology, group dynamics, and the concept of action research. He argued that social research should be based on the actions groups take to improve their conditions. Social research should not focus on controlled experiments, removed from real conditions. As people plan changes and engage in real activities, fact finding should determine whether success is being achieved and whether further planning and action are necessary (Lewin, 1948, p. 206).

Stephen Corey applied Lewin's concept of action research to education. He argued that traditional research is done mainly by researchers outside the public school and has little influence on school practice. Corey wrote:

> Learning that changes behavior substantially is most likely to result when a person himself tries to improve a situation that makes a difference to him . . . when he defines the problem, hypothesizes actions that may help him cope with it, engages in these actions, studies the consequences, and generalizes from them, he will more frequently internalize the experience than when all this is done for him by somebody else, and he reads about it. . . . The value of action research . . . is determined primarily by the extent to which findings lead to improvement in the practices of the people engaged in the research. (1953, p. 9)

Thus, action research in education is study conducted by colleagues in a school setting of the results of their activities to improve instruction. Although an individual teacher can conduct action research, in most cases it is best done as a cooperative endeavor by faculty attempting to improve on a common instructional concern (see Calhoun, 2002).

As Richard Sagor (1993) wrote, "By turning to *collaborative* action research . . . we can renew our commitment to thoughtful teaching and also begin developing an active community of professionals" (p. 10). Action research implies that the practitioners are the researchers. The objectivity and rigor of research methodology can be questioned by classical researchers, but the benefits of the process for students and teachers seem to outweigh the loss of experimental purity.

In addressing the power of teacher-led research, Hubbard and Power (1993, p. xiii) wrote: "Teachers throughout the world are developing professionally by becoming teacher-researchers, a wonderful new breed of artists-in-residence. Using our own classrooms as laboratories and our students as collaborators, we are changing the way we work with students as we look at our classrooms systematically through research." Table 20.1 compares traditional research with action research.

How Is Action Research Conducted?

In the first phase of action research, a focus area is selected—an area of teaching and learning in need of improvement. Second, a needs assessment gathers data on the focus area. The purposes of data gathering at this stage are to understand the problem and how it might be solved and to gather baseline data to help with the evaluation of improvement efforts. The third phase of action research is to design an action plan for solving the problem. The plan includes activities for evaluating the success of improvement efforts. The fourth phase is the implementation of the plan. The fifth phase of action research is the evaluation: data on the action plan's

TABLE 20.1	Comparison of Traditional Research and Action Research	

	Traditional Research	**Action Research**
Usually led by	Outside expert	Practitioners
Purpose	Develop new knowledge	Solve practical problem, improve practice
Types of data gathered	Quantitative or qualitative	Quantitative or qualitative
Purpose of gathering and analyzing data	Gain better understanding of phenomenon, develop or test hypotheses	Explore practical problem, guide action planning, evaluate results
Standard for quality research	Peer review of methods and results	The research results in desired change
Primary audience(s)	Other researchers, the profession, government or private agencies	Members of the school community

effects are gathered and analyzed. Based on the evaluation, action plan objectives and activities may be continued, expanded, revised, or discontinued.

If these five phases sound suspiciously similar to the development of action plans with individual teachers in Chapter 16 (direct assistance), you have won the first round of the supervision concentration game. The aim of direct assistance to teachers is to promote increased thought, choice, and responsibility in individual teachers, and this can be done through cycles of classroom action research. The supervisor's role is to determine what type of assistance the individual teacher needs (directive informational, collaborative, or nondirective), depending on the developmental levels of the teacher with respect to the particular topic. Figure 20.1 depicts the five phases of action research.

A Developmental Approach to Action Research

The developmental model we have discussed throughout this text can be applied to action research. Of the four supervisory approaches discussed in Part III, the directive informational, collaborative, and nondirective approaches are appropriate for supervising action research. Since teacher action research involves teachers

| Phase 1 |
| Select Focus Area |

| Phase 2 |
| Conduct Needs Assessment |

| Phase 3 |
| Design Action Plan |

| Phase 4 |
| Carry Out Action Plan |

| Phase 5 |
| Evaluate Effects and Revise Action Plan |

FIGURE 20.1 *Five Phases of Action Research*

making their own decisions about inquiry and instructional improvement, controlling directive supervision is inappropriate for such research.

Teachers of *very* low levels of development, expertise, and commitment are probably not ready to engage in action research. They will need to receive intensive direct assistance and staff development to help them develop the minimal decision-making capacity and motivation necessary for successful action research. They might be asked to read and discuss articles about action research, shadow a teacher or group engaged in research, or attend a workshop to develop action research skills. For teachers of *fairly* low levels of development, expertise, and commitment, the supervisor can use directive informational supervision while suggesting alternative goals, data-collection and analysis methods, and action plans, and then asking teachers to choose from the alternatives. Since this type of action research involves limited teacher decision making, the supervisor will wish to move toward collaborative action research as soon as teachers are ready to assume more decision-making responsibility (McBee, 2004).

The supervisor can engage in collaborative action research with teachers of moderate or mixed levels of development, expertise, and commitment. In this approach, the supervisor engages in joint decision making with teachers during the goal identification, action planning, implementation, evaluation, and revision phases of action research. Even collaborative action research is a transitional form of teacher inquiry. The ultimate goal is for teachers to reach levels of development, expertise, and commitment that allow teacher-driven research, in which the supervisor uses nondirective supervision to facilitate teacher decision making during each of the five phases of action research. Houser (1990) described full-fledged "teacher-researchers": "They initiate every aspect of the research project. They are responsible for formulating the questions, selecting the (research) tools, and collecting, analyzing, and interpreting the data" (p. 58).

Decisions about Action Research

Collective action research can integrate direct assistance, group development, professional development, and curriculum development. Prior to the beginning of action research, the supervisor chooses an appropriate entry strategy for working with an action research team. The choice of interpersonal approach is shown in Table 20.2.

TABLE 20.2	Choosing an Interpersonal Approach
Interpersonal Behaviors	**Decision**
Nondirective: Listening Reflecting Clarifying Encouraging	High teacher/low supervisor
Collaborative: Presenting Problem solving Negotiating	Equal teacher/equal supervisor
Directive informational: Presenting Problem solving Directing alternatives	Low teacher/high supervisor

Characteristics of Teachers

Levels of development
Expertise
Commitment

First, the team conducts a needs assessment of faculty and collects baseline data to determine common goals for improvement of instruction. Techniques for conducting a needs assessment can be chosen from the following list:

- Eyes and ears
- Systematic classroom and school observations
- Official records
- Review of teacher and student work products
- Third-party review
- Written open-ended survey
- Check and ranking lists
- Delphi technique
- Nominal group
- Cause and effect diagrams
- Flowcharts
- Pareto charts

Explanations of each assessment technique can be found in Chapter 13.

Second, the team brainstorms activities that will cut across supervision tasks. The team can respond to these four questions corresponding to supervisory tasks:

1. What type and frequency of direct assistance must be provided to teachers to reach our instructional goals?
2. What meetings and discussions need to be arranged as part of group development for faculty to share and reach our instructional goals?
3. What professional development opportunities, such as lectures, workshops, demonstrations, courses, and visits, need to be provided for faculty to reach our instructional goals?
4. What is the necessary curriculum development in terms of course content, curriculum guides, lesson plans, and instructional materials to reach our instructional goals.

These tasks of supervision are explained in Chapters 16, 17, 18, and 19.

Third, the team makes a plan relating activities to goals. Techniques for writing plans are as follows:

- Affinity diagrams
- Impact analysis chart
- Gantt chart
- Force field analysis
- PDSA cycle
- Strategic planning

A description of each planning device can be found in Chapter 13.

Fourth, the team determines ways to observe the progress of the action plan as it is implemented in classrooms. Observations can be made with the use of the following instruments:

- Categorical frequency
- Performance indicator
- Visual diagramming
- Space utilization
- Verbatim or selective verbatim
- Detached open-ended narrative
- Participant open-ended observation
- Focused questionnaire
- Educational criticism
- Tailored observation systems

Use of these instruments is explained in Chapter 14.

Fifth, the team chooses an evaluation design that will enable them to analyze data, determine whether objectives have been met, and decide what further actions need to be taken. The design can be quantitative, qualitative, or a combination of both. Questions to be asked in the evaluation include the following:

- What is the purpose of the evaluation?
- Who will evaluate?
- What questions need to be answered?
- What and how will data be gathered?
- How will the data be analyzed?
- How will the evaluation be reported?

To understand the components of a comprehensive evaluation, refer to Chapter 15.

Action Research: Vehicle for a Cause beyond Oneself

Previously, each task of supervision (direct assistance, group development, professional development, and curriculum development) was discussed separately. In reality, any effort to improve instruction must relate each task to the others. It is time to soften the boundaries between the tasks and show how action research can be the vehicle for their integration.

Action research is focused on the need to improve instruction, as perceived by the faculty. As instructional improvements are identified, faculty and supervisor plan related activities to be implemented in each of the tasks of supervision (see Figure 20.2).

Direct-
Assistance
Activities

Professional
Development
Activities

Action Research
Plan for
Instructional
Improvement

Group-
Development
Activities

Curriculum-
Development
Activities

FIGURE 20.2 *Action Research as the Core of Related Supervisory Activities*

Think of action research as a huge meteor falling into the middle of the supervision ocean. As it hits, it causes a rippling of water that activates the four seas of direct assistance, professional development, curriculum development, and group development. The rippling of water continues to increase in force until a giant wave gathers and crashes onto all instructional shores, sweeping away the old sand of past instructional failures and replacing it with the new sand of instructional improvement. Stepping away from the beach, let's look at some examples of action research related to supervisory activities.

Example of Action Research

Matthews Elementary School is located in the heart of Austin, Texas. Matthews serves students from 32 different cultures. The student population includes children from the local Salvation Army shelter and city children's center. Matthews also serves the children of an international community of professors and graduate students from a nearby university. Approximately 50 percent of the students are classified as at-risk. The goal of action research at Matthews was to improve the school's balanced reading program. Needs assessment data included student results on two reading tests, indicating that a large number of students were reading below grade level. Data on teacher perceptions of the reading program were gathered through surveys and interviews. Based on the needs assessment, the action plan called for acquisition of additional resources for the reading program, professional development for teachers, and more effective monitoring of the program.

In the first component of the action plan teachers participated in discussion groups to identify needed resources. In response to these meetings, new nonfiction and fiction books, books on tape, and a variety of new instructional materials were added to the program. The professional development component included monthly meetings of support groups in which teachers learned new strategies, discussed concerns, and shared ideas. Balanced reading also was discussed at general faculty and vertical team meetings. A supervisor served as a mentor for new teachers, providing them assistance as they implemented balanced reading. Two literacy specialists served as support persons to all teachers, leading support groups, teaching demonstration lessons, and visiting classrooms. Teachers visited other schools to observe balanced reading lessons, participated in district workshops on balanced reading, and attended national reading conferences. The last component of the action plan was improved monitoring of the reading program. This included supervisors and reading specialists observing classrooms to determine if balanced reading was being implemented effectively, and also to make sure that teachers were receiving the resources and support they needed. Teachers played a major role in monitoring. They assessed student progress daily by analyzing student work samples, keeping anecdotal records, and listening to students' oral reading. Additionally, teachers used a standardized reading assessment to measure students' reading levels in September, January, and May.

Year-end evaluation of the action research included teacher surveys and interviews as well as pre-post comparisons of student reading levels. Teachers reported a high commitment to balanced reading, understanding of the reading program, and confidence in their ability to implement the program. The teachers stated that they now had adequate materials to implement balanced reading, and that strategies they learned through professional development enabled them to understand strengths and needs of students and to individualize student learning. Analysis of student achievement data supported teacher perceptions. Over the school years there were increases in the percentage of students—including the percentage of economically disadvantaged students—reading on or above grade level. By the end of the school year 85 percent of all students were reading on or above grade level.

Expanding Boundaries: Alternative Approaches to Action Research

The approach to action research emphasized in this book, as well as in most schools that use action research, is a problem-solving approach. A problem is identified, needs assessment data are gathered to find out more about the problem, an action plan is designed to solve the problem, the plan is implemented, and evaluation data are gathered to determine what progress was made and what revisions in the action plan might be needed. There are alternative approaches to action research that schools may wish to consider. These alternatives include interpretive and critical action research.

Interpretive Action Research

Teachers doing interpretive research are attempting to understand phenomena in schools and the meaning that participants make of those phenomena. Examples of phenomena that might be studied include a school's culture, classroom implementation of a new curriculum, and interactions between teachers and students during classroom discussions of controversial issues. For a more detailed example, let us say a group of teachers decided to carry out an interpretive study on the use of a new inquiry-based science program. Research questions might include the following:

1. What does the teacher experience during inquiry learning?
2. What does the student experience during inquiry learning?
3. How does the teacher describe learning that results from inquiry learning?
4. How does the student describe learning that results from inquiry learning?

To gather data on these questions, interpretive researchers might observe inquiry lessons and take extensive field notes on class activities, interactions between teachers and students and among students, and so on. Additionally, the teacher-researchers might conduct interviews with teachers and students on their experiences with inquiry learning and their interpretation of learning resulting from inquiry lessons. The researchers probably would find that different participants experience the same learning activities differently and construct different interpretations of inquiry learning. Through dialogue on alternative perspectives and interpretations identified in the action research, teachers can gain a more holistic understanding of the phenomena being studied. The dialogue, and increased understanding that results, can be the foundation for improved practice. For instance, based on the results of their interpretive research, teachers in our inquiry-learning example might modify the way they present science problems to students.

Critical Action Research

Critical research examines and challenges established, taken-for-granted ways of doing things that support inequity, with an eye toward changing practice to increase equity. In particular, critical research examines power relationships that lead to inequity. External social, economic, and political forces that cause inequity also are examined, and ways to overcome those forces' negative effects are considered. An important process used by critical researchers is *praxis,* which denotes an interactive cycle of practice and theory building. In critical action research, praxis takes the form of an ongoing cycle of action and reflection aimed at emancipating groups and individuals from inequitable treatment.

Teachers engaged in critical action research on a high school's tracking system could begin the research by formulating a set of critical questions such as the following:

- Whose interests are served by the existence of the tracking system?
- What cultural values are reinforced by the tracking system? What cultural values are delegitimized?
- What power relationships are present in the current tracking system?
- How does the tracking system reflect socioeconomic realities in the community that the school serves?
- How does the tracking system reflect ethnic and racial issues present in society?
- Who decides which students are placed in the various tracks?
- Who is placed at an advantage by the tracking system? Who is placed at a disadvantage?

Teachers who are engaged in critical action research find answers to these questions through repeated cycles of data gathering and dialogue on the meaning of the data. Eventually, the researchers begin to focus on a series of questions about changing the system to increase equity.

- How can we include parents and students in decisions about how best to meet student learning needs?
- How can the diverse learning needs of students be met in an emancipatory way?
- What ways of grouping students will benefit the least advantaged students?
- How can student grouping promote democracy and social justice?
- How can the growth and development of all students be placed in the center of the decision-making process at this school?

Again, teachers would go about finding answers to these questions through repeated cycles of data gathering and dialogue. In time, teachers and other members of the school community would use research results as the basis for changes in decision making, student grouping, curriculum, and instruction. The test for the effectiveness of critical action research is whether equity has been increased in a meaningful way.

Shared Governance
for Action Research

A shortcoming of earlier studies of school improvement and action research has been the lack of descriptions of how individual schools or districts went about the process of change (Fullan, 1985, p. 398). Achieving "a cause beyond oneself" in pursuing collaborative and collective instructional goals for students sounds admirable, but how does a supervisor initiate and sustain such efforts? What follows is one explanation, using case studies from the public schools that are part of the League of Professional Schools (Glickman, 1992). The model of shared governance and schoolwide instructional change has been adapted and used in elementary, middle, and secondary schools in Georgia, South Carolina, Vermont, Michigan, and the United States Department of Defense Dependent Schools in Europe.

Premises

Three declarative premises underlie shared governance. Those premises are:

1. Every professional in the school who so desires can be involved in making decisions about schoolwide instructional improvements.
2. Any professional in the school who does not desire to is not obligated to be involved in making decisions about schoolwide instructional improvements.
3. Once a decision is made about schoolwide instructional improvements, all staff must implement the decision.

Thus, an individual can choose to be or not to be part of the decision-making process. However, once decisions are made, all individuals must implement the agreed-upon actions. Operationalizing these premises allows a school to move forward with people who are interested in participating, without forcing any individual who is not interested into a corner. Afterwards, an individual who did not wish to participate in making decisions has no grounds for complaint about decisions about schoolwide instructional actions. Perhaps when the next issue, concern, or topic is brought up for schoolwide action, nonparticipants who have been disgruntled with previous decisions will have a renewed interest in participating.

Principles

The principles in operating shared governance for instructional improvement are:

1. *One person, one vote.* Each representative has the same rights, responsibilities, and equal vote as any other representative. Each teacher who sits on the representative schoolwide council has the same vote as the school principal or any other administrator or formal supervisor.

2. *Limit decisions to schoolwide instruction within the control and sphere of responsibility of the school.* Action research and shared governance involves the core of a school's existence: curriculum and instruction, or teaching and learning. Areas for decision making should be schoolwide and instructional. Issues of day-to-day administration, contracts, school board policies, other schools, and personnel are not the concerns of shared governance for schoolwide action research. The scope of concerns for deliberations, decisions, and actions is always grounded in the question: What should *we* be doing *here* with *our* school to improve learning for *our* students?

3. *Authentic feedback necessitates small groups.* Large meetings result in input from the most confident, the loudest, and the most powerful persons—who are not necessarily the wisest, most insightful, or most interested persons. A true forum for intellectual discourse is a small group (ideally, 7 to 11 members); so, shared governance in large schools must operate in small groups.

Operational Model

The work of Schmuck, Runkel, Arends, and Arends (1977) has provided the basis for an operational model for shared governance, action research, and school improvement that uses the premises of individual choice of involvement and implementation by all and the principles of one-person, one-vote; focus on teaching; and small groups. The model discussed here is a compilation of various models used by schools in the League of Professional Schools (see Glickman, 1992; Allen and Glickman, 1992). Many schools use comparable models of operation and have their own specific versions. The goal is not to advocate a particular model of shared governance, but rather to achieve the premises and principles of shared governance and action research, leading to a purposeful, collective, and thoughtful school—a school that is the center of inquiry.

The Formal Groups. Shared governance in this model involves three groups (see Figure 20.3). *The executive council* is a 7- to 11-member body, consisting of a majority of teachers with administrators. Parent and student representatives can serve as well. (For more details about representation of other groups, see Glickman, 1993.) Teachers could be democratically chosen from liaison groups (described in the following paragraph) or from among grade-level heads, team leaders, department heads, and union representatives. They could be elected at large from the faculty, or some combination of election and appointment could be used. They hold a term of at least three years and move off the council at staggered times. Teachers serve as chairperson and co-chairperson of the executive council. The principal is a member of the committee with the same rights and responsibilities as any other member. The executive council's responsibility is solely for acting on and monitoring schoolwide instructional improvement recommendations. *The council does not make recommendations;* it is an approving board. Recommendations must

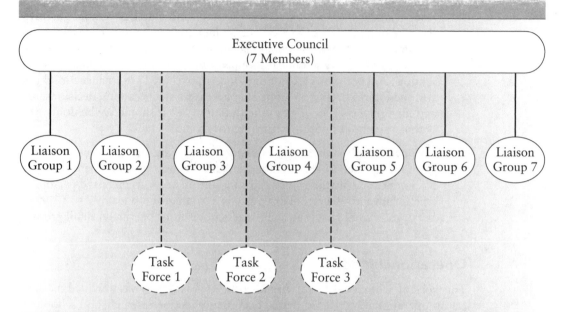

FIGURE 20.3 *Action Research as the Core of Related Supervisory Activities*

come from task force groups within the school. The executive council does not involve itself in administrative matters, community relations, school board policies, personnel matters, or issues that are departmental in nature. It acts on instructional improvement recommendations that the faculty has the legal power to carry out. This differentiation between instructional and administrative responsibilities helps avoid problems that can arise from delving into matters beyond the school's own control.

Liaison groups are formal groups set up as communication links between the faculty and executive council concerning needs, reactions, opinions, and ideas about schoolwide instruction. Liaison groups are an important unit for considering the faculty's ideas and opinions about assessing instructional goals and responding to proposed recommendations. For example, in the case of a school with 50 teachers, there could be 7 liaison groups consisting of approximately 7 faculty members each. An alphabetized list of all faculty names is gathered and each person is assigned a number from 1 to 7. All 1s go to liaison group 1, all 2s go to liaison group 2, and so forth. This assignment procedure ensures that members in each liaison group come from various departments and grade levels. Each liaison group is a microcosm of the entire school. Each group elects a representative to the council. The executive council member can (a) call the liaison group together from time to time for a brief meeting to review a specific recommendation under executive council consideration, (b) gather written opinions about a particular proposal, or (c) simply drop by and talk to the various liaison group members.

Task forces are the last groups shown in Figure 20.3. These ad hoc task groups of volunteers are formed after the executive council has solicited feedback from all the liaison groups about perceived schoolwide instructional needs and reviewed any existing data on schoolwide instruction. The executive council then targets priority instructional areas for the next one to three years. Schoolwide priorities might be such matters as increasing instructional time, coordinating curriculum, improving student attitudes, teaching higher-order thinking, increasing student success rates, improving school discipline, improving school and classroom climate, improving the quality of feedback to students, or improving test scores.

Once the needs for improvement have been selected by the executive council, ad hoc task force groups are formed by recruiting volunteers who have an interest in and a commitment to the particular topic. At least one executive council member serves on each task force, but this person normally does not serve as chair of the task force. The task force volunteers meet, review their task, select their own chairperson, schedule meetings, and set a time line for making a final recommendation for schoolwide action to the executive council. Depending on the topic, one task force might meet three times over three weeks to make a recommendation, whereas another task force might meet every other week for five months before making a recommendation.

Decision-Making Procedures. When the task force is ready to make a recommendation, it makes its report in three parts: (1) goals and objectives, (2) action plan (What will be done, by whom, and when?), and (3) evaluation (How will the success of actions be known?). The executive council discusses the recommendations and either makes an immediate decision to approve (most councils use a consensus vote to approve a first-time recommendation) or, without the required vote, tables the recommendation until the next meeting. During the interim, the executive council members can discuss the recommendation and check with their respective liaison groups to gather input from the entire faculty. At the next meeting, a second vote can be taken. (Most councils use a two-thirds vote to approve a tabled recommendation.) By the second vote, the council will have a good sense of total faculty receptivity and the chances of successful implementation. Some issues are deemed so important by the council that the final decision is made by going back to the entire faculty, parents, and students.

Implementation. After a decision has been made, the executive council (with the task force) announces the approved plan to the school. The task force then disbands, and the executive council implements the plan. It becomes the responsibility of the executive council (including the principal) to enforce the schoolwide decisions and to oversee action research that monitors and evaluates the results.

Suggestions for Assisting Action Research

Our work with schools using action research leads to additional suggestions for increasing the quality of teacher research. First, it is important that teachers receive basic preparation in gathering and analyzing data. Here we are not talking about making every teacher an expert in research design and statistical analysis. Rather, teachers should be introduced to a variety of simple data-gathering methods, both quantitative and qualitative. Also, teachers need to learn simple methods for reviewing and summarizing data, and drawing data-based conclusions. Second, to assure that no teachers or students are placed at academic, social, or emotional risk, the school governance body should establish a set of ethical guidelines for action research, along with a process for reviewing research proposals to make sure they comply with the guidelines. Third, resources need to be provided for action research teams. The most important resource needed by teacher-researchers is *time* to plan action research, gather and analyze data, and implement action plans. Finally, teachers should be provided opportunities to share action research with the school community, and even with teachers from other schools. Sharing action research gives recognition to the teacher-researchers, serves as a basis for reflective dialogue among teachers, and provides other teachers with ideas for improving instruction in their own classrooms and schools.

CONCLUSION: FOCUS, STRUCTURE, AND TIME FOR DEVELOPMENT

Supervision provides a focus, structure, and time for teachers to be engaged in dialogue, debate, research, decisions, and actions about instruction. Without focus, teachers will not discuss teaching, because it has not been an accepted norm for discussion in most schools. Without structure, there are no clear apparatus, procedures, and rules for how decisions are made and implemented. Without time, there is no functional or symbolic expression that teachers have the capacity to make collective and wise instructional decisions on behalf of students.

PRACTITIONER REFLECTION

An Instructional Leader's Experience with Action Research

Jane Ross, *Assistant Principal, Pearce Middle School*

For many school-based educators, including myself, the term *external* often carries with it connotations of fiats, mandates, outsiders, power, and distrust. External "fixes" or external research-based models are viewed as not considering the level context that can only be understood from working on, or closely with, a school campus. The idea that research entities—whether people or institutions—*beyond* schools carry the answers to problems *within* schools can resonate both disempowerment and distrust in the capabilities of the adults and children on the campus to identify areas needing improvement and meaningful solutions. For a profession in which external mandates, external solutions, and external research thrive, action research provides a welcome relief to instructional leaders who believe that educators, parents, and students have the intelligence, context knowledge, and resources to examine issues and respond to them through in-depth inquiry, assessment, and action. In my experience as an instructional leader who trusts the commitments and capacities of school-based adults and students, individual and collaborative action research takes problem solving and research to the fine-tuned level that is hard to reach without a deep understanding of situational variables. Although many externally generated solutions may incorporate the voices of school-based individuals, the voices rarely are those of the specific school to which the research is being applied.

Action research is an effective tool for tapping into educator potential and responding to issues through practitioner-centered inquiry. Indeed, it is difficult for me to imagine any educator or educational system not gravitating toward it as a tool for improvement. The areas of focus in action research are developed organically from those directly affected by a situation, and therefore the features of action research are unique and varied. For example, a group of teachers and I engaged in action research focused on reducing the teacher attrition rate at our middle school. Another time, we used action research to improve student writing on our campus through the use of rubrics and criteria charts. The research incorporated the ongoing and evolving experiences, data, and input of students and teachers, and their voices were interwoven throughout the action steps and program evaluation. The action research positively affected the entire campus.

The preceding two examples were cases in which my educational peers, students, and I engaged in action research on our campus; however, I also have facilitated action research on a different campus through the lens of critical friend. Although school-based inquiry centers on situated context, the contributing human and research resources are not necessarily exclusively internal. In fact, action research, which honors both internal and external perspectives, works in harmony by considering both subjective and objective views of the focus areas. Recently, I had the privilege of serving as a critical friend to Cornerstone Middle School as the educators engaged in a collaborative and comprehensive action research inquiry. They graciously welcomed me as a critical friend to their team, and together we brainstormed ideas about their focus area and how to authentically engage the entire school. After extensive discussion, data gathering, and reflection, the campus reached consensus that improving school culture and climate would be the area of focus. Through further faculty, student, and parent input—including surveys, focus groups, climate inventories, and a review of archival data—three objectives and accompanying action steps emerged within the larger focus area of improving school climate: improving safety, improving productivity, and improving collegiality. The team agreed that these areas affected all aspects of the campus.

For the purpose of planning, organizing, and evaluating, the faculty developed qualitative and quantitative data-collection tools and analysis processes. As an instructional leader and the critical friend throughout their action research journey, I assisted the school by reviewing feedback forms; attending faculty and teacher leader meetings; co-facilitating professional development; collecting and analyzing data from faculty, parents, and students; reviewing progress; and providing ongoing feedback. In addition to on-site visits, we met throughout the year at off-site National Center for School Improvement (NCSI) meetings during which we reflected on progress and challenges as we developed the next steps. The regular meetings with NCSI, which focused on school-based inquiry for school improvement, further evidenced that action research does not discount outside support; rather, it utilizes external resources and perspectives while facilitating campus-based practitioners' empowerment.

I viewed my role as being flexible, and I adapted in response to the needs of the campus. Some of my key goals were to assist the school in developing, organizing, reorganizing, and evaluating their activities in a recursive model. The principal, an exceptional instructional leader, provided time, resources, and support as the research unfolded. Her leadership set the tone for the risk taking, trust, empowerment, and innovation that helped form the foundation of the action research. We continuously reviewed the school's progress, and the team often was surprised by the high quality and positive effects of their improvement strategies. Too often, instructional leaders become so focused on the multifaceted day-to-day operations that they do not notice the effects of their hard work. One of my roles was to encourage the team to find time to reflect on their research. It was motivating to watch everyone finally "pat themselves on the back" with pride when they took the time for deep individual and collaborative reflection. We kept our documentation organized and updated to provide clear evidence of the school's progress toward improved safety, collegiality, and productivity. Although some of the strategies and activities evolved throughout the year, the overarching focus area and goals did not change. The faculty viewed the action research process as a long-term journey that would span many years.

We reached consensus on our key successes and challenges and celebrated the "living" action research plan. Progress was based on the school's unyielding commitment to examining and improving the culture and climate through problem identification, individual and collaborative planning, organization, data-based evaluation, and multidimensional action steps. The action research resulted in dramatic improvements in the school's culture and climate. Instructional leaders who utilize action research as a tool for engagement, inquiry, and professionalism increase the likelihood that school improvement will be substantive and sustained.

PRACTITIONER REFLECTION

Using Developmental Supervision with Action Research

Dana Bashara, *Principal, Cambridge Elementary*

One of my first goals as a new principal was to determine my staff's levels of development and expertise. I spent time in classrooms observing teachers' instruction, interactions with students, classroom management, and other practices as a basis for the needs assessment I felt was essential with a "changing of the guard" in leadership at our school. It was obvious to me that we had a wide range of talents and areas of expertise as I visited the classrooms. To unite our work as a staff, I decided that it would be important for us to have one instructional area of focus that would allow us to share the same kinds of learning opportunities, professional development, and professional language as we talked about best practices for our school.

I included the entire campus in deciding what the focus of our action would be. This area of focus for our school became the implementation of balanced literacy in all classrooms.

My first steps in leading this action research included a variety of staff discussions about defining the characteristics and components of a classroom environment that promotes balanced literacy instruction. We met as a staff to define guided reading, shared reading, word work, and writing structures that would be most beneficial to literacy learning for our students. Next, teachers had to identify where they were professionally in offering these kinds of opportunities to their students to develop their own professional development plan.

The developmental supervision aspect came into play when I met with teachers to determine where they viewed themselves professionally in these areas. I then provided them with feedback on areas that I saw as strengths and helped each teacher decide on a year-long professional development goal consistent without our schoolwide action research. Based on their professional development goals, teachers worked with study groups to learn, discuss, and implement new strategies. These groups provided members with support as they engaged in their new learning. Some of my teachers needed more direct supervision with this task than others, but what was most beneficial was that each of them was able to develop individually while participating in a schoolwide effort to improve our practices!

EXERCISES

Academic

1. Assume you have been assigned the task of speaking in favor of a proposal to provide funding for action research at the next school board meeting. Write your speech, telling how you and your staff will carry out such research and what the benefits will be. To attempt to convince the school board, include in your speech references to sources other than this book.

2. Describe two action research projects that have been reported in the literature and not discussed in this book.

3. Select an objective for instructional improvement that can be adapted to action research. Based on that objective, prepare a written plan for an action research project. Make sure that procedures for conducting action research listed in this chapter are addressed in your plan.

4. Briefly describe an action research project that might be carried out by a small group of teachers facilitated by a supervisor. Next, describe the knowledge and skills the supervisor would need in order to lead the group successfully in the action research. Rely on previous chapters of this book for your answer.

5. Create a model for evaluating action research projects. Components of the model should provide for evaluation of needs assessment, objectives, planning and

sequencing of activities, implementation of activities, measurement techniques, and data analysis. Each component should be accompanied by critical questions to be asked concerning the appropriate phase of the action research project.

Field

1. Plan and carry out a short-term, individual action research project. Report on the action research, its results, your conclusions, and your recommendations.

2. Observe, evaluate, and report on an action research project currently being carried out in a school setting. Include a discussion of whether all four of the other tasks of supervision have been integrated in the action research.

3. Describe an instructional improvement recently introduced in a school with which you are familiar. Suggest how the innovation could have been tried out as action research before being fully implemented. Your suggested plan should meet all the requirements (necessary procedures, integrated supervision tasks) for authentic action research.

4. Determine an instructional improvement that would benefit a school with which you are familiar. Suggest how each of the following four tasks of supervision would be carried out as a part of an action research project intended to meet the instructional improvement objective:

    a. What direct assistance would have to be provided to facilitate the instructional improvement?

    b. What types of group development would faculty need?

    c. What professional development activities would be necessary?

    d. What curriculum development would be necessary?

5. Interview faculty and supervisors of a clearly successful school to determine whether action research is carried out in that school. If so, do faculty members participate collectively in planning for action research? What is the mechanism for such participation (curriculum council, research committees, circle groups)? What are some examples of action research that have been carried out?

    If the selected school does not conduct action research, are teachers allowed opportunities for professional interaction, discussion of ideas for instructional improvement, and reflective and collective thinking? If so, how are such opportunities provided? Prepare a report on your interviews.

Developmental

1. Volunteer to supervise or participate in a long-range group action research project within an educational setting.

2. Take advantage of future opportunities to hold discussions with those involved in school action research. Such discussions can help you generate your own ideas for action research projects and effective supervision of action research.

3. Continue to explore the literature and research on action research. Begin a file of articles appropriate for sharing with educators interested in action research.

REFERENCES

Allen, L., and Glickman, C. D. 1992. School improvement: The elusive faces of shared governance. *NASSP Bulletin, 76*(542), 80–87.

Calhoun, E. F. 2002. Action research for school improvement. *Educational Leadership, 59*(6), 18–24.

Corey, S. M. 1953. *Action research to improve school practices.* New York: Teachers College, Columbia University.

Fullan, M. 1985. Change processes and strategies at the local level. *Elementary School Journal, 85*(3), 391–421.

Glickman, C. D. 1992. The essence of school renewal: The prose has begun. *Educational Leadership, 50*(1), 24–27.

Glickman, C. D. 1993. *Renewing America's schools. A guide for school-based action.* San Francisco: Jossey-Bass.

Houser, N. O. 1990. Teacher-researcher: The synthesis of roles for teacher empowerment. *Action in Teacher Education, 12*(2), 55–60.

Hubbard, R. S., and Power, B. M. 1993. *The art of classroom inquiry: A handbook for teacher-researchers.* Portsmouth, NH: Heinemann.

Lewin, K. 1948. *Resolving social conflicts.* New York: Harper and Brothers.

McBee, M. T. 2004. The classroom as laboratory: An exploration of teacher research. *Roeper Review, 27*(1), 52–58.

Sagor, R. 1993. *How to conduct collaborative action research.* Alexandria, VA: Association for Supervision and Curriculum Development.

Schaefer, R. 1967. *The school as the center of inquiry.* New York: Harper and Row.

Schmuck, R. A., Runkel, P., Arends, J. H., and Arends, R. I. 1977. *The second handbook of organizational development in schools.* Palo Alto, CA: Mayfield.

SUGGESTED READINGS

Calhoun, E. F. 1993. Action research: Three approaches. *Educational Leadership, 51*(2), 62–65.

Calhoun, E. F. 1994. *How to use action research in the self-renewing school.* Alexandria, VA: Association for Supervision and Curriculum Development.

Calhoun, E. F. 2002. Action research for school improvement. *Educational Leadership, 59*(6), 18–24.

Hendricks, C. 2005. *Improving schools through action research: A comprehensive guide for educators.* Boston: Allyn and Bacon.

Houser, N. O. 1990. Teacher-researcher: The synthesis of roles for teacher empowerment. *Action in Teacher Education, 12*(2), 55–60.

Hubbard, R. S., and Power, B. M. 1993. *The art of classroom inquiry: A handbook for teacher-researchers.* Portsmouth, NH: Heinemann.

Johnson, A. P. 2004. *A short guide to action research* (2nd ed.). Boston: Allyn and Bacon.

Russell, T., and Munby, H. (Eds.). 1992. *Teachers and teaching: From classroom to reflection.* London: Falmer.

Sagor, R. 1993. *How to conduct collaborative action research.* Alexandria, VA: Association for Supervision and Curriculum Development.

Sagor, R. 2004. *The action research guidebook: A four-step process for educators and school teams.* Thousand Oaks, CA: Corwin.

part six

Function of SuperVision

The chapters in Part VI address aspects of supervision that transcend traditional knowledge, skills, and tasks of supervision. Chapter 21 focuses on the change process. Change is viewed from both the supervisor's and the teacher's perspectives. Chaos theory is discussed in relation to change and applied to schools and classrooms. Cultures of change are described, and we argue for changing the conditions of teaching. Chapter 22 discusses democratic and moral purpose. Ten moral principles of the "good school" are presented. The moral dilemma brought about by the No Child Left Behind Act is examined, and short- as well as long-term strategies for addressing No Child Left Behind are proposed.

chapter 21

SuperVision, Change, and School Success

Although not all change represents progress, progress—by definition—is not possible without change. Facilitating change necessary for instructional improvement is a supervisory function that cuts across all five tasks of supervision. Initiating a clinical supervision program (direct assistance), assisting teachers in deciding on schoolwide instructional improvement goals (group development), delivering a skill-development program in which teachers learn new models of teaching (professional development), moving from a discipline-based to an interdisciplinary curriculum (curriculum development), and assisting teachers as they conduct research on a new classroom management system (action research) are all examples of facilitating change. In this chapter, we will look at assumptions about change, change from the teacher's view, a developmental view of change strategies, creating a culture for change, changing the conditions of teaching, the role of supervision and supervisors in school improvement, and school success.

Assumptions about Change

After many years of research and reflection on change in schools, Michael Fullan (1991) proposed 10 assumptions about change. Our own experience with change efforts in schools leads us to agree with Fullan's assumptions:

1. Do not assume that your version of what the change should be is the one that should or could be implemented. On the contrary, assume that one of the main purposes of the process of implementation is to exchange your reality of what should be through interaction with implementers and others concerned. Stated another way, assume that successful implementation consists of some transformation or continual development of initial ideas. . . .

2. Assume that any significant innovation, if it is to result in change, requires individual implementers to work out their own meaning. Significant change involves a certain amount of ambiguity, ambivalence, and uncertainty for the individual about the meaning of change. Thus, effective implementation is a process of clarification. . . .

3. Assume that conflict and disagreement are not only inevitable but fundamental to successful change. . . .

4. Assume that people need pressure to change (even in directions that they desire), but it will be effective only under conditions that allow them to react, to form their own position, to interact with other implementors, to obtain technical assistance, etc. . . .

5. Assume that effective change takes time. Unrealistic or undefined time lines fail to recognize that implementation occurs developmentally. Significant change in the form of implementing specific innovations can be expected to take a minimum of two to three years; bringing about institutional reforms can take five or more years. Persistence is a critical attribute of successful change.

6. Do not assume that the reason for lack of implementation is outright rejection of the values embodied in the change, or hard-core resistance to all change. Assume that there are a number of possible reasons: value rejection, inadequate resources to support implementation, insufficient time elapsed.

7. Do not expect all or even most people or groups to change. The complexity of change is such that it is impossible to bring about widespread reform in any large social system. Progress occurs when we take steps (e.g., by following the assumptions listed here) that increase the number of people affected. . . .

8. Assume that you will need a plan that is based on the above assumptions and that addresses the factors known to affect implementation. . . . Evolutionary planning and problem-coping models based on knowledge of the change process are essential. . . .

9. Assume that no amount of knowledge will ever make it totally clear what action should be taken. Action decisions are a combination of valid on-the-spot decisions, and intuition. . . .

10. Assume that changing the culture of institutions is the real agenda, not implementing single innovations. Put another way, when implementing particular innovations, we should always pay attention to whether the institution is developing or not. (pp. 105–107)*

Change from the Teacher's View

Gene Hall and Shirley Hord (1987) have extended the work of Frances Fuller (1969) on teacher concerns (discussed in Chapter 4) and described seven stages of concern about school innovations (numbered from stages 0 through 6). Figure 21.1 describes each of these stages. Note that awareness, informational, and personal concerns about the innovation relate to Fuller's self-concerns; management concerns about the innovation relate to Fuller's task concerns; and consequence, collaboration, and refocusing concerns about the innovation relate to Fuller's impact concerns. Teachers are not likely to move to higher stages of concern until their lower-stage concerns have been addressed.

To help us better understand stages of concern, Hord and associates (Hord, Rutherford, Huling-Austin, and Hall, 1987) have provided "expressions of concern" made by individuals at each stage of concern. Table 21.1 lists stages and expressions of concerns. The supervisor's role is to facilitate teachers' movement through stages of concern—*and* implementation of the innovation—by (1) assessing individual and group stages of concern and (2) meeting the needs of teachers and groups at various stages. The supervisor can assess teachers' stages of concern through conferencing, open-ended concerns statements, and questionnaires (see Hall and Hord, 1987).

Chaos Theory and Change

Chaos theory cuts across a wide number of disciplines, including biology, chemistry, mathematics, meteorology, and physics. The "new science" of chaos has two foci. The first is the exploration of the hidden order that exists within chaotic systems. The second is the study of how self-organization emerges from chaos (Hayles, 1990). Chaos theory involves a number of related concepts, not all of which are relevant to change in schools and classrooms. Several aspects of chaos theory that have significance for educational change are reviewed here.

---

*Reprinted by permission of the publisher from M. Fullan, *The New Meaning of Educational Change* (New York: Teachers College Press, © 1991 by Teachers College, Columbia University. All rights reserved.)

Impact	6	REFOCUSING: The focus is on exploration of more universal benefits from the innovation, including the possibility of major changes or replacement with a more powerful alternative. Individual has definite ideas about alternatives to the proposed or existing form of the innovation.
	5	COLLABORATION: The focus is on coordination and cooperation with others regarding use of the innovation.
	4	CONSEQUENCE: Attention focuses on impact of the innovation on student in his or her immediate sphere of influence. The focus is on relevance of the innovation for students, evaluation of student outcomes, including performance and competencies, and changes needed to increase student outcomes.
Task	3	MANAGEMENT: Attention is focused on the processes and tasks of using the innovation and the best use of information and resources. Issues related to efficiency, organizing, managing, scheduling, and time demands are utmost.
Self	2	PERSONAL: Individual is uncertain about the demands of the innovation, his or her inadequacy to meet those demands, and his or her role with the innovation. This includes analysis of his or her role in relation to the reward structure of the organization, decision making, and consideration of potential conflicts with existing structures or personal commitment. Financial or status implications of the program for self and colleagues may also be reflected.
	1	INFORMATIONAL: A general awareness of the innovation and interest in learning more detail about it is indicated. The person seems to be unworried about himself or herself in relation to the innovation. She or he is interested in substantive aspects of the innovation in a selfless manner such as general characteristics, effects, and requirements for use.
	0	AWARENESS: Little concern about or involvement with the innovation is indicated.

FIGURE 21.1 *Stages of Concern about the Innovation*

Source: Adapted from *Change in Schools, Facilitating the Process* edited by Gene E. Hall and Shirley M. Hord. Reprinted by permission of the State University of New York Press. © 1987, State University of New York. All rights reserved.

TABLE 21.1	Stages and Expressions of Concern

Stages of Concern		Expressions of Concern
I M	6 Refocusing	I have some ideas about something that would work even better.
P A	5 Collaboration	I am concerned about relating what I am doing with what other instructors are doing.
C T	4 Consequence	How is my use affecting kids?
T A S K	3 Management	I seem to be spending all my time getting material ready.
S E	2 Personal	How will using it affect me?
L	1 Informational	I would like to know more about it.
F	0 Awareness	I am not concerned about it (the innovation).

Source: S. M. Hord, W. L. Rutherford, L. Huling-Austin, and G. E. Hall, *Taking Charge of Change.* Alexandria, VA: Association for Supervision and Curriculum Development, 1987, p. 31. Reprinted with permission of S. M. Hord.

Nonlinearity

In a linear system simple cause and effect relationships exist; A causes B which causes C, and so on. A linear system is analogous to tipping over the first in a line of dominoes. The falling first domino knocks down the second, the second knocks down the third, and so on. A chaotic system is nonlinear. A nonlinear system is analogous to throwing a bowling ball toward a set of pins. Myriad variables come into play and interact with each other. The slightest variation in how the bowling ball is released may result in a strike in one frame, and a split or a gutter ball in the next.

Complexity

Chaotic systems take complex forms, making their precise measurement difficult if not impossible. Chapter 5's discussion on measuring the coast of Britain is an example of the problem with measuring complex forms; the method of measurement affects the measure. If one uses 200 mile-long rulers, the coast of Britain is 1,600 miles long. If the rulers are 25 miles long, the length increases to 2,550 miles (Smith, 1995). As the length of the rulers becomes shorter, the length of the coast of Britain increases, on to infinity (Briggs and Peat, 1989).

Butterfly Effect

This phenomenon is technically known as *sensitive dependence on initial conditions*. This means that a small and seemingly unrelated event in one part of a system can have enormous effects on other parts of the system. Theoretical meteorologist Edward Lorenz made the term *butterfly effect* famous when he argued that a butterfly stirring its wings in Bejing today could unleash powerful storms in New York City next month. One implication of sensitive dependence of initial conditions is the impossibility of predicting not only next year's weather but also the long-term future of any chaotic system.

Fractals

A fractal is a geometric shape that is similar to itself at different scales. Mid-sized branches of a tree are remarkably similar in shape to the larger branches from which they come. Smaller branches, in turn, are the same shape as the mid-sized branches from which they come, and so on. Other examples of fractals include coastlines, mountains, clouds, rivers, weather patterns, and the human vascular system. Complex social systems can also reveal self-similarity on different scales: At each level of the system, specific patterns of organization and culture reappear.

Feedback Mechanisms

Chaotic systems contain feedback loops enabling outputs to feed back into the system as input. Feedback can bring stability or turbulence to a system. For example, a thermostat is a feedback mechanism that causes temperature stability. Conversely, when the sound from a loudspeaker feeds back through a microphone, it is rapidly magnified to create a disruptive shriek (Gleick, 1987). Feedback can also cause a system to move toward greater levels of complexity. Physicist Joseph Ford, for example, has referred to evolution as "chaos with feedback."

Turbulence

Turbulence can be caused from disturbances inside or outside of a system. Consider a river, flowing smoothly until it runs through a bed of rocks. The water is perturbed and becomes unstable. Turbulence can also be caused by a heavy rain that greatly increases the volume of water flowing through the river bed. The more complex a system is, the more subject it is to instability due to turbulence. If instability becomes great enough, a point of phase transition is reached; sudden, radical change takes place, resulting in either reorganization or disintegration.

Strange Attractors

Chaotic systems are not truly random. Rather, they possess patterns that are extremely complex and unpredictable, but that stay within certain parameters. Strange attractors are "deeply encoded structures" within chaotic systems (Hayles, 1990).

The discovery that chaos possesses deep structures of order is all the more remarkable because of the wide range of systems that demonstrate this behavior. They range from lynx fur returns to outbreaks of measles epidemics, from the rise and fall of the Nile River to eye movements in schizophrenics. (Hayles, 1990, p. 10)

To summarize, chaos theory informs us that order and chaos are not opposites. Rather, in the words of Margaret Wheatley (1992) they are "mirror images, one containing the other" (p. 11).

Chaos Theory Applied to School Change

School improvement efforts traditionally have treated the change process as linear, with each step in the change effort affecting the next step in a simple cause and effect relationship. But, despite linear organization charts and improvement plans, schools are not linear systems; they are *nonlinear*, chaotic systems. An implication for this reality is that, rather than viewing a change effort as a blueprint to be drawn and followed, it should be viewed as an organic process:

> Here the metaphor for change is the growth and development of a complex organism (for example a human being) rather than the operation of a simple machine. A complex organism begins life at a relatively small stage. Its development is not completely predictable. Its health requires interdependence, consistency, and balance among its various subsystems. Finally, organisms that flourish tend to be adaptable to changing environments. In fact, they are themselves in a constant state of change or "becoming." (Gordon, 1992, p. 73)

The fact that schools are nonlinear systems means that change cannot be controlled from above. It can only be nurtured by promoting a culture for change. The supervisor attempting to nurture such a culture needs to remember Fullan's admonition not to believe that the change the supervisor envisions is the one that should or even could be implemented. Rather it is the interaction of the supervisors ideas about change with ideas from other members of the school community— and the interaction of the change process with many other variables within the school culture—that will determine the direction of change.

The *complexity* of schools means that neither external research on effective schools, nor legislated standards, nor the results of standardized achievement tests can, by themselves, precisely measure improvement needs or the level of success of improvement efforts. Keedy and Achilles (1997) argued that local educators must ask the questions:

1. Why they want to change;
2. What they want to achieve; and
3. How to go about the change process. (p. 116)

We would argue that local educators need to ask a fourth question as well: *how to measure success*. Keedy and Achilles recommended that supervisors and teachers reach consensus on these questions through collaborative, critical inquiry informed by awareness of the change process.

The *butterfly effect* applies to school change: It is impossible to predict the long-term effects of school improvement efforts. This does not mean that formal planning for school change should not take place. It does mean that a different type of planning is needed. Planning in a chaotic system like a school should be medium range (one to two years) rather than long range (five to ten years). It should emphasize general goals, broad guidelines, and built-in flexibility (Gordon, 1992). Formal planning in an unpredictable system needs to focus on process rather than product, with the goal of producing "a stream of wise decisions designed to achieve the mission of the organization" (Patterson, Purkey, and Parker, 1986).

Like *fractals* in nature, schools reveal self-similarity in different scales. For example, a schoolwide staff-development day, a department meeting, a classroom lesson, and a hallway interaction between a teacher and student might all reveal the same cultural characteristic. Thus reflective inquiry at the school, team, classroom, and individual level can help educators better understand their school culture, needed change, and pathways to improvement.

Once school improvement efforts are underway, feedback becomes essential for monitoring and assessing change. *Feedback mechanisms* need to be created and maintained. Feedback can take the form of student performance data, survey results, quality circles, third-party reviews, and so forth. The important thing is that meaningful data on the results of change efforts be made available to teachers, and that they be given opportunities to reflect on the data and redirect their change efforts accordingly.

All complex systems experience *turbulence,* but efforts at change tend to increase its frequency and intensity. Turbulence is not always negative. Without some perturbance, the system would remain in a steady state and improvement would not be possible. However, too much turbulence (from outside or inside the school) can cause school improvement efforts to disintegrate. Keedy and Achilles (1997, p. 115) have written that supervisors and teachers should construct a normative consensus—"a collective, critically-examined, and contextually-based agreement" of essential school norms that they can hold fast to during times of turbulence. The authors have maintained that it is this normative consensus (referred to earlier in this text as a "cause beyond oneself") that can hold a school together during the change process.

Finally, *strange attractors,* those deeply encoded structures within chaotic systems, have implications for school change. Is it possible for supervisors and teachers to create strange attractors within schools that will—albeit in unpredictable ways—create permanent patterns leading to school improvement? Policy makers have attempted to do just that, mandating such structures as site-based management, shared decision making, and parent choice (Keedy, 1995). However, these structures have all failed to lead to patterns of improvement. According to Keedy

(1995), the design that should be embedded throughout the social fabric of schools—for our purpose a "strange attractor"—is *student-centered learning.* He also believes that embedding this design within traditional schools is an extremely difficult task, and that the best chance for making student-centered learning a school's underlying pattern is the design of new schools around that concept.

Implications of Chaos Theory at the Classroom Level

Chaos theory has implications beyond the school level. Classrooms and even individual students can be considered chaotic systems (the reader smiles and nods in agreement)! All joking aside, chaos theory is consistent with recent research that the brain learns in *nonlinear* ways. This calls into question a host of traditional classroom practices, including grouping students by age, separate subjects, a sequential curriculum, and discrete behavioral objectives (Rockler, 1990–1991; Tygestad, 1997; Bloch, 2005). Nonlinearity supports constructivist teaching and learning as discussed in Chapter 5.

Complexity implies that student learning can take many different forms and can be expressed in different ways. This means that teachers should place less emphasis on any single indicator of student aptitude or achievement. It especially calls into question use of the standardized achievement test as the sole measure of student growth (Rockler, 1990–91; Stiggins, 2002; Coladarci, 2002; Clark and Clark, 2000; Newell, 2002; Behuniak, 2002). Complexity suggests the use of multiple measures of student learning, matching different assessment measures to different learning goals. It also supports the use of authentic assessment methods. Finally, complexity gives credence to the idea of allowing students to participate in planning assessment, and in making self-evaluation part of the assessment process.

The *butterfly effect* means that a wide variety of factors seemingly unrelated to a lesson plan (whether a student argued with a parent the night before, ate breakfast, or made a new friend on the school bus that morning) can lead to significant differences in what takes place in the classroom when the lesson is taught, and how the lesson affects an individual student's learning. The butterfly effect assures that no lesson will ever go completely as planned, or have the same effect on any two students. It indicates the need for teacher flexibility in teaching, as well as the need for individual attention to students, each of whom is experiencing a given lesson within his or her own personal context.

If the butterfly effect accounts for differences in classroom interactions and student outcomes, *fractals* are a metaphor for patterns that can be observed on different scales within the classroom. Systematic classroom observation can record behaviors and effects that cut across whole-class, small-group, and individual levels. Additionally, patterned behaviors and interactions can be observed from lesson to lesson. Reflective inquiry into classroom practice, whether in the form of clinical supervision, peer coaching, or action research, can help the teacher to identify patterns that foster and hinder student learning, and to alter the learning environment accordingly.

Feedback mechanisms can have positive or negative effects on classroom teaching and learning. For example, high-stakes testing (much to the chagrin of those who design the tests) can become a negative mechanism. In many cases, feedback on student performance on high-stakes tests has led teachers to ignore curriculum not measured by the test, and teach to the test through "drill and kill" methods focused on practice test items. With all of the the unpredictability present in classrooms, beneficial feedback is critical for both teachers and students. For teachers, student performance data, direct student feedback, and classroom observation data can all assist teachers to improve classroom instruction. Skill at what Donald Schon calls "reflection in action" enables teachers to receive and analyze feedback and respond to that feedback while in the act of teaching. For students, feedback on their cognitive and affective performance—from teachers, parents, and peers—is an essential part of the learning process. The fact that in chaotic systems like classrooms output becomes input means that the artificial distinctions we often draw between learning and assessment need to be removed: In reality, learning and assessment cannot be separated.

Turbulence, like nonlinearity, supports constructivist teaching and learning. Tygestad (1997) has pointed out that new knowledge, like turbulence, causes instability ("disequilibrium") before it is assimilated into a new conceptual scheme. The teacher's task is to first present perturbations that cause instability and activate conceptual change (Luffiego, Bastida, Ramos, and Soto, 1994), and then to support student reconstruction (Doll, 1996).

Finally, the improvement of teaching—like whole-school improvement—is dependent on the ultimate *strange attractor,* student-centered learning. Additional patterns within the fabric of classroom practice can foster student-centered learning, including reflective inquiry, instructional dialogue, and collegial support. It is not possible to predict precisely how these embedded patterns will change classroom instruction in the long run. Rather, they are designed to facilitate a process of continuous improvement.

And so ends our brief journey into the world of chaos, a world that elicits different reactions from those who enter it.

> Those who feel comfortable with order and reason, with symmetry, equilibrium, and stasis, will find life in the world of dynamic complexity quite challenging. On the other hand, those who are comfortable with being in the process, the flow of the system, those who can see the larger patterns beyond the endless change and dynamisms, those who can tolerate ambiguity and unpredictability, those people will find being in a complex system at the edge of chaos to be stimulating and rewarding. (McAndrew, 1997, p. 40)

Does not all that is said in the above quote about chaotic systems apply as well to modern schools and classrooms?

Creating a Culture for Change

The traditional literature on organizational culture treats culture and change as polar opposites, with one purpose of the culture being to *resist* change. Such resistance indeed seems to be part of the typical school culture. However, some school cultures actually foster positive change. What characteristics do these school cultures have that are not present in most schools? Those who have studied "cultures for change" have described very similar characteristics. Little (1982); Rosenholtz (1989); Fullan, Bennett, and Rolheiser-Bennett (1990); Fullan (2001, 2002); and Harris (2002) all cite shared purpose, collegiality, and a spirit of continuous improvement. Simpson (1990) Fullan (2001, 2002), and Harris (2002) described sharing and collegiality, teacher empowerment, and participative/collaborative leadership. Leithwood (1992) described "transformational leadership" that fosters school reform through maintaining collaborative cultures, fostering teacher development, and improving group problem solving.

Saphier and King (1985) described 12 cultural norms that foster school improvement:

1. Collegiality
2. Experimentation
3. High expectations
4. Trust and confidence
5. Tangible support
6. Reaching out to the knowledge bases
7. Appreciation and recognition
8. Caring, celebration, and humor
9. Involvement in decision making
10. Protection of what's important
11. Traditions
12. Honest, open communication (p. 67)

Rather than viewing school culture as a wall impeding change, a better way to define it is as a set of commonly held beliefs, values, norms, and assumptions that can result in change being resisted *or* embraced. Empowered individuals and groups are more likely to develop beliefs, values, norms, and assumptions that are congruent with risk taking, experimentation, and continuous improvement rather than with the status quo. Given the many problems facing our schools today, creating a culture for change has become a critical imperative for supervision and supervisors.

Changing the Conditions of Teaching

Any discussion on change in education would be incomplete if it did not address the conditions of teaching across the nation over the last several years. To say the least, these conditions have not been optimal. All of the research on change now available will be of little value if changing the conditions of teaching is not a central goal of both external and internal school improvement efforts.

- Change is needed, *away from* treating teachers as technicians expected to transmit curriculum developed by bureaucrats, using canned methods published by commercial interests, and measuring student learning through one-size-fits-all tests mandated by policy makers; *toward* treating teachers as professionals invited to make professional decisions about curriculum, instruction, and student assessment.
- Change is needed, *away from* overloading teachers to the extent that they are unable to develop the teacher-student relationships, engage in the reflective planning, and perform the critical self-assessment required for effective teaching; *toward* the manageable class and student load that are prerequisites for quality teaching.
- Change is needed, *away from* the physical and psychological isolation caused by outmoded school structures and norms of individualism; *toward* structures and norms that provide opportunities for professional dialogue and collaborative work.
- Change is needed, *away from* bureaucratic organizations in which teachers are overwhelmed by regulations and paperwork, or—worse yet—mistreated by authoritarian organizations more representative of old-style dictatorships than modern democracies; *toward* democratic school communities in which supervisors promote shared decision-making, collegiality, and teacher leadership.
- Change is needed, *away from* policies that treat teachers as part of the problem and consider education a low priority in the allocation of resources; *toward* policies that value teachers as part of the solution and provide the human and material resources teachers need to improve schools and provide all students with a quality education.
- Change is needed, *away from* teaching as an unstaged career with minimal extrinsic rewards; *toward* teaching as a career in which teachers are properly inducted into the profession and are provided new responsibilities, appropriate support, increased recognition, and significantly increased salary at each career stage.
- Change is needed, *away from* diversity as a combination of colors and symbols; *toward* a vision of practice that values and honors respect and dignity as well as shared power and decision making.

Early in the twenty-first century, although many teachers face negative conditions, there are also efforts to improve the conditions of teaching. Many members of the business community, concerned citizens' groups, and policy makers are working to improve external conditions, and many supervisors have worked from the "inside" to make schools centers of democracy, inquiry, and dialogue. The door for improving external and internal conditions will never close; it's simply a matter of whether or not we care to step in and make a difference.

What Is School Success?

Ironically, the definition of school success has been left to near the end of this book. This has been done for a reason, however. The rationale for a school faculty making its own collective definition of school success should be apparent. In referring to studies of successful schools to support many of the propositions of this book, we mentioned schools that were achieving what they had set out to do, regardless of what those goals were. Some schools prioritize academic learning and achievement as their criteria for success. Some prioritize creativity and self-directed learning. Other schools prioritize problem solving, community involvement, and social cooperation as their criteria for success. Many schools want it all: They want to be successful in academics, creativity, self-directed learning, problem solving, community involvement, and social cooperation (Goodlad, 1984, pp. 33–60). Schools should strive to educate all students well, in ways consistent with education in a democratic society (Barber, 1993). Although we personally prefer schools that strive to have it all, that decision should be a local school matter. It is in the clarity of common purpose that action to improve instruction takes place.

With an understanding of what is meant by improved instruction and school success, we can fill in the remaining circle on the diagram of supervision for successful schools that has served as the map of this book (see Figure 21.2).

PRACTITIONER REFLECTION

The Heart of School Change—
Teachers Working Together

Barbara F. Lunsford, *Principal, Berkmar Middle School*

As the instructional leader of a school of 1,000 students from a variety of countries, my major responsibilities include facilitating the work of 110 staff members. Our focus is on student achievement, and we strive to provide students with authentically engaging work that is relevant and purposeful.

The Context of One School's Effort at School Improvement

As I have participated in and observed school improvement efforts and attempts to make substantive changes in the way schools educate students, I have seen a variety of approaches and rationales over the last 25 years. There have been efforts to change governance at local and district levels, curriculum, assessment of students, assessment of teachers, preparation of teachers, certification of teachers, school culture, school calendars, school schedules, and amount of time to be spent in various content areas, just to name a few. The improvement initiatives have come from federal, state, and district levels as well as the local school level. Although each of these efforts was genuine in trying to address the need to provide an education for all students to be successful academically and socially, the actual work of students in the classroom was not always impacted.

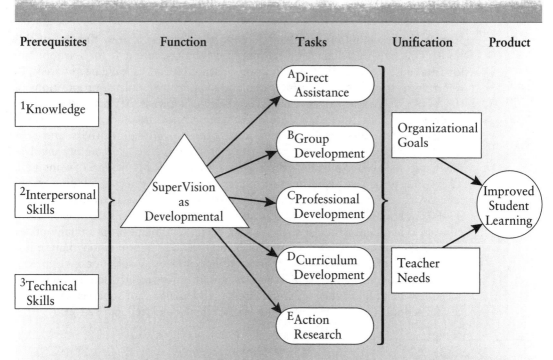

| Prerequisites | Function | Tasks | Unification | Product |

FIGURE 21.2 *SuperVision for Successful Schools*

As we at Berkmar Middle School began to work with a diverse population and a high level of poverty, we began to ask ourselves the following questions:

What are the academic needs of our students?

How are we currently addressing these needs?

In order for our students to be more successful, what do we need to change?

It became clear that, although we were working extremely hard at meeting student needs, we were continuing to use practices that had not proven to be successful in closing the much talked about and very real achievement gap among students of various backgrounds. We discovered that our students in special education and English for Speakers of Other Languages programs were being removed from rigorous classroom instruction to be given small-group instruction. Although this practice was done for all the right reasons, we were not serving these students in a manner that accelerated their rate of learning and prepared them to be successful in the standard curriculum.

At first glance, this problem seems to impact a small percentage of the population, but our investigation as a faculty proved otherwise. We initially looked at this issue as a scheduling problem or something that could be addressed through better management. The more we moved into the real issue, the more it became apparent that this was a critical issue of teacher expectations, instructional practice, knowledge of assessment, and a clear definition of what quality student work looked like. This unfolding of reality and sharing of various perspectives has proven to be the beginning of a change process that has many implications.

As a result of many conversations, review of current literature, and analysis of individual student achievement data, we decided we would make a substantive change in the way we organize the day of our students, and the way teachers use their time as well. Ultimately, we found we needed to change the way teachers plan and work together. Teachers are now in the process of opening up their planning process, their classrooms, their method of assessment, and their willingness to "share" their students. This change for school improvement is certainly a work in progress and we are discovering something new every day. This is the type of change that cannot be driven by federal, state, or even district mandates. In reality, this type of change can't be successful unless there is the commitment and willingness of teachers to reflect, analyze, and decide to take action.

What We Have Learned

Trying something new moves everyone out of his or her comfort zone. Teachers suddenly feel incompetent in doing the things they used to do automatically. Planning becomes something that is inclusive of others and therefore cannot be done on the fly. Lessons that may have been used for years are suddenly not appropriate and there is a certain "first-year" panic when a new approach is tried.

Issues about control and turf must be dealt with openly. For this type of collaborative work to be successful, the teachers have to develop a trusting working relationship. In most of our situations, who works with whom is driven by student needs. This results in teachers sharing their classrooms with people they have not previously known. The whole process of individual style has to be addressed. Teachers working together also need to have a system of effective communication, common goals for students, a willingness to talk with each other about what is working and what is not, and a willingness to work through conflicts in a professional matter.

Individual interests may need to become secondary to the needs of the students. For example, the natural tendency is to think of the support teacher as the "visitor" in the classroom, and this has been something we are in the process of working through. Our support teachers are passionate about their field and about their individual students. We are learning that some of the "protective instinct" is not in the best interest of the students. The most common comment by our support teachers has been, "I didn't know my students could do this well."

There are typical implementation issues that need to be addressed and solved in a professional manner. We realize that this model of instruction is not appropriate for every student and we must be willing to reevaluate how students are doing on a regular basis. It has been important for the teachers to develop a relationship in which concerns can be discussed and resolutions sought. Individuals cannot go in their classroom and think, "I'll just do my own thing."

Implications for Supervisors

Supervisors must be willing to support those willing to take a risk and buffer any repercussions as a result of the staff's actions. Any time a change occurs in a school, there are skeptics both from within and outside. I have viewed my role as one of giving teachers time and permission to work through this process without bearing the brunt of the questions or criticisms. They need to have a safe environment in which to learn.

The supervisor needs to be prepared to serve as a facilitator willing to address issues from all perspectives. Providing opportunities for all involved to have time to work through the issues that arise and to plan together is a primary role the supervisor can play. As the principal, I have the authority and responsibility to direct funds, schedule time, and provide support for the teachers to do this work.

The creation of this disequilibrium has a ripple effect on the daily routine of the school. We have experienced a general sense of anxiety and stress, and continue to work at the process of changing our daily instruction while still having a sense of order and normalcy. Knowing when to keep pushing, when to say "relax," and when to intervene is another role the supervisor needs to be cognizant of as the change process occurs.

In conclusion, this brief example of one school's effort to bring about instructional improvement by changing practice identifies many issues experienced by teachers and supervisors. Throughout the process, open communication is the most essential component. People of goodwill wanting to do what is best for students will prevail if the teachers and supervisors can talk about the real issues and collaboratively seek solutions.

EXERCISES

Academic

1. Find in the literature a description of an educational leader who has turned an unsuccessful school into a successful one. Which of the change strategies discussed in this chapter did the supervisor use? Report on actions related to each of the five tasks of supervision that he or she carried out while turning the school around.

2. If Boyer (1983, 1988) or Goodlad (1984) were asked to write a three-page paper on "What Makes Effective and Successful Schools," what would each of them say in his essay? Assume the role of one of these authors and, on the basis of reading their studies, write such a paper.

3. Prepare a report comparing and contrasting the views of three authors who have written about educational change.

4. Prepare a report on recent efforts by individuals and groups outside of education and government to provide concrete assistance to education and educators. What have they proposed, and what is being done?

5. Diagram your own model for effective supervision. Provide a written explanation of each component of your model. Explain the scope, arrangement, sequence, and relationship of model components.

Field

1. Interview a supervisor on practical problems that must be considered to bring about change within a typical public school system. Prepare a report on your interview. Include your own ideas on how appropriate knowledge, skills, roles, functions, processes, tasks, and strategies discussed in this book can be applied to overcome or reduce problems described by the interviewee.

2. Prepare a photo and/or written essay about schools, students, teachers, and supervisors that has as its theme "A Cause beyond Oneself" and that reflects the meaning this book attaches to this phrase. Share the essay with others.

3. Interview five teachers concerning a program innovation that is being proposed or introduced in their school. On the basis of the interviews, attempt to classify each teacher according to his or her stage of concern about the innovation.

4. Create a collage in which the key ideas of the text are represented. Share the collage with others who have read this text.

Developmental

1. Begin a file of newspaper, magazine, and journal articles describing ideas and efforts of individuals and organizations both in and outside of education for achieving success in education.

2. Use selected readings from other texts on educational supervision to compare authors' ideas on specific issues you consider crucial to your own education and development in supervision.

3. Use opportunities as they arise to test out this book's ideas on supervision within your own particular work setting. Through such exploration, determine which of the proposals and suggestions are of most value to your own development and that of others.

REFERENCES

Barber, R. R. 1993. America skips school. *Harpers, 287*(1722), 39–46.

Behuniak, P. 2002. Consumer-referenced testing. *Phi Delta Kappan, 84*(3), 199–207.

Bloch, D. P. 2005. Complexity, chaos, and nonlinear dynamics: A new perspective on career development theory. *The Career Development Quarterly, 53*(3), 194–207.

Boyer, E. L. 1983. *High school: A report on secondary education in America.* New York: Harper and Row.

Boyer, E. L. 1988. *Report card on school reform: The teachers speak.* Princeton, NJ: Carnegie Commission for the Advancement of Teaching.

Briggs, J., and Peat, F. D. 1989. *Turbulent mirror: An illustrated guide to chaos theory and the science of wholeness.* New York: Harper and Row.

Clark, D.C., and Clark, S. N. 2000. Appropriate assessment strategies for young adolescents in an era of standards-based reform. *The Clearing House, 73*(4), 201–204.

Coladarci, R. 2002. Is it a house or a pile of bricks? Important features of a local assessment system. *Phi Delta Kappan, 83*(10), 772–774.

Doll, W. E. 1996. Prigogine: A new sense of order, a new curriculum. *Theory into Practice, 25*(1), 10–16.

Fullan, M. 1991. *The new meaning of educational change.* New York: Teachers College Press.

Fullan, M. 2001. *Leading in a culture of change.* San Francisco: Jossey-Bass.

Fullan, M. 2002. The change leader. *Educational Leadership, 59*(8), 16–20.

Fullan, M. G., Bennett, B., and Rolheiser-Bennett, C. 1990. Linking classroom and school improvement. *Educational Leadership, 47*(8), 13–19.

Fuller, F. F. 1969. Concerns of teachers: A developmental conceptualization. *American Educational Research Journal, 6*(2), 207–266.

Gleick, J. 1987. *Chaos: Making a new science.* New York: Penguin Books.

Goodlad, J. I. 1984. *A place called school: Prospects for the future.* New York: McGraw-Hill.

Gordon, S. P. 1992. Paradigms, transitions, and the new supervision. *Journal of Curriculum and Supervision, 8*(1), 62–76.

Hall, G. E., and Hord, S. M. 1987. *Change in schools: Facilitating the process.* Albany: State University of New York Press.

Harris, A. 2002. *School improvement: What's in it for schools?* New York: Routledge Falmer.

Hayles, N. K. 1990. *Chaos bound: Orderly disorder in contemporary literature and society.* Ithaca, NY: Cornell University Press.

Hord, S. M., Rutherford, W. L., Huling Austin, L., & Hall, G. E. 1987. *Taking charge of change.* Alexandria, VA: Association for Supervision and Curriculum Development.

Keedy, J. L. 1995. Teacher practical knowledge in restructured high schools. *Journal of Educational Research, 89*(2), 76–89.

Keedy, J. L., and Achilles, C. M. 1997. The need for school-constructed theories in practice in U.S. school restructuring. *Journal of Educational Administration, 35*(2), 102–121.

Leithwood, K. A. 1992. The move toward transformational leadership. *Educational Leadership, 49*(58), 8–12.

Little, J. W. 1982. Norms of collegiality and experimentation: Workplace conditions of school success. *American Educational Research Journal, 19*(3), 325–340.

Luffiego, M., Bastida, M. F., Ramos, F., and Soto, J. 1994. Systemic model of conceptual evolution. *International Journal of Science, 16*(3), 305–313.

McAndrew, D. A. 1997. Chaos, complexity, and fuzziness: Science looks at teaching English. *English Journal, 86*(7), 37–43.

Newell, R. J. 2002. A different look at accountability: The EdVisions approach. *Phi Delta Kappan, 84*(3), 208–211.

Patterson, J. L., Purkey, S. C., and Parker, J. V. 1986. *Productive school systems for a nonrational world.* Alexandria, VA: Association for Supervision and Curriculum Development.

Rockler, M. J. 1990–1991. Thinking about chaos: Non-quantitative approaches to teacher education. *Action in Teacher Education, 12*(4), 56–62.

Rosenholtz, S. 1989. *Teachers' workplace: The social organization of schools.* White Plains, NY: Longman.

Saphier, J., and King, M. 1985. Good seeds grow in strong cultures. *Educational Leadership, 42*(6), 67–74.

Simpson, G. W. 1990. Keeping it alive: Elements of school culture that sustain innovation. *Educational Leadership, 47*(8), 34–37.

Smith, R. D. 1995. The inapplicability principle: What chaos means for social science. *Behavioral Science, 40*(1), 22–40.

Stiggins, R. J. 2002. Assessment crisis: The absence of assessment for learning. *Phi Delta Kappan, 83*(10), 758–765.

Tygestad, J. 1997. *Chaos in the classroom: An application of chaos theory.* Paper presented at the Annual Meeting of the American Educational Research Association, Chicago, March.

Wheatley, M. J. 1992. *Leadership and the new science: Learning about organization from an orderly universe.* San Francisco: Berrett-Koehler.

SUGGESTED READINGS

Barth, R. S. 1991. *Improving schools from within.* San Francisco: Jossey-Bass.

Brandt, R. (Ed.). 1990. *Educational Leadership, 47*(8). Theme issue on "Creating a Culture for Change."

Fullan, M. 1991. *The new meaning of educational change* (2nd ed.). New York: Teachers College Press.

Fullan, M. 1996. Turning systematic thinking on its head. *Phi Delta Kappan, 77,* 420–423.

Fullan, M. 2001. *Leading in a culture of change*. San Francisco: Jossey-Bass.

Fullan, M., and Miles, M. 1992. Getting reform right: What works and what doesn't. *Phi Delta Kappan, 73*, 745–752.

Glatthorn, A. A. 1992. *Teachers as agents of change*. Washington, DC: National Education Association.

Harvey, T. R. 1990. *Checklist for change*. Boston: Allyn and Bacon.

Joyce, B. R. 1995. School renewal: An inquiry, not a formula. *Educational Leadership, 52*(7), 51–55.

Larson, R. L. 1992. *Changing schools from the inside out*. Lancaster, PA: Technomic.

Moran, J. J. 2001. *Collaborative professional development for teachers of adults*. Malabar, FL: Krieger Publishing Company.

Patterson, J. L. 1993. *Leadership for tomorrow's schools*. Alexandria, VA: Association for Supervision and Curriculum Development.

Schlechty, P. C. 2005. *Creating great schools: Six critical systems at the heart of educational innovation*. San Francisco, CA: Jossey-Bass.

chapter 22

SuperVision for What? Democracy and the Good School*

> We first must reaffirm our commitment to education's public purpose and weave it into the fabric of our schools.
>
> —*National Commission on Service Learning, 2002*

All children have the right to experience the joy of learning. We believe it is time for a new commitment to education reform in our country with the goal of giving every child the opportunity to be a part of a learning community that engages and inspires them to reach their full potential.

> —*Civil Society Institute, 2003*

These two quotes taken from two broad-based nonpartisan national commissions have struck a timely chord. Currently in state after state across the United States,

---

*Portions of the introduction and the entire section "The Good School and Moral Principles" originally were published in Gordon, S. P. (2001). The good school, *Florida Educational Leadership, 1* (2), 13–15.

the measure of school success or failure is how students perform on high-stakes achievement tests. These tests, usually consisting of multiple-choice items measuring cognitive learning at the lower level of Bloom's taxonomy, have become state legislatures' primary tool for bringing about school reform. The vision of many educational leaders is a higher percentage of students passing the test. Curricula are aligned with the test, teachers are teaching to the test, and increasingly, students' promotion or graduation depends on their test performance.

In this age of legislated learning enforced by legislated testing, there seems to be little room for a broader vision of school success. Yet, in times like this, it is more critical than ever to make a clarion call for what many would consider a different and better vision of a successful school. This vision is not new, just currently unpopular. It is a vision of a school that is focused not solely on externally imposed standards and tests scores, but on the overall well-being, growth, and development of all students, indeed of all members of the school community. The vision is based on the premise that each individual possesses intrinsic worth as a human being and should, therefore, be afforded the educational opportunities prerequisite to a meaningful and fulfilling life (Baez, 2005).

Reform around Purpose

Listen to the voices of teachers talking about the same group of regular students they have during the schoolday:

Mr. A: The kids here are where the problem is today. These kids are just unteachable. There's nothing wrong with the curriculum. . . . If I could just get the right students, I could teach and everything would be wonderful.

Ms. B: These students are just not real smart, and they don't want to learn. They're just putting in time.

Mr. C: There are kids here who really want to do a good job, but they have seen so much and heard so much that they often are distracted. Their perspective is gone. But they are basically really good kids.

Ms. D: My guys. They're very, very clever and brave kids. It's amazing how they are always figuring out what is going on around them. It is a job to keep up with their energy and channel it into learning experiences.

Without arguing over perception versus reality as reflected in those attitudes toward students, let us ask which views you heard are consistent with the founding principles of U.S. society.

All men [and women] are created equal, that they are endowed by their Creator with certain inalienable Rights; that among these are Life, Liberty, and the pursuit of Happiness; that to secure these rights, Governments are instituted among men, deriving their just powers from the consent of the governed, that whenever any form of government becomes destructive of these ends, it is the Right of the People to alter or abolish it. (Declaration of Independence, 1776)

Take those previous words by teachers about their students and change a few words and you have the central purpose of public education.

All students are created equal; that they are endowed by their Creator with certain inalienable Rights; that among these are an education that will accord them Life, Liberty, and the pursuit of Happiness; that whenever any public school becomes destructive of preparing students for these ends, it is the Right of the People to alter or abolish it.

In essence, the reason we have public education is to enculturate students into the values of our democracy! To summarize Thomas Jefferson, public education has two corollary purposes: (1) to provide for an educated citizenry to participate in decisions about promoting the future good of our democratic society and (2) to allow for leadership in a democratic society to develop from the merits, abilities, and talents of the individual. Leadership in a democratic society should not be accorded based on family privilege, economic wealth, religion, race, or group privilege (Lee, 1961).

The central question for all who educate is:

What should we be doing in our schools, our curriculum, our placement and our scheduling of students, our allocations of resources, and our teaching to give every child his or her inalienable rights to life, liberty, and the pursuit of happiness? What is just, what is fair, what is democratic?

Schools in the United States are indeed better than they've ever been in reaching all students. But the challenge of U.S. schools is not primarily that of achieving economic superiority in the world or of focusing on subject area achievement. The challenge is to rise to the far more demanding and crucially important standard of educating all students to be knowledgeable, proactive, resourceful, and responsible members of our democratic society.

Public schools must ensure a democratic threshold of learning experiences that give all students the knowledge, skills, compassion, and understanding to participate in human affairs. It is these requisites for democratic living that we should be returning to in determining decisions about standards, assessments, curriculum, professional development, placement, and grouping of students, as well as the ways that adults themselves function with each other. The supreme irony of public schools is that the only institution in the United States with the explicit purpose of preparing students for a democracy often operates in ways that demonstrate the lack of belief in such collective participation. Most schools do not include faculty, students, and parents in democratic decision making. Indeed, in many cases, where formal leaders wish for such involvement, many faculty, students, or parents would rather not be involved. Schools in the United States all too often operate in accord with dependency and hierarchical relations, not democratic ones. How can we, as a country, continue to sacrifice the lives of young men and women to protect and extend democracy as the best way of determining the common good while we stand unwilling to use the same beliefs in how we make decisions and set standards about the learning of our youth?

The Good School and Moral Principles

Few will argue with the central purpose of education, but, if we begin to reflect seriously on it, then it leads to a set of moral principles that present a distinct challenge to conventional practice. These principles are in direct conflict with the essentialist philosophy, narrow curriculum, and restricted learning that accompany the standards and high-stakes emphasis of today. Let us, therefore, consider 10 moral principles which, taken together and taken seriously, foster development of a school much more likely to prepare students to use their education well in contributing to a better society.

Compassion

Truly effective leaders and teachers are fired by a spirit of compassion for all other members of the school community. Compassion should not be interpreted as maudlin sympathy, but rather as genuine empathy combined with a concern for the overall well-being of colleagues and students. In a "school of compassion," there is a great deal of interpersonal communication intended to understand the personality, needs, concerns, and interests of others, as well as commitment of time and energy to assist individuals to realize their human potential. Leaders are more concerned about the growth and development of individual teachers and students than just the latest composite test report. Teachers first teach students, not test objectives.

Wholeness

Authentic compassion for students leads to the realization that one cannot separate different aspects of student growth. The good school is concerned with all levels represented in Bloom's taxonomy. In addition to concern for cognitive growth, the good school is committed to students' physical, emotional, creative, social, and moral development. Not only is growth in all of these areas necessary for the development of the whole person, the different domains of learning are interactive and interdependent; growth in one domain is enhanced by growth in the others.

The principle of wholeness applies to adult members of the school community as well. For example, the school needs to concern itself with teachers' pedagogical growth but also with their physical and emotional well-being, and with their creative, social and moral development.

Connectedness

Schools have an obligation to break down artificial barriers to natural relationships in students' lives and learning. For example, the education provided to students must be relevant to both their present and their future, not focused on one at the expense of the other. Connections between different content areas must be made. And, the world of the classroom needs to be connected to life outside the school, including the local, national, and world communities (National Commission on Service Learning, 2002). The principle of connectedness also means that members of the school community should not be restricted to a single role. Administrators, teachers, and students should all engage in leadership, teaching, and learning, albeit at different levels and with different emphases.

Inclusion

Inclusion, as a moral principle, combines the beliefs in equality and equity. It begins with equality; all students are of equal worth as human beings and as members of the school community. A belief in equality leads to a commitment to equity. Those who have physical, cognitive, emotional, or social disabilities need special assistance, including extraordinary measures if necessary, to enable then to remain members of the community and to lead fulfilling lives as students and later as adults. Additionally, the good school *reaches out* to all categories of students (e.g., from low socioeconomic backgrounds, minorities, migrants, international students, non-English speaking students, gay and lesbian students, and even students with serious behavioral problems).

Justice

Teaching about social justice certainly has its place in the school curriculum, but here we mean *providing justice* as a means of facilitating teaching and learning. Justice includes holding teachers accountable for effective instruction and holding students accountable for learning, but in an *educational* context accountability ought to mean the provision of feedback on one's performance and assistance for improving future performance, not the issuing of rewards and punishments.

As its core, justice means treating members of the school community in a fair and consistent manner. By being just with students, educators to some extent can counter the injustice that students may have been dealt by their families, communities, or the larger society. By modeling justice, educators can teach students to treat others justly. Such justice, repeated daily, can facilitate student learning in all areas and eventually lead to a more just society. Justice must also be provided to all adults in the school community. Adults who are treated justly learn better how to treat students justly. A school will very likely provide its students no more justice than it provides its staff.

Peace

Student misbehavior is one of the major school problems reported by supervisors and teachers. Especially troublesome is misbehavior that interferes with the right of other students to learn. Worse yet, in recent years there has been a frightening increase in student violence. Perhaps one way to approach this problem is to change from a school characterized by "effective student discipline" to a "school of peace." Moving toward this vision will require the supervisors, teachers, and students to develop or enhance communication, collaboration, and conflict management skills. But it also will require that administrators, teachers, and students develop new self-concepts; that they begin to view themselves not just as leaders or teachers or students but as *healers* and *peacemakers*. For those who argue that we cannot afford to spend school time learning about healing and peacemaking, our response should be that considering the growing incivility in our communities and schools, we can no longer afford *not* to engage in such learning.

Freedom

Learning and freedom—freedom to dream, to explore, to take risks, and to learn from failures—go hand in hand. Educators need freedom to grow professionally, and likewise, students need freedom to develop to their full potential. Granted, students and adults function at varying stages of development and thus possess varying capacities for responding to freedom. For some, freedom may need to be introduced gradually, initially presented as restricted choice. But it is the *directionality* of the school's efforts that is the important thing; all members of the school community should be moving toward increased freedom of choice in what they learn, how they learn, and how they demonstrate learning. This is a particularly difficult principle to accept for those who equate school reform with external control, an ironic phenomenon in a democratic society.

Trust

Consistent efforts on behalf of compassion, wholeness, connectedness, inclusion, justice, peace, and freedom can lead to trusting relationships among members of the school community. Trust is both a product of adhering to the other principles and a requirement for those principles to flourish over the long run. Authentic learning is based not only on the transmission of knowledge and skills but also on personal relationships, and trust is the ground on which those relationships are built. For all its importance, however, personal trust is not the only type of trust present in the good school. There also is trust in the moral principles to which the school is committed; trust that these principles, if adhered to, will result in a better education and more fulfilling lives for students, and a better future for society.

Empowerment

As a moral principle, empowerment certainly includes involving members of the school community in decisions about matters that affect them. But it goes beyond this standard definition. It also means changing assumptions, norms, roles, and relationships that act as barriers to educators' and students' growth toward self-reliance and self-actualization. It includes not only an invitation to become involved in decisions concerning leadership, teaching, and learning but also to acquire the information and skills necessary to engage in effective decision making in each of these areas. Finally, empowerment means instilling in educators and students a commitment to facilitate the empowerment of *other* members of the school community.

Community

We've referred to the "school community" throughout this book. The good school is a community of leaders, teachers, and learners, with individual members assuming all three roles. *Community* itself can be a moral principle if we understand the term as a group committed to the overall well-being, growth, and development of each member. An authentic community will develop values, norms, relationships, and practices consistent with this common purpose. Community members will engage in collective and individual actions for the well-being of both the community and its individual members. Collegiality and collaboration become a way of life. An additional aspect of community is *celebration*. The community celebrates its progress toward its vision, but also engages in anticipatory celebration of what it wants to be—it celebrates the future!

Priorities

Following these 10 moral principles does not mean that a school ignores legislated standards of learning, externally mandated teacher evaluation systems, or high-stakes tests. What it does mean is that educators realize that schools need to go well beyond these well-intentioned, largely ineffective, and often counterproductive efforts to ensure that all students experience the growth and development necessary to become contributing members of society and to lead fulfilling lives. Educators in the good school realize that leadership, teaching, and learning based on moral principles offer the best chance for students to reach their human potential. What we are talking about then is a question of priorities. Educators committed to moral principles believe that if we base school reform on those principles, we will optimize meaningful student learning. They also realize that in some situations, the most efficient or immediate means of meeting external, simplistic measures of student learning may contradict moral principles. In such situations, they are prepared to choose the long-term good over expedient compliance.

Applying Moral Principles to a Moral Dilemma: No Child Left Behind

The No Child Left Behind Act (NCLB) was enacted for the purpose of holding schools accountable for their students' academic progress and eliminating achievement gaps among student subgroups. The NCLB Act mandates annual testing in reading and math for grades 3 through 8 and at least once in grades 10 through 12, with annual tests in science given once for grades 3 through 5, 6 through 9, and 10 through 12, beginning in 2007. States must set adequate yearly progress goals for districts, schools, and student subgroups, and use the state tests to determine whether schools are making adequate yearly progress toward 100 percent proficiency for all students by the school year 2013–2014. No Child Left Behind requires state assessment results to be disaggregated by economic status, race, ethnicity, and limited English proficiency. The act mandates that all teachers be fully certified and licensed for the subjects they teach and that paraprofessionals have at least two years of college or pass a "rigorous" exam.

Districts and schools that meet or exceed adequate yearly progress goals or close achievement gaps are eligible for State Academic Achievement Awards. Districts and schools that fail to reach their adequate yearly progress goals are subject to "improvement, corrective action, and restructuring" measures. Failing schools must allow students to transfer to a "better" school within the district and the district must pay for the students' transportation to the new school. Districts with schools that fail to meet standards for three out of four years must use a portion of their Title I funds to purchase supplemental educational services for eligible students. Eventually, failing schools may have their staff replaced or be taken over by the state.

At the surface level, NCLB seems to be a positive approach to problems facing public education today. After all, everyone can agree that all students deserve a quality education, achievement gaps among groups of students should be eliminated, and districts and schools should be held accountable for student learning.

On closer examination, however, several aspects of NCLB are problematic. First, NCLB is severely underfunded, in general, and the additional funds provided to poor districts are far from adequate for assisting poor schools to meet NCLB mandates. Second, the long-term requirements of NCLB may be impossible for most schools (including many effective schools) to reach. Some experts predict that as many as 75 percent of all schools eventually will be placed in the "needs improvement" category (Karp, 2002/2003). Third, the strategies that NCLB uses to measure student progress are seriously flawed. The law does not provide for measuring yearly progress of the same group or subgroup of students. Neither the size of the achievement gaps among groups nor the size of gains by underachieving groups are relevant when determining adequate yearly progress. Finally, the primary tool for measuring student progress under NCLB, the high-stakes test, has produced a number of negative effects that have called into question its use as the sole measure of progress.

Most teachers do not believe that high-stakes testing is an accurate measure of student learning or school effectiveness (Reese, Gordon, and Price, 2004), yet they are under intense pressure to meet state testing goals (Brighton, 2002). Due to this pressure, many teachers spend more time than they wish teaching minimal skills and test-taking strategies (Jones et al., 1999; Reese, Gordon, and Price, 2004). The teaching of higher-order thinking and problem solving tends to be deemphasized (Jones et al., 1999). As a result of the pressure to improve test scores, teachers become stressed and anxious, even when their students do well on the test (Jones et al., 1999). They feel frustrated and disappointed when students do poorly (Reese, Gordon, and Price, 2004). The negative effects of testing on their teaching and their students make many teachers feel powerless (Costigan, 2002). One study concluded that standards and high-stakes testing now is the number-one reason experienced teachers leave the profession (Tye and O'Brien, 2002).

Teachers are not the only educators negatively affected by high-stakes testing. Well-respected principals have been dismissed without warning solely due to low scores on a single set of tests (McGhee and Nelson, 2005). School counselors, who often coordinate the administration of state tests, report that testing has negative effects on their role as counselors. Many believe their role in testing inhibits their ability to provide counseling services and damages their relationships with teachers and students (Brown, Galassi, and Akos, 2004).

The most important effects of high-stakes testing, of course, are the effects on students. There is a growing body of evidence that improved scores on state tests do not mean increased student learning (Amrein and Berliner, 2002), and a narrowing of gaps on state test scores between Whites and minority students may actually mask increasing gaps between Whites and minorities on other measures of student learning (Klein et al., 2000). High-stakes testing does not increase students' motivation to learn (Reese, Gordon, and Price, 2004). Rather, the test causes stress, anxiety, and fear among many students (Brown, Galassi, and Akos, 2004), and the constant emphasis on test preparation can cause student burnout on testing (Reese, Gordon, and Price, 2004). The effects of testing on low-income minority students have been especially negative. Test prep materials and drill have replaced the normal curriculum in many schools serving primarily low-income minority students (McNeil, 2000). The oral drill, worksheets, practice tests, and frequent review that characterize test preparation for many minority students is reminiscent of the "pedagogy of poverty" written about by Haberman (1991) more than a decade prior to NCLB. This type of instruction leads to students' passive resentment and poor performance. It is not surprising, then, that graduation rates of African American and Hispanic students have decreased considerably during the era of high-stakes testing (Haney, 1999; Horn, 2003; Madaus and Clarke, 2001).

It is not difficult to identify serious conflicts between the moral principles of the good school and NCLB. The *principle of compassion* calls for us to be more concerned about the growth and development of individual teachers and students than the latest set of test scores. The *principle of wholeness* requires us to teach the whole student, not just teach the narrow proficiencies typically measured by high-stakes tests. The *principle of connectedness* calls for connecting content from different subject areas and connecting students to the real world, not for the narrow curriculum and the artificial world of test preparation that NCLB has led us to. The *principal of inclusion* is inconsistent with the pedagogy of poverty that forces low-income minority students to spend their schooldays in repetitive drill on minimal skills. The *principal of justice* cries out against the triage strategy used in many schools in which teachers focus intensive efforts on "bubble students" while spending less time and effort on students either likely to pass the test or perceived to have little chance of passing. We could go on. As currently written, despite the good intentions of those who made it the law of the land, NCLB contradicts all 10 of the moral principles described earlier.

The problems with NCLB that we have described place supervisors and teachers across the nation in one of the great moral dilemmas of our time. They cannot simply declare NCLB immoral and refuse to help students prepare for their state's high-stakes test. This course of action would put their students at a disadvantage, help bring down sanctions on their school, and eventually result in their dismissal, after which they would no longer be of any value to their students. On the other hand, large numbers of supervisors and teachers believe that NCLB is doing many of our children more harm than good. Isn't it wrong simply to comply with a system that has such negative effects? How should educators who believe that NCLB is harmful to students respond? Brighton (2002) noted that many teachers respond to this dilemma by attempting to "straddle the fence" between what they believe to be sound instructional practices and test preparation strategies. This approach attempts to create a balance between best practice and test practice. Although we believe there is some merit in this approach, we also believe that supervisors and teachers have a moral (and extremely difficult) obligation to directly confront the harmful effects of NCLB and work for changes in its provisions. Therefore, we propose both short-term and long-term strategies for educators to address NCLB, with both types of strategies to be carried out simultaneously.

Short-Term Strategies

These short-term strategies are intended to help schools meet the requirements of NCLB in ways that are consistent with the moral principles discussed earlier. The first set of short-term strategies is suggested for all schools:

- *Develop curriculum:* Embed state standards and test objectives into a comprehensive curriculum that includes more holistic and meaningful learning opportunities. Brighton (2002) noted that standards can be integrated within meaningful units of study and used as scaffolding for larger concepts. Once the curriculum is developed, the larger curriculum goals rather than the discreet standards and test objectives must remain the focus of teaching and learning.

- *Don't eliminate nontested subjects:* Subjects such as social studies, art, health, and physical education are important aspects of students' education, and thus schools have a moral obligation to include those subjects in their curriculum. Moreover, schools that maintain a rich curriculum tend to do better on high-stakes tests than schools that narrow the curriculum to tested content (Reese, Gordon, and Price, 2004).

- *Strive for authentic instruction:* Authentic instruction, including "higher-order thinking, deep knowledge and substantive conversation" as well as "connection to the world beyond the classroom" (Wehlage, Newmann, and Secada, 1996, p. 32) results in increased student learning as measured by both standardized tests and authentic assessment (Marks, Newmann, and Gamoran, 1996). Authentic instruction can lead to significant improvement in academic performance for lower-performing as well as higher-performing students. Many of the "best practices" discussed in the literature are consistent with authentic instruction. These include "concept-based instruction, interdisciplinary connections, student-generated topics of study, authentic assessment, flexible grouping, and differentiated instruction" (Brighton, 2002, p. 31).

- *Make extensive use of formative assessment:* In effective schools, teaching is planned and modified based on ongoing and extensive gathering of informal data on students' daily progress. Teachers observe students' classroom performance, review student work products, engage in diagnostic discussion with students, and revise instruction accordingly.

- *Differentiate instruction:* The one-size-fits-all drill and kill that many schools resort to in order to prepare students for the high-stakes test is neither good teaching practice nor an effective way to raise test scores. Teachers need to use a variety of instructional strategies to meet different student needs, including multiple strategies within the same lesson.

- *Limit test-taking practice:* Students who are not taught test-taking strategies are placed at a disadvantage to students who are, so some preparation for taking a high-stakes, multiple-choice test is necessary. The preparation needed, however, is a far cry from the common practice of using the test format day after day in lessons and assignments. Schools need to set limits on the amount of time and materials used to teach test-taking skills.

- *Provide professional development:* School-focused professional development possessing the characteristics described in Chapter 18 is essential to the improvement of teaching and learning. All professional development programs should include a teacher induction program as well as ongoing professional development assisting teachers with curriculum development, authentic instruction, informal assessment, differentiated instruction, and so on. Professional development also should deal directly with how to address the conflicts between NCLB and best practice.

The strategies discussed so far apply to all schools. Let us now consider additional short-term strategies that are especially relevant for low-income districts and schools.

- *Recruit and retain quality teachers:* Provide incentives, resources, and rewards to attract and keep high-quality teachers in schools serving low-income students.
- *Develop partnerships:* Collaborative partnerships are important to all districts and schools; however, schools serving low-income students must make special efforts to develop collaborative relationships with parents and other community members. This includes parent and community participation in school leadership and school improvement. Partnerships with higher education and business are other key ingredients for school improvement.
- *Focus on analysis and improvement:* Rather than pressuring, threatening, transferring, and dismissing principals and teachers in low-income schools with poor test scores, district leaders should collaborate with school personnel to complete a thorough data-based analysis of why scores are low, and work with the school to plan and implement a long-term, data-driven school improvement plan. A variety of data (not just state test results) should be used to plan for school improvement, and continued data gathering and analysis should guide ongoing school improvement efforts.

Long-Term Strategies

We believe that the short-term strategies just outlined will do much to ameliorate the harmful aspects of NCLB, improve test scores on high-stakes tests, and, most importantly, improve student learning. However, when attempting to follow moral principles that lead to better schools, amelioration of harmful policies is not enough. We believe that the stakes for public education and public school students are so high that K–12 supervisors and teachers need to become directly involved in efforts to change public policy. They will not be able to do it alone, but will need to become part of a coalition of K–12 educators, parents, university educators, and enlightened business persons and policy makers who recognize the critical need for change. Members of this coalition will need to educate the general public, the corporate world, and politicians on the need for change, and push directly for new legislation at the sate and federal levels. Specific changes that should be on the reform agenda include the following:

- Develop at national and state levels more realistic long-term school improvement goals, with the involvement of various educational groups in the establishment of these goals.
- Shift from reliance on the high-stakes achievement test as the sole measure of school effectiveness to the use of multiple measures, with the examination of the local school context a critical part of the assessment process.
- Employ higher-level learning as a measure of student progress. Students, for example, could be assessed on their ability to solve real-world problems.
- Measure academic progress of the same groups and subgroups of students over time, with gains by the same group and subgroups used as indicators of school improvement.
- Separate research-based teaching methods and school improvement strategies from ideological-based methods and strategies; fund research on teaching/learning using a variety of research methods; and promote teaching methods that are supported by multiple types of evidence gathered over time.
- Provide adequate resources for smaller school units, smaller classes, and professional development programs to foster high-quality teaching.
- Provide additional resources to low-income schools, allowing those schools to bridge the gaps with wealthier schools in quality of professional staff, physical facilities, and instructional materials.
- Provide additional resources, including adequate time, for underachieving schools to gather and analyze data on the causes of underachievement, and to plan and implement long-term school improvement programs focused on specific improvement targets.

The use of moral principles to guide us toward "good schools" across the nation, as illustrated by these recommendations, does not consist of embracing romantic abstractions. Rather, the road to the "good school" includes concrete actions to do what we can to improve schools within present limitations while we work together with others to remove these limitations and empower schools to be all that they can be. We will close this discussion of NCLB with two questions for readers to ponder, either individually or in dialogue with one another:

1. What can I do in the short term, either by myself or in collaboration with others, to protect students from external factors that are interfering with student learning?
2. What can I do in the long term, either by myself or in collaboration with others, to change external factors that are interfering with student learning?

CONCLUSION

SuperVision and Instructional Leadership is foremost about the ideas of goodness, purpose, and hope for all of our students. We have provided knowledge, technical and interpersonal skills, and domains, structures, and applications for achieving a purposeful school dedicated to the continuing improvement of teaching and learning. Please remember that competence without clear purpose results in directionless change, and purpose without competence provides inefficiency and frustration. We hope that you the reader, in whatever role of instructional leadership, will add coherence and congruence to the education of all students in your own schools and districts. After all, this is the primary reason for why we chose to be educators—to practice what we believe.

PRACTITIONER REFLECTION

Democracy at Its Best

Daniel Kaufman, *Director, Student Services,*
Vashon Island School District

The dialogue about No Child Left Behind (NCLB) is an emotionally charged and divisive one for educators. The focus on standards and accountability has crept into discussions in school districts across the country, even ones like ours, where students are fairly successful. Administrators and teachers alike have varied personal and professional feelings about the standards imposed by the law, including the assessment requirements associated with it and the definition of what and how a "good school" teaches its students.

Gaps in performance between student groups and demands for more challenging standards for high-performing students in our district has resulted in many parents and other community members raising the question of what we as educators are doing to meet these challenges. As educators, our mission is to teach young people and prepare them for the world that they will face. Historically, in our district, these challenges have not been addressed directly, or systematically, as we continued to operate in a business-as-usual way without reflection or dialogue with our communities. As a result, we have opened ourselves to both professional and moral questioning about our roles and our efficacy.

I believe that as educators we have not been as proactive as we could have been in evaluating, designing, and implementing changes in our practices to meet the challenges that face us. It is therefore inappropriate simply to bemoan the many problems associated with NCLB and the unfair pressures that it places on educators and students. Rather than defending ourselves against the requirements that have been imposed, making us appear uncaring and unresponsive to student needs, we must move forward with our own initiatives with an emphasis on what we believe the "good school" looks like. We must address both the democratic values that we feel are important and, at the same time, provide specific recommendations for how these values and practices can address the challenges we face.

Each educator is, I believe, responsible for reflecting on whether or not he or she is meeting the needs of his or her students and for addressing gaps between goals for students and their actual performance. Here is where supervision is so important. We, the district administrators, as supervisors and as members of our learning community, have committed ourselves to publicly reflecting on the gaps between our goals for our teachers and their actual performance much as we have asked them to do in relation to their students.

If we are to act responsibly, then we are also responsible for meeting the intent of the law. We may not agree with it in part, or at all, but we have a legal and ethical obligation to address its intent. Being a citizen in this country means that there will be times when we do not agree with existing politics, politicians, or political agendas. Yet the freedom we are privileged with must include the knowledge and acceptance that the democratic process is what is most important.

As responsible citizens and as professional educators our job is to find ways to address both our differences with the ethics of those in power and the challenges that face our young people. Many authors have written about the ethics of justice, critique, and care as lenses through which we may address the moral issues that face us in our practice. In our district we believe that, as supervisors, we can model the use of these lenses in our mutual and authentic interactions with teachers as a means of sharing both the frustrations associated with the current power structure and developing the new initiatives necessary to shift the balance of power. We can, in our interactions with teachers, address the belief that all children can and should learn, acknowledge and deconstruct the inequities that result from current power differentials, and use our caring relationships as the springboard for change. Engaging teachers in authentic dialogue about these issues and challenging them to formulate their own solutions moves them from feelings of powerlessness to feelings of power and from being part of the problem to being part of the solution.

In our district we are fighting hard to create opportunities for supervisors to dialogue about learning and to develop the skills necessary to support teachers. Each of us learns from one another and supports one another in our own growth as leaders and supervisors. It is not an easy job. We have adopted a leadership model in which we, as supervisors, are developing and modeling skills aimed at helping to mediate thinking and learning in our teachers so that they can mediate thinking and learning in their students. The goal of developing a learning community requires that everyone be engaged in learning, reflection, and dialogue about our practices, whether school board member, administrator, teacher, parent, or student.

I am hopeful that we can earn the trust of our community and that educators around the country can earn the trust and respect of their own communities. Supervisors have a tremendous burden on their shoulders as they set goals for themselves and the teachers with whom they work. Our administrative team has taken the challenge and recognizes that we need look no further than ourselves when searching for answers to how to respond to the issues with which we are faced. Reflection, authentic communication and pedagogy, and a constant emphasis on helping our children, not only to be ready to face the world they will enter into but also to make it a better place, are the responsibilities that we must shoulder. There is no better way to do this than by modeling how the democratic process works best.

REFERENCES

Amrein, A. L., and Berliner, D. C. 2002, March 28. High-stakes testing, uncertainty, and student learning. *Education Policy Analysis Archives, 10*(18). Retrieved October 29, 2005 from http://epaa.asu.edu/epaa/v10n18.

Baez, B. 2005. Schools and the public good: Privatization, democracy, freedom, and "government." *JCT, 21*(2), 63–82.

Brighton, C. M. 2002. Straddling the fence: Implementing best practices in the age of accountability. *Gifted Child Today, 25*(3), 30–33.

Brown, D., Galassi, J. P., and Akos, P. 2004. School counselors' perceptions of the impact of high-stakes testing. *Professional School Counseling, 8*(1), 31–39.

Civil Society Institute. 2003. Draft statement for a national conversation about school reform and public education. Newton Centre, MA. (draft available at www.civilsocietyinstitute.org)

Costigan, A. T. 2002. Teaching the culture of high stakes testing: Listening to new teachers. *Action in Teacher Education, 23*(4), 35–42.

Gordon, S. P. 2001. The good school. *Florida Educational Leadership, 1*(2), 13–15.

Habermann, M. 1991. The pedagogy of poverty versus good teaching. *Phi Delta Kappan, 73,* 290–294.

Haney, W. 1999. *Study of Texas Education Agency statistics on cohorts of Texas high school students.* Boston: Center for the Study of Testing, Evaluation, and Educational Policy.

Horn, C. 2003. High stakes testing and students: Stopping or perpetuating a cycle of failure? *Theory into Practice, 42*(1), 30–41.

Jones, M. G., Jones, B. D., Hardin, B., Chapman, L., Yarbrough, T., and Davis, M. 1999. The impact of high stakes testing on teachers and students in North Carolina. *Phi Delta Kappan, 81,* 199–203.

Klein, S., Hamilton, L., McCaffrey, D., and Stetcher, B. 2000. *What do test scores in Texas tell us?* Santa Monica: RAND Corp.

Lee, G. C. 1961. The precious blessings of liberty. In G. Lee (Ed.), *Crusade against ignorance: Thomas Jefferson on education.* New York: Columbia University (pp. 27–28).

Madaus, G., and Clarke, M. 2001. The impact of high-stakes testing on minority students. In M. Kornhaber and G. Orfield (Eds.), *Raising standards or raising barriers: Inequality and high stakes testing in public education* (pp. 85–106). New York: Century Foundation.

Marks, H. M., Newmann, F. M., and Gamoran, A. 1996. Does authentic pedagogy increase student achievement? In F. M. Newmann and Associates (Eds.), *Authentic achievement: Restructuring schools for intellectual quality* (pp. 49–73). San Francisco: Jossey-Bass.

McGhee, M. M., and Nelson, S. 2005. Sacrificing leaders, villainizing leadership: How educational accountability policies impair school leadership. *Phi Delta Kappan, 86*(5), 361–372.

McNeil, L. M. 2000. Creating new inequalities: Contradictions of reform. *Phi Delta Kappan, 81,* 728–734.

National Commission on Service Learning. 2002. *Learning in deed.* Battle Creek, Michigan: W. K. Kellogg Foundation and the John Glenn Institute for Public Service (Available from the W. K. Kellogg Foundation (800) 819-9997, wkkford@ iserv.net)

Olson, L. 2002. "Inadequate" yearly gains are predicted. *Education Week, 21*(29): 1, 24–26.

Reese, M., Gordon, S. P., and Price, L. R. 2004. Teachers' perceptions of high-stakes testing. *Journal of School Leadership, 14,* 464–496.

Tye, B. B., and O'Brien, L. 2002. Why are experienced teachers leaving the profession? *Phi Delta Kappan, 84,* 24–32.

Wehlage, G. G., Newmann, F. W., and Secada, W. G. 1996. Standards for authentic achievement and pedagogy. In F. M. Newmann and Associates (Eds.), *Authentic achievement: Restructuring schools for intellectual quality* (pp. 23–48). San Francisco: Jossey-Bass.

SUGGESTED READINGS

Fullan, M. 2005. *Leadership and sustainability: System thinkers in action.* Thousand Oaks, CA: Corwin.

Glickman, C. D. 2003. *Holding sacred ground: Essays on leadership, courage, and endurance in our schools.* San Francisco, CA: Jossey-Bass.

Kohlberg, L. 1981. *Essays on moral development: The philosophy of moral development* (Vols. 1 and 2). New York: HarperCollins.

Lightfoot, S. L. 1983. *The good high school: Portraits of character and culture.* New York: Basic Books.

Meier, D., and Wood, G. (Eds.). 2004. *Many children left behind: How the No Child Left Behind Act is damaging our children and our schools.* Boston: Beacon Press.

Sergiovanni, T. J. 1992. *Moral leadership: Getting to the heart of school improvement.* San Francisco, CA: Jossey-Bass.

Sizer, T. R. 2004. *The red pencil: Convictions from experience in education.* New Haven, CT: Yale University Press.

Starratt, R. J. 1994. *Building an ethical school: A practical response to the moral crisis in schools.* London and Washington, DC: Falmer Press.

Waite, D., and Allen, D. (in press). Corruption and democracy in educational leadership. In P. Jenlink (Ed.), *Democracy and education reconsidered: Critical perspectives on educational leadership for the new millennium.* Lanham, MD: Scarecrow Education.

Waite, D., Waite, S. F., and Fillion, S. (in press). Duplicity, democracy and domesticity: Educational leadership for critical democratic action. In R. E. White and K. Cooper (Eds.), *The practical critical educator.* Dordrecht, The Netherlands: Kluwer.

Zinn, H. 2005. *Howard Zinn on democratic education.* Boulder, CO: Paradigm.

What Is Your Educational Philosophy?

Instructions

Please check the answer under each item that best reflects your thinking. You may also want to check more than one answer for any one of the questions.

1. What is the essence of education?
   A. The essence of education is *reason* and *intuition.*
   B. The essence of education is *growth.*
   C. The essence of education is *knowledge* and *skills.*
   D. The essence of education is *choice.*

2. What is the nature of the learner?
   A. The learner is an experiencing organism.
   B. The learner is a unique, free choosing, and responsible creature made up of intellect and emotion.
   C. The learner is a rational and intuitive being.
   D. The learner is a storehouse for knowledge and skills, which, once acquired, can later be applied and used.

Source: Patricia T. Jersin, "What Is Your EP: A Test Which Identifies Your Educational Philosophy," *Clearing House, 46,* pages 274–278, January 1972. Reprinted with permission of the Helen Dwight Reid Educational Foundation. Published by Heldref Publications, 1319 Eighteenth St., N. W., Washington, D.C. 20036-1802. Copyright © 1972. (You may note that Jersin has identified four philosophies. Since educational practice is reflected in three, we would subsume her philosophies in this way—Perennialism (belief in changeless knowledge) grouped with Essentialism, Progressivism as Experimentalism, and Existentialism as itself.)

3. How should education provide for the needs of man?
   A. The students need a passionate encounter with the perennial problems of life; the agony and joy of love, reality of choice, anguish of freedom, consequences of actions, and the inevitability of death.
   B. Education allows for the needs of man when it inculcates the child with certain essential skills and knowledge which all men should possess.
   C. The one distinguishing characteristic of man is intelligence. Education should concentrate on developing the intellectual needs of students.
   D. Since the needs of man are variable, education should concentrate on developing the individual differences in students.

4. What should be the environment of education?
   A. Education should possess an environment where the student adjusts to the material and social world as it really exists.
   B. The environment of education should be life itself, where students can experience living—not prepare for it.
   C. The environment of education should be one that encourages the growth of free, creative individuality, not adjustment to group thinking or the public norms.
   D. Education is not a true replica of life, rather, it is an artificial environment where the child should be developing his intellectual potentialities and preparing for the future.

5. What should be the goal of education?
   A. Growth, through the reconstruction of experience, is the nature, and should be the open-ended goal, of education.
   B. The only type of goal to which education should lead is to the goal of truth, which is absolute, universal, and unchanging.
   C. The primary concern of education should be with the development of the uniqueness of individual students.
   D. The goal of education should be to provide a framework of knowledge for the student against which new truths can be gathered and assimilated.

6. What should be the concern of the school?
   A. The school should concern itself with man's distinguishing characteristic, his mind, and concentrate on developing rationality.
   B. The school should provide an education for the "whole child," centering its attention on all the needs and interests of the child.
   C. The school should educate the child to attain the basic knowledge necessary to understand the real world outside.
   D. The school should provide each student with assistance in his journey toward self-realization.

7. What should be the atmosphere of the school?
    A. The school should provide for group thinking in a democratic atmosphere that fosters cooperation rather than competition.
    B. The atmosphere of the school should be one of authentic freedom where a student is allowed to find his own truth and ultimate fulfillment through nonconforming choice making.
    C. The school should surround its students with "Great Books" and foster individuality in an atmosphere of intellectualism and creative thinking.
    D. The school should retain an atmosphere of mental discipline, yet incorporate innovative techniques which would introduce the student to a perceptual examination of the realities about him.

8. How should appropriate learning occur?
    A. Appropriate learning occurs as the student freely engages in choosing among alternatives while weighing personal responsibilities and the possible consequences of his actions.
    B. Appropriate learning takes place through the experience of problem-solving projects by which the child is led from practical issues to theoretical principles (concrete-to-abstract).
    C. Appropriate learning takes place as certain basic readings acquaint students with the world's permanencies, inculcating them in theoretical principles that they will later apply in life (abstract-to-concrete).
    D. Appropriate learning occurs when hard effort has been extended to absorb and master the prescribed subject matter.

9. What should be the role of the teacher?
    A. The teacher should discipline pupils intellectually through a study of the great works in literature where the universal concerns of man have best been expressed.
    B. The teacher should present principles and values and the reasons for them, encouraging students to examine them in order to choose for themselves whether or not to accept them.
    C. The teacher should guide and advise students, since the children's own interests should determine what they learn, not authority or the subject matter of the textbooks.
    D. The teacher, the responsible authority, should mediate between the adult world and the world of the child since immature students cannot comprehend the nature and demands of adulthood by themselves.

10. What should the curriculum include?
    A. The curriculum should include only that which has survived the test of time and combines the symbols and ideas of literature, history, and mathematics with the sciences of the physical world.

B. The curriculum should concentrate on teaching students how to manage change through problem-solving activities in the social studies . . . empirical sciences and vocational technology.

C. The curriculum should concentrate on intellectual subject matter and include English, languages, history, mathematics, natural sciences, the fine arts, and also philosophy.

D. The curriculum should concentrate on the humanities; history, literature, philosophy, and art—where greater depth into the nature of man and his conflict with the world are revealed.

11. What should be the preferred teaching method?

A. *Projects* should be the preferred method whereby the students can be guided through problem-solving experiences.

B. *Lectures, readings,* and *discussions* should be the preferred methods for training the intellect.

C. *Demonstrations* should be the preferred method for teaching knowledge and skills.

D. *Socratic dialogue* (drawing responses from a questioning conversation) should be the preferred method for finding the self.

Scoring the Test

This test is self-scoring. Circle the answer you selected for each of the questions checked on the test (Table A.1). Total the number of circles below each column.

TABLE A.1	**What Is Your EP?**			
	Progressivism	**Perennialism**	**Essentialism**	**Existentialism**
1	B	A	C	D
2	A	C	D	B
3	D	C	B	A
4	B	D	A	C
5	A	B	D	C
6	B	A	C	D
7	A	C	D	B
8	B	C	D	A
9	C	A	D	B
10	B	C	A	D
11	A	B	C	D

Implications

The four answers selected for each of the questions in this multiple-choice test represent positions on educational issues being taken by hypothetical advocates of the major educational philosophies heading each column—Progressivism, Perennialism, Essentialism, and Existentialism. If, in scoring your test, you find that a majority of your choices, no matter how much doubling up of answers, falls in a single column, you are selecting a dominant educational philosophy from among the four. For example, if you find your totals: Progressivism (9), Perennialism (1), Essentialism (3), and Existentialism (2); your dominant educational philosophy as determined by this test would be *Progressivism* (9 out of 15 choices being a majority). If you discover yourself spread rather evenly among several, or even all four, this scattering of answers demonstrates an eclectic set of educational values. Indecisiveness in selecting from the four positions could indicate other values and beliefs not contained within one of these major educational systems.

In all formal systems of philosophy, an important measure of the system's validity is its consistency. Your consistency in taking this test can be measured by comparing the answer you selected for item #1 that identifies *essence* with your other answers. The more of the remaining 10 responses you find in the same column where you circled item #1, the more consistent you should be in your educational philosophy. The fewer of the other 10 responses in the same column as item #1, the more you should find your responses contradicting one another—a problem inherent in eclecticism. Again, keep in mind, lack of consistency may also be due to valuing another set of educational beliefs, consistent in themselves, but not included as one of the possible systems selected for representation here.

Skill Practices Using Directive Control, Directive Informational, Collaborative, and Nondirective Approaches

B1: Directions for All Skill Practices

1. Each conference will have the same identical three phases.

   Phase One: Goal Identification

   Gathering information and descriptions of situation

   Finding a focus for improvement

   Stating a goal

   Phase Two: Plan

   Exploring alternative actions

   Anticipating consequences for various alternatives

   Selecting and specifying those actions likely to achieve the goal

   Writing the plan

Phase Three: Critique

Supervisor asking for feedback on his or her behaviors

Discussing ways the supervisor could improve further conferences with supervisee

2. Each conference will produce a simplified plan of action to include:

   I. Goal to be achieved
   II. Specific actions to be taken

   (A more detailed plan could include objectives, activities, resources, and evaluation.)

3. Each skill practice should be a *real* conference dealing with an *actual* professional concern, problem, or situation that the supervisee wishes to act on and that is *within* his or her control to do something about. Situations that are dependent on actions by persons outside of the supervisee's sphere of influence should not be used in these skill practices.

4. An authentic and original plan that will be implemented should be the outcome of the conference. Once again, supervisor and supervisees are not pretending to be somebody else—they are to be themselves, engaged in real professional discussion about goals and actions.

5. The only difference is that one person is responsible for conducting the conference according to a particular approach. The person conducting the conference is called the supervisor, responsible for moving through the three phases and seeing that an action plan is derived. The supervisee is the person who comes to the conference with a professional goal or concern for which he or she wishes to establish a plan.

6. At the conclusion of each skill practice, it is illuminating to ask the *supervisees*, in writing, to rate the value of their plans (how good is the plan for reaching your goal) on a scale from 1 (not of value) to 10 (of great value) and then, also in writing, to describe with three adjectives the personal experience of having a (directive control, directive informational, collaborative, or nondirective) approach used. Ask the supervisor to describe with three adjectives the personal experience of using a (directive control, directive informational, collaborative, or nondirective) approach. Each person should write independently, and then the instructor can solicit responses to each question with the entire group. Some fascinating discussions about the use and misuse of a particular approach usually ensue, with an opportunity at the end to compare all four approaches.

7. Each skill practice session will need about 30 to 40 minutes for the actual conference and 20 to 30 minutes for debriefing—a total of 50 to 70 minutes for each approach.

8. It might help to reproduce the skill practice guides on the next two pages as overheads. Explain the approach to be used, ask participants to pair off, designate supervisor and supervisee, and time (announcing start and stop) through each step of the conference.

Conferences
Goal-Identification Phase
Information and Descriptions
Focus for Improvement
Goal Statement

Plan Phase
Alternative Actions
Consequences
Selecting and Specifying
Writing Plan

Critique Phase
Feedback on Supervisor's Behaviors
Feedback on Ways to Improve Next Conference

Written Action Plan
Goal Statement
Actions to Be Taken
   1.
   2.
   3.
Signed _____

B2: Directive Control Skill Practice

Directions: Review Chapter 8. (Remember that the supervisor assumes full responsibility for developing the plan. In this case, the supervisor already has information about the problem. The supervisor identifies the problem at the beginning of the conference, but allows teacher input before determining the best solution.)

I. Goal-Identification Phase
   A. Supervisor identifies problem—2 minutes.
   B. Supervisor asks for supervisee input.

    C. Supervisor states goal, asks if teacher understands goal, and clarifies if necessary—3 minutes.

    D. Supervisor writes statement of goal—1 minute.

II. Plan Phase

    A. Supervisor tells supervisee at least three expectations and rationale for each expectation—3 minutes.

    B. Supervisor asks supervisee for input into expectations—3 minutes.

    C. Supervisor modifies expectations, if necessary, and provides specific details of each expectation—6 minutes.

    D. Supervisor reviews and writes goal and expectations—4 minutes.

III. Critique Phase—3 minutes

    A. Supervisor asks, "What feedback can you give me on how I conducted this conference?"

    B. Supervisor asks, "What might we do next time to make these observations and conferences more helpful?"

    C. Supervisor summarizes what he or she has learned, for use in later conferences.

B3: Directive Informational Skill Practice

Directions: Review Chapter 9. (Remember that the supervisor is the source of information and direction in developing the plan. In this case, the supervisor does not have prior information about the situation or possible goals, so he or she gathers feedback to identify the goal. Eventually, the supervisor will provide the arena of choice for the supervisee in developing the final plan.)

I. Goal-Identification Phase

    A. Supervisor tells supervisee, "Describe to me the situation that you are facing"—3 minutes.

    B. Supervisor asks for additional information about the situation—2 minutes.

    C. Supervisor asks questions to understand the supervisee's goal—2 minutes.

    D. The supervisor states his or her understanding of the goal and asks supervisee to react to the statement—1 minute.

    E. Supervisor writes statement of goal—1 minute.

II. Plan Phase

    A. After writing the goal, the supervisor thinks of possible actions and says, "Based on my experience (knowledge), I believe that you might do the following . . . . The supervisor gives at least three specific actions and re-views the anticipated consequences of using each action—4 minutes.

B. Supervisor asks supervisee to respond to the proposed actions: "What do you think?"—2 minutes.

C. After hearing the supervisee's response, the supervisor now modifies, revises, or expands the alternatives and directs the choices. "These appear to be realistic actions that you might take. You could do the following . . . ." Supervisor then asks "Which one of these makes the most sense to you?" and "Which will you use?"—4 minutes.

D. After the supervisee makes his or her choices, the supervisor affirms, "I understand that you will do . . ." and writes actions on plan—4 minutes.

III. Critique Phase—3 minutes

A. Supervisor asks, "What feedback can you give me on how I conducted this conference?"

B. Supervisor asks, "What might we do next time to make these observations and conferences more helpful?"

C. Supervisor summarizes what he or she has learned, for use in later conferences.

B4: Collaborative Skill Practice

Directions: Review Chapter 10. (Remember that the supervisee and supervisor have equal influence in determining the goal and plan. So as not to exert undue influence, the supervisor should allow the supervisee to lead first in each phase of the conference. Before beginning, they should pick a topic of concern that is of mutual interest.)

I. Goal-Identification Phase

A. *Describe the situation* (both parties). Supervisor asks supervisee to explain the current situation that he or she wishes to improve. Supervisor paraphrases and checks for accuracy, and then explains how he or she sees the situation, asks for a paraphrase, and gives feedback on accuracy—7 minutes.

B. *Ask for further information.* Supervisee asks questions of supervisor and supervisor asks questions of supervisee, to gather further information to determine a common goal—5 minutes.

C. *State the goal.* Supervisor states the common goal, checks for accuracy and agreement, and writes it down on the first part of the plan—2 minutes.

II. Plan Phase

   A. *Brainstorm possible actions* (let supervisee lead). Supervisor asks supervisee to brainstorm at least three possible alternative actions and then offers his or her own possibilities of actions—2 minutes.

   B. *Ask questions and discuss consequences.* Supervisor and supervisee question each other about consequences of various proposed actions and look for commonalities and differences—5 minutes.

   C. *Negotiate.* Supervisor and supervisee determine actions that they both agree will help reach the goal—2 minutes.

   D. *State a jointly agreed action.* Supervisor and supervisee specify the agreed upon actions so that each knows exactly:

   > Who will do what?
   > How will it be done?
   > When will it be done?
   > When will it be reviewed?—3 minutes.

   E. *Write the plan.* Supervisor writes the agreed-upon actions in the plan. (No action is recorded unless both parties fully agree to it.)—5 minutes.

III. Critique Phase—3 minutes

   A. Supervisor asks, "What feedback can you give me on how I conducted this conference?"

   B. Supervisor asks, "What might we do next time to make these observations and conferences more helpful?"

   C. Supervisor summarizes what he or she has learned, for use in later conferences.

B5: Nondirective Skill Practice

Directions: Review Chapter 11. (Remember that the supervisor's responsibility is to facilitate the supervisee's own thinking and decision making and not to impose his or her own ideas.)

I. Goal-Identification Phase

   A. Supervisor begins, "Could you explain the current concern that you need to take action on?"

   Supervisee talk—3 minutes

   Paraphrase by supervisor—45 seconds

   Accuracy of paraphrase (check by supervisor)—30 seconds

   B. Supervisor asks questions to gather further information—2 minutes.

   C. Supervisor states perceived goal and checks for accuracy. Supervisor writes goal on first part of plan—3 minutes.

II. Plan Phase

    A. Supervisor asks supervisee to brainstorm possible alternative actions (at least three)—5 minutes.

    B. Supervisor asks supervisee to weigh pros and cons of alternatives—3 minutes.

    C. Supervisor asks, "What will you do?" Paraphrase: "Then I understand you will . . . ."—2 minutes.

    D. Supervisor now writes a plan of action as dictated by supervisee (make sure actions are clear and specific)—3 minutes.

III. Critique Phase—3 minutes

    A. Supervisor asks, "What feedback can you give me on how I conducted this conference?"

    B. Supervisor asks, "What might we do next time to make these observations and conferences more helpful?"

    C. Supervisor summarizes what he or she has learned, for use in later conferences.

Name Index

Subject Index